Cocoa® Programming Developer's Handbook

Cocoa® Programming Developer's Handbook

David Chisnall

Addison-Wesley

Upper Saddle River, NJ • Boston • Indianapolis • San Francisco
New York • Toronto • Montreal • London • Munich • Paris • Madrid
Capetown • Sydney • Tokyo • Singapore • Mexico City

Cocoa® Programming Developer's Handbook

ISBN-13: 978-0-321-63963-9
ISBN-10: 0-321-63963-4

Library of Congress Cataloging-in-Publication Data

Chisnall, David.
Cocoa programming developer's handbook / David Chisnall.
p. cm.
Includes index.
ISBN 978-0-321-63963-9 (pbk. : alk. paper) 1. Cocoa (Application development environment) 2. Object-oriented programming (Computer science) 3. Application program interfaces (Computer software) 4. Mac OS. I. Title.
QA76.64.C485 2010
005.26'8—dc22

2009042661

Printed in the United States on recycled paper at Edwards Brothers in Ann Arbor, Michigan.

First Printing December 2009

Trademarks

All terms mentioned in this book that are known to be trademarks or service marks have been appropriately capitalized. Pearson cannot attest to the accuracy of this information. Use of a term in this book should not be regarded as affecting the validity of any trademark or service mark.

Warning and Disclaimer

Every effort has been made to make this book as complete and as accurate as possible, but no warranty or fitness is implied. The information provided is on an "as is" basis. The author and the publisher shall have neither liability nor responsibility to any person or entity with respect to any loss or damages arising from the information contained in this book.

Bulk Sales

Pearson offers excellent discounts on this book when ordered in quantity for bulk purchases or special sales. For more information, please contact us by phone or email:

U.S. Corporate and Government Sales
1-800-382-3419
corpsales@pearsontechgroup.com

For sales outside of the U.S., please contact the International Sales group:

International Sales
international@pearson.com

Editor-in-Chief
Mark L. Taub

Managing Editor
John Fuller

Full-Service Production Manager
Julie B. Nahil

Technical Reviewer
Gregory Casamento

Book Designer
Gary Adair

Composition
David Chisnall

Contents

List of Figures

List of Tables

Preface

This book aims to serve as a guide to the Cocoa APIs found on Mac OS X. The core frameworks are described in detail, as are many of the other components used to build rich applications.

These APIs are huge. In most Cocoa programs, you include the Cocoa.h header, which imports the two core frameworks that make up Cocoa. This header, when preprocessed, including all of the headers that it references, is well over 100,000 lines long. If you printed the preprocessed header out, you would get something over twice as long as this book, and you would still only have the core APIs, and not any of the more advanced parts discussed in later parts of this book.

This book aims to provide a guided tour, indicating features of interest to help visitors find their way around this enormous family of APIs. As with many travel books, this aims to include the same 'must-see' destinations that everyone will visit as well as some of the more interesting but often-overlooked parts.

Deep familiarity with something like Cocoa only comes from years of practice using the classes that are included as part of the frameworks. This book provides an introduction, but you will only become an expert OS X developer if you take the information contained in these pages and apply it, developing your own applications.

Who Should Read This Book

This book is aimed at people wanting to learn how to develop applications using the rich Cocoa APIs on OS X. It is not aimed at people wanting to learn iPhone development. The iPhone SDK is designed to be easy to learn for seasoned Mac programmers, and shares a lot of core concepts and frameworks with the desktop APIs, but it is a separate system. Reading this book will make it easy for you to learn iPhone development later and care has been taken to point out places where the desktop and mobile APIs diverge; however, this book does not cover the iPhone APIs directly.

If you want to learn how to develop rich applications for Mac OS X then this book will help you. This includes coverage of the core APIs that have remained largely unchanged since the early 1990s on NeXT workstations up to the latest additions for integration with an internetworked environment and handling rich multimedia content.

This book assumes some general knowledge of programming. The first chapters include an introduction to the Objective-C, which should be sufficient for readers already familiar with languages like C or Java. This section is not intended as a general introduction to programming concepts.

Overview and Organization

This book is divided into seven parts. Each covers part of the Cocoa APIs.

Introducing Cocoa covers the background of Cocoa, how it fits into OS X, and where it came from. This part introduces and describes the Objective-C language and provides the reader with an overview of the tools used to create Cocoa applications.

In *The Cocoa Frameworks* you will be introduced to the Foundation and Application Kit frameworks that form the core of the Cocoa APIs. Foundation provides low-level, core functions, while the Application Kit is layered on top and provides the features needed to build rich applications. This part introduces both, giving an overview of how they fit together and how to begin creating applications using them. You will see the basic concepts that underlie the Cocoa application model, including how events are delivered and how the drawing model works. By the end of this part you will understand how to create simple applications using Cocoa.

Cocoa Documents covers developing document-driven applications with Cocoa. A document driven application is one that creates identical windows representing some persistent model, typically a file. Cocoa includes a lot of code to support this kind of application. You will also be introduced in this part to the Core Data framework, which handles automatic persistence for documents.

Part IV, *Complex User Interfaces* goes deeper into the Application Kit. You will learn about the more advanced view objects that interact with your program via a data source and will learn how to provide data dynamically to them. You will also see how to create new view objects.

The next part, *Advanced Graphics*, builds on top of this knowledge by exploring some of the more complex graphical capabilities of Cocoa. This includes the Core Animation framework, found on both desktop and iPhone OS X, which enables you to create intricate animated effects with only a small amount of code. This part will also take a small diversion from the visual into the audio world and discuss how to provide audible feedback to your user interface. This includes using the speech recognition and synthesis APIs on OS X. By the end of this part, you should be able to write complex multimedia Cocoa applications.

User Interface Integration focusses on the parts of OS X that make an application feel like a part of the environment, rather than an isolated program. This includes integration with the systemwide search facilities as well as the various shared data stores, such as the address book and calendar.

The final part, *System Programming*, covers the low-level features of Cocoa, including network programming and concurrency. This ranges from creating sockets to fetching data from a remote URL, and explores the distributed objects system in the Foundation framework.

This book is not intended as a replacement for Apple's excellent documentation. Every class in Cocoa has an accompanying reference available both online and in the XCode environment. Many also include guides covering how a small set of classes relate to each other. This comes to a total of several tens of thousands of pages of material.

You will not find detailed descriptions of every method in a class in this book. If you want to learn exactly what a class can do, look it up in the Apple documentation. Instead, you will find descriptions of the most important and commonly used features of classes and how they relate together. The Apple documentation, while thorough, can be overwhelming. Reading this book will help you find the subset that you need to solve a particular problem.

The example programs provided by Apple are similarly different to the ones provided by this book. Each of the examples included with this book is intended to demonstrate a single aspect of the Cocoa API. In contrast, the Apple examples tend to be complete applications demonstrating a complete API. The TextEdit application included with OS X is one such example. This is a full-featured rich text editor, and is several thousand lines of code. If you want to see a detailed example of how all of the parts of the Cocoa document support and text system fit together, it is an invaluable resource, but trying to understand the whole of the code can be very difficult if you are not already quite familiar with Cocoa.

Typographical Conventions

This book uses a number of different typefaces and other visual hints to describe different types of material.

Filenames, such as `/bin/sh`, are all shown in `this font`. This is also used for commands that you might type into a terminal.

Variable or function names, such as `example()`, used in text will be typeset like this. Objective-C message names will be prefixed with a plus sign if they are indented to be sent to classes or a minus if they are sent to instances, for example, `+alloc` and `-init`.

This book contains two kinds of code listing. Short listings appear like this:

```
eg = example_function(arg1);
```

This kind of listing is intended to highlight a simple point and may contain shorthand or depend on variables or functions that are not given. You should not expect to be able to copy these listings into a source file and compile them; they are intended to aid understanding.

Longer listings will have line numbers down the left, and a gray background, as shown in Listing 1. In all listings, bold is used to indicate keywords, and italicized text represents strings and comments.

Listing 1: An example listing [from: example/hello.c]

```
#include <stdio.h>

int main(void)
{
    /* Print hello world */
    printf("Hello World!\n");
    return 0;
}
```

Listings that are taken from external files will retain the line numbers of the original file, allowing the referenced section to be found easily by the reader. The captions contain the original source in square brackets. Those beginning with example/ are from the example sources that accompany this book. You should be able to compile and run any of these on a modern OS X system.

Output from command-line interaction is shown in the following way:

```
$ gcc hello.c
$ ./a.out
Hello World!
```

A $ prompt indicates commands that can be run as any user, while a # is used to indicate that root access is likely to be required. Most of the time, example programs are intended to be compiled using XCode. A few single-file examples are intended to be compiled from the terminal.

Part I

Introducing Cocoa

Chapter 1

Cocoa and Mac OS X

Since its release in 2001, Mac OS X has grown in market share slowly until, eight years later, it occupies almost ten percent of the desktop market. A lot of factors have contributed to this success: the solid, UNIX, underpinnings of the system, the simple and clean GUI (complete with eye-candy where required), and the attention to detail in all aspects of the system.

One feature is constantly lauded by third-party Mac developers: Cocoa. A set of clean, object-oriented, APIs, with a history of constant refinement dating back to the 1980s. Cocoa is what makes OS X easy and fun to develop for, but what exactly is Cocoa, and how does it fit with th rest of the system?

1.1 Understanding When to Use Cocoa

Cocoa is not the only way of developing for OS X and is not always the best choice. This section will look at some of the alternatives and when they might be used. The choice of development framework is not always an either-or choice. You can mix Cocoa, Carbon, and other frameworks in the same application, with some limitations. You can also mix languages, developing the performance-critical parts of your application in C or Objective-C and the rest in a higher-level scripting language.

1.1.1 Carbon

Before Mac OS X, there was Classic MacOS (called Apple System for most of its life, and Mac OS for the last few releases). This dated back to 1984 and contained a lot of incremental updates along the way. It was ported from Motorola's 68000 series architecture to Apple, IBM, and Motorola's PowerPC and contained an emulator for running old code. The early PowerPC machines were slower than the fastest Motorola 68040 machines at the time because much of the operating system and most of the applications ran in emulation.

The first versions contained user interface routines in ROM, known as the Macintosh Toolbox. This was replaced with a version loaded into RAM in later models, when RAM became more plentiful.[1]

When it became clear that MacOS was going to be retired, the days of the Toolbox were numbered. To ease the transition, Apple released a cleaned-up version of the API called Carbon. This ran on MacOS 8.1 and later.

The Carbon APIs and the old Toolbox shared a large common subset. For some applications, switching from Toolbox to Carbon was a simple recompile, while for most it required a set of relatively minor changes. This process was known colloquially as *carbonization*.

Carbon and Cocoa were both supported as first-class citizens on OS X 10.0. Some core applications, such as the Finder, were written in Carbon. Early versions had some limitations, such as the inability to access *services* from Carbon. Mixing Carbon and Cocoa was also difficult, since they had different event models. These limitations were gradually removed. For a long time it looked as if Carbon would be a permanent fixture of OS X.

The change came in 2007, when it was announced that Carbon would not be making the switch to 64 bit. Apple had released 64-bit CPUs earlier in the form of the PowerPC G5. With the PowerPC architecture, it makes little sense for most code to be 64 bit. Pointers become longer (increasing cache usage), but there are few other differences. After the switch to Intel, however, this changed. The x86-64 architecture contains a number of improvements over the 32-bit version, including faster calling conventions, a simpler memory model, more registers, and better floating-point support.

Although Carbon is not going away, it is relegated to the ghettos of Mac OS X. One of the improvements for OS X 10.6 is a rewritten, Cocoa, Finder, replacing the old Carbon Finder with a new Cocoa one. XCode 3.2, which shipped with OS X 10.6, no longer has project templates for Carbon applications, frameworks, and so on, and very few of the newer features are exposed to Carbon. This, effectively, makes Cocoa the only "native" application framework for OS X. Carbon is now only recommended when porting applications from Mac OS 9 or earlier, and there are very few of these still around that are worth porting but haven't been.

The Apple documentation sometimes uses the term "Carbon" to describe any C APIs on OS X and not just those that are part of the Carbon framework. The same inconsistent usage applies to Cocoa, which sometimes refers to just the Foundation and Application Kit frameworks and sometimes any Objective-C

[1]The original Mac had only 128KB of RAM, making it a very scarce resource.

libraries on OS X. Some parts of OS X are still only accessible via C APIs. These are not going to go away; it is only the Carbon framework that is disappearing.

1.1.2 Java

Java is a language most commonly associated with cross-platform code. When Apple bought NeXT, it gained a lot of experience with Java. NeXT, at that time, made a lot of its money selling the WebObjects web application platform. This was originally written in Objective-C but was ported to Java with version 5. Newer versions are now free and included with the XCode developer tools.

Programmers wanting to use Java on OS X have two choices. They can stick to Pure Java™ and not make use of any of the Apple-specific code. This is an obvious solution for porting code from other platforms.

Historically, OS X was one of the better places to run Java code. Apple was among the first to implement a VM capable of sharing class files between multiple apps, and it spent a lot of effort prior to the first release of OS X adding theming support to Swing and making Java apps look like Mac apps.

In addition to Java GUI libraries, Apple provided a bridge to a number of Cocoa objects. This bridge allowed Cocoa to be used from Java. The result was colloquially known a *Mocha* (Java + Cocoa). This had a few advantages. More developers were familiar with Java than Objective-C, and Java had a few features that Objective-C lacked, such as garbage collection. The converse was also true. Java did not gain support for proxies until 1.3.

Unfortunately, over the intervening years, Apple lost interest in Java. As of 10.3, Apple deprecated Mocha and no APIs introduced in Cocoa since then have been exposed via the bridge. This decision was largely caused by developer apathy. Cocoa is a big API, and Objective-C is a small language. If you are going to go to the effort of learning Cocoa, learning Objective-C is not much additional work and has the benefit of being the language Cocoa was designed for.

Java has much more limited support for reflection than Objective-C. Apple has spent a lot of time optimizing parts of the Objective-C runtime library so that you can write programs that use introspection-driven mechanisms for keeping model and view objects synchronized. Doing the same in Java would be a lot harder.

1.1.3 Cocoa

When OS X was introduced, it was a fusion of two operating systems: Apple's MacOS 9 and NeXT OPENSTEP 4. Carbon came from the MacOS heritage and Cocoa from the NeXT side of the family. The APIs that became known as Cocoa date back to the early NeXTSTEP APIs.

In NeXTSTEP, most of the low-level programming was done in C, with a GUI toolkit written in Objective-C. This platform was very popular with the few developers who could afford it. Perhaps the most well-known piece of software to have been developed with this framework was WorldWideWeb, a simple program written by physicist Tim Berners-Lee, working at CERN. This was the first ever web browser.

NeXT sold most of its machines to universities, and a few ended up at Stanford, where they were used to write HippoDraw, a statistical data analysis tool. When the authors wanted to port it to other platforms, rather than rewriting it, they wrote a compatibility library, *libobjcX*, which implemented the NeXT GUI functions on top of the X Window System.

Another admirer of the systems was a hacker at MIT, Richard Stallman, who was inspired by NeXT system and based a number of parts of the GNU operating system on ideas from it.

The NeXTSTEP frameworks, with their strong focus on object orientation and GUI builder tools were among the first *Rapid Application Development* (*RAD*) tools. Around 1993, they attracted the interest of Sun Microsystems, which entered into a joint venture with NeXT to produce an improved version.

The result of this collaboration was the *OpenStep* specification. OpenStep defined two libraries, the *Foundation Kit* and the *Application Kit*. The first contained core objects that would be useful to any program, while the second was aimed at GUI applications. *Display PostScript* was also specified, although few programmers used it directly.

The OpenStep specification was implemented on the next version of NeXTSTEP, which was renamed OPENSTEP (note the different capitalization) to reflect this. NeXT also began selling an implementation of it for Windows NT and Sun included an implementation with Solaris. Sun shifted their focus toward Java at around this time and largely abandoned OpenStep on Solaris.

After the specification was released, libobjcX was adopted as a GNU project and renamed *GNUstep*. The GNUstep project implemented complete compatibility with the OpenStep specification some years ago. It now seeks to track changes introduced by Apple in Cocoa.

GNUstep received little attention during the NeXT years. Most people who used OPENSTEP loved it, but few could afford the $499 price tag for the i486 version, or the $4999 price of the cheapest workstation NeXT sold. With the release of Mac OS X, a lot more developers were exposed to OpenStep via Cocoa, and GNUstep garnered increased attention.

The NeXT heritage is still visible in Cocoa. Programs written for OpenStep will mostly compile out-of-the-box on OS X, although a few of the less common classes were removed. All of the Cocoa classes still have names that start "NS" for NeXT-Sun (the two companies involved in creating the OpenStep specification).

Very occasionally, you will come across references to classes that date back to even earlier versions. These use the NX prefix, for NeXT. Apple has kept the NS prefix for the core Cocoa classes and uses framework-specific prefixes for other code.

1.1.4 UNIX APIs

Since version 10.5, OS X has been UNIX™. This means that it is certified by The Open Group as conforming to the *Single UNIX Specification* (*SUS*). Technically, this only applies to OS X on Intel Macs. The certification only applies to a specific version of the operating system on specific hardware, and Apple did not pay to have OS X certified on PowerPC hardware.

This certification ended a trademark lawsuit initiated by The Open Group against Apple, which had been describing OS X as UNIX in spite of lacking the certification. The *Single UNIX Specification* (*SUS*) is a superset of the *Portable Operating System Interface* (*POSIX*) standard. POSIX defines a set of interfaces that can be implemented by any operating system, and the SUS provides an extended set of definitions that only make sense for UNIX-like systems.

Because OS X is certified as being UNIX, it can run any programs that are written to the published UNIX specifications. These provide a rich set of application-level interfaces, although they do not include any support for graphics.

Apple provides an optional X server, X11.app, which implements the X11 protocol used by most other UNIX systems for communicating with displays. X11 is designed to be network-transparent, meaning that you can run applications on one system and display their interface on another. This lets you use OS X as a client for remote UNIX applications, as well as running them locally.

If you write an application using X11, then it is unlikely to be accepted by most Mac users. X11 applications are definitely second-class citizens on a Mac desktop. They don't use the same menu bar or Dock in the same way as other applications and only have limited support for the standard OS X pasteboards.

X11 has the advantage of being supported on a lot of other systems, and so it can be used as a starting point for porting UNIX software to OS X. If you start by compiling the software with minor modifications, you can run it in OS X under X11 and check that it works. You can then write a new GUI layer for it. This is very easy for applications that are designed with clear separation between their models and views, but harder for others.

If you are writing server applications, then you may want to stick to the standard UNIX interfaces. Alternatively, you can use the Foundation library on OS X and one of the open source implementations of this framework when you port your application elsewhere.

1.1.5 Other Choices

Although these are the main toolkits for GUI development, there are a number of other options. Cross-platform toolkits, such as WxWidgets and Qt, for example, are relatively popular on *NIX and Windows. They are much less common on OS X due to the strength of the platform's *Human Interface Guidelines* (*HIG*). These, and the way in which the developer tools make it easy to follow them, mean that most Cocoa and Carbon applications look and, more importantly, behave in a certain way that users expect. There are a number of examples of this, such as the placement of buttons in dialog boxes, the orders of menus, and even the shortcuts used to jump around in a text field.

Using a cross-platform toolkit often mirrors the look, but not the feel, of a native application. In many ways, this is the worst possible combination, because users miss out on the visual clues that an application will not behave as they expect. One of the worst offenders in this respect has been the Qt framework from Trolltech, which managed to provide an Aqua look for applications but, for many releases, got basic things like the shortcut keys for skipping forward and backward in a text field wrong. This is very jarring for users and is likely to make them dislike your application, even if they can't quite identify why.

Because of this, there are far fewer successful applications on OS X using cross-platform GUI toolkits than on other systems. This is not to say that cross-platform development is not a good idea, however. It is possible to implement many applications with a clean abstraction layer between the GUI and the rest of the code, allowing a different GUI to be plugged in on every platform. A good example of this is the VLC media player, which is popular on Windows, *NIX, and Mac OS X. It has a number of user interfaces, including a Cocoa GUI and even a small web server allowing it to be controlled remotely.

If you can separate out your application in this way, it is possible to make a portable application that looks and feels polished on all platforms. If you use GNUstep on other platforms, then you can use the Cocoa Foundation libraries in your core logic and either use GNUstep or write a native GUI for each other platform you choose to support. Alternatively, you can use a framework that you are more experienced with for your core logic and just write a Cocoa GUI on top of it.

Not every application needs to have a graphical interface, of course. OS X contains a rich set of developer tools for building command-line systems. Pure C, Python, Ruby, or shell scripts designed for UNIX-like systems will often run unmodified on the system.

1.2 Understanding Cocoa's Role in Mac OS X

Cocoa is a large and important part of development on Mac OS X, but it is not the only part. It is important to understand how it fits in to the larger picture. Figure 1.1 gives a simple overview of how the major components of OS X fit together. As a developer, you can choose to ignore most of the details of the layers underneath Cocoa, but understanding them will help you to write better programs.

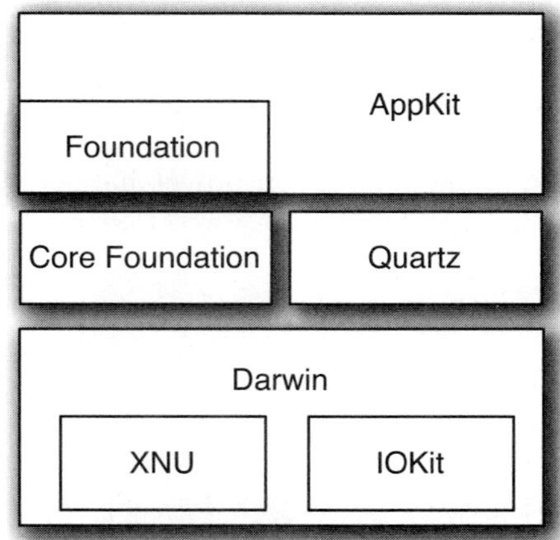

Figure 1.1: An overview of the major components of OS X.

1.2.1 Cocoa

Cocoa is the top level of the application developer's stack. It provides two, layered, frameworks: Foundation and AppKit. The first provides standard data types, such as strings, and collection classes. It also includes a lot of lower level functionality, such as interfaces to the filesystem and the network.

One of the most powerful parts of Foundation is the *Distributed Objects* framework. This uses the proxy facilities of Objective-C and the serialization capabilities of the Foundation objects to allow different objects running in different processes, or on different machines, to interact as if they were local.

The most important part of the Foundation library is the memory management code. Prior to OpenStep, NeXT code used a C-like allocate and free mechanism, where objects all had an owner and needed to be explicitly freed by this owner.

Tracking ownership was a major source of bugs. With OpenStep, objects maintained an internal reference count, making this a much simpler problem. Reference counting isn't perfect, and recent versions of Cocoa incorporate a tracing garbage collector. This doesn't completely eliminate memory management problems—even some of Apple's own applications still manage to leak memory—but it can make life a lot easier.

On top of this is the Application Kit, or AppKit for short. This contains all of the GUI-related code and a lot of other things. It is closely integrated with the Foundation framework, and there are lots of examples of classes declared in Foundation and either extended or wrapped in AppKit.

One such example is the run loop. `NSRunLoop` is a class defined in Foundation that handles a simple loop calling methods on objects in each iteration. In AppKit, this is extended by having the application object handle event delivery for each run-loop iteration.

Cocoa and the iPhone

In 2007, Apple introduced the iPhone and iPod Touch, handheld devices running a cut-down version of OS X. These run the Foundation part of Cocoa, but not AppKit. Instead, they use UIKit, a framework designed for small form-factor devices. UIKit is based on a lot of the same concepts as AppKit, and a lot of AppKit classes have direct analogues in UIKit.

Unlike desktop OS X, iPhone OS X does not need to support legacy applications. It is a completely new platform, and Apple took this opportunity to break a lot of legacy features. You can think of UIKit as a cleaned-up version of AppKit. New additions to AppKit share a lot more in common with UIKit than they do with older parts of AppKit. Because UIKit and AppKit have a large overlapping subset, it is easy for developers familiar with one to move to the other. It is also easy to port code between the two.

A number of the more advanced desktop frameworks are not available on the iPhone version of OS X, and neither are some newer features like garbage collection, which would not run well on low-powered devices like the iPhone. You can expect future versions of desktop and iPhone OS X to converge. Although it is unlikely that they will ever share exactly the same APIs, there is an increasingly large common subset that works on both.

Another case is the `NSAttributedString` class. This is defined in Foundation as a simple class that stores mappings from ranges in a string to dictionaries of attributes. In Foundation, the attributes are arbitrary key-value pairs. AppKit extends this by defining meanings for certain keys, such as the "font" key for the typeface of the text range.

A large number of other frameworks are now included under the slightly amorphous Cocoa brand. Some of these relate to system integration, such as the Address Book framework. This provides support for storing arbitrary data about people, allowing instant messaging, email, and other communication tools to share a single store. Others, such as Core Data, make managing data in your application easier.

The term Cocoa is used to mean two things. The Cocoa framework is a simple wrapper that includes just the Foundation and AppKit frameworks. Often, however, people who say "Cocoa" mean "Objective-C frameworks included with OS X." There are a huge number of these and an even bigger collection of third-party frameworks available to developers.

1.2.2 Quartz

NeXTSTEP used *Display PostScript* (*DPS*) for the display. This made the platform very attractive for desktop publishing, since the output to the display and printer were the same.

PostScript is a very complex language. It is Turing-complete, meaning that it can implement any algorithm. This was convenient for printing, since it allowed complex programs to be sent to the printer and generate complex documents. It is less convenient for on-screen drawing. If you send a PostScript program to the printer that infinite loops, you just turn the printer off and on again and resubmit your jobs. If you do the same with a display server, you have a problem. A well-designed Display PostScript implementation can kill widgets that run for too long, but defining "too long" is nontrivial.

Most users didn't use much of the power of DPS. They used bezier curves and simple drawing commands, but wrote all of the control structures in C or Objective-C. This removed one of the main advantages of a DPS-like environment. Sun produced a similar PostScript-based windowing system called *NeWS*, which competed with the X Windowing System in the early days of graphical UNIX. The main advantage of NeWS over X was that graphical objects were written in PostScript and sent over the network to the display. When you clicked on a button on an X GUI, it sent a "mouse clicked" event to the remote machine, which then sent X commands back to handle updating the UI. With NeWS, the PostScript UI processed the event, drew the pressed button image, and sent a "button pressed" event to the remote machine. This enabled much lower-latency remote display. NeXT, however, never pushed remote display for DPS and so this capability was not exploited.

When it came time to produce OS X, Apple investigated using X11 instead of

DPS, since it was standard on other UNIX-like platforms at the time (and still is). They found that it lacked a number of features they needed, such as good support for antialiased fonts, color calibration, and compositing. DPS didn't support all of these things either, so Apple wrote a new system.

Since no one was using the DPS flow control structures, these were the first to go. Adobe had already created a PostScript-like language without flow control: *Portable Document Format* (*PDF*). The new windowing system adopted the PDF drawing model and integrated compositing support from the start and is sometimes referred to as *Display PDF*. Earlier windowing systems—X11, DPS, NeWS, and the Windows GDI—were all created in an era when RAM was very expensive. Buffering every single window on a display could easily take tens of megabytes of memory. The framebuffer alone for the original NeXT workstations was almost 2MB (1120×832 in 16-bit color), and buffers for overlapping windows could easily have filled the 12MB of RAM the color version included. When OS X was introduced, the target machine had at least 64MB of RAM, 16MB of video RAM, and a similar sized display. This made buffering everything a lot more attractive, since the cost was relatively small and the benefit was reducing the CPU used for redrawing and eliminating tearing.

The first versions of OS X were relatively slow for large graphics updates, since all of the compositing was performed on the CPU. Later versions offloaded this to the GPU that could perform composting operations much faster. The updated version was called *Quartz Extreme*.

With 10.4, Apple attempted to offload even more to the GPU. Somewhat ironically, the most expensive graphical operation on OS X is rendering text. *Quartz GL*, formerly *Quartz 2D Extreme*, accelerated this by rendering each font glyph as an antialiased outline to a texture and then drawing them by compositing these together. This was a lot faster than drawing the bezier curves of each glyph for every character. When it was introduced, Quartz 2D Extreme was less reliable than its predecessor and so was not enabled by default. It can still be enabled by the end user with the *Quartz Debug* utility, which is included with the developer tools bundle.

It is often said that Quartz uses OpenGL. This is not true. Quartz may use the 3D hardware, but it does so via its own interface. Both OpenGL and Quartz are built on top of the 3D hardware drivers. Quartz windows may contain OpenGL contexts, allowing OpenGL to be used on OS X. The deformations on Windows and compositing operations are all implemented directly by Quartz and the window server.

The programmatic interface to the Quartz is called *Core Graphics*. This provides low-level drawing functions following the PDF model. You can use Core Graphics to draw antialiased bezier curves, filled shapes, and composited bitmaps. These functions are also wrapped by AppKit APIs. The iPhone, which does not use AppKit, does have an implementation of Core Graphics, so drawing code using these APIs will work on both systems.

1.2.3 Core Foundation

While Quartz provides the low-level display primitives, *Core Foundation* provides low-level data manipulation primitives. Both Cocoa and Carbon use Core Foundation for a number of things, including representing strings and collections.

When you inspect a Cocoa object in the debugger, you may find that the real object has a CF prefix, instead of (or in addition to) the NS prefix. This is because Core Foundation implements a simple version of the Objective-C object model for C, and some of the common objects are implemented in this way. This allows them to be used easily as C opaque types in Carbon and as Objective-C objects in Cocoa. You can see this when you create an Objective-C string object. This appears in your code as an instance of the `NSString` class, but in the debugger as an `NSCFString`. A C programmer will create these using macros and will see them as instances of the `CFString` opaque type.

The phrase *toll-free bridge* is used to describe this arrangement. This means that you can pass the Cocoa and Core Foundation objects to functions or methods that expect the other form, and it will all work without any additional overhead. There is some deep voodoo used to implement this in practice. Core Foundation objects all have their class pointer set to a value less than 0xFFFF, and the message dispatch functions treat these values as special.

Every Objective-C object is a structure whose first element is a pointer to the class. This is used by the message sending functions to look up the correct method to call. Core Foundation types set this pointer to a value that is invalid as a pointer, allowing their methods to be called by message sending functions or directly. Unlike Objective-C methods, Core Foundation functions take the object, but not the selector (method name), as arguments. This means that some of the more advanced features of Objective-C, such as message forwarding, are unavailable to Core Foundation types.

The Core Foundation functions are used directly from Carbon applications, and Cocoa developers can use equivalent methods. A number of parts of the userland, such as Launchd, make use of Core Foundation. All of the data types that can be serialized in property lists are implemented by Core Foundation, allowing pure C applications to be use property lists created by Cocoa applications. This is relatively common in OS X, where system dæmons use Core Foundation but the GUIs responsible for their configuration use Cocoa.

In the Core Foundation documentation, you will often see the term "class" used in relation to Core Foundation types. This means roughly the same thing that it does for Objective-C. The biggest difference is that a Core Foundation class is purely an abstract concept; it has no run-time existence. You can get a pointer to an Objective-C class and inspect it, but a Core Foundation class is identified by an integer and all of its behavior is hard-coded.

> **CFLite**
>
> In addition to the full version of Core Foundation, Apple have released an open source subset of it, called CFLite. This does not implement the toll-free bridging support, since this is a feature of the Apple Objective-C runtime; however, it does implement all of the C APIs. This means that code that only uses the Core Foundation libraries can be ported to other platforms relatively easily. Note, however, that CFLite is not used by GNUstep, and so it does not aid in porting code that mixes Core Foundation and Cocoa calls, unless the objects used for each are entirely separate.

1.2.4 Darwin

The core of OS X is the Darwin operating system. The original NeXTSTEP system was based on CMU's Mach operating system, with a single BSD server providing a lot of the services usually associated with a kernel. Mach is a microkernel, a very simple kernel that tries to do as little as possible. There are two ways of using a microkernel. The intended design is to decompose the kernel into a set of different components, called *servers*, each providing some aspects of the operating system's functionality. The other alternative is to run a single server that does everything. The latter approach is used by OS X. For efficiency reasons, the single BSD server runs inside the kernel's address space, eliminating a lot of the performance problems that plagued early Mach-based systems at the cost of most of the stability advantages that Mach brought over traditional UNIX-like systems.

When Apple acquired NeXT, it began updating the core operating system with code from NetBSD, and later from FreeBSD. The early userland contained a mixture of utilities from NeXTSTEP, FreeBSD, and GNU. A lot of the older NeXTSTEP code has now been removed. The init system and a number of related systems such as cron and inetd were rolled into Launchd, and the NetInfo directory service from NeXTSTEP was replaced with LDAP and a simpler local directory system based on property lists.

The current userland is very similar to a FreeBSD system, with some Apple embellishments. A few changes were made to make Linux users feel more at home, for example, including the GNU shell, `bash`, rather than a C shell, as the default. Several other GNU utilities are also included, replacing the FreeBSD equivalents.

The biggest difference between Darwin and most other open-source UNIX-like systems is that it does not use the GNU binary utilities. While other systems use the *Executable and Linking Format* (*ELF*) for binaries, Darwin uses the *Mach-O* format. These are roughly equivalent in terms of capabilities. To support this format, Darwin uses its own linker and loader, as well as its own tools for inspecting binaries.

If you are familiar with other UNIX systems, you may be used to using ldd to inspect shared libraries. This does not exist on Darwin; its functionality is subsumed into the otool program, which provides a number of options for inspecting binary objects in Mach-O format.

As well as the binary utilities, OS X provides its own C++ standard library and a C library based on the FreeBSD version.

As of 10.5, OS X was certified by The Open Group as compliant with the Single Unix Specification 2003. This means that it has the right to be described as UNIX™, something Apple was doing already for marketing purposes. Note that the certification is per platform, as well as per version. Technically speaking, OS X on Intel is UNIX, while OS X on PowerPC is not.

Apple has released the core Darwin code as open source under a variety of licenses. Most Apple-original parts are under the *Apple Public Source License* (*APSL*), while others are under whatever license their original authors picked.

It is possible to run Darwin as a stand-alone operating system, although this is not a popular choice. Until 10.5 (Darwin 9), kernel performance was markedly inferior to other open source UNIX-like systems. There are also some limitations. On most other UNIX systems, sound is generated by writing to /dev/dsp or a similar location. On OS X, there is no low-level access to the sound hardware from userspace, all sound goes through Core Audio, which is not open source. This means sound is not easily supported by Darwin unless you want to go to the trouble of writing a replacement that interfaces to the top layers of the drivers directly. A similar situation exists for 3D graphics.

Note, by the way, that Darwin version numbers correspond directly to version numbers from NeXTSTEP and OPENSTEP. The first release of OS X was Darwin 5, following on from OPENSTEP 4.

1.2.5 XNU

The core of Darwin is the XNU kernel. This is a single-server Mach microkernel with a BSD server derived largely from FreeBSD. The distinction between Mach and BSD in the XNU kernel is largely academic, since they both run in the same process. Mach in XNU fills a similar rôle to the HAL in Windows. It is a small layer of platform-specific code that is easy to port to new architectures. It handles memory and process-related activities, but higher-level interfaces are all handled by the BSD layer. In addition, the BSD layer is responsible for providing a POSIX interface to the Mach functionality.

The Mach microkernel is responsible for handling threads, processes, and interprocess communication. Everything else is implemented by the BSD layer. Some things are shared between the two. Although it is possible to interact with Mach threads directly, most of the time developers choose to use the POSIX functions. The BSD subsystem is responsible for maintaining UNIX process structures that are implemented in terms of Mach tasks and allowing UNIX-like system calls to control the kernel.

Device drivers for OPENSTEP were written using DriverKit, an Objective-C framework. It is worth noting that, on a platform with a 25MHz Motorola 68040 CPU, Objective-C was regarded as being fast enough for writing device drivers. On OS X, DriverKit was replaced with IOKit. This framework has a similar design, but is implemented in Embedded C++, a very small subset of C++ omitting a large amount of the language to make it suitable for embedded work.

1.3 Overview

The OS X system is built in layers, each of which builds on top of the one below. At the core is the XNU kernel, providing a feature-complete UNIX03 system. This is surrounded by the Darwin core userland, on which runs the Quartz display. The APIs are built in a similar way, with the C standard library being used by Core Foundation to produce a set of abstract data types for use by all programs. These are then wrapped and extended by the Cocoa Foundation framework to provide a friendly set of Objective-C APIs, which are further extended by the Application Kit.

None of these layers replaces the lower ones. It is possible to make calls to the C standard library, Core Foundation, Foundation, and AppKit from the same program. Sometimes the lower-level functionality is used where speed is critical, while the more abstract interfaces are used for their flexibility. One of the major strengths of the platform is the ability to choose at a very fine granularity how much you want to trade speed for convenience.

Chapter 2

Cocoa Language Options

When most people think of Cocoa, they think of Objective-C. In the NeXT days, Objective-C was the only way of developing for OpenStep. With OS X 10.0, Java was supported as well, and with recent releases other languages have had support added, but Objective-C remains the standard language for Cocoa development.

Objective-C itself has evolved a lot over the years. Under the direction of NeXT, it remained relatively static, but each release of OS X has introduced new versions. Java-like keywords for exception handling and synchronization were added over the years, and 10.5 introduced a complete break in compatibility and a new version of the language: Objective-C 2.0. 64-bit Cocoa and Objective-C 2.0 are both only supported on 10.5 and later, and using either means that you are using a completely new Objective-C runtime library. This incorporates a number of changes to make it easier to improve in the future.

2.1 Object Orientation

Alan Kay, who coined the term *object orientation* described it as:

> Simple computers, communicating by message passing.

Dan Ingalls, who implemented most of the original *Smalltalk* system, proposed the following test:

> Can you define a new kind of integer, put your new integers into rectangles (which are already part of the window system), ask the system to blacken a rectangle, and have everything work?

Smalltalk was the first pure object-oriented language, and one from which Objective-C gains a lot of inspiration. Both the object model and syntax of Objective-C come directly from Smalltalk. It has sometimes been referred to affectionately as "the bastard child of C and Smalltalk."

The Smalltalk model is very simple. Objects are simple models of computers that send and receive messages. How they handle these messages is entirely up to them, but most use a *class* as a template. An object has a pointer to its class and delegates the mapping from message names to methods to this class. The class may delegate it again to another class. This delegation between classes is known as *inheritance*.

If the chain of classes does not know how to implement a specific method, then the object is sent a `doesNotUnderstand:` message containing an object encapsulating the original message as an argument. In Cocoa, the equivalent message is `forwardInvocation:`, which receives an `NSInvocation` object as an argument. This is referred to as the *second-chance dispatch* mechanism. When a class has failed to find a method, the object gets a second chance to try to handle the method. On OS X, this is around 600 times slower than a direct message send, so it should not be used in performance-critical code, but it does add a lot of flexibility where required.

Because everything is an object in Smalltalk, classes are also objects. They can receive messages and respond to them. In both Smalltalk and Objective-C, message lookup for a class is handled by a *metaclass*; a class for a class. Smalltalk does more with this abstraction than Objective-C. It is very rare to deal with a metaclass directly in Objective-C. In implementation an Objective-C `MetaClass` is just a **`typedef`** for a **`Class`**, although a flag is set in the body of the class to indicate that it is a metaclass.

It is important to understand the distinction between sending a message in the Objective-C or Smalltalk sense, and calling a method in the C++ or Simula sense. When you call a method, you are effectively calling a function, with a hidden pointer to the object. If the function is declared as virtual, then you may get a different function for each class, but the mapping is static.

Sending a message is a higher-level abstraction than this. The mapping between method names (*selectors*) and methods is dynamic. It does not depend on what the caller thinks the class is, only on what the class really is and whether the object implements second-chance dispatch.

A dialect of Smalltalk called F-Script is available for scripting on OS X, and Étoilé contains a Smalltalk compiler that allows it to be used for OpenStep programming with GNUstep, although it currently only supports the GNU Objective-C runtime and so is not available on OS X.

2.2 Objective-C

Objective-C is a pure superset of C created by Brad Cox and Tom Love in 1986. They licensed the language to NeXT in 1988, and for a long time NeXT was the only major supplier of tools for the language.

The Free Software Foundation often quotes Objective-C as a success story for the GPL. Steve Naroff wrote initial support for Objective-C in the *GNU Compiler Collection* (*GCC*), but NeXT did not wish to distribute this code. Instead, it shipped a binary object file and required users to link it to their copy of GCC, attempting to circumvent the requirements of the GPL. The Free Software Foundation eventually forced NeXT to release its code.

The story, unfortunately, does not end here. The compiler is only half of the problem. Objective-C also requires a runtime library, which handles things like module loading, class lookup, and message sending. The compiler is little more than a C preprocessor that turns Objective-C syntax into calls to this library. The first Objective-C compilers and the open source *Portable Object Compiler* (*POC*) worked in this way.

NeXT did not release its own runtime library, so the Free Software Foundation was forced to write its own. They did and included a few small improvements, making the two incompatible. The Objective-C support in GCC began to fill with **`#ifdef`** statements for the GNU and NeXT runtimes. Over the next decade, these interfaces diverged more and more, until eventually there was very little shared code. NeXT (later Apple) never incorporated the code for the GNU runtime into its GCC branch, and so incorporating improvements made by Apple was increasingly difficult.

In 2005, Apple started working with the *Low-Level Virtual Machine* (*LLVM*) project and hired some of its lead developers. They used it for the CPU-based OpenGL shader implementation on 10.5 and began using it for code generation with GCC. This was motivated in part by GCC's switch to GPLv3. In 2007, they began working on a new front end. Like LLVM itself, the new front end, called *Clang*, is BSD licensed. I wrote the original implementation of code generation for Objective-C with this compiler, and it has maintained a clean separation between the runtime-specific and runtime-agnostic parts. The GNU runtime back end is under a thousand lines of code, making it much easier to maintain and keep feature parity with the Apple implementation. This means that, in the long run, Objective-C support on other platforms is likely to improve.

Objective-C was created at a time when Smalltalk was seen as powerful but too slow. The hardware required to run the Smalltalk-80 environment was very expensive. Objective-C was a compromise. It removed some of the features of Smalltalk, most notable closures and garbage collection, and added the rest to C. Since Objective-C had flow control constructs from C, closures were less important.

In Smalltalk, they were the only way of doing flow control; if you wanted an if statement, you'd send an `ifTrue:` message to a value with a closure as an argument, and it would execute it or not, depending on whether its value were true. Objective-C lost some of this flexibility but gained a lot of speed in return. Apple added blocks with 10.6, but they are considerably less flexible than Smalltalk blocks and do not support reflection.

Because Objective-C is a pure superset of C, every C program is a valid C program. Some new types are defined, such as **`id`** (any object) and **`Class`**, but these are defined as C types in a header and so are subject to the same scoping rules as other C types. This is in contrast with C++, where `class` is a keyword. A C program with a variable named `class` is not a valid C++ program.

In addition to the types, Objective-C includes a small number of new keywords. All of these are prefixed by the `@` symbol, preventing them from clashing with existing C identifiers.

2.2.1 Objective-C Compiler Choices

The original Objective-C "compiler" was really a preprocessor that turned Objective-C code into C, which was then compiled with a C compiler. NeXT integrated this into the GNU Compiler Collection and produced a real compiler. Another project, the Portable Object Compiler, kept the old preprocessor model but has since evolved the language in a different direction, which has made it incompatible with GCC.

With the introduction of OS X 10.6, GCC is seen as a legacy compiler. Although Apple will continue to support it for a while, it is not a good choice for new code. Due to licensing restrictions, none of the improvements to the code generation facility in the main branch of GCC will be incorporated into Apple's version.

OS X 10.6 includes two other compilers, both built on top of LLVM. The first is LLVM GCC. This was created by taking the front-end code from Apple's branch of GCC and compiling it to LLVM's intermediate representation, which is then optimized and converted to native code by LLVM.

The main aim of LLVM GCC is to act as a transitional step. It uses LLVM for code generation, optimization, and so on but uses the parser from GCC. This means that it can, with a few small restrictions, compile anything that GCC can compile and, in most cases, generate better code. One of the benefits that LLVM introduces is *link-time optimization* (*LTO*).

Traditionally, C (and, therefore, Objective-C) code is compiled one preprocessed file at a time. These separate compilation units are entirely independent and are only combined later, by the linker. With LLVM the front-end compiler emits files containing LLVM bitcode, which are then combined together by an

LLVM-enabled linker, optimized, and only then converted to native code. This means that optimizations can be aware of much more of the program. A trivial example of this is function inlining. If you have a very short function in one file, and you call it in another, a traditional C compiler cannot inline it, while one that performs LTO can.

LLVM incorporates a large number of optimizations that benefit from being run at link time. One example is function specialization, which generates a specialized version of a function for a specific input. If you are calling a function with a constant as an argument, then LLVM can generate two versions of the function: one that accepts any arguments, and one that has had one of the arguments removed and the constant value propagated to everywhere where the argument was used. Calls to the function with that constant value argument will then be updated to call the other function. In some cases, this will result in the called function becoming very small (for example, by removing conditional branches based on the removed argument) and allowing it to be inlined. This turns a function call to a complex function into a few inline instructions, which can be a big improvement.

Clang, the third compiler, uses the same back end as LLVM GCC, but is a completely rewritten parser. If you compile on the command line, you will see that clang provides much more helpful error messages than GCC. It features a unified parser for C, Objective-C, and C++. At the time of writing, C++ (and, therefore, Objective-C++) support is very immature and even trivial C++ programs fail to compile with Clang, although it is expected to be supporting most of C++ by late 2010. Because it uses the same back end as LLVM GCC, you can use Clang for C and Objective-C, LLVM GCC for C++ and Objective-C++ (until Clang is more mature) and still benefit from cross-module optimizations performed by LLVM.

Clang was designed to be modular. One of the problems that Apple had with GCC was that it was very difficult—both technically and legally—to separate out the parser and semantic analysis parts to use for things like syntax checking and highlighting in an IDE, or for static analysis. Parts of Clang are used extensively in Apple's tools, not just for compiling. One example of this is the static analyzer, which can find bugs in a lot of C and Objective-C programs. This is also available on non-Apple platforms.

In general, you should use Clang if it can compile your code, LLVM GCC if not, and GCC if all else fails. Clang is seeing the most active development. Apple's branch of GCC is receiving few improvements. LLVM GCC is being synchronized with Apple's GCC at the front end, but LLVM is in active development, so it receives continual improvements to the code generation. That said, GCC is still the most mature of the three compilers, and still the only one to support some relatively obscure GNU extensions, such as the `__builtin_apply()` family, making it the best choice in some cases. It is the default in current versions of Apple's tools, because it is the most compatible, but this may change in the future.

2.2.2 Differences from Java and C++

While many people think of Java as being close to C++, this is not really true. The syntax is vaguely like C++, but semantically it inherits a lot from Objective-C. This is not surprising, since a lot of the people who worked on Java came from NeXT or were involved with OpenStep at Sun.

Java was designed as a language for "average programmers," incorporating an object model similar to Objective-C and syntax from C++. If you have used Java, Objective-C will be familiar to you. The type system is similar, with object types identified by interfaces and a few primitive or intrinsic types. Objective-C class methods became Java static methods. Objective-C protocols became Java interfaces. Objective-C categories are not present in Java.

The differences between Objective-C and C++ are much more profound. Objective-C was created by adding Smalltalk-like extensions to C. C++ was created by adding Simula-like extensions to C. Although Simula is often called the first object-oriented language, it fails Ingalls' test.

C++ classes are not real objects. You cannot use them as you would objects, and the dispatch mechanism is very different. At first glance, it appears that message dispatch in Objective-C is similar to calling a virtual method in C++. This is not the case, however. C++ supports multiple inheritance, and to do this implements some very complex casting rules. When you cast a pointer to an object in Objective-C to a pointer to another object, no code is generated by the compiler. In C++, the result of a pointer cast can be a different address. When you call a `doSomething()` virtual method in C++, you are doing this kind of pointer cast on the vtable.

A vtable is the closest thing C++ gets to a class object, although it's not exposed at the language level. A vtable is simply an array of function pointers. Each virtual method in a class has an offset in the vtable and an entry. When you create a subclass in C++, you get a new vtable for each superclass. When you then cast the object to one of these superclasses (implicitly or explicitly), you get a structure containing a pointer to this vtable. Calling methods then calls the function at the specified offset.

This means that you can have two objects implementing virtual methods with the same name, but if they don't have a common superclass that declares that method as virtual, you can't call them both the same way.

In Objective-C, method lookups depend on just the class of the receiver and the message name. You can use two objects interchangeably if they implement the same methods, even if they do not share a common superclass. This eliminates a lot of the need for multiple inheritance.

While the semantic differences are the most important, the syntactic differences are the most obvious. C++ and Java borrow syntax from C structures for method calls. Objective-C, in contrast, uses Smalltalk syntax enclosed in square brackets. The following is an example of inserting an object into a Java `Dictionary` object and a Cocoa `NSMutableDictonary`:

```
// Java
aDict.put(a, b);
// Objective-C
[aDict setObject: b forKey: a];
```

The Java code is shorter, but a lot less readable. Without checking the documentation, or being familiar with the API in question, you wouldn't know that `a` is the key and `b` is the value. In contrast, you can't read the Objective-C code without being aware of this (as long as you can read English).

This is one of the things that makes Cocoa nicer to use than many competing frameworks. Because the language forces you to name every parameter, code using large APIs is much easier to read without having to become intimately familiar with every single class and method. It also makes it very easy to learn the API; you will never find yourself having to consult the documentation for the order of parameters if you can remember the method names. There's no reason that Java couldn't have used `putKeyValue()` or similar as the method name, but it didn't. Cocoa always does.

2.2.3 Objective-C 2.0

With 10.5, Apple released a new version of Objective-C, dubbed *Objective-C 2.0*. While versions with earlier versions of OS X had added a few new features, they had retained binary-compatibility with the older versions. You can take a framework from OS X 10.0 and still use it on any newer version. Objective-C 2, however, provided a clean break.

With OS X 10.5, there are two runtime libraries for Objective-C, described by Apple as the "modern" and "legacy" runtime libraries. 64-bit code, and code compiled for the iPhone, will use the modern library, while 32-bit code uses the legacy library. All versions of OS X prior to 10.5 use the legacy library and only support 32-bit Cocoa applications.

Although the modern runtime is often called the Objective-C 2.0 runtime, this is not entirely true. Almost all of the features of Objective-C 2.0 can be used with the legacy runtime on Leopard. Some, such as *fast enumeration*, do not require any support from the runtime, but are limited to being useful on 10.5 since they require support from objects that is only provided in newer versions of Foundation.

If you are writing 32-bit code, you can still use frameworks compiled on earlier versions of OS X with Objective-C 2, although you probably won't be able to use the biggest new feature: garbage collection. The addition of garbage collection in Objective-C 2 means that you don't have to worry about memory management at all. This is an obvious advantage, although it comes with certain costs. The most obvious one is portability, since code using the garbage collector can only run on OS X 10.5 or newer, not on older versions of OS X and currently not on other platforms. In particular, this includes (current versions of) the iPhone. If you think you might want to port your code to the iPhone in the future, do not use garbage collection.

The other features are generally useful. Properties allow you to define a standard interface for accessing data on objects, and fast enumeration allows you to quickly get at all of the objects in a collection. Calling Objective-C 2.0 a new version is a little misleading, since properties and fast enumeration are really just syntactic sugar and garbage collection is optional. The additions added in 10.3 for structured exception handling were, arguably, as significant a set of changes and did not warrant a new version number.

2.3 Ruby and Python

Ruby is increasingly used for Cocoa development. Ruby has a Smalltalk-like object model with Perl-like syntax. The object model means that it is a good fit for Cocoa, although the syntax is an acquired taste.

There are two versions of Ruby available for OS X. RubyCocoa uses the standard Ruby implementation and provides a bridge to Objective-C, allowing the use of Objective-C objects. MacRuby is a new implementation that compiles Ruby objects to use the same underlying object model as Objective-C.

Python can also be used, via the PyObjC bridge. This is similar to RubyCocoa, in that it uses the existing Python implementation and simply provides access to Cocoa objects via a bridge. The biggest issue when implementing this kind of bridge is that Objective-C, like Smalltalk, uses infix parameters. The most common convention is to replace the colons in Objective-C method names with underscores. This is used in the Python and JavaScript bridges.

Implementing a new bridge from a dynamic language is relatively easy. You can create a simple bridge using the `NSProxy` class to represent objects in your language on the Cocoa side and use the C foreign function call capability of your language to call the Objective-C runtime functions or send messages like `performSelector:`

from `NSObject`. Damien Pollet and I implemented a simple bridge from GNU Smalltalk in an afternoon using this mechanism.

2.4 Summary

There are a number of language options for programming on OS X, but the Cocoa frameworks are written with Objective-C in mind. If you want to get the full power and flexibility from Cocoa, then you should use Objective-C.

Bridges or interfaces to a number of other languages exist, however, and provide varying capabilities. If you are more familiar with one of these languages, or need to integrate with other code written in them, then you may prefer to use them.

The rest of this book will use Objective-C for examples; however, any language with a Cocoa bridge can be used to send the same messages and could be used to reimplement most of them. If you are thinking of using another language with Cocoa, then rewriting some of the examples from this book in your language of choice might be a good start.

Chapter 3

Using Apple's Developer Tools

Before they were bought by Apple, NeXT's business was almost entirely selling developer tools. Its hardware lines had been discontinued and their operating system was not widely used. Its developer tools, however, were very well regarded by the few who could afford them.

When OS X was first released, it contained *Project Builder* and *Interface Builder*, the two cornerstones of NeXT's development environment, in an almost unmodified form. Although Apple machines had a reputation for being very expensive, the most expensive Mac sold at the time cost around the same amount as NeXT had been charging for the Windows version of OpenStep and the accompanying developer tools.

Over the years, Apple has rewritten a lot of these. Interface Builder got a complete rewrite with 10.5 and prior to that Project Builder was evolved into *XCode*. In recent versions of XCode, Apple has started using the new LLVM C, Objective-C and C++ front end, *Clang*, not just for for compilation, but also for refactoring and static analysis, as well as syntax highlighting. One of the design goals for Clang is to be able to parse and perform semantic analysis on source code files fast enough to be run in the background periodically by a code editor and provide real-time diagnostic information and syntax highlighting.

Most code editors don't really do syntax highlighting; they do lexical highlighting. They tokenize the input file and color keywords and comments. A full syntax highlighter allows XCode to color class names differently from other types, and color variables differently depending on their scope, for example. A big advantage of this approach is that a full parser understands the C preprocessor, a feature that is currently very problematic for code editors.

3.1 Obtaining Apple's Developer Tools

The install DVD that came with your Mac is likely to contain an old version of the developer tools. Although this was current when the DVD was created, Apple releases new versions fairly often. Since the update mechanism for these tools involves downloading the complete new version and installing that, it is worth checking if you have a recent version before installing it.

The developer tools can be downloaded from the Apple developer site, at `http://developer.apple.com/mac/`. The package labeled XCode contains all of the required tools for OS X development. This may require you to sign up for a free *Apple Developer Connection* (*ADC*) account. This involves agreeing to some terms and conditions that you may or may not find acceptable. If you do not wish to do this, it is possible (although much harder) to build software for OS X using Free Software tools, which we will look at in Section 3.3.4.

3.2 Interface Builder

Interface Builder is probably the worst-named application on OS X. If Apple had followed this naming convention elsewhere, iTunes would have been called CD Ripper and OS X itself would have been named TextEdit Launcher.

While building interfaces is something that Interface Builder is able to do, and very good at, it is only a small subset of its functionality. GNUstep provides a less polished equivalent, the *Graphical Object Relationship Modeller* (*GORM*), which is a more accurate, if more cumbersome, name. GORM can be used for producing UIs for OS X on other platforms, although if you have access to OS X you will find Interface Builder much more user-friendly.

Interface Builder produces *nib files*. The original extension comes from NeXT Interface Builder. These are used in a lot of places in Cocoa. A nib contains a serialized object graph. These objects are often user interface objects, but not always. Even in a user interface nib, it is common to include instances of *controllers* in addition to *views*. Prior to OS X 10.5, Interface Builder used nib files internally. More recent versions use *xib files*, which use a simple XML format to represent the same information and are converted to nib files when the program is built.

The entire nib can be instantiated from within the program. This provides a very simple and convenient way of creating new copies of commonly used sets of objects. The most common use is in document-driven applications, where a nib

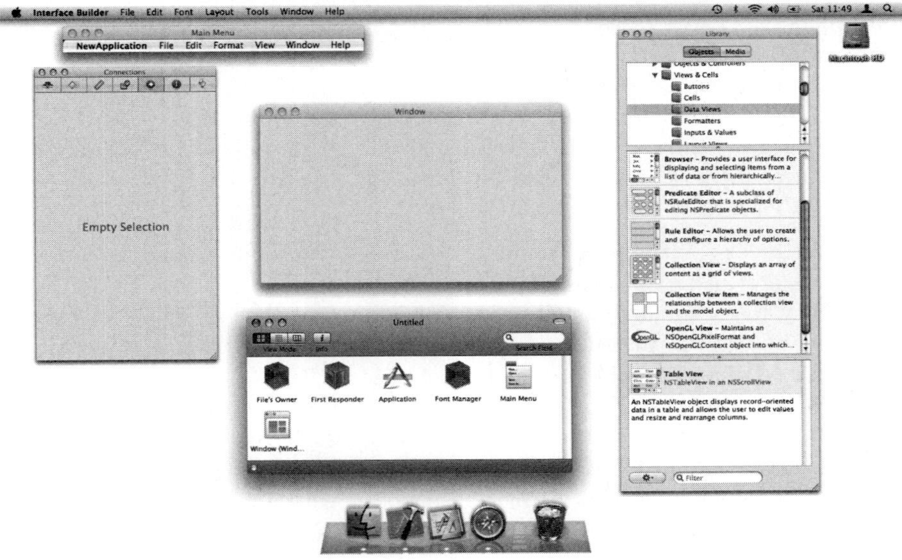

Figure 3.1: Interface Builder with a new application project.

will contain all of the objects required for a single instance of the document. It can then be created with a single line of code.

> **Model-View-Controller**
>
> The *model-view-controller* (*MVC*) pattern is used all over Cocoa. Views are objects that present a user interface and contain only a small amount of state. Models are objects that represent some abstract data, such as a document or a part of a document. Controllers are the glue used to join the two together. In recent versions of Cocoa, *bindings* make it possible to avoid the need for controllers in a lot of cases.
>
> Following the MVC model means that your application logic and user interface are completely separated. This makes porting an application to another platform much easier. Moving a well-designed Cocoa application to the iPhone, for example, is just a matter of writing a new UI optimized for the device's small screen; most of the code can be shared.

The `NSNib` class is the programmatic interface to nib files. Loading nibs with this class is a two-step process. Creating an instance of the class loads the file into memory ready for use but does not actually create the objects. Subsequent calls to the object will produce new copies of the objects stored in the nib. You can use this to quickly create a collection of objects.

Most of the time, you won't use `NSNib` directly. The application object will load the main nib for the application and instantiate all of the objects in it. The `NSWindowController` class provides an interface for loading nibs that represent windows. When you create an `NSWindowController` with a nib file, it will set itself as the owner of the nib and create a copy of all of the objects in the nib.

Every nib has a pseudo-object, shown in IB as the *file's owner*. This object is not part of the nib; it must be created outside of the nib and passed in to `NSNib` when creating the object graph. In the common use, where the nib contains a window, a set of views in the window, and a set of controllers for those views, the file's owner will be the `NSWindowController` subclass used as the controller object for the window.

3.2.1 Outlets and Actions

You can create any object in a nib, irrespective of whether it supports archiving. Objects are connected together by two kinds of interface: *outlets* and *actions*. Outlets are instance variables that are set to objects when a nib is loaded. Actions are methods that are sent when some action occurs.

There are two ways of a view notifying a controller of a change. The first is via an action; the second is via a *delegate*. Actions are fairly simple. They are implemented by `NSControl` and provide a simple mechanism for telling the controller that something has happened. When the view is created by the nib loading system, it will have two methods called on it: `-setTarget:` and `-setAction:`. The first of these tells it which object should be sent the action. The second tells it which method on the object it should call. These can be connected visually in Interface Builder. Figure 3.2 shows the inspector used to select which outlet or action to connect.

This mechanism is used to deliver button presses and other simple events. The action method receives the sender as its argument. This is fine for simple things like button presses, but it's not ideal for more complex views, where a number of different interactions are possible.

For these, a delegate is used. A delegate is a controller object that responds to a set of messages defined by the view. Because Objective-C allows late-binding and introspection easily, it is not always necessary to implement all of the methods defined for a delegate. Java programmers may be familiar with classes that implement some of the `Listener` family of interfaces and have a number of methods containing no code, just to satisfy the interface specification. In Cocoa, this never happens; the view will check which messages the delegate responds to and only send those ones.

Delegates are an example of an outlet. This is another feature made possible by the introspective capabilities of Objective-C. It is possible to introspect a class at runtime and find out what instance variables it has, and what their types and offsets are from the start of an object. This is exactly what happens when a nib is loaded. The offset of the named instance variable is checked and then the instance variable is set to the object in question. This is another example of *loose coupling.* You can recompile the object and change its in-memory layout without modifying the nib. As long as it still has an instance variable with the correct name and type, then the nib will continue to work.

This kind of loose coupling is found all over Cocoa. It has two advantages. First, it means that changes to one part of a program rarely require recompiling other parts, allowing for a very fast write-compile-test cycle. This is less relevant now than it was on a 25MHz system, but still important for large projects. The other advantage is that it means that Cocoa code is very likely to be generic and reusable, which cuts down development time a lot.

3.2.2 Cocoa Bindings

OS X 10.3 introduced two related mechanisms. The first was *key-value coding* (*KVC*). This is a fairly simple mechanism providing a unified interface to accessing

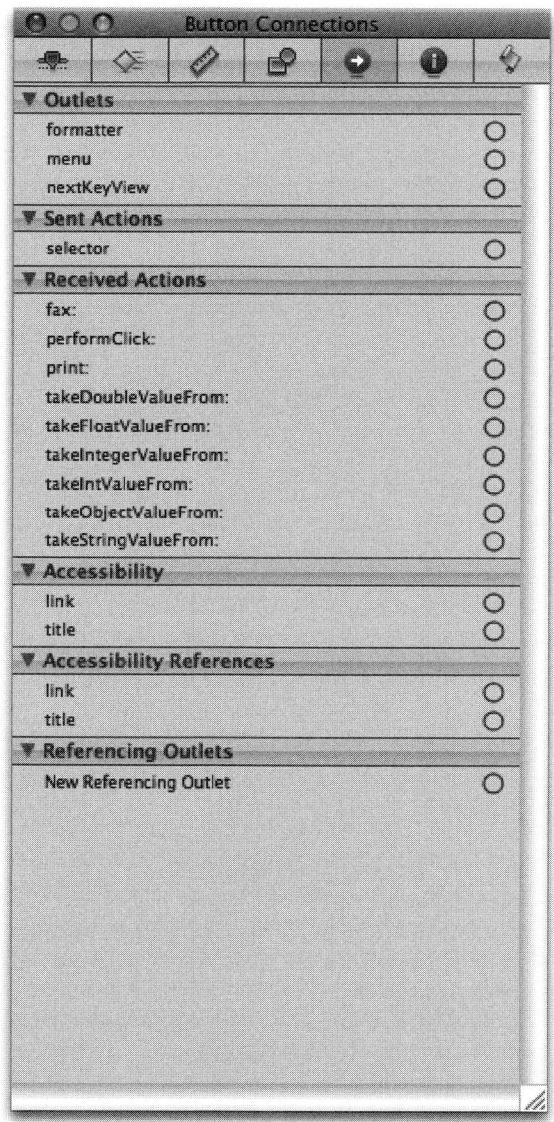

Figure 3.2: The outlet and action inspector in Interface Builder.

properties of an object. It provides two methods: one for setting values and another for getting them. Under the hood, it provides mechanisms for directly accessing instance variables, calling set and get methods, and calling a fall-back mechanism.

While KVC is a convenient abstraction mechanism, the real magic is made possible by *key-value observing* (*KVO*). This allows other objects to request to be notified when the value associated with a specific key is changed. These two mechanisms are supported by a lot of Cocoa classes, and the `NSObject` root class implements the skeleton mechanisms required to easily support them in your own classes.

The combination of KVC, KVO, and a little bit of Interface Builder, is referred to as *Cocoa bindings*. Bindings use a combination of KVC to set a property in one object whenever a property in another object changes. This mechanism makes it possible to eliminate the need for a lot of controller objects. If a model object supports KVO and a view supports KVC, then the view can automatically be updated when the model changes. Similarly, if the model supports KVC and the view supports KVO, then the model can be updated transparently when the view changes. When the Delicious Library application was updated to use bindings, the authors deleted around a thousand lines of code in a single day and got more functionality and some bug fixes for free by reusing the generic bindings code in place of their custom controller objects.

The generic nature of bindings does come with a cost. They are significantly slower than direct message sending operations and require a bit of extra space. For user interface code, however, they are very unlikely to be the bottleneck. Drawing a simple text string on a window is much slower than the operations performed by bindings.

Instruction Cache Performance

One of the reasons why it is very difficult to write fair benchmarks these days is that performance of code is now highly dependent on cache usage. Accesses to memory are incredibly slow compared to accesses to registers or cache, taking hundreds of cycles to complete. Generic code that is slow in microbenchmarks can end up being faster in real usage. If the generic code is used in a lot of places, then it is likely to stay in the CPU's instruction cache and so may run to completion while the CPU would still have been waiting for the highly optimized code to load from memory. Remember this when you think about writing hand-optimized specialized routines; you may end up making your program use more memory and run more slowly, which is probably not a good use of your time.

3.2.3 Drawing a Simple Application

The loose coupling in Objective-C makes it possible to create simple behaviors, and some quite complex ones, without needing to write any code. When you start Interface Builder, you are confronted with an empty window and a palette. You can draw views onto the window by simply dragging them from the palette and resizing them.

Figure 3.3 shows a selection of views. The button in the bottom-right part of this panel allows you to alter how the views are listed. While you are learning Cocoa, you may find the mode that shows both icons and descriptions more convenient, since this allows you to quickly read all of the descriptions. After you are familiar with the available objects, switching to the icon-only view makes finding the correct one faster.

For this simple example, drag a text field and a horizontal slider to the window.

With these two views embedded in the window, you can now try joining them together. Hold down the Control key and drag the mouse from one to the other. When you release the button, a list of outlets and actions should appear in a pop-up translucent window, as shown in Figure 3.4. Select the `takeIntegerValueFrom:` action from the list of received actions and then do the same thing in the other direction.

Now, whenever the value in one of the views changes, it will send a `takeIntegerValueFrom:` message to the other. Because this is an action message, it takes the sender as the argument. The receiver will send an `integerValue` message to the sender and set its value to be equal to whatever is returned.

Neither object needs to know anything about the other. The action message is not hard-coded into either; it is set when the nib is loaded. Neither knows anything about how the other represents its data internally. The slider stores its position as a floating point value and the text field as a string, but since both implement an `integerValue` method, they can both be interrogated by the other to determine an integer version of their value.

You can test the UI from inside Interface Builder by pressing Command-R. This should show a window like the one in Figure 3.5. When you move the slider, the number in the text box will change. When you enter a number in the text box, the slider position will change.

This shows two things. Firstly, it demonstrates that it is often possible to get away without righting code in Cocoa. This is good because any new code is likely to contain bugs, while old code is likely to have been more thoroughly tested, especially if the old code is from the Cocoa frameworks and used all over OS X.

The second point is that this is a real set of objects. When the nib is loaded, real Cocoa view objects are created and connected together. Although no new code was written here, the objects created are instances of Cocoa classes. Their connections

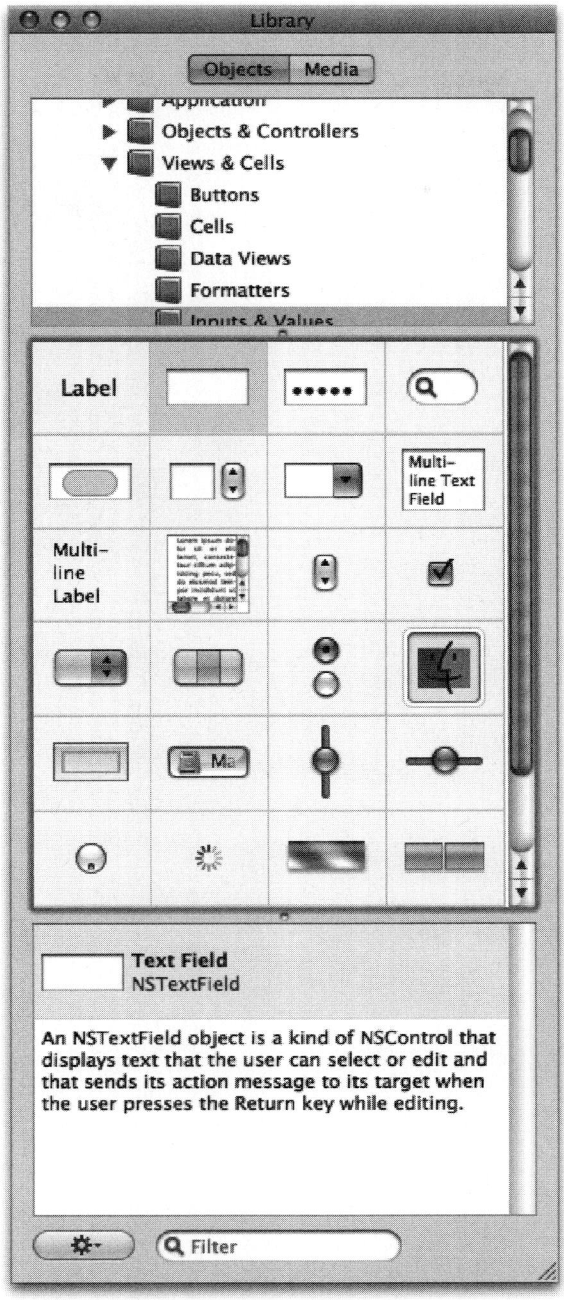

Figure 3.3: Views palette in Interface Builder.

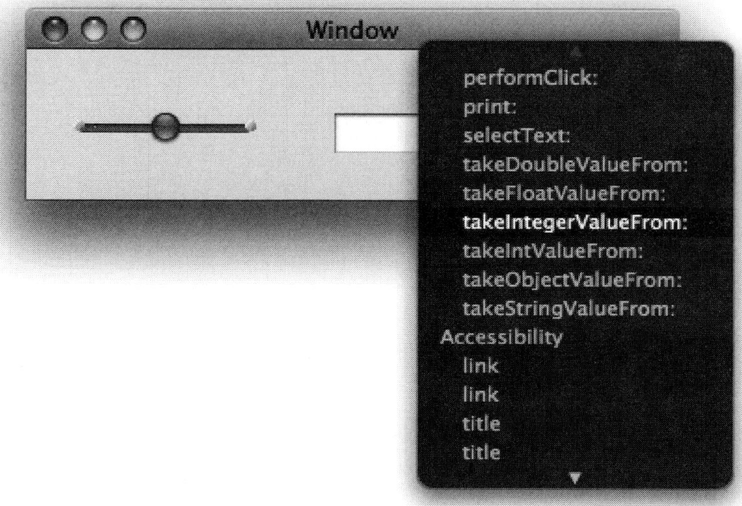

Figure 3.4: Connecting an action.

Figure 3.5: Running a simple UI.

are handled via Objective-C, not via any scripting language layered on top. This also highlights the strength of Objective-C for promoting code reuse. Neither of the two classes that are communicating has any special code for interacting with the other. You could easily replace either with your own view object and use the same mechanisms.

3.3 XCode

OS X 10.3 included a large number of improvements to the development environment. These included extensions to the Objective-C language, large changes to the Cocoa objects, and new developer tools. In particular, Project Builder was replaced by the XCode IDE.

XCode provides a build system, a code editor, and a debugger. Interface Builder remains a separate application, although the two interact quite closely. The debugging facilities are built on top of the *GNU debugger* (*GDB*). This is a command-line application, which XCode talks to via a pipe. You can send commands directly to it, which is sometimes useful since XCode doesn't expose all of its capabilities via the GUI. Spending some time reading the GDB manual can save you a lot of effort later on.

3.3.1 Creating a Simple Project

When you create a new project, you will be greeted by the window shown in Figure 3.6. This provides a large collection of template projects. For most cases, you will want to select a Cooca Application or a Cocoa Document-based Application. This will ask you for a location to save the files and then produce a skeleton project in this directory.

The skeleton project contains a small number of files that are needed by every project. It will contain a MainMenu.xib, which contains the main menu and window for the application and will be compiled to MainMenu.nib when you build the program. You can customize this in Interface Builder.

The only source file created by a Cocoa Application is the main.m file, which provides the application entry point. You will rarely modify this. Instead, you will create additional classes and connect them up to your application object via your main nib file. Creating a new file presents you with the options shown in Figure 3.7.

If you create a new Objective-C file, you will have the option of having an accompanying header file created as well. Most often, this is what you want. Cocoa will put a skeleton implementation in the .m file and a skeleton interface in the .h file.

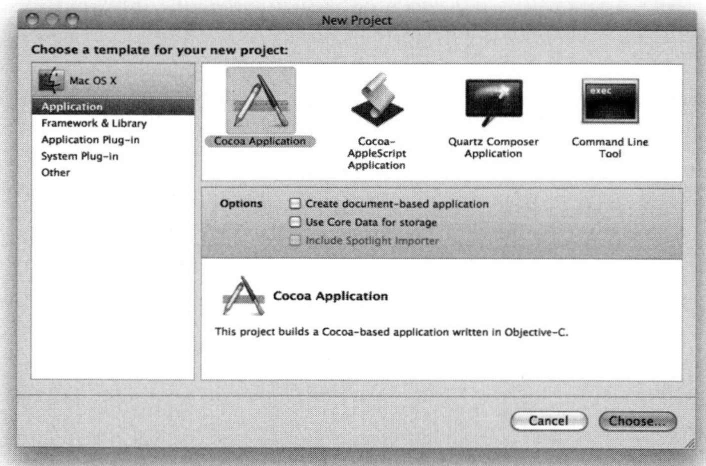

Figure 3.6: Creating a new project with XCode.

The main window of XCode is shown in Figure 3.8. This has three panes. The one on the left shows all of the things in the current project. Not all of these are source files. An application can have different *targets*, which correspond to sets of rules for building *products*, which are typically applications or frameworks. You can also create smart groups here, which are sets of files in the project matching certain user-defined criteria. When you select a group in the left pane, the contents will appear in the top-right pane.

You can use XCode in two ways, either with a single editor for the project or with one for each file. If you double-click on a file, it will be opened in a new editor. Single-clicking on it will cause it to be opened in the attached editor. This also applies in other windows provided by XCode, such as the debugger and build windows.

If you are not using the attached editor pane, then you can collapse it, giving more space for the other panes. There is one very convenient set of keyboard shortcuts that is worth memorizing when you are using the Cocoa code editor. If you hold down the Command and Option keys, then you press an arrow key, you will get a different file. The up arrow key toggles between interface and implementation files of the same name. If you are editing `MyObject.m` and press Command-Option-up, then you will switch to `MyObject.h`. Each file has a separate

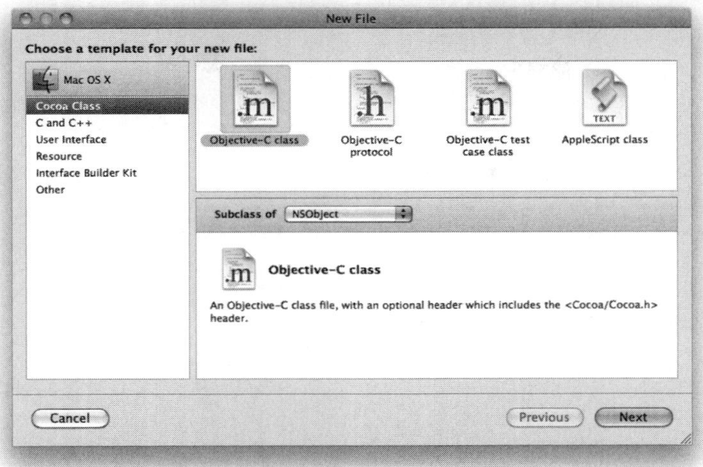

Figure 3.7: Creating a new file in XCode.

undo buffer, so doing this does not lose the ability to undo changes in another file. The text editor also maintains a history of all of the files that you have edited in it. The left and right arrows, when Command and Option are held down, allow you to quickly skip forward and backward in this history.

3.3.2 OpenStep Bundles

One of the defining features of Classic MacOS was the idea of *forks* in the filesystem. From the start, the HFS filesystem supported two forks for every file: a data fork and a resource fork. The data fork contained the usual stream of bytes that files on other systems would contain, while the resource fork contained a structured set of resources. Common uses for this included storing icons and other resources.

Forks were a very nice model from the point of view of the user, since they meant that applications (and other types of document) were single files, even though they may have contained a lot of other components. You could drag them to another disk and not worry about having left some parts behind.

NeXT considered this model but abandoned it because it was too dependent on special support in the filesystem. If you copied an application to a DOS disk, or shared it over NFS, then the resource fork would be lost. Instead, they used

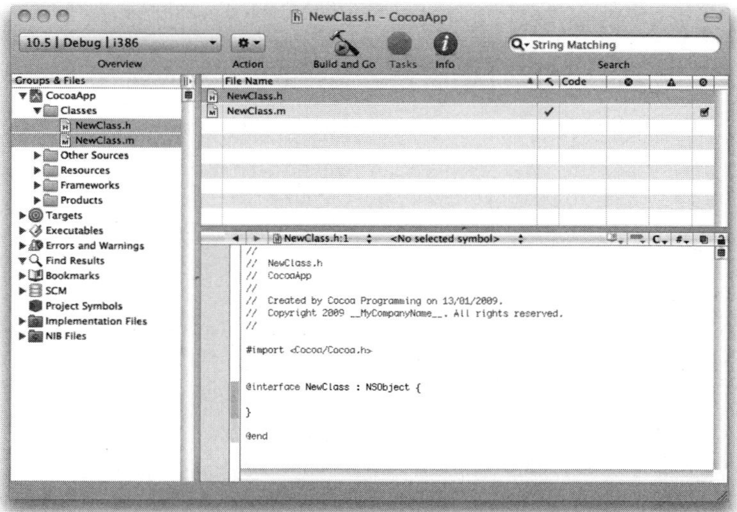

Figure 3.8: The XCode main window.

bundles. A bundle is, from the filesystem's perspective, just a directory. If you copy or modify them on a system that doesn't know about bundles, then nothing will be lost.

HFS+ does have some special support for bundles, however. One bit in the metadata is used to indicate whether a directory is a bundle or not. You can see the HFS+ flags using the GetFileInfo tool:

```
$ GetFileInfo example.key/
directory: "/Users/CocoaProgramming/example.key"
attributes: avBstclinmEdz
```

This shows the attributes for a keynote bundle. The lowercase letters represent flags that are not set; the uppercase ones represent flags that are set. For this bundle, the B and E flags are set, meaning that this directory is a bundle and the extension (.key) should be hidden in the Finder. You will note that these are not set on applications:

```
$ GetFileInfo TextEdit.app/
directory: "/Applications/TextEdit.app"
attributes: avbstclinmedz
```

This is because OS X is designed to work on other filesystems, so all of the standard bundle formats, like .app, have special logic in the Finder for handling them. If a directory has one of the known bundle extensions or has the correct flag set, the Finder will show it as a file and try to open it with the workspace functions rather than showing the contents when it is double clicked.

Bundles are used all over OS X, and if you are creating a document-driven application, then you may want to define your own bundle type.

As a developer, one of the most common bundles you will encounter are *frameworks*. These are bundles containing a library and the header files required to use it. They can also contain resources, such as sounds and images, that can be accessed from the code using `NSBundle`.

3.3.3 Developer Examples

When you install the XCode developer tools, you will find that the Developer/Examples directory is populated with a lot of examples. These are all very permissively licensed; you can do whatever you want with them, including incorporating them in proprietary or open source software, as long as you don't distribute modified versions as Apple sample code.

Each of the directories in this folder contains examples relating to a particular part of the OS X. Some of the most important ones are in the AppKit folder. This contains examples relating to the Cocoa application kit framework, which is at the core of almost every Cocoa application.

You will also find examples for using different languages on OS X. The Java, Perl, Python, and Ruby directories all contain examples for using these languages on OS X. More are found in the wxWidgets folder, which contains Perl and Python examples using the cross-platform wxWidgets framework for developing applications on OS X.

Some of the examples here are very low level; for example, the IOKit directory contains examples related to writing device drivers on OS X. Others relate to specific frameworks, such as WebKit, the HTML-rendering framework developed for Safari and used in a number of places in OS X.

It is worth spending a little while playing with the examples in this directory. Just compiling and running them will give an overview of what you can do with OS X. Note that the permissions on the examples are set such that you can only compile them if you are an administrator, since you need to write files into the Build directory. If you are running as a normal user, copy them somewhere else before building them.

3.3.4 Building Without XCode

Project Builder on NeXT platforms and early versions of XCode used the *GNU Compiler Collection* (*GCC*) for compiling.[1] The version included with OS X is not quite the same version that the Free Software Foundation releases, although it is developed in a branch in the Foundation's version control system. The two are often referred to as Apple GCC and GNU GCC to differentiate them. Some features appeared in one version before the other, so testing for compiler features using the version macros can cause problems when moving code between the two.

Starting with XCode 3, Apple also included a new compiler, *LLVM GCC*. This uses a modified version of GCC for parsing and the *Low-Level Virtual Machine* for code generation. This was the only compiler supported for iPhone development in the initial SDK. GCC is not really designed for separating out and using in this way, so Apple is also working on a new front end, *Clang*, which will parse C, Objective-C, and C++ code. This switch is due partly to technical and partly to legal reasons. As of 4.3, GNU GCC is released under version 3 of the *GNU General Public License* (*GPL*). Apple is not distributing any code released under this license, and so its branch of GCC can no longer incorporate changes from the mainline version.

Both of these compilers can be used from the command line. If you come from other UNIX platforms, you will probably be familiar with GCC and its various command-line options. OS X adds one more: -framework. This specifies a framework to link the application against. Since frameworks can include both headers and libraries, this works as a combination of both -I, -L, and -l.

Although you can build applications on OS X using make, this is not easy to integrate with XCode.[2] It is possible to build XCode projects from the command line with the xcodebuild utility. This utility is also used by XCode when it builds your projects; the output from xcodebuild is what you see in the build window if you opt to view details.

Unlike make, xcodebuild differentiates between targets and actions. A target is a set of build products, while an action is something that is done with a target. The three most commonly used actions are build, install, and clean. These create the target, install it, and delete intermediate results, respectively.

You can run xcodebuild from a folder containing a single XCode file with no options:

```
$ xcodebuild
=== BUILDING NATIVE TARGET Presenter OF PROJECT Presenter WITH THE
```

[1] Unlike Linux and BSD systems, OS X includes its own linker and does not use GNU ld.

[2] If you wish to build applications on OS X with make, GNUstep Make has predefined rules for doing this relatively easily.

```
DEFAULT CONFIGURATION (Release) ===

Checking Dependencies...

{lots of output}

** BUILD SUCCEEDED **
```

This will build the project in the default configuration, as set in XCode. There are lots of other command-line options for this tool, which are all documented in the `man` page. If you want to automate a nightly build, then you should consider using it, but for most people clicking on the build button in XCode is more convenient.

3.4 Objective-C

Objective-C is a pure superset of C designed to allow Smalltalk-like object-oriented programming and to promote code reuse. There are a few core principles that are reflected by the language:

Compatibilty. Everything valid in C is valid in Objective-C. This makes it very easy to reuse existing code. You don't need `extern "C"` declarations, just call or embed the C code directly. All of the new keywords are prefixed with an at (@) sign, so they don't conflict with existing identifiers.

No magic. The Objective-C compiler is quite simple and just replaces calls to the runtime library. All of the mechanisms are exposed to the programmer, and anything the compiler can do you can do in your own code. Nothing goes in the language that can be done in the library.

No unnecessary complexity. Objective-C is meant to be easy to learn and easy to use. Unlike C++, the language is tiny and can be learned by a C programmer in an afternoon.

New semantics mean new syntax. Objective-C does not overload existing syntax with new meanings. If new functionality is added that is not present in C, it gets new keywords or other new syntactic elements.

One effect of the "no magic" rule is that introspection is available all through the language. Almost everything the compiler knows, the programmer can find out. You can enumerate the methods and instance variables of a class and even create new classes at run time if you need to.

3.4.1 Why Learn Objective-C?

Objective-C is a set of Smalltalk-like object-oriented extensions to C. The language is very simple, with only one major syntactic addition (message sending) and a handful of new keywords. Contrary to popular belief, using Objective-C does not lock you in to using Apple platforms. Apple shipped two Objective-C compilers, gcc and llvm-gcc, with OS X 10.5. Both of these are open source, although llvm-gcc only compiles Objective-C on OS X. A third compiler, clang, was introduced with XCode 3.2, which ships with OS X 10.6. Clang is currently the only compiler that can compile programs that use newer Objective-C features on non-Apple platforms.

Objective-C was created to provide the flexibility of Smalltalk to C programmers on cheap computers. Brad Cox, the language's creator, wrote a number of papers on component-based software in the early 1980s, and Objective-C was designed to encourage the development of independent components.

The potential of the language was seen early on by Steve Jobs after leaving Apple. His goal at NeXT was to produce the closest approximation of the perfect computer possible with the current technology, and a dynamic, modular system was a major part of this goal. NeXT, with later collaboration from Sun, produced the APIs that are now known as Cocoa. They are implemented by Apple on OS X and by other projects, such as GNUstep and Cocotron, on other platforms.

Although Objective-C is not the only language you can use with Cocoa, it is the one that Cocoa was designed for. Most other languages are implemented via bridges, or use some mappings that are less than perfect. Objective-C is also the only language supported on all of the platforms where the Cocoa APIs are implemented.

3.4.2 Additions to C

As a pure superset of C, Objective-C can be defined by its changes from C. The most common parts will look familiar to anyone who has seen Smalltalk code, but a few are unique to Objective-C and help integrate the Smalltalk object model with C syntax.

This chapter will give an overview of Objective-C and an introduction to most of its features.

Not all of the additions provided by Objective-C are to the C language itself. In particular, one is to the preprocessor. The `#import` directive is a version of `#include` that ensures that the header is only imported once into the compilation unit. This means that Objective-C headers do not need to be protected by `#ifdef` blocks; they will always only be included once.

The simplest things Objective-C adds are some new types. These are imple-

> ## Which C?
>
> There are three main dialects of C in use. The original, pre-standardization C, often called *K&R C* after its creators is now mainly used in legacy code and should be avoided for new projects. There are two standard dialects of C, named *C89* and *C99* after the year in which they were standardized. A new version, *C1X*, is due to become a standard soon.
>
> Objective-C is a superset of C, but exactly which dialect of C is up to you. XCode allows you to pick the one you want, although there is very little reason not to pick C99.

mented as **typedef**s in a header, and so don't really count as additions to the language, but are important. The **id** type is used to represent a pointer to an object. You can also use an explicit type, like `NSObject*` to specify a pointer to an object of a specific type.

This includes some additional casting rules. The **id** type is roughly equivalent to the **void*** type in C, with the extra condition that the pointee must be an object. You can implicitly cast an **id** to or from any other object type. Additionally, you can implicitly cast an object pointer to a pointer to any of its superclasses. Any other casts between object pointers require an explicit cast, just as in C.

The other two types added to C are **Class**, representing a pointer to a class structure, and **SEL** representing *selectors*. A selector is an abstract form of a message name. When you send a message in Objective-C, the lookup is performed based on the selector. You can generate selectors at compile time using the `@selector()` directive, like this:

```
SEL newsel = @selector(new);
```

This gives the selector for the message named "new." You can also look up selectors from strings at run time using the `NSStringFromSelector()` function.

Message Sending

The most important part of Objective-C is message sending. All interactions between Objective-C objects happens via message sending. By default, messages are delivered synchronously, just like function calls, although there are some advanced cases where you can allow them to happen asynchronously.

A message send is a higher-level version of a function call. Unlike a function call, messages are late-bound. This means that the code run in response to a given message (the *method*) is not defined until the message is sent. This is in contrast to calling a C function, where the code to run is defined at load time or compile time.

Methods and Messages

Often the phrases "send a message" and "call a method" are used interchangeably when talking about Objective-C code. In most cases they are roughly equivalent. Sending a message will result in the method of the same name being called. This is not always the case, however; in some cases sending a message will result in that message being saved or sent across the network, or a method in an entirely different object being called.

Because message sending is semantically different to calling functions, it gains new syntax. At first glance, this makes Objective-C seem more "foreign" than C++, but in the long run it makes the code easier to read. Consider the following C++ line:

```
object.doSomething();
```

This has three possible meanings:

1. If `object` is a C structure, then this is a call to the function identified by the function pointer in the `doSomething` field.

2. If `object` is a C++ object and `doSomething` is not declared virtual, then this is a call to the `doSomething()` method in whichever class the caller thinks `object` belongs to, with a hidden `this` parameter set to a pointer to `object`.

3. If `object` is a C++ object and `doSomething` is declared virtual, then this is a call to the `doSomething()` method, dynamically looked up from the class of `object`, with a hidden `this` parameter set to a pointer to `object`.

Deciding which of these is really the case requires reading a lot of code. Even worse, if the `object.` prefix was not there then it could be either of the last two called on the current object, or a C function. Objective-C has no equivalent of non-virtual methods in C++, since these are semantically equivalent to C functions. There is no difference between how these two lines are implemented in C++ (if `doSomething()` is non-virtual):

```
doSomething(object);
object.doSomething();
```

The second can be thought of as syntactic sugar on the first, but since it is one more character to type (two if `object` is a pointer) it is more accurately considered syntactic salt. Objective-C uses Smalltalk-like syntax for message sends. The equivalent would be

```
[object doSomething];
```

Messages that take parameters have them interspersed with the message name, like this:

```
[dict setObject: anObject forKey: aKey];
[dict removeObjectForKey: aKey];
```

The square brackets are a deviation from Smalltalk syntax. They make it easier for the compiler to spot the boundary between pure-C and Smalltalk-like syntax. They also explicitly group messages together, so you can easily tell that both `setObject:` and `forKey:` are part of the same message.

The square bracket syntax was strongly advocated by Tom Love, one of the original designers of Objective-C. He described the notation as "a gear shift into the object land," meaning that everything outside of it was C and everything inside was Smalltalk-like. This makes Objective-C much clearer to read than a language like C++; you can clearly spot the difference between a message send and a function call in Objective-C, but in C++ you need to know the code and libraries well to differentiate between a function call and a method invocation.

Message sends have three components: the *receiver*, *selector*, and (optionally) *arguments*. The receiver is the object that receives the message, in this example `dict`. The selector is a unique version of the method name. Objective-C adds a new keyword, **`@selector`**, for getting a selector from a string at compile time. You can also use the `NSSelectorFromString()` function to look one up from a string constructed at run time.

There is one special case for sending messages. If you send a message to `nil` (or some other zero pointer), the result will be `nil`, zero, or a structure filled with zeroes, depending on what the caller expects.

Classes

The two major additions to C by Objective-C are classes and message sending. In Objective-C, an object is a structure whose first element is a pointer to a class. Prior to 10.5, the class structure was public. As you can see in Listing 3.1, it is still visible in 10.5 if you are compiling with Objective-C 1, but not with Objective-C 2.

With Objective-C 2, the class structure became an opaque type. You can still manipulate it, but now you have to go via runtime library functions. This makes it possible for Apple to add new fields to classes in the future, without breaking the ABI.

Although this structure is liable to change in the future, it gives a good overview of the kind of data that is stored for a class. Three of these end with

Listing 3.1: The Objective-C class structure. [from: /usr/include/objc/runtime.h]

```
struct objc_class {
    Class isa;

#if !__OBJC2__
    Class super_class OBJC2_UNAVAILABLE;
    const char *name OBJC2_UNAVAILABLE;
    long version OBJC2_UNAVAILABLE;
    long info OBJC2_UNAVAILABLE;
    long instance_size OBJC2_UNAVAILABLE;
    struct objc_ivar_list *ivars OBJC2_UNAVAILABLE;
    struct objc_method_list **methodLists OBJC2_UNAVAILABLE;
    struct objc_cache *cache OBJC2_UNAVAILABLE;
    struct objc_protocol_list *protocols OBJC2_UNAVAILABLE;
#endif

} OBJC2_UNAVAILABLE;
```

`_list` as a suffix. These are lists of the three types of attribute of a class: *methods*, *protocols*, and *instance variables* (*ivars*).

The `isa` pointer points to a *metaclass*. Just as objects have a class defining messages that can be sent to them, classes have metaclasses defining messages that they understand. Objective-C classes are objects, and so you can send them messages just as you would an object. The `isa` pointer should not be confused with the `super_class` pointer. This defines the class that this class inherits from. If you send a message to an object, first methods in its class, then methods in its superclass, and so on, will be looked up. The metaclass is only involved when sending messages to the class, not to instances of it.

The other fields are mostly metadata. The most important is the `instance_size` field, which defines how big an instance of the class is. When you instantiate a class, this field is used to allocate enough space for it.

Creating these structures directly was possible before Leopard and can be done on 10.5 via the `objc_allocateClassPair()` function, but this is not terribly convenient. Most of the time you will use Objective-C syntax for defining them and have the compiler, or the runtime library, construct these structures for you.

This is done in two phases. The first is to describe an interface to the object. This typically lives in a header file but might go in an implementation file for objects that do not need to publish their interfaces. Listing 3.2 shows an interface to a simple class.

The interface is bracketed by **`@interface`** and **`@end`** keywords. The first line

Listing 3.2: An Objective-C interface. [from: examples/SimpleObject/simpleObject.m]

```
3 @interface SimpleObject : NSObject {
4     int counter;
5 }
6 - (void) addToCounter:(int) anInteger;
7 - (int) counter;
8 @end
```

gives the name of the class (`SimpleObject`) and its superclass (`NSObject`). Recall that Objective-C does not support multiple inheritance and so there is only ever one superclass. Specifying `NSObject` as the superclass is redundant on OS X, since this class will be used if no superclass is specified, but it is good style.

The block following this contains the list of instance variables defined in this class. Every instance of this class will be a structure containing all of the instance variables defined in this class, and each of its superclasses, as fields. It's worth noting that the pointer to the class (the `isa` pointer) is not in any way special; it is simply an instance variable defined by `NSObject`.

The remaining lines, 6 and 7, are method declarations. The - prefix is because they are *instance methods*, as opposed to *class methods*, which would be prefixed with a + symbol. An instance method is one that is attached to the class, while a class method is attached to the metaclass. This means that instances of the class will respond to instance methods, and the class itself will respond to class methods.

The next step in defining a class is to define the implementation. Listing 3.3 shows the corresponding implementation. Each of the methods declared in the interface must be declared in the implementation, but methods not declared may also be defined.

Objective-C does not enforce run-time private methods; however, attempts to call a method not defined in a class's interface will result in a compile-time warning.

One thing to note is that the counter is never initialized. This is because every instance variable in an Objective-C object is initialized to 0 automatically when the object is created. If this is a sensible initial value for an instance variable, you do not need to explicitly set it.

Listing 3.3: An Objective-C class implementation. [from: examples/SimpleObject/simpleObject.m]

```
@implementation SimpleObject
- (void) addToCounter:(int) anInteger
{
    counter += anInteger;
}
- (int) counter
{
    return counter;
}
@end
```

Protocols

The Java object model was closely modeled after Objective-C, and Java interfaces are very similar to Objective-C protocols. One difference is that, unlike interfaces, protocols are objects, specifically instances of the `Protocol` class.

A protocol is a list of messages that must be implemented by a class that conforms to the protocol must understand. Listing 3.4 contains a modified version of the interface from Listing 3.2 where the methods are now declared in a protocol, which is adopted by the class. Protocols that a class conforms to are listed in angle brackets, separated by commas, after the superclass.

Listing 3.4: An Objective-C interface using a protocol. [from: examples/SimpleObject/simpleObject2.m]

```
@protocol SimpleObject
- (void) addToCounter:(int) anInteger;
- (int) counter;
@end

@interface SimpleObject : NSObject <SimpleObject> {
    int counter;
}
@end
```

You can test for protocol conformance at run time by sending a `-conformsToProtocol:` message to the object, like this:

```
[obj conformsToProtocol:@protocol(SimpleObject)];
```

This presents a small implementation problem. The compiler doesn't need to be able to see the definition of the `SimpleObject` protocol at this point. The protocol might not even be linked in to the current compilation unit. The solution was to just create a new `Protocol` object with the name set to "SimpleObject" if the protocol definition is not available at compile time.

Two protocols are considered identical at run time if they have the same name. The methods they list are not tested. Care must be taken to ensure that a program does not contain two protocols with the same name and different definitions.

Categories

One of the most interesting features of Objective-C is the idea of *categories*. A category is a group of methods. Like a class, it can contain both an interface and an implementation. Unlike a class, a category is just a collection of methods, not of instance variables, and is attached to an existing class.

Categories provide a mechanism for extending a class where you don't have access to the source code. They also provide a way of splitting an object up into conceptually different parts. Since Objective-C classes must have all of their methods between an **`@implementation`**...**`@end`** block, they can only be split between files using the preprocessor.

Categories provide an alternative to this. Core methods can be implemented in the class and others can be defined in categories. Listing 3.5 shows a trivial example of this.

This implementation of `SimpleObject` is equivalent to the two we have seen already. In this version, the `-counter` method is both declared (lines 8–10) and defined (lines 18–23) in a category. The name of the category, given in both the declaration and definition, is mainly for documentation. Both the interface and implementation are optional for categories.

A category interface with no corresponding implementation can be used to expose "private" methods in an object.

Informal Protocols

Categories are sometimes used to define *informal protocols* by adding empty implementations of all of the methods to `NSObject`. This allows the messages to be sent to any object without first testing for conformance. Adding methods to `NSObject` should be avoided where possible, since it can slow down method lookups on all objects and can cause problems if two different libraries both try to add the same method.

Listing 3.5: An Objective-C class split into two parts. [from: examples/SimpleObject/simpleObject3.m]

```
@interface SimpleObject : NSObject {
    int counter;
}
- (void) addToCounter:(int) anInteger;
@end
@interface SimpleObject (GetMethod)
- (int) counter;
@end

@implementation SimpleObject
- (void) addToCounter:(int) anInteger
{
    counter += anInteger;
}
@end
@implementation SimpleObject (GetMethod)
- (int) counter
{
    return counter;
}
@end
```

3.4.3 Exceptions and Synchronization

Starting with 10.3, Apple introduced a small number of Java-like additions to the Objective-C language. In keeping with the idea that nothing should be done in the language that can be done in the library, Objective-C did not include any exception handling primitives.

Exception handling in OpenStep is accomplished by a set of macros and the `NSException` class. The macros allow blocks like this:

```
NS_DURING
    // Code throwing an exception.
    NS_VALUERETURN(YES, BOOL);
NS_HANDLER
    return NO;
NS_ENDHANDLER
```

These macros are implemented by a complex combination of **goto**s and setjmp()/longjmp() calls. The setjmp() function saves the current register set and the longjmp() call restores it.

This approach had two major disadvantages. The first is that setjmp() had no way of calling cleanup code in intervening stack frames. This means that any stack frame between where the exception is thrown and where it is caught must be aware of the possibility of exception throwing and ensure that it is in a state where it can return abruptly before every call. The second problem is speed.

Exceptions, by their very nature, should only happen in exceptional circumstances. An ideal exception mechanism costs nothing unless an exception is really thrown. This implementation is the exact opposite; throwing an exception is quite cheap, but the setjmp() call at every NS_DURING macro is very expensive.

There are also some minor problems. Only NSException instances could be thrown and were identified by localException in the handler block. Additionally, you cannot use a **return** statement in an exception block, or it will not be removed from the exception handler stack and will cause problems later. The NS_VALUERETURN and NS_VOIDRETURN macros must be used instead.

With 10.3, Apple introduced three new keywords for exception handling: **@try**, **@catch**, and **@finally**. These behave exactly as their Java counterparts. Exception blocks now look like this:

```
@try {
    // Something that might throw an exception
} @catch(NSException *e) {
    // Handle the exception
} @finally {
    // Clean up
}
```

The old exception-handling macros were re-implemented in terms of these keywords, as shown in Listing 3.6. The addition of the **@finally**() block made it easier for cleanup code to be run, and the ability to specify multiple **@catch**() blocks made it possible to throw different types of object.

Listing 3.6: Exception macros from 10.6. [from: NSException.h]

```

#define NS_DURING        @try {
#define NS_HANDLER       } @catch (NSException *localException) {
#define NS_ENDHANDLER      }
#define NS_VALUERETURN(v,t) return (v)
```

The big problem, the cost of **@try** blocks, was not solved. These were still compiled down to setjmp()/longjmp() calls, for compatibility with older code. With 10.5, however, Apple had the opportunity to break the ABI without anyone complaining. When you compile 64-bit code, or code targeting the Objective-C 2 runtime, you are using a new exception model.

This is based on the Itanium 'zero-cost' exception handling system. Functions in a simple executable are just streams of instructions. If you compile with debugging support, there will also be some DWARF data describing the layout of data in these functions, allowing the debugger to access variables by name, and get the current line in the source file. The zero-cost exception system extends this debugging information by providing the address and some type information of a `@catch()` statement for every call in a `@try` block.

When you throw an exception, the unwinding library moves up the stack, calling a *personality function* for each frame. One of these is provided for every language that supports unwinding. This includes C, although the C version just progresses to the next frame. The personality function reads the debugging data for the stack frame and checks whether it has any cleanup code that needs to run, or whether it knows how to handle the exception.

As you might imagine, this is quite an expensive operation. A personality function needs to be called for each stack frame, and it needs to call additional functions to parse the DWARF data. The big advantage is that this only needs to happen when an exception is thrown. When no exception is thrown, none of this code runs. The unwinding information is statically emitted, so it increases the size of the executable slightly, but a `@try` block costs nothing in terms of execution speed.

If your code throws enough exceptions to be slower in the new model, then the code was probably wrong to start with.

The other nice benefit of this model is that it uses the same unwinding code as C++. Both languages have different personality functions and different types, so you cannot catch an exception thrown in one language with the other. If, however, some C++ code calls some Objective-C code, which calls some C++ code, then exceptions thrown and caught in the C++ code will still cause the cleanup code in the Objective-C stack frames to be called.

The underlying implementation of this mechanism provides support for foreign exceptions, so it is possible that future versions will implement an `NSCXXException` class or similar that will allow C++ exceptions to be caught in Objective-C.

In addition to the extra keywords for exception handling, Apple added the `@synchronized()` directive. This is used for mutual exclusion, much as the equivalent Java keyword. In a modern Java VM, a huge amount of effort is spent optimizing this mechanism, for example, by completely removing locking when it can prove that no two CPUs will be executing code locking on the same object. This requires accurate garbage collection and the ability to rewrite the native binary, neither of which is available to an Objective-C compiler. As such, this keyword is very inefficient.

When you lock an object like this, it looks up a POSIX recursive mutex for the object, locks it at the start of the block, and unlocks it at the end. The lookup can be relatively expensive, and recursive mutexes are the most expensive locking primitives provided by the POSIX threading library, making this very expensive.

The main benefit of **`@synchronized`** is that it integrates with the exception handling mechanism. If an exception is thrown inside the block, then it will be caught, the lock released, and the exception re-thrown. If you know that no exceptions will be thrown across your critical section, then there are much more efficient forms of locking that you can use in Objective-C.

3.4.4 Introspection

Objective-C provides a lot of introspection information. Every object in Objective-C is an instance of a class and has a pointer to the structure used to represent the class. This is different from languages like C++, where an object might just be a structure with no knowledge of its own structure. This pointer is crucial to how Objective-C works. Its existence means that every object is responsible for knowing how to handle messages sent to it. It also means that any object knows about its own structure.

Reflection

The term *reflection* is often used when people mean introspection. This can be confusing. Introspection refers to the ability of an object to look inside itself and see its own structure and capabilities. Reflection refers to this and also to the ability of an object to modify its structure. Introspection is a subset of reflection. Objective-C supports reflection via the runtime library APIs. For more information, see Chapter 25.

Every class has two main attributes: a list of methods and a list of instance variables. The instance variables describe the structure of the object. Every instance variable has three properties:

- The name of the instance variable.
- The type of the variable.
- The offset of the instance variable from the object. Given a pointer to an object, this value can be used to get a pointer to the instance variable.

Prior to the new runtime library shipped with Leopard, all of these were fixed at compile time. With Leopard, the offset is not fixed until load time. This has two negative side effects. First, it makes accesses to instance variables slightly slower, since they need to go via a layer of indirection. Second, it prevents the **@defs()** directive from working. With other runtimes, you can define a structure like this:

```
struct MyObjectStruct
{
    @defs(MyObject);
};
```

You can then cast a pointer to an instance of `MyObject` to a `struct MyObjectStruct*` and access the instance variables from C. This no longer works, since the layout of a class can no longer be determined at compile time. The big advantage from this change is that adding an instance variable to a class no longer requires its subclasses to all be recompiled.

Another change made as part of the new runtime was to hide the class structure as an opaque type. You now get the offset of an instance variable as a two-step process:

```
Ivar ivar = class_getInstanceVariable([obj class], "aVariable");
ptrdiff_t offset = ivar_getOffset(ivar);
```

`Ivar` is another opaque type in the new runtime, while in the old one it was a `struct` containing three fields for the three attributes just listed. The type is in the form of an *Objective-C type encoding*. This is a string constructed from the characters shown in Table 3.1.

Arrays, structures, and unions are built out of these. An array is encoded in square brackets, with the number of elements followed by the type of a single element. An `int[12]` would be [12i]. Structures are formed by listing the types inside braces. The encoding {Point=ff} would correspond to this structure:

```
struct Point
{
    float x;
    float y;
};
```

Note that the name of the structure is preserved, but the names of the fields are not. Objective-C type encodings are used in a lot of places. You can generate a type encoding at compile time by using the `@encode()` compiler directive. For example, `@encode(int)` will be evaluated to the constant string "i" at compile time. You can use `@encode()` in the same situations where you would use `sizeof()`.

A slightly more complex form of type encodings is used with methods. The `addToCounter:` method from the earlier example will have a type encoding of either "v12@0:4i8" or "v20@0:8i16" depending on whether it is built on a 32- or 64-bit

Type Encoding	C Type
c	**char**
C	**unsigned char**
s	**short**
S	**unsigned short**
i	**int**
I	**unsigned int**
l	**long**
L	**unsigned long**
q	**long long**
Q	**unsigned long long**
f	**float**
d	**double**
B	`bool` (C++) or `_Bool` (C99)
v	**void**
*	**char** *
@	**id**
#	**Class**
:	**SEL**
^type	`type*`

Table 3.1: Objective-C type encodings.

platform. The first character represents the return type of the function, in this case **void**. The next number then represents the total size of all of the arguments. There are then a series of three pairs of arguments and their offsets in an argument frame. The arguments are **self**, **_cmd**, and `anInteger`. The **self** and **_cmd** arguments are hidden arguments that are passed to every Objective-C method, and so they will be found in the encodings of every method, whether it takes any explicit arguments or not.

Although the runtime library provides some low-level introspection functions, which technically count as being part of Objective-C, since they are C and C is a subset of Objective-C, they are not always very friendly. Objective-C also specifies the existence of two classes, `Protocol` and `Object`. The `Object` class implements some wrappers around these. In Cocoa, you typically use `NSObject`, which provides similar functionality. In particular, you can query an object for the methods and protocols it implements and its position in the class hierarchy.

Given an object, you can ask whether it is an instance of a specific class by sending it a `-isMemberOfClass:` message. This takes a **Class** as an argument and returns YES if the receiver is an instance of that class. The -isKindOfClass: method relaxes this constraint slightly and also returns YES if the receiver is an instance of any class that is a subclass of the argument.

To test for protocol conformance, you can send -conformsToProtocol: messages to the class or the instance. More useful is the ability to test whether an object can handle a specific message. This is useful when dealing with *delegates*. A common pattern in Cocoa is to have some code like this:

```
if ([delegate respondsToSelector: @selector(delegateMessage:)])
{
    [delegate delegateMessage: anArgument];
}
```

In a real implementation, you would probably cache whether the delegate responds to the selector, rather than test it every single time, but this shows the basic idea. This capability is why most delegates and event handlers do not have protocols; they are free to implement or not implement methods for any messages that might be sent to them, and it is the responsibility of the caller to first check whether they really do.

3.4.5 Objective-C in C

One of the nice side effects of Objective-C's no magic policy is that you can do everything you would normally do in Objective-C in plain C. When you send a message to an object on OS X, you are really calling the objc_msgSend() function. Objective-C methods are compiled down to C functions with two hidden parameters. The following will generate the same code:

```
- (int) aMethod
...
int aFunction(id self, SEL _cmd)
...
```

The method will be added to whichever class it is declared in, but the executable component will be the same. You can look up the function for a particular method by sending the object a -methodForSelector: message. This calls the corresponding runtime library function, which on Leopard is class_getMethodImplementation().

Listing 3.7 shows how you can write a simple Objective-C program in C. Lines 7 and 8 look up two classes that will be used. Lines 10–12 look up some selectors that will be used. In compiled Objective-C code, all of this will be done by the module load function and cached per compilation unit.

The real code starts on line 14, which creates a new autorelease pool. Line 16 creates a new NSObject instance. Both of these are done by sending a +new message to the class objects. Note how, at the implementation level as well as the abstract level, there is no difference in how a message is sent to an object and a class. On line 21 exactly the same function is used to send a message to an `NSString` instance.

Listing 3.7: A simple Objective-C program written in C. [from: examples/ObjCinC/objc.c]

```
1  #include <objc/Runtime.h>
2  #include <stdio.h>
3  
4  int main(void)
5  {
6      // Look up the classes we need
7      Class NSObject= (Class)objc_getClass("NSObject");
8      Class NSAutoreleasePool = (Class)objc_getClass("NSAutoreleasePool");
9      // Cache some selectors.
10     SEL new = sel_getUid("new");
11     SEL description = sel_getUid("description");
12     SEL UTF8String = sel_getUid("UTF8String");
13     // Create the autorelease pool
14     objc_msgSend(NSAutoreleasePool, new);
15     // Create the NSObject instance in two steps.
16     id obj = (id)objc_msgSend(NSObject, new);
17     // id descString = [obj description];
18     IMP descMethod = class_getMethodImplementation(obj->isa, description);
19     id descString = descMethod(obj, description);
20     // char *desc = [descString UTF8String];
21     char *desc = (char*)objc_msgSend(descString, UTF8String);
22     printf("Created␣object:␣%s\n", desc);
23     return 0;
24 }
```

On lines 18 and 19 the other mechanism for calling a method is shown. This first looks up the *instance method pointer* (*IMP*), a pointer to a function implementing the method, and then calls that function. This is slower on OS X, which uses some optimized assembly for the `objc_msgSend()` function, and inlines it when it's generated from Objective-C. It has the advantage that you can cache the result. This is known as *IMP caching* and means that you only have to perform the method lookup once; subsequent calls are as fast as calling a C function pointer.

When we compile and run this program, we get the following output:

```
$ gcc objc.c -framework Foundation  && ./a.out
Created object: <NSObject: 0x10032a0>
```

Not a lot of result for the amount of effort, and this is why it's uncommon to want to do this. It can sometimes be useful for writing C interfaces to Objective-C functions, however.

Note that this example uses calls specific to the Leopard Objective-C runtime. It will not work with the GNU Objective-C runtime library or older versions of the NeXT / Apple one. These libraries provide equivalent functionality, but with different interfaces.

3.4.6 Objective-C 2.0

With OS X 10.5, Apple introduced a new version of Objective-C. This introduced a large number of new features. This was accompanied by a new Objective-C runtime library, completely rewritten and not binary-compatible with the older one. The new one has much cleaner interfaces to introspection features, making it easier for Apple to change the implementation in future.

Garbage Collection

The biggest one was the introduction of *garbage collection*. Objective-C 1 uses manual memory management, with reference counting added by the Foundation framework.

Objective-C 2 adds write barriers when you assign an object pointer to an instance variable or a global. These are calls to functions in the runtime library that update the state of the garbage collector.

The big change with the addition of garbage collection is the addition of *weak references*. A weak reference is one that is ignored by the garbage collector. An object can be freed if there are weak references to it, but not if there are strong references. By default, all object pointers are strong pointers. A weak pointer is qualified by prefixing it with `__weak`, like this:

```
__weak id delegate;
```

If an object referenced via a weak reference is freed, then the weak reference will be set to `Nil`. (Actually it will be set to `nil` on the next access.) This means that they can be used for any kind of pointer where you don't want the pointer to point to some invalid memory, but you don't care if the object is freed. These are often used for delegates or for objects in collections.

With garbage collection, the code for cleaning up an object is changed slightly. Most objects implement a `-dealloc` method, which is called to free the object. Most of the time, this method does nothing other than reduce the reference count of objects referenced by the object being freed. This is not required by a garbage collected program. Instead, a `-finalize` method can be implemented, which will

Tracing versus Reference Counting

There are two ways of implementing garbage collection, which are both forms of the same generalized algorithm. One is automatic reference counting. This is not enough by itself, since two objects that have references to each other will never be freed. To turn reference counting into full garbage collection, you need to add a cycle detector. This visits some subset of objects and removes extra references that come from cycles.

The other option is *tracing*, and this is what the *autozone* collector Apple provided with Objective-C 2 does. Both approaches have advantages and disadvantages. Reference counting typically has a slightly higher cost per assignment and uses more memory. Tracing provides less deterministic run times, making it harder to reason about code, and doesn't interact nicely in low-memory conditions that cause swapping (since the tracing code needs to visit each object in turn, even ones that have been swapped out) and doesn't work very nicely with objects in different address spaces, as can be the case with distributed objects.

It is unclear quite why Apple decided to use tracing, rather than add automatic reference counting and a cycle detector to the existing manual reference counting already provided.

be called when an object is about to be freed by the garbage collector. This can be used to close file handles and free pointers to C or C++ data.

There are three options when it comes to garbage collection in Cocoa. The first is simply not to use it. This is the best option for compatibility, since garbage collected code will not work on OS X 10.4 and earlier and is currently difficult to port to other implementations of the Cocoa APIs. The second option is to turn it on and use it for everything. This is the easiest if you are just starting with Cocoa programming and don't care about compatibility.

There is also a middle road. If you write your code using the older-style reference counting mechanism, then you can still take advantage of garbage collection. The `-fobjc-gc` option to GCC, or selecting "Supported" as the option for garbage collection in the XCode project properties, will enable the garbage collector on code not explicitly written for it. This will cause all reference counting messages to be ignored but still allows them to be used. This option is particularly useful for frameworks, since it permits them to be linked against any applications, irrespective of whether they use garbage collection.

Properties

The other big addition to Objective-C with Leopard is *properties*. These are a means of declaring instance variables that are accessed in a uniform way. This is effectively a thin layer for declaring and calling setter and getter methods. Properties are first declared in a class interface, like this:

```
@property int counter;
```

This declares that there is a property called `counter` that is an integer. This is equivalent to declaring the following two methods:

```
- (int) counter;
- (void) setCounter: (int)anInteger;
```

You can access properties without using any special syntax, simply by sending the corresponding messages. Alternatively, a new syntax is provided that makes them look more like fields in a structure. The following two pairs of lines show two equivalent syntactic forms for the same operation:

```
// Using property syntax
obj.counter = 12;
int c = obj.counter;
// Using ObjC 1 syntax
[obj setCounter: 12];
int c = [obj counter];
```

The new syntax breaks a few of the rules of Objective-C, since it reuses existing structure field accessing syntax for very different behavior. It is a lot simpler when you are accessing deeply nested properties, however.

One of the nice things about properties is that they allow you to hide implementation details a lot better than you could without them. The **`@synthesize`** directive is used to create implementations of a property. This can be used to create set and get methods for an existing instance variable, or to add a new instance variable. (The latter behavior is only available with the 64-bit or Objective-C 2 runtime.) You can also use the `@dynamic` directive to specify a property that you will provide your own implementation for.

Properties provide a lot of hints about their implementation. These are declared in a comma-separated list in their declaration, like this:

```
@property(nonatomic, readonly) id object;
```

The first of these is probably the most important. By default, properties use atomic operations for assignment, making them thread safe. If this is not required then it is faster to create a non-atomic property.

The next one in this list, `readonly`, specifies that only the accessor method should be generated. No `-setObject:` method would be set in this example. You can also specify the names of the methods to be used, if you don't want to use the defaults, by using `setter=` and `getter=` in your property declaration. This is useful for ensuring that your property matches the conventions used by key-value coding, such as having the accessor methods for boolean values start with "is."

You can also specify the semantics for set methods generated with the `@synthesize` directive by putting `assign`, `retain`, or `copy` in your property declaration. The first of these is usually the default and emits a method that generates a simple assignment. This is the only one that is valid for non-object types. For objects, when not using garbage collection, there is no default and one must be explicitly stated. You rarely want `assign` since this makes it easy for an object to be released while you still have a pointer to it, resulting in your later dereferencing an invalid pointer. The `retain` and `copy` options both result in the old value being released (having its reference count decremented) and the new one either being sent a `retain` or `copy` message. The former increments the reference count; the latter returns a copy (or the original object for immutable objects).

3.4.7 Blocks

Blocks are not technically part of Objective-C; they are an Apple-designed extension to C, introduced with OS X 10.6. For quite a while, GCC has supported nested functions. These allow you to define functions inside functions, with access to the enclosing scope's variables. This lets you do things like this:

```
void function(void)
{
    int count=0
    id nested(id object)
    {
        count++;
        return [object permute];
    }
    array = mapArray(array, nested);
    return count;
}
```

This should be familiar to anyone who has done any programming in a functional or dynamic language. The inner function is passed by pointer to the `mapArray()` function, which (presumably) will call it on every object in a collection and return a new array generated from it.

Apple disabled these by default in its version of OS X. The reason for this is potential security problems with their implementation. When these are compiled, they are emitted as two separate functions. When you take the pointer to the inner function, you really get a pointer to a trampoline on the stack. This is a short snip of machine code that loads the address of the stack frame in which the pointer was taken from just behind the start of the trampoline code and then jumps to the real function.

Because you need to execute code on the stack, you need to have your stack both writable and executable. This is generally considered a very bad idea from a security standpoint, since it makes it trivial to turn stack buffer overflows into arbitrary code execution vulnerabilities.

Unfortunately, nested functions are quite useful, and a lot of people complained when Apple disabled them. Its solution was to create a new language feature: *blocks*. This involved adding a calling convention and pointer type to C. Function pointers declared with a caret (^) instead of an asterisk (*) are fat pointers. They contain both a function pointer and a data pointer. The data pointer is passed as a hidden argument into the function. This is the same mechanism used for method pointers in some C++ compilers. With blocks, you can do things like this:

```
void call_a_block(void (^blockptr)(int))
{
    blockptr(4);
}

void test()
{
    int X = 8;
    call_a_block( ^(int y){ printf("%d\n", X+y); });
}
```

Blocks and Blocks

The terminology for blocks is quite confusing. In C, it is common to refer to a region of lexical scoping—an area between braces—as a block. The new language feature is named after the equivalent Smalltalk construct. In Smalltalk, blocks fulfill both rôles. Lexical scopes in Smalltalk are really closure literals, just like the blocks described in this section.

This will print 12 to the screen. The argument to `call_a_block()` is a block, a new kind of function that takes a hidden argument. This argument points to a structure that contains a copy of `X`. This block can access the value of `X` from the time it was created, but it can't assign to it.

As well as the new pointer type and way of declaring functions, they also added a new modifier on variable declarations, which you can see here:

```
__block int shared = 12;
void (^nested)(int) =
    ^(int y)
    {
        shared += y;
    };
```

The shared variable, because it is declared __block, will be copied into a reference-counted structure that will be referenced from the data associated with nested() here. Each call to nested() will increment this value, and the stack frame will also be able to refer to it. From the perspective of a programmer, the shared variable will be the same both inside and outside the block and can be modified in both cases.

These blocks are first-class closures. You can't use them interchangeably with function pointers, but you can use them in exactly the same way. They allow you to quickly generate functions that refer to scoped variables, and so can be used for things like map and fold operations on collections.

Blocks implement something a lot like Objective-C's retain/release mechanism. If you want to keep a pointer to a block, you need to do something like this:

```
savedBlock = Block_copy(aBlock);
// Some time later:
Block_release(savedBlock);
```

This will either copy the block or increment its reference count, depending on whether the block is still on the stack.

You can expect future versions of Cocoa to make heavy use of blocks, in collection classes and elsewhere. A number of these methods were added in OS X 10.6, and we'll take a look at some of them in the next chapter. Blocks complement the Objective-C model, because they are effectively objects with a single method defined on them but are much faster to write than full-fledged objects. You can implement a complete object model with a dictionary of blocks, although it will be slower than using real objects.

As with Smalltalk, blocks are also objects. Rather than calling the two functions for reference counting, you can send them -retain and -release messages. You can also use them in any situation where you would otherwise use objects. This makes some very flexible flow control available. You can, for example, store a set of blocks as values in a dictionary and call the corresponding block for each input you receive.

Adding blocks to objects as methods is a possibility. This will extend Objective-C to support *Lieberman prototypes* in the same way that JavaScript and Self do. This is very convenient for quickly customizing a class, particularly for user interface work. Even without direct support for this from Apple, you can implement it using the second-chance dispatch mechanism to call blocks, although this would be very slow, or via a trampoline function.

3.4.8 Objective-C++

Objective-C is a set of extensions to C. These extensions are largely orthogonal to C. When the same extensions are added to C++, they are known as Objective-C++. Not every Objective-C program is a valid Objective-C++ program, just as not every C program is a valid C++ program; however, every C++ program is a valid Objective-C++ program.

There aren't many cases where Objective-C++ is useful, since C++ has very few advantages over Objective-C. The main advantage is when you need to interface with a large body of existing C++ code. The most well-known example of this is the *WebKit* framework. This began life as a fork of the KDE project's KHTML library, written in C++. The public interfaces on OS X are all written in Objective-C, with Objective-C++ serving as the bridge between the two languages.

If you are porting a C++ application to OS X, then Objective-C++ will allow you to use Cocoa without having to write C interfaces between the C++ and Objective-C code.

3.5 Cocoa Conventions

Conventions are important for consistency in an API. Learning patterns that are used throughout Cocoa is a lot easier than learning the intimate details of every single class and function. The Cocoa APIs are huge, and memorizing everything is impossible for most programmers. The important thing is to be able to easily find the correct class or method, either by using autocompletion in XCode or by checking in the documentation.

3.5.1 Naming

A good language is a nice start when producing a friendly API, but naming conventions are also very important. One of the biggest complaints about Java 1.0, for example, was the inconsistent ordering of parameters in functions. Consistent usage of conventions throughout an API makes it easier to remember how to use an API, since you are just remembering general patterns, rather than the details of every element.

One of the things that often irritates people who start learning Cocoa is how verbose Cocoa tends to be. Class and method names can often be over a dozen characters each, with some method names being much longer. This is rarely a problem when using a code editor that supports autocompletion. In XCode, you rarely have to type more than the first few characters of a name before the editor will complete it for you.

Prefixes

Every class in a framework in Objective-C typically has a short prefix. All of the Cocoa standard classes have the `NS` prefix, indicating their NeXTStep heritage. This is due to the lack of namespaces in Objective-C. All Objective-C classes linked to a program live in the same namespace. This means that two frameworks implementing classes with the same name cannot be linked together without problems.

The solution to this is for classes in frameworks to have a short prefix unique to the vendor or the framework. Apple uses `NS` a lot, but some frameworks have their own prefixes, such as `AB` for the AddressBook framework.

These prefixes are not just used on classes. Functions, constants, and anything else in a global namespace should use them. The exception is methods, since methods are attached to a specific class.

Class Names

Class names for simple classes are usually generated by appending a noun to the prefix. Examples of this are `NSObject` or `ABPerson`. Subclasses often add adjectives between the prefix and the noun, such as `NSMutableArray`, a subclass of `NSArray` that adds mutable behavior.

Class names should always express the functionality of the class. Most classes encapsulate some kind of data and their names should reflect this. For example, it is obvious what a `NSDate` represents, or a `PDFPage`.

Naming of protocols is slightly different. A protocol describes a behavior, while a class describes an object. As such, protocols are typically named with verbs, such as `NSCopying` or `NSLocking`. The exception to this is when a protocol describes the important methods of a class. This is the case with the `NSObject` protocol, which describes the methods that the `NSObject` class implements and which any other base class needs to implement to be used by objects in Cocoa. This protocol is adopted by the other base class in Cocoa, `NSProxy`.

If you are defining a class that is a default implementation of a general idea, this pattern is worth following. In other code, you should require objects that adopt the protocol, rather than instances of the class, allowing other people to create their own versions without subclassing or explicit casting.

Method Names

Method names should start with lowercase letters. They usually start with a verb and have a noun for each parameter. Methods that don't take any parameters are usually just verbs if they perform some action, like `-retain` or `-log`. If they take a parameter they will be verb-noun pairs, like `-addObject:`.

For methods with more than one argument, the rules are slightly more complicated. Each subsequent parameter should generally be a noun or an adjective-noun pair. For example, `setObject:forKey:`, which is verb-noun for the first parameter then adjective-noun for the second. Often the adjective is omitted, such as in `-initWithString:calendarFormat:` because it would be redundant. In contrast, a method like `-rangeOfUnit:inUnit:forDate:` has adjectives for all parameters, even the first one. This is because it is querying data from the object, not performing any action. Calling this method `-rangeOfUnit:unit:date:` would be far less self-documenting.

Most methods that return some part of the object's state are single words, such as `-count` or `-length`. The main exception is methods that return a **`BOOL`**, which usually start with `is`, as in `-isEnabled`. This makes the method easier to read. You can read the following line of code aloud as if it were just an English question:

```
if ([anObject isEnabled])
```

Method names can often be very long, and you may end up needing to wrap them over multiple lines. Convention in Objective-C is to line up the colons when doing this. In Étoilé, we have adopted the convention that the spacing after the indent should be done using spaces, and the indent itself should be inserted using tabs. This gives the following layout:

```
	[NSAlert alertWithMessageText: @"Example"
	                defaultButton: @"Continue"
	              alternateButton: @"Abort"
	                  otherButton: nil
	    informativeTextWithFormat: @"An example long line"];
```

The advantage of this approach is that it allows anyone reading your code to set the indent size to whatever they prefer without breaking the alignment. Unfortunately, XCode does not differentiate between indenting and alignment and so will not indent to this style automatically.

One thing to be careful of is that selectors in Apple's implementation of Objective-C are untyped. Imagine that you define these two methods with the same name in two different classes, with different parameter types. When some other code has a pointer to an object and sends a message with this name to an object, the compiler has to generate code for the call frame. If the pointer is to

> ### "Get" in Names
>
> A lot of toolkits use `get` as a prefix for methods that return a property and `set` for methods that set it. Cocoa uses the `set` prefix, but not `get`. The only methods or functions that should have `get` in their names are ones that take a pointer as an argument and use it to return a value by reference.

a specific object type, then the version of the method declared on that object (assuming it is visible to the compiler) will be chosen. Otherwise, it can pick either.

If both types are different kinds of object, this is not a problem. Either the argument will respond to the correct messages, or a run time exception will be thrown. If, on the other hand, they are different primitive types, or one is a primitive type and one is an object type, then the stack frame may end up being the wrong size. This can lead to stack corruption, security holes, and crashing.

To avoid this problem, a lot of methods have the type of their arguments in their name, for example `-addObject:`, or `-setIntValue:`. This is a good habit to get into. If your objects end up in a framework, then it may link against another framework that implements other classes with conflicting selector names, and this problem can appear long after either framework was written.

Function Names

Function names follow a mixture of the conventions of classes and methods. If they are not part of a public API, then they should be declared **`static`**. Doing this prevents them entering the global namespace and makes their name less important. For functions that cannot be declared **`static`**, you should always begin with a prefix. Cocoa functions, like Cocoa classes, all begin with `NS`.

In general, there are two kinds of functions in Cocoa: those that do something and those that perform translations. Specifically, some are called because of their side effects, and some are called because of their return value. The later kind is usually named `NSTypeFromOtherType()`. These return a value that is a different representation or a property of the parameter. Examples of this include `NSClassFromString()` and `NSEventMaskFromType()`.

Functions that are called because of their side effects generally have a verb after the prefix, such as `NSAllocateObject()`.

Functions in Cocoa that refer to an opaque type generally have the type name in the function name, usually immediately after the prefix. Examples of this include `NSMapInsert()` and `NSDecimalAdd()`. A few have the verb before the prefix, such as `NSFreeMapTable()` and `NSMakePoint()`. Unfortunately, there is quite a lot of inconsistency in names for Foundation functions.

3.5.2 Memory Management

Classic (pre-NeXT) Objective-C used manual memory management, of the kind found in C and C++. You can see this in the `Object` class, which is provided with the Objective-C runtime library. The interface to this is in /usr/include/objc/Object.h, although it is very rarely used. This class provides `+new` and `-free` methods, which correspond directly to the C `malloc()` and `free()` functions.

This has some problems. Objects are very commonly aliased—multiple objects have pointers to them—and this makes it difficult to decide who should free an object. Typically this is done by assigning an owner to each object and having complex rules to decide which objects should own which others, and copying objects more than you need to when you aren't sure.

Reference Counting

Cocoa, with Objective-C 1, uses reference counting. When you want to keep a reference to an object, you send it a `-retain` message. In almost all cases, this returns the object. In a very small number of cases, however, it returns a new object, and so you should always keep the object returned from this:

```
obj = [obj retain];
```

This can happen when the object is stored in some transient location that will not be valid later on. The inverse of `-retain` is `-release`. When you are no longer using an object, you should send it a `-release` message.

There is one tricky thing to remember. When you are implementing a set method for an instance variable, then you might think that the obvious way of doing it would be

```
- (void) setFoo:(id) anObject
{
    [foo release];
    foo = [anObject retain];
}
```

This works fine in most cases, but what happens when `anObject == foo` and when the reference count is one? In this case, the `release` message will cause the object to be freed; the `retain` message will be sent to an invalid memory location. If the object's memory hasn't been returned to the operating system yet, then the new value for `foo` will be the same as the old value, only now it will be an invalid pointer that will cause subtle bugs later. If it has been returned, then this will cause a segmentation fault immediately. The solution is to do the `-retain` first, like this:

```
id tmp = [anObject retain];
[foo release];
foo = tmp;
```

This is slightly cumbersome. GNUstep provides an `ASSIGN()` macro that does this. You might consider implementing something similar for your own code. This can be defined simply like this:

```
#define ASSIGN(var, obj) do {\
    id _tmp = [obj retain];\
    [var release];\
    var = _tmp;\
} while(0)
```

Autorelease Pools

Simple reference counting is enough for a lot of cases, but there are some problems. The most common one is what happens when you return a temporary object from a method or a function? You don't want to keep a reference to it, so you want to release it; only this would destroy it before the caller has an opportunity to retain it.

The Cocoa solution to this problem is the autorelease pool. At any point in a Cocoa program, there should be a valid instance of `NSAutoreleasePool`. If you send an object an `-autorelease` message, instead of `-release`, then it will look up the current autorelease pool and add itself. When the current pool is destroyed, it will send a `-release` message to every object registered with it.

Autoreleasing an object means that you don't want it anymore, but someone else might soon, so don't destroy it quite yet. Commonly, you will autorelease an object created in a function or method immediately before returning it.

If you use a garbage collected environment, then you don't need to worry about retaining and releasing objects. The rest of this book will continue to do so in examples, since code written with manual retain and release management can be compiled for garbage collection, while the converse is not true. If you wish to support older versions of OS X than 10.5, the iPhone, people using frameworks that have not been compiled with garbage collection, or other OpenStep implementations, you should avoid depending on garbage collection.

GNUstep has supported garbage collection via the *Boehm garbage collector* for a few years, and uses `RETAIN()` and `RELEASE()` macros, which are removed by the preprocessor when compiled with garbage collection. It might be good practice to use something similar in your own code. At some point in the future, it will almost certainly become pointless maintaining support systems without garbage collection, and this provides a simple way of removing the overhead of the (ignored) `retain` and `release` messages.

3.5.3 Constructors and Initializers

With classical, pre-NeXT, Objective-C, objects were created with a Smalltalk-style `+new` message, which simply wrapped `malloc()`. To support more complex memory management systems, NeXT split this into two methods. When you send a `+new` message to a class, it invokes a method that calls `+alloc` and then `-init` on the result.

The `+alloc` method, declared in `NSObject`, calls `+allocWithZone:`, which allocates an instance of the object in a `NSZone`. On Cocoa, this is an opaque type indicating a region of memory. Currently only two sorts are supported, heap-like and stack-like allocations. The latter type must be freed all in one go, and so is useful when you are creating a large number of objects with a short lifespan.

In NeXTSTEP `NSZone` was used very heavily to squeeze performance out of the slow machines of the time. With Cocoa it is much more rarely used. Unfortunately, most of the benefits of `NSZone` only apply when all of the code is written with zones in mind, and this is almost never the case. Zones are also not available when using garbage collection.

The main legacy of this is that you almost never override `+alloc`, but you do override `-init`. This is slightly harder than it sounds. Simply calling `-init` in the superclass is not always enough. An object is not required to return itself from `-init`, it may instead return a singleton or some other value, or initialization may fail and it may return `nil`. Listing 3.8 shows the correct way of implementing a `-init` method.

The first step is to send a `-init` message to the superclass and assign the result to **`self`**. This handles initialization of any state specific to the superclass. Assigning to **`self`** may seem strange, but remember that **`self`** is just another parameter in Objective-C and follows exactly the same rules as any other function argument.

If this operation has set **`self`** to `nil`, then any attempts to set instance variables will result in a segmentation fault and the program will crash. You should then perform any per-class initialization. In most classes, there is nothing here that can fail. In some cases, initializing a class will acquire some resource, such as a file or a network socket, which can fail. In this case, the object should release itself and return nil from the initializer.

In addition to `-init`, classes can also implement a `+initialize` method. This will be called automatically by the runtime when the first message is sent to a class. This is a good way of lazily initializing file-static variables and improves

Listing 3.8: An object initialization method.

```
- (id) init
{
    self = [super init];
    if (self == nil)
    {
        return nil;
    }
    // Do initialization specific to this class.
    if (someInitializationFailureCondition)
    {
        [self release]
        self = nil;
    }
    return self;
}
```

the start time for Objective-C programs by reducing the amount that needs to be done at load time. The `+initialize` method will always be called before any instances of the class have been created. Most commonly, the first message sent to a class will be `+alloc` and so the initialization for the class will run just before the first instance is created.

Note that your `+initialize` method may be called from a subclass. Sometimes you may want to do something for every subclass, but more often you will just want to run this method once. Listing 3.9 shows how to do this.

Listing 3.9: A class initialization method.

```
1 + (void) initialize
2 {
3     if (self == [MyClass class])
4     {
5         // Do initialization
6     }
7     [super initialize];
8 }
```

Since this is a class method, **self** will be the class, rather than an instance of the class. The test in line 3 will only succeed once—when `+initialize` is called on `MyClass`—not on any subclass invocations. The last line calls the superclass, which will probably have a similar block to this and therefore ignore the message.

Note that this method, unlike object initializers, returns **void**. This is because it is invoked by the runtime library, rather than user code. If it did return a value, there is nothing sensible that the caller could do with it.

The Objective-C runtime also provides special behavior for a `+load` method. This will be called when the class is loaded. Because library load order is not well defined, this means that it can only depend on its superclasses having been loaded by this stage, not any others. In practice, you can usually depend on Cocoa classes having been loaded before your own ones, but this is generally bad practice.

The most common reason to implement a `+load` method used to be to make use of *class posing*, where one class replaces another at run time. This was an alternative to categories with the advantage that the new implementation of a method could call the old one. This is deprecated with the new runtime, although it is still possible to achieve the same effect by replacing method implementations. This must be done with `+load` instead of `+initialize` because it must happen before the superclass is instantiated.

Because it runs at load time, code in `+load` will increase the application launch time, and so is generally bad from a user interface perspective. Because the state of the executable is not well defined, they are not a very good option for many kinds of initialization. I have written `+load` methods a grand total of two times, and both were in very low-level code that replaced a chunk of Foundation's functionality.

In addition to the default initialization methods, a lot of objects implement named initializers and constructors. An example of this is `NSArray`'s `+arrayWithObject:` and `-initWithObject:` methods. The first calls the latter after allocating an object.

Each class has a *designated initializer*, which is the method that subclasses should call on **`super`** when they are initializing. This is usually `-init`, but not always. Some *class clusters* do not have a designated initializer; subclasses should not send any message to **`super`** during initialization.

When calling named constructors, the returned object will be autoreleased. The following two lines are equivalent:

```
[NSArray arrayWithObject: anObject];
[[[NSArray alloc] initWithObject: anObject] autorelease];
```

The first form is usually just a wrapper around the latter, although in some class clusters it may avoid allocating a placeholder object that is then replaced by a subclass instance in the initializer. In some cases, only one form will be available.

3.6 Summary

This chapter has given an introduction to Objective-C and to the Apple developer tools. The only way of becoming fluent in either is practice. XCode follows a lot of the conventions of other Mac applications and so should be relatively easy to learn. In particular, it uses inspectors very widely, and most things you can click on can be inspected. Spend some time browsing the various inspectors and take a look at the examples provided as part of the developer tools bundle, and browse the collection of objects available in Interface Builder's palette.

If you already know C, then you might want to try writing some simple Objective-C programs without using much of the Cocoa libraries. If you have implemented your own object model for a simple C library, try modifying it to use `NSObject` instead. This doesn't require much knowledge of Cocoa, just replace each of your type definitions with an Objective-C **`@interface`**, use the `-retain` and `-release` methods for memory management, and turn your functions into methods. Don't spend too much time on this though. In the next part of this book, we will look at the standard objects provided by Cocoa, which will make using Objective-C a lot easier.

Part II

The Cocoa Frameworks

Chapter 4

Foundation: The Objective-C Standard Library

The "core" Objective-C language only defines two classes: Object and Protocol. It is rare to use Objective-C without an implementation of OpenStep Foundation, whether it's GNUstep, Cocoa, libfoundation, or Cocotron. The Portable Object Compiler provides its own set of core objects, but it is not widely used.

The OpenStep Foundation is the closest thing that Objective-C has to a standard library, the equivalent of the C standard library or C++'s STL. Of course since Objective-C is a pure superset of C, the C standard library can also be used. The original idea was to do exactly this, and use Objective-C for building components from C software.

Foundation was only introduced with OpenStep to hide the differences between NeXTSTEP's Mach-based operating system and Solaris, and to make it easier to write endian-independent code. Most of Foundation is endian-independent, which was a huge benefit when Apple moved from the big-endian PowerPC to the little-endian x86 architecture.

4.1 General Concepts

Although the Foundation framework is very large, it is quite easy to learn. A lot of the classes share common design principles. When you understand these shared concepts, you can learn how to use each of the individual classes quickly.

4.1.1 Mutability

Objective-C does not have a concept of constant objects. This is not quite true; the `const` keyword from C still exists, but it only applies to direct access to instance variables. Methods cannot be marked as mutators and so any messages sent to an object may modify it, irrespective of whether the object pointer is `const`-qualified.

In many cases, however, it is useful to have mutable and immutable versions of objects. This is often done in object-oriented systems by having mutable and immutable classes. Strings are a common example. If you create an Objective-C string literal `@"like_this"` then you are creating a constant string. The compiler will put this string in the constants section of the binary—attempting to modify it will cause a segmentation fault. Having to create a new string and copy can make a program very slow, however. This is one of the reasons Java code has a reputation for being slow; Java's `String` class is immutable, and since it is declared `final` you can't use Cocoa's solution to the problem, a mutable subclass.

The `NSString` object is an immutable string. It has a subclass, `NSMutableString`. Because the mutable version is a subclass, it can be used anywhere that the immutable version can. It implements all of the same methods.

The distinction between mutable and immutable objects is most apparent in the implementation of the `-copy` method. When you send a `-copy` message to an immutable object, you often get the same object back (but with the retain count incremented). Because you cannot modify either "copy" they can never become different from each other.

This ability is one of the reasons why Objective-C programs are often faster than C++, in spite of microbenchmarks showing the opposite. In a C++ program, the equivalent with `std::string` objects would result in a real copy. A C++ string might be copied half a dozen times, whereas a Cocoa string will only have its reference count incremented and decremented.

4.1.2 Class Clusters

Although `NSString` is the class for immutable strings, your string literal will not really be an `NSString`. Instead, it will be an `NSConstantString` or similar. This class is a private subclass of `NSString`, used for a specific purpose.

This is very common in Cocoa. There might be half a dozen or so different implementations of common classes, such as `NSDictionary`, all optimized for different uses. When you initialize one, you will get back a specific subclass, rather than the abstract superclass.

There are two ways in which this can be done. The first is to return a different subclass from each constructor or initializer. The second is to use the same instance variable layout and use a trick known as *isa-swizzling*. The `isa` pointer, the pointer to the object's class, is just another instance variable. In keeping with the "no magic" philosophy of Objective-C, there is nothing special about it. You can assign a new value to it if you wish. As long as both the new and old classes have the same layout in memory, everything will keep working. (If they don't, you will get some difficult-to-debug memory corruption.)

Class clusters make subclassing slightly difficult. Typically, each of the hidden classes in a cluster implements only a small number of primitive methods. In `NSString` these are `-characterAtIndex:` and `-length`. All of the others are implemented in the superclass in terms of these. If you want to create a new `NSString` subclass, you must implement these methods yourself. It is common to do this by having a concrete instance as an instance variable and delegating to it, although you can implement the primitive methods yourself.

Of course, there is nothing stopping you from implementing more than just these two primitive methods. You may be able to implement more efficient versions of some of them.

More isa-swizzling

The `isa`-swizzling trick is useful in a lot of cases, not just class clusters. It can be used for debugging use-after-free memory problems, by having the `-dealloc` method simply change the class to one that throws an exception if it receives any messages. You can also use it to implement state machines, where each state is in a separate subclass of a common class. To enter a new state, simply change the `isa` pointer to that pointer's class.

You can implement class clusters of your own very easily. Typically, you will have a set of different initializers in the public class, and each of these will return an instance of a different subclass. To demonstrate this, we will define a simple class encapsulating a pair of values. Listing 4.1 shows this interface. Note that no instance variables are declared here.

In the implementation file, we define two concrete subclasses of the `Pair` class, one for storing integers and one for floating point values. These are shown in Listing 4.2. Neither of these defines any new methods. Since these interfaces are private, there would be no point in adding new methods since no one would know to call them. They do, however, define the structure. Class clusters implemented like this allow entirely different data layouts for different implementations.

The implementation of the public class, shown in Listing 4.3, is very simple. Most of the methods just return simple default values, since they should not be called. A more robust implementation might throw an exception.

The important thing to note is the `[self release]` line in both initializers.

Listing 4.1: The public interface to the pair class. [from: examples/ClassCluster/Pair.h]

```
@interface Pair : NSObject {}
- (Pair*) initWithFloat:(float)a float:(float)b;
- (Pair*) initWithInt:(int)a int:(int)b;
- (float) firstFloat;
- (float) secondFloat;
- (int) firstInt;
- (int) secondInt;
@end
```

Listing 4.2: The private interfaces to the concrete pair classes. [from: examples/ClassCluster/Pair.m]

```
@interface IntPair : Pair {
    int first;
    int second;
}
@end
@interface FloatPair : Pair {
    float first;
    float second;
}
@end
```

Listing 4.3: The implementation of the public pair class. [from: examples/ClassCluster/Pair.m]

```
@implementation Pair
- (Pair*) initWithFloat: (float)a float: (float)b
{
    [self release];
    return [[FloatPair alloc] initWithFloat: a float: b];
}
- (Pair*) initWithInt: (int)a int: (int)b
{
    [self release];
    return [[IntPair alloc] initWithInt: a int: b];
}
- (float) firstFloat { return 0; }
- (float) secondFloat { return 0; }
- (int) firstInt { return 0; }
- (int) secondInt { return 0; }
@end
```

Typically, an object will be created by first sending `+alloc` to the `Pair` class and then sending the result the initialization message. The object returned from `+alloc` is not required, and so is released here and a new object returned instead.

Listing 4.4 shows the implementations of the private pair classes. Each of these only implements a single constructor, the one relevant to its data type. The accessor methods then either return instance variables or casts of instance variables, allowing both kinds of pair to return **`int`**s or **`float`**s. One method from `NSObject` is implemented by both, `-description`, which provides a human-readable description of the object. Note that neither of these call the designated initializer in the superclass; this is quite bad style, but was done to simplify the example.

Listing 4.4: The implementation of the private pair classes. [from: examples/ClassCluster/Pair.m]

```
@implementation IntPair
- (Pair*) initWithInt: (int)a int: (int)b
{
	first = a;
	second = b;
	return self;
}
- (NSString*) description
{
	return [NSString stringWithFormat: @"(%d,␣%d)",
		first, second];
}
- (float) firstFloat { return (float)first; }
- (float) secondFloat { return (float)second; }
- (int) firstInt { return first; }
- (int) secondInt { return second; }
@end
@implementation FloatPair
- (Pair*) initWithFloat: (float)a float: (float)b
{
	first = a;
	second = b;
	return self;
}
- (NSString*) description
{
	return [NSString stringWithFormat: @"(%f,␣%f)",
		(double)first, (double)second];
}
- (float) firstFloat { return first; }
```

```
- (float) secondFloat { return second; }
- (int) firstInt { return (int)first; }
- (int) secondInt { return (int)second; }
@end
```

Users of the pair class now don't have to be aware of either of the private classes. A simple test program that creates one of each can demonstrate this. Listing 4.5 shows a short program that just creates two pair objects and logs them. The format string provided to `NSLog` will cause the `-description` method in each to be called.

Listing 4.5: Demonstrating the pair classes. [from: examples/ClassCluster/test.m]

```
#import "Pair.h"

int main(void)
{
    [NSAutoreleasePool new];
    Pair *floats = [[Pair alloc] initWithFloat:0.5 float:12.42];
    Pair *ints= [[Pair alloc] initWithInt:1984 int:2001];
    NSLog(@"Two␣floats:␣%@", floats);
    NSLog(@"Two␣ints:␣%@", ints);
    return 0;
}
```

Running this program gives the following output:

```
2009-01-14 14:27:55.091 a.out[80326:10b] Two floats: (0.500000, 12.420000)
2009-01-14 14:27:55.093 a.out[80326:10b] Two ints: (1984, 2001)
```

A more full implementation of this cluster would have named constructors, such as `+pairWithInt:int:`, which would avoid the need to allocate and then free an instance of the `Pair` object. The alternate way of avoiding this, as mentioned earlier, is to use `isa`-swizzling. The `Pair` class might have two instance variables that were unions of an **`int`** and a **`float`**. Implemented in this way, the initializers would look like this:

```
- (Pair*) initWithFloat: (float)a float: (float)b
{
    isa = [FloatPair class];
    return [self initWithFloat: a float: b];
}
```

This first line in this implementation sets the class pointer to the subclass, and the second calls the method again. Because the class pointer has changed, the second call will invoke the subclass implementation of this method. Each subclass would then refer to the correct field in the union.

4.2 Core Foundation Types

The *Core Foundation* (*CF*) library contains a set of C opaque types that have a similar interface to a number of Cocoa Foundation objects. This similarity is not accidental. The aim of Core Foundation was to produce a rich common set of fundamental types that both Cocoa and Carbon applications could use. This is no longer important, since Carbon did not make the 64-bit switch, but Core Foundation is still used in a lot of low-level parts of OS X, such as Launchd.

Although C does not have a notion of inheritance on types, Core Foundation types are built into a hierarchy. At the root is `CFType`, which implements basic memory management for CF types. Just as Cocoa objects are reference counted with `-retain` and `-release` messages, Core Foundation types are reference counted by calling the `CFRetain()` and `CFRelease()` functions with them as an argument.

Many of the Core Foundation types use the *toll-free bridging* mechanism to interoperate with their Cocoa equivalents. The first field in any CF structure is an `isa` pointer, just as with an Objective-C object. Unlike Cocoa objects, however, this value is always between 0 and 2^{16}, a region of memory where no Objective-C classes will be. When you send a message to a CF object, the message send function will use a special case for class pointers in this range.

Similarly, when you call a Core Foundation function with a Cocoa object, it will test that the `isa` pointer is greater than 0xFFFF and, if it is, then call the Objective-C runtime functions for method dispatch, bouncing the call back to Objective-C. This allows you to use the Core Foundation types and Cocoa objects interchangeably.

A lot of the Cocoa Foundation objects have Core Foundation analogues. The most common is probably `CFString`, the equivalent of Cocoa's `NSString`. In fact, both `NSString` and `NSMutableString` are class clusters on Cocoa, meaning that their instances may not really be versions of that class. Under the hood, all three types are implemented by the `NSCFString` type. This is true for a lot of class clusters in Cocoa.

4.3 Basic Data Types

Foundation provides a number of data types, some as primitive C types, and some as object types. Some of these represent some kind of structured data, such as a string or a date, while others are collections of arbitrary types.

Any nontrivial Cocoa program is likely to make heavy use of some of these. All of them provide a rich set of methods for manipulating them, and so you should take care to check the documentation carefully before implementing new features for them.

4.3.1 Non-Object Types

OpenStep was originally designed to work on very slow computers by today's standards. One of the big improvements in performance over Smalltalk came from the judicious use of non-object types. The most obvious of these are the various primitive integer and floating point types. There are also a small number of structures, such as `NSRange`, which are used throughout the Foundation frameworks.

There are several reasons why these are not objects. The first is their size. Most of these structures are pairs of values. A range is a start and a length, for example. Adding on four bytes for an `isa` pointer and four bytes for a reference count would double their size. By making them structures, they can be passed by value in registers, which makes calling methods (and functions) that use or return them faster. Finally, they are rarely aliased. When you set a range or a point or rectangle somewhere, you want to set a copy.

The most common structures used in Cocoa are

- `NSRange`, a pair of positive integers representing an offset and length in a sequence. These are most commonly used with `NSString`s for defining substrings, but can be used with arrays and other similar data structures.

- `NSPoint`, which contains two floating-point values representing x and y coordinates.

- `NSSize`, which is structurally equivalent to `NSPoint`. The difference between `NSSize` and `NSPoint` is that the values for a size should never be negative. As a structure it is unable to enforce this constraint; however, assigning a negative value to either field may cause exceptions or subtle failures.

- `NSRect`, an aggregate of an `NSPoint` and an `NSSize` that allows a rectangle to be defined in 2D space.

Note that the last three of these are all most commonly used for drawing functions in AppKit, even though they are defined in Foundation.

CGFloat, NSUInteger, and Friends

Prior to 10.5, most of these structures used **`int`**, **`float`**, and similar types. With 10.5, Apple redefined a lot of types and functions to use the `CGFloat` and `NSUInteger` types. The new `NSUInteger` and `NSInteger` types are identical to C99's `uintptr_t` and `intptr_t` respectively. They are provided for compatibility with code using C89 or older dialects. `CGFloat` is defined as a **`float`** on 32-bit platforms and a **`double`** on 64-bit.

Foundation also includes a number of other primitive data types, including a large number of enumerated types. Common examples of these include `NSComparisonResult`, which defines `NSOrderedAscending`, `NSOrderedSame`, and `NSOrderedDescending`, and is used to define how two objects should be ordered. If you sort a collection of Cocoa objects, the order will be defined by calling a function or a method that returns one of these three values on pairs of objects in the collection.

4.3.2 Strings

One of the most commonly used classes in Foundation is `NSString`. Technically speaking, this means subclasses of `NSString`, since it is a *class cluster* and is never directly used.

Each concrete subclass of `NSString` must override at least two of the methods defined by this class: `-length` and `-characterAtIndex:`. The first of these returns the length of the string, and the second returns a unicode (32-bit) character at a specified index. Note that the internal format of the string may be in any format. The class cluster design allows 8-, 16-, and 32-bit strings to all be stored internally when a given string does not include any characters from outside the set that can be expressed with these. The programmer can be largely oblivious to this and use these strings interchangeably: The `NSString` subclass will transparently handle any conversion required.

Although these are the only methods that need to be overridden, most of the methods in `NSString` will call `getCharacters:range:`, which writes a substring into a buffer provided by the caller. Subclasses that implement this directly, rather than using the superclass implementation that repeatedly calls `-characterAtIndex:`, will be much faster.

Note that this method name begins with the `get` prefix. This is a common Cocoa idiom for methods that return a value into space provided by the caller. Contrast this with the `length` method, which does not have the `get` prefix, and just returns the length.

Although it is possible to create your own subclass of `NSString`, it is generally a better option to compose objects without subclassing. An example of this in the Foundation framework is `NSAttributedString`. This responds to `-stringValue` messages to return the string for which it stores attributes, but cannot be used directly in place of a string. We will look at this class in a lot more detail in Chapter 8.

`NSString` has one public subclass (which is also a class cluster), for representing strings that can be modified: `NSMutableString`. This adds methods for modifying characters. Only seven new methods are added by this class, with six being defined in terms of the one primitive method: `replaceCharactersInRange:withString:`.

The `NSString` class has a huge number of methods, and 10.5 added a lot more. A lot of these are to do with path handling. One of the problems that OS X developers encountered a lot in the early days was the fact that MacOS and OPENSTEP had different ways of representing paths. MacOS used a multi-routed file hierarchy, with one file for each disk, with path components separated by colons. OPENSTEP used a UNIX-style file hierarchy, with a single root and path components separated by slashes. Mac OS X applications often had to deal with both.

Fortunately, this was a problem that NeXT had already encountered. OpenStep applications were able to run on Solaris, OPENSTEP, and Windows. Windows file paths were similar in structure to classic MacOS paths. `NSString` has a set of methods for adding and deleting path components and splitting paths apart in a way that is independent of the underlying filesystem representation. It is good practice to use these, rather than manually constructing paths.

Recent versions of OS X have begun to move away from using file paths entirely, with a lot of methods now using *URLs* in the file:// namespace instead of file paths. There are fewer methods on `NSString` for dealing with these; however, the `NSURL` class provides a lot more.

4.3.3 Boxed Numbers and Values

The advantage of using primitive types is speed. The disadvantage is that they don't integrate well with collections that expect objects. There are three classes that are provided for working around these. Each of them boxes a specific kind of primitive value.

> **Boxing**
>
> Boxing is a term used to describe wrapping a primitive value in an object. High-level languages like Lisp and Smalltalk perform auto-boxing, and so you can interact with primitive values as if they were objects. Objective-C requires manual boxing.

The most general boxing class is `NSValue`, which can contain any primitive type. This is most commonly used for encapsulating the Foundation **`struct`** types, such as `NSRange` and storing them in collections. This class has a subclass (actually, a class cluster), `NSNumber`, which is used to store single numerical values. Any value from a **`char`** to a **`long long`** stored in one of these, and it will correctly cast the result if any of the `-somethingValue` family of methods is called. For example, you can create an `NSNumber` from a primitive **`unsigned int`** like this:

```
[NSNumber numberWithUnsignedInt: myInt];
```

It could then be stored in a collection, retrieved, passed to another method, and then turned into a 64-bit value like this:

```
[aNumber longLongValue];
```

Be careful when doing this, however. If you do the reverse operation—create an `NSNumber` with a 64-bit value and then retrieve a 32-bit or smaller value—then there will be silent truncation of the result.

Decimal Arithmetic

In addition to the standard binary types inherited from C, and their boxed equivalents, Foundation defines an `NSDecimal` structure and a `NSDecimalNumber` boxed equivalent. These can be used for performing decimal floating point arithmetic. Some decimal numbers, such as 0.1, cannot be represented as finite binary values. This is problematic for financial applications, where a fixed number of decimal digits of precision is required. The `NSDecimal` type can be used to accomplish this.

There is one remaining boxed value, which is often overlooked. `NSNull` is a singleton—only one instance of it ever exists—representing a boxed version of `NULL`.

The Many Types of Zero

In C, `NULL` is defined as `(void*)0`; a pointer value of zero. Because the `void*` type can be silently cast to any pointer, the `NULL` value can be used for any pointer. Objective-C adds two new types of zero; `nil` and `Nil`, meaning `(id)0` and `(Class)0` respectively. In addition, there is the boxed version, `NSNull` and zero values boxed in `NSValue` and `NSNumber` objects. This means that there are a lot of different ways of expressing zero in Cocoa, depending on the use.

Unlike many of the other classes in Foundation, there is no `NSMutableNumber` or `NSMutableDecimalNumber`. If you need to modify a boxed value, you need to first unbox it, then perform primitive operations on it, and then box it again. This makes sense, since operations on primitive values are typically a lot faster than message sends. In a language like Smalltalk or Lisp, the compiler would try to transparently turn the object into a primitive value and do this for you, but Objective-C compilers are not (yet) clever enough to do so.

4.3.4 Data

In C, arbitrary data is typically represented in the same way as strings; by `char*`s. In Cocoa, using string objects would not work, since they perform character set conversion. The `NSData` class exists to encapsulate raw data. You can think of it as a boxed version of `void*`, although it also stores a length, preventing pointer arithmetic bugs from overwriting random memory locations.

You can get a pointer to the object's data by sending it a `-bytes` message. It may seem that this will be more efficient; however, this is not always the case. In some cases, the underlying representation may be a set of non-contiguous memory regions, or data in a file that has not been read into memory. When you call `-bytes` the object is required to ensure that all of the data is in a contiguous memory region, which may be an expensive operation. Subsequent operation on the data will, in the absence of swapping, be very fast.

You can use `NSData` and its mutable subclass, `NSMutableData`, for doing simple file I/O operations. Data objects can be initialized using the contents of a file, either using file reading operations or using `mmap()`. Using a memory-mapped `NSData` object is often a very convenient way of doing random access on a file. On 32-bit platforms you can exhaust your address space fairly quickly doing this, but on 64-bit systems you have a lot of spare address space for memory mapped files.

One big advantage of accessing files in this way is that it is very VM-friendly. If you read the contents of a file into memory and then the system is low on RAM, then it has to write out your copy to the swap file, even if you haven't modified it. If you use a `NSData` object created with `dataWithContentsOfMappedFile:` or similar, then it will simply evict the pages from memory and read them back from the original file when needed.

Since `NSData` objects can be initialized from URLs, they provide a very simple means of accessing the system's URL loading services. OS X has code for loading data from a wide variety of URL types, including files, HTTP, and FTP.

4.3.5 Caches and Discardable Data

Memory conservation is an important problem for a lot of modern applications. In recent years, the price of memory has fallen considerably, and so it becomes increasingly tempting to use some of it to store results from calculations or data received over the network. This suddenly becomes a problem when you want to port your code to a device that has a small amount of memory, like the iPhone, or when everyone is doing it.

With OS X 10.6, Apple introduced the `NSDiscardableContent` protocol. This defines a transactional API for working with objects. Before you use an object that implements this protocol, you should send it a `-beginContentAccess` message.

If this returns **`YES`**, then you can use the object as you would and then send an `-endContentAccess` message when you are finished. Other code may send the object a `-discardContentIfPossible` message, and if this message is received outside of a transaction, then the receiver will discard its contents.

This is easiest to understand with a concrete implementation, such as that provided by a new subclass of `NSMutableData` called `NSPurgeableData`. This behaves in exactly the same way as `NSMutableData`, but also implements the `NSDiscardableContent` protocol. When it receives a `-discardContentIfPossible` message, it will free the data that it encapsulates unless it is currently being accessed.

You may want to combine objects that uses the `NSDiscardableContent` protocol with existing code. The `-autoContentAccessingProxy` method, declared on `NSObject`, lets you do this safely. This returns a proxy object that calls `-beginContentAccess` on the receiver when it is created, and `-endContentAccess` when it is destroyed, passing all other messages on to the original object. This prevents the contents of the object from being freed as long as the proxy exists.

This is useful for storing cached data, for example, images rendered from other data in the application, that can be regenerated if required. The object remains valid, but its contents do not. This means that you can use it as a form of zeroing weak reference in non-garbage-collected environments. It is more flexible than a weak reference, however, because it provides fine-grained control over when it can be freed.

Most commonly, you will use objects that implement this protocol in conjunction with `NSCache`. This class is conceptually similar to a dictionary but is designed for storing discardable content. When you add an object to a cache, you use the `-setObject:forKey:cost:` method. The third argument defines the cost of keeping this object in the cache. When the total cost exceeds the limit set by `-setTotalCostLimit:`, the cache will attempt to discard the contents of some objects (and, optionally, the objects themselves) to reduce the cost.

Most commonly the cost is memory. When using `NSPurgeableData` instances, you would use the size as the limit. You might also use caches to limit the number of objects holding some other scarce resource, such as file handles, or even some remote resources hosted on a server somewhere.

4.3.6 Dates and Time

Time on POSIX systems is stored in `time_t` values. In a traditional UNIX system, this was a 32-bit signed value counting seconds since the UNIX epoch (the start of 1970). This means that there will be a new version of the Y2K bug some time in 2038, when this value overflows. On OS X, the `time_t` is a **`long`**, meaning that it is 32 bit on 32-bit systems and 64 bit on 64-bit systems. If people are still using

OS X in three hundred trillion years, when this overflows, then they probably will have had enough time to port their software to some other system.

Since the implementation of `time_t` is implementation-dependent, it was not a good fit for Cocoa. On some platforms it is an integer, on others a floating point value. Cocoa defines a `NSTimeInterval` type, which is a **`double`**. As a floating point value, the accuracy of an `NSTimeInterval` depends on the size of the value. A **`double`** has a 53-bit mantissa and a 10-bit exponent. If the least significant bit of the mantissa is a millisecond, then the value can store 9×10^{12} seconds, or around 285,427 years. If you use a range of under around a hundred thousand years, it will store half milliseconds, and so on. For any value that could be stored in a 32-bit `time_t`, the value will be accurate to under a microsecond, which is usually more accurate than is needed. The time slicing quantum for most UNIX-like systems is around 10ms, meaning that you are very unlikely to get timer events more accurately than every few tens of milliseconds.

As with other primitive values, Foundation defines both the basic primitive type and a number of classes for interacting with them in a more friendly way. These gain a little more precision by using the start of 2001 (the year OS X was publicly released) as their reference date.

Date handling is much more complex than time handling. While an `NSTimeInterval` can represent a time four hundred years ago easily, getting the corresponding calendar date is much more complex. The Gregorian calendar was introduced in 1582, but Britain didn't switch over until 1752 and Russia didn't switch until 1918. The existence of leap years and leap seconds further complicates matters, meaning that a `NSTimeInterval` may represent different dates in different locales. And all of this is before you get into the matter of time zones.

The `NSDate` class is a fairly simple wrapper around a time interval from some reference date (2001 by default, although the UNIX epoch and the current timestamp are other options). The `NSCalendarDate` subclass provides a version in the Gregorian calendar, although its use is discouraged.

With 10.4, Apple introduced the `NSCalendar` class, which encapsulates a *calendar*. A calendar is a mechanism from mapping between time intervals and dates. Early calendars were simple means of mapping between fixed dates, such as the summer and winter solstices, and seasons. Modern calendars map between time intervals and more complex dates. Cocoa understands a number of different calendars, including the Gregorian, Buddhist, Chinese, and Islamic calendars.

If you create an `NSCalendar` with `+autoupdatingCurrentCalendar`, then the calendar will automatically update depending on the currently specified locale. This means you should avoid caching values returned from the calendar, since they may change at arbitrary points in the future.

A `NSCalendar` allows you to turn a `NSDate` into an `NSDateComponents` object. This object is roughly equivalent to the POSIX **`struct`** `tm`. It allows the year, month, day, day of the week, and so on to be extracted, based on the interpretation of an `NSDate` in a specified calendar.

In general, you should always store dates in `NSDate` objects and only convert them to a given calendar when you want to display them in the user interface. This is one of the reasons why using `NSCalendarDate` is discouraged—as an `NSDate` subclass it is very tempting to use it for long-term storage—the other being that it is limited to the Gregorian calendar, making it unsuitable for use in Japan, China, and much of the rest of the world outside the Americas and Europe.

4.4 Collections

A big part of any language's standard library is providing collections, and Foundation is no exception. It includes a small number of primitive collection types defined as opaque C types and then uses these to build more complex Objective-C types.

In contrast with the C++ standard template library, Cocoa collections are heterogeneous and can contain any kind of object. All objects are referenced by pointer, so the amount of space needed to store pointers to any two objects is always the same: one word.

4.4.1 Comparisons and Ordering

For ordered collections, objects implement their own comparison. While almost any object can be stored in an array, there are more strict requirements for those that are to be stored in a set (which doesn't allow duplicates) or used as keys in a dictionary. Objects that are stored in this way must implement two methods: `-hash` and `-isEqual:`. These have a complex relationship.

1. Any two objects that are equal must return **`YES`** to `isEqual:` when compared in either order.

2. Any two objects that are equal must return the same value in response to `-hash`.

3. The hash of any object must remain constant while it is stored in a collection.

The first of these is somewhat difficult to implement by itself. It means that the following must always be true:

```
[a isEqual: b] == [b isEqual: a]
```

If this is ever not true, then some very strange and unexpected behavior may occur. This may seem very easy to get right, but what happens when you compare an object to its subclass or to an object of a different class? Some classes may allow comparisons with other classes; for example, an object encapsulating a number may decide it is equal to another object if they both return the same result to `intValue`.

An example of when this can cause problems is in the use of objects as keys in dictionaries. When you set a value for a given key in a dictionary, the dictionary first checks if the key is already in the dictionary. If it is, then it replaces the value for that key. If not, then it inserts a new value.

If `[a isEqual: b]` returns **YES** but `[b isEqual: a]` returns **NO**, then you will get two different dictionaries depending on whether you set a value for the key `a` first and then the value for the key `b`. In general, therefore, it is good practice to only use one kind of object as keys in any given collection (most commonly `NSString`s).

Listing 4.6 gives a simple example of this. This defines three new classes. The first, `A`, is a simple superclass for both of the others, which returns a constant value for the hash. It implements `copyWithZone:` in a simple way. Since this object is immutable (it has no instance variables, therefore no state, therefore no mutable state), instead of copying we just return the original object with its reference count incremented. This is required since the dictionary will attempt to copy keys, to ensure that they are not modified outside the collection (more on this later).

Listing 4.6: An invalid implementation of `isEqual:` [from: examples/isEqualFailure/dict.m]

```
#import <Foundation/Foundation.h>

@interface A : NSObject {}
@end
@interface B : A {}
@end
@interface C : A {}
@end
@implementation A
- (id) copyWithZone: (NSZone*)aZone { return [self retain]; }
- (NSString*)description { return [self className]; }
- (NSUInteger)hash { return 0; }
@end
@implementation B
- (BOOL) isEqual: (id)other { return YES; }
@end
@implementation C
- (BOOL) isEqual: (id)other { return NO; }
@end

```

```
int main(void)
{
    id pool = [NSAutoreleasePool new];
    NSObject *anObject = [NSObject new];
    NSMutableDictionary *d1 = [NSMutableDictionary new];
    [d1 setObject: anObject forKey: [B new]];
    [d1 setObject: anObject forKey: [C new]];
    NSMutableDictionary *d2 = [NSMutableDictionary new];
    [d2 setObject: anObject forKey: [C new]];
    [d2 setObject: anObject forKey: [B new]];
    NSLog(@"d1: %@", d1);
    NSLog(@"d2: %@", d2);
    return 0;
}
```

The two subclasses, `B` and `C`, have similarly trivial implementations of the `-isEqual:` method. One always returns **`YES`**; the other returns **`NO`**. In the `main()` function, we create two mutable dictionaries and set two objects for them, one with an instance of `A` and one with an instance of `B` as keys.

When we run the program, we get the following result:

```
$ gcc -framework Foundation dict.m &&./a.out
2009-01-07 16:54:15.735 a.out[28893:10b] d1: {
    B = <NSObject: 0x1003270>;
}
2009-01-07 16:54:15.737 a.out[28893:10b] d2: {
    B = <NSObject: 0x1003270>;
    C = <NSObject: 0x1003270>;
}
```

The first dictionary only contains one object, the second one contains two. This is a problem. In a more complex program, the keys may come from some external source. You could spend a long time wondering why in some instances you got a duplicate key and in others you got different ones.

Equality on objects of different classes makes the hash value even more tricky, since both objects must have the same hash value if they are equal. This means that both classes must use the same hash function, and if one has some state not present in the other, then this cannot be used in calculating the hash. Alternatively, both can return the same, constant, value for all objects. This is simple, but if taken to its logical conclusion means all objects must return 0 for their hash, which is far from ideal.

The third requirement is the hardest of all to satisfy in theory, but the easiest in practice. An object has no way of knowing when it is in a collection. If you use an object as a key in a dictionary, or insert it into a set, then modify it, then its hash might change. If its hash doesn't change, then it might now be breaking the second condition.

In practice, you can avoid this by simply avoiding modifying objects while they are in collections.

4.4.2 Primitive Collections

As mentioned earlier, Foundation provides some primitive collections as C opaque types. As of 10.5, these gained an `isa` pointer and so can be used both via their C and Objective-C interfaces. The biggest advantage of this is that they can be stored in other collections without wrapping them in `NSValue` instances. Most of the time, if you use these, you will want to use them via their C interfaces. These are faster and provide access to more functionality. The object interfaces are largely to support collections containing weak references in a garbage-collected environment. If you are not using garbage collection, or wish to use the primitive collections to store other types of value, then the C interfaces are more useful.

The simplest type of collection defined in Foundation, beyond the primitive C types like arrays and structures, is `NSHashTable`. This is a simple hash table implementation. It stores a set of unique values identified by pointers. A hash table is created using a `NSHashTableCallBacks` structure, which defines five functions used for interacting with the objects in the collection:

- `hash` defines a function returning hash value for a given pointer.
- `isEqual` provides the comparison function, used for testing whether two pointers point to equal values.
- `retain` is called on every pointer as it is inserted into the hash table.
- `release` is the inverse operation, called on objects that are removed.
- `describe` returns an `NSString` describing the object, largely for debugging purposes.

All of these correspond to methods declared by `NSObject`, and you can store these in a hash table by using the predefined set of callbacks called `NSObjectHashCallBacks` or `NSNonRetainedObjectHashCallBacks`, depending on whether you want the hash table to retain the objects when they are inserted.

The hash table model is extended slightly by `NSMapTable`. An `NSMapTable` is effectively a hash table storing pairs and only using the first element for comparisons. These are defined by two sets of callbacks, one for the key and one for the value.

Unlike other Cocoa collections, both of these can be used to store non-object types, including integers that fit in a pointer, or pointers to C structures or arrays.

4.4.3 Arrays

Objective-C, as a pure superset of C, has access to standard C arrays, but since these are just pointers to a blob of memory they are not very friendly to use. OpenStep defined two kinds of arrays: mutable and immutable. The `NSArray` class implements the immutable kind and its subclass `NSMutableArray` implements the mutable version.

Unlike C arrays, these can only store Objective-C objects. If you need an array of other objects, you can either use a C array directly or create a new Objective-C class that contains an array of the required type.

`NSArray` is another example of a class cluster. The two primitive methods in this case are `-count` and `-objectAtIndex:`. These have almost identical behavior to their counterparts in `NSString`, although the latter returns objects instead of unicode characters.

As with strings, immutable arrays can be more efficient in terms of storage than their C counterparts. When you create an array from a range in another array, for example, you may get an object back that only stores a pointer to the original array and the range—a view on the original array—avoiding the need to copy large numbers of elements.

Since Cocoa arrays are objects, they can do a lot of things that plain data arrays in C can't. The best example of this is the `-makeObjectsPerformSelector:` method, which sends a selector to every single element in an array. You can use this to write some very concise code.

With 10.5, Apple added `NSPointerArray`. This can store arbitrary pointers (but not non-pointer types). Unlike `NSArray`, it can store `NULL` values and in the presence of garbage collection can be configured to use weak references. In this case, a `NULL` value will be used for any object that is destroyed while in the array.

Variadic Initializers

Most Cocoa collections have a variadic constructor and initializer. Examples of this include `+arrayWithObjects:` and `+dictionaryWithObjectsAndKeys:`. These take a variable number of arguments, terminated with `nil` and return a constant array or dictionary with the named elements. These can be very useful for quickly constructing collections where the number of elements is known at compile time.

The Cocoa arrays are very flexible. They can be used as both *stacks* and *queues* without modification since they allow insertion at both ends with a single method. Using an array as a stack is very efficient. A stack is defined by three operations: push, pop, and top. The first of these adds a new object to the top of the stack. `NSMutableArray`'s `-addObject:` method does this. The pop operation removes the last object to have been pushed onto the stack, which is exactly what `-removeLastObject` does. The remaining operation, top, gets the object currently on the top of the stack (at the end of the array) and is provided by `NSArray`'s `-lastObject` method.

Using an array as a queue is less efficient. A queue has objects inserted at one end and removed from the other. You can cheaply insert objects at the end of the array, but inserting them at the front is very expensive. Similarly, you can remove the object from the end of an array very efficiently, but removing the first one is more expensive. The `removeObjectAtIndex:` method may not actually move the objects in the array up one if you delete the first element, however. Since `NSMutableArray` is a class cluster, certain implementations may be more efficient for removing the first element, but there is no way to guarantee this.

4.4.4 Dictionaries

Dictionaries, sometimes called *associative arrays* are implemented by the `NSDictionary` class. A dictionary is a mapping from objects to other objects, a more friendly version of `NSMapTable` that only works for objects.

It is common to use strings as keys in dictionaries, since they meet all of the requirements for a key. In a lot of Cocoa, keys for use in dictionaries are defined as constant strings. Somewhere in a header file you will find something like:

```
extern NSString *kAKeyForSomeProperty;
```

Then in a private implementation file somewhere it will say

```
NSString *kAKeyForSomeProperty = @"kAKeyForSomeProperty";
```

This pattern is found all over Cocoa and in various third-party frameworks. Often you can just use the literal value, rather than the key, but this will use a bit more space in the binary and be slightly slower, so there isn't any advantage in doing so.

As you might expect, the mutable version of a dictionary is an `NSMutableDictionary`, which adds `-setObject:forKey:` and `-removeObjectForKey:` primitive methods, and a few convenience methods.

Dictionaries can often be used as a substitute for creating a new class. If all you need is something storing some structured data, and not any methods on this data, then dictionaries are quite cheap and are very quick to create. You can create a dictionary in a single call, like this:

```
[NSDictionary dictionaryWithObjectsAndKeys:
    image, @"image",
    string, @"caption", nil];
```

This is a variadic constructor that takes a `nil`-terminated list of objects as arguments and inserts each pair into the dictionary as object and key. You can then access these by sending a `-objectForKey:` message to the resulting dictionary.

Cocoa uses this in quite a few places. Notifications store a dictionary, with a specific set of keys defined for certain notification types. This makes it easy to add additional data in the future.

4.4.5 Sets

Just as `NSDictionary` is an object built on top of the primitive `NSMapTable`, `NSSet` is an object built on top of the primitive `NSHashTable`. As in mathematics, *sets* in Cocoa are unordered collections of unique objects. Unlike an array, an object can only be in a set once.

The rules for determining whether two objects are equal are very simple. Objects in a set are first split into buckets using their hash, or some bits of the their hash for small sets. When a new object is inserted, the set first finds the correct bucket for its hash. It then tests it with every object in that bucket using `-isEqual:`. If none of them match it, then the new object is inserted.

For a `NSSet`, this is only done when the set is initialized from an array or a list of objects as arguments. `NSMutableSet` allows objects to be added to an existing set and will perform this check every time. As you might imagine, this is very slow ($\mathcal{O}(n)$) if all of the objects have the same hash value.

In addition to basic sets, OpenStep provided `NSCountedSet`. This is a subclass of `NSMutableSet` and so is also mutable. Unlike normal sets, *counted sets* (also known as *bags*) allow objects to exist more than once in the collection. Like sets, they are unordered. Another way of thinking of them is unordered arrays, although an array allows distinct-but-equal objects to exist in the same collection, while a counted set just keeps a count of objects.

With 10.3, `NSIndexSet` was also added. This is a set of integers that can be used as indexes in an array or some other integer-indexed data structure. Internally, `NSIndexSet` stores a set of non-overlapping ranges, so if you are storing sets containing contiguous ranges, then it can be very efficient.

`NSIndexSet` is not very useful by itself. It is made useful by `NSArray` methods such as `-objectsAtIndexes:`, which returns an array containing just the specified elements. Since the indexes are all within a certain range, operations on an `NSArray` using an index set only require bounds checking once, rather than for every lookup, which can make things faster.

4.5 Enumeration

The traditional way of performing enumeration on Foundation collections is via the `NSEnumerator`. This is a very simple object that responds to a `-nextObject` message and returns either the next object, or `nil` if there is no next object. To enumerate a collection using an enumerator, you simply call a method like `-objectEnumerator` on the collection and then loop sending `-nextObject` to the returned enumerator until it returns `nil`.

With 10.5, Apple added a fast enumeration system. This uses a new **for** loop construct, part of Objective-C 2.0, which handles collections.

A lot of the time, however, you don't need to use enumeration directly at all. You can use something like `NSArray`'s `-makeObjectsPerformSelector:` method. Listing 4.7 shows an example of all three ways of sending a single message to all objects in an array.

Listing 4.7: The three ways of sending a message to an object in Cocoa.[from: examples/Enumeration/enum.m]

```
#import <Foundation/Foundation.h>

@interface NSString (printing)
- (void) print;
@end
@implementation NSString (printing)
- (void) print
{
    fprintf(stderr, "%s\n", [self UTF8String]);
}
@end

int main(void)
{
    [NSAutoreleasePool new];
    NSArray* a =
        [NSArray arrayWithObjects: @"this", @"is", @"an", @"array", nil];

    NSLog(@"The␣Objective-C␣1␣way:");
    NSEnumerator *e=[a objectEnumerator];
    for (id obj=[e nextObject]; nil!=obj ; obj=[e nextObject])
    {
        [obj print];
    }
    NSLog(@"The␣Leopard␣way:");
    for (id obj in a)
```

```
27         {
28             [obj print];
29         }
30         NSLog(@"The simplest way:");
31         [a makeObjectsPerformSelector: @selector(print)];
32         return 0;
33 }
```

Lines 20–24 show how to use an enumerator. This is quite complex and easy to make typos in, so in Étoilé we hide this pattern in a `FOREACH` macro (which also does some caching to speed things up slightly). A simpler version is shown in lines 26–29, using the fast enumeration pattern. This is both simpler code and faster, which is quite a rare achievement. The final version, on line 31, is even simpler. This is a single line. If you want to send more than one message, or messages with more than one argument, then this mechanism is unavailable.

Running this code, we get

```
$ gcc -std=c99 -framework Foundation enum.m && ./a.out
2009-01-07 18:06:41.014 a.out[30527:10b] The Objective-C 1 way:
this
is
an
array
2009-01-07 18:06:41.020 a.out[30527:10b] The Leopard way:
this
is
an
array
2009-01-07 18:06:41.021 a.out[30527:10b] The simplest way:
this
is
an
array
```

4.5.1 Enumerating with Higher-Order Messaging

An additional way of performing enumeration, among other things, was proposed by Marcel Weiher. The mechanism, called *higher-order messaging* (*HOM*) uses the proxy capabilities of Objective-C. It adds methods like `-map` to the collection classes. When these are called, they return a proxy object that bounces every message sent to them to every object in the array.

Listing 4.8 shows a `-map` method added as a category on `NSArray`. This is taken from the EtoileFoundation framework, with the Étoilé-specific macros removed.

This framework is available under a BSD license, and so you can use it in your own projects if you wish.

Listing 4.8: A example of a map method implemented using higher-order messaging. [from: examples/HOM/NSArray+map.m]

```
@interface NSArrayMapProxy : NSProxy {
    NSArray * array;
}
- (id) initWithArray:(NSArray*)anArray;
@end

@implementation NSArrayMapProxy
- (id) initWithArray:(NSArray*)anArray
{
    if (nil == (self = [self init])) { return nil; }
    array = [anArray retain];
    return self;
}
- (id) methodSignatureForSelector:(SEL)aSelector
{
    for (object in array)
    {
        if([object respondsToSelector:aSelector])
        {
            return [object methodSignatureForSelector:aSelector];
        }
    }
    return [super methodSignatureForSelector:aSelector];
}
- (void) forwardInvocation:(NSInvocation*)anInvocation
{
    SEL selector = [anInvocation selector];
    NSMutableArray * mappedArray =
        [NSMutableArray arrayWithCapacity:[array count]];
    for (object in array)
    {
        if([object respondsToSelector:selector])
        {
            [anInvocation invokeWithTarget:object];
            id mapped;
            [anInvocation getReturnValue:&mapped];
            [mappedArray addObject:mapped];
        }
    }
```

```
    [anInvocation setReturnValue:mappedArray];
}
- (void) dealloc
{
    [array release];
    [super dealloc];
}
@end

@implementation NSArray (AllElements)
- (id) map
{
    return [[[NSArrayMapProxy alloc] initWithArray:self] autorelease];
}
@end
```

The `-map` method itself is relatively simple; it just creates an instance of the proxy, associates it with the array, and returns it. You would use this category like this:

```
[[array map] stringValue];
```

This would return an array containing the result of sending `-stringValue` to every element in `array`. When you send the `-stringValue` message to the proxy, the runtime calls the `-methodSignatureForSelector:` method. This is used to find out the types of the method. This implementation simply calls the same method on every object in the array until it finds one which returns a value.

Next, the `-forwardInvocation:` method will be called. This has an encapsulated message as the argument. The body of this method sends this message to every object in the array and then adds the result to a new array.

Unlike the `-makeObjectsPerformSelector:`, messages sent to objects using higher-order messaging can have an arbitrary number of arguments. Exactly the same mechanism can be used to implement a variety of other high-level operations on collections, such as folding or selecting.

Although the use of the forwarding mechanism makes this relatively slow, compared with other enumeration mechanisms, the fact that it preserves high-level information in the source code can make it attractive. It results in less duplicated code and code that is easier to write. HOM is used a lot in modern Smalltalk implementations, although the initial implementation was in Objective-C.

Higher-order messaging is not limited to enumeration. It is also used for a wide number of other tasks, including sending messages between threads. We'll look more at how to use it for asynchronous messaging in Chapter 23.

4.5.2 Enumerating with Blocks

OS X 10.6 added blocks, which we looked at in the last chapter, to the C family of languages. Blocks by themselves are quite useful, but their real power comes from their integration with the rest of the Foundation framework. This integration comes from a number of new methods, such as this one on `NSArray`:

```
- (void)enumerateObjectsUsingBlock:
        (void (^)(id obj, NSUInteger idx, BOOL *stop))block;
```

The argument is a block taking three arguments: an object, the index at which that object appears in the array, and a pointer to a boolean value to set if enumeration should stop. We could rewrite the same enumeration example that we used earlier with a block as:

```
[a enumerateObjectsUsingBlock:
        ^(id obj, NSUInteger idx, BOOL *stop) { [obj print]; } ];
```

The requirement to put the types of the block arguments inline makes this quite difficult to read, but you could split it up a bit by declaring the block separately and then calling it. In this example, the block doesn't refer to anything other than its arguments, so using a block is equivalent to using a function pointer, with the exception that a block can be declared inline.

The method shown above is a simplified version. The more complex variant includes an options parameter that is an `NSEnumerationOptions` value. This is an enumerated type that specifies whether the enumeration should proceed forward, in reverse, or in parallel. If you specify `NSEnumerationConcurrent`, then the array may spawn a new thread or use a thread from a pool to split the enumeration across multiple processors. This is usually only a good idea for large arrays or blocks that take a long time to execute.

Foundation defines two other kinds of blocks for use with collections: *test blocks* and *comparator blocks*. A test block returns a **`BOOL`**, while a comparator is defined by the `NSComparator` **`typedef`**:

```
typedef NSComparisonResult (^NSComparator)(id obj1, id obj2);
```

Comparator blocks are used everywhere that sorting might be performed. Both mutable and immutable arrays can be sorted with comparators but so can sets and dictionaries. This includes some quite complex methods, such as this one from `NSDictionary`:

```
- (NSArray*)keysSortedByValueUsingComparator: (NSComparator)cmptr;
```

The argument to this method is a comparator block that defines the ordering of two objects. This will be called with all of the values in the dictionary, and the method will return an array containing all of the keys in the order that their values are listed. This can then be used to visit the values in this order by sending `-valueForKey:` messages to the dictionary.

Test blocks are used for filtering. Unlike comparators, they do not have a specific type associated with them because each class defines the arguments that a test block takes. For example, `NSIndexSet` test blocks take an `NSUInteger` argument, while tests for `NSDictionary` take both the key and value as arguments.

Most collection classes, including those outside of Foundation, such as those managed by the *Core Data* framework support `NSPredicate` as a means of filtering. As of OS X 10.6, you can also create `NSPredicate` instances from test blocks. You can also create `NSSortDescriptor` instances, which are heavily used in conjunction with *Cocoa bindings* from comparator blocks and, using the `-comparator` method turn an `NSSortDescriptor` object into a comparator block.

4.5.3 Supporting Fast Enumeration

From time to time, you will want to implement your own collection classes, and want to use them with the new **`for...in`** loops. If your collection can create enumerators, then you can use the enumerator as the enumerator's support for fast enumeration, but this is slightly unwieldy and slow. Full support requires collections to conform to the `NSFastEnumeration` protocol and implement the following method:

```
- (NSUInteger)countByEnumeratingWithState: (NSFastEnumerationState*)state
                                  objects: (id*)stackbuf
                                    count: (NSUInteger)len;
```

Understanding this method requires understanding the `NSFastEnumerationState` structure. This is defined in the NSEnumerator.h Foundation header, as shown in Listing 4.9.

Listing 4.9: The fast enumeration state structure. [from: NSEnumerator.h]

```
typedef struct {
    unsigned long state;
    id *itemsPtr;
    unsigned long *mutationsPtr;
    unsigned long extra[5];
} NSFastEnumerationState;
```

The first time this method is called, it should initialize the `mutationsPtr` field of this structure. This must be a valid pointer to something at least as big as a **`long`**. The caller will automatically cache the pointed-to value when the method is first called and then compare this on every subsequent iteration through the loop. If it has changed, then an exception will be thrown. In contrast, an `NSEnumerator` has no way of knowing if the collection it is enumerating has changed.

The second argument is a pointer to a buffer allocated by the caller, and the third is the size of this buffer. If the collection stores objects internally in a C array, it can return a pointer to this directly by setting `state->itemsPtr` to the array and returning the number of elements. Otherwise, it copies up to `len` elements into `stackbuf` and returns the number it copies. The compiler currently sets `len` to 16, and so only a single message send is required for every 16 items enumerated. In contrast, at least 32 will be required when using an enumerator (one to the enumerator and one from the enumerator to the collection). It is easy to see why Apple calls this the 'fast enumeration' system.

To see how you can support fast enumeration in your own collections, we will create two new classes, as shown in Listing 4.10. These both conform to the `NSFastEnumeration` protocol. One is mutable and the other immutable. Supporting fast enumeration is done slightly differently for mutable and immutable objects.

Listing 4.10: Integer array interfaces. [from: examples/FastEnumeration/IntegerArray.h]

```
#import <Foundation/Foundation.h>

@interface IntegerArray : NSObject<NSFastEnumeration> {
    NSUInteger count;
    NSInteger *values;
}
- (id)initWithValues: (NSInteger*)array count: (NSUInteger)size;
- (NSInteger)integerAtIndex: (NSUInteger)index;
@end

@interface MutableIntegerArray : IntegerArray {
    unsigned long version;
}
- (void)setInteger: (NSInteger)newValue atIndex: (NSUInteger)index;
@end
```

The most noticeable difference in the interface is that the mutable version has a `version` instance variable. This is used to track whether the object has changed during enumeration.

The immutable version is shown in Listing 4.11. The first two methods are very simple; they just initialize the array and allow values to be accessed. The array is a simple C buffer, created with `malloc()`. The `-dealloc` method frees the buffer when the object is destroyed.

The fast enumeration implementation here returns a pointer to the instance variable, on line 28. This code is written to support partial enumeration, where the caller only requests some subset of the total collection. This is not currently supported by the compiler, but, because this is just an Objective-C method, you cannot guarantee that it will not be called directly by some code wanting just the

Listing 4.11: A simple immutable integer array supporting fast enumeration.

[from: examples/FastEnumeration/IntegerArray.m]

```
@implementation IntegerArray
- (id)initWithValues: (NSInteger*)array count: (NSUInteger)size
{
    if (nil == (self = [self init])) { return nil; }
    count = size;
    NSInteger arraySize = size * sizeof(NSInteger);
    values = malloc(arraySize);
    memcpy(values, array, arraySize);
    return self;
}
- (NSInteger)integerAtIndex: (NSUInteger)index
{
    if (index >= count)
    {
        [NSException raise: NSRangeException
                    format: @"Invalid index"];
    }
    return values[index];
}
- (NSUInteger)countByEnumeratingWithState: (NSFastEnumerationState*)state
                                  objects: (id*)stackbuf
                                    count: (NSUInteger)len
{
    NSUInteger n = count - state->state;
    state->mutationsPtr = (unsigned long *)self;
    state->itemsPtr = (id*)(values + state->state);
    state->state += n;
    return n;
}
- (void)dealloc
{
    free(values);
    [super dealloc];
}
@end
```

values after a certain element. The `state` field will be set to the first element that the caller wants. In normal use, this will be either 0 or `count`. The items pointer is set to the correct offset in the instance variable array using some simple pointer arithmetic.

The `state` field is updated to equal the index of the last value and the array is returned. Any **`for...in`** loop will call this method twice. After the first call the `state` field will have been set to `count`. In the second call, the value of `n` will be set to 0 and the loop will terminate.

Note that the mutations pointer is set to **`self`**. Dereferencing this will give the `isa` pointer. This class does not support modifying the values, but some other code may change the class of this object to a subclass that does. In this case, the mutation pointer will change. This is very unlikely; for most cases the **`self`** pointer is a convenient value because it is a pointer that is going to remain both valid and constant for the duration of the loop.

The mutable case is a bit more complicated. This is shown in Listing 4.12. This class adds a method, allowing values in the array to be set. Note that on line 42 the version is incremented. This is used to abort enumeration when the array is modified.

The enumeration method in this class sets the mutation pointer to the address of the `version` instance variable. The initial value of this is cached by the code generated from the loop construct, and every loop iteration will be compared against the current value to detect changes.

Listing 4.12: A simple mutable integer array supporting fast enumeration. [from: examples/FastEnumeration/IntegerArray.m]

```
39 @implementation MutableIntegerArray
40 - (void)setInteger: (NSInteger)newValue atIndex: (NSUInteger)index
41 {
42     version++;
43     if (index >= count)
44     {
45         values = realloc(values, (index+1) * sizeof(NSInteger));
46         count = index + 1;
47     }
48     values[index] = newValue;
49 }
50 - (NSUInteger)countByEnumeratingWithState: (NSFastEnumerationState*)state
51                                   objects: (id*)stackbuf
52                                     count: (NSUInteger)len
53 {
54     NSInteger n;
55     state->mutationsPtr = &version;
56     n = MIN(len, count - state->state);
57     if (n >= 0)
58     {
59         memcpy(stackbuf, values + state->state, n * sizeof(NSInteger));
60         state->state += n;
61     }
62     else
```

```
63      {
64          n = 0;
65      }
66      state->itemsPtr = stackbuf;
67      return n;
68  }
69  @end
```

Because the mutable array's internal array can be reallocated and become invalid, we copy values out onto the stack buffer. This is not technically required; the collection is not thread-safe anyway, and so the array cannot be accessed in a way that would cause problems, but it's done here as an example of how to use the stack buffer.

The stack buffer has a fixed size. This is typically 16 entries. On line 56, we find which is smaller out of the number of slots in the stack buffer and the number of elements left to return. We then copy this many elements on line 59. The items pointer is then set to the stack buffer's address.

Using the stack buffer is entirely optional. Our immutable array didn't use it, while this one does. It is there simply as a convenient place to put elements if the class doesn't use an array internally.

To test these two classes, we use the simple program shown in Listing 4.13. This creates two integer arrays, one mutable and one immutable, and iterates over both of them using the fast enumeration **for...in** loop construct.

Listing 4.13: Testing the fast enumeration implementation. [from: examples/FastEnumeration/test.m]

```
#import "IntegerArray.h"

int main(void)
{
    [NSAutoreleasePool new];
    NSInteger cArray[] = {1, 2, 3, 4, 5, 6, 7, 8, 9, 10, 11, 12, 13, 14,
        15, 16, 17, 18, 19, 20};
    IntegerArray *array = [[IntegerArray alloc] initWithValues: cArray
                                                          count: 20];
    NSInteger total = 0;
    for (id i in array)
    {
        total += (NSInteger)i;
    }
    printf("total:␣%d\n", (int)total);
    MutableIntegerArray *mutablearray =
        [[MutableIntegerArray alloc] initWithValues: cArray
```

```
17                                          count: 20];
18     [mutablearray setInteger: 21 atIndex: 20];
19     for (id i in mutablearray)
20     {
21         total += (NSInteger)i;
22     }
23     printf("total: %d\n", (int)total);
24     for (id i in mutablearray)
25     {
26         total += (NSInteger)i;
27         printf("value: %d\n", (int)(NSInteger)i);
28         [mutablearray setInteger: 22 atIndex: 21];
29     }
30     return 0;
31 }
```

Note that the type of the element in these loops has to be an **id**. This is only a requirement of the type checker. The compiler does not insert any message sends to the returned objects, so as long as they are the same size as an **id** they can be returned.

On line 28, we modify the collection inside a loop. This is exactly the kind of thing that the fast enumeration structure's mutation pointer field is intended to detect. If we have written the implementation correctly, then an exception will be thrown. Running the program, we see that this does happen:

```
$ gcc -framework Foundation *.m && ./a.out
total: 210
total: 441
value: 1
2009-02-21 16:24:56.278 a.out[4506:10b] *** Terminating app
due to uncaught exception  NSGenericException , reason:
 *** Collection <MutableIntegerArray: 0x1004bb0> was mutated
while being enumerated.
```

We didn't have to do anything explicit here to raise the exception. Just modifying the `version` instance variable did it. Note that the exception was raised after the first loop iteration, even though the first 16 values were all returned at once. This is why the mutation pointer is a pointer and not just a value. If it had been a simple value that we had set to the value of the `version` ivar in each call, the loop would not have been able to detect the mutation until the next call. Because it is a pointer, it can be dereferenced and tested very cheaply at each loop iteration and so the mutation is caught the first time the caller tries to load a value from the array that has since changed.

Because we modified the version counter before making any changes to the array, we guaranteed that the mutation will always be caught. If you add any other mutation methods to the class, just remember to add `version++` at the start, and this will keep working.

4.6 Property Lists

Property lists (*plists*) are a feature of OPENSTEP and OS X that crop up in a lot of places. The simplicity of the form and its utility have caused a number of other systems to implement support for property lists.

The original NeXT property lists were a simple ASCII format with single characters representing the borders of different types of collection. This had a few limitations. It was difficult to extend, and relatively difficult to embed in other formats. To address these problems, OS X added an XML format for property lists. This can store a few more formats than the original format and, with proper namespacing, can be embedded in any XML format.

Unfortunately, XML is a very verbose format. Parsing it is relatively expensive and storing it requires a lot of space. To address this, Apple added a third format, which is a proprietary (and undocumented) binary encoding. This encoding is very fast to parse and very dense.

The NeXT format is largely deprecated on OS X, although a few command-line tools (such as the defaults utility) still use it since it is the most human-readable. The XML format is primarily used for interchange and the binary format is used for local storage. Table 4.1 shows a comparison of the XML and OpenStep property list formats. In particular, you will see how much more verbose arrays and dictionaries are in the new XML format.

It is worth noting that GNUstep has extended the OpenStep format to allow `NSValue` and `NSDate` objects to be stored, making GNUstep OpenStep-style property lists as expressive as XML ones, at the cost of interoperability.

The plutil tool can convert to the XML and binary formats. It can also convert from the original NeXT format, but not to it. This is due to the fact that this format is less expressive than the new versions—for example, it cannot store `NSDate` objects—and so the tool cannot guarantee that property lists can be safely converted. As well as converting, the -lint option to the tool causes it to check a plist file and report errors. This is very useful if you ever need to edit a property list by hand.

Type	Cocoa Class	NeXT	XML
String	NSString	"a string"	<string>a string </string>
Boolean	NSNumber	N/A	<true /> or <false />
Integer	NSNumber	12	<integer>12</integer>
Floating Point	NSNumber	12.42	<real>12.42</real>
Date	NSDate	N/A	<date>2009-01-07T13:39Z </date>
Binary data	NSData	<666f6f>	<data>fooZm9v</data>
Arrays	NSArray	("a")	<array> <string>a</string> </array>
Dictionaries	NSDictionary	{"key" = "value";}	<dict> <key> <string>key</string> </key> <value> <string>value</string> </value> </dict>

Table 4.1: The data types that can be stored in OpenStep (NeXT) and XML (Apple) property lists.

4.6.1 Serialization

The main use for property lists is to store collections of data in a format that can be easily written out and read back in. Table 4.1 showed the Cocoa objects that correspond to various elements in a property list, but because only a relatively small set of general formats of data are supported, Cocoa is not the only system that can handle plists.

The Core Foundation library also supports all of the data types, and so does CFLite. This means that property lists can be used by simple C applications without requiring all of Cocoa or even Core Foundation. There are other libraries available for parsing property lists. NetBSD's proplib is a BSD-licensed C library for handling XML property lists without any Apple code.

This means that Cocoa can be used to create configuration or simple data files in a format that is easy to parse and usable by non-Cocoa apps using a variety of toolkits. A lot of core configuration information for OS X is stored in property lists and accessed long before any Cocoa applications start.

The Cocoa collections can be written to property list files directly and read from them with a single call. Listing 4.14 shows an example of this. The program creates a simple array, writes it to a file, and reads it back into a new array. Logging the two arrays shows that they are equivalent.

Listing 4.14: Storing an array in a property list. [from: examples/PropertyList/plist.m]

```
#import <Foundation/Foundation.h>

int main(void)
{
    [NSAutoreleasePool new];
    NSArray *a = [NSArray arrayWithObjects:@"this", @"is", @"an", @"array",
        nil];
    [a writeToFile:@"array.plist" atomically:NO];
    NSArray *b = [NSArray arrayWithContentsOfFile:@"array.plist"];
    NSLog(@"a:␣%@", a);
    NSLog(@"b:␣%@", b);
    return 0;
}
```

When we run this program, we can verify that it works correctly:

```
$ gcc -framework Foundation plist.m && ./a.out
2009-01-07 19:13:15.299 a.out[34155:10b] a: (
    this,
    is,
    an,
    array
)
2009-01-07 19:13:15.300 a.out[34155:10b] b: (
    this,
    is,
    an,
    array
)
```

Although this simple example just contains strings, the same code will work on an array containing any of the types that can be stored in a property list.

This basic functionality is enough for a lot of uses, but for more advanced cases the `NSPropertyListSerialization` class is helpful. This provides the ability to validate property lists, and to load and store them from `NSData` objects in memory, rather than from files. The plutil utility mentioned earlier is a very simple wrapper around this class.

To create a property list with `NSPropertyListSerialization`, you would use this method:

```
+ (NSData *)dataFromPropertyList: (id)plist
                          format: (NSPropertyListFormat)format
                errorDescription: (NSString**)errorString;
```

The `plist` object is an object that will be turned into property list form. The format can be either `NSPropertyListXMLFormat_v1_0` for the XML format, or `NSPropertyListBinaryFormat_v1_0` for binary property lists. There is also `NSPropertyListOpenStepFormat` defined by the `NSPropertyListFormat` enumeration, but this is only valid for reading OpenStep property lists—OS X no longer has the capability to write them. The final parameter is a pointer to a string that will be used to return an error message.

This method is quite unusual in taking a pointer to a string as a parameter for returning an error. This is due to its age. It was introduced with OS X 10.2. Prior to this, exceptions were always used for returning errors and methods that could soft-fail returned a **`BOOL`**. With 10.2.7 (or earlier versions with Safari installed), Apple introduced the `NSError` class. A pointer to a pointer to an instance of this class is often passed in as a final argument, and set to non-`nil` on return, but this method was written just a few months too early to take advantage of it.

For deserializing property lists, the converse method is

```
+ (id)propertyListFromData: (NSData*)data
         mutabilityOption: (NSPropertyListMutabilityOptions)opt
                   format: (NSPropertyListFormat*)format
         errorDescription: (NSString**)errorString
```

Most of the parameters are the same here. The `format` is now an output parameter, which is set to the format of the property list, which is autodetected. The new parameter, `opt`, defines whether deserialized objects should be mutable. Property lists do not store mutability options—an `NSString` and an `NSMutableString` will be stored in the same way—so you must specify this when deserializing. You can define whether everything (`NSPropertyListMutableContainersAndLeaves`), only containers (`NSPropertyListMutableContainers`), or nothing (`NSPropertyListImmutable`) should be mutable.

4.6.2 User Defaults

One of the problems on any system is how to store preferences for an application. Numerous solutions have been suggested for this problem, from individual configuration files to a centralized registry. OS X picks a path somewhere in the middle. Each application has a property list file containing a dictionary associated with it.

This is accessed via the `NSUserDefaults` class, which also handles notifying parts of an application of changes to individual keys.

This combines most of the benefits of both approaches. You can treat user defaults as a system-maintained database. The `defaults` command-line tool can browse and modify the defaults for any application. Since they are just property lists, you can also modify them outside of the defaults system and delete them for unwanted applications.

To get a user defaults object for your application, you do

```
[NSUserDefaults standardUserDefaults];
```

This returns a singleton object. You can call this as many times as you want from your application and still be using the same object. It maintains a copy of the defaults in memory and periodically synchronizes it with the copy stored on disk. Alternatively, you can explicitly synchronize it by sending a `-synchronize` message.

The shared defaults object is similar to an `NSMutableDictionary`. It has a `setObject:forKey:` and an `objectForKey:` method, which set and get objects, respectively. There are also some convenience methods, like `boolForKey:` that fetches the boxed value, unboxes it, and returns a **`BOOL`**.

Since user defaults supports *key-value coding* (*KVC*), you can also use the standard KVC methods to access defaults. In particular, this includes the `valueForKeyPath:` method. This is very useful when you have a set of attributes stored in a dictionary in defaults. You can get at a nested key with a single call:

```
[[NSUserDefaults standardUserDefaults] valueForKeyPath: @"dict.key"];
```

As long as the user defaults system contains a dictionary called "dict" that contains a key called "key," this will return the corresponding value. You can use this for even deeper-nested dictionaries using a longer key path. Unfortunately, using the corresponding `setValue:forKeyPath:` method will cause a run-time exception.

Defaults and the Command Line

The user defaults system searches for values in a set of *defaults domains*. One of the most often overlooked is `NSArgumentDomain`. This can be very useful as a way of getting values from the command line. If you start a Cocoa application from the command line, you can override user defaults settings by specifying them on the command line in the form `-default value`. You can also use this as a quick and easy way of defining command-line options for tools that use the Foundation framework. To do this, you just need to pass the name of the command-line option as the key when loading a value from defaults.

There are a few difficulties with mutable collections in defaults. This is not directly supported, and so you must do it by creating a new copy of the collection and inserting this back into defaults. This typically involves the following steps:

```
NSUserDefaults *defaults = [NSUserDefaults standardUserDefaults];
NSMutableDictionary *d = [[defaults dictionaryForKey: aKey] mutableCopy];
// Some operations on d
[defaults setObject: d forKey: aKey];
```

This is somewhat clumsy, and so it is common to wrap it up in a method. In particular, you should remember that categories allow you to add methods to `NSUserDefaults`. If your application stores a dictionary of sounds, then you might consider adding a `-setSound:forAction:` or similar method that sets an entry in the sounds dictionary in defaults.

User defaults only supports storing objects that can be saved in property lists. A notable exception to this is the `NSColor` object. Apple suggests adding a category on `NSUserDefaults` for storing these, using the `NSArchiver` mechanism.

`NSArchiver` allows objects that support creating a serialized form of objects that implement the `NSCoding` mechanism. If the object you want to store in defaults implements these, then `NSArchiver` can turn it into a `NSData` instance and `NSUnarchiver` can restore it. This provides a mechanism for storing the object in defaults, since the defaults system can handle `NSData` instances.

Often, a more lightweight approach is possible. Some objects, like `NSURL` can easily be stored as strings. Listing 4.15 shows a simple category for storing URLs as strings in defaults. If your object already implements `-stringValue` and `-initWithString:` methods, then you might find this mechanism simpler than implementing `NSCoding`.

Listing 4.15: A category for storing URLs in defaults. [from: examples/URLDefaults/urldefaults.m]

```
@implementation NSUserDefaults (NSURL)
- (void) setURL: (NSURL*)aURL forKey: (NSString*)aKey
{
    [self setObject: [aURL absoluteString] forKey: aKey];
}
- (NSURL*) URLForKey: (NSString*)aKey
{
    return [NSURL URLWithString: [self stringForKey: aKey]];
}
@end
```

Either mechanism can be used for your own objects, depending on their complexity.

4.7 Interacting with the Filesystem

Most nontrivial programs need to interact with the filesystem in some way. On most UNIX-like systems, including OS X, the filesystem is the only persistent storage facility provided. User defaults is just a high-level interface to a small part of the filesystem, providing access to specific files via a dictionary-like interface.

How you want to interact with the filesystem depends a lot on the task at hand. Cocoa provides a number of facilities exposing files as UNIX-style streams of bytes, or as structured data of some kind. Which you should use depends on your requirements.

4.7.1 Bundles

Bundles are a very important part of OS X. They were used on NeXT systems and have gradually replaced resource forks from earlier versions of Mac OS. The big advantage is not needing any special filesystem support.

Applications on OS X are bundles and can have other resources as well as the code. On NeXT systems, application bundles were used to store different versions of the executable for different platforms; you could have a single .app on an NFS share and run it on OPENSTEP, Solaris, or any other platform that it supported. This legacy is still found in OS X today. The binary is in the Contents/MacOS directory inside the bundle. In theory, you could add binaries for other platforms, although this is not currently supported by the Apple tools.

Prior to the release (and naming) of OS X, the in-development successor to Classic MacOS was called *Rhapsody*. Three "boxes" were announced by Apple. Two eventually became part of OS X. *Blue box* was the virtualized compatibility layer for MacOS that was called *Classic* on early versions of OS X and is not present on Intel Macs. The *yellow box* was the OpenStep environment that was later rebranded Cocoa. The final box, the *red box*, never made it to a shipping product and was a Windows environment for OS X similar to WINE. There was also a planned Windows version of the yellow box, based on the *OPENSTEP Enterprise* (*OSE*) product from NeXT, including Project Builder and Interface Builder and allowing Cocoa applications to be developed for Windows.

It seems likely that Apple still maintains descendants of the Windows version of the yellow box internally and uses them for porting applications like Safari to Windows, although Apple does not use the bundle architecture for these applications. Although the red box was not shipped, it was seen as a possible future product for long enough for OS X to retain the ability to run application bundles with executables in entirely different formats.

OS X, like OPENSTEP, uses the *Mach-O* binary format, which supports different format executables in the same binary files (sharing constants and data when the endian is the same). This is more efficient than having independent binaries for each version and allows Intel and PowerPC, 32-bit and 64-bit executables to be included in the same file. NeXT called these *fat binaries*, while Apple opted for the more politically correct *universal binaries*.

Because applications are bundles, every application has at least one bundle that it will want to load resources from. In a very simple application this happens automatically. The main nib for the application will be loaded when it starts and connected to the application delegate and any other objects.

Other resources can be loaded from the application bundle with the `NSBundle` class. In general, you will have one instance of this class for each bundle you want to interact with. You can get the application bundle with

```
[NSBundle mainBundle];
```

Be careful when doing this. At some point in the future you may decide that your class is very useful and that you want to reuse it. When you do this, you will move it and a framework—another kind of bundle containing a loadable library, headers, and resources—along with any resources it might want to load. When you get the main bundle from your class, you will get the application bundle for the application that linked against the framework, rather than the framework bundle. If you are getting a bundle to load resources that are included with the class then this is not what you want. Instead, you should use

```
[NSBundle bundleForClass: [self class]];
```

This is relatively slow, so it is best done in the `+initialize` method for the class and cached in a file-static variable, like this:

```
static NSBundle *frameworkBundle;
+ (void) initialize
{
    frameworkBundle = [[NSBundle bundleForClass: self] retain];
}
```

In real code, you would probably want to wrap this in a check to ensure that it was only being called on the correct class, as shown in Chapter 3. Because this is a class method, it only needs to pass `self`, rather than `[self class]` as the parameter. You can also use `+bundleWithIdentifier`, which is generally faster. This loads the bundle that has the identifier provided as the argument. The bundle identifier is set in the bundle's property list by the CFBundleIdentifier key.

Once you have a bundle, you can load resources from it. This is a two-step process. The first is to find the path of the resource, using a method like this:

```
- (NSString*)pathForResource: (NSString*)name
                      ofType: (NSString*)extension
                 inDirectory: (NSString*)subpath
             forLocalization: (NSString*)localizationName
```

There are two wrapper versions of this method where the last parameters are filled in with default values. The simplest form just has the first two and finds resources using the user's preferred localization in the top-level resource directory in the bundle.

If you want to load all of the resources of a specific type in a bundle, there is a form that returns an array instead of a string:

```
- (NSArray*)pathsForResourcesOfType: (NSString*)extension
                        inDirectory: (NSString*)subpath
```

This, and the version that specifies a localization, finds all of the resources of a specific type, for example, all of the png files in a theme directory in the Resources directory in the bundle.

In addition to resources, you can load code from bundles, too. Listing 4.16 shows a simple framework loader. Because frameworks are just another kind of bundle with a well-known layout, the standard bundle loading code can be used to load them.

This example is taken from Étoilé's LangaugeKit and is used to allow scripts loaded and compiled by a running program to specify frameworks that they depend upon, without requiring the program that loads them to link against every possible framework that a script might want.

This example shows a number of Cocoa features. The first is the file manager, which we will look at in the next section. This is used in line 24 to test whether the framework exists at a given path. If it does, then `NSBundle` is used on lines 27 and 28 to load the code in the framework.

Listing 4.16: A simple framework loader. [from: examples/Loader/simpleLoader.m]

```
7  @implementation SimpleLoader
8  + (BOOL) loadFramework: (NSString*)framework
9  {
10     NSFileManager *fm = [NSFileManager defaultManager];
11     NSArray *dirs =
12         NSSearchPathForDirectoriesInDomains(
13             NSLibraryDirectory,
14             NSAllDomainsMask,
15             YES);
```

```
16     FOREACH(dirs, dir, NSString*)
17     {
18         NSString *f =
19             [[[dir stringByAppendingPathComponent: @"Frameworks"]
20                 stringByAppendingPathComponent: framework]
21                     stringByAppendingPathExtension: @"framework"];
22         // Check that the framework exists and is a directory.
23         BOOL isDir = NO;
24         if ([fm fileExistsAtPath: f isDirectory: &isDir]
25             && isDir)
26         {
27             NSBundle *bundle = [NSBundle bundleWithPath: f];
28             if ([bundle load])
29             {
30                 NSLog(@"Loaded␣bundle␣%@", f);
31                 return YES;
32             }
33         }
34     }
35     return NO;
36 }
37 @end
```

The function on line 11 is one of the most useful, and most overlooked, parts of Cocoa, since it allows you to avoid hard-coding paths in a lot of instances. Line 19 shows some of `NSString`'s path manipulation code. This is used to assemble the correct path by appending the Frameworks directory, then the framework name as path components, and then the .framework extension. This could be done with `-stringWithFormat:` for OS X, but doing it this way means that it will continue to work if you try to move your code to a different platform with different path formats.

4.7.2 Workspace and File Management

Cocoa provides two ways of interacting with the filesystem, `NSFileManager` and `NSWorkspace`. The latter is part of AppKit and provides a higher-level interface. The `NSWorkspace` class does file operations in the background and posts a notification when they are done, while `NSFileManager` works synchronously. Both classes are *singletons*; you will only ever have (at most) one instance for each in an application.

We saw an example of one of the things you can do with a file manager in Listing 4.16. This used the `-fileExistsAtPath:isDirectory:` method, to see if a file existed. The second argument to this is a pointer to a **BOOL**, which is set to **YES** if the file is found and is a directory.

Most other common file manipulation operations are supported by the file manager, such as copying, moving, and linking files and directories. It can also enumerate the contents of folders and compare files. Most of NSFileManager's functionality is exposed by a single method in NSWorkspace:

```
- (BOOL)performFileOperation: (NSString*)operation
                      source: (NSString*)source
                 destination: (NSString*)destination
                       files: (NSArray*)files
                         tag: (NSInteger)tag
```

This takes a source and destination directory as arguments and an array of files. It performs move, copy, link, destroy, or recycle operations and sets the value of the integer pointed to by tag to indicate whether the operation succeeded.

Most of NSWorkspace's functionality deals with higher-level operations on files. While NSFileManager is for dealing with files as UNIX-style streams of bytes, NSWorkspace is for dealing with files as a user-level abstraction, representing documents or applications. Methods like openFile: are examples of this. This method opens a specified file with the default application and is used to implement the command-line open tool.

The low-level file manager methods are very easy to use. Listing 4.17 shows a simple tool for copying a file. This uses the user defaults system to read command-line arguments and then uses the file manager to copy the specified file.

Note that this example code does not check whether the input file exists or that the output is a valid destination. The file manager will call a delegate method in case of an error, but we did not set a handler on line 12, and so this will not allow error checking either. Implementing the handler is not required, it simply allows you to track the progress of the operation and to decide whether to proceed in case of an error. The return value from this method is a boolean indicating whether the copy succeeded. You can run this simple tool like this:

```
$ gcc -framework Foundation FileCopy.m -o FileCopy
$ ./FileCopy -in FileCopy -out CopyOfFileCopy
$ ls
CopyOfFileCopy FileCopy        FileCopy.m
```

Note that the file manager automatically resolved relative paths. These are treated as being relative to whatever the file manager returns from -currentDirectoryPath. You can alter the working directory for a running program by sending the file manager a -changeCurrentDirectoryPath: message. The working directory is much more important for command-line tools than it is for

Listing 4.17: A simple tool for copying files. [from: examples/FileCopy/FileCopy.m]

```
#import <Foundation/Foundation.h>

int main(void)
{
    [NSAutoreleasePool new];
    NSUserDefaults *defaults = [NSUserDefaults standardUserDefaults];
    NSString *source = [defaults stringForKey: @"in"];
    NSString *destination  = [defaults stringForKey: @"out"];
    NSFileManager *fm = [NSFileManager defaultManager];
    [fm copyPath: source
          toPath: destination
         handler: nil];
    return 0;
}
```

graphical applications. A command-line tool inherits its current working directory from the shell. The concept of a current directory does not make sense for an application invoked via the Finder or from the Dock.

Starting with 10.5, Apple began using the *uniform type identifier* (*UTI*) system for identifying file types. A UTI is a hierarchical arrangement of types. `NSWorkspace` is used to map between file extensions and UTIs.

4.7.3 Working with Paths

When working with filesystem paths, there are a number of helpful methods provided by `NSString`. These allow you to decompose paths into components and create various individual components without worrying about the kind of path that is represented.

On UNIX platforms, a tilde (~) is commonly used as a shorthand for the user's home directory. You can get this explicitly by calling `NSHomeDirectory()` but often users will enter strings containing this shorthand and expect it to work. If you select Go to Folder in the Finder's Go menu, then enter "~/Documents" then it will open a new window showing the Documents folder in your home directory.

The `NSString` class provides a convenient method for strings that may contain a tilde. If you send the string a `-stringByExpandingTildeInPath` message, then you will get back a new string containing the absolute path, without a tilde. Although less useful, it is also possible to go the other way by sending a full path a `-stringByAbbreviatingWithTildeInPath` message. If the path points to something inside the user's home directory, then it will be collapsed to only use a tilde character for this part of the path.

When interacting with the filesystem, you very often need to decompose a path into three parts: the file name, the file extension, and the path of the directory containing the file. You can do all of these from `NSString`, like this:

```
NSString *fullPath = @"/tmp/folder/file.extension";
// ext = @"extension";
NSString *ext = [fullPath pathExtension];
// file = @"file";
NSString *file = [[fullPath lastPathComponent]
    stringByDeletingPathExtension];
// dir = @"/tmp/folder";
NSString *dir = [fullPath stringByDeletingLastPathComponent];
```

There are also methods for constructing a path from individual parts, including appending components and setting the extension. Before you start writing code for parsing path strings yourself, make sure that `NSString` doesn't already have methods for doing what you need.

4.7.4 File Access

While `NSFileManager` lets you interact with the filesystem, and `NSWorkspace` lets you open files in other applications, neither provides a means of accessing the contents of files.

There is nothing stopping you from using the C library and POSIX functions for doing this, but they are not very convenient. Cocoa includes a wrapper around them in the form of the `NSFileHandle` class. This wraps a file handle as would be returned by `open()`. Four singleton instances exist, representing the C standard input, output and error streams, and a placeholder that discards all data written to it. Additional file handles can be created for reading, writing, or updating, with named constructors.

You can use the `NSFileHandle` class anywhere you have a C file handle using this initializer:

```
- (id)initWithFileDescriptor: (int)fileDescriptor
              closeOnDealloc: (BOOL)flag
```

The file descriptor is any C file descriptor, for example, the kind returned by `open()` or `socket()`. Whether the resulting object supports reading or writing depends on the underlying file descriptor. If you set `flag` to **`YES`**, then you can use this as a simple way of tracking how many parts of your program are using the file and ensuring that it is closed at the correct point. As long as you then only use the file descriptor with the object, it will stay open as long as some parts of your program are using it and close itself when it is no longer required.

If all you want to do is read data from a file, NSData objects can be created from a file using this method:

```
+ (id)dataWithContentsOfFile: (NSString*)path
                     options: (NSUInteger)mask
                       error: (NSError**)errorPtr
```

This creates a new NSData object from the contents of the file pointed to by path and sets the errorPtr to an NSError instance if it fails. The mask parameter allows two options to be set: NSMappedRead and NSUncachedRead. The first uses mmap() instead of file reading operations. As discussed earlier, this is a good idea if you know that the file is not going to be modified, for example, for read-only resources in an application bundle. If the system is low on memory, it can very cheaply free mapped data and load it back from the original file, while data read in will have to be written out to the swap file, even if they have not been modified. The second option allows the data to bypass the operating system's cache. If you know that you are just going to read the data once and then discard it, then it can improve performance. Otherwise it will use less RAM, but require more disk accesses.

NSData can also be used to write data back to a file. For small file output, using an NSMutableData to construct the file in memory and then using the writeToFile:atomically: or writeToURL:atomically: methods to output it is very simple. The second parameter to each of these is a **BOOL**, which, if set to **YES**, will write the data first to a temporary file and then rename the temporary file, ensuring on-disk consistency.

4.8 Notifications

Notifications are another example of *loose coupling* in Cocoa. They provide a layer of indirection between events and event handlers. Rather than every object keeping a list of objects that need to receive events, they go via the *notification center*, embodied by the NSNotificationCenter class. Objects can request notifications with a specific name, from a specific object, or both. When the specified object posts the named notification, the observer will receive a message with an NSNotification object as an argument.

This mechanism makes it very easy to join parts of your application together without explicitly hard-coding the connections. It is also a good example of the layering of Foundation and AppKit. Foundation defines notifications, but AppKit uses them heavily. A lot of view objects will post notifications when some user interaction has occurred, as well as delivering the message to their delegate. This allows multiple objects to be notified when some part of the user interface changes, with very little code.

By default, notifications are delivered synchronously. An object sends the notification to the notification center, and the notification center passes it on to all observers. Sometimes this is not the desired behavior. For asynchronous delivery, the `NSNotificationQueue` class integrates with the run loop and allows delivery of notifications to be deferred until the run loop is idle, or until the next iteration of the run loop.

4.8.1 Requesting Notifications

There are, generally speaking, two things you can do with notifications: send them and receive them. Receiving a notification is a two-step process. First, you tell the notification center what you want to receive, and then you wait.

Listing 4.18 shows a simple class for receiving notifications. This implements a single method, `receiveNotification:`, which takes a notification as an object. This is a very simple method that logs the name of the notification and the value associated with a key in the *user info dictionary*. The user info dictionary is what makes notifications so flexible. Any notification sender can attach an arbitrary set of key-value pairs to any notification. Because it is a dictionary, a receiver doesn't even need to know the specific keys; it has the option of enumerating every single key and doing something with all of the items in the dictionary, or it can simply ignore any keys it doesn't know about.

When the object is created, the default notification center is told to deliver notifications with the name "ExampleNotification" to its `receiveNotification:` method, from any object. It is also possible to specify a specific object to receive notifications from. In this case, you may leave the `name:` argument as `nil` and get every notification sent by that object.

Listing 4.18: Notification receiver object. [from: examples/Noti↓cations/notify.m]

```
@interface Receiver : NSObject {}
- (void) receiveNotification: (NSNotification*)aNotification;
@end

@implementation Receiver
- (id) init
{
    if (nil == (self = [super init]))
    {
        return nil;
    }
    // register to receive notifications
```

```
    NSNotificationCenter *center =
        [NSNotificationCenter defaultCenter];
    [center addObserver: self
               selector: @selector(receiveNotification:)
                   name: @"ExampleNotification"
                 object: nil];
    return self;
}
- (void) receiveNotification: (NSNotification*)aNotification
{
    printf("Received␣notification:␣%s",
            [[aNotification name] UTFString]);
    printf("Received␣notification:␣%s",
        [[[aNotification userInfo] objectForKey: @"message"] UTFString]);
}
- (void) dealloc
{
    NSNotificationCenter *center =
        [NSNotificationCenter defaultCenter];
    [super dealloc];
}
@end
```

There is one remaining part of handling notifications that is very important. You must remember to send the notification center a `removeObserver:` message when your object is destroyed. For this reason, it is good practice to ensure that the object that is registering as an observer in notifications is always **`self`**. This makes it very easy to make sure you call `removeObserver:` at the right time; just put the call in the `-dealloc` method. In a garbage-collected environment, the notification center should keep weak references to observers, so they will be automatically removed when no longer valid.

In this simple example, notifications are identified by literal strings. It is more common when creating public notifications to use shared global objects, initialized in one file and declared **`extern`** in a header.

4.8.2 Sending Notifications

The other half of the equation, sending messages, is even simpler. Listing 4.19 shows a simple object that sends a notification in response to a `sendMessage:` message. The string argument is inserted into the user info dictionary and delivered via a notification.

This is the companion of the `Receiver` class from the Listing 4.18. The these two classes communicate without either having a direct reference to the other.

Listing 4.19: Sending a notification. [from: examples/Notifications/notify.m]

```
@interface Sender : NSObject {}
- (void) sendMessage: (NSString*)aMessage;
@end
@implementation Sender
- (void) sendMessage: (NSString*)aMessage
{
    NSNotificationCenter *center =
        [NSNotificationCenter defaultCenter];

    NSDictionary *message =
        [NSDictionary dictionaryWithObject: aMessage
                                    forKey: @"message"];
    [center postNotificationName: @"ExampleNotification"
                          object: self
                        userInfo: message];
}
@end

int main(void)
{
    [NSAutoreleasePool new];
    // Set up the receiver
    Receiver *receiver = [Receiver new];
    // Send the notification
    [[Sender new] sendMessage: @"A␣short␣message"];
    return 0;
}
```

The `main()` method creates an instance of each class and calls the `sendMessage:` method on the sender. This posts a notification that is received by the receiver:

```
$ gcc -framework Foundation notify.m && ./a.out
Received notification: ExampleNotification
Message is: A short message
```

4.8.3 Sending Asynchronous Notification

Normally, sending a notification is a synchronous operation. You send a `-postNotification:` message to the notification center, it iterates over all of the objects that have registered to receive that notification, sends the notification to them, and then returns.

Every thread has its own notification center, and it also has a notification queue, an instance of `NSNotificationQueue`. This functions in a similar way to the notification center, but defers delivery of notifications until a future run-loop iteration.

Notification queues are particularly useful if you are generating a lot of the same sort of notification in quick succession. Often, the observers do not need to run immediately. Consider something like the spell checker in a text box. This could send a notification every time the user types a character. The spell checker could register for this notification, receive it, see if the typed word is valid, and update the display. This has two drawbacks. First, a word will be checked several times as it is typed, which is not always needed. Second, the spell checking will interrupt the typing.

A better design would flag the text box as needing spell checking as soon as the user typed something, but defer the actual checking until later. The notification queue does two things that help here. First, it performs *notification coalescing*, turning multiple identical notifications into a single one. This means that you can send a notification for every key press, but the spell checker will only receive one. The other useful feature is deferred delivery. When you post a notification via a queue, you can decide whether it should be delivered now, soon, or when the thread has nothing else to do. A typical program spends most of its time doing nothing. The notification queue allows you to defer handling of notifications until one of these times, for example, only running the spell checker when the user stops typing. In practice, no user types fast enough to keep a modern CPU busy, but this system applies equally to other data sources, such as the disk or network, which can provide data fast enough to keep a processor busy for a while.

A notification queue is a front end to a notification center. You insert notifications into the queue and it then sends them to the notification center, which sends them to the observers. This combination means that objects listening for a notification do not have to know whether the sender is using a notification queue or sending notifications synchronously.

There are two ways of getting a pointer to a notification queue. The most common way is to send a `+defaultQueue` message to the class. This will return the notification queue connected to the thread's default notification center. Notifications posted to this queue will be delivered in the thread that sent them.

Alternatively, you can explicitly create a queue for a given center. You can have different queues, as shown in Figure 4.1. Each object can send notifications to one or more notification queues, or to the notification center directly. The notification queues will coalesce the notifications and then pass them on to the notification center, which then distributes them to all of the registered observers.

Having multiple notification queues allows you to control how notifications are coalesced. You may want to have all notifications from every instance of a particular class to be coalesced, but to be delivered separately from notifications of the same kind delivered from other objects, you can create a new notification queue for the class. You must attach the queue to a notification center when you initialize it, by sending it an `-initWithNotificationCenter:` message.

You send a notification through a queue by sending it either this message or one of the simpler forms that omits one or more argument:

```
- (void)enqueueNotification: (NSNotification*)notification
               postingStyle: (NSPostingStyle)postingStyle
               coalesceMask: (NSUInteger)coalesceMask
                   forModes: (NSArray*)modes;
```

The first argument is a notification. You have to create this yourself; there are convenience methods for constructing them as there are on the notification center. You will typically do this by sending a `+notificationWithName:object:userInfo:` message to the notification class.

The second argument defines when the notification should be delivered. You have three options here. If you specify `NSPostNow`, then the behavior is similar sending the message directly to the notification center. The notification will be posted synchronously, but it will first be coalesced. You can use this to flush a set of notifications. If you have a set of operations that may all trigger a particular kind of notification, then you can have them all send their notifications into a queue and then send a notification with the posting style set to `NSPostNow` to ensure that exactly one notification will be sent.

The other options defer posting of the notification until a future run-loop iteration. If you specify `NSPostASAP`, then the notification will be posted as soon as possible. This may not be at the start of the next run-loop iteration, because there may be other notifications with the same priority already waiting for delivery, but it will be soon. If the notification is not very important, then you can set the posting style to `NSPostWhenIdle`. This will cause it to be delivered only when there are no more pressing events waiting for the run loop's attention.

Coalescing works best the longer notifications are allowed to stay in the queue. If everything is posted with `NSPostNow`, then the queue never has a chance to coalesce them. If everything is posted with `NSPostWhenIdle`, then notifications may stay in the queue for a long time, and will have a lot more opportunities for being combined.

The coalescing behavior is configured with the third argument. This is a mask formed by combining flags specifying whether notifications should be coalesced if they are from the same sender or of the same type. Most often you will specify either both of these flags, or neither. Coalescing notifications from the same sender

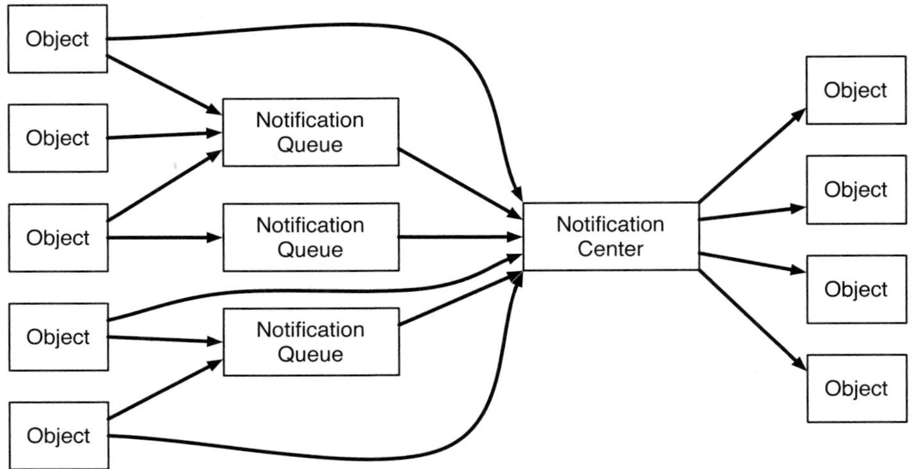

Figure 4.1: The flow of notifications in a Cocoa program.

but with different types may cause some very strange behavior. You can coalesce notifications of the same type from different senders, but this is generally not recommended either.

The final argument specifies the run-loop modes in which the notification will be delivered. You can use this to prevent notifications from being handled in certain modes, or to define new modes for handling certain kinds of notification and keep them queued until you explicitly tell the run loop to enter that mode. This provides a fairly simple way of deferring notification delivery until you explicitly decide you want to handle them.

Notification queues are very powerful, but rarely need to be used. They are most commonly treated as an optimization technique. If you profile your code and find that it is spending a lot of time handling duplicate notifications, then consider adding a notification queue.

4.8.4 Distributed Notifications

Notifications aren't solely subject to use in a single process. The `NSDistributedNotificationCenter` class is a subclass of `NSNotificationCenter` built using the *distributed objects* (*DO*) mechanism. This makes them the simplest form of *interprocess communication* (*IPC*) to use on OS X.

Although less flexible than using DO directly, distributed notifications provide

> **Notifications and Signals**
>
> If you come from a UNIX programming background, you may find notifications quite similar, conceptually, to UNIX signals. When combined with notification queues, they work in a similar way to signals sent using the POSIX realtime extensions to signal support. They are delivered asynchronously, can be enqueued, and carry something the size of a pointer as extra data with them.

a very simple way of communicating between different processes. In principle, distributed notifications could be integrated with *Bonjour* for sending notifications across the local network segment. The `-notificationCenterForType:` constructor hints at future possibilities for distributed notifications; however, it only supports `NSLocalNotificationCenterType` on OS X. The GNUstep implementation also supports `GSNetworkNotificationCenterType` for delivering notifications over the network using distributed objects, but there is currently no equivalent provided by Apple.

Registering to receive a distributed notification is almost the same as registering to receive a normal one. The main difference is the last parameter. Note the different method prototypes for registering observers in a notification center and a distributed notification center:

```
// NSNotificationCenter
- (void)addObserver: (id)notificationObserver
           selector: (SEL)notificationSelector
               name: (NSString*)notificationName
             object: (id)notificationSender;
// NSDistributedNotificationCenter
- (void)addObserver: (id)notificationObserver
           selector: (SEL)notificationSelector
               name: (NSString*)notificationName
             object: (NSString*)notificationSender;
```

The last argument is a pointer to the object from which you want to receive the notifications. In a distributed notification center, senders are identified by name, rather than pointer. The reason for this should be obvious: Distributed notifications can come from other processes, and pointers are only valid in the current process's address space.

Sending distributed notifications has the same change. The same method can be used, but the sender must be a string instead of an object. Typically, this is the name of the application sending the notification.

There are also some restrictions placed on the user info dictionary when sending distributed notifications. Because the notification is sent over DO, all of the objects in the dictionary must conform to the `NSCoding` protocol, allowing them to be serialized and deserialized in the remote process. Since the deserialization can potentially be done in a large number of listening processes, it is a good idea to keep notifications small.

4.9 Summary

In this chapter, we've gone through the most important aspects of the Foundation framework. This framework covers the core functionality of the Cocoa development environment and even provides a number of features that would typically be thought of as part of the language, such as reference counting and message forwarding.

We spent some time examining the core concepts of the Foundation library. In subsequent chapters, you will see examples of all of the things we've discussed here.

We looked at the collection classes provided by Foundation—sets, arrays, and dictionaries—and how enumeration of these types works. We saw the basic value types used to store non-object values in collections.

The most important aspects of the Foundation framework were covered in this chapter. This should not be taken as an exhaustive reference. The framework contains a large number of classes and functions. If you printed out just the class references from the Foundation framework, you would end up with something longer than this entire book, and many of the method descriptions would still be single-line comments.

In-depth understanding of all of the details of the Foundation library is almost impossible. The purpose of this chapter was to highlight the most important parts to look at. Familiarity with the classes discussed in this chapter goes a long way toward making a good Cocoa programmer.

Chapter 5

Application Concepts

An application, in Cocoa terminology, is a process that displays a graphical user interface and runs in an interactive mode. While the Foundation library provides classes that are likely to be useful for any kind of program, AppKit is focused on producing interactive GUIs. A lot of the core functionality for building applications is found in Foundation and extended in AppKit.

5.1 Run Loops

The core of any Cocoa application is the run loop. This provides a simple implementation of *coroutines*. Each iteration through the run loop is triggered by an event. Handlers for this event are then triggered and run until completion.

The mapping between events and their handlers is rarely explicit in Cocoa. For events triggered by the user doing something, a complex set of delivery rules handle calling the correct object. These will be discussed in Section 5.3. Others are routed explicitly, by setting an object and selector pair.

We have already seen one object that interacts with the run loop. The `NSDistributedNotificationCenter` class delivers Objective-C messages in response to remote messages. These are delivered through the distributed objects mechanism. When this happens, a remote object injects an event into the application's event queue. This is then delivered to the distributed notification center, which then performs the required calls.

This kind of abstraction is common in Cocoa. It is possible to write quite complex Cocoa applications without ever interacting directly with the run loop or event classes directly. Most often, the raw events will be handled by one of the built-in Cocoa classes and then delivered to objects that have requested notification. Most of the time, you will interact with the run loop via two mechanisms: *timers* and *notifications*.

A timer is an instance of the `NSTimer` class. This registers an object-selector pair to be sent a message after a specified time interval has elapsed.

Before we start taking advantage of the friendly wrappers that AppKit provides, let's take a look at how we can use the run-loop mechanism from within a command-line tool by building a simple version of the UNIX `talk` utility on top of distributed notifications. This example will include three classes:

- `LineBuffer` will receive a notification from `NSFileHandle` whenever there is some data ready to read, and send one notification for each complete line.
- `Sender` will receive line notifications and deliver a distributed notification including the user's name and his or her message.
- `Receiver` will listen for chat message distributed notifications and print each one to the screen as it arrives.

None of these classes will hold references to each other; they will all communicate via notifications. The addition of a run loop makes this a purely *event-driven* application; there is no polling by any component, they all respond to events and then wait for the next one.

The first part of this program is the `LineBuffer` class, shown in Listing 5.1. This takes a file handle as an argument when it is created and listens for notifications that this file handle has data to deliver. The message sent to `NSNotificationCenter` on lines 101–104 has all of the arguments set to non-`nil` values. In this particular instance, the object only wants to be notified of notifications delivered by a specific object with a specific name. On Line 105 it instructs the file handle to spawn a new thread that waits until there is some data to read and then deliver a notification.

The real work of this class is done in the `-readData:` method. This is called in response to the notification that is requested during initialization. First, it reads the data from the file handle and constructs a string from it (lines 110–114). It then appends this string to the internal buffer and splits it into an array of strings separated by newlines.

Listing 5.1: The line buffer class. [from: examples/Notifications /distributedNotify.m]

```
88 @interface LineBuffer : NSObject {
89     NSMutableString *buffer;
90 }
91 - (id) initWithFile: (NSFileHandle*)aFileHandle;
92 @end
93 @implementation LineBuffer
94 - (id) initWithFile: (NSFileHandle*)aFileHandle
```

```
{
    if (nil == (self = [self init]))
    {
        return nil;
    }
    buffer = [[NSMutableString alloc] init];
    NSNotificationCenter *center =
        [NSNotificationCenter defaultCenter];
    [center addObserver: self
               selector: @selector(readData:)
                   name: NSFileHandleDataAvailableNotification
                 object: aFileHandle];
    [aFileHandle waitForDataInBackgroundAndNotify];
    return self;
}
- (void) readData: (NSNotification*)aNotification
{
    NSFileHandle *handle = [aNotification object];
    NSData *data = [handle availableData];
    NSString *str =
        [[NSString alloc] initWithData: data
                              encoding: NSUTF8StringEncoding];
    [buffer appendString: str];
    [str release];
    NSArray *lines =
        [buffer componentsSeparatedByString: @"\n"];
    NSNotificationCenter *center =
        [NSNotificationCenter defaultCenter];
    // The last object in the array will be the newline string
    // if a new line is found, or the unterminated line
    for (unsigned int i=0 ; i<[lines count] - 1 ; i++)
    {
        NSDictionary *line =
            [NSDictionary dictionaryWithObject: [lines objectAtIndex: i]
                                        forKey: @"Line"];
        [center postNotificationName: LineInputNotification
                              object: self
                            userInfo: line];
    }
    [buffer setString: [lines lastObject]];
    [handle waitForDataInBackgroundAndNotify];
}
- (void) dealloc
{
```

```
    NSNotificationCenter *center =
        [NSNotificationCenter defaultCenter];
    [center removeObserver: self];
    [buffer release];
    [super dealloc];
}
```

The array of strings returned by `NSString`'s `componentsSeparatedByString:` method will always contain at least one string. If there are no separators, it will contain just the input string. If it ends with the separator, then the last string will be the empty string (`@""`). If it doesn't end with the separator, then the last entry will be non-empty. This means that all except the last object in the array will be complete lines, and the last object will either be an empty string or a partial line.[1] For each one of these lines, the object fires a new notification.

These notifications are received by the `Sender` class, shown in Listing 5.2. On lines 57–60, this class also registers to receive a notification; the notification sent by the line buffer. In this case, however, it does not specify a source. In a more complex program, there might be different objects sending notifications with this name, but in this simple example we can use *loose coupling* between the two classes.

Listing 5.2: The sender class for distributed notifications. [from: examples/Notifications/distributedNotify.m]

```
42 @end
43
44 @interface Sender : NSObject {
45     NSString *name;
46 }
47 - (id) initWithName: (NSString*)aName;
48 @end
49 @implementation Sender
50 - (id) initWithName: (NSString*)aName
51 {
52     if (nil == (self = [self init]))
53     {
54         return nil;
55     }
56     name = [aName retain];
57     NSNotificationCenter *center =
58         [NSNotificationCenter defaultCenter];
59     [center addObserver: self
```

[1]In fact, `NSFileHandle` will only send complete lines when used in this way, although this behavior is not guaranteed.

```
60                   selector: @selector(sendMessage:)
61                       name: LineInputNotification
62                     object: nil];
63     return self;
64 }
65 - (void) sendMessage: (NSNotification*)aNotificaton
66 {
67     NSNotificationCenter *center =
68         [NSDistributedNotificationCenter defaultCenter];
69     NSString *line =
70         [[aNotificaton userInfo] objectForKey: @"Line"];
71     NSDictionary *message =
72         [NSDictionary dictionaryWithObject: line
73                                     forKey: @"message"];
74     [center postNotificationName: ChatMessageNotification
75                           object: name
76                         userInfo: message];
77 }
78 - (void) dealloc
79 {
80     NSNotificationCenter *center =
81         [NSNotificationCenter defaultCenter];
82     [center removeObserver: self];
83     [name release];
84     [super dealloc];
85 }
86 @end
```

This class both sends and receives notifications. It receives local notifications that a line has been read, and posts distributed notifications containing the line. Line 75 shows the main difference between sending distributed and local notifications; the sender for the distributed notification is a string, in this case the name of the person sending the chat message, which was set when the object was created.

The final class in this example, the `Receiver`, is shown in Listing 5.3. Again, this registers for a notification when it is created. Unlike the other two classes, this registers to receive a distributed notification. Every time it receives a notification, it prints it to the screen. Note that it uses the C function `printf()` here. There is nothing wrong with using pure C in parts of Objective-C programs. Many C++ programmers feel that using the C standard library makes their code in some way unclean, but Objective-C was designed to add functionality to C, not replace it, and sometimes the simplest way of working is to use C functions.

Once we have these three classes, we need to join them together. Listing 5.4 shows the `main()` function for this little program. Note that the user defaults system is used for looking up the name. This is a quick and simple way of getting command-line options. The `NSUserDefaults` class allows any default to be overridden with a command-line option, and so we can specify the user name with a `-name` parameter on the executable. If none is specified, we just use "anon."

Listing 5.3: The receiver class for distributed notifications. [from: examples/Notifications/distributedNotify.m]

```
@interface Receiver : NSObject {}
- (void) receiveNotification: (NSNotification*)aNotification;
@end

@implementation Receiver
- (id) init
{
    if (nil == (self = [super init]))
    {
        return nil;
    }
    // register to receive notifications
    NSNotificationCenter *center =
        [NSDistributedNotificationCenter defaultCenter];
    [center addObserver: self
               selector: @selector(receiveNotification:)
                   name: ChatMessageNotification
                 object: nil];
    return self;
}
- (void) receiveNotification: (NSNotification*)aNotification
{
    printf("%s: %s\n",
        [[aNotification object] UTF8String],
        [[[aNotification userInfo] objectForKey: @"message"] UTF8String]);
}
- (void) dealloc
{
    NSNotificationCenter *center =
        [NSDistributedNotificationCenter defaultCenter];
    [center removeObserver: self];
    [super dealloc];
```

Line 162 is where the run loop is started. Every thread has its own run-loop object, although initially it is not doing anything. When you send it a `-run` message, it sleeps until it receives an event, delivers the event, and then returns to sleep.

You may have noticed that this program contains a number of autoreleased objects. For example, the array returned when splitting the string is an example of this. We don't explicitly free it ever; it will be freed when the current autorelease pool is freed. We only explicitly create one autorelease pool, however, on line 149, and we never destroy it. The array will not leak, however, due to `NSRunLoop`. At the start of every run-loop iteration, a new autorelease pool is created, and then it is destroyed at the end. This means that, if you are using run loops, you can just autorelease objects and never worry about managing pools yourself.

If you are using garbage collection, then this is less relevant. The run loop will still provide some assistance even with garbage collection, by attempting to trigger collection between events.

Listing 5.4: The `main()` function for the chat tool. [from: examples/Noti↓cations/distributedNotify.m]

```
147 int main(void)
148 {
149     [NSAutoreleasePool new];
150     // Set up the receiver
151     Receiver *receiver = [Receiver new];
152     NSString *name =
153         [[NSUserDefaults standardUserDefaults]
154             stringForKey: @"name"];
155     if (nil == name)
156     {
157         name = @"anon";
158     }
159     [[Sender alloc] initWithName: name];
160     [[LineBuffer alloc] initWithFile:
161         [NSFileHandle fileHandleWithStandardInput]];
162     [[NSRunLoop currentRunLoop] run];
163     return 0;
164 }
```

When we compile and run this tool, we get a simple chat system, where every line we type is sent to every running instance of the program (and any other program that requests it).

```
$ gcc -framework Foundation -std=c99 distributedNotify.m
$ ./a.out  -name David
Thomas: Hello
Hi
David: Hi
How are you?
```

```
David: How are you?
Thomas: Fine thanks.
```

Meanwhile, in another terminal:

```
$ ./a.out -name Thomas
Hello
Thomas: Hello
David: Hi
David: How are you?
Fine thanks.
Thomas: Fine thanks.
```

Messages from both instances are displayed by both. The run loop has allowed us to create a simple event-driven application with two event sources—the keyboard and other instances of the chat program—and distributed notifications have allowed simple peer-to-peer communication.

5.2 Applications and Delegates

All of examples we've used so far have had a C-style `main()` function. This is required by all Cocoa applications, since Objective-C does not specify any additional entry points. In most Cocoa applications, this will be a skeleton created by XCode and not modified, containing just this line:

```
return NSApplicationMain(argc, argv);
```

The OpenStep specification describes this function as being equivalent to the following:

```
void NSApplicationMain(int argc, char *argv[])
{
    [NSApplication sharedApplication];
    [NSBundle loadNibNamed: @"myMain" owner: NSApp];
    [NSApp run];
}
```

This is a slight oversimplification. The name of the main nib is not hard-coded; it is really looked up from a property list in the application bundle. Apart from this, however, it is mostly correct. The first line creates the shared application object. `NSApplication` is a singleton; only one instance exists per application. The first time that this method is called, it sets the global `NSApp` variable to point to the shared instance, so after the application has started, this global can be used instead.

The nib is loaded and its owner set to the application object. This provides a simple way of connecting objects constructed from your main nib to objects described elsewhere in your application. The application delegate is typically set in the nib file, although it is possible to set it from code before loading the nib. Finally, a `-run` message is sent to the application object.

When an application is running, the default `NSRunLoop` instance is collecting messages from the system and dispatching them. By default, `NSApp` will register for most user input messages and then dispatch them using the *responder chain* described in the next section.

It is possible to subclass `NSApplication`, although this is generally a very bad idea. The delegate, set with `-setDelegate:` or in the nib file, is called by the application object for almost everything it does, and allows modification of the application's behavior in a much cleaner and safer way.

The application delegate contains the main entry point for your application. There are two methods that a delegate may choose to implement for this:

```
- (void)applicationWillFinishLaunching: (NSNotification*)aNotification;
- (void)applicationDidFinishLaunching: (NSNotification*)aNotification;
```

This is a common pattern in Cocoa, where events have a "should," and "will," and a "did" form. The "should" form asks the delegate if the event should proceed, the "will" form indicates that it is about to occur, and the "did" form indicates that it has completed.

In this case, there is no "should" form, since it is assumed that if an application has started to launch it should always launch. The `-applicationWillFinishLaunching:` delegate method is called when the run loop is initialized. If the application was started by dragging some files on to it, then these will then be opened, and finally the `-applicationDidFinishLaunching:` method will be called, before normal event processing starts.

Note that both of these methods take a notification as an argument. It is also possible for other objects to receive these as notifications. If you create an object before sending the application a `-run` message, and register it to receive a notification named `NSApplicationDidFinishLaunchingNotification`, then it will also be notified when the application has launched. The same is true of many of the other application delegate methods. You may choose to handle them either in the delegate itself, or in another bit of code. For example, the `-applicationDidHide:` message is not particularly useful in a delegate. Few applications need to do anything specific when they are hidden, but an individual view object might, for example, stop updating its contents until the application is unhidden. In this case, each view would register to receive the corresponding notification and the delegate would not implement the method.

Notifications, although part of Foundation, are vastly more important in AppKit. A lot of AppKit objects send at least one kind of notification. Most follow the same pattern as `NSApplication`, by sending all notifications to specific methods in their delegate and also delivering them to the notification center. The delegate is a simpler mechanism, since you just need to implement the correct method, but has the limitation that there can only be one delegate per object.

Recall that Cocoa uses introspection on delegates. Your delegate object is not required to implement any of the methods documented as delegate methods for `NSApplication`. Before calling any of them, the application object will send your delegate a `-respondsToSelector:` message, and only send the delegate message if this returns **`YES`**. Some objects that take delegates will cache the set of messages that the delegate understands, and so if you use any runtime tricks to alter the methods the delegate responds to, then you should call `setDelegate:` again to ensure that the cache is updated.

5.3 The Responder Chain

There are two sorts of events in Cocoa. We have already seen high-level events, which are instances of the `NSNotification` class. The low-level events from the windowing system are encapsulated by the `NSEvent` class.

You very rarely have to interact with events (as opposed to notifications and messages). A large proportion of AppKit exists to hide them from you. For example, when you type a key, an event will be generated, but you will only receive a notification that the text represented by a text view has changed, or get an Objective-C message from a button or menu item that was activated.

In general, view classes handle `NSEvent`s. They then call delegate methods or send action messages to targets in their controllers, or fire notifications. Controllers handle action messages and call into their model objects. Models send notifications.

5.3.1 Event Delivery

Event delivery is orthogonal to notification delivery. An arbitrary number of objects may handle a notification, but only one should handle an event. Events enter the system by being sent to the application's `-sendEvent:` method. You can override this in a custom `NSApplication` subclass to perform some custom event interception, although this is quite rare. This method takes an `NSEvent` as an argument and is the most primitive form of event dispatch in Cocoa. Events at this layer encapsulate actions such as a key press or a mouse movement.

Starting with OS X 10.6, Apple introduced a mechanism for inspecting or transforming events before they are delivered to the application. The `-addLocalMonitorForEventsMatchingMask:handler:` method on `NSEvent` takes a block as the second argument. Before any event is delivered it is passed to this block, and the event that the block returns is the one actually delivered to the application. You can use this, for example, to add mouse gestures to your application by catching mouse events and replacing them with keyboard events. You might also find it useful for debugging, to get a notification when a particular kind of event is delivered to the application.

Most events will need to be delivered to a specific window. `NSApplication` does this by calling the `-sendEvent:` method in the *active window*. This will be an instance of `NSWindow`.

From here, event delivery becomes a little more friendly. Each window maintains a *first responder* pointer. This is a view object that accepts keyboard events. Keyboard events will be delivered to this object. Mouse events will be delivered to the view on which the mouse event occurred. Figure 5.1 shows the default objects in a nib file created by Interface Builder. Note the existence of the First Responder object here. This allows the first responder to be set as the target for actions. Doing this allows the target/action mechanism to deliver messages to the responder chain. An example of where this is used is for the cut, copy, and paste menu items, which send an action message to the first responder.

The *responder chain* is responsible for deciding which object should handle an event from here. The responder chain begins with the first responder and then travels up the view hierarchy. The view hierarchy can be quite complex. Figure 5.2 shows a moderately complex window. This contains a text view, a browser view, and a button. Although this appears simple, the view hierarchy is not nearly so trivial. Interface Builder allows us to see this in an outline view. Figure 5.3 shows all of the views in this window.

At the deepest level, there are six nested views. If the text view is the first responder, then each of these will be given the opportunity to handle the event. In common cases, the text view will handle the event itself. If it does not, then it will delegate it to the bordered scroll view, which will delegate it to the split view and so on until it reaches the window.

If the window doesn't handle it, then it will first pass it to its delegate and then to its controller. Finally, the application object, and then the application object's delegate will be given a chance to handle it. In document-driven applications, both the `NSDocument` and `NSDocumentController` instances will be given an opportunity to handle events, too.

Conceptually, you can think of your windows being in the view hierarchy inside the application and of every item in the view hierarchy first trying to handle an event itself, then passing it to its delegate, then its controller (if they are different),

Figure 5.1: Default objects in an application nib.

and then to its parent in the view hierarchy. This is a simplification of what really happens but is close enough in most cases.

You can subvert the responder chain in two ways. If you create a custom view, you do not have to delegate events up the view hierarchy; although you need to think carefully about where you will send them. Alternatively, you can grab them before they enter the responder chain from an `NSApplication` or `NSWindow` subclass by overriding the `-sendEvent:` method, like this:

```
- (void)sendEvent:(NSEvent *)event
{
    if ([event type] == NSKeyDown)
    {
        // Intercept events
        return;
    }
    [super sendEvent: event];
}
```

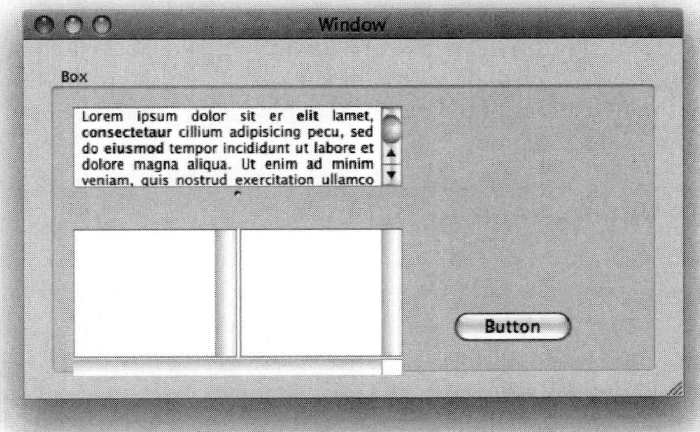

Figure 5.2: A window containing nested views.

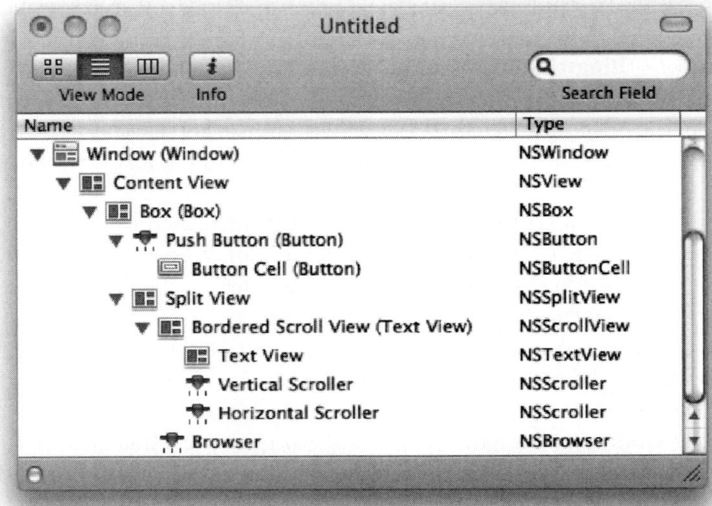

Figure 5.3: The view hierarchy for the window in Figure 5.2.

This simple version will ignore all key events delivered to the window. You can do this to intercept just some events and either handle them in a special way or prevent them from entering the responder chain. This would be used in something like Keynote's presenter display, where all key events are intercepted, rather than passed on to the objects used to draw the display, and are either used to control the slide show or silently ignored.

5.3.2 Targets and Actions

A lot of views use the *target-action pattern* for notifying their controller that something has happened. An action is a special kind of message that takes the sender as an argument. There are two ways of telling Interface Builder about them. The first is via the inspector; the second is in header files. In the Cocoa headers, you will find this macro defined:

```
#define IBAction void
```

You use this in code by defining action methods like this:

```
- (IBAction)doSomething: (id)sender;
```

When compiling, the preprocessor will simply replace `IBAction` with **`void`**, so this method should not return anything. If you load the header into Interface Builder, it will know that instances of your class expect to receive this kind of action.

The simplest thing that you can do with actions is connect them to a specific target, but this is not the most flexible way of using them. They can also be connected to the responder chain. If you set the target as the First Responder proxy, then messages will be delivered along a modified form of the responder chain.

Delivery of action messages is slightly more complex than delivery of normal event messages. Each event message is defined in `NSResponder` with a default implementation that simply calls the next responder in the chain. If you send a `doSomething:` message to the first responder, however, you will get an exception saying that the first responder does not understand this kind of message.

Action delivery is really handled by `NSApplication`'s `-sendAction:to:from:` method. It starts in the first responder of the key window and then moves up the responder chain until it gets to the key window. It then moves to the first responder of the main window (if the main window is not also key) and then up its responder chain.

For each potential target for the action, it sends a `-respondsToSelector:` message to see if it understands the message. If it does, then it will deliver the action; if not, then it will go up the responder chain. As with normal responder chains, `NSApp` and its delegate will try handling it if no views are able to.

This mechanism is used to automatically enable and disable menu items. You can send a `-targetForAction:` message to `NSApp` with the action's selector as an argument. If something in the current responder chain recognizes that selector, then it will return the object; otherwise, it will return `nil`. When you set the target for a menu item to the first responder, then this mechanism will be used when the menu is displayed to see if the menu item can be used. If nothing in the chain responds to the action, then it will be grayed out.

5.3.3 Becoming First Responder

First responder status is taken automatically by some existing views in response to mouse events. If you implement a subclass of `NSView`, then all you need to do to adopt this behavior is override the `-acceptsFirstResponder` method to return **`YES`**. This method will be called to see whether the method should be asked to become first responder. This should generally return a constant; if a view doesn't want to take first responder status at a specific time, then it has another opportunity to reject it later.

When a view is selected to become the new first responder, it is sent a `-becomeFirstResponder` message. It should do any setup required for being first responder here, such as drawing borders around itself, and return **`YES`** if it accepts first responder status.

Before another view is about to become first responder, the current one must relinquish this status. The `-resignFirstResponder` method is called. An object can refuse to lose first responder status by returning **`NO`** here, but this is rare.

You should never call these methods yourself. The window object tracks the first responder, and so trying to set it manually will break things that ask the window for the first responder and confuse event delivery. Instead, use `NSWindow`'s `-makeFirstResponder:` method, which will call these methods in the right order and track the change correctly.

5.4 Run Loops in Applications

At the start of this chapter we looked at the basic idea of a run loop. An `NSRunLoop` waits for events and fires off messages when they occur. It is possible to use run loops in any project that uses Foundation, including command line and web applications, but when writing applications that use AppKit they become much more important.

The run-loop class in Foundation is closely integrated with distributed objects. The original run-loop model comes from the Mach kernel architecture on NeXTSTEP. The only event sources that the run loop understood were *Mach ports*. These are the fundamental mechanism for Mach applications to communicate outside their process.

Mach, as a microkernel, does very little itself. It provides two abstractions: memory objects and ports. A memory object is simply a region of memory with some permissions, while a port is a connection over which messages can be delivered. Two models were used for building complex operating systems on top of this. The pure microkernel approach, also known as a *multi-server microkernel*, involved a number of processes, providing the services traditionally associated with an operating system. Each device driver would run as its own process, with some memory objects allocated over the device I/O range. The network stack might have separate processes for TCP, IP, Ethernet, and network card drivers, all of which would communicate by passing messages over ports.

Although this design scales very well to multiple processors, it had one significant disadvantage. Sending a message through a Mach port costs about ten times as much as making a system call. This made the multi-server model very slow on single-processor machines. The alternative was a *single-server microkernel*. This ran an existing kernel, typically 4BSD, as a process on top of Mach. The low-level parts of the kernel were rewritten to call Mach primitives instead of using platform-specific assembly, and most userspace processes just talked to this server.

OS X and NeXTSTEP are examples of the single-server approach. In NeXTSTEP, however, Mach ports were still very widely used for *interprocess communication* (*IPC*). Because of the microkernel design, Mach ports can be used both for messages from other processes and from the operating system, or rather from the BSD server that implements most of the functionality typically associated with the operating system.

The run-loop model was designed around the idea that all events would come from outside the process as Mach messages. When OpenStep was implemented on top of other platforms, this was generalized slightly, but the basic idea remains the same. Even sources are encapsulated in `NSPort` objects. Some of these are hidden from the programmer, in particular the connection to the window server that sends mouse and keyboard events. Connections from other processes using distributed objects will be handled via an `NSPort` subclass wrapping either a Mach port or a network socket.

The run loop provides two methods for managing event sources:

```
- (void)addPort: (NSPort*)aPort forMode: (NSString*)mode;
- (void)removePort: (NSPort*)aPort forMode: (NSString*)mode;
```

Each of these takes a port as the first argument. This is an abstract class that encapsulates a communication channel. The second argument is the *run-loop mode*. In Foundation, only two modes were traditionally defined;

`NSDefaultRunLoopMode` and `NSConnectionReplyMode`. The second of these is for ports that are part of the distributed objects mechanism, while the first is for all other event sources. A port will only be used as an event source when the run loop is in a mode that matches one for which the port was added.

This is another good example of AppKit building on functionality provided by Foundation. You can define your own run-loop modes when programming with Foundation, to limit the messages that you will receive when your program is in a certain state. When you use AppKit you will find two new modes defined for you. These are `NSModalPanelRunLoopMode` and `NSEventTrackingRunLoopMode`. If you run a modal dialog box, then only messages destined for that window will be delivered in the first of these modes. The second allows for synchronous tracking of mouse movements, for example, when drawing a shape in a box or selecting a region of text. Implementing these with purely asynchronous event delivery would be very difficult.

When your application starts, `NSApp` will start the main thread's run loop in the default mode and register to receive messages from the window server. Figure 5.4 shows an example flow of event messages in a Cocoa application. The window server will send messages to the process in the form of Mach messages[2] that are encapsulated in a port message object. This is delivered to the run loop, which turns it into an `NSEvent` instance and passes it to `NSApp`'s `-sendEvent:` method. The application object sends it to the correct window, which passes it to the first responder, using the correct method for this kind of event. In this case, the first responder doesn't handle it, and delegates it up the responder chain. The superview then passes it to its delegate, which does handle it.

Delivering events in this way is a very complex process, which, in almost all cases, you can ignore. If you want to implement a view object, you just subclass `NSResponder` or (more likely) one of its existing subclasses. If you want to implement a controller, then you simply set your object as a delegate or register for notifications. In both cases, you will just have to implement some Objective-C methods for specific high-level actions.

A number of Cocoa classes hide the details of run-loop modes from you. A simple example of this is `NSAlert`. This represents a model dialog box, which can either be application-modal or attached to a specific window. These are implemented in two quite different ways. The first sets the run loop to enqueue all events that are not destined for the window representing the alert. The second delivers events as normal, but instructs the window not to process any other events until the dialog has exited.

The first of these methods allows a simple synchronous programming style (although a worse user experience). You simply call the `-runModal` method on the

[2]Or, potentially, some other form of IPC.

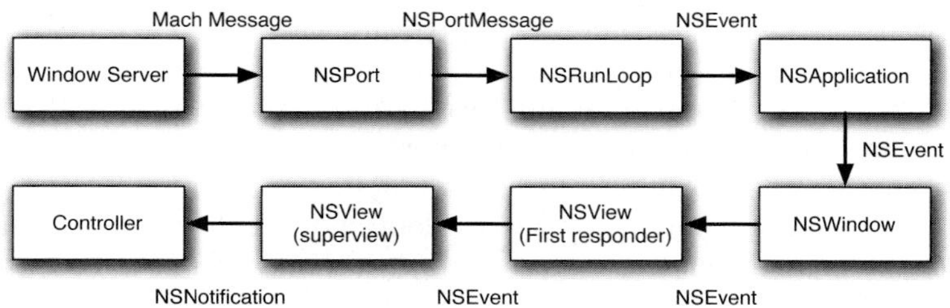

Figure 5.4: Example message flow in a Cocoa application.

alert object and get the button that was pressed as a return value. The second is slightly more complex. You need to call this method on the alert:

```
- (void)beginSheetModalForWindow: (NSWindow*)window
                   modalDelegate: (id)modalDelegate
                  didEndSelector: (SEL)alertDidEndSelector
                     contextInfo: (void*)contextInfo
```

This specifies the window that the sheet should be attached to and some information for the call-back. The delegate and selector follow the standard target-action pattern; the method will be called on the object when the dialog finishes. Unlike normal actions, this selector must take three arguments: the alert object that completed, the return code identifying the button, and the `contextInfo` passed in.

A number of other panels follow this pattern. If you wish to display an "open" dialog box in your application, the `NSOpenPanel` object has methods for running as a modal and a non-modal dialog box. In general, you should only ever use the modal form for prototyping and quick hacks, and favor the non-modal version for real applications.

There is one event source that we haven't looked at much yet. The `NSTimer` class provides a simple interface to timers, and is closely related to the run-loop class. Timers, when added to the run loop, are stored in a queue, with the first one defining how long the run loop will block while waiting for external events. Most commonly, you will create a timer with this method:

```
+ (NSTimer*)scheduledTimerWithTimeInterval: (NSTimeInterval)seconds
                                    target: (id)target
                                  selector: (SEL)aSelector
                                  userInfo: (id)userInfo
                                   repeats: (BOOL)repeats;
```

The first parameter defines how many seconds in the future the timer fires. If the `repeats` parameter is set to **`YES`**, then the timer will continue firing periodically after the same interval. Recall that `NSTimeInterval` is a **`double`** so this accepts fractions of a second. You can use timers firing several times a second for simple animations. The remaining three parameters are the same as for most other Cocoa methods that involve calling back. The selector must take one argument, which will be the `NSTimer` instance itself. As with a notification, this responds to a `-userInfo` message to get back the object passed in with the fourth argument.

5.5 Delegates and Notifications

Most view objects in Cocoa have delegates. These can be set by calling their `-setDelegate:` method, but more usually you will define them in Interface Builder.

If you hold down the Control key when dragging between two objects in Interface Builder, you will see a line drawn between them, as shown in Figure 5.5. The endpoints will both be highlighted, which is very useful when attempting to join an object to a sub-view. In this example, one of the objects is in a window and another is just represented by its icon in the project window. If you click on the outline view mode icon in the project window, then you will get an outline of the view hierarchy, which is sometimes more convenient for connecting objects that are deeply nested in the view hierarchy.

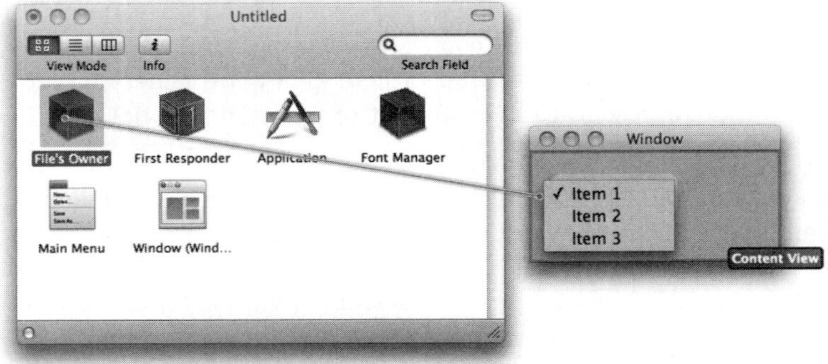

Figure 5.5: Connecting outlets and actions in Interface Builder.

When you release the mouse button, you will get a list of all of the *actions* and *outlets* that can be connected. Each object may send at most one action (although it can receive as many as it wishes) and may have one object set for each of the

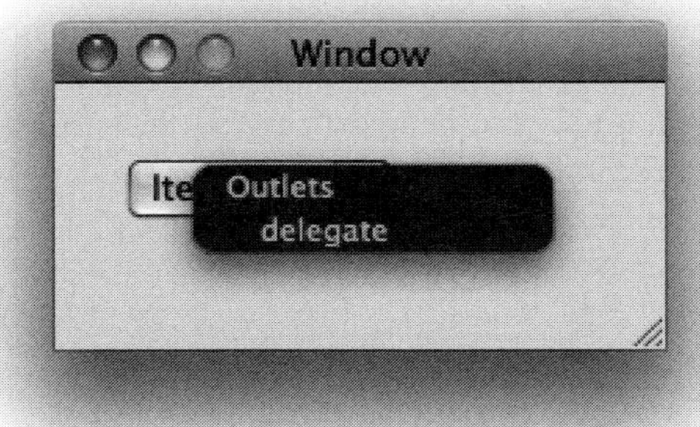

Figure 5.6: Setting a delegate in Interface Builder.

outlets it defines. Figure 5.6 shows the outlet defined for a drop-down box: the delegate. The object connected to this will be sent any of the delegate messages defined by the object.

> **Controls and Views**
>
> In some GUI toolkits, all visual components are referred to as *controls*. In Cocoa, these are a sub-category of *views*, which is the term used to refer to all user interface components. A control is a simple kind of view that simply wraps the behavior of a certain kind of cell. They are generally very simple components that represent a small amount of unstructured data.

There are two kinds of messages a delegate may receive. The simplest kind is equivalent to notifications, and generally take a notification as an argument. The other kind require some action by the delegate. A lot of these are defined in `NSControl`, the superclass for all simple controls in Cocoa. The delegate methods supported by this object include the following pair for editing text:

```
-       (BOOL)control: (NSControl*)control
textShouldBeginEditing: (NSText*)fieldEditor;
- (void)controlTextDidBeginEditing: (NSNotification*)aNotification;
```

The first of these returns a Boolean value indicating whether the control should allow the text to be edited at this point. If the delegate chooses to implement this method, then it can control the behavior of the view. In contrast, the second method is simply a notification that something has happened. The return value is **void** because the delegate is not required to make any kind of decision at this point. In addition to this method being called, the control will also post a `NSControlTextDidBeginEditingNotification`. An arbitrary number of other objects can listen for this notification and can handle it in any way they want. This is not true of the delegate methods that require a response; they can only be handled by a single object.

Many of the more complex view objects have a second kind of delegate known as their *data source*. While the delegate controls the user interaction behavior of a view, the data source controls the view's interaction with the model object. Data sources are often required to implement at least some of their methods, unlike delegates that can generally ignore any message that they don't have a specific need for. A data source is required to populate the view with data and so the return values from calls to it are important and cannot be replaced by default values.

The `NSTableView` class is a good example of a class that uses a data source. The methods that should be implemented are described by the `NSTableDataSource` informal protocol. Only two methods in this protocol must be implemented by a data source:

```
- (NSInteger)numberOfRowsInTableView: (NSTableView*)aTableView;
-           (id)tableView: (NSTableView*)aTableView
objectValueForTableColumn: (NSTableColumn*)aTableColumn
                      row: (NSInteger)rowIndex;
```

The first of these returns the number of rows of data and the second returns an object for a specified column-row combination. Note that these also take the view object as an argument, meaning that the same data source object can be used for multiple views, returning different data to them.

The most common optional method in this data source protocol is the converse of the second one, used for setting values:

```
- (void)tableView: (NSTableView*)aTableView
   setObjectValue: (id)anObject
   forTableColumn: (NSTableColumn*)aTableColumn
              row: (NSInteger)rowIndex;
```

If this method is not implemented, then the table view will not support writing data back to the model object, even if it is set to editable. Other methods in this protocol relate to drag and drop. Sometimes, data source methods can be used to provide nicer user interaction. The data source protocol for `NSComboBox` has an optional method for auto-completion. If a data source object implements this, then the combo box will automatically try to auto-complete text typed by the user.

We will look at data sources in more detail in Chapter 11.

5.6 The View Hierarchy

The *view hierarchy* is used for event delivery, but also provides a semantic grouping of related view objects and a set of incremental coordinate transforms. Each view has its own coordinate system, which is defined as a transform on its parent's coordinates.

5.6.1 Windows

The top level of the view hierarchy is the window. A window, conceptually, is a virtual display. The job of the operating system is to allow different programs to share hardware resources without having to be aware of each other. It shares the speakers by mixing sound streams from every program. It shares the keyboard by allowing each application to have access to them exclusively when the user chooses. It shares the CPU by allocating each application time slices and it shares RAM by partitioning it. It shares the screen by allowing each application to create virtual screens and displaying them on the real one.

In Cocoa, *screens* are represented by `NSScreen` objects. These are not part of the view hierarchy, although conceptually you might expect them to be the top level. A screen is a very simple object providing information about the display device, but not handling any of the real work of drawing on it. This is done by the *window server*. When you draw in a window, you are sending commands to the window server. Depending on the version of OS X you are using and the capabilities of the hardware, these may then run code on the CPU or the GPU to perform drawing operation into an off-screen buffer. The window server is then responsible for compositing these buffers together to provide the contents of the screen.

Windows in Cocoa are instances of the `NSWindow` class. This class is responsible for delivering events to views and for handling drawing inside itself. Every window has exactly one `NSView` instance representing its contents. This view may contain other views, and usually does.

In any Cocoa application, there are two important windows, the *main window* and the `key window`. The main window is the window representing the user's attention. This is typically the window for the current document, or the main user interface window in an application that is not document driven. The key window is the window that receives key events. These are often the same, but not always. Often a document will have various ancillary windows floating around it, such as panels or inspectors. These may become key—for example, when the user wants to type something in a text field on one of them—but will not become the main window.

There is one subclass of `NSWindow` that is commonly used in AppKit; `NSPanel`.

This represents floating panels. These are used by the standard dialog boxes in Cocoa and cannot become the main window. Panels mainly work by overriding methods in `NSWindow` that return one value and returning another. An example of this is the `-hidesOnDeactivate` method. In both classes, this returns a configurable flag; however in windows it defaults to **`NO`** and in panels it defaults to **`YES`**. This means that panels will be hidden when an application stops being active, while windows will not. This helps to reduce screen clutter in OS X and should generally not be overridden.

Each window typically has an associated controller, an instance of a subclass of `NSWindowController`. This does a little bit more than other controller objects and is intimately involved in the nib loading process. Most commonly, you create a window instance by sending an `-initWithWindowNibName:` message to a `NSWindowController` object. This loads the nib in the application's bundle with the specified name and sets itself as the owner. Typically the main window in the nib will set its window controller to the file's owner.

5.6.2 Views

Cocoa *views* are usually subclasses of `NSView`. Since the Objective-C type system and dispatch mechanism do not depend on the class hierarchy, it is possible to have view objects that are subclasses of some other class, but this would involve massive amounts of duplicated effort and so is not a good idea.

Views are part of the responder chain, and inherit much of this behavior from `NSResponder`, the superclass of `NSView`. Most of the additional behavior implemented by the view class is related to drawing.

The main method related to drawing is `-drawRect:`. This takes an `NSRect` as an argument and draws the part of the view that is within that rectangle. This rectangle is in the receiver's coordinate system. Every view has its own, local, *coordinate system*. The bottom-left corner of a view is the (0, 0) coordinate—the origin—and coordinate values increase toward the top-right corner of the view.

Before calling `-drawRect:` in a subview, the superview will modify the graphics state so that the subview's coordinate system is valid, and then restore the old coordinate system afterward. This means that drawing in a view is relatively simple. The view can be largely oblivious to its superview and the related coordinate systems.

Cocoa includes a number of standard view classes. If possible, you should use these instead of defining your own. Part of the consistency of Mac applications comes from the good selection of user interface components that are used by most applications. If you define a new view object that implements similar functionality to an existing view, then you may confuse users. Some of the most common views include

- `NSButton`, a class encapsulating a simple button with a large number of options.
- `NSImageView`, which is used to draw images.
- `NSTextField` and `NSTextView`, which provide basic and full-featured text drawing functionality, respectively.
- `NSMovieView`, a wrapper around QuickTime, which is used for displaying video in a window.
- `NSOpenGLView` manages the setup of an OpenGL context and allows the OpenGL APIs to be used for drawing in a Cocoa window.

There are many others, most of which can be drawn in Interface Builder and configured there without needing any code. Note that there isn't a direct correspondence between classes and selectable items in the Interface Builder palette. Some classes, such as `NSButton`, appear a large number of times with different sets of default options.

Pixels and Points

All drawing in Cocoa is done using the PostScript display model. Distance units in Cocoa are PostScript points. There are 72 PostScript points in an inch. In older versions of OS X, there was an implicit assumption that the display was 72dpi, so one pixel was always one point. This is not a good assumption; modern displays can be over 150dpi. Code should not make any assumptions about the size of a point in pixels.

5.6.3 Cells

A lot of views, such as the table view, contain a lot of smaller components. A relatively small table might contain ten rows and ten columns. At each intersection, something needs to be drawn, and there may also be column headers, giving a total of 110 subviews. This would consume a lot of memory. On 10.5, `NSView` is 80 bytes when compiling as 32-bit code, and 152 bytes in 64-bit mode. For the table view, we would need 16KB of RAM for the view objects. Scaling this up to a 100 by 100 table gives almost 1.5MB just for the view instances. In a real program you would use some subclass of `NSView`, making this even larger.

The solution to this is to use *cells*—subclasses of `NSCell`—which are much lighter than full-blown views. On Leopard, `NSCell` is 20 or 32 bytes, for 32-bit and

64-bit targets, respectively. For the 100 by 100 table example, with one cell instead of one view at each intersection, you would save over 1MB of RAM. Cells, unlike views, do not maintain their own coordinate system or any setup code related to this; instead, they draw into a specified view. One side effect of this is that you can reuse a cell for drawing a number of times on a view.

A table view typically only has one cell per column and uses this for each visible row. Typically this is done by calling the `-setObjectValue:` method on the cell for the value returned by the data source and then the `-drawWithFrame:inView:` method to tell the cell where to draw itself in the view.

The best way of thinking about a cell is like an ink stamp. An ink stamp allows you to draw the same shape in different colors on a page by dipping it in different colors of ink and then stamping. Similarly, a cell allows you to draw the same kind of representation of an object, with different objects, by setting its value and then drawing it.

A number of view objects use cells. The simplest is `NSControl`. This is a very simple class that uses a single cell for drawing. A lot of the basic user interface components in Cocoa are subclasses of this with a specific cell. A good example is `NSButton`, which is a `NSControl` subclass using a `NSButtonCell` for drawing. A slightly more complex example is `NSMatrix`, which contains a two-dimensional matrix of cells.

If you are creating a new kind of view, then you might consider using the cell abstraction and putting your drawing code in a `NSCell` subclass and then wrapping this in a `NSControl` subclass. This allows you to use your new UI component in table views, outline views, browser views, and matrices, as well as inserting it directly in the view hierarchy.

5.7 Summary

This chapter has given a brief guided tour of the AppKit concepts. We looked at the types of events delivered in Cocoa and how they are delivered. We saw how AppKit extends Foundation in various ways, and looked at how the view hierarchy is designed.

All of the concepts explored in this chapter are central to the design of Cocoa applications. We will look in more detail at how each of these is used in future chapters. We've seen how events are delivered to views on the screen and then to model objects, and how this can trigger drawing.

Chapter 6

Creating Graphical User Interfaces

Although AppKit contains a lot of classes, for a variety of purposes, a significant proportion of the framework is responsible for creating graphical user interfaces. This chapter will explore the concepts behind Cocoa GUIs and some of the classes used to create them.

6.1 Positioning Views

Cocoa, like most other GUI toolkits, uses a Cartesian coordinate system for drawing. Points are described by the `NSPoint` structure, which contains two `CGFloat`s; either **`float`**s or **`double`**s, depending on whether you are on a 32- or 64-bit system. This structure has the same layout as the `CGPoint` structure, and the two can be used mostly interchangeably.

> **Core Text**
>
> The Core Text framework is new with OS X 10.5. It provides a C interface closely modeled after the Cocoa text system, discussed in Chapter 8. Earlier versions of OS X used *Apple Type Services for Unicode Imaging* (*ATSUI*), a framework dating back to MacOS 8.5.
>
> Code using the Cocoa classes does not require modification to move between the two underlying frameworks, since AppKit abstracts the details of the one in use away from the developer.

The CG prefix on the latter definition is short for *Core Graphics*, the name Apple gives to the programmatic interface to *Quartz*, the PDF-like display system on OS X. Core Graphics is a set of C APIs that define ways of drawing bitmaps and polygons on the screen. On top of this sits *Core Text*, another C API that uses the primitive bezier curve drawing facilities in Core Graphics to render text. Cocoa exposes the functionality of both via AppKit objects.

Coordinates in Cocoa have their origin at the bottom-left corner of the drawable region. Figure 6.1 shows how this works in practice. The screen, window, and views all have independent coordinate systems. Note in particular the *flipped view*, which has its y axis the opposite way up to all of the other views.

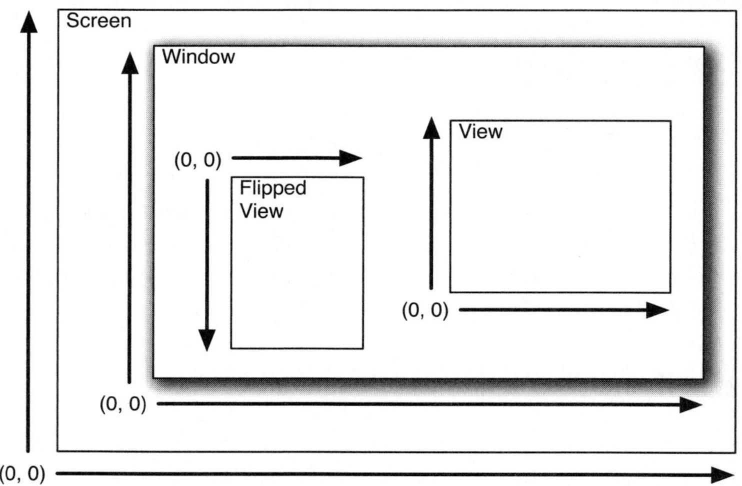

Figure 6.1: Coordinate systems in Cocoa.

In some views it is very inconvenient to have the coordinates start at the bottom. You want to start drawing at the top and have things grow downward. Text views are a good example of this, where you start rendering text at the top and the layout and position of all subsequent text depends on the words already placed in the view.

You can do this in a normal view, but it requires constantly calculating distances based on the offset from the bottom, which is time consuming and error prone. Cocoa simplifies this by allowing any view to be flipped—to have its coordinate system inverted—putting the origin in the top-left corner of the view. This is more natural for some visual content, and less natural for other kinds.

Any coordinate system for a view is implemented via an *affine transform*, a transform between two coordinate systems, implemented by the `NSAffineTransform` class. This is a 3×3 that is multiplied by the coordinate vector to give a point in a new coordinate space. The general formula for this is

$$\begin{pmatrix} x & y & 1 \end{pmatrix} \times \begin{pmatrix} m_{11} & m_{12} & 0 \\ m_{21} & m_{22} & 0 \\ t_x & t_y & 1 \end{pmatrix} = \begin{pmatrix} x' & y' & 1 \end{pmatrix}$$

Note that a number of these values are always zero or one. The Cocoa and Core Graphics classes structures do not store these values; points are only defined by two values and transformations by six. The remaining values can be used for normalization, but in Cocoa they are always stored in their normalized form.

Transformation matrices defined in this way can represent rotations, translations, and scaling. They can be composed by matrix multiplication to give a combined transform matrix. This means that coordinates in any view, irrespective of the number of transforms that have been applied to define it, can be performed by a single matrix multiplication on the results.

This is why flipped views are more efficient than calculating the coordinate offsets manually; they simply require an additional set of transforms to be applied to the matrix and this to be applied to the result. This is a slight oversimplification, since often you need to reflect the drawn shape before drawing it in a flipped view, making flipped views slower that non-flipped views. If you are trying to draw something and find you are constantly manually calculating the distance from the top of the view, then a flipped view will be more efficient. Otherwise, it should be avoided.

When you place a view using Interface Builder, you can select its position using direct manipulation; just drag it and resize it where you want. You can also explicitly set the coordinates using the inspector, shown in Figure 6.2.

This inspector also allows setting resizing rules for the view to be defined. The behavior of a view when its parent is resized depends on six attributes. Four define whether the distance from the view to the top, bottom, left, and right of the superview can be changed. The remaining two define whether the width or the size can be changed.

Some combinations of these don't make sense. For example, if you set that the distance from the left and right edge of the superview can change and the view can be resized horizontally, this does not give enough information to sensibly place the view. More commonly, you will set a view to be a fixed distance from one side and either allow it to resize or keep it fixed.

Figure 6.3 shows the effect of resizing a window containing a text view and three buttons. The buttons keep their position relative to the top-right corner of the window, while the text view is resized to fit the remaining space.

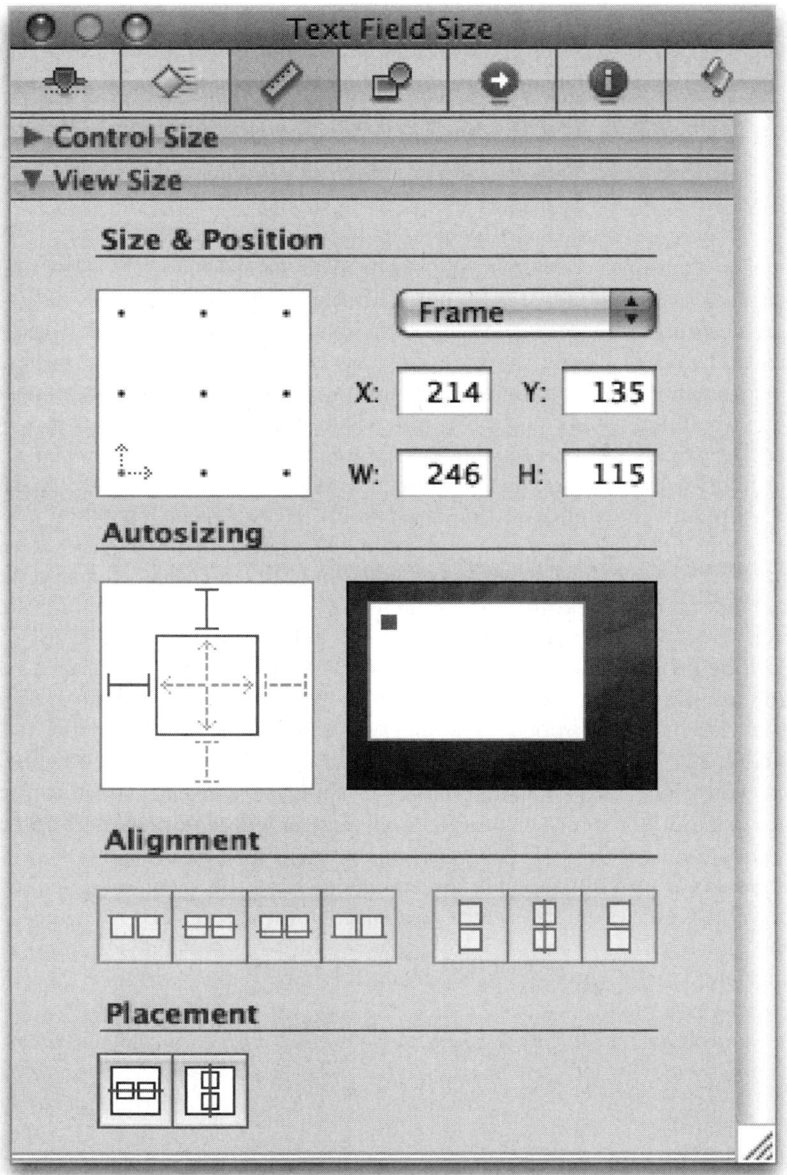

Figure 6.2: The view size inspector in Interface Builder.

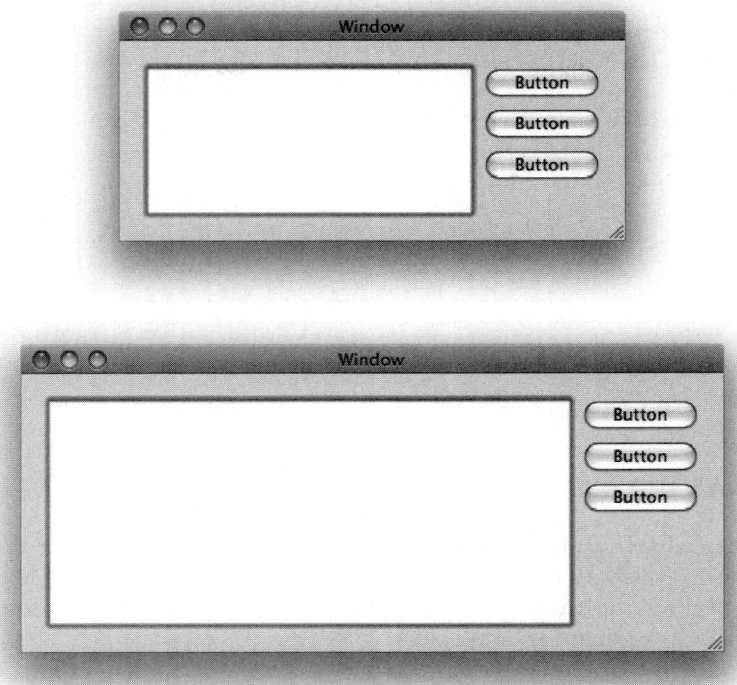

Figure 6.3: Resizing a window containing three buttons and a text view.

This is accomplished with the resizing rules shown in Figure 6.4. The left image shows the configuration for the buttons. The center of the square is empty—the buttons may not resize—and they are linked to the top and right of the window. When you resize the window, these buttons will stay the same size and remain fixed in position relative to the top-right corner.

The right image shows the resizing rules for the text view. This has all of the options selected. The distance between all of the borders of the text view and the sides of the window are constant, and the view can be resized in the horizontal and vertical dimensions. This means, among other things, that the distance between the buttons and the view will remain constant. The left edge of the buttons is fixed because the location of their right edge and their width is fixed.

You might have noticed a limitation of this approach. What happens if we have two resizable views in a single window? There is no way of resizing a view relative to the view next to it, only to the view that contains it. There is a solution to this, although it's not particularly elegant. You can embed the two resizable views in another view, have that view resize relative to the parent, and the subviews resize relative to the nested view. We'll look at exactly how you do this in the next section.

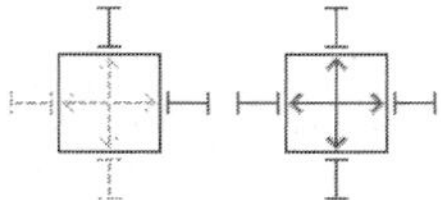

Figure 6.4: Autosizing rules for the views in Figure 6.3.

6.2 Nested Views

Views are arranged in a hierarchy. Views are typically subclasses of `NSView`, which implements support for maintaining the *view hierarchy.* Whenever a view is drawn, the superview sets up the coordinate transform, as described in the last section, and instructs it to draw.

Although any view can contain other views, some are explicitly designed to do so. These typically expose some extra methods for manipulating the child views. Cocoa provides some very easy-to-use views that are designed to contain other views. The simplest of all is the `NSView` class itself, which can contain children in arbitrary locations. When you create a new window, it will have a `NSView` as its content view, and all of the views you drag into it in Interface Builder will be set as parents of this view. Others provide a little more functionality than this, such as clipping, scrolling, or automatically hiding their children.

Many of the more complex view objects in Cocoa are implemented in collaboration with some of the views described in this section.

6.2.1 Clipped Views

Very often, you want to display a large document in a small window. To do this, you have to do one of two things: either zoom or clip the document. Clipping is an ability inherent in most Cocoa views. When a view needs to be drawn, it is sent a `-drawRect:` message, which specifies a rectangle in the view that should be drawn. A well-optimized view will restrict itself to only drawing the parts that need drawing.

Not all views will completely restrict themselves in this way, however. A view may simply draw all of its contents, or it may draw shapes that are partially in the rectangle. The `NSClipView` class contains another view and clips its drawing. The clip view does not perform the clipping itself; it merely sets the clipping rectangle in the drawing context before calling the `-drawRect:` method on the subview. The drawing context then discards any drawing commands that are outside of this rectangle. You can do this in your own view by calling the `NSRectClip()` and `NSRectClipList()` functions. These set the clipping region to either a single rectangle or a list of rectangles, respectively.

As well as handling the clipped drawing, the clip view is responsible for tracking which part of the subview to draw. This is done by sending it `-scrollToPoint:` messages. These take an `NSPoint` as an argument and instruct the clip view to set that point in the subview to its origin. This point will be drawn at (0, 0) in the clip view's coordinate system. The width and height of the subview that are drawn are taken automatically from the clip view's size.

For optimization, you might want to call the clip view's `-setCopiesOnScroll:` method. If this is passed **`YES`** as an argument, then scrolling will cause the clip view to copy the pixels from the old view into their new location and only request that the subview draws the newly revealed part. For complex views, this can be hugely more efficient. If the subview is drawing a lot of text, for example, then redrawing will cause it to have to render each glyph and composite them together, while copying can be done purely on the graphics card. If the view contains a lot of empty space, however, then copying may be slower than simply issuing a single fill command.

6.2.2 Scroll Views

Scrolling in Cocoa is implemented using the clip view. This is responsible for showing a small part of a larger view, in an efficient way. Drawing the scroll bars and other user interface components is the responsibility of the *scroll view*, implemented by `NSScrollView`.

A view that is surrounded by scroll bars will be quite deeply nested in the view hierarchy. At a minimum, the hierarchy will be likely to contain

1. The window's contents view, typically a `NSView` that contains arbitrarily placed subviews.
2. The scroll view, which draws the scroll bars.
3. The clip view, which handles clipping of the real view and is controlled by the scroll view.
4. The real subview, which is rendering the document the user is interested in.

The scroll bars are also views, instances of `NSScroller`. If horizontal and vertical scroll bars are both visible, then you have four extra views between your view and the window's view related to scrolling. Most of the time, however, you can ignore these completely.

When you set the document view for the scroll view, either using `-setDocumentView:` or by dragging another view inside it in Interface Builder, the default scroll behavior will work correctly. When the user moves the scroll bars, the scroll view will send `-scrollToPoint:` messages to the clip view it contains, causing the document to scroll.

Both the scroll view and the clip view are quite simple objects. The separation of concerns between the two means that you can implement your own replacement for the scroll view easily. As long as you provide some kind of user interface for scrolling, the clip view will handle the scrolling.

The scroll view is just a simple view connecting the scrollers to the clip view. Because of this, you can customize it easily, rather than replacing it outright, if you want different kinds of scroll bars. Simply implement a subclass of `NSScroller`. This is done by the open source chat client Colloquy, which implements a subclass of `NSScroller` called `JVMarkedScroller`. This subclass puts marks down the scroll bar indicating locations in the back buffer where your name was mentioned. It also adds action methods for jumping to the next and previous mark. These just call the relevant methods in the scroll and clip views. This simple customization of a core Cocoa UI element does a lot to increase usability in this particular application and is a good example of how to extend Cocoa to improve your application.

6.2.3 Tab Views

A more conventional form of nested view is the *tab view*, implemented by the `NSTabView` class. This contains a set of independent subviews. Each subview is associated with a label, which is shown at the top of the view. The appearance of tab views has changed a lot since the initial release of OS X. Rather than appearing like a set of folder tabs, they are just boxes with a row of buttons along the top. This is more aesthetically pleasing than older versions but removes the visual clue relating them to pages in a folder. Figure 6.5 shows the new look for tab views.

The tab view has two important components: the row of tabs at the top, and the contents view at the bottom. The row of buttons is part of the tab view, but the view at the bottom is a subview and can contain any other views.

Tab views use a helper class, `NSTabViewItem`, which encapsulates a single tab. This contains a label, an identifier, and a view. The *identifier* model is used in a number of places in Cocoa. It is used to uniquely identify the tab. You can display a tab for a specific identifier. This allows you to have different human-readable

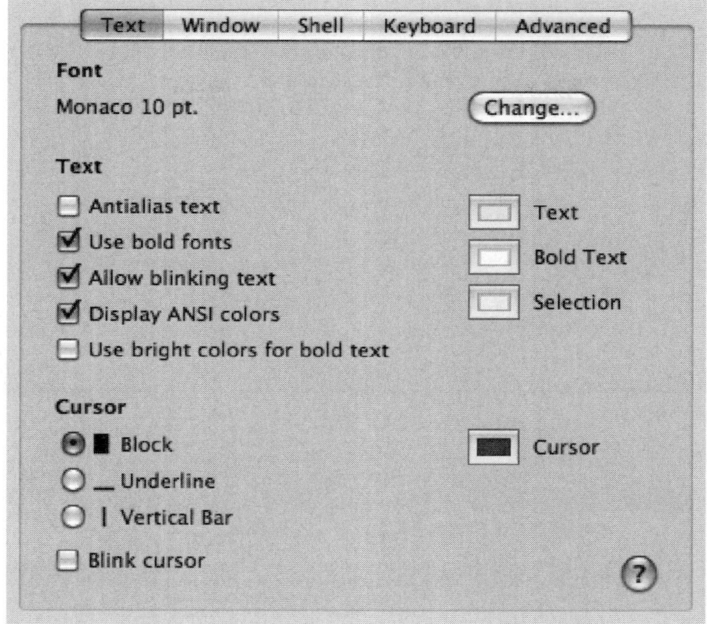

Figure 6.5: A tab view in recent versions of OS X.

labels and internal labels, which helps with *localization*. You will find this pattern in most Cocoa view objects that manage a collection of elements.

6.2.4 Split Views

Split views are a simple kind of container view. Each split view contains subviews divided either horizontally or vertically by a bar that the user can resize.

This is the easiest solution to the problem mentioned earlier where you need two or more resizable views in a window. By embedding each in a split view, you can have them resize both relative to each other and relative to the parent view.

Figure 6.6 shows the earlier example modified so that the left side now contains a split view, rather than a single text view. This contains a people view from the Address Book framework and a text view. Now, when the window is resized the two views on the left are resized without any issues.

Remember that split views are views themselves, which means that they can be used as contents views in other split views. You will see an example of this

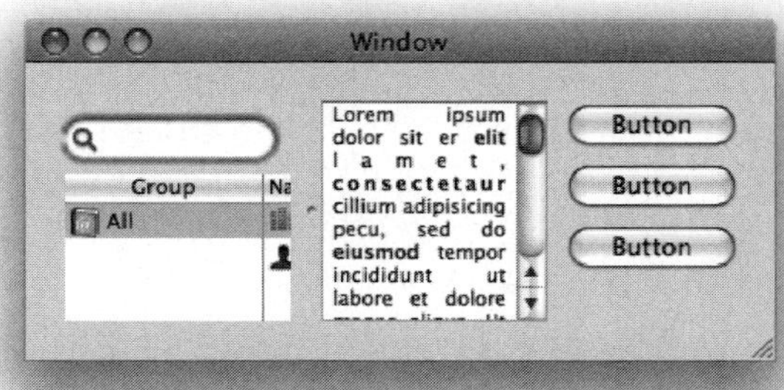

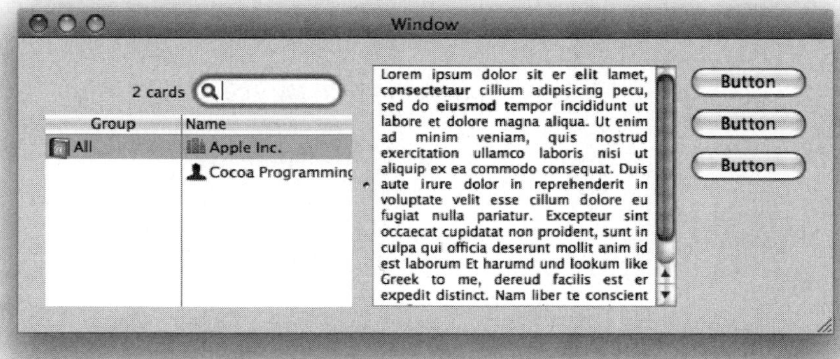

Figure 6.6: Resizing a window containing a split view.

all of the time when you are developing on OS X since XCode uses nested split views for its user interface. At the top level is a vertical split view containing the outline view of the project on the left and a horizontal split view on the right. The second split view contains the file list and the editor. This same three-pane layout is found in Mail.app, and a number of other applications.

The split view allows the subviews to be collapsed against the side by double-clicking on the divider. As with a number of other parts of Cocoa, this is controlled via a *delegate*. The delegate for a split view controls a number of aspects of the behavior of the object, in particular what happens when the user clicks and drags on the divider (the only part of the split view that it is responsible for drawing).

The split view can contain more than two subviews, although this is not obviously apparent in Interface Builder. When you create a split view, you can set the child views by dragging a new view to one of the panes. To add a third child view, drag a new view to the dividing line between the two. The view will then split further. This allows you to have long runs of views that can be resized relative to each other.

6.2.5 Boxes

The simplest kind of nested view is the box, `NSBox`. This just draws a border around a collection of subviews. Using boxes is generally discouraged. They are not intrinsically bad but were heavily over-used by a lot of early Cocoa applications. Boxes allocate a lot of screen space to something that does not provide any user interaction, which is rarely ideal.

The main reason for boxes is to provide a semantic grouping of view objects as a hint for the user. In many cases it is better to split views using some other mechanism, such as putting them on different panels or in different tabs. If views are designed to be used together, then they shouldn't be in different boxes. If they are designed to be used at different times, then they shouldn't be in the same pane.

There are obvious exceptions to this. Preference panels often have sets of preferences that are related but distinct. An example of this is the System Preferences panel for Exposé, which contains boxes for setting key shortcuts and hot corners. These belong on the same pane because they both relate to shortcuts for activating Exposé, but they go in different boxes because they relate to distinct activities.

The Apple *Human Interface Guidelines* (*HIGs*) have this to say about boxes:

> Although group boxes are very useful for separating logical collections of content, avoid nesting them when possible; nested group boxes use a lot of space, and it can be difficult to perceive individual boundaries when group boxes are nested too deeply. Instead, consider using a separator or white space to group content within a group box.

Using boxes in Cocoa is easy. For the most part, you can ignore their existence and simply treat them as a decoration drawn on the window, rather than anything with programmatic significance.

6.3 Creating Views

Most of the time, you will create views simply by dragging them onto a window in Interface Builder. Creating views in code is very rare in Cocoa. It is worth noting that you can put parentless views in a nib file. This allows you to draw UIs that are not attached to any specific window and later insert them into the view hierarchy. You will need to do this if you want to create an application that runs full-screen, for example, since there is no way of creating a full-screen window in Interface Builder.

The interface palette contains all of the Cocoa view objects, some of them more than once. This is because Interface Builder creates views with some parameters defined. A number of Cocoa views can have very different visual behavior with different flags set. Figure 6.7 illustrates this. Every object in this panel is an instance of the same class.

6.3.1 Buttons

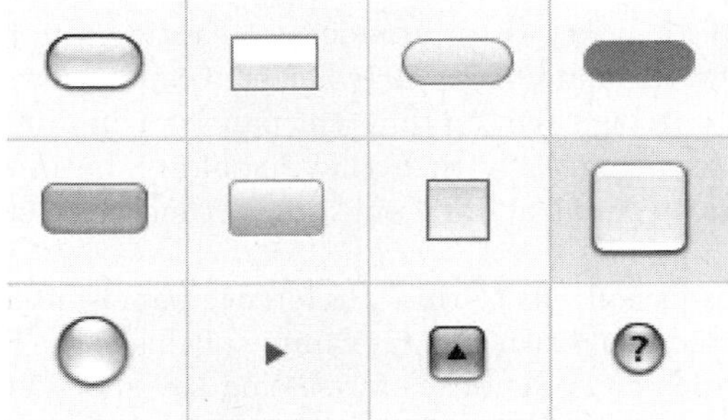

Figure 6.7: Buttons available in Interface Builder.

The simplest kind of view, conceptually if not in terms of implementation, is the button. These are instances of `NSButton`. All of the objects you can see in Figure 6.7 are instances of this class.

A button is a view that understands mouse down events and sends an action in response to them. For a button to be usable, it generally changes its image in some way while it is being pressed.

The `NSButton` class does almost nothing itself. It inherits view-like behavior from its superclass, `NSControl`, and adopts button-like behavior from an `NSButtonCell` instance. Most of the messages sent to a button will be passed on to its cell.

The button cell inherits a lot of its behavior from the `NSActionCell` superclass. This class handles mouse tracking and sending actions in response to mouse and keyboard events. It also handles some basic drawing.

Buttons may display text, an image, or both. The text can be set either as a plain string, via `-setTitle:`, or an attributed string with rich text attributes via

`-setAttributedTitle:`. The image is set via `-setImage:`. How they are displayed in relation to each other is defined by `-setImagePosition:`.

There are a large number of other methods that are used to configure buttons, and you can spend a long time reading the documentation for them and how they relate to each other if you need to generate buttons in code. Fortunately, this is very rare. Interface Builder provides the inspector shown in Figure 6.8 to allow button customization from within a nib. Even though there are a range of predefined button types in the palette (12, as of OS X 10.5, with more being added with every version), these are not really required. You can create any of the buttons from the palette by selecting any of the others and customizing it in the inspector.

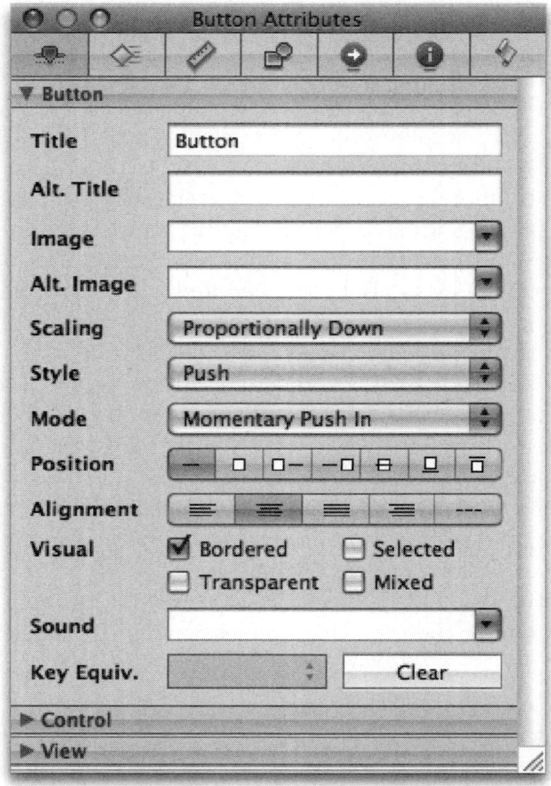

Figure 6.8: Configuring button attributes in Interface Builder.

When a button is pressed the method defined by its target and action will be called. We looked at how to set these from Interface Builder in Chapter 3. Just control-drag from the button to the controller object and select the action from the list that appears.

Remember that you can use the same action for several buttons, since each one will be passed as a parameter to the action method. You can compare this against the pointer value of an instance variable representing the button, or define a different method for each. Which option makes more sense depends a lot on the application. Two actions that are unrelated should never be handled by the same method, but two that are slight variations might be best implemented by the same method.

6.3.2 Text Views

The most complex views in Cocoa relate to drawing text. We will look at these in a lot more detail in the next chapter. There are generally three ways of interacting with text in Cocoa. The simplest object responsible for text rendering is the `NSCell` class, which has the ability to render text.

There is a slightly more advanced cell for editing text, the `NSTextField`, which adds options like placeholder strings—strings that are shown in light gray when the field is empty—and modifying the background color. This is wrapped in a view by the `NSTextField` class. Both the cell and the control have "secure" subclasses (`NSSecureTextField` and `NSSecureTextFieldCell`) that display a placeholder for each character that is typed, rather than the character itself.

All of the cell classes use a `NSText` object for editing. There is a shared instance of this class that is used whenever text editing is required. The `NSText` class is a general interface to text editing objects. If you try to instantiate it, you will actually get an instance of the `NSTextView` class.

`NSTextView` is the most powerful part of the Cocoa text system. It implements everything needed for a simple word processor, including the ability to represent embedded images, complex layouts, pagination, rules, and so on. The TextEdit application, included with OS X, uses an `NSTextView` for its main document view. You will find the source code for this application in /Developer/Examples/AppKit/TextEdit.

6.3.3 Data Views

The most complex views to work with on Cocoa are those that require a *data source*. These implement the view part of the *model-view-controller* (*MVC*) pattern. They retain a small amount of state, corresponding to what is currently being displayed, but nothing more. When you visit a different part of the data, they query their data source.

There were three of these in Cocoa:

- The `NSBrowser` class implements the browser view found in the Finder and its NeXT counterpart. This presents hierarchical data in columns, with the selection in each column defining the content of the one to the right.
- Tables of two-dimensional data are represented by the `NSTableView`. This is used for displaying records and has a data source that gets objects for each row and then displayable data from each object for every visible row.
- The table model is refined to allow hierarchical data by the `NSOutlineView` class. This can display the same data as the table view if no hierarchy is defined, but is most commonly used to display data in a tree form.

These are all designed to display large amounts of data provided by another source. One thing to watch out for is that they do not retain the objects that the data source provides. This means that the data source is required to ensure that the object persists for longer than the view holds a reference to it. Unfortunately, there is no way of telling how long this is. Since this behavior is highly undesirable, it may be fixed in future versions of OS X.

To demonstrate how to use these, we'll build a simple outliner. This will use an `NSOutlineView` object for the view and a tree of objects for the model. We will create three new classes for this project:

- `OutlineItem` will be a simple class representing a single item in the tree and containing references to its children.
- `OutlineDataSource` will act as the data source for the view and maintain a tree of `OutlineItem` objects.
- `OutlineDocument` will be an `NSDocument` subclass representing the document.

We will look at document-driven applications in more detail in Chapter 9 and revisit this example then to expand the document object. For now we will ignore most of its functionality; the outliner will not support loading or saving yet.

The simplest class is `OutlineItem`. This contains an `NSString` representing the title and an `NSMutableArray` of children. Listing 6.1 shows the interface to this class. No methods are declared, only two instance variables and two properties.

The properties each correspond to one of the instance variables. If we were happy to support only Leopard and newer systems, then we would not need to declare these instance variables. Apple's modern Objective-C runtime library allows instance variables that are not declared in the header, but for compatibility with the legacy runtime we declare them anyway.

The two properties are both declared `retain` so that they just keep a reference to new versions, `nonatomic` because we don't care about them being accessed concurrently from multiple threads, and `readwrite` so that they can be both accessed and set.

Listing 6.1: Outline item interface. [from: examples/Outliner/OutlineItem.h]

```
#import <Cocoa/Cocoa.h>

@interface OutlineItem : NSObject {
    NSString *title;
    NSMutableArray *children;
}
@property (retain, nonatomic, readwrite) NSString *title;
@property (retain, nonatomic, readwrite) NSMutableArray *children;
@end
```

The implementation, shown in Listing 6.2, is almost as simple. This synthesizes the two properties, which creates accessor methods for them both, and then sets some initial values. We don't actually need to set an initial value for the title, but doing so makes it more obvious that everything is working in the user interface.

Listing 6.2: Outline item implementation. [from: examples/Outliner/OutlineItem.m]

```
@implementation OutlineItem
@synthesize children;
@synthesize title;
- (id)init
{
    if (nil == (self = [super init]))
    {
        return nil;
    }
    children = [NSMutableArray new];
    title = @"New Item";
    return self;
}
- (void) dealloc
{
    [children release];
    [title release];
    [super dealloc];
}
@end
```

Listing 6.3 shows the data source interface. Again, this is very simple, only declaring single property. This property is the root node for the outline tree. `NSOutlineView` supports multi-rooted hierarchies, but this version of the outliner doesn't. As a simple exercise, you could try replacing this with an `NSMutableArray` and supporting more than one root object.

Although this class implements a number of methods, it doesn't declare any in its interface. This is because the methods are all called by the view object, which performs run-time testing to determine which messages it responds to. No code needs to be aware of the implemented methods at compile time, so there is no need to publish them in the interface.

Listing 6.3: Outliner data source interface. [from: examples/Outliner/OutlineDataSource.h]

```
#import <Cocoa/Cocoa.h>
#import "OutlineItem.h"

@interface OutlineDataSource : NSObject {
    OutlineItem *root;
}
@property (nonatomic, retain) OutlineItem *root;
@end
```

The implementation of this class, shown in Listing 6.4, is much more complicated. The initializer is fairly simple, just creating a new root node for the hierarchy and setting its title to a default value.

All of the other methods are defined by the `NSOutlineViewDataSource` informal protocol. They all take the outline view objects as their first argument and query the data source for information about a specific part of the hierarchy.

Listing 6.4: Outliner data source implementation. [from: examples/Outliner/OutlineDataSource.m]

```
#import "OutlineDataSource.h"

@implementation OutlineDataSource
@synthesize root;
- (id)init
{
    if (nil == (self = [super init]))
    {
        return nil;
    }
    root = [OutlineItem new];
    root.title = @"Root";
    return self;
```

```
}

- (id)outlineView:(NSOutlineView *)outlineView
            child:(NSInteger)index
           ofItem:(OutlineItem*)item
{
    if (nil == item)
    {
        return root;
    }
    return [item.children objectAtIndex:index];
}
- (BOOL)outlineView:(NSOutlineView *)outlineView
   isItemExpandable:(OutlineItem*)item
{
    if (item == nil)
    {
        return YES;
    }
    return [item.children count] > 0;
}
- (NSInteger)outlineView:(NSOutlineView *)outlineView
  numberOfChildrenOfItem:(OutlineItem*)item
{
    if (item == nil)
    {
        return 1;
    }
    return [item.children count];
}
-          (id)outlineView:(NSOutlineView *)outlineView
objectValueForTableColumn:(NSTableColumn *)tableColumn
                   byItem:(OutlineItem*)item
{
    return item.title;
}
- (void)outlineView:(NSOutlineView *)outlineView
     setObjectValue:(id)object
     forTableColumn:(NSTableColumn *)tableColumn
             byItem:(OutlineItem*)item
{
    item.title = object;
}
- (void) dealloc
```

```
{
    [root release];
    [super dealloc];
}
@end
```

The first of these to be called will be `-outlineView:numberOfChildrenOfItem:`. This will initially be called with `nil` as the second argument. This is a placeholder for the root node of the outline view. If this only has one child, then a single root will be visible to the user. If it has more than one, then the view will appear to contain multiple root objects. Since we only support a single-rooted outline, we return one in this case. For every other case, we look up the `children` property of the item and return the number of elements it has.

The next method to be called will be `-outlineView:child:ofItem:`. This requests the child with a specific index of the item. Since there is only one child of the root item—our displayable root—we ignore the `index` parameter when `item` is `nil` and just return the root object. In other cases, we look up the children array and get the child at the correct index. The value returned here will be used as the `item` parameter in future calls to the data source for navigating down the hierarchy and displaying data in columns.

The simplest method here is used for setting the value of object: `-outlineView:setObjectValue:forTableColumn:byItem:`. This is called whenever a value in the outline view is edited. If you don't implement this, then any changes will be discarded immediately. It would be nicer if the outline view disabled editing automatically if the data source did not support this, but unfortunately this is not the case.

Note that for all of these methods we set the type of the `item` parameter to be `OutlineItem*`, although the data source protocol says it should be **`id`**. This is because we know that every item that we get from here will be an outline item object and so we can provide the compiler with a little more information. This will give us compile-time warnings if we try doing anything with the item that our outline item class doesn't support. Since we don't access any instance variables on this object directly, we will also get a run-time exception if, for some reason, this is not an outline item.

Listing 6.5 shows the interface to the document. This has two `IBOutlets` and one `IBAction`. These can be connected up to objects and actions in the nib file in Interface Builder.

The implementation of this object contains a lot of placeholder code for document-related methods. Listing 6.6 shows the action method. This adds a new child to the currently selected item in the outline, or to the root node if none exists.

Listing 6.5: Outliner document class interface. [from: examples/Outliner/OutlineDocument.h]

```
@interface OutlineDocument : NSDocument {
    IBOutlet OutlineDataSource *dataSource;
    IBOutlet NSOutlineView *view;
}
- (IBAction)addItem: (id)sender;
@end
```

Listing 6.6: Outliner document method for adding children. [from: examples/Outliner/OutlineDocument.m]

```
44 - (IBAction) addItem: (id)sender
45 {
46     OutlineItem *item = [view itemAtRow: [view selectedRow]];
47     if (nil == item)
48     {
49         item = dataSource.root;
50     }
51     [item.children addObject: [OutlineItem new]];
52     [view reloadItem: item];
53 }
54 @end
```

The `-selectedRow` method on the view returns the index of the currently selected row. This is then translated to an object by calling `-itemAtRow:`. This may involve calls to the data source, but the view should have cached references to the object when it displayed the row, so, unless something is wrong with the outline view implementation, it shouldn't.

Note that line 52 only updates the single item, rather than the whole table. Depending on where the new line is, this may require a redisplay of most of the table, but the view will only have to fetch the modified items from the data source.

Now that all of the classes are built, the next step is to connect them up in Interface Builder. Because this is a document-driven application, we have two nib files. One is for the entire project; the other is per-document. We only need to modify the second one. The first thing to do is put a couple of objects into the window. We need a button for adding new rows, and an outline view. Figure 6.9 shows what it should look like.

We also need one other object that is an instance of the data source. We don't have to create this in code, just drag a `NSObject` instance to the project window. You then have to set the class of this in the class pane of the object inspector. While you are there, also make sure that the class of the File's Owner is set to

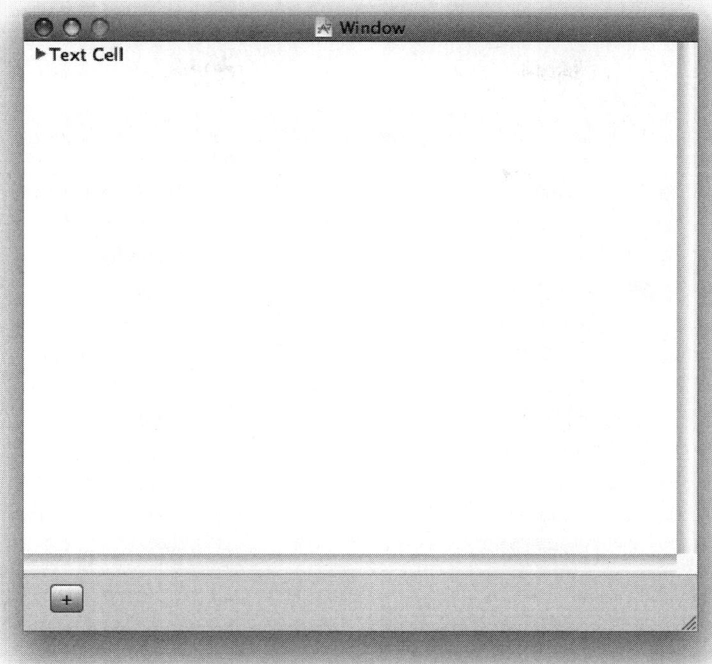

Figure 6.9: The Outliner Window.

`OutlineDocument`. Once you have done this, you should have the objects shown in Figure 6.10.

Now that all of the object exist, they need to be connected together. The data source should be attached to the `dataSource` outlet in both outline view and the document (File's Owner). The outline view also needs to be connected to the document's `view` outlet, since the `-addItem:` action needs to reference it to find out the currently selected item. This action should be connected to the button.

Once all of these connections are made, the application should be ready to run. When you create a new document, the code from `NSDocument` will automatically instantiate a new copy of the nib, creating a new data source that, in turn, creates a new root outliner item. It will also connect everything together. You should get a window like the one in Figure 6.11.

This outliner is very simple. It doesn't allow multiple roots, multiple columns,

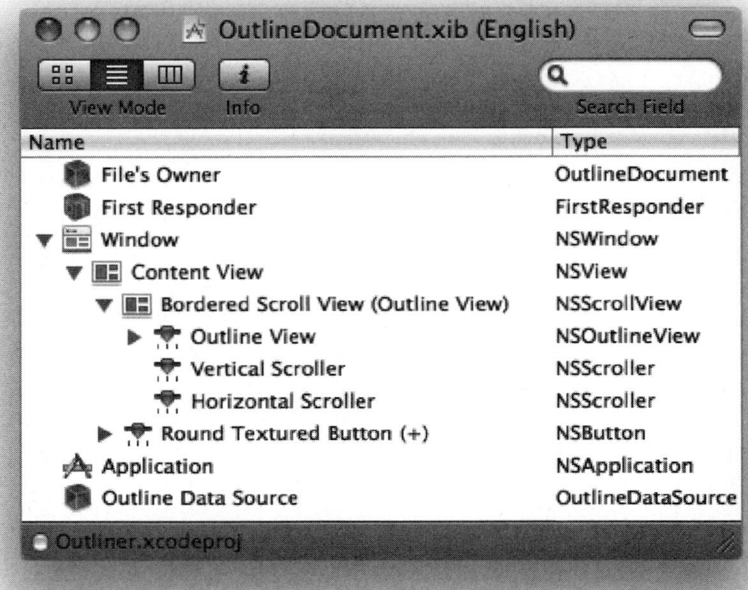

Figure 6.10: The Outliner document nib window.

or anything other than plain text. It also doesn't allow sorting. These are all supported by the outline view.

Some of these are very simple to add. To support multiple roots, you need to change the data source's `root` property to an array and modify the cases in the data source methods where it is passed a `nil` item.

Supporting multiple columns is not much harder. You would need to modify the item to store a dictionary instead of a string. You then need to modify the document's `-outlineView:objectValueForTableColumn:byItem:` method. The current version of this ignores the column parameter. To support multiple columns, you would need to get the column's identifier and return the value in the dictionary corresponding to that key. Adding the ability to add columns to a specific document would be more difficult, but still possible.

Adding any of these extra features would make a good exercise for familiarizing

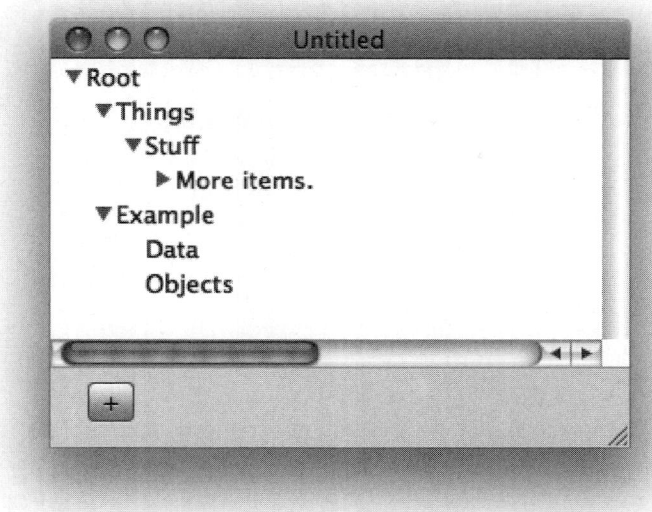

Figure 6.11: Running the simple outliner.

yourself better with the outline view. You could also try modifying it to use a `NSBrowser` instead. This also displays hierarchical data, but in a different view. The data source protocols for both classes are very similar, since they both require the same information for their views.

6.3.4 Menus

One of the most important parts of a graphical user interface is the menu. Since its debut in 1984, the menu bar at the top of the screen has been the most recognizable feature of the Mac GUI. The NeXT style was somewhat different. The application menu was arranged vertically, as in Figure 6.12.

There are good reasons for putting the menu bar at the top of the screen. The time it takes to click on an object on screen is given by *Fitts' Law*. In simple terms, it is the sum of the time taken to move the mouse to the object and the time taken to stop. If you imagine a line that intersects the current mouse location to the center of the target, the stopping distance is defined by the amount of this line that is over the target. When you move the mouse to the edge of the screen, however, it stops, meaning that from a lot of angles the size of the target along

Figure 6.12: NeXT-style menus were vertical.

the line the mouse will move is effectively infinite. The other factor is defined by the angle from the pointer to edges of the target, which defines how easy it is to hit. Menus at the top of the screen are very easy to hit because of this.

Looking at the NeXT menu, you might think it is pretty much the exact worst design possible. This is almost true. The saving feature was that right-clicking anywhere where a context menu was not defined caused a copy of the main menu to pop up. Moving the mouse to something that has just appeared immediately under it is, obviously, very easy. They could also be used as floating palettes, since submenus could be pulled off and positioned somewhere convenient. This feature, unfortunately, was lost with OS X.

Menus in OS X applications should contain every option that the application exposes. Apart from text entry, everything else in your user interface should be a shortcut for items in a menu. Because of this, there is a potentially huge number of menu items that you might want. Fortunately, menus are hierarchical, and so you can add a lot of them without cluttering your application too much.

Menus can be created graphically in Interface Builder. When you create a new project, the MainMenu.nib will contain your application's main menu. You can also define new menus for other purposes, such as context menus. The NeXT menu design accounts for the classes used with menus. When you look at a Mac menu bar, you see something very different to the things that pop up when you click on a menu title, and so you might expect them to be different classes. In contrast, NeXT menus look the same irrespective of their depth in the hierarchy, and so it is clear that they should be the same.

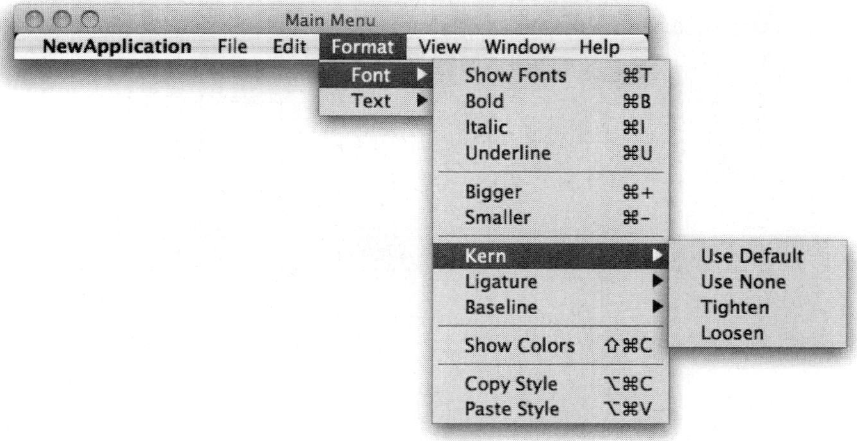

Figure 6.13: An OS X menu in Interface Builder.

There are two classes used to describe the menu bar. `NSMenu` defines a menu and `NSMenuItem` defines an item on the menu. The top-level menu, any context menus, and all submenus are all instances of `NSMenu`. Everything that appears on these is a menu item. Figure 6.13 shows the menu bar created by default in Interface Builder.

Some of the menu items you can see here pop up submenus when they are clicked. This is one of the standard configurable behaviors provided by `NSMenuItem`. You can also configure a menu item to display a toggle next to it.

All menu items use the *target-action pattern*. When they are clicked, they fire an action in their target. This makes it very easy to connect them to controllers. All of the standard menu items are already connected in this way. You can see in Figure 6.14 how the Copy menu item is set up by default.

When you click on the copy menu item, a `-copy:` action message is delivered to the first responder. Menus use their target to automatically determine whether they should be enabled or not.

If a menu has a fixed target set, it will be enabled if the target responds to the message defined by the action. If not, then when the menu is displayed it will query the responder chain to determine the target and disable itself if that object doesn't respond to the target message.

Alternatively you can implement the `-validateMenuItem:` or

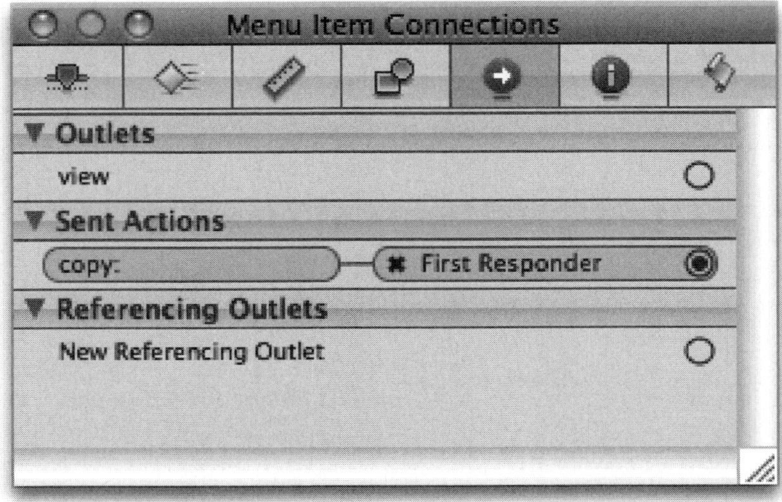

Figure 6.14: The target and action for the standard copy menu item.

`-validateUserInterfaceItem:` methods in an item that might become first responder. The latter works on other kinds of user interface elements as well. This is the mechanism used to disable menu items automatically when the first responder does implement a method for the action message, but can't handle it right now. Sending a `-action` message to the argument of `-validateUserInterfaceItem:` will return the selector.

You can also manually enable and disable menu items by sending a `-setEnabled:` message to them after sending a `-setAutoenablesItems:` message to turn off the automatic behavior.

6.4 Cocoa Bindings

Cocoa bindings make working with data sources slightly easier, since they allow common model types to be used without custom controllers. You can connect generic controllers to both the model and view objects and have them translate between the interfaces that they use. This is done using a combination of two technologies introduced with OS X 10.3. These provide a simple model for getting, setting, and watching properties of objects. When the model supports them, a generic controller can be used to interface between the model and the view.

This mechanism was introduced in 10.3, and expanded slightly in 10.4 by the addition of some new controller objects, in particular the `NSTreeController`, for representing hierarchical data.

6.4.1 Key-Value Coding

The simpler half of the bindings mechanism is *key-value coding* (*KVC*). This defines two simple generalized methods for accessing and setting properties on objects:

```
- (id)valueForKey: (NSString*)key;
- (void)setValue: (id)value forKey: (NSString*)key;
```

This provides a uniform mechanism for treating objects like dictionaries. By itself, this is not particularly useful. Each class could implement these methods, but that would be a lot of work. For every `-setFoo:` method you would need to add a special case to `-setValue:forKey:`. This would be a lot of effort, and few people would bother.

Fortunately, this is not required. The implementations of these methods in `NSObject` make heavy use of runtime introspection. Consider the following line:

```
[anObject valueForKey: @"aProperty"];
```

If the object implements its own version of `-valueForKey:`, then this will be called, but in most cases the version in `NSObject` will be invoked.

The first thing this does is test to see whether it implements a `-aProperty` method. If so, then it calls it. If not, then it sends a `+accessInstanceVariablesDirectly` message to its class. If this returns **YES**, then it uses the runtime library metadata functions to look up the instance variable and returns its value directly. If this fails, then it calls `[self valueForUndefinedKey: @"aProperty"]`. The implementation of this in `NSObject` simply throws an exception. Subclasses can implement their own versions.

The `-setValue:forKey:` method does almost the same thing. First, it will look for a set method. This is a very useful pattern outside of KVC. The EtoileXML framework implements a SAX-like XML parser that uses it for adding a parsed XML element to its parent. In this framework, each XML element is parsed by a separate class, which is passed a key when it is constructed. When the close tag is encountered, the parser calls `-addChild:forKey:` in the generated object. The implementation of this method is shown in Listing 6.7.

This is a very simple version of the KVC set method. It first constructs a string by adding a prefix to the key. KVC uses the `set` prefix and also capitalizes the first letter of the string. This string is then turned into a selector. The object then checks whether it responds to that selector and invokes it if it does.

Listing 6.7: A KVC-like mechanism used in the EtoileXML framework.

```
- (void) addChild: (id)aChild forKey: (id)aKey
{
    NSString * childSelectorName =
        [NSString stringWithFormat:@"add%@:", aKey];
    SEL childSelector =
        NSSelectorFromString(childSelectorName);
    if([self respondsToSelector:childSelector])
    {
        [self performSelector:childSelector
                   withObject:aChild];
    }
}
```

This mechanism is very simple to implement, so you may find other cases where it's useful. The KVC version is much more heavily optimized than the one shown here and calls runtime library functions directly.

Implementing the second part of the KVC mechanism yourself is also quite easy. The runtime library provides this function:

```
Ivar object_getInstanceVariable(id obj, const char *name, void **outValue);
```

The second parameter to this is the name of an instance variable, and the third is a pointer to the instance variable:

```
id ret;
object_getInstanceVariable(sel, [aKey UTF8String], &ret);
return ret;
```

Note that this short snippet assumes that the instance variable is an object. The `object_getInstanceVariable()` function returns an `Ivar`. For more robust code, you should pass this to `ivar_getTypeEncoding()` and ensure that the result is `"@"` (recall the type encodings from Chapter 3).

The rules for the methods and instance variables that the KVC system will try to look up are quite simple. For accessors, it will look for a method with the same name as the key, or the same name prefixed by an underscore (_), although the latter is deprecated. It will also look for these with `is` in front of the key, since properties like `isEnabled` are common for Boolean values. For the key "property" the following will be checked:

1. `-property` method

2. `-_property` method (deprecated)

3. `_property` ivar

4. `_isProperty` ivar

5. `property` ivar

6. `isProperty` ivar

7. `valueForUndefinedKey:` method

Remember that the instance variables will only be directly accessed if the class implements a `+accessInstanceVariablesDirectly` method that returns **`YES`**. When setting values, a similar search path is followed. The main difference is that it capitalizes the initial character in the property name, giving the following list:

1. `-setProperty:` method

2. `_property` ivar

3. `_isProperty` ivar

4. `property` ivar

5. `isProperty` ivar

6. `setValue:forUndefinedKey:` method

KVC is now integrated quite closely with *declared properties*. If you declare a property with **`@property`**, then the property generated will automatically support KVC unless you specify a name for the accessor method yourself and do not respect these rules.

Validating Properties

Although this is a very useful mechanism by itself, this is not all that KVC does. Before any key is set, the receiver has the option of validating it. This is done by implementing a method with a prototype like this:

```
-(BOOL)validateProperty: (id*)aValue error: (NSError**)outError;
```

This will not be called in response to a `-setValue:forKey:` message with `@"property"` as the key. Code wishing to validate properties should call this method before calling the `-setValue:ForKey:` method:

```
- (BOOL)validateValue: (id*)ioValue
               forKey: (NSString*)key
                error: (NSError**)outError;
```

The return value of this is used to decide whether to proceed with setting the value. If you return **NO** here and `outError` is not `NULL`, then you should also set the error message indicating why it failed.

Because the new value is passed in by pointer, you can also modify it and then return **YES**, meaning that the caller can set the value with the new version. Because of this, care should be taken with what pointer you pass in to this. Do not pass a pointer to an object that you need to release later, because the validation method will perform straight assignment and you will lose it. Similarly, do not pass a pointer to an instance variable or a global unless you don't mind losing the old value.

Validation is rarely invoked manually. It is used in a lot of places by Cocoa Bindings, however, to validate input from the user interface before inserting it into the model object.

Primitive Types with KVC

So far everything we have seen with KVC has used objects as values. This is simple to do, since objects have run-time introspection capabilities and a constant size. Supporting primitive values is a bit harder. What do you think would happen if someone called `[obj valueForKey:@"property"]` and the object implemented the following method?

```
- (int)property;
```

The obvious answer is that KVC would get an **int**, think it was an **id**, and the first time you tried sending a message to it you'd get a segmentation fault. Fortunately, this is not the case. When KVC looks up the method, it checks the return type. Recall that methods have an associated type string stored in the class structure. On a 32-bit system, this one would be "i8@0:4". The important part is the first letter, the "i", which indicates that the return type is an integer.

The KVC code knows about all of the primitive C types and the common foundation structure types. When accessing a property that is one of these types, it will automatically create an `NSValue` or `NSNumber` object encapsulating the returned value.

More useful is the behavior when setting these. The argument to `-setValue:forKey:` has to be an object. The KVC code will call the `-intValue` method on this to get the primitive integer version. Other standard methods, like `-pointValue`, will be used to get `NSPoint` and similar structure values.

This mechanism is intended to allow you to pass an `NSNumber` in as a value for setting numbers. The message dispatch mechanism in Objective-C makes this slightly more flexible, however. You can pass any object that responds to a `-intValue` message in to set an **int** property. This means that you can set values using some view objects directly, since they can give an integer representation of themselves.

As of 10.5, KVC supports arbitrary primitive types. These are always boxed as `NSValue` instances, using the `-valueWithBytes:objCType:` and unboxed with the `-getValue:` method. These do not do anything special for object pointers in structures, so you should be careful to retain and release objects correctly when using this mechanism.

The one thing that KVC can't do automatically is map a `nil` object to a structure. If you want to be able to set some value that corresponds to `nil` for a non-object primitive, you should implement the `-setNilValueForKey:` method. This is called whenever `-setValue:forKey:` is called with a nil value for a key representing a scalar quantity.

KVC and Collections

As well as simple one-to-one relations, KVC supports one-to-many mappings, where one key corresponds to a number of different objects. The simplest case of this is when an instance variable is an array. More complex versions may be stored in some other way but still want to be exposed as a set of objects corresponding to a single key.

There are two kinds of to-many mappings that KVC understands: ordered and unordered. These can be accessed as arrays and sets, respectively, by two general methods:

```
- (NSMutableArray*)mutableArrayValueForKey: (NSString*)key;
- (NSMutableSet*)mutableSetValueForKey: (NSString*)key;
```

These both return a proxy object that handles sending KVC messages to the real object, allowing its properties to be exposed as a mutable array or set even if this is not how they are implemented directly.

To support ordered to-many collections for something not stored internally as an array, you should implement three methods. These correspond to the primitive methods in `NSArray` and `NSMutableArray`. The first of these returns the number of objects. The remaining two insert and remove objects at a specified index. To support the "toMany" property, you would implement these:

```
- (unsigned int)countOfToMany;
- (id)objectInToManyAtIndex: (unsigned int)index;
- (void)insertObject: (id)anObject
    inToManyAtIndex: (unsigned int)index;
```

Other code can then set and get these properties via the `NSMutableArray` subclass that it receives. Any interactions with this proxy will result in messages being sent to the original receiver of the `-mutableArrayValueForKey:` message.

Unordered mappings were added with 10.4. To support these on the @"toMany" key, you just need to implement these methods, corresponding to the primitive methods in NSMutableSet:

```
- (void)addToManyObject: (id)anObject;
- (void)addyObject: (id)anObject;
```

Note that you can't use the unordered collection methods to enumerate or access the objects in the set. They were added for use by Code Data (see Chapter 10) and are not widely useful outside this framework.

The proxies returned by these methods demonstrate the power of the *class cluster* approach. The NSMutableArray class is a class cluster and so you never actually get an instance of it. It only defines three primitive methods—methods that subclasses must implement—and the subclass returned from these methods implements these by calling KVC methods in the original object.

Key Paths

You might be wondering what the point of one-to-many mappings is, since you can just get the collection or call the underlying methods directly. The answer is the final part of KVC: *key paths*. A key path is a string of keys, separated by dots. This allows you to get at deeply nested properties in a collection.

Key paths are useful for bindings since they allow a particular UI component to be connected to some property at an arbitrary depth in the model object with a standard mechanism.

6.4.2 Key-Value Observing

The other half of bindings is *key-value observing* (*KVO*), a mechanism closely related to KVC. The KVO mechanism allows an object to observe a specific key and be notified whenever it changes.

Registering to receive notifications of changes to a key path is remarkably similar to registering with a NSNotificationCenter to receive notifications. The method used is

```
- (void)addObserver: (NSObject*)anObserver
         forKeyPath: (NSString*)keyPath
            options: (NSKeyValueObservingOptions)options
            context: (void*)context;
```

The options specified by the third argument are a mask indicating whether the observer should be given the new value, the old value, or both when it is notified of the changes. Unlike registering for a notification, you do not specify a selector to KVO. The same method will be called for all KVO notifications:

```
- (void)observeValueForKeyPath: (NSString*)keyPath
                      ofObject: (id)object
                        change: (NSDictionary*)change
                       context: (void*)context;
```

The `change` dictionary contains a lot of information about the change. If you specified `NSKeyValueObservingOptionNew` when registering the observer, then the `NSKeyValueChangeNewKey` key will correspond to the new value. Similarly, if you specified `NSKeyValueObservingOptionOld`, then there will be a `NSKeyValueChangeOldKey` key corresponding to the old value. If you OR'd these two options together, then both keys will be present.

If you change an attribute on an object via KVC, then all of the objects that have registered to observe that key will be notified. The same will happen when you use the KVC-compliant accessor methods.

This works by another instance of *isa-swizzling*. When you add an observer, a new class will be created at run time and the object's `isa` pointer will be set to point to it. This class adds methods, replacing the set methods that KVC will call. They call the superclass implementation, but also invoke methods in the observers. When the observer is removed, they will be removed.

Within a class it is common to modify instance variables directly, rather than via their methods (which are considerably slower). Doing this will cause the observers to miss their notifications. Fortunately, you can send the notifications manually.

If you intend to support KVO in your class—and not all classes need to—then you should bracket direct accesses to instance variables that contain values for keys that might be observed with notification calls.

Two notifications are sent for each modification, the same two that happen for a lot of AppKit operations: will and did. The first is sent just before a key changes and the second afterward. Methods for sending both of these notifications are implemented by `NSObject` and should be called on **`self`**, like this:

```
[self willChangeValueForKey: @"anAttribute"];
anAttribute = newValue;
[self didChangeValueForKey: @"anAttribute"];
```

Sometimes you will want to use the manual mechanism in place of the automatic system. Before installing handlers for automatic notification, `+automaticallyNotifiesObserversForKey:` will be called with the key name as an argument. The implementation of this in `NSObject` returns **`YES`** unconditionally. You can override this class method to return **`NO`** for a specific key.

There are a few reasons for doing this. It may be that you want to implement a transaction mechanism in your class. By disabling the automatic mechanism, you can defer notification delivery until a complete transaction has completed.

Alternatively you might set two observable keys directly in your set method and want to combine the notifications, or avoid sending notifications if the new object matches some condition, such as being equal to the old value.

In most complex applications, attributes are related. If you change one, this may cause others to change. Prior to 10.5 you had to manually register each of these dependencies, using a technique that had some serious limitations. Leopard introduced a new method:

```
+ (NSSet*)keyPathsForValuesAffectingValueForKey: (NSString*)key;
```

This returns a set of all key paths that may cause `key` to be updated. This method is called when installing the observer methods for a key. It will also install an observer for each of the key paths returned here.

This is most useful for attributes that are computed, rather than stored. If setting one attribute causes another to be set, then the second should not list the first one as affecting it. For example, you might have three attributes: `mass`, `volume`, and `density`, where `density` is automatically calculated from the first two. There are two ways of implementing this. The first is to have the methods for setting the mass or volume also set the density. This should be done using the standard KVO mechanisms for setting an attribute: either calling a KVC-compliant set method or by manually sending KVO notifications. The other option is to have `-density` compute the density whenever it is called. In this case, there is no set method, but someone might still want to observe the value. In this case, your class would provide the following implementation:

```
+ (NSSet*)keyPathsForValuesAffectingValueForKey: (NSString*)key
{
    NSSet *paths = [super keyPathsForValuesAffectingValueForKey: key];
    if ([@"density" isEqualToString: key])
    {
        paths = [paths setByAddingObjectsFromSet:
            [NSSet setWithObjects: @"mass", @"volume", nil]];
    }
    return paths;
}
```

This will allow density to be watched just like any other attribute of the class. Note the call to **super** here. This is not necessary in this specific case, but is in the general case. If the property is present in the superclass and is calculated, in part, by sending some messages to **super**, then the superclass might know of some other keys that the class depends on.

As with other KVC/KVO methods, there is also a variant that takes the key name as part of the selector. In this instance, you could also implement

```
+ (NSSet*)keyPathsForValuesAffectingDensity
{
    return [NSSet setWithObjects: @"mass", @"volume", nil];
}
```

Note that this doesn't call **super**. While the general method will always be present in the superclass (returning an empty set in `NSObject`), this method will only be present in the superclass if the superclass has a density attribute. Calling it otherwise will generate a run-time exception.

6.4.3 Exposing Bindings

KVC and KVO are the two mechanisms used by Cocoa bindings to interact with model and view objects. In principle, you could set your model object to use KVC to set values in the view and KVO to be notified of changes. This is quite repetitive code to write, and one of the core principles of Cocoa is that repetitive code should be implemented once in a generic fashion. This is done through the `NSKeyValueBindingCreation` informal protocol.

A binding, in the general sense, is a connection between two attributes in different objects. We saw an example of this back in Chapter 3, where the actions of two view objects were connected together. While this makes a nice demo, it's not really very useful in the real world. Most often you would want one view to modify the model and then the other view to take the new value from the model. You can do this using the target-action pattern, but it becomes cumbersome. If the model object supports KVC and KVO, then it should be simpler. You should just be able to connect some property of the view to a property in the model and have the two kept in sync using these two mechanisms. This is exactly what Cocoa Bindings do.

When a class that supports bindings is initialized, it calls `+exposeBinding:` on itself for every property that it wants to expose for bindings. The bindings system is then able to retrieve an array of all bindings by sending an `-exposedBindings` message to an instance of the class. Bindings to the exposed properties are then created using a single call:

```
- (void)bind: (NSString*)binding
    toObject: (id)observableController
 withKeyPath: (NSString*)keyPath
     options: (NSDictionary*)options;
```

This tells the receiver to bind the key path in the specified object to the attribute exposed by the binding. There are lots of options that can be set, such as whether the view should set its enabled state depending on information from the binding. For a full list, see the `NSKeyValueBindingCreation` informal protocol documentation. To remove the binding later, simply call `-unbind:` with the name of the binding.

Note that each property exposed in this way can only have one binding. This makes sense, since a view cannot represent the state of two models in the same interface component. A typical property exposed for binding might be the position of a slider or the value of a text field. If this were bound to multiple models, then the behavior would be very strange when the models were not identical.

The converse is not true, however. A single model object can have two view objects bound to the same property. This also makes sense, since you commonly have the same attribute of a model visible in two or more different places in a user interface. A typical example of this is iTunes, where the currently playing song is visible at the top of the window, in the library view, and sometimes in the cover art view as well.

Although the view needs to implement these bindings methods, the model does not. It simply needs to ensure that it is KVC- and KVO-compliant for the properties that might be connected via bindings.

Bindings and the iPhone

Although bindings are very useful, they have one major disadvantage: They are not supported on the iPhone. Only AppKit, not UIKit, allows bindings. That said, both KVC and KVO are supported on the iPhone, so making your model objects KVC-compliant will make your life easier if you decide to port your application from desktop to handheld OS X.

Since AppKit and UIKit are subtly different, and the screen on the iPhone is much smaller, you will need to rewrite your UI code anyway when doing this kind of port. Being able to share model objects across implementations saves a lot of work, even if you need different controllers.

6.4.4 Generic Controllers

Connecting views directly to models like this is not particularly flexible. Often a model object will have some specific layout for its data, and the view object will want a slightly different version.

The traditional answer to this problem of tight coupling is the model-view-controller pattern, where a controller provides some glue between model and view objects, allowing both to have interfaces that more closely represent their own needs. In the Outliner example, the data source object was a controller, which mapped between the tree of outliner item objects (the model) and the outline view.

Controllers are the least interesting part of any program to write. The model is important because it defines the kind of data and operations that the application supports. The views are important, because the user interacts with them directly. Controllers are just glue between the two, and are very tedious code that often just implements one method calling another one with almost identical behavior but slightly different parameters.

As of OS X 10.3, Apple introduced the `NSController` class hierarchy. These are closely tied to Cocoa bindings. Each controller exposes properties via KVC and KVO and so can be bound to properties in views. It also supports binding to model objects.

The basic controllers are simple wrappers around an object. The view object uses KVC and KVO to set and observe changes in the controller, and the controller uses the same mechanism to interact with the model. They allow mapping from simple keys for the view to complex key paths in the model. This, by itself, is not very useful. They also provide a number of convenience functions, such as managing the selected object and implementing placeholders for `nil` values.

Value Transformers

One of the common functions of a controller is turning data from one form into another. Bindings provide a general mechanism for doing this in the form of *value transformers*. These are subclasses of the `NSValueTransformer` class and implement a `-transformedValue:` method. This turns the argument into an instance of different class. You can use these to avoid your model objects needing to be able to export strings and numbers directly.

6.4.5 Bindings and User Defaults

One of the most useful general controllers is the `NSUserDefaultsController` class. This is an `NSController` subclass that wraps the *user defaults* system. Binding this to a user interface element allows the defaults system to be direly accessed from the user interface.

A simple use of this is in a preference pane, where a particular user default would be bound to a control for setting it. You can also use it for getting user-interface-related settings from defaults and automatically setting parameters on some view to use them.

Since the bindings mechanism handles automatic updates in both directions, doing this means that you will not need any code to have the views that depend on a user defaults setting update whenever it is changed.

6.4.6 Using Bindings in Interface Builder

So far we've seen how to set bindings in code. This is occasionally useful, and lets you see how they really work, but is not how you use bindings most often. The point of bindings, along with much of the rest of Cocoa, is to avoid writing code. The golden rule for Cocoa programming is never write the same code twice, and having a load of initialization methods setting up bindings would be counter to this.

Instead, you set up bindings in Interface Builder. Every object has a bindings inspector that allows you to control what it binds to. To demonstrate how this works, we'll modify the Outliner example to use bindings instead of a custom data source object.

The nice thing about this example is that there is no new code for you to read. Modifying the outliner to use bindings did not require writing a single line of new code. Looking at the line counts for the various files shows a stark contrast:

```
$ wc -l Outliner/*.{m,h}
      58 Outliner/OutlineDataSource.m
      54 Outliner/OutlineDocument.m
      16 Outliner/OutlineItem.m
      14 Outliner/main.m
       8 Outliner/OutlineDataSource.h
       9 Outliner/OutlineDocument.h
       9 Outliner/OutlineItem.h
     168 total
$ wc -l BindingsOutliner/*.{m,h}
      44 BindingsOutliner/OutlineDocument.m
      16 BindingsOutliner/OutlineItem.m
      14 BindingsOutliner/main.m
       5 BindingsOutliner/OutlineDocument.h
       9 BindingsOutliner/OutlineItem.h
      88 total
```

The `wc -l` command gives the number of lines in a set of files, giving a quick (if not totally accurate) way of comparing the complexity of different source files. The `OutlineDataSource` class, which made up almost 40% of the code in the outliner example, is gone completely. The `OutlineItem` class is unmodified, and the `OutlineDocument` class is simplified.

You will notice that the document class header shrunk by four lines. This is because the outlets and actions defined in it are removed. The bindings now perform all of the controller actions that this object used to do.

Because we used *declared properties* to define the attributes of our model object, we can already get at them in a KVC-compliant way and so we don't need to do anything more to them.

Figure 6.15 shows the contents of the document nib for the version of the outliner that uses bindings. There are a few changes here from the previous one. The most obvious addition is the `NSTreeController` object. This was added with 10.4 and uses bindings to access a tree of KVC-compliant objects. The hierarchical view objects can use this as a data source. The addition of this object is the reason that the `OutlineDataSource` class is no longer required.

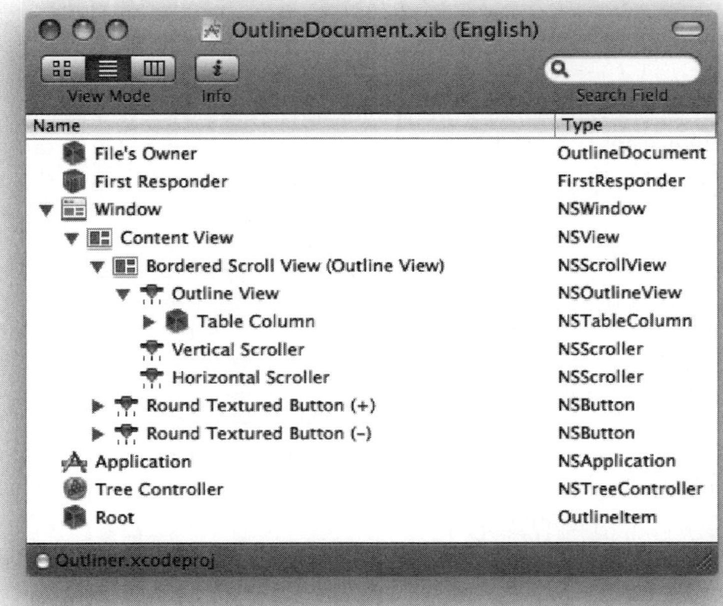

Figure 6.15: Bindings Outliner nib contents.

The other additions are relatively small. Root is an instance of the `OutlineItem` class that is used as the root item in the tree. Recall that the root item in an outline view just has children; it is not displayed itself, to allow multi-rooted and single-rooted trees. In a real outliner you would probably have a document object that has a children attribute containing the real elements. We cheat here and just use a hidden root.

The final addition is the second button. This is for removing items from the outline. This was not supported by the old version of the outliner, but we'll add it here since it doesn't require writing any new code.

The important part of this example is the connection of the bindings, so once these objects are created the next place to visit should be the bindings inspector. Figure 6.16 shows two of these for the outline view and the table column it contains. Note that we have to bind both of these to the tree controller.

The outline view will use the bound object to get the layout of the items in the hierarchy. The table column will use it to get the text it should display for each item. You will recall that a similar two-stage process was required in the data source.

Since the table column needs a specific attribute of the returned object, it needs the *model key path* attribute set. This is set to "title" since we want the title property of the outline view to be shown.

The outline view is bound to the tree controller twice in this example. The first binding is for getting the content. The second is for maintaining the selection. When you select an object in the outline view, the tree controller will track this selection. This is used when inserting and removing items.

The two buttons are connected (not using bindings) to the tree controller's `-addChild:` and `-remove:` actions. These both operate on the selection, the former adding a new child to the current selection and the latter removing the current selection. Take a look at the inspector for the controller, shown in Figure 6.17.

This has some fields at the bottom for defining a class. This is how the controller is able to add new children. Whenever it receives an `-addChild:` message, it calls `-newObject` on itself. This is implemented by its superclass, `NSObjectController`, and returns a new instance of the class set here. This doesn't perform any custom initialization, it just calls `+alloc` and `-init`. If you want a different kind of object, then you should subclass `NSTreeController` and override the `-newObject` method to return a new instance of your class.

Note that the tree does not have to be filled with the same kind of object. It does, however, need to be filled with objects that all present the KVC attributes that the controller expects.

In this example, the controller is set to use the children key for accessing the children of the tree node, and the table column uses the title attribute for the display text. Since these are accessed via KVC they don't need to be implemented in the same way. A custom node might implement `-objectInChildrenAtIndex:`

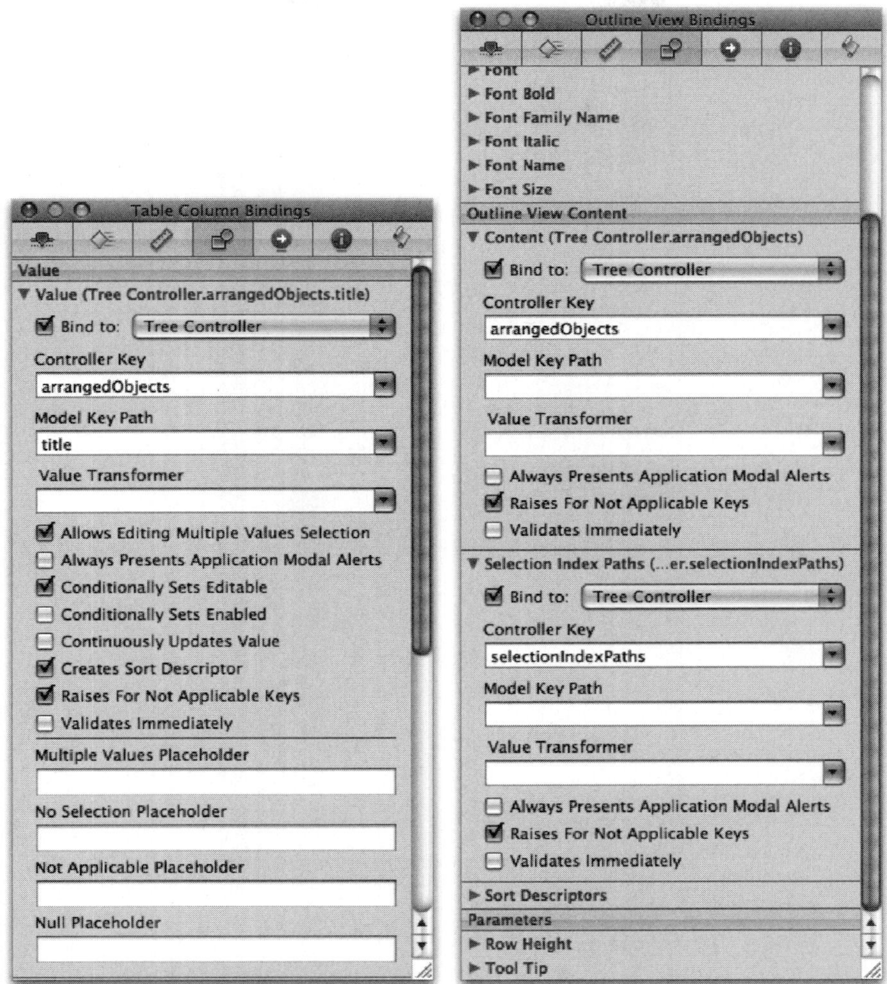

Figure 6.16: Bindings inspectors for the outline view.

and the related methods while storing child nodes in a C array or some other data structure. The controller and view would be unaware of this change.

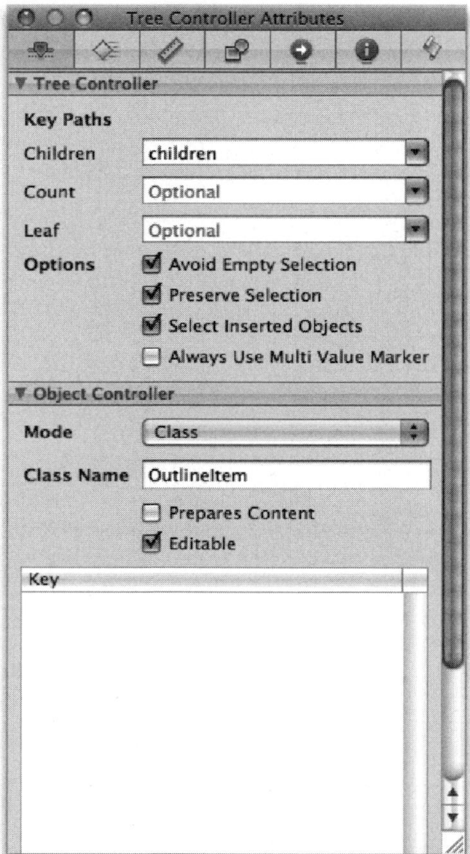

Figure 6.17: The properties of the tree controller.

For this example, we only set one key path. For efficiency, you can also set one that gives the number of children of a node, although doing this prevents some of the nice automatic features of the tree controller from working.

You can also set a key that indicates if a node is a leaf (i.e., it has no children). Doing this speeds things up since the controller doesn't need to enumerate the

Key Paths and Bindings

All of the bindings settings work with a key path, rather than a specific key. This allows access to nested properties in an object. You are not limited to working with a single object. In this example, the title property is a top level element of the node, but it doesn't have to be. You might have a dictionary containing different attributes of the node and set the key path to "display-Attributes.title" instead. As long as the dictionary contained a value for the `@"title"` key, then it would continue working.

available children for leaf nodes, which typically make up a significant proportion of an outline.

Because this last property is accessed via KVC, like the others, it does not need to be stored in an instance variable. You could implement a separate subclass for leaf nodes that implemented this method:

```
- (BOOL) isLeaf { return YES; }
```

Since this is a KVC-compliant accessor for the `@"leaf"` key, it will be accessed correctly, as long as the superclass implements a version returning **NO**. If your leaf nodes don't support adding children, this is all you need. Alternatively, you will need to change the return value when a child is added. You can do this easily using `isa`-swizzling, by setting the object's `isa` pointer to the superclass. Most of the time this is a lot more complexity than you need.

When we run the outliner, we get a window like the one in Figure 6.18. This looks a lot like the old version, but is implemented in about half as much code and now has working deletion of tree nodes.

Doing the same thing in half as much code is always good. Doing more in less code is even better. Bindings, due to the large number of layers of indirection they use, are relatively slow. The KVC and KVO mechanisms have been optimized a lot by Apple, but they are still much slower than direct message sends.

The speed of KVO is difficult to judge. Without it, you would need some equivalent mechanism to notify the views that the model has changed. Doing this in an ad-hoc basis is likely to be faster for simple models and slower for complex ones. KVO inserts hidden classes directly into the class hierarchy, at run time. This makes it quite efficient and is sufficiently difficult that most custom observer mechanisms would opt for something simpler (and slower) instead.

The earlier comment about instruction cache usage applies to bindings especially. Shrinking the code size of an application by 50% means that a lot more of the application's logic will fit into the instruction cache, which may make using a slower mechanism faster overall.

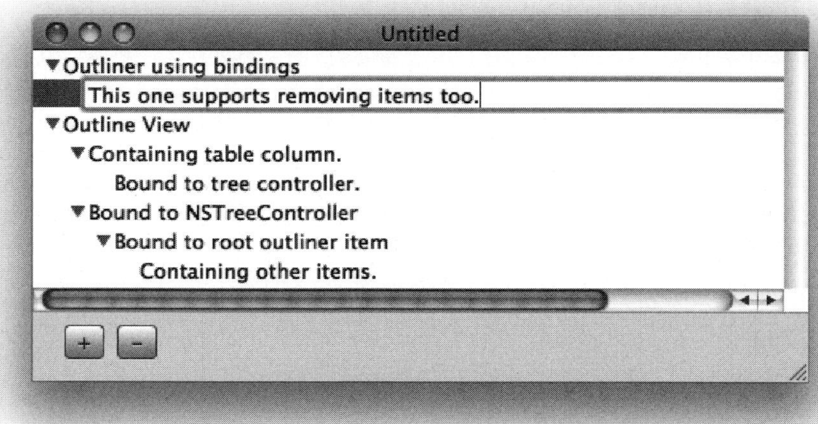

Figure 6.18: Running the new version of the Outliner.

The way we bound the tree controller to the outline view is not the only possible way. Try experimenting with some of the other ways. As an exercise, you might consider adding a panel containing a `NSBrowser` and making the small changes required to use our existing model with it. Then you can run the outliner example and have the contents of the browser view updated automatically. Don't worry if this is too hard; we'll look at using a single model with multiple views in more detail in Chapter 11.

6.5 Summary

In this chapter, we've looked at the core GUI concepts in Cocoa. We've seen how views are arranged in a hierarchy with coordinate transforms used to map them into their parent and looked at the common view objects in Cocoa.

We saw how action messages and events are delivered, and contrasted the three kinds of events that Cocoa uses.

We've also seen how the KVC and KVO mechanisms, in combination with Cocoa Bindings, can dramatically simplify the creation of user interfaces. This extends the target-action pattern seen earlier to provide a way of having multiple user interface elements tracking and updating the same model object automatically.

Chapter 7

Windows and Menus

Every application on OS X has two user interface components: menus and windows. These two elements have been part of the Mac UI since 1984, with the horizontal menu bar being the most recognizable part of the Macintosh interface for all of this time.

The concept of having windows is not unique, or even original, to the Mac user interface, but it was a key selling point for the early models. The Mac interface is an example of a *window, icon, menu, pointing device* (*WIMP*) system. The acronym WIMP is not very common anymore, because such systems have become the norm, rather than the exception. It is worth noting, because it highlights the four aspects that were considered important on Mac-like systems:

Windows allow the user to have several applications or, more importantly, documents, on screen at once.

Icons represent choices with images, rather than text, allowing fast selection.

Menus provide a single location from which all of an application's features can be accessed.

Pointing devices such as the mouse or trackpad give an on-screen equivalent of the user's hand, allowing direct manipulation of on-screen objects.

Because windows and menus are such an important part of the OS X user interface, it is worth spending some time understanding them fully.

7.1 Understanding Windows

The basic idea of a window is a virtualized screen. On the Apple II and other computers of the same era, the operating system did not multiplex the screen. Applications drew their user interface by writing directly to the display hardware, which was often little more than a region of RAM that acted as a frame buffer.

Windowing systems moved this interaction through an abstraction layer. There are two general approaches to implementing windows. The simplest version is to have a single task acting as a coordinator, assigning regions of the screen to individual applications. The applications just get a list or rectangles from this application and then draw their contents into the frame buffer where they should. This is how *QuickDraw* worked on Classic Mac OS. This is typically quite fast, but causes synchronization problems when lots of applications are drawing. The other alternative is to have the screen owned by a single application, typically called a *window server* and make this do all of the drawing. When an application wants to draw things on the screen, it sends messages to the window server telling it what to draw.

Most modern windowing systems adopt the latter approach, and OS X is no exception. If you run activity monitor, you can see the window server process, as shown in Figure 7.1. This has a very large virtual memory allocation because it maps the video card's memory into its own address space. It also uses shared memory regions to communicate with other processes.

When you do any drawing in Cocoa—or with any of the other graphical toolkits on OS X—you are sending commands to the window server. If you are drawing a lot of lines, these can easily be sent as simple drawing commands. Copying images every time they needed to be sent to the window server would be very slow, and so a shared memory region is typically used for this case.

Fortunately, as a developer using a high-level language, you are abstracted from all of these issues. You are free to treat every window as if it were your own private screen with a very intelligent display controller.

The Quartz window server shipped with OS X is an example of a *compositing window server*. This means that every application draws into an off-screen buffer and then the window server composites them all together immediately prior to drawing. This avoids the synchronization problems of earlier windowing systems. Every application can implement double buffering, where it draws into one buffer while the other is being displayed and swap them over when it has finished drawing, and the window server can combine the finished buffers into an on-screen display.

The cost of this is a much greater memory requirement. With the old Mac OS windowing system, there was no compositing system. Applications could implement double buffering themselves, but the front buffer was always drawn straight to the screen. Most applications on systems like this simply draw regions when

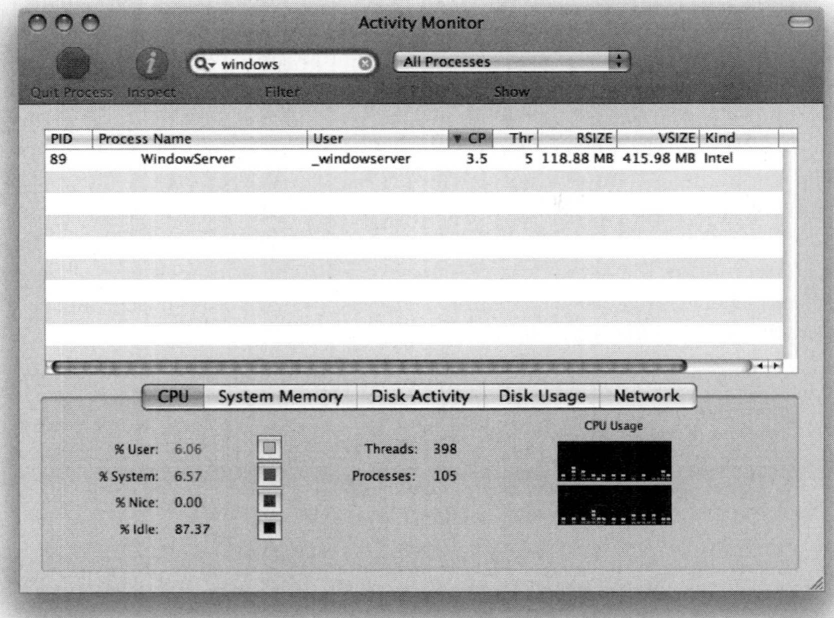

Figure 7.1: The window server process on OS X 10.5.

they are needed. When you move a window away from another, it generates an expose event. The newly visible window then sends drawing commands to fill in the exposed region. The total amount of memory used is the size of the screen—the number of pixels multiplied by the number of bits per pixel—for any number of windows. When you add compositing, you also need to store copies of the windows. I currently have open enough windows to completely cover my screen around six times, so I am using at least six times as much memory due to composting as I would have been with an older windowing system.

This extra memory cost has only recently become acceptable. The old NeXT systems did not support compositing, because they ran on systems with a tiny fraction of the memory that even something like the iPhone has now. Moore's Law says that the number of features on an integrated circuit, for a fixed monetary investment, doubles every 18 months. This means that, twenty years after the first release of NeXTSTEP, the same amount of money buys us over eight thousand

(2^{13}) times as much memory. An application now that wastes as much memory as the NeXTStation had total RAM will not even be noticed by a modern computer user, and so systems that provide benefits—such as translucent windows—at the cost of a bit of memory are suddenly very attractive.

You might be surprised at the number of windows that you have on your system. If you run the Quartz Debug application and select Show Window List from the Tools menu, you will get a window like the one in Figure 7.2 displayed. This shows a list of all of the windows and the application that owns them. You might expect that the Dock only owns one window, but in fact all of the elements in the Dock window have separate identities with the window server. So do all menus, and everything else that appears on-screen in its own rectangle. Even icons on the desktop are separate windows.

Application	PID	CID	WID ▲	KB	Origin	Size	Type	Encodin	On	Share	Fad	Lev
Terminal												
▼Finder												
Finder	214	29091	21	0.7	0/0	1*1	NonRetained	-1 BPS-A	No	No	100%	-21
Finder	214	29091	22	0.7	0/0	1440*900	NonRetained	-1 BPS-A	Yes	No	100%	-21
Finder	214	29091	23	12.9	80/212	90*74	Buffered	32 BPS-A	Yes	Yes	100%	-21
Finder	214	29091	24	16.9	69/304	113*74	Buffered	32 BPS-A	Yes	Yes	100%	-21
Finder	214	29091	25	20.9	1132/464	147*89	Buffered	32 BPS-A	Yes	Yes	100%	-21
Finder	214	29091	26	16.9	59/120	133*74	Buffered	32 BPS-A	Yes	Yes	100%	-21
Finder	214	29091	27	12.9	84/396	82*74	Buffered	32 BPS-A	Yes	Yes	100%	-21
Finder	214	29091	28	12.9	1309/740	104*74	Buffered	32 BPS-A	Yes	Yes	100%	-21
Finder	214	29091	29	16.9	204/304	154*89	Buffered	32 BPS-A	Yes	Yes	100%	-21
Finder	214	29091	30	20.9	208/212	147*89	Buffered	32 BPS-A	Yes	Yes	100%	-21
Finder	214	29091	31	20.9	1151/740	108*89	Buffered	32 BPS-A	Yes	Yes	100%	-21
Finder	214	29091	32	12.9	79/740	93*74	Buffered	32 BPS-A	Yes	Yes	100%	-21
Finder	214	29091	33	12.9	1316/832	91*74	Buffered	32 BPS-A	Yes	Yes	100%	-21
Finder	214	29091	34	60.9	1299/120	149*89	Buffered	32 BPS-A	Yes	Yes	100%	-21
Finder	214	29091	35	12.9	74/832	103*74	Buffered	32 BPS-A	Yes	Yes	100%	-21
Finder	214	29091	36	16.9	1159/731	102*74	Buffered	32 BPS-A	Yes	Yes	100%	-21
Finder	214	29091	37	12.9	393/120	88*74	Buffered	32 BPS-A	Yes	Yes	100%	-21
Finder	214	29091	38	36.9	1307/212	109*74	Buffered	32 BPS-A	Yes	Yes	100%	-21
Finder	214	29091	39	16.9	225/396	113*74	Buffered	32 BPS-A	Yes	Yes	100%	-21
Finder	214	29091	40	24.9	216/120	131*89	Buffered	32 BPS-A	Yes	Yes	100%	-21
Finder	214	29091	41	16.9	1310/832	103*74	Buffered	32 BPS-A	Yes	Yes	100%	-21
Finder	214	29091	42	12.9	245/28	73*74	Buffered	32 BPS-A	Yes	Yes	100%	-21
Finder	214	29091	43	16.9	984/120	131*74	Buffered	32 BPS-A	Yes	Yes	100%	-21
Finder	214	29091	44	60.9	60/559	149*89	Buffered	32 BPS-A	Yes	Yes	100%	-21
Finder	214	29091	45	16.9	213/740	136*89	Buffered	32 BPS-A	Yes	Yes	100%	-21
Finder	214	29091	46	16.9	536/28	115*74	Buffered	32 BPS-A	Yes	Yes	100%	-21
Finder	214	29091	47	12.9	423/753	94*74	Buffered	32 BPS-A	Yes	Yes	100%	-21
Finder	214	29091	48	16.9	1341/829	147*74	Buffered	32 BPS-A	Yes	Yes	100%	-21
Finder	214	29091	49	36.9	1305/120	112*74	Buffered	32 BPS-A	Yes	Yes	100%	-21
Finder	214	29091	50	20.9	1221/613	134*89	Buffered	32 BPS-A	Yes	Yes	100%	-21
Finder	214	29091	51	20.9	59/856	133*89	Buffered	32 BPS-A	Yes	Yes	100%	-21
Finder	214	29091	52	12.9	1334/304	54*74	Buffered	32 BPS-A	Yes	Yes	100%	-21
Finder	214	29091	53	16.9	1131/814	153*74	Buffered	32 BPS-A	Yes	Yes	100%	-21

Figure 7.2: The list of windows currently attached to the window server.

Some of the windows in this list will be colored blue. This indicates that they are compressed. If you don't modify a window for a while, the window server will compress its buffer in memory, saving some space. Compressed windows can still be composited to the screen quickly, but they cannot be drawn to without decompressing, modifying, and compressing the new version. For this reason, it does not make sense to compress windows that are frequently updated.

7.1.1 Types of Windows

Over the years, OS X windows have gone through several different themes. In the worst days, from a user interface consistency viewpoint, there were four different sets of visual appearance in common use in OS X. The classic "pin-striped" windows, were first introduced with 10.0, and gradually had their stripes faded until they vanished completely with 10.5. These were joined by the brushed metal look, which was intended to be for applications that didn't expose anything like a document metaphor, but were generally used throughout OS X. The iLife and Pro suites from Apple introduced their own sets of visual themes.

All of these windows are the same underlying types. The visual appearance of a window gives hints about, but does not define, its purpose. There are three common types of windows on OS X:

Windows have a large title bar and typically contain something that looks and behaves like a document.

Panels have a thin title bar and typically are never the focal point for a user's attention even when they are receiving key events. They are used for palettes and inspectors, providing extra information about the document.

Sheets are a special kind of window that is attached to another. They are most commonly used to provide window-modal dialog boxes and cannot exist separately from their parent window.

There are a few other kinds that are less common. Some windows don't fit into any of these categories. The Dock and the menu bar, for example, are windows from the perspective of the window server, but are not thought of as windows by most users.

Both windows and panels were present in the original OpenStep specification, and had equivalents in the Classic Macintosh Toolbox, but sheets are new. Sheets are typically used where dialog boxes would be used on other systems. When you want to create a dialog box, you have three options. The best is to make it completely independent of the rest of the application. It runs and receives events just like any other window and then does something when it is closed.

The worst kind of dialog box, from a user interface perspective, is the *modal dialog*. These put the application into a different mode, where the only thing the user can do is interact with the dialog. They are generally considered bad, because they interrupt the user's flow. Sheets fit somewhere between these two extremes. They block a user from interacting with one window, but leave the rest of the application alone. They are usually used for dialog boxes that have a special relevance to a particular window, for example, a save dialog that will save the attached window.

The distinction between windows and panels is somewhat more flexible. A panel is really a special case of a window, rather than a separate kind of drawable object. This is reflected by the fact that the `NSPanel` class is a subclass of `NSWindow`.

You can do anything with a window that you can with a panel. The distinction exists in Cocoa as a convenience, to avoid the need for every programmer to reinvent the panel. Every application has two special windows, the *key window* and the *main window*. The key window, as its name implies, is the window that will receive key events. When you type on the keyboard, you generally only want the letters you type to go to a single window, or text input would quickly get very confusing.

The definition of the main window is more fuzzy. The main window is the one that the user is thinking about, which may not be the one that he is looking at or interacting with. In a document-driven application, the main window is usually the one containing the current document. In other applications it is up to the programmer to decide which window is main.

7.2 Creating Windows

There are several ways of creating windows in Cocoa. The simplest is to simply drag them from the palette in Interface Builder. This will create a new `NSWindow` or `NSPanel` instance in the current nib file. You can then draw view objects inside the window to construct the view hierarchy.

The other option is to create the windows yourself. This is not something you will do very often, but we will look at it now to understand what is being done for you automatically when you instantiate a window from a nib file.

7.3 Creating Window Objects

When you create a window in code, you are creating instances of the `NSWindow` class or some subclass. This object wraps all of the interaction with the window server and presents you with a Cocoa graphics context for drawing into. The main initializer for windows is this method:

```
- (id)initWithContentRect: (NSRect)contentRect
                styleMask: (NSUInteger)windowStyle
```

```
backing: (NSBackingStoreType)bufferingType
  defer: (BOOL)deferCreation
 screen: (NSScreen*)screen;
```

One thing you might notice about this method is that only one of the parameters is an object, and that one is optional. The screen specifies which physical screen to display the window on, and can be `nil` to default to the screen containing the current key window, or the screen containing the menu bar if no window is currently key.

The important part of any window is its contents. This is a region of the screen where the window is allowed to draw (unless it is obscured by another window). The first parameter describes this region. This is specified in the screen's coordinate system. When the window is created, its contents view will cover this region of the screen.

The window style describes some of the properties of the window. The simplest kind of window is created with the `NSBorderlessWindowMask` constant here. This creates a window with none of the usual decoration that an OS X window shows. This includes the resize indicator in the corner and the title bar. You can turn on each of these and the close and minimize buttons by applying other flags here. OS X 10.2 introduced the brushed metal look, which was specified with `NSTexturedBackgroundWindowMask`. This look has now gone away, but the behavior that accompanied it—the ability to move the window by dragging anywhere—remains.

The third parameter is largely around for legacy reasons. It is very rare to use anything other than `NSBackingStoreBuffered` as the argument here. This will create an off-screen buffer for the window to draw into and allow the window server to composite it. There are two other options here, although their use is not recommended. Retained windows were supported on OPENSTEP as a compromise between buffered and unbuffered windows. The window would only use an off-screen buffer for portions that were obscured by other windows. This allowed it to be quickly redrawn but not use as much memory as full double-buffering. As of OS X 10.5, retained windows are no longer supported and will be silently turned into buffered ones. The final kind of backing store is the nonretained window, which draws directly into the frame buffer. These do not work correctly with Quartz Extreme and will slow down the drawing system a lot. They were originally provided on OS X to support the Classic environment, which allowed applications written for earlier versions of Mac OS to run.

The remaining option is a Boolean flag indicating whether the window's creation should be deferred. If you set this, the window will buffer all of the commands that need to be sent to the window server to create it and set its location and contents until it is displayed, and then send them all at one time. The main reason for doing this is to create panels that exist as objects as long as the application is running, but are not always visible. You can create these when the application launches but not use any window server resources until later.

This is important because the *interprocess communication* (*IPC*) limits imposed by the XNU kernel are relatively low. When you have a lot of windows attached to the window server, it is possible to exhaust the allowed amount of shared memory. If this happens, then the window server will be unable to create new windows and drawing methods will start throwing exceptions. The most obvious symptom of this is windows failing in the middle of drawing and suddenly turning white. XCode typically creates a number of windows as it performs common tasks, and so it will be obviously hit if you reach this limit. Most users will not encounter this problem, but keeping the number of created windows low helps reduce the probability that any of your users will encounter it.

7.3.1 Displaying Windows

When you have created an `NSWindow` object, you still won't see anything on the screen, even if you didn't tell it to defer creation of the window server's portion. It will not be drawn on the screen until you send it a message that tells the window server where to place it in the depth dimension. The most common message for doing this is the `-makeKeyAndOrderFront:` action. This adds the window to the screen on front of all other windows and makes it the key window.

Quite often you don't want the newly created window to become the key window. In particular, a window should only become the key window in response to some user action, for example, selecting a menu item or clicking on a window. Something like an instant messaging application might create windows in response to other events, like a remote user initiating a chat. If you create these windows and make them key, then it's easy for the user to accidentally send the other person something that they meant to type in another window. This can be embarrassing if it's something the user typed in another chat window, but if the other window was an Internet banking site's login page, it can be much worse.

When you just want to display a window, you can do so by sending it either a `-orderFront:` or `-orderBack:` message, to insert it in front of, or behind, all of the other windows.

Every window in the system has a level associated with it. When you inspect windows in Quartz Debug, you will see levels in a large range. When you set a window level, you will do so in a much narrower range and have it scaled automatically.

The window level defines allowed orderings of windows on the screen. You can think of the window server as a ring binder full of transparent page jackets. Each jacket contains some scraps of paper. These scraps of paper are your windows and the jackets are the window levels. You can slide them around inside the jacket and move them in front of each other, but they will never move from one jacket to another unless you explicitly tell them to.

When you send a -orderFront: or -orderBack: message, you are moving a window around in its current level. You can move it in front of, or behind, any windows that have the same level. For more fine-gained movement, you can use this method:

```
- (void)orderWindow: (NSWindowOrderingMode)orderingMode
        relativeTo: (NSInteger)otherWindowNumber;
```

This allows you to move a window either in front of, or behind, some other window. The other window is identified by a number. There are three ways of identifying a window in Cocoa. One is by the associated NSWindow object. This usually uniquely identifies the window, although there are a few very unusual corner cases where the same window can have multiple window objects. Within the application, the number returned by sending a -windowNumber message to the window object gives a unique value. This is the number that should be used when ordering windows with the method shown previously.

You cannot use this window number to globally identify the window. If you send it to another process, and that process asks for the window with that number, then it will not get the same window object back. The global identifier that the window server uses to uniquely identify windows is not exposed to Cocoa, although it can be accessed via Core Graphics calls.

Moving a window between layers is fairly rare. Typically, you will set the level of a window when you create it, and leave it there for the window's life cycle. You do this by sending the window object a -setLevel: message. This takes an integer representing the level as the argument.

The window levels defined by Cocoa are all defined as macros pointing to Core Graphics constants. These, in turn, are all defined as macros that look up the value for keys in the _CGCommonWindowLevelKey enumeration. When you set a window level in Cocoa using one of these macros, you are not setting the level to a constant. The macro you pass to the -setLevel: method looks up the real window level—the level that the window server will use—at run time.

A lot of the valid constants are not provided by Cocoa, although they are available in the Core Graphics framework. You are discouraged from using any of the values that are not part of the Cocoa API, but you may find it interesting to see the ones that are available in the CGWindowLevel.h file. Several of these are not intended for use by third-party developers. In general, you should consider any that are not exposed via Cocoa macros to be private, and potentially unsupported in future versions of OS X. You can look up level values using the

`CGWindowLevelForKey()` function. This takes one of the values in the enumeration as an argument and returns a window level.

This enumeration defines window levels for all of the system window types. The `kCGDesktopIconWindowLevelKey` level, for example, is used for icons on the desktop. As mentioned earlier, every icon on the desktop is a separate window. You can create something that looks exactly like a desktop icon by setting this as the level for your window. A few people have used this to provide something similar to Microsoft's Active Desktop, where their application provides widgets that appear to be present on the desktop, rather than floating as normal windows. This can confuse the user, because the application, rather than the Finder, will display its menu bar when this object is selected.

7.3.2 Hiding Windows

When you have finished with a window, you have several options. Closing a window is a fairly complex procedure. There are three steps in the process, not all of which are required:

1. Remove the window from the display.
2. Remove the window from the window server.
3. Remove the window object from the program.

Each of these steps depends on the previous ones, and will implicitly make the earlier steps happen if you don't do them in order. If you just want to remove a window from the display, you send it a `-orderOut:` message. This always removes it from the screen but may not remove it from the window server.

Each window in Cocoa has an attribute that defines whether it should be removed from the window server when it is hidden. This is set by calling the `-setOneShot:` method. A one-shot window will be removed from the window server as soon as it is removed from the screen. As the name implies, this behavior is appropriate for windows that have a single, short, use.

Common examples of one-shot windows include dialog boxes. These are constructed, displayed, interacted with, and then removed. Removing the resources that they use when they are finished makes sense. Other windows, like inspectors or palettes, may be hidden frequently but then brought back at a later date.

Whether a window is one-shot or not makes little difference from the perspective of the programmer. A one-shot window costs more to make visible but uses less memory when it is not being displayed. If a window is likely to spend a lot of its time invisible, or is very cheap to draw, then making it one-shot is likely to be a better choice.

Removing a window from the window server does not destroy the window object in the program. Even a one-shot window can be removed from the screen and then put back by sending it a `-orderOut:` message followed by a `-orderFront:` message. The only difference is that the one-shot message will be asked to redraw its contents view, while the other window will simply have the off-screen buffer added back to the list that the window server composites to give the final desktop view.

Hiding and closing a window are very similar. From the perspective of the user, a hidden window is one that can come back in the future, while a closed one has been destroyed. Even this distinction is not entirely clear-cut. You can close a document in an application and then reopen it, re-creating a closed window.

From the perspective of a programmer, they are overlapping operations. Both will remove the window from the display. Either may remove the window from the window server. Closing is more likely to destroy the window object, but this is optional in both cases. You might, for example, chose to support an "undo close window" operation, in which case you would defer destroying the window for a while.

Windows are usually closed by sending a `-performClose:` action message to the window object. This gives the window's delegate a chance to intervene. If the delegate may need to prevent the window from closing, it should implement this method:

```
- (BOOL)windowShouldClose: (id)window;
```

This returns a boolean value, indicating whether the close operation should proceed. If it returns **`YES`**, then the window will next send itself a `-close` message. You can also send this message directly to the window, rather than `-performClose:`, to close a window unconditionally. This is usually the wrong thing to do, but occasionally it is useful. Note that `-close` is not an action message. It does not take the sender as an argument. This is an intentional design choice to make sure that developers do not connect the `-close` method to something in the user interface. User actions should always trigger `-performClose:`.

The `-close` method will post a `NSWindowWillCloseNotification` notification just before the window closes. This can be used to free up any resources associated with, but not owned by, the window by sending them `-autorelease` messages. (Don't send `-release` messages, or they may be freed before the window is really gone.)

A lot of windows are self-owned. They are retained when they are created, but the reference is not stored. Windows like this may not be referenced from anywhere else in your program but should not be freed until they are closed. You can send a window a `-setReleasedWhenClosed:` message to tell it to release itself when it is closed. This is very good for one-shot windows that are created in some code and then left to run on their own. By setting a window to release when closed, you can forget about it and have it automatically cleaned up when the user closes the window.

7.3.3 Understanding Window Controllers

Most of the time, you won't interact with window objects directly. The `NSWindowController` class was added to OpenStep to support the document system that we will look at in Part III. Since then, their use has grown far beyond the document system, and most windows now have a window controller associated with them.

The window controller is associated with a window when it is initialized. This is done either with an existing window, or with the name of a nib file, typically with one of this pair of initalizers:

```
- (id)initWithWindow: (NSWindow*)window;
- (id)initWithWindowNibName: (NSString*)windowNibName;
```

The second is the more interesting of the two. It handles the creation and instantiation of a window from a nib file. This is the most common way of creating windows in Cocoa programs. You create a template window in Interface Builder and then create copies of it in your program using a window controller.

7.3.4 Creating a Simple Window Factory

To demonstrate how all of this fits together, we will write a simple window factory application. This will allow the user to create windows with various different settings. You can see the result in Figure 7.3.

This simple application will also show how to create a window from a nub using a window controller. It defines two action methods, in the class shown in Listing 7.1. This class is connected to the check boxes (`NSButton` instances) shown in the user interface and to the text field, and uses the values of these to construct a window when the first button is pressed. The second button is connected to the `-createWindowFromNib:` action method, which creates a window from a nib file. Note that this leaks memory when the window is closed.

Listing 7.1: A simple window factory. [from: examples/WindowFactory/WindowFactory.m]

```
#import "WindowFactory.h"

@implementation WindowFactory
- (IBAction)createWindowFromNib: (id)sender
{
    // Note: This leaks.
```

```
7       NSWindowController *controller =
8           [[NSWindowController alloc] initWithWindowNibName: @"Window"];
9       [controller showWindow: self];
10  }
11  - (IBAction)createWindowInCode: (id)sender
12  {
13      NSUInteger style = NSClosableWindowMask;
14      if ([isTitled state] == NSOnState)
15      {
16          style |= NSTitledWindowMask;
17      }
18      if ([isTextured state] == NSOnState)
19      {
20          style |= NSTexturedBackgroundWindowMask;
21      }
22      NSRect frame = [[sender window] frame];
23      frame.origin.x += (((double)random()) / LONG_MAX) * 200;
24      frame.origin.y += (((double)random()) / LONG_MAX) * 200;
25      NSWindow *win =
26          [[NSWindow alloc] initWithContentRect: frame
27                                      styleMask: style
28                                        backing: NSBackingStoreBuffered
29                                          defer: NO];
30      if ([isOpaque state] == NSOffState)
31      {
32          [win setOpaque: NO];
33          [win setAlphaValue: 0.5];
34      }
35      [win setHasShadow: ([hasShadow state] == NSOnState)];
36
37      [win setTitle: [title stringValue]];
38      [win orderFront: self];
39  }
40  @end
```

The other method creates a window manually, without using a nib as a template. The window is created in the middle of this method, on lines 25–29. Some of the attributes of the new window are set before it is created, some after.

In general, the ones set before the window is created define the type of the window, while the ones defined later are dynamic attributes that may change as the program runs. The window style is defined by applying style masks before the window is created. Two of these can be configured in our simple program. The first indicates whether the window should have a title bar. If this is not set, then the window's entire area will be used for its contents view.

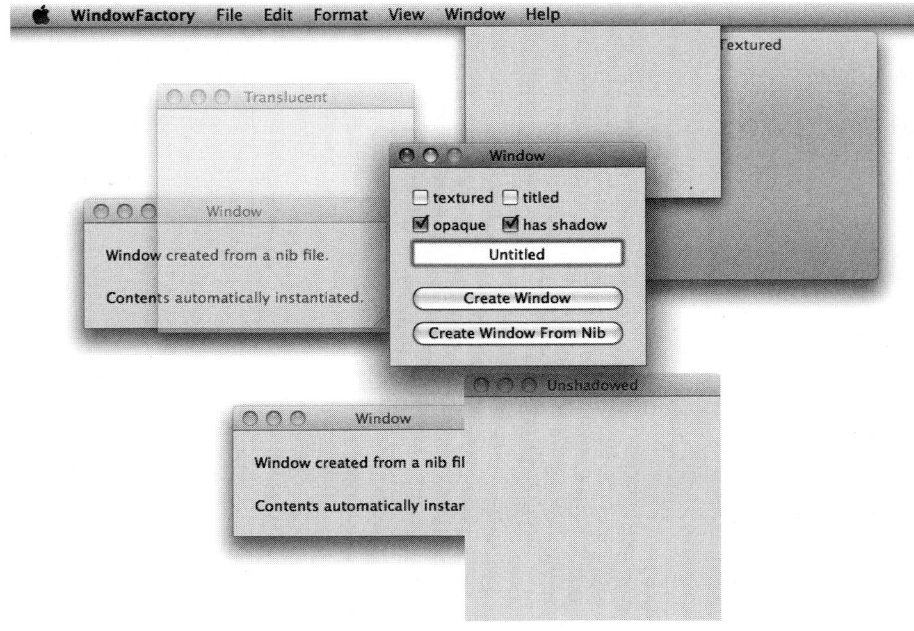

Figure 7.3: A simple window factory.

Windows without title bars are most commonly used for temporary floating notifications. You can use these to display simple notifications that float above your application and then fade away. The screen brightness and volume indicators that pop up when you adjust these settings from the keyboard are good examples of these. They pop up a transparent, borderless, window and gradually fade it away. This window is set to ignore key events and floats on top of all others. This is a much better way of presenting alerts that don't require any special user handling than popping up a dialog box.

The other attribute that we can set in this program is the textured flag. This indicates whether the window has the newer behavior, where dragging on any part of the window will allow it to be moved.

On lines 22–24, we define a frame for the new window. This is done by displacing the current window's frame by a small random amount. Most of the time, you will create a new window with a predefined frame. The random displacement is done here to avoid all of the new windows appearing on top of each other.

The final two flags are set after the window is created, but before it is displayed. The first defines whether the window is opaque or not. This sets two different attributes of the window. The first defines whether the window, as a whole, is opaque. This determines whether the window buffer has an alpha channel associated with it. If a window is not opaque, this doesn't make it translucent. A non-opaque window can still have opaque views inside it. To understand this, you need to remember that there are two or three compositing steps between a view and the screen:

1. Views draw into layers, which are off-screen buffers representing some part of the window. This can involve compositing operations, such as overlaying lines, images, and text.
2. Layers are composited together to produce the window contents.
3. The windows are composited together to produce the final desktop.

The middle step is omitted if you are not using *Core Animation* and the results of the first step are drawn directly into the buffer used by the third. When discussing window opacity, the third step is the important one. The first two steps usually involve compositing various components that have alpha channels. If the background for the window is opaque, however, or a large number of translucent views are overlaid, then the result by an opaque buffer.

By default, windows will draw an opaque background. You can adjust this by setting a translucent color. The line will make a non-opaque window fully transparent, as shown in Figure 7.4, except where views inside it draw something opaque:

```
[window setBackgroundColor: [NSColor clearColor]];
```

In Figure 7.4, you can see a button in the middle of a window. Both the title bar and the button are opaque, but the rest of the window is transparent. Note how the drop shadow is visible around the button. This is part of the window's shadow.

The other value that we set for non-opaque windows in this example affects the final compositing step, when the windows are drawn to the screen. This is independent of whether the window's contents are opaque. When the window is composited to the screen, the value passed as the parameter to `-setAlphaValue:` will be used in the compositing operation. The windows we create in this example have an opaque background but are still translucent because the window server is applying an alpha value of 0.5 when it composites them to the screen. You can use this property to fade windows.

Figure 7.4: A window with a transparent background.

Windows have a lot more adjustable parameters. If you think of some visual effect or behavior that you want from a window, check the `NSWindow` class reference. You may find that it is already supported.

7.3.5 Saving a Window's Position

OS X tries hard to avoid the user having to be aware of the distinction between running and exited programs. When a program is in the dock, ideally, the only difference between clicking on it when it is running and clicking on it when it is not is the time taken to respond. In some cases, even this doesn't apply; when an application has been inactive for a long time and has been swapped out, it can be faster to relaunch it.

Running and not-running states are examples of a *modal user interface*, which is usually a bad design. From the perspective of an operating system, there is a clear difference between applications that are running and those that aren't, but for a user this distinction should not be important.

One of the ways you can help keep this illusion is to make sure that windows do not move in between program invocations. If you place a window somewhere on the screen, it should stay there until you move it somewhere else. Exiting and relaunching the window should not affect this.

The NSWindow class provides a simple way of storing the window's frame in the *user defaults* system. You can associate a name with a window, and it will automatically synchronize its frame with a set of values in defaults. You can see how this is used in other applications by looking in the defaults system:

```
$ defaults read com.apple.terminal | grep NSWindow
"NSWindow Frame Inspector" = "401 163 268 435 0 0 1280 832 ";
"NSWindow Frame NSColorPanel" = "490 339 201 309 0 0 1440 878 ";
"NSWindow Frame NSFontPanel" = "231 -4 320 221 0 0 1280 832 ";
"NSWindow Frame RunCommand" = "417 498 499 112 0 0 1280 832 ";
"NSWindow Frame TTAppPreferences" = "449 291 590 399 0 0 1440 878
```

Each line is the stored frame for a different window. The eight values give the origin and size of the window. The ones shown here describe floating panels, but other named windows controlled by the application also have their frames saved. This is particularly important for document-driven applications. If the user finds that a document has moved when it is reloaded, then this destroys motor memory and makes interacting with it slower.

Fortunately, supporting this is very easy. You just need to send a -setFrameAutosaveName: message to the window. The argument is the name of the window, which must be unique among windows in the system.

When a window receives this message, it will first check whether another window already has this name. If it does, then the call will fail. Next, it will check whether a frame with this name is stored in user defaults already. If it is, then the window will load it and set its frame to the stored value. Whenever the user resizes or moves the window, it will update the version in user defaults to correspond to the new value.

You can also control this via a window controller, by sending it a -setWindowFrameAutosaveName: message.

7.4 Panels

Panels are a special kind of window. All of the techniques that we have looked at for windows also apply to panels. Panels are typically used for floating palettes, inspectors, and similar windows.

Panels are normally used to contain parts of the user interface that are not central to the current model. If windows contain nouns, panels contain verbs and adjectives. They provide information about the current document, and things to do with it, but are not the focus of the user's attention for a long time.

Because of their special rôle, panels have a set of different default values to windows. When an application ceases to be the active application, by default every window will remain visible and every panel will be hidden. You can alter this behavior for any specific window or panel by sending it a `-setHidesOnDeactivate:` message.

The `NSPanel` class extends `NSWindow` to provide three new optional sets of behavior. We looked earlier at how to set the level of a window. Most of the time, you won't want to do this explicitly. Panels are an exception. A lot of panels ought to float above other windows in your application. Consider something like the font panel. Most of the time you use this, you want to select some text and then apply a style to it. If selecting the text caused the panel to disappear behind the window containing the text, it would not be very useful. The solution to this is to set the panel's level so that it floats above all of the other windows in your application.

The `-setFloatingPanel:` method on `NSPanel` is a convenience method for doing this. It toggles between `NSNormalWindowLevel` and `NSFloatingWindowLevel` as values for the window level. Be circumspect when creating floating panels. They are very convenient when used correctly, but if too much screen space is taken up with them, then the user will spend more time shuffling windows around than actually doing any work.

Another attribute of the font panel is related to the way in which it is used. When you are adjusting some attribute of the current font, you typically click on the font panel and then return to typing in the main window. Most of the time, the font panel does not need to become the key window. (As a panel, it never becomes the main window.) The `-setBecomesKeyOnlyIfNeeded:` method lets you implement this behavior for your panels. If it is set, then the panel will only become the key window when a view that wants accept text input is clicked on. Pressing a button or moving a slider will not cause the window to become key.

The final addition to this is the ability for a panel to work while another window is modal. This is controlled via the `-setWorksWhenModal:` method. When you set this, modal run loops will continue to dispatch events destined for the panel. This uses the same mechanism that keeps the menu working when a window is modal. A better solution in most cases is to not use modal windows. They are almost always avoidable, and the non-modal alternative provides a better user interface.

7.4.1 Displaying Standard Palettes

There are two standard palettes that you might want to use. These are implemented by the `NSFontPanel` and `NSColorPanel` classes. They both have a number of similarities. To highlight some of the differences, we'll use them both in a simple application, shown in Figure 7.5. This will display both panels and allow the user to control the font and background color of the text field.

Most of the time that you use these panels, you won't interact with them directly. The font panel is automatically displayed by the text-editing views in Cocoa when it is invoked from the menu, and the new font automatically applied.

The color panel is usually displayed by an `NSColorWell`. This can display a color panel when clicked and will send an action message whenever the color is changed. This is generally much simpler than using the panel directly. You can configure the target of the action in Interface Builder and not have to worry about setting it in code.

The example in Listing 7.2 shows how to display both yourself. The most common reason for doing this is to implement a new view that needs to use one or other of the panels. If you are implementing something that displays text, but is not an `NSTextField` or `NSTextView` subclass, you may want to display the font panel yourself to alter its font.

Listing 7.2: Displaying the standard palettes. [from: examples/StandardPalettes/PaletteController.m]

```
@implementation PaletteController
- (IBAction)showFontPanel: (id)sender
{
    NSFontPanel *panel = [NSFontPanel sharedFontPanel];
    [panel orderFront: self];
    NSFontManager *manager = [NSFontManager sharedFontManager];
    [manager setTarget: self];
    [manager setAction: @selector(fontChanged:)];
}
- (IBAction)showColorPanel: (id)sender
{
    NSColorPanel *panel = [NSColorPanel sharedColorPanel];
    [panel orderFront: self];
    [panel setTarget: self];
    [panel setAction: @selector(colorChanged:)];
}
- (void)fontChanged: (NSFontManager*)manager
{
    [text setFont: [manager convertFont: [text font]]];
}
- (void)colorChanged: (NSColorPanel*)panel
{
    [text setBackgroundColor: [panel color]];
}
@end
```

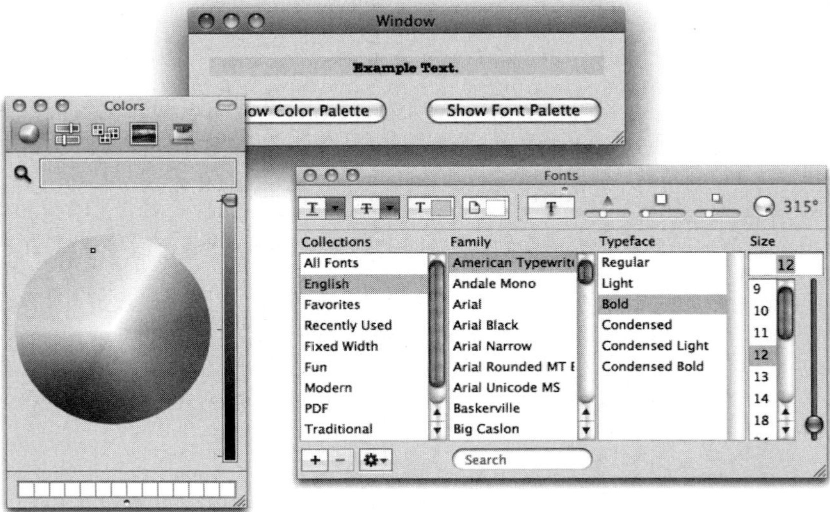

Figure 7.5: Displaying the standard palettes.

This class defines two action methods, one for each kind of panel. Much of the structure of these is the same. They first get the shared instance of the panel from the class. Each of these panels is an example of the *singleton pattern*. There is only one instance of each in the system. Because they are hidden when they are deactivated, it appears as if there is only one instance in the entire system, although it can move around when you switch between applications, destroying this illusion.

The panel is then displayed just like any other panel. They are both floating panels so they will automatically be in front of all windows except other floating panels. Sending an `-orderFront:` message moves the panel in front of all other panels, but more importantly makes sure it is displayed on the screen, and not hidden.

Once the panel is displayed, we see the difference between the two. The color panel sends action messages when its value changes. These are handled on line 23. The current color is found by sending the panel a `-color` message. The color panel will keep sending action messages to the target until some other object claims it. This is sometimes a problem when using color wells. A lot of simple bugs can cause a color panel to become disconnected from its color well, and cause the updates to get lost.

The font panel is more complicated. It sends updates to the *font manager*. This is a central part of the Cocoa text system, responsible for handling interaction with font conversions. When you adjust a property in the font panel, it does not create a new font description. The font panel and `NSFontManager` keep track of the changes that have been made to the font. On line 21, we make use of this by sending a `-convertFont:` message to the font manager. This causes the font manager to apply all of the changes that have been made in the panel to the font. The return value is a new `NSFont` instance created by modifying the old font. You can see how this works by moving the size slider in the font panel without setting the font.

Most of the time when you use a font panel, you will first call this method in the font manager:

```
- (void)setSelectedFont: (NSFont*)aFont isMultiple: (BOOL)flag;
```

This sets the font that will be displayed in the panel. If the second argument is **YES**, then the font will be ignored and a placeholder for multiple selection will be displayed in the box. In this example, we did not initialize the font panel with any sensible value. This was intentional. When the font panel is displayed, its contents will most likely not match the current font. You can change various elements independently and see that the font conversion is working.

7.5 Sheets

A sheet is a special kind of panel that is attached to another window. Unlike normal panels, a sheet has no independent existence. It cannot be moved independently of the window it is attached to, and it does not exist beyond the life of the attached window.

7.5.1 Creating Sheets

Sheets are created just like any other panel. You can construct them in Interface Builder or in code. Figure 7.6 shows the settings you should use when creating a sheet in Interface Builder. The most important part of this is the Document Modal flag. This indicates that the panel will be used as a sheet and should be drawn in an appropriate style. If you create a sheet in code, you should pass `NSDocModalWindowMask` as the style mask to have the equivalent effect.

At first glance, the mechanism for running a sheet seems quite strange. Rather than sending a message to the window that will host the sheet, you call this method on the application object:

```
- (void)beginSheet: (NSWindow*)sheet
   modalForWindow: (NSWindow*)docWindow
    modalDelegate: (id)modalDelegate
   didEndSelector: (SEL)didEndSelector
      contextInfo: (void*)contextInfo;
```

The reason for this is largely historical. Sheets were not part of the original OpenStep specification. On OpenStep platforms that predate OS X, and most other platforms today, window-modal dialogs had a much worse user interface. They would be displayed as free-standing windows, and attempting to do anything with their parent window would beep or silently fail. When creating a window like this, you create a modal run loop with `NSApplication`. Sheets have a similar implementation and are used in a similar way, so the method for constructing them was added to the application object, rather than the window.

Listing 7.3 shows a simple class that displays a sheet. This sheet is configured in Interface Builder using the settings shown in Figure 7.6. Note that this sheet is intended to be attached to a single window and so is set not to release when closed and not to be visible when the nib file is loaded. More often, you will create sheets in separate nib files and instantiate a new copy when the sheet needs to be run, allowing the same sheet to be added to different windows. Alternatively, you might create one instance of the sheet for each document window in the document nib.

Figure 7.7 shows the sheet that this class displays. It contains two buttons, both connected to the action method on line 18. Each of these buttons has its tag set in Interface Builder to the value shown in the button title. This provides a simple and quick way of identifying the button in a localization-friendly way.

Note that, when you display a custom sheet, you are responsible for both triggering the end message and for hiding the sheet. In this example, the sheet is just hidden, rather than destroyed, so it can be used again.

When the application receives the `-endSheet:returnCode:` message, it will send the message defined on lines 8 and 9 indicating to the sheet delegate that the sheet has ended. You are not required to use this mechanism; you can use any other way of notifying the creator of the sheet that it has ended you want, for example, posting a notification. This is just provided as a simple convenience. If all you need to return is some kind of index, for example, an indication of which button was pressed, then you can use it; otherwise, feel free to use notifications or some other mechanism.

7.5.2 Showing Standard Sheets

Several of the standard panels that are available in Cocoa are designed to work as sheets. For example, `NSSavePanel` is always used to save a specific document and

Figure 7.6: Configuring a panel in Interface Builder.

Listing 7.3: Running a custom sheet. [from: examples/SheetWindow/SheetRunner.m]

```
#import "SheetRunner.h"

@implementation SheetRunner
- (IBAction)runSheet: (id)sender
{
    [NSApp beginSheet:sheet
       modalForWindow: [sender window]
        modalDelegate: self
       didEndSelector: @selector(sheetDidEnd:returnCode:contextInfo:)
          contextInfo: NULL];
}
- (void)sheetDidEnd: (NSWindow*)sheet
         returnCode:(int)returnCode
        contextInfo:(void *)contextInfo
{
    [result setIntValue: returnCode];
}
- (IBAction)endSheet: (id)sender
{
    [NSApp endSheet: [sender window]
         returnCode: [sender tag]];
    [[sender window] orderOut: self];
}
@end
```

so should be attached as a sheet to the window containing that document. The same is true of the print panel, the `NSPrintPanel` class.

All of the standard panels have interfaces designed to display them in a convenient way without having to call the `NSApplication` methods directly. They can also generally be used in at least two different ways: as sheets or as modal dialogs. The open panel can be used as a non-modal dialog as well.

Listing 7.4 shows how to create all three kinds of open panel. An instance of this class is connected to a window containing three buttons and a text field. When any of the dialogs completes, the selected file is displayed in the text field. Figure 7.8 shows this simple example running. Note how several non-modal open panels can be displayed independently. You might want to adjust this behavior yourself by creating a singleton open panel for non-modal use and just sending it an `-orderFront:` if it is invoked a second time.

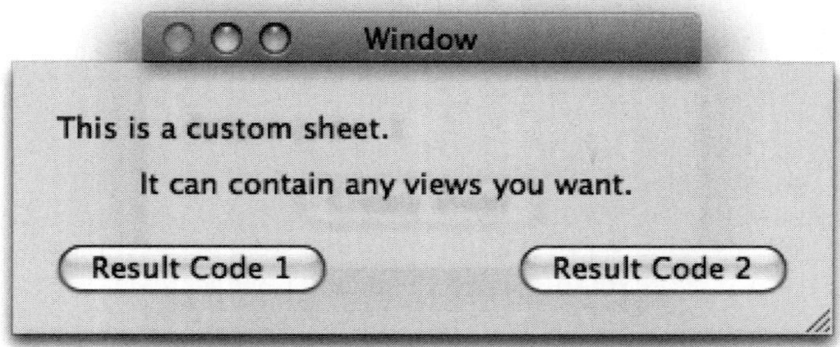

Figure 7.7: Displaying a custom sheet.

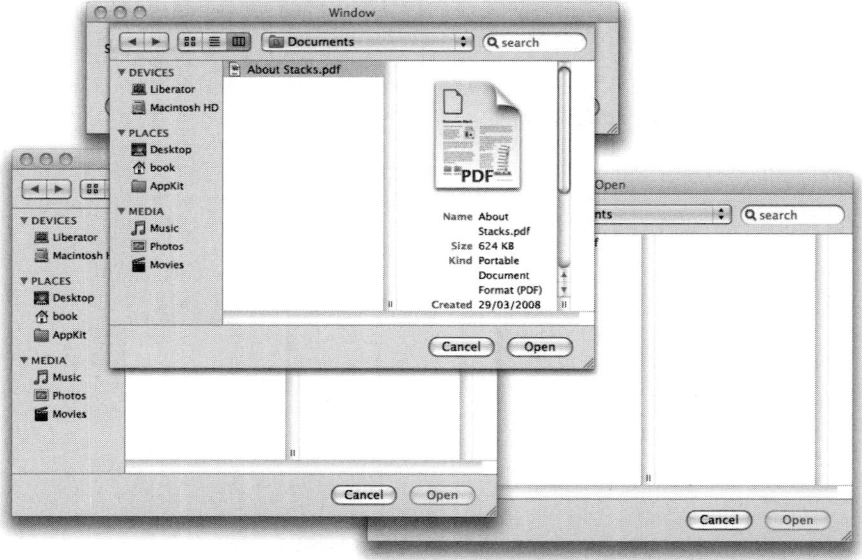

Figure 7.8: Displaying open panels.

Listing 7.4: Creating and displaying open panels. [from: examples/OpenPanel/OpenPanel-Controller.m]

```
#import "OpenPanelController.h"

@implementation OpenPanelController
- (void)openPanelDidEnd: (NSOpenPanel*)panel
             returnCode: (int)returnCode
            contextInfo: (void *)contextInfo
{
    [filename setStringValue: [panel filename]];
    [panel release];
}
- (IBAction)runSheet: (id)sender
{
    NSOpenPanel *panel = [[NSOpenPanel alloc] init];
    [panel beginSheetForDirectory: nil
                             file: nil
                   modalForWindow: [sender window]
                    modalDelegate: self
                   didEndSelector: @selector(openPanelDidEnd:returnCode:
                       contextInfo:)
                      contextInfo: NULL];
}
- (IBAction)runModal: (id)sender
{
    NSOpenPanel *panel = [[NSOpenPanel alloc] init];
    int returnCode = [panel runModal];
    [self openPanelDidEnd: panel
               returnCode: returnCode
              contextInfo: NULL];
}
- (IBAction)runModeless: (id)sender
{
    NSOpenPanel *panel = [[NSOpenPanel alloc] init];
    [panel beginForDirectory: nil
                        file: nil
                       types: nil
            modelessDelegate: self
              didEndSelector: @selector(openPanelDidEnd:returnCode:
                  contextInfo:)
                 contextInfo: NULL];
}
@end
```

The simplest way of displaying this dialog is the modal panel. This simply blocks execution of this run loop and creates an inner run loop for the panel. Most of the time, you should avoid doing this, although it can sometimes be useful for prototyping. If you were just displaying a modal version, you would replace the call on lines 25–27 with the body of the method. As you can see, this is only very slightly simpler than the non-blocking version.

The modeless version, shown on lines 29–38, creates the panel in exactly the same way and then instructs it to run itself. This does almost the same thing as the modal version, with a gap in the middle for processing other events. Rather than blocking and then calling the method on line 4, it returns immediately and only calls this method when it has finished running.

The sheet version is called in exactly the same way as its modeless counterpart. The only difference is that it will block events from being delivered to the window underneath the sheet.

All of the standard panels have various configurable options. You can specify the types of files to select, the initial path, and various other settings. If you are using the Cocoa document architecture, you don't need to interact with the open and save panels directly at all. They will be displayed automatically and the selected file names passed to high-level methods in your `NSDocument` subclass. For more information about this, read Chapter 9. We'll look at the print panel in more detail in Chapter 13.

7.6 Alert Dialogs

For simple messages, creating a window in Interface Builder or in code can be more time-consuming than you want it to be. A lot of applications need to prompt the user occasionally to make a choice. These can be created easily with the `NSAlert` class.

Alerts can be created with `+alloc/-init`, but are often created with this constructor that allows you to set most of the properties at once:

```
+ (NSAlert*)alertWithMessageText: (NSString*)messageTitle
                   defaultButton: (NSString*)defaultButtonTitle
                 alternateButton: (NSString*)alternateButtonTitle
                     otherButton: (NSString*)otherButtonTitle
       informativeTextWithFormat: (NSString*)informativeText, ...;
```

This creates an alert dialog box with a title, a description, and between one and three buttons. You can specify `nil` for any of the button titles. A `nil` value for the second or third button will cause that button to be omitted from the dialog box. The first button will always be displayed, but will have the local variant of "OK" as its title if it is not specified explicitly.

Be very careful about creating alerts with a single button. If the user is not presented with a choice, you should ponder why you are asking for any interaction. Most of the time, alerts like this are a sign of a bad user interface. You should also avoid things like "Yes" or "No" as dialog button text.

Figure 7.9 is an example of a good alert panel. You would set up buttons with the same layout like this:

```
[NSAlert alertWithMessageText: saveChangesTitle
                defaultButton: @"Save..."
              alternateButton: @"Don t␣Save"
                  otherButton: @"Cancel"
    informativeTextWithFormat: saveChangesMessage];
```

The title contains the question that is being asked, and the informative text gives the warning about what will happen if you do the wrong thing. The buttons are arranged in a different order depending on the locale. For left-to-right reading order locales, such as English-speaking countries, the default button will go on the right with the alternate button on the left. These should correspond to forward and backward actions. Selecting the option on the right should never result in any data being lost.

Note that all of the button titles are descriptive. Most users will not read the text carefully, they will scan a few key words and then look at the buttons. If the dialog buttons said "Yes" and "No" then some users would think the question is "do you want to save changes?" and some would think it is "are you sure you want to discard changes?" In this version, it is impossible to make this mistake; no one will click on a button labeled "Save..." thinking that it will discard their changes, and vice versa. This dialog could be improved slightly by changing the leftmost button to read "Discard changes" so that there is no shared text on the two buttons with opposite meanings.

Another visual clue about the different actions is provided by the ellipsis at the end of the save button. This is used on menus as well, and indicates that taking this action will require more interaction, in this case with the save dialog.

This constructor is very convenient for simple alert boxes, but its use is discouraged in the more general case. For more complex alert panels, you should use the standard allocation mechanism and then set the individual attributes separately.

There are two ways of running an alert. Alerts are always modal, but you can decide whether they should be application-modal or window-modal (sheets). The simplest way of running an alert is to send it a `-runModal` message. This will synchronously display the alert as an application-modal dialog and return when the user clicks on a button.

The return value from a modal dialog depends on how the object was created. For simple alerts created with the constructor shown previously, the return value

Figure 7.9: An alert panel from TextEdit.

will be `NSAlertDefaultReturn`, `NSAlertAlternateReturn`, or `NSAlertOtherReturn` depending on which button was pressed. Other alerts will return a number computed by adding 1000 to the button index. There are constants of the form `NSAlertFirstButtonReturn` provided for the first three buttons.

Application-modal dialog boxes are almost always a bad idea. More often, you will want to attach an alert to a specific window, using this method:

```
- (void)beginSheetModalForWindow: (NSWindow*)window
                   modalDelegate: (id)modalDelegate
                  didEndSelector: (SEL)alertDidEndSelector
                     contextInfo: (void*)contextInfo;
```

This attaches the alert to the specified window as a sheet and returns immediately. The window will then be blocked from receiving events until the user presses a button, but everything else in the application will continue to work as expected. When the alert ends, the delegate will be sent a message corresponding to the provided selector, which should take three arguments:

```
- (void) alertDidEnd: (NSAlert*)alert
          returnCode: (int)returnCode
         contextInfo: (void*)contextInfo;
```

The first of these is the alert itself. The third argument here is the same pointer passed as the fourth argument when the sheet was displayed. You can use this to provide some extra information about the alert, for example, the document being closed.

7.7 Menus

The menu bar at the top of the screen is the most instantly recognizable part of the Mac user interface. It has been there since the original Mac in 1984 and, although the look has changed several times, is still there on a modern OS X system.

A menu in a restaurant is a list of all of the dishes that are served. Often, it will be broken down into various sections—appetizer, main course, and so on—giving a hierarchical set of options to users of the restaurant. A menu in an application should be no different. Everything that you can do with the application should be exposed via the menu system.

In most applications, this rule is bent slightly. A few things can only be done via floating palettes and inspectors. Applications that do this usually try to make up for it by placing the inspectors in prominent positions in the menu system.

7.7.1 The Structure of a Menu

Menus are constructed from three classes:

- `NSMenu` represents a menu. This is a collection of items drawn in a special kind of window. Most instances display a vertical menu; however, the top-level application menu is also an `NSMenu` and is drawn across the top of the screen horizontally.
- `NSMenuItem` represents a single item in a menu.
- `NSMenuItemCell` is responsible for drawing the menu item.

Typically, you only interact with the first two of these. The cell can be used for drawing menu-like views, but otherwise can be ignored. The `NSMenuItem` class exposes all of the features of the cell that you are likely to need for implementing menus.

The menu hierarchy is defined by assigning submenus to menu items. A menu item does one of two things when you click on it. It either sends an action message, like a button, or it displays a submenu.

If you are creating menus in Interface Builder—which you will in almost all cases—you can create submenus simply by dragging them from the palette and adding new items. There is no technical limit to the depth of menu nesting allowed, although going beyond two layers is generally considered to be very difficult to use.

Menu items work a lot like buttons. They send an action message when they are clicked, either to a specific object or, more commonly, to the first responder proxy. The first responder is very important for menus because, unlike almost all other user interface elements, menus are not associated with a specific window or element in the view hierarchy. When you click on a menu item, the first responder can be any view in the application.

The visible attributes of a menu item are its title and *key equivalent*. Menus have special interaction with the event delivery mechanism. Both views and menus are allowed to register key equivalents. The application will send `-performKeyEquivalent:` messages to every view in the hierarchy. If they all return `NO`, then it will try sending it to the menu items in the menu bar.

The easiest way of setting a key equivalent is to press the corresponding buttons while Key Equiv. box in the Interface Builder inspector is first responder. You can also set them in code. This is a two-step process and usually requires you to call both of these methods on the menu item:

```
- (void)setKeyEquivalent: (NSString*)aString;
- (void)setKeyEquivalentModifierMask:(NSUInteger)mask;
```

The first of these sets the string containing a sequence of unicode characters representing the key to be pressed. Most of the time, this will be a single character, and always will in most English locales. The user must be able to type the entire string with a single key press. Some keyboards have keys for short sequences of unicode characters, and these are allowed to be used as menu equivalents.

The default modifier for key equivalents created in this way is the command key. If you set the key equivalent string to `@"s"` then the menu will be invoked when the user hits command-s. If you want to set some other combination of modifiers, call the second method.

There are two ways of setting a combination using a shift or option modifier. These both alter the character that is typed, and so you can just set that modified character as the key equivalent string. Alternatively, you can set the lowercase letter and assign the modifier keys.

If every one of your users has the same type of keyboard as you, then these two will be equivalent. Other layouts, however, are likely to have different key combinations used for non-ASCII unicode characters. Some may not be available at all on other keyboards. If you wanted to create a shortcut that was command-option-2, you might set it to the trademark symbol as a string. Someone using a British keyboard will then have to enter command-option-shift-2 to achieve the same thing. If you had set it as the numeral 2 and applied the modifiers, it would be in the same place for both users.

Some applications, such as video players, need to hide the menu bar. This is done by sending a `+setMenuBarVisible:` message to `NSMenu`. Make sure, if you do this, that there is some way of bringing the menu back again afterward.

Default Keys

Be careful when assigning key equivalents that you don't clash with any system defaults. A large part of the consistency in the Mac user interface comes from the fact that all applications use the same set of standard shortcut keys for common operations, like saving, printing, copying, pasting, and so on. If you use one of these key equivalents for something else, then you will confuse users of your application and may make their use of other applications slower if they get used to your version.

You should also beware of using the command-shift modifier combination. This is used for system services (see Chapter 20) and so may conflict with global shortcuts.

Although it is possible to define shortcuts that don't include the command modifier, this is almost always a bad idea. The command key is named because it is intended to be used with all commands. If you define a command shortcut without using the command key, then it is confusing.

7.7.2 Populating the Window Menu

Almost all OS X applications have a Window menu. This menu contains a set of standard operations for controlling the active window, and a list of windows. If you have looked in the Window menu for any of the examples so far, you will have noticed that the main window has always been listed.

The Window menu is managed by the shared application object. Any window will be automatically added to the menu if it meets both of these conditions:

- The window can become the main window. Windows that cannot become the main window are usually floating palettes and should be excluded.
- The window returns **NO** to `-isExcludedFromWindowsMenu` messages.

You can override this standard behavior in several ways. By default, `NSWindow` instances will return **NO** to this and `NSPanel`s will return **YES**. You can exclude a window by sending it a `-setExcludedFromWindowsMenu:` message.

Adding a panel to the window list is harder. This cannot be done with a standard panel; you need to subclass `NSPanel` and override the `-isExcludedFromWindowsMenu` method to return **NO**. You must also add windows manually by calling this method on the application object:

```
- (void)addWindowsItem: (NSWindow*)aWindow
                 title: (NSString*)aString
              filename: (BOOL)isFilename;
```

This creates an entry in the Window menu with the specified title, pointing to the specified window. This can be any kind of window, even a panel that would normally be excluded. There are a few good reasons for doing this. Most of the time, this method will be called automatically by a window when it is added to the screen. If you call it yourself, you should be aware that it can have some strange effects, such as making non-activating panels the main window. Most of the time, you should stick to using the higher-level mechanisms for populating the Window menu, and let them call this method.

7.7.3 Dock Menus

The menu bar is not the only place in OS X where you find menus. Every application has a menu attached to its dock icon as well. This has a small number of default entries, such as Hide and Quit. Any windows that appear on the window menu will also appear here.

It is also possible for the application to provide its own menu. This is done by a few Apple applications. Figure 7.10 shows the dock menu for Apple's X server. This is divided into three sections. The top part shows the open windows (currently none), the bottom part shows the standard menu, and the middle contains the custom menu. This menu has a single item, pointing to a submenu that the application populates itself. You are not limited to a single menu item here. iTunes, for example, installs a small collection of entries in its menu for controlling playback.

Providing a dock menu is very easy. When you create an application nib file, the file's owner will be an `NSApplication` instance. This has three outlets, one of which is called `dockMenu`. Any menu you connect to this outlet will automatically be shown in the dock.

For some applications, it is more convenient to provide a dock menu dynamically. These might display different dock menus depending on their active state, or simply change the menu over time. When the dock menu is about to be displayed, the application will send this message to its delegate:

```
- (NSMenu*)applicationDockMenu: (NSApplication*)sender;
```

The sender will always be `NSApp` and the return value should be the menu to display. You can use this to override the menu defined in the nib file. The returned menu can come from any source; you can create it in code or load it from another nib file.

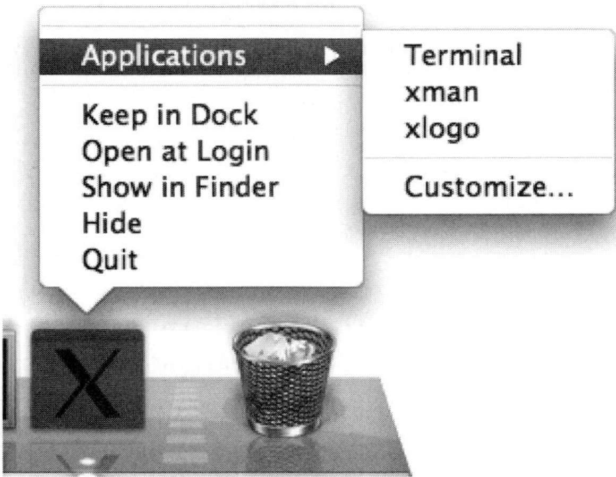

Figure 7.10: The dock menu for Apple's X11 application.

7.7.4 Validating Menu Items

Every menu item has two states: enabled and disabled. You can set the state by sending a menu item a `-setEnabled:` message. Every time the first responder changes, the set of menu items that make sense also changes. If every responder had to send a message to every menu item to define its state, then even very simple applications would quickly become incomprehensible.

Fortunately, with Cocoa, manually enabling and disabling menu items is considered a last resort. Often, automatic validation of menu items works with no additional code in the views. Objective-C introspection allows a menu to determine if the target of its action responds to a given message. If the target of the menu item's action doesn't respond to the selector chosen for the action message, then it will automatically be disabled.

Some views support different menu items at different times. The Copy menu item, for example, only makes sense when something inside a view is selected. You would support this in a custom view by implementing a method like this:

```
- (BOOL)validateUserInterfaceItem: (id<NSValidatedUserInterfaceItem>)anItem
{
    if ((@selector(copy:) == [anItem action])
        &&
        (nil == [self selectedItem]))
    {
```

```
        return NO;
    }
    return [super validateUserInterfaceItem: anItem];
}
```

This will be called for each menu item just before the menu is displayed. This simple version tests whether the selector is `-copy:` and the selected item of the view is `nil`. The default superclass implementation will cause all other menu items to be enabled if the object responds to the action message. You only use this method for disabling menu items; using it to enable menu items that send action messages that your view doesn't understand does not make sense. Note that this method can also automatically disable other kinds of user interface components, such as buttons, which send action messages.

You can turn off this automatic validation by sending a menu a `-setAutoenablesItems:` message with `NO`. This will prevent it from automatically validating any of the items. You typically only want to do this for context menus or menus in pop-up buttons.

7.7.5 Context Menus

The menu at the top of the screen contains all of the commands that can be applied anywhere on the screen, but sometimes it is useful to display a menu that is only applicable to a certain view, or object inside that view. When you right-click or control-click on a view, it will be sent a `-menuForEvent:` message by the default mouse-down handler.

This method will first see if the menu attribute is defined, and if so return that. If not, it will send its class a `+defaultMenu` message and return the result.

This gives three opportunities to define the context menu that a view will display. You can define a menu for the class, a menu for the instance, or a menu for a region. If you are writing a new view that has a meaningful context menu layout for all instances, you should override `+defaultMenu`. Some of the standard Cocoa views do this, in particular `NSTextView`, which displays a simplified version of the Edit menu as a context menu.

The horizontal menu at the top of the screen is easy for the user to reach—he just needs to throw the mouse at the top of the screen—but the context menu is even easier. Invoking the context menu doesn't require moving the mouse, just clicking on a button. Selecting the top item from the context menu is one of the fastest user interactions possible. Selecting others is slightly slower, and becomes progressively more slow as the menu size and complexity increases.

A lot of views implement a hybrid context menu, where some elements are defined statically by the class, and some are dependent on the selected region. Often these views will query the model object when displaying the context menu.

The text view, for example, populates its context menu with spelling suggestions for the word under the cursor.

To demonstrate how to use these together, we will create a new view that displays the context menu shown in Figure 7.11. This menu is composed of three parts. The top menu item is not really a menu item in the conventional sense, it is purely informative, giving the coordinates within the view of the menu click. The middle section is created using the view's `menu` outlet, inherited from `NSView`. This is connected in Interface Builder to a simple example menu. All of these menu items are enabled because they are connected to random actions in `NSApp`. The final part is defined on a per-class basis. The code for this is shown in Listing 7.5.

Figure 7.11: Displaying a context menu for a custom view.

The first method in this class creates a standard menu for all instances. Note the **`@synchronized`** line in the initializer and the double-test. Because this is a class method, users will expect it to be thread-safe. If two threads called this without the **`@synchronized`** directive, then both threads would create the object and one copy would leak. This isn't a major problem, because it's a small object, but it's worth avoiding anyway. The inner test is required for the same case. If two threads call this method at once, then they will enter the **@synchronized** block sequentially. When the second one enters this block, the default menu has already been created, so it doesn't need to create it again.

Listing 7.5: Creating a context menu. [from: examples/ContextMenuView/ContextMenuView.m]

```
#import "ContextMenuView.h"

static NSMenu *defaultMenu;

@implementation ContextMenuView
+ (NSMenu*)defaultMenu
{
    if (nil == defaultMenu)
    {
        @synchronized(self)
        {
            if (nil == defaultMenu)
            {
                defaultMenu = [NSMenu new];
                [defaultMenu addItemWithTitle: @"Copy"
                                       action: @selector(copy:)
                                keyEquivalent: @"c"];
                [defaultMenu addItemWithTitle: @"Paste"
                                       action: @selector(paste:)
                                keyEquivalent: @"v"];
            }
        }
    }
    return defaultMenu;
}
static BOOL addItemsToMenuFromMenu(NSMenu *menu, NSMenu *template)
{
    for (NSMenuItem *item in [template itemArray])
    {
        NSMenuItem *itemCopy = [item copy];
        [menu addItem: itemCopy];
        [itemCopy release];
    }
    return [menu numberOfItems] > 0;
}
- (NSMenu*)menuForEvent: (NSEvent*)theEvent
{
```

```
38     NSPoint click = [self convertPoint: [theEvent locationInWindow]
39                               fromView: nil];
40 
41     NSMenuItem *locationMenuItem =
42         [[NSMenuItem alloc] initWithTitle: NSStringFromPoint(click)
43                                    action: NULL
44                             keyEquivalent: @""];
45     [locationMenuItem setEnabled: NO];
46     NSMenu *menu = [NSMenu new];
47     [menu addItem: locationMenuItem];
48     [locationMenuItem release];
49     [menu addItem: [NSMenuItem separatorItem]];
50     if (addItemsToMenuFromMenu(menu, [self menu]))
51     {
52         [menu addItem: [NSMenuItem separatorItem]];
53     }
54     addItemsToMenuFromMenu(menu, [[self class] defaultMenu]);
55     return [menu autorelease];
56 }
57 @end
```

The default menu is set up on lines 15–20 to contain items equivalent to the standard Copy and Paste commands. These will deliver their actions to the first responder, and so will always be disabled for this view. Subclasses of the view, however, can implement the `-copy:` and `-paste:` action messages and have the menu items work correctly. This menu is constructed using a convenience method that implicitly creates the menu item. If you don't need to customize the item in any way, this is very convenient.

The function on line 26 is a small helper for adding the items in one menu to another. It allows you to use menus as templates. Note that menu items are not allowed to appear on more than one menu. This function copies all of the menu items from the template menu and adds them to another menu. Copying is made easy by the fact that menu items implement the `NSCopying` protocol and so can be duplicated by just sending them a `-copy` message. This function returns a boolean value indicating whether the template menu contained any items.

Whenever the user right-clicks on this class, the method on line 36 is called. This is responsible for constructing the context menu. The first item displays a simple string representation of the click location. You will see this in the context menu for some graphics editors. Often, views will intersect the click location with rectangles of important components and create context menu items specific to these components. You can do this using exactly the same mechanism used to construct this first item.

On lines 50 and 54, the menu has the instance and class context menus' items added. Note that a `+defaultMenu` message is sent to the class to get the default menu, rather than using the `defaultMenu` variable directly. This is to allow subclasses to provide their own default menus.

In this example, the view has a menu connected to its outlet in Interface Builder, but this might not always be the case. If a particular instance of the view doesn't have a context menu defined, then we don't want to display two separators next to each other. The test on line 50 ensures that we only add the second menu separator if we have added some menu items after the first one. The separator is a simple `NSMenuItem` instance that just displays a line and doesn't send any action messages. You can create them in Interface Builder or, as shown here, by sending a `+separatorItem` message to `NSMenuItem`.

This example shows all three ways of adding menu items to the context menu, and demonstrates how to create menus at run time both purely in code and using a template. Subclasses of this view can extend the context menu by overriding `+defaultMenu` or `-menu`. Try creating a new subclass and experimenting with this.

Context Menus and Touch Screens

At the time of writing, no shipping Macs include a touch screen. The iPhone, obviously, does, but it does not use AppKit. This does not mean that future OS X systems will not include touchscreens, or that users will not connect desktop Macs to touch-screen devices.

On newer, multitouch, screens, right-clicking can be emulated by tracking two-fingered taps. On older, or cheaper, screens, this is not possible. The user can emulate a right-click by control-clicking, but this requires one hand to be on the keyboard, which is much less common with touch screen users than with mouse and trackpad users.

If you put important functionality on a context menu, then your application becomes inaccessible to these users. You should view the context menu as a shortcut, only containing copies of commands available in other parts of the user interface.

7.7.6 Pop-Up Menus

Cocoa provides a special kind of button that displays a context menu whenever you click on it. This is conceptually similar to a context menu. Unlike a context menu, it appears with a normal click on the button, rather than a control-click or right-click.

The `NSPopUpButton` class is a subclass of `NSButton`. When you click on it, it displays a menu, usually created in Interface Builder and attached to its `menu` outlet. The button title is set to the last-selected value from the menu.

As with any other kind of button, this sends an action message when the user has interacted with it. Usually the method this calls will send a `-selectedItem` message to its sender to get the menu items that the user clicked on.

You can use the cell responsible for this behavior when implementing other kinds of pop-up menus. Because this is a cell, it can be used to draw a menu attached to any view. The simple `NSView` subclass in Listing 7.6 shows how to do this. When the view is loaded it creates a new `NSPopUpButtonCell` to display the menu. This class also declares a `clickMenu` outlet, which contains the menu to be displayed. As a simple demonstration, this is connected to the application's main menu in the nib file, as shown in Figure 7.12. Note that, unlike views, menus are allowed to be displayed in different places at the same time.

Listing 7.6: Displaying a menu in response to a click. [from: examples/ClickMenu/ClickMenuView.m]

```
#import "ClickMenuView.h"


@implementation ClickMenuView
- (void)awakeFromNib
{
    cell = [NSPopUpButtonCell new];
}
- (void)mouseDown: (NSEvent*)theEvent
{
    NSRect frame;
    frame.origin = [self convertPoint: [theEvent locationInWindow]
                             fromView: nil];
    frame.size = NSZeroSize;

    [cell setMenu: clickMenu];
    [cell performClickWithFrame: frame
                         inView: self];
}
@end
```

When this view receives a mouse down event, it displays a menu. This is done by sending the `-performClickWithFrame:inView:` message to the cell. This method is intended to be called by an `NSPopUpButton`. The frame passed as the first parameter would be the control's frame in normal use. The menu would then be aligned with the control. Passing this view's frame would cause the menu to be displayed along one side, which is not what we want. Instead, we create a new

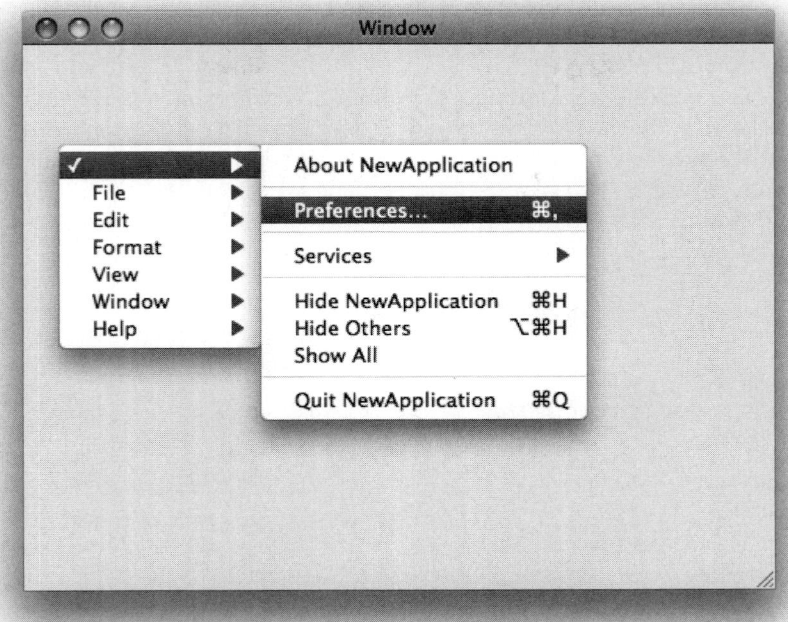

Figure 7.12: Displaying a pop-up menu in response to a click.

zero-sized rectangle at the mouse click location. The menu will then be displayed as if it were attached to a control at this point.

Note that we don't configure the action for this cell. Each menu item has its own, independent, target and action. The pop-up menu functions just like any other. Because we are reusing the application menu for this example, any of the menu items that work normally will continue to work here.

7.8 Summary

In this chapter we have looked at two of the most fundamental parts of the Mac UI: windows and menus. Both are fundamental to almost any graphical application on OS X.

We discussed the difference between windows, panels, and sheets and how to create all three. OS X provides several standard panels and sheets and we saw how to create these, as well as how to set various properties on them and load windows from nib files.

Next we looked at the various places in OS X where menus are used; at the top of the screen, in the dock, in response to a right-click, and attached to pop-up buttons. We saw how to create menus for all of these and how to populate them with items.

After reading this chapter, you should understand how windows and menus are created and displayed in a Cocoa application.

Chapter 8

Text in Cocoa

In spite of the complex graphical capabilities of OS X, most applications still spend a lot of their time processing text. Cocoa provides several classes for doing this, collectively known as the *text system*.

Text processing is a surprisingly complex activity. Even displaying a simple string on the screen involves several steps. First, what is a string? In C, it's a sequence of bytes. Everything inside the computer is a sequence of bytes, so that's a good place to start. For sequences of bytes to have any meaning as text, you need the concept of *character sets*. When you load a text file, it will be in a character set like UTF-8 or Mac OS Roman. Internally, it will probably be converted into UTF-32. Now the sequence of bytes is a sequence of 32-bit characters.

Characters correspond to some abstract idea of a letter, unlike bytes, which simply represent numbers. The character 65 might represent the uppercase letter A. At this stage, we still have a fairly abstract representation of the text. Characters have no concept of their representation; they are just identifiers. The spoken and written forms of a letter would be identified by the same character.

To draw them on the screen, we need *glyphs*. A glyph is a picture used to represent a character, often stored as a sequence of curves. Before they can be drawn on the screen, they must be turned into pixels. (Often this stage can be done in the GPU on modern systems.) Figure 8.1 illustrates this text pipeline.

This is a simplification of what happens in Cocoa. For example, it does not cover how different attributes on a string, such as bold, italic, red, or really big, are defined. It also does not cover how the glyphs are drawn on the screen in relation to each other. In a simple text system only supporting monospaced text, this is simple; the next character is always drawn n pixels after the current one. Cocoa, however, supports proportional fonts, ligatures, and a host of other typographic features.

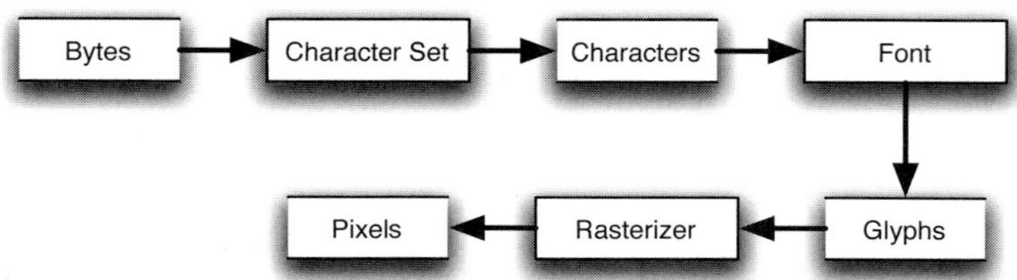

Figure 8.1: A simple text rendering pipeline.

8.1 Constructing and Deconstructing Strings

The bottom layer of Cocoa's text system is the string, as embodied by `NSString` and its mutable subclass `NSMutableString`. These store sequences of characters, a slightly higher-level abstraction than C's sting-of-bytes representation. When you create a Cocoa string using one of these classes, you have to specify the character encoding used. A typical method for doing this is `-initWithCString:encoding:`. All of the methods in this family take an `NSStringEncoding` as an argument. This is just an integer, used to identify the encoding. There are a large number of these, specified by an enumerated type. The most common one OS X is `NSUTF8StringEncoding`, since most applications default to using UTF-8 for storage.

Once a string has been created, you can assign its contents to other strings without worrying about the encoding. Irrespective of how the string object is actually storing the data, it will expose it as an array of `unichar`s, 32-bit unicode characters.

You can also create strings from most objects by sending them either a `-stringValue` or a `-description` method. The first of these means "represent your contents as a string," while the second is used to provide a summary of the object for a debugger. We've looked at a few examples that use this implicitly in `NSLog` statements, like this:

```
NSLog(@"An object: %@", anObject);
```

The first argument to `NSLog` is a *format string.* This is a special kind of string containing placeholders prefixed by a percent (%) character. If you have ever used the C library functions `printf()` and `scanf()`, then this kind of format string will be familiar to you. This one just uses a single such placeholder: "%@". This is a Cocoa-specific extension to the set that is supported by `printf()`. When a string is constructed from a format string like this, each placeholder is replaced by a string representation of one of the arguments. If it is a primitive type, then there are some fixed rules for representing it. Objects, however, must define their own way of being represented. This is done by implementing the -description method, which returns an NSString.

Format strings can be used to construct complex strings; they are not just used for logging. NSString has a +stringWithFormat: method, and NSMutableString adds an -appendFormat: method. These are examples of *variadic methods*, since they take a variable number of arguments after the number that is fixed by the method description. You can use these in almost exactly the same way as printf():

```
[NSString stringWithFormat: @"int:␣%d,␣float:␣%f,␣object:␣%@",
    anInt, aDouble, anObject];
```

Note that you do not need to null-terminate the argument list, since the number of arguments expected is defined by the format string. If you provide too many arguments, the excess will be ignored. If you provide too few, you will corrupt your stack.

The inverse of printf() is scanf(), but Cocoa does not have a direct analog of this. Instead, it provides the NSScanner class. This is a very simple, but powerful, tokenizer. It takes a string as input and then allows components of the string to be consumed if they match certain patterns. A scanner is created by passing it a string to scan:

```
[NSScanner scannerWithString: aString];
```

Unlike scanf(), which uses a format string for scanning, you send the NSScanner instance one message for each component you want to scan. For example, to read an integer from the string, you will send it a -scanInt: message. This takes a pointer to an integer as an argument (just like scanf() with a %d in the format string) and attempts to parse an integer from the current string. If it succeeds, it will set the variable pointed to by the argument to the integer it parsed. In this example, twelve will be set to 12 and success to **YES**:

```
NSScanner *scanner= [NSScanner scannerWithString: @"12"];
int twelve;
BOOL success = [scanner scanInt: &twelve];
```

The most powerful method in NSScanner's arsenal is -scanCharactersFromSet:intoString:. This takes an NSCharacterSet as an argument. NSCharacterSet is a set of characters. There are some predefined ones, such as the alphanumeric characters. An identifier in C is defined as a letter followed by an alphanumeric string. You could parse C identifiers by calling this method twice, once with [NSCharacterSet letterCharacterSet] and once with [NSCharacterSet alphanumericCharacterSet] as arguments, and then joining the two resulting strings together.

There are lots of other ways of using character sets with strings. You can divide a string into components separated by characters in a given character set with `NSString`'s `-componentsSeparatedByCharactersInSet:` method, which returns an array of strings. You can also implement this very easily using an `NSScanner`. Character sets can be inverted by sending them a `-invertedSet` message. You would alternate scanning for the separator set and the inverse set until you reached the end of the string, and store every string found by matching the resulting array. You can also use this mechanism to process each component individually, rather than waiting for the whole string to be split.

8.2 Annotating Strings

The next step toward drawing a string on the screen is to provide it with annotations. *Attributed strings* are represented by `NSAttributedString` objects. These contain a string and a set of annotations on ranges of the string.

These annotations can be any key-value pairs. All the class handles is a set of mappings from `NSRanges` to `NSDictionary` instances associated with a given string. What goes in these dictionaries is entirely up to the developer. For example, someone writing a code editor might set entries in the dictionary indicating whether a range represents a keyword, or what the scope of a variable is. Alternatively, an HTML viewer might only display the character data, and store the tag and tag attribute values as attribute runs.

The full power and flexibility of attributed strings is very rarely explored. Most applications use them simply to store visual information to allow the parts of AppKit responsible for rendering text how to display it.

For accessing attributes in a given range, `NSAttributedString` provides this method:

```
- (NSDictionary*)attributesAtIndex: (NSUInteger)index
             longestEffectiveRange: (NSRangePointer)aRange
                           inRange: (NSRange)rangeLimit;
```

An `NSRangePointer`, as you might imagine, is a pointer to an `NSRange`. This is an output parameter. You pass in a pointer to a range here and the `location` and `length` fields are filled in. This returns a dictionary of attributes that are present at the specified index, and then looks along the range limit to find how many subsequent characters have the same attributes, returning this via the range pointer.

In many cases, you don't actually need the longest possible range. A simpler version of this method is also provided, which is not guaranteed to give the longest possible range:

```
- (NSDictionary*)attributesAtIndex: (NSUInteger)index
                    effectiveRange: (NSRangePointer)aRange;
```

Internally, an attributed string may store a sorted list of range-dictionary pairs. When new pairs are inserted into this list, it may compact the list, merging together adjacent ranges with the same dictionary, or it might not. If it does, then this method will return the longest effective range. If not, then it will return a shorter effective range. This means that, in the worst case, this method will be no slower than the longest effective range version, and it will often be faster.

You can also test for the presence of a specific attribute using this method, or its longest effective range variant:

```
- (id)attribute: (NSString )attributeName
        atIndex: (NSUInteger)index
 effectiveRange: (NSRangePointer)aRange;
```

This looks up the attributes at a specified index and tests in the returned dictionary whether the named attribute is set. If it is, then the value of the attribute is returned. Otherwise, it is ignored.

The longest effective range variant of this method is often considerably slower. A single attribute may have a much longer effective range than the dictionary it contains. For example, consider a paragraph of text in a single font with a number of words underlined. Each underlined section will have the same font attributes, but a different underline attribute type. This means that finding the longest effective range for the font attribute will involve looking up the font attribute for each range and then comparing it to the first one (not a cheap comparison, since fonts have a large number of attributes). Try not to use this method unless you really need to.

As with most Foundation classes, there is a mutable subclass, `NSMutableAttributedString`. This provides methods for modifying the underlying string as well as the attributes. You can get an `NSMutableString` instance back by sending a `-mutableString` message to a mutable attributed string. This is not the same class as a mutable string you might construct by sending messages to `NSMutableString`. It is a proxy class that sends messages to the attributed string and the underlying string, to ensure that any changes to the string also have the attribute mappings updated.

Most of the methods on mutable attributed strings are fairly simple. One pair is worth noting, however. The `-beginEditing` and `-endEditing` methods allow groups of edits to be consolidated into a single operation. This will defer notifying observers of changes until a complete set has been completed. These methods are not particularly important on `NSMutableAttributedString` itself, but can make interactions with some of its more complex subclasses a lot faster. If you are making a lot of changes to a rich text object that is being displayed in a GUI, then wrapping these changes in begin and end editing messages can make things a lot faster.

The attributed string objects in Foundation are fairly abstract. AppKit contains a set of additions to this class in the form of a category and a set of constants. In particular, they provide mechanisms for creating attributed strings from HTML or RTF and vice versa. Other methods are convenience methods for setting and testing the presence of attributes used by the text system for rendering, including things like ruler dimensions and so on.

RTFD

One of the most common document bundle formats on OS X is the .rtfd format. *Rich Text Format (RTF)* is a format defined by Microsoft for document interchange between word processors. One of the big limitations of the format was that it was unable to contain complex embedded images. The .rtfd format extended this by using a special code in the RTF document to indicate an attachment, which was then stored as a separate file in the bundle. This allowed PDF or other complex, scalable, images to be embedded in the documents. This format can be written and read by attributed string objects using methods provided in AppKit.

8.3 Localization

The English-speaking world is an increasingly small part of the global computer-using community. At some point it is very likely that your application will need translating into other languages.

APIs that generate user interfaces from code or from abstract definitions typically load strings at the same time. Cocoa does not. The nib file mechanism is intended to allow graphical designers to create user interfaces visually and then have programmers connect the created views up to controllers.

This means that a nib file has many hard-coded sizes in it, designed to look correct in a single language. If you replaced the strings with translated versions, you would get something quite ugly looking. You should create a new nib file for each language you want to support.

The text is not the only thing that should be changed in localized nib files. You may also want to change the button order and visual metaphors. For example, in English nib files you put the “proceed” action button on the right because that makes sense in a left-to-right reading order. For a right-to-left reading order locale, you would want the opposite.

Re-creating a nib entirely from scratch is quite time consuming. To make it easier, Cocoa provides the ibtool command-line utility. This can perform a large number of refactoring tasks on nib files, but one of the most useful is dumping and reimporting the strings. The two commands for exporting and importing a strings file are

```
$ ibtool --generate-strings-file MainMenu.strings en.lproj/MainMenu.nib
$ ibtool --strings-file es.lproj/MainMenu.strings \
--write es.lproj/MainMenu.nib en.lproj/MainMenu.nib
```

This will create a new Spanish nib file based on the English one, with the translated strings file. In between these two steps, someone needs to create the es.lproj/MainMenu.strings file, by translating the English into Spanish. Unfortunately the tools are not capable of doing this automatically yet.

8.3.1 Localization Macros

Very often there will be bits of code in your program where you set the string value of a view. Cocoa provides several simple functions for localizing strings. Most of these work via `NSBundle`. This class implements the following method:

```
- (NSString*)localizedStringForKey: (NSString*)key
                             value: (NSString*)value
                             table: (NSString*)tableName;
```

This looks up a string in the specified bundle. Note that strings are not the only resources that you can localize; any file that your application loads from a bundle can have localized versions. You can have localized images, for example, to contain culturally relevant icons.

The first argument that this method takes is the key in a strings table. Often this will be the English version of the string. The `value` parameter is a default value. This will be returned if the key is not found in the table. The final parameter is the name of the dictionary to use. If this is `nil`, then the default strings file will be used.

There are helper functions that wrap this method on the application's main bundle. The most commonly used one is

```
NSString *NSLocalizedString(NSString *key, NSString *comment);
```

This simply calls the `NSBundle` method with the first parameter set to `key` and the other two as `nil`. The comment is a description of the string, used to provide clues to translators. This is used so often that GNUstep declares this macro to wrap it:

```
#define _(X) NSLocalizedString (X, @"")
```

You might consider using this macro in your own code, even if you are not using any of the other bits of GNUstep. Supporting localization in your code is then just a matter of writing things like this:

```
// Not localized
[cell setStringValue: @"A string"];
// Localized
[cell setStringValue: _(@"A string")];
```

Note that you don't have to do this everywhere where you use a constant string in your code, only in places where the string will end up in the user interface.

These helper functions, unfortunately, only work on the main bundle. If you are writing a framework that needs localizing, then you need to either call the bundle method directly or one of the more complex convenience functions that includes a bundle as an argument. This shows the general way of looking up a string in a framework:

```
NSBundle *bundle = [NSBundle bundleForClass: [self class]];
NSString *str = [bundle localizedStringForKey: @"A string"
                                         value: @"A string"
                                         table: nil];
```

Note that `-bundleForClass:` is very expensive. Ideally you would either use `-bundleWithIdentifier:` instead, or get the bundle in `+initialize` and cache it. You could also cache the strings; this is not perfect, since the user's locale settings may change during the application's run, but very few applications handle this particularly gracefully. It is generally accepted that a new locale setting will only affect new applications.

8.3.2 Strings Files

Strings files in Cocoa are simple dictionaries. They map from a set of abstract strings to strings in a specific language. Strings files are one of the few places in OS X where the old OpenStep property list format is still actively used. Strings files typically contain comments and key-value pairs like this:

```
??/* This is the verb form, not the noun */
"Print" = "Imprimer"
```

When you call `NSLocalizedString()`, the second argument is ignored. It exists for the genstrings tool. This scans a source file and generates strings files from the localization functions. You can see this in operation by writing a simple program containing a line like this:

```
#import <Foundation/Foundation.h>

int main(void)
{
    [NSAutoreleasePool new];
    NSLog(NSLocalizedString(@"A␣log␣message",
        @"Used␣to␣demonstrate␣genstrings:"));
    return 0;
}
```

When you run genstrings on the source file containing this line, you will get a Localizable.strings file emitted, like this:

```
$ genstrings str.m
$ cat Localizable.strings
??/* Used to demonstrate genstrings: */
"A log message" = "A log message";
```

For tools, the main bundle will point to the directory of the tool binary, so you can experiment with this by editing the strings file in place. For applications, you will create a separate strings file in each of the lproj subdirectories.

8.3.3 Localizing Format Strings

One of the biggest problems with localization comes with word order. If you are translating simple constant phrases like the examples we have seen so far, then there is no problem. More often you will translate strings like `@"file␣%@␣not␣found`.

The real problem happens when you have two or more extra parameters being inserted into the format string. You might want to translate nouns and adjectives separately to reduce the translators' workload. Unfortunately, if you translate into a language like French or Russian you will find that your format strings are no longer accepting parameters in the correct order.

Imagine a simple vector drawing program with an inspector showing the selected object. It might display messages like "red rectangle" or "blue ellipse." You would start by constructing these with the following code:

```
msg = [NSString stringWithFormat: @"Selected:␣%@␣%@",
    [selected shapeName], [selected colorName]];
```

When you localized these, you would wrap all three of these strings in `NSLocalizedString()` calls. Translating the shape and color names is relatively easy, but how do you translate the format string into a language that puts the adjective after the noun? Fortunately, this problem was solved a long time ago for `printf()`, and all of the Cocoa. You would put an entry like this in your strings like:

```
"Selected: %@ %@" = "Choisi: %2$@ %$1@"
```

The format string now reads the second parameter before the first one. You can even use this kind of rule to construct general, reusable, sentence fragments. For example, you might have an entry like this:

```
"SUBJECT VERB OBJECT %@ %@ %@" = "%@ %@ %@"
```

This is a simple placeholder for any string containing a subject, a verb, and an object. In English, the three arguments go in this order. On other languages they might be reversed. This kind of general grammar rule is mostly only of academic interest. When you get to providing general rules expressive enough for the kind of real phrases you will use in your program, you are likely to find that it is much easier to translate every phrase you do use than try to provide generalizations.

8.4 Text Storage

When using AppKit, it is common to use `NSTextStorage`, a subclass of `NSMutableAttributedString`. This is the main model object for the text system, used to represent text displayed in an `NSTextView` or similar view class.

In addition to the functionality of `NSMutableAttributedString`, the text storage object manages a set of layout managers. This brings it one step closer to displaying text on the screen or a printed page. By itself, an attributed string contains some markup indicating attributes of characters, but nothing about how they are laid out on the page.

The `NSLayoutManager` class provides a way of laying out text. Figure 8.2 shows the relationship between these classes:

Attributed Strings contain mappings from ranges in a string to dictionaries of attributes.

Text Storage objects provide attributed characters to one or more layout managers.

Text Containers provide geometry information for pages, text boxes, and other places where text might be stored.

Layout Managers handle loading glyphs and generating coordinates for drawing them in each text container they are responsible for.

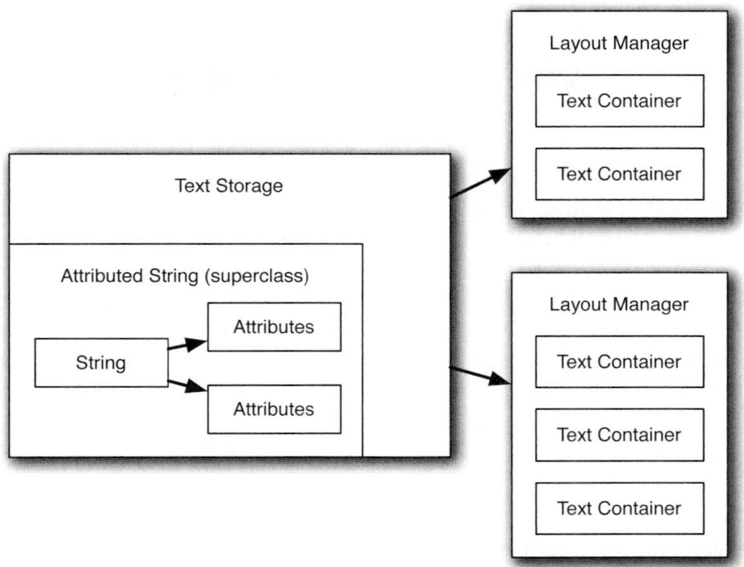

Figure 8.2: The relationship between text storage and layout managers.

A simple text box, or a single page of text, might only have a single text container. More complex layouts, particularly for printing, might contain a lot more.

8.5 Understanding Fonts

The text that an `NSTextStorage` object contains is a set of strings and attributes. One of the most important attributes, for the purpose of display, is the *font* associated with a particular set of characters. A font, represented by `NSFont`, is a way of mapping from characters to glyphs.

Fonts are identified in Cocoa by a font descriptor. This encapsulates the typeface name and any attributes. Dealing with fonts directly can be very complicated. The `NSFontManager` class exists to simplify a lot of common font tasks. It has a single shared instance for the entire program, which is responsible for providing an interface to the underlying system font services.

You can construct font objects either directly or via the font manager. `NSFont` has a number of class methods for getting scaled instances of the system fonts, such

Fonts and Typefaces

You will often hear people say "font" when they mean "typeface." This is not helped by the fact that the Font Manager application on OS X manages type faces, not fonts, and has a Font column in the middle that lists typefaces.

A typeface is a set of character shapes. An example of a typeface would be something like Times or Helvetica. These are grouped together in families, such as sans serif. Each typeface contains a number of different fonts.

A font is a way of representing characters in a given typeface, and includes the font's size. The `NSFont` class encapsulates a font, not a typeface.

The simplest way of distinguishing between a font and a typeface is to remember that a font has at most one glyph image for any given character, while a typeface can have any number. This distinction is blurred slightly by cheap, low-quality, TrueType or OpenType fonts, which use the same vector outline and metrics for all sizes.

as `+systemFontOfSize:`, but creating a specific font object can be more complicated. You must provide either a font name or a font descriptor to `NSFont`'s constructor. Font names must be complete PostScript-style names. In most cases where you wish to create a specific font object, it is easier to do so using the font manager, with this method:

```
- (NSFont*)fontWithFamily: (NSString*)family
                   traits: (NSFontTraitMask)fontTraitMask
                   weight: (NSInteger)weight
                     size: (CGFloat)size;
```

Most of the arguments to this should be self-explanatory. The family is the simple name of the font, such as Helvetica or Monaco. The size is the height of the glyphs, in points. Recall that PostScript points[1] are the standard unit of measurement in Cocoa, equal to $\frac{1}{72}$ inch. The weight defines the thickness of the line, on an arbitrary scale from 0 to 15, with 5 being defined as normal weight and 9 being the customary bold weight. Good fonts will have separate glyph descriptions for their normal, fine, and bold versions, but many common versions use the same outlines and just adjust the width of the lines.

The traits are defined as a set of attributes, such as bold or italic. These are used as filters when trying to locate a version of the font to use. Some traits have

[1] The point, as a unit of measurement for typographical systems, was invented in France in the 18th century. Inches, at the time, were not an internationally standardized measurement, and so over the years various differing definitions of the size of a point appeared. The only one still in common use today is the PostScript point.

flags to explicitly block and require their existence. For example, `NSItalicFontMask` and `NSUnitalicFontMask` specify that the returned font either must, or must not, be italic. If neither is specified, then the returned font might be italic, but probably won't. Some typefaces do not include a definition for all combinations of traits. If a font file only contains italic glyphs, then you will get the italic version if you don't specify either of these masks, or `nil` if you specify `NSUnitalicFontMask`.

8.5.1 Converting Fonts

A more interesting—and useful—feature of the font manager is the ability to modify existing fonts. It is quite rare to want to construct a new font object from scratch, but a lot more common to want to add a particular trait to a font, or create a new font in a particular typeface but taking all of its other attributes from an existing font object.

This kind of conversion happens very often if user interface elements expose font attributes. A simple rich text editor might have a drop-down list of fonts and a text field for the font size. When you select a font from the font list you expect the selected text to adopt this font but not change its size of any other attributes. When you press a bold button, you expect the text to become bold faced, but not change in any other way.

A lot of the time, you don't have to write this code yourself. Figure 8.3 shows the font menu that can be created in Interface Builder by dragging it from the palette. You can also create this in code by sending a `-fontMenu:` message to the font manager. The argument to this message is a flag indicating if the object should be created.

Some of the items in this menu are connected directly to the `-addFontTrait:` action method in the font manager. This, in turn, sends a `-changeFont:` action message to the first responder, which should reply by sending a `-convertFont:` message back to the font manager. The font manager will then send itself a `-convertFont:toHaveTrait:` message with the tag of the original sender as the second argument.

The result of this complex procedure is to apply a new set of font attributes to the currently selected text in the first responder. You can reuse this mechanism to support font formatting yourself by sending this message and setting the tag correctly in the sender. Alternatively, you can call the underlying methods and do the font conversion yourself.

The font manager has a selection of methods for converting a font to a similar font with some modified properties. These all take two arguments. The first is the original font, and the second is the new value of the property to modify. This operation will not always succeed; it is possible to request combinations of attributes that cannot be created with fonts installed in the system.

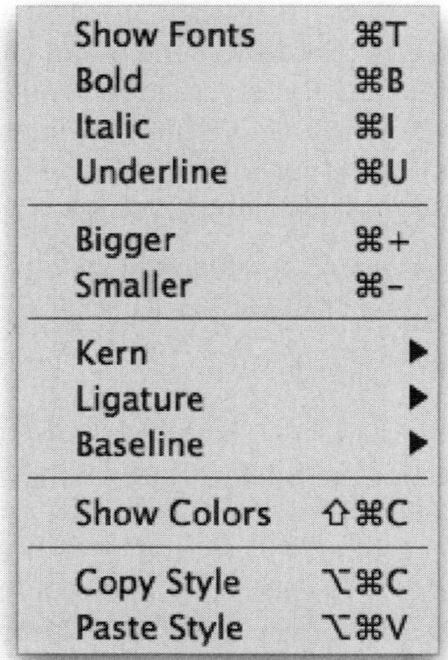

Figure 8.3: The Font menu in Interface Builder.

To demonstrate how to use these methods, we will write a simple font factory, which will modify the font of a text field. Note that this example does not show the best way of implementing this functionality. If you were adding something similar to a real application, then you would use the `-addFontTrait:` method described earlier, and similar calls. This example is intended to demonstrate how to use the font manager's conversion functions manually. You would typically use these for parsing a custom rich text format or similar activities.

The controller defined for this application is shown in Listing 8.1. This defines three action methods that all modify the text field's font. The controls that send these messages are shown in Figure 8.4. The font name and size boxes are connected to the first two methods, and the check boxes are all connected to the last one.

The structure of all of the methods is similar. They get the current font, tell the font manager to transform it, and then set the new font in the text field.

The first two methods are almost identical. They simply get the value from the control that called them and use these to set the font family and size. The last method is more complicated.

The check boxes are defined as toggles. They either add or remove a font

Listing 8.1: Modifying font properties. [from: examples/FontFactory/FontController.m]

```
#import "FontController.h"

NSFontManager *fm;

@implementation FontController
- (void) awakeFromNib
{
    fm = [NSFontManager sharedFontManager];
}
- (IBAction)setFontName: (id)sender
{
    NSFont *font = [text font];
    font = [fm convertFont: font
                  toFamily: [sender stringValue]];
    [text setFont: font];
}
- (IBAction)setFontSize: (id)sender
{
    NSFont *font = [text font];
    font = [fm convertFont: font
                    toSize: [sender doubleValue]];
    [text setFont: font];
}
- (IBAction)setFontAttribute: (id)sender
{
    NSFont *font = [text font];
    NSFontTraitMask attribute = [sender tag];
    if ([sender state] == NSOnState)
    {
        font = [fm convertFont: font
                 toHaveTrait: attribute];
    }
    else
    {
        font = [fm convertFont: font
              toNotHaveTrait: attribute];
    }
    [sender setState: ([fm traitsOfFont: font] & attribute)];
    [text setFont: font];
}
@end
```

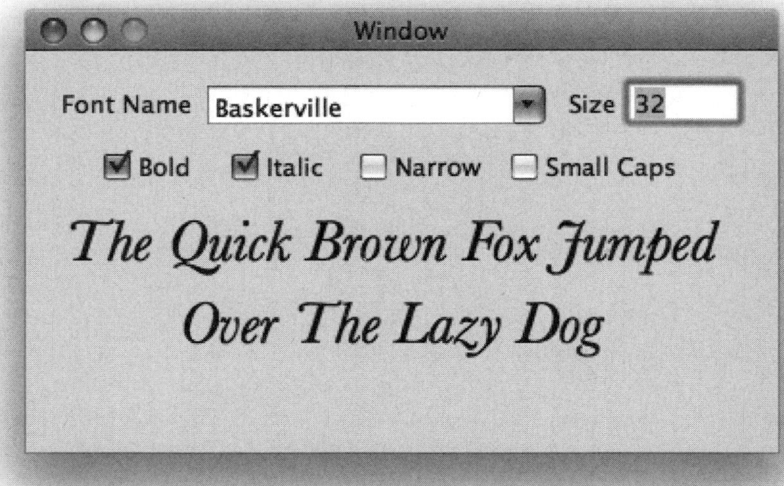

Figure 8.4: Modifying font properties.

attribute. Because this method may be called from various different controls, we use the sender's tag to provide the font mask. These were all set in Interface Builder using the constants in the `NSFontManager` documentation.

The font manager operation is defined by the state of the sender. Each check box sets its state when it is clicked, before sending the action message. This can then be read back, as it is on line 28, and used to determine whether we should be adding or removing the associated trait.

Because applying a font trait can fail, the last step is to update the sender's state to reflect whether the change actually worked. A lot of fonts don't support the small caps or narrow variants and so these are quite likely to fail. If they do, then the test on line 38 will set the check box state to reflect this failure. Note that this simple version doesn't provide any checking for the other user interface elements, so until you set their value they may not correspond to the real font.

8.5.2 Enumerating Fonts

The options in the drop-down list box in the last example are filled in by binding the contents of the box to the font manager's `-availableFontFamilies` key. This returns an array of all of the font families in the system.

This is part of the other rôle of the font manager. As well as creating and converting fonts, it is responsible for managing the set of fonts installed on the system. One of the common uses for this is to get a list of all of the font families that support a particular combination of traits. The `-availableFontNamesWithTraits:` returns an array of font names for fonts that can be constructed with the specified set of names.

You can use this to populate user interface elements with a list of fonts that are compatible with a selected set of options. Try modifying the example in the last section so that it updates the font list to only contain the ones compatible with the selected options. You can do this by defining an array instance variable and binding the contents of the drop-down list to it instead of directly to the font manager. You would then update this whenever the attributes are modified.

8.6 Displaying Text

Cocoa provides a large number of ways of displaying text, all layered on top of each other. These begin with simple methods for drawing text into a view and extend up to complex view objects that handle layout and modification of large text documents.

8.6.1 Primitive Drawing

The lowest level text drawing functions relate to drawing a set of glyphs on the screen. These don't do any line breaking; they just draw shapes corresponding to the text. The low-level parts of these are in Core Text and are not technically part of Cocoa. These are C APIs, wrapping a slightly simplified Objective-C-style object model.

The class typically used for drawing in Cocoa is `NSBezierPath`. This allows rendering glyphs at a specific point along a path. Most of the time, you will not need to use these methods at all, although we will look at them in Chapter 13.

Near the bottom level of Cocoa drawing is a set of primitive functions for displaying attributed strings. These are the simplest text model object with enough information to display on screen. You can also display `NSStrings` directly, although these must have attributes defined for them and so are turned into a form of attributed string when they are drawn.

When you display an attributed string, the conversion to a set of glyphs is done for you automatically. The `NSAttributedString` additions in AppKit define a set of attribute semantics that allow mapping from attributes on a character to glyphs. The most obvious of these is the font.

Figure 8.5 shows a simple window displaying the text "Hello World." This is rendered by a custom view class, using one of the two methods on `NSAttributedString` related to drawing.

Listing 8.2 shows how this is implemented. This is the draw method from the `HelloView` subclass of `NSView`. The nib file accompanying this class has the window's content view class set to `HelloView`, so the view hierarchy is very simple, with just a single entry.

Listing 8.2: Drawing an attributed string. [from: examples/He so ew.m]

```
1  - (void)drawRect:(NSRect)rect {
2      NSString *text = @"Hello␣World";
3      NSMutableAttributedString *str =
4          [[NSMutableAttributedString alloc] initWithString:text];
5      NSFont *font = [NSFont fontWithName:@"Times"
6                                     size:32];
7      NSDictionary *attributes =
8          [NSDictionary dictionaryWithObject:font
9                                      forKey:NSFontAttributeName];
10     [str setAttributes:attributes
11                  range:NSMakeRange(0, [text length])];
12     [str drawInRect:rect];
13 }
```

Whenever the window needs to be displayed, this method will be called. All we do here is construct a simple attributed string and display it. There are two parts to an attributed string: the string and the attributes. We set the string on line 17 and the attributes on line 23. Because this is a very simple example, we just define one set of attributes for the entire string.

Attributes are defined by a dictionary. Here we create a dictionary with a single entry, containing a font. The key used here, `NSFontAttributeName`, is defined in AppKit and must have an instance of `NSFont` as its value.

The drawing is done in the final line. This assumes that a drawing context is already set up, and so should only be called in a view's draw method, or a method intended to be called from a view's draw method.

Most of the time you will not draw text in this way. These mechanisms can be used when creating a new view, but often even they are more low-level than you need. Listing 8.3 shows an alternate implementation of this class using an `NSCell` instance.

Figure 8.5: Hello World in Cocoa.

Listing 8.3: Drawing a string using a cell. [from: examples/HelloCocoaCell/HelloView.m]

```
@implementation HelloView
- (void) createCell
{
    cell = [[NSCell alloc] initTextCell:@"Hello World"];
    [cell setFont:[NSFont fontWithName:@"Times"
                                  size:32]];
}
- (void) awakeFromNib
{
    [self createCell];
}
- (id)initWithFrame:(NSRect)frame
{
    if (nil != (self = [super initWithFrame:frame]))
    {
        [self createCell];
    }
    return self;
}
- (void)drawRect:(NSRect)rect
{
    [cell drawWithFrame:rect inView:self];
}
@end
```

Note that there are two possible ways in which this object can be created, depending on whether the view is instantiated from a nib or not (and the way in which it is stored in the nib). The `-createCell` method is called in both cases and creates the `cell` instance variable.

If you create an instance of this view in code, you will call the designated initializer to create it with a specific frame. This may also be called in some cases when loading a nib, but this is quite rare and is specific to subclassing more complex views. The `-awakeFromNib` method will be called when the class has been loaded from a nib, however, and can be used to create the cell. We did not have to do this in the last version, since it did not have any state.

The drawing method in this class is now very simple; it just tells the cell to draw itself. You can draw the cell somewhere else in the view easily. The internal state of the cell contains everything it needs to draw the string but does not store anything about where it should be drawn. This means you can use the same cell several times in a view's draw method. You can also change the text or the attributes of the cell easily.

If you have an attributed string from some other source that you want to display, you can either draw it directly or use `NSCell`'s `-setAttributedString:` method and then draw it using the cell.

Prior to 10.4, the attributed string drawing methods were very slow. Whenever you called one of these methods, it created a new layout manager instance and other supporting classes from the text system. With 10.4, there are singleton instances of these that are reused for every call, speeding up the process a lot.

This improved a lot in 10.4, although they are still likely to be slightly slower than the implementation in `NSTextView`. This is unlikely to matter, since you generally don't draw the same volume of text using these methods as you would using a text view. If you need to draw large amounts of text, you should consider using a text view as a subview of your view (or directly). An example of a class that does this can be found in TextEdit. When you are in wrap to page mode, this uses a custom text drawing class that creates a text view for each page.

8.6.2 Layout Managers

Drawing a single character is very simple. You turn it into a glyph, create a bitmap from this glyph, and composite that with the window's buffer. Drawing a string is more complicated. Strings are sequences of characters, and the placement of the characters relative to each other is very important when generating attractive text.

The layout manager is one of the most complicated classes in AppKit. It is responsible for almost everything between the attributed string and the contents of the view.

The first thing a layout manager is responsible for is determining the glyphs to be used for the text. In some langauges, this is a very simple mapping operation from a font and character index to an outline. In others, particularly English, the rules are a lot more complicated. Consider the word in Figure 8.6. This contains four letters, but only three glyphs. In other cases, you might have more glyphs than characters. Some characters, like æ or é are not present in all fonts, but can be generated by combining two other glyphs.

Figure 8.6: An example ligature.

Once a sequence of glyphs is generated the layout manager is responsible for working out where they should go. This is the part of its task that gives it its name. Much of this is delegated to another class, a concrete subclass of the `NSTypeSetter` abstract class.

The typesetter is responsible for laying out lines. There is a shared instance of one of these classes per program that can be obtained by sending the class a `+sharedSystemTypesetter` message. Since it returns a different implementation of the class for every version of OS X, you might find that text saved on one version and loaded on another is laid out differently. To avoid this, there is also a `+sharedSystemTypesetterForBehavior:` that requests a typesetter with a set of defined behavior. One of these can be created for each previous version of OS X, allowing the same layout to be generated as with older versions.

The typesetter is also responsible for inserting line breaks. This is one of the most important parts of any typesetting system. When I am writing this paragraph, the entire thing is a single line. I am using text editor with a simple, greedy, line-breaking strategy, so I see a line break at the first space before the word that overlaps with the width of the window. This looks quite ugly. When you read this, the same text will have been passed through the *Knuth-Plass line-breaking algorithm*. This uses a dynamic programming approach to find the optimal line break position. The difference between the two approaches is very obvious. In left-aligned text, the greedy algorithm will have lines with quite different lengths. In justified text, the size of spaces will be very different on subsequent lines. This makes reading the text quite tiring, even if it is not something you consciously notice.

In addition to choosing a gap between words for a line break, a typesetter can also insert hyphens when there is not a break in a sensible place. Doing this well is more difficult for English than for almost any other language. The rules for English allow a hyphen to be inserted between any pair of root words, or between a root word and a prefix or suffix, and finally between syllables. Since English takes common words from a relatively large number of other languages, detecting these automatically is very hard. The best algorithm for doing this to date is the *Knuth-Liang hyphenation algorithm*.

You might have noted that both of the typesetting algorithms I've mentioned are named after Donald Knuth. He was displeased with the output from existing typesetters in the 1970s, when working on *The Art of Computer Programming*, and took a few years out to fix it. Franklin Mark Liang was one of his PhD students during this time and developed the hyphenation algorithm used by Knuth's TeX typesetting system.

The hyphenation code in Apple's typesetter implementation is controlled via a hyphenation factor. This is a floating point value from 0 to 1 used to decide whether hyphenation should be attempted. By default, it is zero. Text Edit allows this to be toggled between two values, 0 and 0.9. The higher the value, the more the typesetter will favor hyphenated lines over ragged ones, with zero, hyphenation will be completely disabled. Figure 8.7 shows the same sentence typeset by Text Edit with hyphens enabled and disabled.

If this is enabled, then the typesetter can insert hyphens, specifically hyphen glyphs. This is an example of the case where the typesetter modifies the glyph stream. It may also do this at any other point, as may the layout manager. This is important, since it allows a custom typesetter to perform glyph substitutions. You might, for example, want a custom typesetter that inserted old-style s ligatures into your text in the letter combinations where they are valid.

Once a typesetter has found a line fragment that it thinks should be typeset in one time, it passes it to the layout manager. Each `NSTextContainer` represents a region in which text can be typeset. The default implementation is rectangular, although you can create subclasses representing other shapes. The main job of the text container is to implement this method:

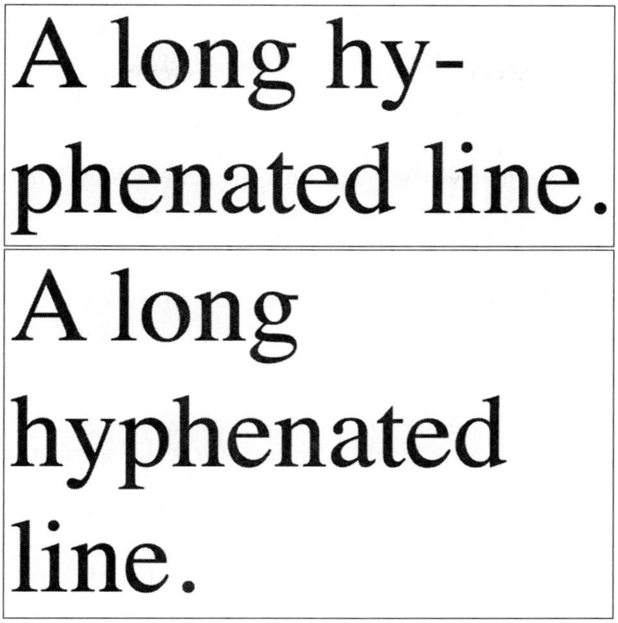

A long hy-
phenated line.

A long
hyphenated
line.

Figure 8.7: Automatic hyphenation in Cocoa.

```
- (NSRect)lineFragmentRectForProposedRect: (NSRect)proposedRect
                            sweepDirection: (NSLineSweepDirection)
                                sweepDirection
                         movementDirection:(NSLineMovementDirection)
                             movementDirection
                             remainingRect: (NSRectPointer)remainingRect;
```

This is called by the typesetter when it has a first approximation of a line. The proposed rectangle is where the typesetter wants to draw a line fragment. The next two arguments indicate the direction of characters in a line and the direction of line in a page (left to right and top to bottom, respectively, for English).

The text container then returns the largest rectangle that is within this text container. This can be done by trimming the right end of the rectangle for left-to-right reading order typesetters. If this will not result in any space, it can move it in the direction of lines, down for English. For example, the proposed rectangle might be off the top of the page. In this case, the container would move it down until it was entirely on the page, and trim it down if the right edge went over the right margin.

Some containers may have holes in the middle. A simple desktop publishing application, for example, would have figures placed at arbitrary locations and allow text to wrap around them. A proposed rectangle might contain regions on the left and right sides of the page where it's possible to put text. The text container would decompose this into three sections. The first rectangle would be returned and used for text. The second rectangle, the section that intersects with the object in the middle where no text is allowed, would be discarded. The final section, to the right of the gap, is a potential place to write additional text and so would be placed in the rectangle pointed to by the last argument. The typesetter should then try to insert the next region into this rectangle.

You will probably not want to implement your own typesetter. The one provided by Apple is very powerful and produces attractive output. You are much more likely to want to create `NSTextContainer` subclasses to support text wrapped to non-rectangular shapes.

The typesetter is responsible for laying out lines, but the overall shape of the page is defined by the layout manager. When the layout manager sends a sequence of glyphs to the typesetter, they must all be in the same paragraph. The style of this paragraph is defined by an `NSParagraphStyle` object. This contains a number of attributes, such as the line spacing, line height, indent, and tab positions.

Each paragraph is contained in a page. The shape of the page is defined by the layout manager itself, and includes attributes such as the location of the margins and so on.

8.6.3 Attachments

One extra complication in the text system comes from the fact that not everything in an attributed string is really a character. There is a special character, `NSAttachmentCharacter`, which does not map to a glyph. This is a placeholder meaning "some other kind of data" and is defined as the *object placement character* in unicode.

The attributes for this character must contain a key named `NSAttachmentAttributeName` mapping to an instance of the `NSTextAttachment` class. This attribute defines how the character will really be inserted. This contains a file wrapper pointing to the embedded file. If you loaded some text from an `.rtfd` bundle, then each of these will point to another file in the bundle. Additionally, it contains a cell implementing the `NSTextAttachmentCell` protocol.

The cell is responsible for drawing the attachment and handling mouse events. The default cell simply draws the file's icon, although you can substitute others that display the file's data.

When text is typeset containing the object placement character, the cell will be queried for its dimensions. This is used in place of a glyph's geometry when rendering text containing attachments.

This mechanism only allows for attachments to be rendered as part of the text. Most text layout systems allow for floating section as well. If you want to implement something like this, then you will need a custom subclass of `NSTextContainer` that reserves space for the attachment and ensures that the typesetter draws text around it. You will also need to provide some mechanism for getting these attachments and determining where to place them.

8.6.4 Text Views

Most of the time, when you want to display some text, you will use either an `NSTextField` or an `NSTextView`, depending on how complex the text is.

The `NSTextField` view is a simple wrapper around an `NSTextCell` and should be used for simple text drawing. The most common uses for this are labels and fields in a form. This is traditionally only used for single-line text boxes, although it does support line wrapping. In the last section we saw how to draw a simple text string using a cell. The text field class is implemented in a similar way, although it supports editing as well, while the simple example view ignored all incoming events.

For more complex text, you should use `NSTextView`. This class is the main interface to the Cocoa text system. When you create one, you will also get a text storage object and a layout manager created. This makes implementing text editing very easy. The view creates all of the objects you need to interface with the text system. Sometimes, however, it is desirable to create this hierarchy manually.

When you create a text view in Interface Builder, you get a lot of objects. On the view side, you will get a scroll view and two scroll bars surrounding the text view itself. Often it is convenient to add a text view outside of the scroll view. Unfortunately, Interface Builder tends to assume that this isn't what you want and will sometimes prevent you from doing it. It does allow you to create text views outside of a window, however, so you can create the view like this and then insert it into the view hierarchy in code later.

As well as the scroll view, you will get a text container, a layout manager, and a text storage object created. These are all required for the view to function. Each view must have a text container that represents the drawable region inside it. Although these objects always come as a pair, layout managers and text storage objects can have several views associated with them, so the view will not always need a unique one. We'll take a look at how to use several views on the same text model later on in this chapter.

If you want to implement a simple (rich) text editor, you can just drag a text view into your document window and add a call to the text storage object's methods for creating and loading `.rtfd` files.

8.6.5 Text Cells

If you are rendering a small amount of text in your own view, then you will typically want to keel an `NSCell` around to help you. This is a simple object that allows an attributed string to be drawn as a specified location in a view.

If you need to provide the ability to edit text in your view, you can still do this via text cells. Every window has a lazily created `NSTextView` instance associated with it called the *field editor*. This is used to provide text editing capabilities to cells. Only one cell per window can be using the field editor at any given time. This is not a limitation, since only one view can be first responder at a given time.

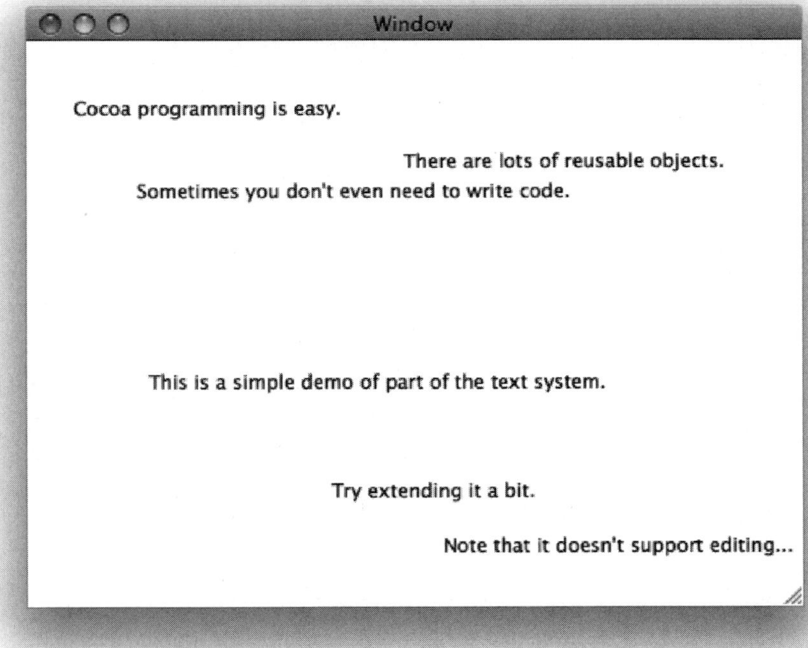

Figure 8.8: The click text example.

The field editor is implicitly added as a subview of the view that owns the cell and performs editing.

We will write a simple example using this, which lets you write text anywhere in a window. The final result is shown in Figure 8.8.

The view will store the text in an array. In a proper view object, you would delegate the storage to some kind of data source object. Later, you might want to try extending this view to support using a data source.

The view's interface is shown in Listing 8.4. This contains three instance variables: an array of text clippings, the location of the current text clipping, and a cell used for drawing.

Listing 8.4: The click text view interface. [from: examples/ClickText/ClickTextView.h]

```
#import <Cocoa/Cocoa.h>

@interface ClickTextView : NSView {
    NSMutableArray *texts;
    NSPoint currentLocation;
    NSCell *cell;
}
@end
```

The implementation of this class is shown in Listing 8.5. The first thing to notice is the private class defined on lines 3–21. This is being used in much the same way as a C **struct**. The difference is that this knows its type (so it's easier to debug) and it can be stored Foundation collections, specifically the `NSMutableArray` instance variable of the view.

Listing 8.5: The click text view implementation. [from: examples/ClickText/ClickTextView.h]

```
1  #import "ClickTextView.h"
2
3  @interface TextClip : NSObject {
4  @public
5      NSString *text;
6      NSPoint location;
7  }
8  @end
9  @implementation TextClip
10 - (NSString*) description
11 {
12     return [NSString stringWithFormat:@"clip␣(%@)␣at␣%@",
13            text,
14            NSStringFromPoint(location)];
15 }
```

```
- (void) dealloc
{
    [text release];
    [super dealloc];
}
@end

@implementation ClickTextView
- (void) awakeFromNib
{
    texts = [[NSMutableArray alloc] init];
    cell = [[NSTextFieldCell alloc] initTextCell:@""];
    [cell setEditable:YES];
    [cell setShowsFirstResponder:YES];
}
- (void)mouseDown:(NSEvent *)theEvent
{
    currentLocation = [self convertPoint:[theEvent locationInWindow]
                                fromView:nil];
    NSText *fieldEditor = [[self window] fieldEditor:YES
                                           forObject:self];
    [cell endEditing:fieldEditor];
    [fieldEditor setString:@""];
    [cell setStringValue:@""];
    NSRect frame = {currentLocation, {400, 30}};
    [cell editWithFrame:frame
                 inView:self
                 editor:fieldEditor
               delegate:self
                  event:theEvent];
}
- (BOOL) isFlipped
{
    return YES;
}
- (void)drawRect:(NSRect)rect
{
    NSRect frame = rect;
    [[NSColor whiteColor] set];
    [NSBezierPath fillRect:rect];
    for (TextClip *clip in texts)
    {
        [cell setStringValue:clip->text];
        frame.origin=clip->location;
```

```
60          [cell drawWithFrame:frame inView:self];
61      }
62  }
63  - (void) textDidEndEditing: (NSNotification *)aNotification
64  {
65      NSText *text = [aNotification object];
66      TextClip *clip = [[TextClip alloc] init];
67      clip->text = [[text string] copy];
68      clip->location = currentLocation;
69      [texts addObject:clip];
70      [clip release];
71
72      [cell endEditing:text];
73      [self setNeedsDisplay:YES];
74  }
75  - (void) dealloc
76  {
77      [texts release];
78      [cell release];
79      [super dealloc];
80  }
81  @end
```

This, like many views, does two things. It responds to events and it draws data. We'll look at the drawing component first. This is found on lines 51–62. The first thing the drawing method does is clear the background. This is done using `NSColor` to set the color of the current *graphics context* to white, and then using `NSBezierPath` to draw a rectangle in this color.

Note that the dimensions of the rectangle drawn are defined by the region needing redisplay, rather than the region covered by the view. This is a small efficiency saving, rather offset by the fact that the view doesn't check whether the text clips it draws are inside the rectangle, and so still does the expensive operation even when it's not needed. You could try storing the dimensions of each rendered text clip the first time you draw it and then only draw it again if it is in the updated rectangle.

After setting the background, this method iterates over every clip in the array, in the loop that starts on line 56. The same `NSCell` is used to draw every single string, simply by setting the value. You could also draw attributed strings in the same way using the `-setAttributedString:` method instead. The cell doesn't maintain its own coordinate transform, so it needs to know which view to draw in and where in this view to draw. The rectangle passed here only specifies the space the cell can use, not the space it must fill, so we can get away with giving it a large size in the correct location.

This is all you need to draw text in a view using a single cell. You can even share the cell between different views, if you have a cluster of related ones; although since cells are only a few dozen bytes this isn't much of a saving.

Editing is slightly trickier. When this view receives a mouse down event, it goes into editing mode for a new text clip. The first thing it does is find the location of the click, in the current coordinate space. This is done on lines 33–34 and requires transforming them from the window's space. These coordinates are then stored. Later, when we have finished editing, we will use them to construct the text clip.

The next thing it needs to do is get a reference to the field editor. This is requested from the window. By default this is an `NSTextView` instance, although `NSWindow` subclasses are free to override this method and provide a custom implementation. Line 37 tells the cell to get out of editing mode if we clicked somewhere without ending editing properly. This is fine for an example, but it's not a very clean way of exiting editing.

There are two places where the field editor can get initial text, from its own text storage object or from the cell. If these two don't match you get some very strange behavior. Finally, we tell the cell to run the field editor. This draws it in the specified frame, in the given view. The delegate will receive all of the standard `NSTextView` delegate messages. The only one of these we handle in this example is the one received when editing is finished. This is handled on line 63.

When the field editor exits, we need to create a new clipping. Note that on line 67 we copy, rather than retain, the field editor's string value. This is because it will return a mutable string that will be reused the next time it is needed. Often, this value does not need to persist for longer than the field editor invocation. If you enter a value in a view connected to a data source then it is likely that a *value transformer* will turn the value into some other form and so there is no need for the field editor to provide a copy of the string to everyone who wants one. The new clip is then added to the array and the view is told that it needs redisplaying.

This example can be expanded a lot. Not all of the delegate methods are implemented, the view doesn't allow editing of existing text snippets, and drawing is highly sub-optimal. It does, however, demonstrate the use of cells in drawing text.

If you want to be able to edit existing text, you will first need to find which drawn clipping the mouse click intersected with. The cell, being stateless with respect to drawing, can't help you here. You will need to track the regions it draws on and then use `NSMouseInRect()` to find out which one it is. You will then need to set up the field editor for the existing string and modify the string in the new place.

If you sent the cell a `-cellSize` message, it will tell you how much space is needed to draw it. You can modify the clipping to store an `NSRect` instead of the point it currently stores, with the size being the result of this call. This can be used to find the clipping that intersects with the mouse and also to optimize the drawing code by calling `NSIntersectsRect()` with the argument of `-drawRect:` to see if the clip needs drawing.

We will look at using cells for drawing in a bit more detail in Chapter 13. A variety of different cell types are available in Cocoa, including images and buttons, as well as the text cells that we have seen in this section.

8.7 Writing a Custom Text Container

One of the most common ways of customizing the text system is to add new text containers. These allow all of the normal text system components to be used to lay out text in non-rectangular spaces.

In this example, we will write a simple text container that lays out text in a wheel shape, a circle with a circular hole in the middle. This provides an example of clipping both the outside and the inside of a text region and so can be generalized to any desired shape. The final result can be seen in Figure 8.9.

To demonstrate this class, we create a window with an `NSTextView` in it and a new menu item to toggle the container. The implementation of the action connected to this menu item is in Listing 8.6.

Listing 8.6: The controller for the text wheel demo. [from: examples/TextWheel/WheelController.m]

```
- (IBAction) toggleLayout:(id)sender
{
    NSTextContainer *oldContainer = [view textContainer];
    Class newContainerClass;
    if ([oldContainer isKindOfClass:[WheelLayout class]])
    {
        newContainerClass = [NSTextContainer class];
    }
    else
    {
        newContainerClass = [WheelLayout class];
    }
    NSTextContainer *newContainer = [[newContainerClass alloc] init];
    [newContainer setHeightTracksTextView:YES];
    [newContainer setWidthTracksTextView:YES];
    [view replaceTextContainer:newContainer];
    [newContainer release];
}
```

This demonstrates a few nice features of Objective-C. The first is introspection, on line 9, where we check whether the existing container is an instance of our new class or not. Since a **Class** is a type in Objective-C, the conditional can just get a pointer to the class we want to instantiate. The code afterward is exactly the same code you would use to instantiate a text container statically, only this time the container class is a variable instead of a constant.

The new container is instantiated on line 17 and added to the text view on line 20. This replaces the existing text container but maintains the mappings between the text view, layout manager, and text storage objects. Before adding it, we set a couple of flags to indicate that the size of the container should change when the size of the view changes. This is most commonly used for simple screen-only text views. If you are planning to print the contents of the view, then you probably want the text container's size fixed relative to the page, rather than the view.

The new container itself is shown in Listing 8.7. This is a fairly simple subclass of `NSTextContainer`, implementing the two methods that almost every subclass needs to.

Listing 8.7: The wheel-shaped text container. [from: examples/TextWheel/WheelLayout.m]

```
#import "WheelLayout.h"

@implementation WheelLayout
@synthesize holeSize;
- (id) init
{
    if (nil == (self=[super init])) { return nil; }
    holeSize = 50;
    return self;
}

- (NSRect)lineFragmentRectForProposedRect:(NSRect)proposedRect
                          sweepDirection:(NSLineSweepDirection)
                              sweepDirection
                       movementDirection:(NSLineMovementDirection)
                           movementDirection
                           remainingRect:(NSRectPointer)remainingRect
{
    NSSize containerSize = [self containerSize];
    // First trim the proposed rectangle to the container
    NSRect rect =
        [super lineFragmentRectForProposedRect:proposedRect
                               sweepDirection:sweepDirection
                            movementDirection:movementDirection
                                remainingRect:remainingRect];
```

```
24     // Now trim it to the rectangle to the width of the circle
25     CGFloat radius = fmin(containerSize.width, containerSize.height) / 2.0;
26     CGFloat y = fabs((rect.origin.y + rect.size.height / 2.0) - radius);
27     CGFloat lineWidth = 2 * sqrt(radius * radius - y * y);
28 
29     NSRect circleRect =
30         NSMakeRect(rect.origin.x + radius - lineWidth / 2.0,
31                    rect.origin.y,
32                    lineWidth,
33                    rect.size.height);
34     if (y < holeSize)
35     {
36         CGFloat right = circleRect.origin.x + circleRect.size.width;
37         circleRect.size.width /= 2;
38         CGFloat holeWidth =  sqrt(holeSize * holeSize - y * y);
39         circleRect.size.width -= holeWidth;
40         if (remainingRect != NULL && circleRect.origin.x < radius)
41         {
42             *remainingRect = circleRect;
43             remainingRect->origin.x = right - circleRect.size.width;
44         }
45     }
46     return circleRect;
47 }
48 
49 - (BOOL)isSimpleRectangularTextContainer
50 {
51     return NO;
52 }
53 @end
```

The method on line 51 indicates that the typesetter must actually call this layout manager with proposed rectangles. If it had returned **YES** here, then the typesetter could simply use its internal code for rendering in a rectangle, which saves a lot of message sends and so is faster. A generalized version of this class, representing an arbitrary layout with an external clipping region and holes in the middle, would return a variable here, returning **YES** if there were not holes and the clipping region was a rectangle.

The real body of the implementation begins on line 12. This is the method that is responsible for clipping a proposed rectangle to the wheel. The first thing this does is call the superclass implementation (lines 19-23). This clips the proposed rectangle to the bounds of the container, which is a good first approximation. We now need to do two things: trim the edges and trim the middle.

Lines 25–33 trim the edges of the rectangle. The first calculate the width of a line of text at the specified distance from the center of the circle and then construct a rectangle to match it. For some lines, this is all you need to do.

If the distance from the center of the circle is less than the size of the hole, then the line needs chopping in the middle. This is a two-step process and depends on where the region being tested is.

If the proposed rectangle starts to the left of the hole, then we just need to crop the right edge. This is done by dividing the width in half and removing space for the hole. This, alone, is enough to make a circle with a slice taken out of it. To

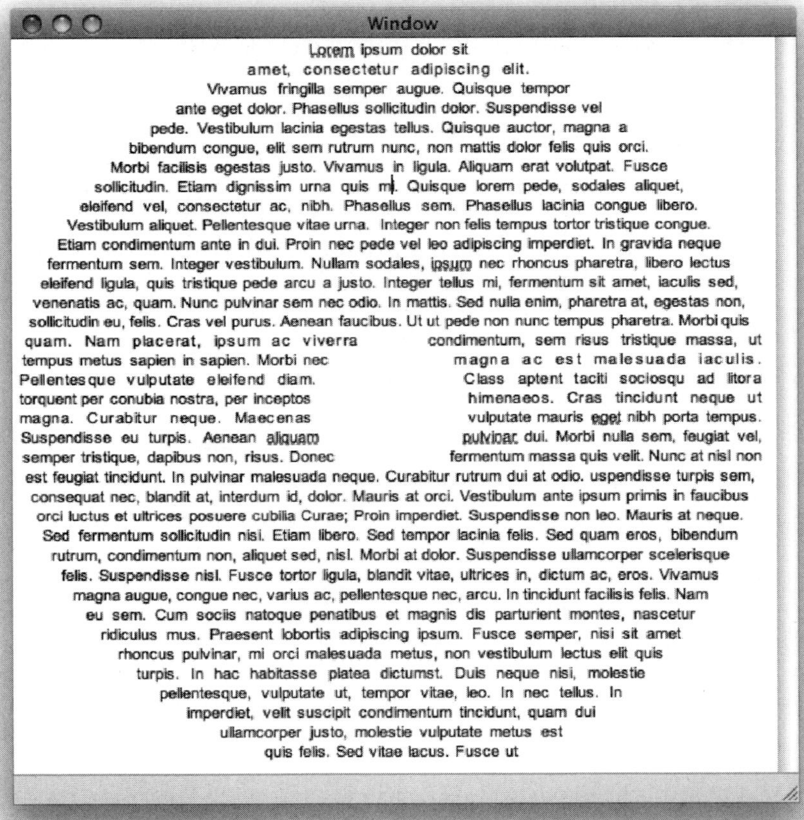

Figure 8.9: A wheel of text in a custom layout manager.

have text drawn on the right side of the hole, we also need to tell the typesetter that it is allowed to draw there. We do this by filling in the `remainingRect` structure, in lines 42 and 43. This is almost the same as the cropped rectangle—the width, height, and y-coordinate, are all the same—but has a different start location.

Returning this rectangle works, and the text is displayed properly in the wheel. This is not quite a full implementation, however, since it will only work for languages with the same reading order as English. Try extending it to support other values for `sweepDirection` and `movementDirection`.

8.8 Using Multiple Text Views

Often you can get a similar result to writing a custom layout manager simply by using more than one. Each text storage object can have as many different layout managers as you want, each providing a different view of the text. Layout managers can similarly have lots of text containers.

Figure 8.10 shows how all of these connect together. We will assemble a simple application that follows this arrangement. There will be a single text storage object with two layout managers. This corresponds to a word processor where you might have a structural and a typeset view on the same document. One would be used for quickly entering text, while the other would show the final version. Since they are both connected to the same storage object, you can edit either and have the others updated automatically.

One of the layout managers will represent the structural view, and just use a single text container in a single text view to display all of the text. The other will have several different views, all showing parts of the document. You can see the final result in Figure 8.11.

Implementing this is surprisingly simple. We will start with a nib file containing a horizontal split view. In the top we will put a vertical split view and in the bottom a text view. Both of these are connected to a controller object via outlets. We will also add a menu item and connect it to an action in our controller. This will be used for adding columns dynamically.

The implementation of the controller is shown in Listing 8.8. This contains two methods: one to initialize its state after being instantiated from a nib, and the other to add columns.

When the nib is loaded and the bottom text view created, we get a text container, a layout manager, and a text storage object all created automatically. Since we want our top views all using the same text storage object as the bottom one, we first get a pointer to the store and then create a new layout manager pointing to it. On line 24, we register the new layout manager with the text

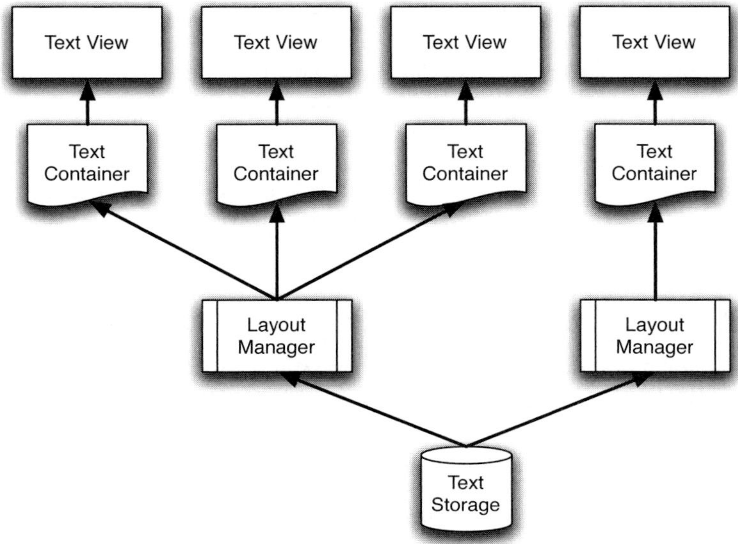

Figure 8.10: The text system arrangement.

storage object. This allows it to be notified of any changes to the store, so when one text view updates the text all of the attached layout managers will be updated.

Note that on line 25 we release the new layout manager after assigning it to the text storage. The arrows in Figure 8.10 show which object retains which other objects. Although the objects toward the top maintain references to the objects lower down, they do not retain them, and so you should take care that you always release references going down this tree. Normally you will not retain references to anything other than the text storage object, and will release this when you want to release the whole tree.

The action method is responsible for creating the new columns. At the start, the window will contain two, but extra ones can be added at run time. Each new view needs a new text container. On line 9 we create one with the bounds of the split view. This is a rough first-approximation, and will be inaccurate for any but the first column. Fortunately, when we add the view as a child of the split view it will be automatically resized. Lines 10 and 11 tell the text container to automatically resize itself when this happens. This also allows the columns to be resized by the user.

Once the container is created, it is associated with the layout manager and

Listing 8.8: The multi-text controller implementation. [from: examples/MultiText/-TextViewController.m]

```
#import "TextViewController.h"


@implementation TextViewController
- (IBAction) addColumn:(id)sender
{
    NSRect frame = [columnView frame];
    NSTextContainer *container =
        [[NSTextContainer alloc] initWithContainerSize:frame.size];
    [container setHeightTracksTextView:YES];
    [container setWidthTracksTextView:YES];
    [secondLayout addTextContainer:container];
    [container release];
    NSTextView *newView = [[NSTextView alloc] initWithFrame:frame
                                              textContainer:container];
    [columnView addSubview:newView];
    [newView release];
}
- (void)awakeFromNib
{
    // Get the store
    NSTextStorage *storage = [bottomView textStorage];
    // Add a second layout manager
    secondLayout = [[NSLayoutManager alloc] init];
    [storage addLayoutManager:secondLayout];
    [secondLayout release];

    // Create the columns
    [self addColumn:self];
    [self addColumn:self];
}
@end
```

released. The release is needed because it is now retained by the layout manager and it would leak if we didn't balance the `+alloc` with a `-release`.

The last three lines of this method creates the new view, associated with the text container, and adds it to the text container. When we run this code, we are presented by a window similar to the one in Figure 8.11. Initially it only has two columns at the top, but additional ones can be added from the Format menu.

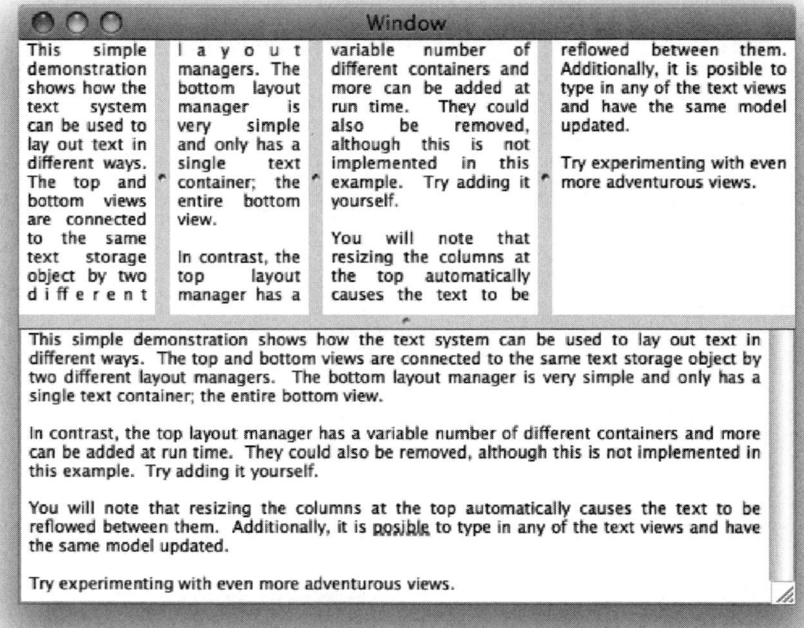

Figure 8.11: Running the multi-text example.

You can use exactly the same pattern as this for a simple desktop publishing application. Rather than putting the new text views in a simple split view, you would allow the user to place them in arbitrary positions. These would then automatically re-flow the text between them. If you also add the ability to insert image views into the parent view, then you can create some quite complex documents with only a very small amount of code. Cocoa already allows you to save RTF text and images in a variety of formats, so all you would need to do is define a bundle format that stores them and output a property list containing the locations of all of the embedded views.

8.9 Summary

The Cocoa text system is an incredibly powerful and complex piece of software. We have seen how the principal classes fit together and how they can be extended to provide custom functionality.

Most of the time, you will not have to construct the text system manually; you will simply create an `NSTextView` in a nib file and rely on it to instantiate the rest of the system. We saw how to combine this approach with manual creation of the text system, so a single model was connected to several different views.

Part III

Cocoa Documents

Chapter 9

Creating Document-Driven Applications

Most user interface toolkits divide applications into *document-driven applications* and all other applications. Documents are some form of user state that is (usually) editable and often maps to a file. The key feature of a document-driven application is that it can have several copies of a set of objects that correspond directly to something that the user thinks of as a document.

The classical example of a document-driven application is a text editor, an application that provides multiple windows, each showing a representation of a text file. A more unusual example would be a web browser. Although the user rarely edits or saves its documents, each browsing session (either a window or a tab) can be considered a document. The browser stores data about the session, such as the history, often persistently, and presents multiple copies of the same interface to the user.

Other applications are harder to categorize. Something like Apple's Garage Band might be thought of as a document-driven application, since it presents a studio editing UI representing an on-disk project. It only presents one instance of the UI at once, however, making it more of an appliance-like application. The simplest example of this kind of application is the calculator.

Both types of application have their uses. The parts of Cocoa we've already looked at contain a lot of useful tools for creating document-driven applications, even though nothing we've done yet has been specific to them. In particular, the nib system is incredibly useful for documents.

The Outliner example from Chapter 6 was a document-driven application, although at the time we ignored this. It had a nib file for each document, which contained the views and skeleton models for generating the document.

Although we wrote no code specific to creating documents in the outliner, we could create several documents, as shown in Figure 9.1, without doing anything special. The skeleton document-driven application specified the name of the nib representing a document and `NSDocument` handled instantiating a new copy of this every time we needed a new document.

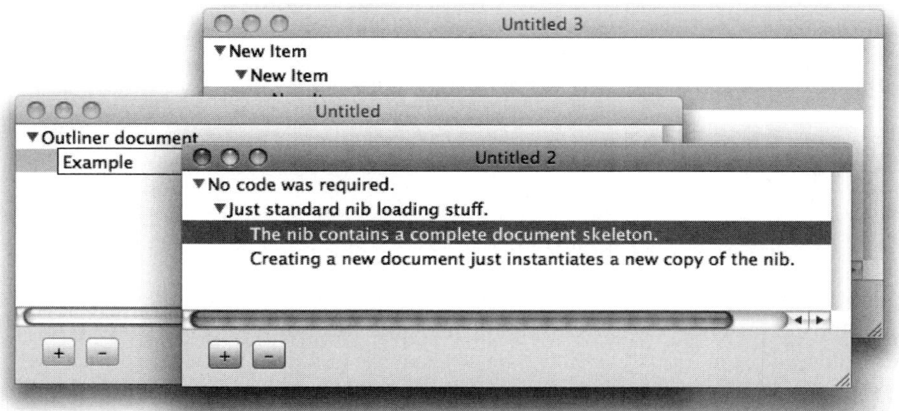

Figure 9.1: Multiple outliner documents.

In this chapter, we'll look at what went on behind the scenes to make all of that work, and how to fill in the missing parts of the outliner to make it into a full-fledged document-driven application.

9.1 The Cocoa Document Model

The document system in Cocoa is built around the `NSDocument` class. Each document-driven application will have a subclass of this, implementing the document model. This is responsible for loading and saving the document and for creating all of the user interface components required to interact with it.

Most complex document-driven applications will provide one or more window controllers, instances of `NSWindowController` or a custom subclass, which are responsible for managing the windows. A simple document only needs one window for representing the document, although there might be some floating panels for modifying it.

The easiest class in the document system to forget about is NSDocumentController. Subclassing this is rare. Most of the time you will just use the default instance that you get for free along with a document-driven application.

In the outliner example, when we selected the New item from the File menu, it was an instance of NSDocumentController that handled the resulting action message. This then created an instance of the **OutlineDocument** class, looked up the nib that this class used, and instantiated a new copy of it with the new document object as its owner.

The document controller is responsible for tracking all of the open documents. When you open or create a new document, you will typically go through this object. It is also responsible for a number of related user-interface book-keeping tasks. These include

- Handling the action messages from New and Open menu items, including displaying the modal Open dialog.
- Creating new document objects when opening a file, from any source, by instantiating the correct NSDocument subclass.
- Updating the recent items submenu.
- Tracking whether the application has unsaved data (used to see if it can quit without prompting the user).

Occasionally you will want to modify some of this behavior and will create an NSDocumentController subclass for your document-driven application. A more common reason for subclassing is to use some of this in an application that does not use NSDocument. In particular, you might want the recent documents menu handling without any of the other standard document handling code. Even this is quite unusual though, and should not be attempted by novice Cocoa programmers.

9.1.1 File Types

A single document-driven application can support as many types of documents as it wants. The Info.plist file in the application bundle is a *property list* that contains a list of the document types that the applications supports, in the CFBundleDocumentTypes key. Listing 9.1 shows an extract from this dictionary for the Preview application that comes with OS X.

This contains a lot of different information. You can see from the NSDocumentClass elements in both dictionaries that this application contains (at

Listing 9.1: An extract from Preview.app's Info.plist. [from: /Applications/Preview.app/Contents/Info.plist]

```
        <dict>
            <key>CFBundleTypeIconFile</key>
            <string>eps.icns</string>
            <key>CFBundleTypeRole</key>
            <string>Viewer</string>
            <key>LSIsAppleDefaultForType</key>
            <true/>
            <key>LSItemContentTypes</key>
            <array>
                <string>com.adobe.encapsulated-postscript</string>
            </array>
            <key>NSDocumentClass</key>
            <string>PVDocument</string>
        </dict>
        <dict>
            <key>CFBundleTypeIconFile</key>
            <string>tiff.icns</string>
            <key>CFBundleTypeRole</key>
            <string>Editor</string>
            <key>LSIsAppleDefaultForType</key>
            <true/>
            <key>LSItemContentTypes</key>
            <array>
                <string>public.tiff</string>
            </array>
            <key>NSDocumentClass</key>
            <string>PVDocument</string>
        </dict>
```

least) two `NSDocument` subclasses. The `PVImageDocument` represents image documents while the `PVPDFDocument` is for PDF-like documents, including postscript. This dictionary also contains the icon to be used for documents of this type, and the rôle of the application—either an editor or a viewer—when it opens the file.

Some of these keys are for use by *Launch Services* (*LS*) and have the corresponding prefix. In particular, not the `LSItemContentTypes` key. This contains the *Uniform Type Identifier* (*UTI*) for this type. This is a hierarchical type string representing a kind of document. UTIs help unify the possible sources of file type information.

On MacOS Classic, there were two kinds of file type information. HFS stored two 32-bit values: a type, and creator code. These were typically rendered as four 8-bit characters, although this was not required. The type indicated the type of the file, and the creator code indicated which application should be used to edit it.

This was not ideal, since it could not be stored on non-HFS filesystems easily. In particular, files coming from MS DOS and Windows systems did not contain type and creator codes. On these systems, a three-character file extension was used to identify file types.

In the 1990s, the Internet grew more common and *Multipurpose Internet Mail Extensions* (*MIME*) types became a common way of identifying files being transferred between systems. These are used by Internet email and by the web for informing the client of the type of a file.

The UTI mechanism provides a unified way of dealing with all of these. The system maintains mappings from file extensions, HFS type codes, and MIME types, to UTIs. UTIs support multiple inheritance and can contain a lot of information about a type in this hierarchy. Figure 9.2 shows the UTI hierarchy for an application bundle on OS X. Knowing nothing else about the type, this hierarchy would allow you to see that this is a kind of executable and that it is a kind of directory. You might try running it—or warning the user that it's potentially unsafe—or looking inside it.

Note that there are two top-level hierarchies here. The public prefix is used for types that are not associated with any specific company. This namespace is reserved for Apple to use. Others here are Apple-specific. These are stored in reverse-DNS format, so Apple uses com.apple, while an open source project might use org.project-name. We saw both kinds in the snippet from Preview's property list, a public type and one defined by Adobe.

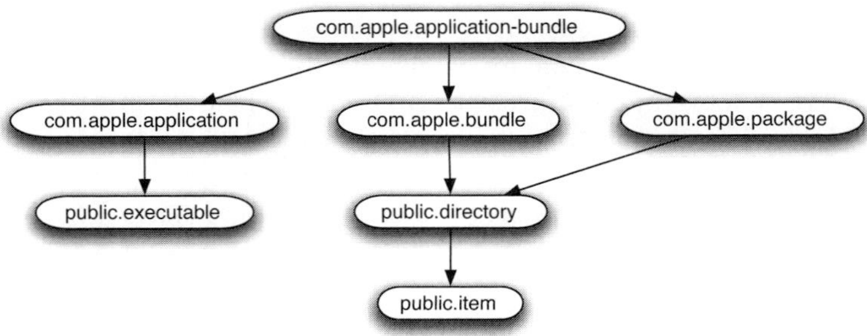

Figure 9.2: The UTI hierarchy for an application bundle.

UTIs are relatively new; they were introduced with 10.3 and greatly expanded in 10.4. If you are creating a new application, you should use them from the start. If you use any of the large selection of UTIs that are provided by the system, then you don't have to worry about file extensions or MIME types.

You still have to worry about saving and loading your file. For some common image and (rich) text formats, you can create `NSTextStorage` or `NSImage` instances directly from the file. Others you will need to parse yourself, often with the aid of a third-party library.

9.1.2 Document Objects

Although the document controller handles a lot of the generic behavior for this kind of application, it delegates a lot to the document objects referenced in the Info.plist file. Every application that uses the Cocoa document architecture will include at least one `NSDocument` subclass.

At a minimum, this is responsible for loading and saving files from disk. The Outliner example just had a skeleton method for doing this that raised a not-implemented error. In this chapter, we will expand the example to provide loading and saving of our outlines.

Loading and saving are implemented in a three-tier system. The core methods load and save a document from data objects. These are wrapped by methods that load and save to files, which, in turn, are wrapped by those that deal with URLs. For simple documents, you only need to implement the first of these and allow the default implementation in `NSDocument` to handle all of the file and URL I/O for you. A more complex document may need saving to a bundle, rather than a single file. In this case you will need to implement the methods for saving and loading into files. The default implementation for URLs saves to a file and then copies the result.

The other main responsibility of the document object is creating the window controllers. These are responsible for managing the windows associated with the document. We've looked at `NSWindowController` a bit before, but it is most useful when used in conjunction with a document object.

Window controllers are responsible for a number of aspects of a window that work better in collaboration with a document. One particular example is closing the window. When you try to close a window that is part of a document-driven application, then you may also be closing the document. This depends largely on how many windows there are for the document. Even if a document allows several views on it to be open at once, one may be considered the main one and close the document when it is closed. This is the case in some word processors, for example, which allow outline summaries of the document in secondary windows.

Alternatively, closing a window might be interrupted by the document, to prevent unsaved data being lost.

9.2 Creating the Application Skeleton

A document-driven Cocoa application is one of the projects that you can create when you create a new project in XCode. When you create one, you will be presented with a skeleton project looking something like Figure 9.3.

This contains a lot of things that you won't touch. The four frameworks are the standard ones for this kind of application. We've discussed AppKit and Foundation before. Cocoa is a simple umbrella that wraps both, allowing you to just include a single header for everything in your files. The *Core Data* framework is important, but we will ignore it for now and look at it in more detail in the next chapter. As before, main.m is a simple stub that jumps into the AppKit code for creating and starting the application. The .pch file is a precompiled header, which saves you from having to parse the massive amount of text found in framework headers every time you recompile.

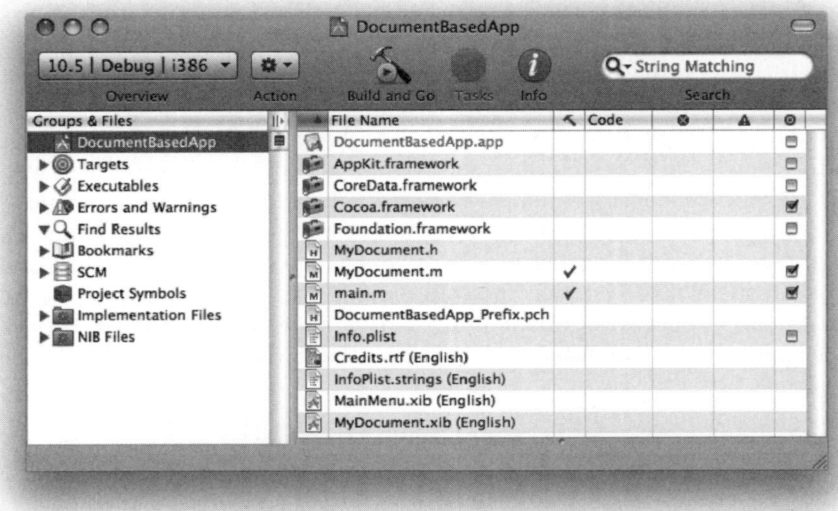

Figure 9.3: A new document-driven application project.

The other remaining entries are important. MainMenu.nib is found in every Cocoa application, whether document-driven or not, and contains the menu and any windows that are created once per application. The other nib, MyDocument.nib, is instantiated once per document. This should contain the document window and any other objects that are needed for it. This doesn't usually include floating palettes. Most of the time these are per-application, not per-document, so they go in MainMenu.nib and send action messages to the first responder proxy. This allows them to modify the current document.

You will probably want to rename MyDocument.nib to something a bit more sensible. The matching MyDocument.h and MyDocument.m files contain a skeleton `NSDocument` subclass. If you rename the document nib file, you need to update the reference to it in the implementation file. By default, you will find this method:

```
- (NSString*)windowNibName
{
    return @"MyDocument";
}
```

The document controller uses this to identify the nib file for this document type when creating a new document. You will probably also want to modify the name of the document class, since `MyDocument` is not very informative. As well as modifying this in the header and implementation files, you also need to update Info.plist. As discussed earlier, this contains a list of classes used for different document types. It also contains a lot of other information about the application. Figure 9.4 shows the default values in XCode's property list editor.

As well as changing the class used for the document type, you probably also want to change the type information. While you are here, you might want to change the bundle identifier—unless you are working on a commercial project and your employer is mycompany—but most of the other information can be left as it is. If you add support for other file types, don't forget to update this file.

The Credits.rtf file contains the information that will be automatically displayed in the application's about box. It is a good idea to change this if you are distributing your application, since the default contents does not look very professional.

If you compile and run this project, you will get the simplest possible document-driven application. It won't be able to open or save anything, and its documents will be empty windows, but all of the infrastructure is in place.

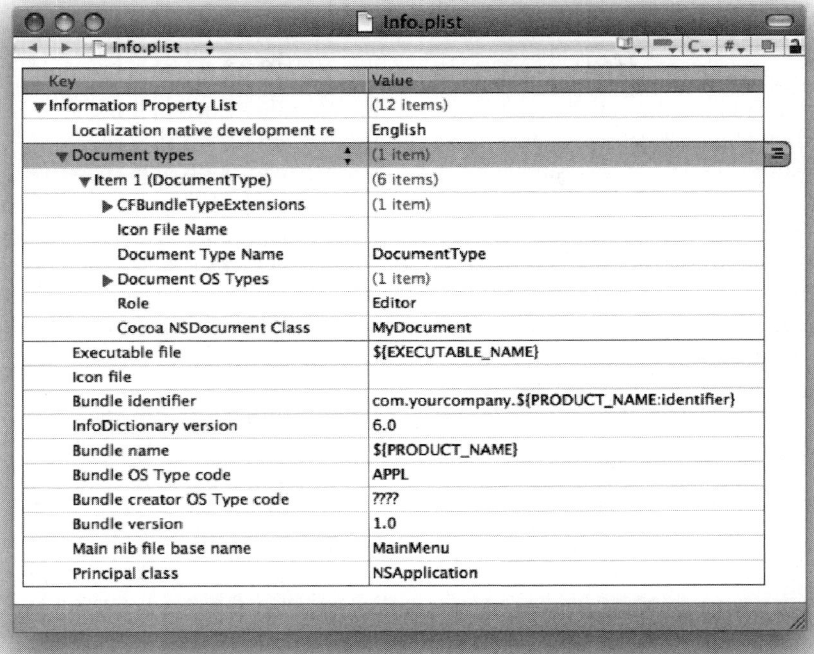

Figure 9.4: A new info property list for a document-driven application.

9.3 Creating the Document

The skeleton document-driven application contains a simple `NSDocument` subclass. This implements some stub methods that you should extend to create a real document.

9.3.1 Loading the Windows

We've looked at one of these already, the `-windowNibName` method that tells the document controller which nib file it should load. This is only used for documents that are represented by a single window. Remember that `NSWindowController` is closely integrated with the document system. When the document controller creates a new document, it calls -makeWindowControllers.

For a nib containing a single window, you will have a single window controller and NSDocument can set this up for you. For more complex documents, you might have multiple windows in a single nib or multiple nibs. Supporting these requires overriding the -makeWindowControllers method.

It would be nice if we could see exactly what needs to be done here by looking at the Cocoa source, but unfortunately this is impossible. The next best thing is to look at the implementation provided by GNUstep. This is often a good way of understanding how Cocoa classes work. The implementations won't be exactly the same, but you will see at least one way of implementing the functionality you see in the documentation. Listing 9.2 shows the important part of the method. There is also an **else** clause after this that throws an exception.

Listing 9.2: A extract from GNUstep's document class.

```
NSString *name = [self windowNibName];

if (name != nil && [name length] > 0)
  {
    NSWindowController *controller;

    controller = [[NSWindowController alloc] initWithWindowNibName: name
                                                              owner: self];
    [self addWindowController: controller];
    RELEASE(controller);
  }
```

The first thing, as you might expect, is a call to -windowNibName. If you are overriding this method it is because a single nib containing a single window controller is not sufficient, so you won't want to call this method yourself. The important bit is inside the inner block. First, a controller is created and used to load a nib. Then it is passed to the -addWindowController: method in NSDocument. The controller is then released. (GNUstep uses a macro for this so it can be turned off when compiled with garbage collection.) Adding the window controller ensures that NSDocument has a reference to it, and so the reference caused by allocating it with +alloc can be discarded.

When you implement this method yourself, you need to create the window controllers and call -addWindowController: yourself on each one. If they are all in separate nibs, then you can create each of them this way. If you want to put more than one window controller in a nib, then you will use a subclass of NSWindowController as the owner of the nib and ensure that it has outlets connected to the others. This is only required if you want to connect the windows closely to each other, which is usually a bad idea. More commonly, you will have separate nib files, one for each window, and have them only interact with each other via the model object.

9.3.2 Building the Document Model

Every `NSDocument` subclass is meant to represent a single document. It is the model object in the *model-view-controller* (*MVC*) pattern. As we saw in Chapter 6, you often don't need to write controllers in Cocoa, and most of the view objects will be standard ones loaded from your nib files. This means that the model object is the single most important part of your project.

The most important feature of a model object is its state. Every model object has to store some data. In Objective-C, this translates to instance variables. Typically, a document model object will be quite large. The document class in TextEdit, for example, has over twenty instance variables and several dozen accessor methods for them.

When you define a new document class, one of the first things you will want to do is define some instance variables for storing the document. In the Outliner example, the first version defined a single instance variable for storing the root object. In the second version we cheated slightly and moved it into the nib file. In this version, the document itself wasn't responsible for managing the model. This only worked because this was a very simple document type and we weren't using the document system very much. In particular, if you tried to close an outliner window it would close immediately. In a proper application it should only do this if the document has been saved.

9.3.3 Loading and Saving Documents

The most important aspect of documents when compared to other kinds of model object is persistence. A document, by definition, is something that the user cares about and so should generally last longer than a single invocation of the program.

You have three options for implementing these. The skeleton document object provides stub implementations for two methods:

```
- (NSData*)dataOfType: (NSString*)typeName
                error: (NSError**)outError;
- (BOOL)readFromData: (NSData*)data
              ofType: (NSString*)typeName
               error: (NSError**)outError;
```

As is common in post-10.3 Cocoa methods, the last parameter is a pointer to an error object that should be set if the operation fails. The stub implementations contain something like this, which sets a not-implemented error when either method is called:

```
if (outError != NULL)
{
    *outError = [NSError errorWithDomain: NSOSStatusErrorDomain
                                     code: unimpErr
                                 userInfo: NULL];
}
```

In spite of setting the error, the default implementation of `-readFromData:ofType:error:` returns **YES**. In a real implementation, you should return **NO** if loading fails. The stub returns **YES** so that you won't need to change it when you have implemented proper loading.

These methods are responsible for transforming between instances of your document class and `NSData` instances. The type parameter is a string defined in your Info.plist. The document type name key for each supported file type defines the value of this parameter.

How you encode the data for your application is entirely up to you. A lot of the Cocoa classes that you might want to use to store some data support various forms of serialization. The two most common forms are using the `NSCoder` system and using property lists.

Classes that implement the `NSCoding` protocol can be passed to an `NSCoder` subclass and serialized. This protocol defines two methods:

```
- (void)encodeWithCoder: (NSCoder*)encoder;
- (id)initWithCoder: (NSCoder*)decoder;
```

A primitive form of this functionality was present in the original versions of Objective-C. The `Object` class implemented `-write:` and `read:` methods that wrote to a `TypedStream` object. Starting with OS X 10.2, Apple introduced two kinds of coders. The first kind, dating back to NeXT, archives objects in a stream, while the second kind has a more dictionary-like interface.

The old interface is implemented by `NSArchiver` and `NSUnarchiver`. These return **NO** to `-allowsKeyedCoding`, indicating that they do not support dictionary-like encoding. Calls to the archiver must appear in the same order as they appear in the unarchiver with this kind of serialization.

The newer form supports keyed archiving. Values are stored in the coder using methods like `-encodeFloat:forKey:`. When deserializing you can look up the value using the corresponding method of the form `-decodeFloatForKey:`. Keyed archivers are more extensible, since you can add new keys without preventing an older version deserializing the subset that it knows about.

To use these for your model, you would implement a method like this in your document object:

```
- (NSData*)dataOfType: (NSString*)typeName
                error: (NSError**)outError
{
    NSMutableData *data = [NSMutableData data];
    NSKeyedArchiver *coder = [[NSKeyedArchiver alloc]
        initForWritingWithMutableData: data];
    [coder archivedDataWithRootObject: rootObject];
    [coder release];
    return data;
}
```

This creates a new data object and serializes `rootObject`, assumed to be the important model object, into it. You might instead pass **self** here and implement the `NSCoding` protocol yourself. In your read method, you would call `+unarchiveObjectWithData:` on `NSKeyedUnarchiver` to get a copy of the object graph back.

For simple models, another option is to use property lists. If your objects are represented by arrays and dictionaries of the kind of data that can be saved in a property list, then you can use `NSPropertyListSerialization` to convert between these types and a `NSData` instance containing property lists.

More complex documents are not best represented by a single file. Although on other systems it is common to use things like zip files or custom binary formats to encode documents containing more than one discrete component, the typical solution on OS X is to use *bundles*. You cannot represent a bundle with a data object, because a data object is unstructured. Instead, you must implement one of the slightly higher-level methods to access the files directly:

```
- (BOOL)readFromFileWrapper: (NSFileWrapper*)fileWrapper
                     ofType: (NSString*)typeName
                      error: (NSError**)outError;
- (NSFileWrapper*)fileWrapperOfType: (NSString*)typeName
                              error: (NSError**)outError;
```

These use `NSFileWrapper` objects to encapsulate the document data. This is a high-level wrapper around some entry in the filesystem hierarchy. It can represent a regular file, a directory, or a symbolic link. You can use any kind of file I/O, including standard C or Foundation classes, to perform the save, and then return a new file wrapper pointing to the file.

The final way of saving, preferred in newer versions of OS X, involves writing to a URL, rather than a file. The simplest methods for doing this are almost identical to the file versions, except that they take an `NSURL` as an argument. The default implementations of these call the file versions and, if the URL is not a file URL, copy the version that was saved in a temporary location there.

Atomic Saving

The default implementation of the saving methods, which use the data objects returned by the custom subclass, will use the atomic operations defined by the `NSFileHandle` class. These create a new file, write to it, and then rename it to the old version.

A simple version of this can be implemented for bundles, by creating a new bundle every time you save. This has two disadvantages. The first is that it is slow if not all of the files have changed. The second is that it will break some revision control systems, like CVS and Subversion, which store hidden files inside the bundle. A better option is to write all changed files to temporaries and then rename them all at the end. When you load a document, scan the bundle for temporaries and rename them before loading.

You can use `NSFileWrapper` to create a bundle by creating a directory file wrapper and adding files to it. If you send it a `-serializedRepresentation` message, then you will get an `NSData` object back. You can return this from the methods described here and Cocoa will write it to the disk for you.

There are more complex versions of the URL saving and loading methods, but these are rarely overridden. To properly support writing to URLs, however, you might want to implement this method:

```
- (NSDictionary*)fileAttributesToWriteToURL: (NSURL*)absoluteURL
                                    ofType: (NSString*)typeName
                          forSaveOperation: (NSSaveOperationType)saveOperation
                       originalContentsURL: (NSURL*)absoluteOriginalContentsURL
                                     error: (NSError**)outError;
```

This allows you to just write the result to a file, but allows the correct attributes to be stored along with it. The save operation allows you to distinguish between save, save as, save to, and autosaving operations. The original location allows you to read an existing set of attributes and copy them, preventing the old versions from being destroyed. This is used for setting HFS+ metadata, encapsulating it in hidden files for non-HFS+ filesystems.

The valid attributes are documented in `NSFileManager`. The most commonly used one of these is `NSFileExtensionHidden`, which indicates whether the Finder should hide the file extension. The default implementation of this method will set this if the save dialog box indicated that it should.

Autosaving

As of 10.4, Apple implemented a very simple mechanism for automatically saving documents. If you send a `-setAutosavingDelay:` message to the document controller, then your documents will periodically be told to save. The location for this is a global temporary directory for unsaved documents, and a different file name in the same directory for manually saved documents.

You can customize the behavior of autosaving, but for simple documents just enabling it will give you as much functionality as you need. Doing this ensures that application crashes and power failures will not result in the user losing very much data.

9.3.4 Document Creation Events

Although `NSDocumentController` will create document instances automatically, with no intervention from you, it is possible to run your own code at a number of places in this process.

The most obvious time to run custom code is when the nib has loaded. Any object in a nib file that responds to a `-awakeFromNib` message will receive one. This will run after all of the objects are loaded from the nib, but the order in which objects will be awoken is not guaranteed, and so you should not depend on other objects in a nib being initialized fully when implementing this, although you can expect all outlets to be connected correctly.

The next point is during the creation of window controllers. This receives two messages, `-windowWillLoad` and `-windowDidLoad`, before and after the nib is loaded. You can use these with a custom window controller class to perform any initialization related to the user interface.

Finally, the `NSDocument` itself provides a number of opportunities for running custom code. It will receive an `-initWithType:error:` message for creating a new document (or an `-initWithContentsOfURL:ofType:error:` message for opening files) when it is created, but before any state has been set. Then it will receive a `-makeWindowControllers` message to initialize the GUI, and finally a `-showWindows` message to display the UI. Any of these can be overridden to run some custom code.

9.4 Extending the Outliner

To illustrate the document concepts, we will extend the Outliner example into a full document-driven application. This will involve creating a simple file format for outliner documents and defining methods for saving them. We will demonstrate two mechanisms for doing this, one using property lists and one using `NSCoder`. This serves to demonstrate the divide between native and supported file formats present in a lot of applications.

For our example, the format dumped with `NSCoder` corresponds to the native file format. This has a very obvious mapping to the internal data structures used for the model. The property list format corresponds to a foreign format. We don't internally store our data in a format that can be dumped to a property list, but we can construct a tree of dictionaries that map to it. This is useful for interoperability, since a lot of other applications understand property lists.

We will also expand the user interface by providing a floating palette in the main nib for the application that can be used to modify properties of the selected outline.

9.4.1 Defining a Native File Format

The native file format is created very easily. Our model is represented by a tree of objects of the same class. These objects contain two other objects, instances of `NSMutableArray` and `NSString`, both of which implement he `NSCoding` protocol. The array only really supports coding if all of the objects in it do. Currently, the outline item class doesn't, so our first step is to remedy this.

As mentioned earlier, there are two kinds of archiver: keyed and unkeyed. We only need to support one, since we are just using this to define a file format, but for completeness we should support both. This will also allow the outline model to be exposed via the distributed objects mechanism.

Supporting the `NSCoding` protocol in our model object requires implementing two methods, one for saving and one for loading. We need to save both instance variables and then load them back later. Listing 9.3 shows the implementation of these.

For each one, we provide two implementations depending on whether the archiver supports keyed coding or not. The keyed version is convenient since it allows us to easily add other properties later. A bit later, we will see how to extend the outliner to support multiple columns and keep backward compatibility with the old file format.

Ideally the non-keyed version would store a version with it, so future versions will only try storing loading objects it knows were saved. We aren't doing this here, since we are only using keyed archiving for our file format. The only time this will be called with a coder that doesn't support keyed coding will be for transient copies, where backward compatibility is not required.

Listing 9.3: Serializing and deserializing the outline items. [from: examples/DocumentOutliner/OutlineItem.m]

```
- (id) initWithCoder:(NSCoder*)coder
{
    if (nil == (self = [super init]))
    {
        return nil;
    }
    if ([coder allowsKeyedCoding])
    {
        children = [coder decodeObjectForKey:@"children"];
        title = [coder decodeObjectForKey:@"title"];
    }
    else
    {
        children = [coder decodeObject];
        title = [coder decodeObject];
    }
    [children retain];
    [title retain];
    return self;
}
- (void) encodeWithCoder:(NSCoder*)coder
{
    if ([coder allowsKeyedCoding])
    {
        [coder encodeObject:children forKey:@"children"];
        [coder encodeObject:title forKey:@"title"];
    }
    else
    {
        [coder encodeObject:children];
        [coder encodeObject:title];
    }
}
```

There are a few things to note here. The `initWithCoder:` method calls `-init` in **`super`**, not in **`self`**. This is because the implementation in **`self`** will set the instance variables to default values, which we do not want.

In general, you should call `[`**`super`**` initWithCoder: coder]` here and `[`**`super`**` encodeWithCoder: coder]` at the start of your encoding method. This allows any state inherited from the superclass to be stored and loaded correctly. We don't do this here because `NSObject`, the superclass of `OutlineItem`, does not conform to the `NSCoding` protocol and so does not implement these two methods.

Note also that the objects we get back from the coder are autoreleased. This means that the pointers to them are valid now, but will become invalid some time between now and the start of the next run loop. If we didn't retain them, then the next iteration through the run loop would cause a segmentation fault in `objc_msgSend()` and the back trace would show a load of AppKit classes. If you see this kind of error, it usually means you have forgotten to retain something. You can't immediately see where this comes from; the malloc_history tool can help. You need to set the MallocStackLogging and MallocStackLoggingNoCompact environment variables for your application. (You can do this from the XCode executable inspector.) After the crash, don't terminate the application; run this command in a terminal:

```
$ malloc_history {pid} {address of segmentation fault}
```

This will give you a stack trace at the point where the memory identified by that address was allocated. You can then quickly go to that bit of your code and check the lifecycle of the relevant object and find where you are failing to retain it.

As well as serializing and deserializing individual objects in the tree, we need to be able to serialize the whole tree. This is done trivially by serializing the root node, which will recursively invoke the encoding method on all of its children implicitly as a result of telling the coder to store the dictionary of children. We do this by calling the encoder from the document object.

9.4.2 Defining a Foreign File Format

The foreign file format we want to use is a property list. We could add methods to our model object for constructing them from a property list, but this would quickly become unmanageable if we needed to do it for every single foreign file type we wanted to support. Instead, we define a transformer that translates from `OutlineItem` trees into `NSDictionary` trees.

Rather than hard code the instance values, we will use `NSClassDescription` to enumerate all of the attributes that the model object exposes to key-value coding and store these in the dictionary, along with a special case for the children. Listing 9.4 shows how the outline item is modified to provide a class description.

Listing 9.4: Exporting a class description for outline items. [from: examples/DocumentOutliner/OutlineItem.m]

```
@interface OutlineItemClassDescription : NSClassDescription
@end
@implementation OutlineItemClassDescription
- (NSArray *)attributeKeys
{
```

```
    return [NSArray arrayWithObject:@"title"];
}
@end

@implementation OutlineItem
@synthesize children;
@synthesize title;
- (NSClassDescription *)classDescription
{
    return [[[OutlineItemClassDescription alloc] init] autorelease];
}
```

This defines a new subclass of `NSClassDescription` for the class, which returns an array of all of the attributes that should be stored. This is slightly more complicated than it needs to be. We could just define a `-peristentProperties` method on the outliner, but doing this demonstrate how to use the class description mechanism that integrates with KVC. This version is not particularly efficient; it creates a new instance of the class every time one is needed, and this, in turn, returns a new copy of the array. Try modifying it so both the array and the class description are singletons.

This class description is used by the `OutlineItemDictionaryTransformer` class, shown in Listing 9.5. This implements two class methods, one for turning a dictionary into a tree of outline items and one for turning a tree of outline items into a dictionary.

Listing 9.5: The outline item dictionary transformer.

```
#import "OutlineItemDictionaryTransformer.h"


@implementation OutlineItemDictionaryTransformer
+ (NSDictionary*) dictionaryForOutlineItem:(OutlineItem*)item
{
    NSMutableDictionary *dict = [NSMutableDictionary dictionary];
    NSArray *properties = [[item classDescription] attributeKeys];
    for (NSString *property in properties)
    {
        [dict setObject:[item valueForKey:property]
                 forKey:property];
    }
    NSArray *children = [item children];
    NSMutableArray *childDictionaries =
        [NSMutableArray array];
    for (id child in children)
    {
```

```
19         [childDictionaries addObject:[self dictionaryForOutlineItem:child
               ]];
20     }
21     [dict setObject:childDictionaries forKey:@"children"];
22     return dict;
23 }
24 + (OutlineItem*) outlineItemFromDictionary:(NSDictionary*)dict
25 {
26     OutlineItem *item = [[[OutlineItem alloc] init] autorelease];
27     NSArray *keys = [dict allKeys];
28     for (NSString *key in keys)
29     {
30         if ([@"children" isEqualToString:key])
31         {
32             NSArray *childDictionaries = [dict objectForKey:key];
33             for (id child in childDictionaries)
34             {
35                 [item.children addObject:[self outlineItemFromDictionary:
                       child]];
36             }
37         }
38         else
39         {
40             [item setValue:[dict objectForKey:key]
41                     forKey:key];
42         }
43     }
44     return item;
45 }
46 @end
```

This does not hard-code very much about the outline item. It requires that the item has a children attribute—which is also required by the bindings—and that every other attribute has a value that can be stored in a property list. Later on we'll extend the outline view to allow rich text to be stored in items and see how to extend this class to support storing other objects.

These methods make extensive use of KVC. The loop on line 9 iterates over every property exposed via the class description and gets it using KVC, then stores it in the dictionary. Similarly, on line 40 we set the value again in the new outline item using KVC. This allows us to save a property to a plist and then reload it with a future version that stores the property in a different way. For the current version, this looks horribly over-engineered, since there is only one property.

Each of these methods recursively calls itself with the new children of the node it's working on. Both return autoreleased instances. The dictionary was created with +dictionary, which is a named constructor so it returns an autoreleased instance, while the item is explicitly autoreleased. Inserting each child into the dictionary retains it, so you don't have to worry about doing this yourself.

9.4.3 Supporting Loading and Saving

Now that we have mechanisms for turning a tree of outline items into a proprietary data representation and a standard property list, we can use this for supporting loading and saving in the outliner.

This requires quite a few changes. First, we need to move the root node in the outline out of the nib. This was a quick hack to make it work with bindings and is no longer required. Listing 9.6 shows the new interface for the document. This exposes the root node as a property.

Listing 9.6: The new outline document interface. [from: examples/DocumentOutliner/OutlineDocument.h]

```
#import <Cocoa/Cocoa.h>
#import "OutlineItem.h"

@interface OutlineDocument : NSDocument {
    OutlineItem *root;
}
@property (retain) OutlineItem *root;
@end
```

Because properties are KVC-compliant by default, we can use them with Cocoa bindings. The only change in the nib file to support this—apart from deleting the old root object—is to update the bindings for the tree controller. Figure 9.5 shows how this is done. Two things need to be changed. The target of the binding is now set to the file's owner. This is a proxy object set when the nib is created. If you recall in Listing 9.2 we saw that, by default, this will be the NSDocument subclass.

The second change requires updating the key path. We now want to set the root object to the children of the document's root object, rather than to the children of the bound object. We add another layer of indirection here, setting the key path to root.children.

The next thing we need to change is the Info.plist file. This now contains two entries for supported document types, as shown in Figure 9.6. The first is for XML property lists; the second is for outliner documents. Both use the same NSDocument subclass, but with different names for the type.

These types are passed in to the document class when loading and saving. Listing 9.7 shows the new version of this class. This now contains a new method,

`-initWithType:error:`, used to create a new document. The root node is initialized here, rather than in `-init`, since `-init` will be called whether the instance is a new document or created by loading an existing one.

The two methods that were originally stubs, those for creating instances from data and data from instances, are now fully implemented. These have a case for each of the types in the Info.plist and a final case that raises a not-implemented error for unsupported types. This final case should never be reached.

When saving in the native file format, we just need a single call to the keyed archiver, since this can generate a data object directly. Property lists are two-step processes, since out translator produces dictionaries, rather than data objects. The `NSPropertyListSerialization` class is then used to translate these into data objects using the standard property list support. The loading code path will work for binary and ASCII property lists as well, although we only support saving to XML property lists.

Figure 9.5: Binding the view to the new model.

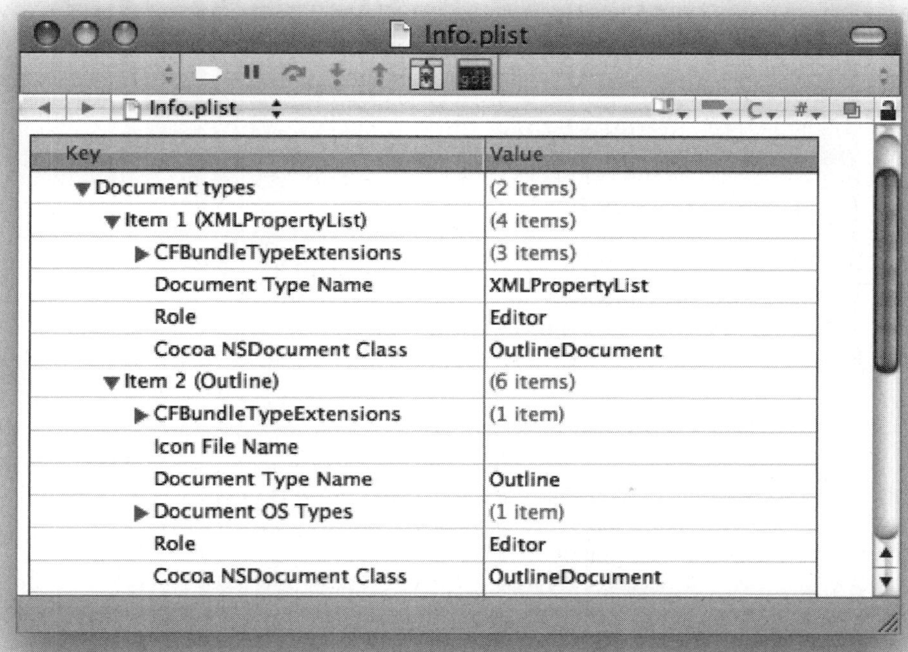

Figure 9.6: Setting the document types.

Listing 9.7: The outliner document class, supporting loading and saving. [from: examples/DocumentOutliner/OutlineDocument.m]

```
#import "OutlineDocument.h"
#import "OutlineItemDictionaryTransformer.h"

@implementation OutlineDocument
@synthesize root;

- (id)initWithType: (NSString*)typeName error: (NSError**)outError
{
    if (nil == (self = [self init]))
    {
```

```
        return nil;
    }
    root = [OutlineItem new];
    return self;
}

- (NSString*)windowNibName
{
    return @"OutlineDocument";
}


- (NSData*)dataOfType: (NSString*)typeName
                error: (NSError**)outError
{
    if ([@"XMLPropertyList" isEqualToString: typeName])
    {
        NSDictionary *dict = [OutlineItemDictionaryTransformer
            dictionaryForOutlineItem:root];
        return [NSPropertyListSerialization
            dataFromPropertyList: dict
                          format: NSPropertyListXMLFormat_v1_0
                errorDescription: NULL];
    }
    if ([@"Outline" isEqualToString:typeName])
    {
        return [NSKeyedArchiver archivedDataWithRootObject: root];
    }
    if (NULL != outError)
    {
        *outError = [NSError errorWithDomain: NSOSStatusErrorDomain
                                        code: unimpErr
                                    userInfo: nil];
    }
    return nil;
}

- (BOOL)readFromData: (NSData*)data
              ofType: (NSString*)typeName
               error: (NSError**)outError
{
    if ([@"XMLPropertyList" isEqualToString: typeName])
    {
        NSDictionary *dict = [NSPropertyListSerialization
```

```
                propertyListFromData: data
                    mutabilityOption: NSPropertyListMutableContainersAndLeaves
                              format: NULL
                    errorDescription: NULL];
            root = [OutlineItemDictionaryTransformer outlineItemFromDictionary:
                dict];
        }
        else if ([@"Outline" isEqualToString: typeName])
        {
            root = [NSKeyedUnarchiver unarchiveObjectWithData: data];
        }
        root = [root retain];
        if (nil == root && NULL != outError)
        {
            *outError = [NSError errorWithDomain: NSOSStatusErrorDomain
                                            code: unimpErr
                                        userInfo: nil];
            return NO;
        }
        return YES;
    }
    - (void) dealloc
    {
        [root release];
        [super dealloc];
    }
    @end
```

Constant String Messages

You might notice that I prefer to use the constant string as the receiver when sending `-isEqualToString:` messages. This is because the compiler knows the class of constant strings at compile time, while it doesn't know the class of the other type. This means it has more potential for optimization, although current compilers do very little with this information.

Once the file types are defined in the property list, the save dialog box will show them correctly. Figure 9.7 shows what happens now when you try to save an outline. Note the pop-up box at the bottom of this sheet. This is automatically populated with the file types that the application claims to be an editor for. (If it claims to be a viewer in the plist, then you can open the file but not save it.)

Some applications will implement some file formats that it can only save, not

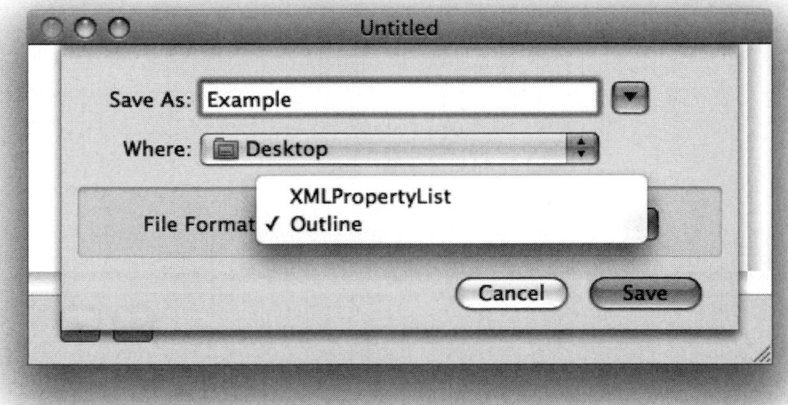

Figure 9.7: The save dialog from the new outliner.

load. PDF is a common example of this, where it loses information that the document model requires and so can only be used as an export target. To implement these, you would add a new menu item for exporting and connect this up to an action method that manually displayed the save dialog. You would not put the file type in Info.plist, because nothing other than the application itself needs to know that it supports exporting.

Once you save a file, you will get a file proxy icon in the title bar, as shown in Figure 9.8. This is set automatically and can be used for *drag and drop*. If you drag this, you will get an alias to the file that can be passed to any drop target that accepts file aliases.

We now have a version of the outliner that supports both loading and saving in two file formats. One thing you will notice is that closing an unsaved document doesn't present a warning. This is fairly bad, and we'll look at fixing it in the next section.

9.5 Supporting Undo

One of the most important aspects of a good application is that it supports undoing user actions. Supporting the *undo* operation is quite difficult. You need to track

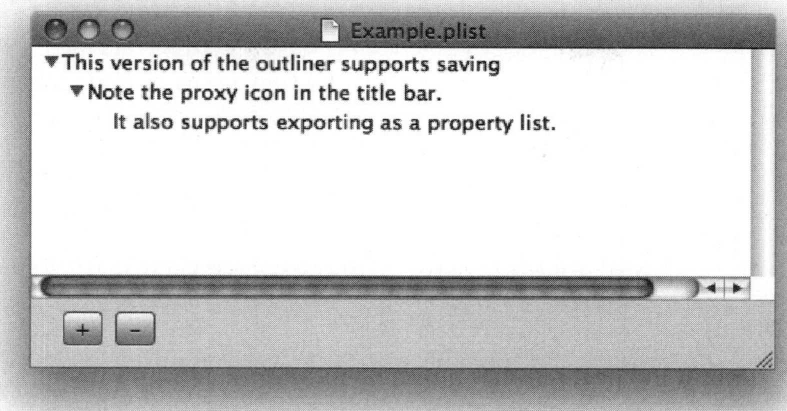

Figure 9.8: The new version of the outliner.

every change and be able to revert to the old state. Doing this yourself would be a huge amount of effort, but fortunately Cocoa provides a lot of help.

The core of the undo system in Cocoa is the `NSUndoManager` class. This is basically a stack. Each entry in the stack contains the operation required to undo and redo the operation. As well as the *undo stack*, the undo manager maintains a *redo stack*. When you undo an operation, the undone operation is pushed on to the redo stack, allowing you to undo all of the undo operations.

If you make new changes after undoing, then the redo stack will be destroyed. If this is not the behavior you want—you want *branching undo*—then you will need to subclass `NSUndoManager`.

It is very easy for Cocoa to record the forward invocations. This can be done using the standard forwarding mechanism from Objective-C. When an object in Cocoa receives a message that it has no method for, it enters the second-chance dispatch mechanism. Some magic[1] in the Foundation library calls `-methodSignatureForSelector:` on the receiver to get the type information and then constructs an `NSInvocation` instance from the call frame. This is a simple class that encapsulates a copy of a call frame. Each parameter will be copied into the object's ivars. This includes object pointers, although the objects themselves

[1]You can see how this is implemented in GNUstep by looking at the GSFFIInvocation.m file. Doing so will make you glad that Foundation does this for you.

will not be copied. It can also retain the objects, allowing the invocation to persist. Some NSObject then calls -forwardInvocation: with the invocation object as a parameter.

At this point the receiver has a copy of the call frame encapsulated in an object and can do anything it likes with it. This mechanism is used by *distributed objects* and a few other bits of Cocoa, and can be used by the undo manager.

This is only half of the problem. Recording invocations allows us to replay the history of the object. In theory, you could record the initial state of an object and all of the invocations and then replay them from the start to get back to an early version. We actually do something close to this with the CoreObject framework for objects that don't implement their own undo functionality, but it's not the most efficient possible implementation.

To efficiently implement undo, you need some mechanism for performing an inverse operation. If drawing a line is a forward operation, then deleting that line is the inverse operation. There is no way of doing this automatically, since it depends on the implementation of the method, although we will see some things in the next chapter that can make it a lot easier.

9.5.1 Registering Undo Operations

When you implement code that makes changes to your model objects, you should also implement code that undoes the operation. This is done by constructing an inverse operation and registering it with the undo manager.

There are two ways of doing this. The first corresponds to NSObject's -performSelector:withObject: method. You register a new selector and object pair that performs the inverse operation to whatever you are currently doing. This only works for methods where the inverse operation is a method that takes a single object as an argument. You would use this method like this:

```
- (void) setStatus: (id)newStatus
{
    [undoManager registerUndoWithTarget: self
                               selector: _cmd
                                 object: status];
    // Actually set the status
}
```

This assumes that the -setStatus: method sets the value of the status variable. Before setting it, it registers the old value and with the undo manager. If you try to undo this operation, then the -setStatus: method will be called again with the old value. This version uses the _cmd implicit parameter to Objective-C methods. This is the selector for the current method. Using it here is less error-prone than specifying a selector by name, and marginally more efficient.

Where to Implement Undo

There are a lot of potential places where you can implement undo functionality. Having each object in your model's object graph implement its own undo is tempting, but then the model objects have to be aware of the undo manager, which complicates things. The document class is already aware of the undo manager, since it is maintained by the superclass. This is another convenient place for it, but in most applications undoing is closely related to the user interface.

The best place for setting up undo objects is usually in a controller. This is somewhat unfortunately if you are using bindings, since you will not have a custom controller object. Fortunately, it is possible to get around this using KVO, as we will see later.

For more complex operations the undo manager provides a *higher-order messaging* mechanism. This is used by calling `-prepareWithInvocationTarget:` on the undo manager. This method returns a proxy (possibly the undo manager itself, possibly something new) that uses the forwarding mechanism described earlier to record the next message sent to it. This is then added to the undo stack.

Using the invocation-based approach, the last example would be implemented as

```
- (void)setStatus: (id)newStatus
{
    [[undoManager prepareWithInvocationTarget: self] setStatus: status];
    // Actually set the status
}
```

This is likely to be slightly slower than the first approach, since it requires constructing an invocation from a stack frame, but is a lot more flexible since any message can be sent here, with any number and any type of arguments.

Any objects passed as message arguments will be retained; however, the target of the message will not be. This is because the target is often the document, which contains a retained reference to the undo manager. Retaining this target would cause a retain cycle, causing a memory leak.

Because the target is not retained, it might be deleted at some point in the future. This can be a problem, since it will mean that future undo operations might send a message to a deallocated object. When you delete an object that has been registered as a target for undo operations, you need to call `-removeAllActionsWithTarget:` on the undo manager to ensure that this doesn't happen.

9.5.2 Creating Undo Groups

Very often messages do not correspond directly to user interface actions. When you type some text, the model object will get an update message for every single character you type. A user typically doesn't want undo to be this fine-grained. Undoing typing one word at a time might be more convenient.

To support this, the undo manager supports the concept of *undo groups*. An undo group is a sequence of actions that corresponds to a single user action. When you perform an undo operation, you will undo a complete group.

A new undo group is automatically started at the beginning of every run loop in Cocoa applications. Most of the time this means you can completely ignore the group mechanism, just as you can ignore autorelease pools. You can turn this off by sending a `-setGroupsByEvent:` message with `NO` as the argument to the undo manager. You might do this in something like a text editor so that you can begin a new group periodically and end one after a word or a sentence has been typed.

Undo groups can contain other groups. A common use for this is in text cells. When you edit a text cell in a larger view, it will talk to the undo manager and register undo operations for the typing. When you press Enter, and leave the text cell, you will revert to the enclosing undo context and can undo the changes to the text cell in one go. This allows you to have a temporary buffer that is used for changing a single item and then a global undo for the whole document.

Undo groups are created by a pair of methods: `-beginUndoGrouping` and `-endUndoGrouping`. These are called at the start and end of the group. All undo operations registered with the undo manager between these calls will be assigned to the group.

9.5.3 Performing Undo Operations

Most of the time you won't perform undo operations manually; you will let the responder chain deliver undo action messages correctly and rely on the user to trigger them. Sometimes it can be useful to deliver them yourself, however.

There are two methods for doing this, `-undo` and `-undoNestedGroup`. The first of these only works when there is just one undo group, while the second should be used when there is more than one. They both close the groups and then rewind the state of the model to the start of the group.

The second one is used for nested undos, such as a text cell. This will undo the current group. The difference is the modifications to the redo stack. You can undo nested groups all in one go by closing them and then calling `-undo`. When you undo all of the nested undo groups at once, then only a single new entry will be pushed on to the redo stack. When you undo them all individually then each of these will cause a new entry to be added. You can go in the opposite direction by calling `-redo`.

When an undo operation is performed, the current groups are finished. This is fine most of the time, since the undo manager is setting this up for you at the start of the run loop. If you have created your own group, it causes problems. An undo group must be ended before it can be used, meaning that you must call `-endUndoGrouping`. For groups that last longer than a single iteration of the run loop, it is possible for the user to trigger an undo in the middle. For other groups, you may trigger the undo in code yourself.

When this happens, the group will be ended and your subsequent call to `-endUndoGrouping` will either end the parent group or raise an internal consistency exception, depending on whether there is a parent group. Neither of these is particularly desirable.

Fortunately, when either undo method is called, it posts an `NSUndoManagerCheckpointNotification`. When you begin a group you should register an observer for this notification on the undo manager. This notification is not just posted when an undo operation is called, it is also posted when any other mechanism opens or closes a group. You can use it to detect whether your group has been closed by some other code and to avoid closing it twice.

9.5.4 The Undo User Interface

The standard Edit menu has Undo and Redo items. These are connected to actions in the first responder. This means that they can automatically disable themselves when nothing in the responder chain understands these messages.

You may have noticed that a lot of Cocoa applications have menu items like the ones in Figure 9.9. These show the name of the top items on the undo and redo stacks in the menu, making it more obvious to users exactly what will be undone or redone.

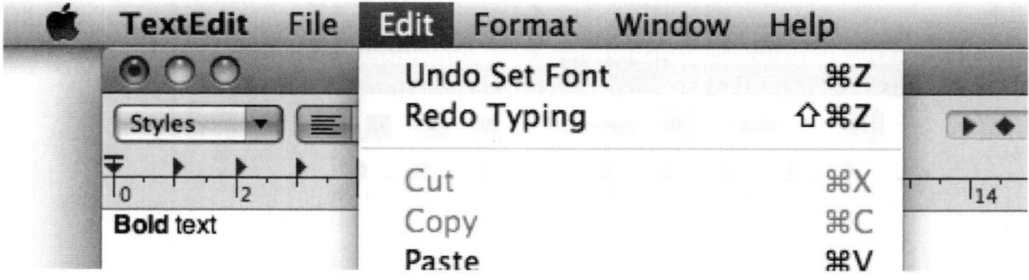

Figure 9.9: The undo menu items in TextEdit.

Implementing these is entirely optional, but will make your application look more polished. The string shown in the menu is set by calling `-setActionName:` on the undo manager when you are setting up an undo action. This should be a localized string suitable for display in a user interface.

Each undo group has a single title associated with it, since undo groups are undone and redone at the same time. Since the name is associated with the group, not with a specific action, it can be set before or after the invocation required to perform the undo action.

The undo manager is also used to decide if a document has unsaved changes. Every time you start an undo group, or perform an undo operation with the document's default undo manager, the document will receive a notification. It will use this to update its change count. This will also update the proxy icon in the title bar and the close button to indicate the unsaved changes.

In some applications you will want to have some actions that can't be undone. These are rare, and usually bad design, but sometimes they are unavoidable. Since these changes will not be entered into the undo manager, you must call `-updateChangeCount:` on the document to manually update the change count if you want them to be registered as unsaved changes.

9.6 Adding Undo to the Outliner

The outliner that we've been working on earlier in this chapter doesn't include any support for undo operations. Since we're using bindings for the user interface, it would be nice to be able to use the same KVO mechanism for detecting changes. To do this we need to register the document object to observe changes in the outline. Unfortunately, there is no simple way of registering for notifications of changes anywhere in a tree. We could do this using the tree controller and make our document object support bindings itself, but that's quite a bit more complexity than we need.

Instead, we replicate the bit of `NSTreeController`'s functionality that we actually need. This is done by adding the four methods to the `OutlineDocument` class shown in Listing 9.8. These form two matched pairs. The first two simply add and remove observers from a single outline node.

Listing 9.8: Registering observers in the outliner document. [from: examples/UndoOutliner/OutlineDocument.m]

```
- (void) registerObserversForOutlineItem: (OutlineItem*)item
{
    [item addObserver: self
           forKeyPath: @"children"
              options: NSKeyValueObservingOptionOld |
```

```
12                              NSKeyValueObservingOptionNew
13                  context: nil];
14      NSArray *properties = [item allProperties];
15      for (id key in properties)
16      {
17          [item addObserver: self
18                 forKeyPath: key
19                    options: NSKeyValueObservingOptionOld |
20                             NSKeyValueObservingOptionNew
21                    context: nil];
22      }
23  }
24  - (void) unregisterObserversForOutlineItem: (OutlineItem*)item
25  {
26      [item removeObserver: self
27                forKeyPath: @"children"];
28      NSArray *properties = [item allProperties];
29      for (id key in properties)
30      {
31          [item removeObserver: self
32                    forKeyPath: key];
33      }
34  }
35  - (void) registerObserversForItemTree: (OutlineItem*)item
36  {
37      [self registerObserversForOutlineItem: item];
38      for (OutlineItem *child in item.children)
39      {
40          [self registerObserversForItemTree: child];
41      }
42  }
43  - (void) unregisterObserversForItemTree: (OutlineItem*)item
44  {
45      [self unregisterObserversForOutlineItem: item];
46      for (OutlineItem *child in item.children)
47      {
48          [self unregisterObserversForItemTree: child];
49      }
50  }
```

Observers are set in two stages. Lines 9–13 and 26–27 add and remove observers for the children key. This is a fixed key that we expect all of our outline nodes to implement. Other keys may be added in future versions, and there are an increasing number of places in our code that depend on these keys. So far, these are

- The outline item object itself, which must expose them and allow them to be serialized.
- The user interface, via bindings, which must display them to the user.
- The dictionary exporter, which must enumerate them and store them as dictionary key pairs.
- The document object for handling undo.

The `-allProperties` call on lines 14 and 28 is a simplified version of the class description code from earlier. This is shown in Listing 9.9. When the outline item class receives its first message, it creates an array of names of properties that it exposes. Each call to `-allProperties` on an instance returns a pointer to this array, which is used for enumerating them elsewhere. The **for** loops in the register and unregister methods enumerate all of these properties and register observers for them.

Currently there is only one public property, so this code is somewhat redundant, but it means that when we add more properties to the outline item, we don't need to make any changes except in the item model itself and the user interface: Our document and the dictionary exporter will automatically adapt. You will find a lot of Cocoa code designed like this, since the language and APIs favor generic code. This is one of the reasons why Cocoa is good for rapid development. It is usually almost as easy to write a generic implementation as it is to write a

Listing 9.9: Supporting property enumeration in outline items. [from: examples/UndoOutliner/OutlineItem.m]

```
static NSArray *allProperties;
+ (void) initialize
{
    if ([OutlineItem class] != self) { return; }
    allProperties = [[NSArray arrayWithObjects:
                        @"title", nil] retain];
}
- (NSArray*) allProperties
{
    return allProperties;
}
```

specialized one, meaning that your legacy code will be very flexible and easy to modify.

The other two methods added to the document here are for recursively adding and removing observers for every item in a tree. These will be used when a document is loaded and when the document is closed. These work in a similar way to the first two, although they iterate over the children instead of the properties array.

Once we've added observers to the document model, we need to actually do something with the notifications we receive. These are sent to the method shown in Listing 9.10. This uses three different methods for registering undo actions.

This method begins with a guard clause, indicating that it should abort immediately if it receives a notification about the wrong kind of object. This should not be needed, but since all KVO notifications are delivered to the same method, it's worth doing for a little additional safety. You might like to turn this off when you are not debugging, or set a break point on the **return** statement so that you can fix it if it is called incorrectly.

The main body of the method is a large **switch** statement on the integer stored in the `NSKeyValueChangeKindKey` key of the change dictionary. This tells you the kind of change that has taken place. There are three options that we support: changing a key, adding a child, and removing a child. There is a third case for replacing an object in a collection, but this is not supported by our model so we don't need to handle it.

The first case is from lines 73–86 (Listing 9.11). This is currently only caused by changes to the title of the item. Looking at this, you might think it is more

Listing 9.10: Managing undo in the outliner document. [from: examples/UndoOutliner/OutlineDocument.m]

```
62 - (void)observeValueForKeyPath: (NSString*)keyPath
63                       ofObject: (OutlineItem*)object
64                         change: (NSDictionary*)change
65                        context: (void*)context
66 {
67     if (![object isKindOfClass: [OutlineItem class]]) return;
68     NSUndoManager *undo = [self undoManager];
69     // Find the type of the change
70     switch ([[change objectForKey: NSKeyValueChangeKindKey] intValue])
71     {
72         // Handle property changes
```

Listing 9.11: Managing undo in item title changes. [from: examples/UndoOutliner/Outline-Document.m]

```
73         case NSKeyValueChangeSetting:
74         {
75             id old = [change objectForKey: NSKeyValueChangeOldKey];
76             // Construct the inverse invocation
77             NSMethodSignature *sig = [object methodSignatureForSelector:
                   @selector(setValue:forKeyPath:)];
78             NSInvocation *inv = [NSInvocation invocationWithMethodSignature
                   : sig];
79             [inv setSelector: @selector(setValue:forKeyPath:)];
80             [inv setArgument: &old atIndex: 2];
81             [inv setArgument: &keyPath atIndex: 3];
82             // Register it with the undo manager
83             [[undo prepareWithInvocationTarget: object] forwardInvocation:
                   inv];
84             [undo setActionName: @"Typing"];
85             break;
86         }
```

complicated than it needs to be. It would be much simpler to replace lines 77-83 with

```
[[undo prepareWithInvocationTarget: object]
                         setObject: old
                            forKey: keyPath];
```

While this is much simpler, it has one significant problem; it doesn't work. If you implemented the method like this, then you would get something like this showing up in your run log:

```
2009-01-20 12:44:44.682 Outliner[27412:813] Error setting value
for key path title of object <OutlineItem: 0x3f70440> (from
bound object <NSTableColumn: 0x3f54ff0>(null)): [<NSUndoManager
0x3f7ead0> setValue:forUndefinedKey:]: this class is not key value
coding-compliant for the key title.
```

This is because of a flaw in the implementation of the undo manager. This ought to return an `NSProxy` subclass from `-prepareWithInvocationTarget:`. `NSProxy` is an alternative root object that conforms to the `NSObject` protocol but implements only a small subset of the methods. It is used for proxy objects, since almost any message sent to it will trigger a `-forwardInvocation:` call allowing forwarding. Unfortunately, `NSUndoManager` returns an `NSObject` subclass here (itself, in fact).

This has an obvious problem; any method implemented in `NSUndoManager` will simply be called when you send it a matching message. The forwarding mechanism will not be invoked.

This is a fairly serious problem when handling undo creation. You cannot use the `-prepareWithInvocationTarget:` mechanism for any method implemented by `NSObject` or by `NSUndoManager`. Since `NSObject` implements the standard KVC mechanisms, you can't use it here.

Fortunately, there is a work-around. All the forwarding mechanism does is have some fall-back code in `NSObject` construct an invocation and pass it to `-forwardInvocation:`. We can't use the code for automatically constructing the invocation, but we can still call `-forwardInvocation:`. Use this slightly cumbersome mechanism whenever you want to send a message implemented by `NSObject` to perform an undo action.

Constructing an invocation is a two-step process. First, we need an `NSMethodSignature`. This is a class that stores the layout of a call frame. The only official way of constructing one of these is to send a `-methodSignatureForSelector:` message to an object that implements the selector. Since this message signature is not going to change during a program invocation, we don't need to construct it here, we could keep one cached somewhere, although the performance gain would be very small.

Lines 78–81 construct the invocation. We don't need to set a target, since the undo manager will add one for us. We do, however, need to specify all of the other arguments. At first glance it is slightly confusing that the arguments we set with `-setArgument:atIndex:` start from 2. Recall that the definition of an Objective-C method pointer is

```
typedef id (*IMP)(id, SEL, ...);
```

The first two arguments are **self** and **_cmd**, the receiver and selector. An invocation object counts the arguments to the function, not to the method, and so the two implicit arguments still count for calculating the index.

Once we've created the invocation, we can call `-forwardInvocation:` directly. On older versions of OS X, calling the `-forwardInvocation:` method on `NSUndoManager` was supported. You could set the target of the invocation and expect it to work. The fact that this was deprecated with 10.5 implies that Apple is planning to make the return value from `-prepareWithInvocationTarget:` into a proper proxy at some point.

Note that this is done in a completely generic way. The inverse operation to setting a value for a key is to set the old value for the same key.

The next block, lines 87–116, is shown in Listing 9.12. This part manages undo for item insertion. This code uses two undo mechanisms.

Listing 9.12: Managing undo in inserting items. [from: examples/UndoOutliner/OutlineDocument.m]

```
87          // Handle child insertion
88          case NSKeyValueChangeInsertion:
89          {
90              NSArray *new = [change objectForKey: NSKeyValueChangeNewKey];
91              for (OutlineItem *child in new)
92              {
93                  [self registerObserversForItemTree: child];
94              }
95              NSIndexSet *changedIndexes =
96              [change objectForKey: NSKeyValueChangeIndexesKey];
97              NSUInteger count = [changedIndexes count];
98              NSUInteger indexes[count];
99              NSRange range = NSMakeRange(0, [changedIndexes lastIndex]+1);
100             [changedIndexes getIndexes: indexes
101                                maxCount: count
102                            inIndexRange: &range];
103             for(NSUInteger i=0; i<count; i++)
104             {
105                 [undo registerUndoWithTarget: object
106                                     selector: @selector(
                                            willChangeValueForKey:)
107                                       object: @"children"];
108                 [[undo prepareWithInvocationTarget: object]
109                    removeObjectFromChildrenAtIndex: indexes[i]];
110                 [undo registerUndoWithTarget: object
111                                     selector: @selector(
                                            didChangeValueForKey:)
112                                       object: @"children"];
113             }
114             [undo setActionName: @"Add␣Item"];
115             break;
116         }
```

The first thing this method does, in lines 90–94, is register for notifications of changes to any properties on the newly added objects. Without this you would not be able to undo any changes to objects other than the root object (for new documents) or for initial items (in loaded documents).

This method is calling the `-removeObjectFromChildrenAtIndex:` method in the outliner item directly. This does not automatically invoke the KVO methods and so we need to bracket it with calls to "will" and "did" notification methods.

This is an example of several actions being part of the same undo operation.

When you undo inserting an item, the undo manager will fire three invocations, equivalent to this snippet:

```
[object willChangeValueForKey: @"children"];
[object removeObjectFromChildrenAtIndex: indexes[i]];
[object DidChangeValueForKey: @"children"];
```

This isn't the whole story though. Note the loop over the contents of the index set. This is because inserting several objects can be part of the same KVO operation. Nothing in our existing code will do this, but we may as well support it now so that we don't add it later and then wonder why the outliner is suddenly breaking. Each iteration through the loop registers these three calls for the newly added object. This means that if multiple objects are added at once, we can remove them with a single call. This is most useful when pasting items—something we don't support yet—since you want the entire paste operation to be undone at once.

The first and last of these three messages is registered with a single call to `-registerUndoWithTarget:selector:object:`. The second one can't be, unfortunately, since it takes a non-object type as an argument. Instead, it uses the same `-prepareWithInvocationTarget:` mechanism we've already seen, but with a simple message send rather than an invocation.

The final case is shown in Listing 9.13 and handles the case where you delete one or more items from the tree. This is almost the exact inverse of the last case. When undoing a delete, you have to re-add the deleted item. Because we need to get the child for a corresponding index, we join the two loops together into a single one.

Listing 9.13: Managing undo of removing items. [from: examples/UndoOutliner/OutlineDocument.m]

```
        // Handle child removal
        case NSKeyValueChangeRemoval:
        {
            NSArray *old = [change objectForKey: NSKeyValueChangeOldKey];

            NSIndexSet *changedIndexes =
                [change objectForKey: NSKeyValueChangeIndexesKey];
            NSUInteger count = [changedIndexes count];
            NSUInteger indexes[count];
            NSRange range = NSMakeRange(0, [changedIndexes lastIndex]+1);
            [changedIndexes getIndexes: indexes
                              maxCount: count
                          inIndexRange: &range];
            for(NSUInteger i=0; i<count; i++)
```

```
            {
                OutlineItem *child = [old objectAtIndex: i];
                [self unregisterObserversForItemTree: child];
                id proxy = [undo prepareWithInvocationTarget: object];
                [proxy insertObject: child
                  inChildrenAtIndex: indexes[i]];
            }
            [undo setActionName: @"Remove Item"];
            break;
        }
```

For each deleted child we first unregister for notifications of changes. The child is not being deallocated here, since it is pushed onto the undo stack, but it might be deleted in the future when it falls off the bottom of the stack so it's easier to unregister here and re-register later.

This version just re-adds the item; it does not post the update notifications. This is not technically correct. To be fully KVO-compliant we should send the notifications here, too. The reason we can get away without it is that the tree controller will receive a notification from the parent and update the view anyway. This means there will be a brief period where the view and the model are out of sync.

This can happen in a lot of Cocoa applications, usually by mistake. It's done here deliberately to demonstrate that it doesn't matter if the view only knows about a subset of the model, but not if it knows about a superset. Try removing the notifications from the previous block and undoing an add child operation. When you do this, the model will have an object deleted from it but the view won't be aware of this, and the program will crash when the view tries to update. In contrast, here there is no observable problem because the view never has references to objects or key paths that are no longer valid.

It is still wrong, however. In a real program you should make sure you have the KVO notifications posted in both directions, or you will encounter some subtle bugs.

The final part of this modification is to ensure that we don't stay registered for any KVO notifications after the registered objects exit. Listing 9.14 shows the cleanup code for this object. In a garbage-collected program, only the first of these two methods will be called. In a program compiled without garbage collection, only the second will be called.

Note the split between these two. The `-dealloc` method only handles memory-related cleanup. It releases the reference to the root node of the outline and frees the object by calling `[super dealloc]`. The `-finalize` method performs the rest of the cleanup, removing the observers that point to the object. This is done before the items are freed, or the code will leak.

Listing 9.14: Cleaning up the document. [from: examples/UndoOutliner/OutlineDocument.m]

```
- (void) finalize
{
    [self unregisterObserversForOutlineItem: root];
}
- (void) dealloc
{
    [self finalize];
    [root release];
    [super dealloc];
}
```

Now that undo is implemented, we can see if it worked. Lines 84, 144, and 138, all called `-setActionName:` on the undo manager. When we undo something and look at the Edit menu, we see something like Figure 9.10. The Undo and Redo menu items now say what operations will be undone or redone as a result of selecting them.

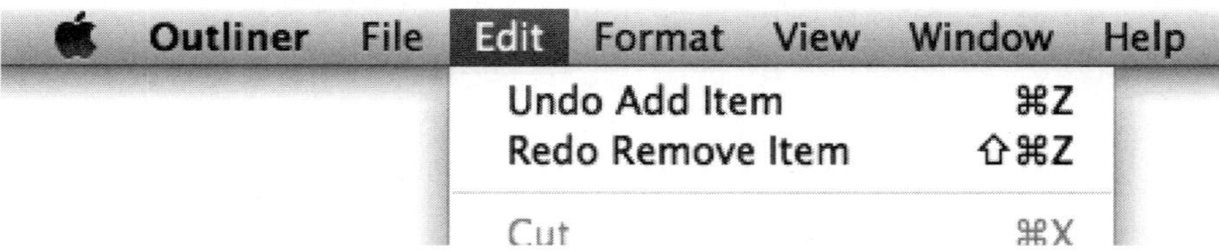

Figure 9.10: The new undo menu items.

Undo works, but we also get a lot of extra functionality for free from supporting undo in the application. Figure 9.11 shows the top of the outliner window after making a change. Note the spot in the middle of the close button and the faded proxy icon. Both of these are visual clues in OS X that the document contains some unsaved data.

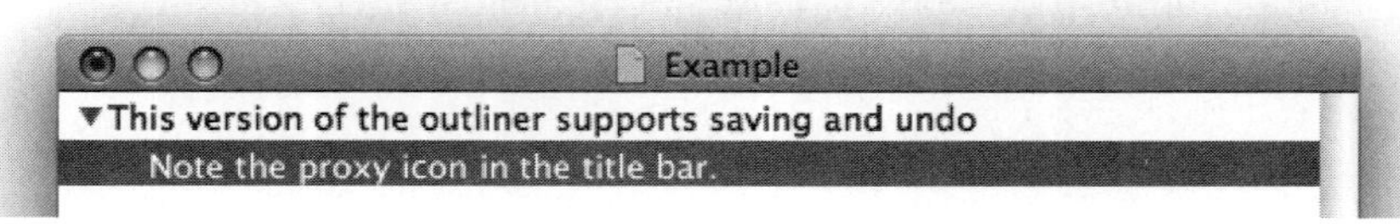

Figure 9.11: An unsaved outliner document.

We didn't need to add anything to support this. Simply implementing undo allowed `NSDocument` to tell when there were unsaved changes. Whenever an item is pushed onto the undo stack, it increments a change counter, and whenever an item is popped off, it decrements it. When the document is saved, it resets this counter to zero. As long as saving and undo work, the document can tell if it has unsaved changes without requiring any new code.

Another side effect of this working is the sheet shown in Figure 9.12. This is displayed automatically when you try to close an outliner window containing some unsaved changes.

Figure 9.12: Trying to close an unsaved outline.

9.7 Summary

In this chapter we have looked at the core document concepts. We created a simple document-driven application that represents an outline and supports loading and saving to both a native and a foreign file format.

We saw how *serialization* worked with both `NSCoder` and `NSPropertyListSerialization`, and how these can be used for persistence.

We extended the outliner to support undo operations using `NSUndoManager` and saw an example of *higher-order messaging* implemented by this class.

Chapter 10

Core Data

Core Data is a new API in 10.4 that provides a persistent data model and a data-object mapping layer. It is based (loosely) on the older Enterprise Object Framework, which provided an object-relations mapping for WebObjects.

> **iPhone**
>
> The Core Data framework is currently not available for the iPhone. Using it will limit your application to the desktop, although it can save you a lot of work. If you think you might want to port your application to the iPhone, consider using Core Data for prototyping; don't make explicit use of any of its advanced features and make sure you can replace it later with manual implementations of your model objects.

Using Core Data, a lot of the code we wrote in the last chapter becomes obsolete. The framework is included with new projects created in XCode by default, and can be used quite easily by new projects.

Rather than defining objects directly with Core Data, you begin by defining an abstract model for your data. This is composed of entities and relations between them. In our outliner example from the last chapter, the outline node is an entity and the children property is a to-many relation.

The central concept for Core Data is a *managed object.* This is a subclass of `NSManagedObject`, a new class introduced for Core Data that adds extra support for persistence.

If you use Core Data for your object model, you get a few things for free:

- Persistent storage on disk

- Automatic undo and redo support
- Full support for bindings for connecting your user interface
- Lazy loading of part of the document

This makes the framework very attractive for new projects. It is slightly harder to migrate existing applications to use Core Data, but still possible. In this chapter we will take a look at how it can be used to remove even more of the need to write code in document-driven applications.

10.1 Introducing Data Modeling

A common technique for persistence in object-oriented programs is *object-relational mapping* (*OR mapping*). This involves mapping a set of objects to a set of rows in a relational database. Typically, you will have one table in the database for each class, with one row for each instance of the class. Attributes (some or all of the instance variables) are mapped to rows in the table.

This allows you to use objects for live data and relational database tables for persistent data and provides several advantages. The main one is interoperability, since any code capable of communicating with the database server can use the same model as the object-oriented code.

NeXT released a framework for doing this in 1994. The *Enterprise Object Framework* (*EOF*) allows mappings from relational databases to objects to be defined and was one of the first pieces of code to use the new OpenStep Foundation library.

EOF was used by a number of companies in conjunction with the other NeXT developer tools to create applications connecting to their existing databases. It was most commonly used in conjunction with WebObjects, released a couple of years later. The combination of the two meant that you could create web applications easily that connected to an existing database.

EOF has been reimplemented by GNUstep in the form of the *GNUstep Database Library 2* (*GDL2*). This was originally developed for use in conjunction with *GNUstepWeb*, the GNUstep reimplementation of WebObjects 4.5 (the last Objective-C version), but can also be used with other Foundation implementations, including Cocoa.

Although EOF was used most often for web applications, it was popular with a few desktop application developers, too. Unfortunately, Apple discontinued the stand-alone version of EOF before releasing OS X and only continued to support the Java version, leaving desktop Objective-C developers without any kind of OR framework.

With 10.4, they introduced Code Data. This is not a direct replacement for EOF. The back end does not have to be an SQL database; it can be a binary or XML file or, with 10.5, a user-defined storage mechanism. These differences are intentional. Core Data is not designed for building multiuser enterprise applications; it is designed for building desktop applications.

While it was important for EOF to be able to connect to a large back-end database for a company, this is not needed for most desktop applications. The automatic persistence features, however, are very useful.

Core Data makes you define your data model in terms of *attributes* and *relations*. Attributes are simple data, such as strings and integers. Relations are references to other objects. They are slightly higher-level than simple pointer ivars, however. A relation can be a relation to one, or to many objects, and maps very closely to KVC, which allowed the same form of definition.

10.2 Understanding Managed Objects

The central object for a Code Data model is the `NSManagedObject`. This is a special KVC-compliant object used to represent model objects by Core Data. This is closely related to `NSEntityDescription`. When you draw a model object in the data modeler, you will create an entity description.

Recall that Core Data uses an *entity-relation* (*ER*) model to represent documents and, like EOF, generates an automatic mapping from this to objects. Each entity in a Core Data model is mapped to an object. Entities have attributes and relations. Attributes are simple data types, such as strings or integers, that are intrinsic to the object. Relations are links to other objects.

You can use this model without Core Data. Both attributes and relations can be represented as instance variables. An instance variable that points to other model objects is a relation. KVC provides some support for relations, allowing both to-one and to-many relations to be represented. In the outliner example from the last chapter we used a to-many relation via KVC and KVO for the children of an outliner node.

Thinking of this model object in terms of attributes and relations gives one of each. The title is an attribute and the children property is a to-many relation.

When you use a managed object, you do not use instance variables for most of these. Each model object will be an instance of `NSManagedObject` or a subclass. These are created from a persistent store, a name, and an entity description.

Each managed object provides KVC access to all of the attributes and relations that are described by the entity description. These are not stored in instance variables; they are stored in the data store associated with the model.

When you create an instance of a managed object, you get something that is really a proxy for accessing the store. This makes them very cheap to create, since they just need to store pointers to the model, the store and their name, and no other data. Accessing their properties is slightly more expensive.

> **Accessing Attributes and Relations**
>
> When Core Data was introduced, attributes and relations had to be accessed via KVC. This is a simple and clean mechanism, but it prevents the compiler from doing any sanity checking. Starting with 10.5, the framework generates a new class for each entity and adds KVC-compliant accessor methods. You can use these directly, which avoids some KVC overhead and allows the compiler to check that for typos in the attribute name.

When you create a managed object, its relationships will not be resolved automatically. The attributes will be loaded from the store, but managed objects for the destination of the relationships will not. When you attempt to dereference a relationship, managed objects for the pointed-to entities will be created if they are not already in memory.

If you have used an *Object-Oriented Database* (*OODB*) such as Gemstone, this will be familiar to you. These typically work by making loaded objects unreadable in memory and then catching segmentation faults and loading the object's properties when they are accessed. Since all Core Data's managed object properties are accessed via KVC, hacks like this are not required; the object can simply load them if they are not already present when it receives an accessor message.

The process by which objects are instantiated from the store is called *faulting*. An object fault in Core Data is analogous to a page fault in the operating system's VM subsystem. If you are using the SQLite store, then this may involve fetching data from the disk as well creating new objects wrapping data.

10.3 Attribute Types

Core Data attributes are more limited than Objective-C instance variables. They can only store a small number of basic types. These are similar to the data types implemented by Foundation, with some C types.

Integer 16 values are 16-bit integers, represented by an `NSNumber`.

Integer 32 values are 32-bit integers, represented by an `NSNumber`.

Integer 64 values are 64-bit integers, represented by an `NSNumber`.

Decimal values correspond to binary-coded decimal data, represented by an `NSDecimalNumber`.

String values are Objective-C strings, represented by an `NSString` subclass.

Boolean values are either true or false, and are represented by an `NSNumber`.

Date values correspond to a date, represented by an `NSDate`.

Binary data values are raw data stored in an `NSData`.

The object types do not necessarily match the internal storage types. An `NSNumber` containing a 16-bit integer is a 16-bit instance variable, a 32-bit or 64-bit `isa` pointer, and probably a reference count and a few other things hidden from the programmer. Storing all of these would not make sense. Instead the persistent store will contain a table of entries with a 16-bit integer field for storing these. When they are loaded, they will be wrapped in objects.

This is not as limiting as it might appear, for two reasons. The first is that most of the complexity of a data model comes from the relations. Relations are roughly equivalent to pointers in a language like C, and when you add pointers to this list of types, you get a richer data representation language than C. Relationships provide more metadata than plain pointers, since they allow to-many and inverse mappings to be defined.

If this is not enough, there is also the option to define *transformable attributes*. These are attributes that are stored as binary data internally, but have a `NSValueTransformer` instance registered with them to handle loading and storing them. Cocoa defaults to using a keyed archiver as a value transformer for doing this, which allows any object that supports keyed coding to be stored automatically. You can also use a custom value transformer, for example, to allow the data to be stored using some custom, efficient, compression scheme.

Occasionally, you might want to use a custom subclass of `NSManagedObject` instead, and implement the attribute yourself. This is still supported, but is not recommended for projects targeting 10.5 or later. Using a custom subclass does not provide any more expressive power than using a value transformer. You need to manage your own "shadow" attribute that manages the persistent store and map it to the public one. This is quite tricky and requires a lot of custom code to do exactly what the value transformer mechanism does for you.

A very common use for transformable attributes is to reference bundle attributes. If you have a document containing a lot of images, then you might consider storing the images in separate files in a bundle and just storing the file names in Core Data. You will then use a value transformer to allow the files to be read into memory when the attribute is accessed. This makes saving and running Time Machine backups faster.

10.4 Creating a Data Model

In this section, we'll put together a simple Core Data document-driven application. This will be a very simple payroll application, which will store an hierarchical set of departments and some employee data for each one.

The first step in any Core Data application is to create a new data model. The model for this application is shown in Figure 10.1. It includes two entities, one for departments and one for employees.

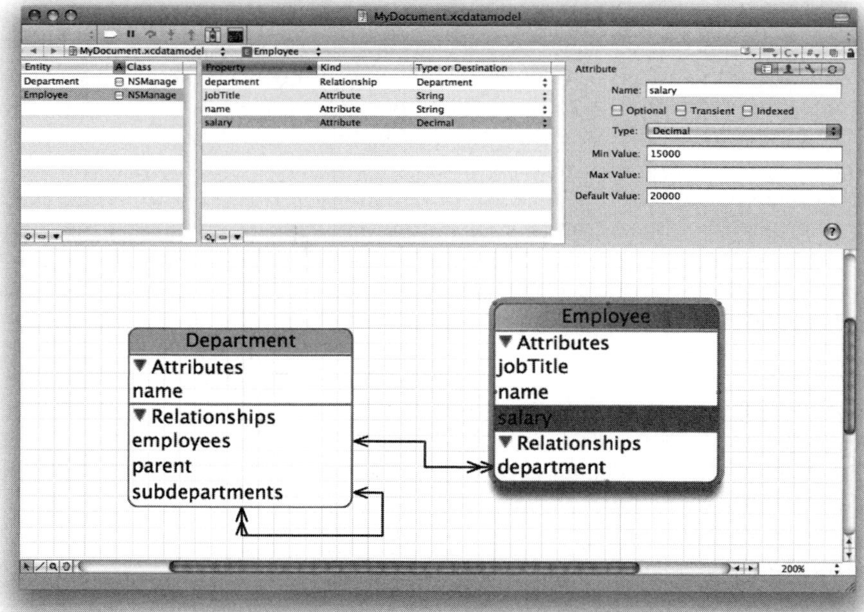

Figure 10.1: The data model for the payroll example.

The XCode data modeler provides a visual representation of the model. Each entity is shown as a rounded box with a list of attributes and relationships. The lines connect relationships to the type of entity that they refer to. A single arrow indicates that the object is referred to, and a double arrow indicates that it is a to-many relation.

You can see an example of both in the arrow between the two relationships. One end starts at employees and the other end starts at department. There is a single arrow at the Department end and a double arrow at the Employee end. This tells us several things:

- The double arrow indicates that employees is a to-many relationship (i.e., one department has many employees).
- The single arrow indicates that department is a to-one relationship (i.e., each employee works for a single department).
- The fact that the line ends at a relation at both ends indicates that one relation is the inverse of the other, so if one holds between two objects, then so will the other.

The other two relationships here allow a hierarchy to be specified. The parent and subdepartments relationships are inverses of each other, allowing navigation up and down a tree of departments. We need the parent relationship for connecting up the tree controller via bindings, as we will see later.

This is a fairly simple data model. We could define it in code quite easily, but Core Data gives us quite a few things for free. To highlight this, take a look at the implementation of the document class, shown in Listing 10.1. This is a subclass of `NSPersistentDocument`, the document class provided by Core Data.

Listing 10.1: The payroll document class. [from: examples/CoreDataPayroll/MyDocument.m]

```
#import "MyDocument.h"

@implementation MyDocument
- (NSString *)windowNibName
{
    return @"MyDocument";
}
@end
```

A category on `NSDocument` that returned `[self classname]` instead of `nil` would make even this short class unrequired in a lot of cases. This isn't the only code we need for the application, but it's not far off.

Our data model stores the salary as a decimal value, so that we can later extend this and perform calculations in a way that is safe for financial data. Unfortunately, we can't present this in a view directly. When the `NSDecimalNumber` is loaded by the text cell, it will have its `-stringValue` method called. When the data view tries setting the new value in the model, however, it will pass the new string instance back to the KVC methods, and this will fail.

To avoid this, we use a *value transformer*, a subclass of `NSValueTransformer`. This transforms between some arbitrary object type and a string. The implementation of this is trivial for `NSDecimalNumber` instances, since it already provides methods for translating from it and a string. We just need to call these from a value transformer, as shown in Listing 10.2.

Listing 10.2: The payroll document class. [from: examples/CoreDataPayroll/DecimalValueTransformer.m]

```
#import "DecimalValueTransformer.h"

@implementation DecimalValueTransformer
+ (Class)transformedValueClass
{
    return [NSDecimalNumber class];
}
+ (BOOL)allowsReverseTransformation
{
    return YES;
}
- (id)transformedValue:(id)value
{
    return [value stringValue];
}
- (id)reverseTransformedValue:(id)value
{
    return [NSDecimalNumber decimalNumberWithString:value];
}
@end
```

The two class methods just specify some basic information about this implementation: that it works on decimal numbers and can translate in both directions. The two instance methods perform the actual translation, simply by calling the relevant methods on the decimal number.

These two files are the sum total of all of the code required for this application. All of the rest of it is defined in terms of Core Data, Interface Builder, and bindings. Figure 10.2 shows the objects that need to be created in the nib file for the payroll.

Most of these objects are views. We create a split view in the main document window. In the left pane we will show all of the departments in an outline view, and in the right pane we will show a table view with the employees in this department. Figure 10.4 shows what it will look like when it's finished. At the bottom of the window we have two pairs of buttons, for adding and removing departments and employees.

The other important objects in the nib are instances of two controller classes, `NSTreeController` and `NSArrayController`. These are used to provide the data to the outline and table views. Figure 10.3 shows the attributes for the tree controller.

This is a little different from the last time we saw a tree controller. This

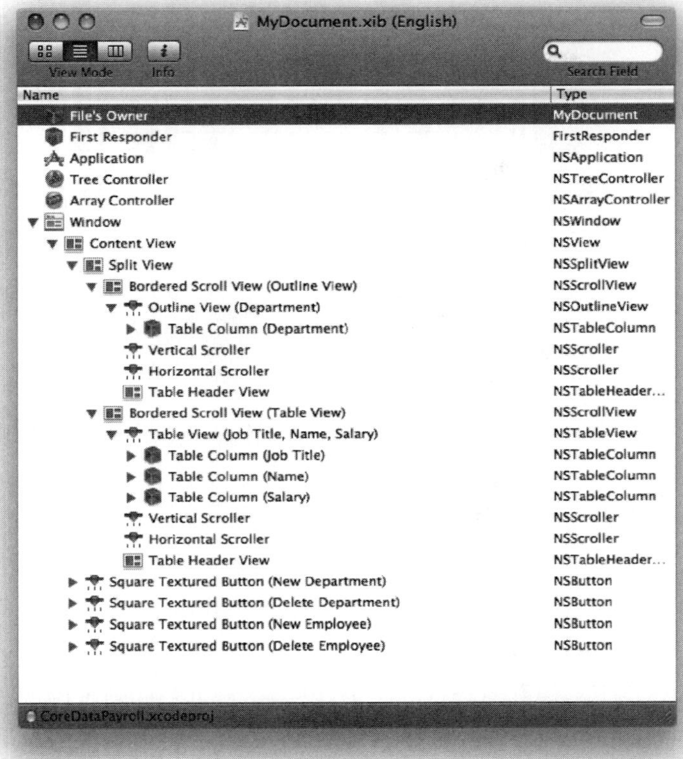

Figure 10.2: The document nib for the payroll example.

time the controller is in Entity mode, which means that it will create managed objects. For this to work, you need to have the controller's managed object context binding connected. In this case we bind it to the managed object context in the file's owner. The persistent document object maintains this context, automatically creating one when it is created.

There are two important things to notice here. The first is that the Prepares Content check box is checked. This was called Automatically prepare content in older versions of Interface Builder and is still referred to by this name in a lot of Apple documentation. This says that when the nib is instantiated the

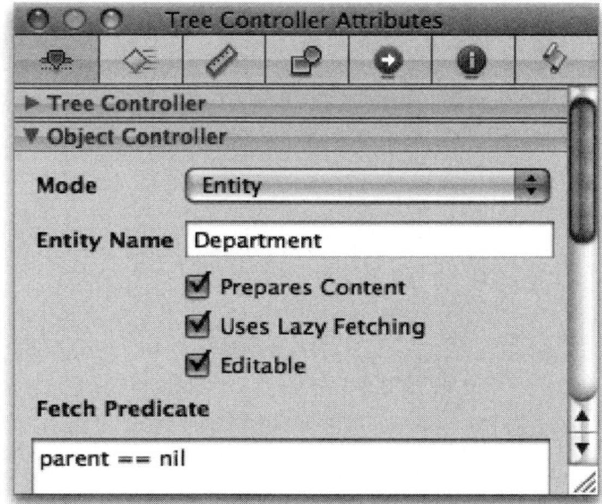

Figure 10.3: Attributes of the payroll tree controller.

controller should automatically try to fetch data to display from the persistent model context.

The other important thing to note is the predicate. The tree controller will treat every object that satisfies this predicate as a root node in the tree. This predicate is written in a simple domain-specific language that is used by `NSPredicate` and is inspired by both SQL and Objective-C.

If we did not have this predicate then every Department entity would be a root node in the tree as well as being in the correct location. You need something like this whenever you use a tree controller with Core Data, or you will find that you get some very strange results.

The array controller also needs to be in entity mode, but it doesn't need any custom predicates. The only thing remaining now is to connect up all of the actions and bindings. The actions for the four buttons are connected to add and remove actions in the two controllers. The bindings are a little more complicated.

Each table column needs to be bound to the correct key path in the correct controller. For the department column this is "name" in the tree controller. For each of the others it is the correct key in the array controller.

The easiest binding to forget is the selection indexes binding from the outline view to the tree controller. Without this the tree controller will not properly track selection. Every new object will be selected automatically, but selection changes will be ignored. When you try to insert new children, you will always get a child of the last-inserted object added.

Debugging Bindings

The unfortunate side effect of not needing to write code is that you have nowhere sensible to insert breakpoints for debugging. You may find it useful when hunting for issues in bindings to use a custom subclass of the controller object and override methods in it that relate to the problem. You can then add break points or debugging statements to them.

The other bindings are between the controllers. This application is a simple example of a *master-detail view*. The outline view on the left is a master view, while the table view on the right shows some detail relating to whatever is selected in the master view.

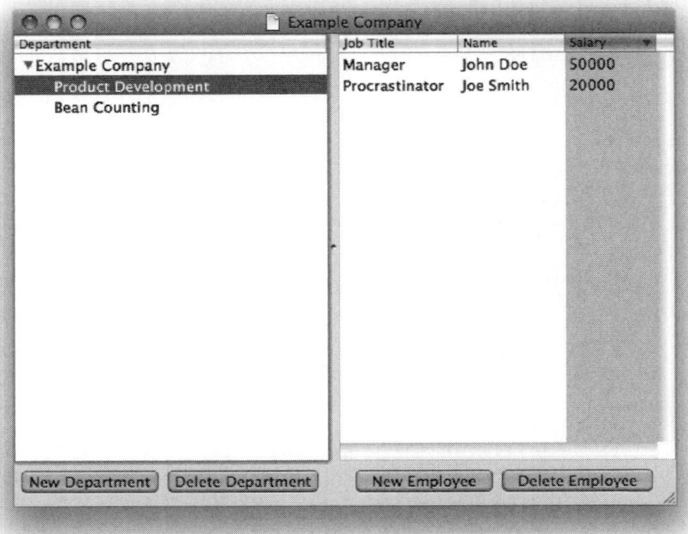

Figure 10.4: Running the payroll example.

For this to work, the array controller's content set must be bound to the tree controller's selection key. The employees model key in this then gives the employees, and keys on these are used to display the table columns. When everything is connected together, you can run it.

The buttons should work and allow you to add and remove both kinds of entity. Selecting an entry in the left pane should update the column on the right. One thing you will notice is that clicking on the columns causes the entries to be sorted, even though we didn't write any code for doing this. This functionality is provided by bindings, which uses the `-compare:` method to find the order between two keys and sorts the objects according to the results. This allows views on collections to be sorted automatically.

Since the basic attribute types supported by Core Data all support comparisons, this works automatically. With this application running, we can try saving a simple model. The save dialog for a default Core Data document provides options for all three on-disk persistent stores supported by the framework. Before shipping a real application you will want to choose one of these, and define a new file type for it. If we save an XML file, we will get something like Listing 10.3.

Listing 10.3: A simple Core Data XML file.

```
<?xml version="1.0"?>
<!DOCTYPE database SYSTEM "file:///System/Library/DTDs/CoreData.dtd">

<database>
    <databaseInfo>
        <version>134481920</version>
        <UUID>4056EE5E-BED5-442D-AD99-2FDFA7CE25F7</UUID>
        <nextObjectID>106</nextObjectID>
        <metadata>
            <plist version="1.0">
                <dict>
                    <key>NSPersistenceFrameworkVersion</key>
                    <integer>186</integer>
                    <key>NSStoreModelVersionHashes</key>
                    <dict>
                        <key>Department</key>
                        <data>
        tyAR5JGVkY+N5wiiWodgVjQ8tOLLbb6rLYORde4NmBg=
        </data>
                        <key>Employee</key>
                        <data>
        9fSlVo3LF6yYn492SYM1JUlnOlABYRfq9qknuIaNeOA=
        </data>
                    </dict>
                    <key>NSStoreModelVersionHashesVersion</key>
                    <integer>3</integer>
```

```
                    <key>NSStoreModelVersionIdentifiers</key>
                    <array></array>
                </dict>
            </plist>
        </metadata>
    </databaseInfo>
    <object type="DEPARTMENT" id="z102">
        <attribute name="name" type="string">Example Company</attribute>
        <relationship name="parent" type="1/1" destination="DEPARTMENT"></relationship>
        <relationship name="employees" type="1/0" destination="EMPLOYEE"></relationship>
        <relationship name="subdepartments" type="0/0" destination="DEPARTMENT" idrefs="z105 z103"></relationship>
    </object>
    <object type="DEPARTMENT" id="z103">
        <attribute name="name" type="string">Bean Counting</attribute>
        <relationship name="parent" type="1/1" destination="DEPARTMENT" idrefs="z102"></relationship>
        <relationship name="employees" type="1/0" destination="EMPLOYEE"></relationship>
        <relationship name="subdepartments" type="0/0" destination="DEPARTMENT"></relationship>
    </object>
    <object type="EMPLOYEE" id="z104">
        <attribute name="salary" type="decimal">20000</attribute>
        <attribute name="name" type="string">Joe Smith</attribute>
        <attribute name="jobtitle" type="string">Procrastinator</attribute>
        <relationship name="department" type="1/1" destination="DEPARTMENT" idrefs="z105"></relationship>
    </object>
    <object type="DEPARTMENT" id="z105">
        <attribute name="name" type="string">Product Development</attribute>
        <relationship name="parent" type="1/1" destination="DEPARTMENT" idrefs="z102"></relationship>
        <relationship name="employees" type="1/0" destination="EMPLOYEE" idrefs="z104 z106"></relationship>
        <relationship name="subdepartments" type="0/0" destination="DEPARTMENT"></relationship>
    </object>
    <object type="EMPLOYEE" id="z106">
        <attribute name="salary" type="decimal">50000</attribute>
        <attribute name="name" type="string">John Doe</attribute>
```

```
60         <attribute name="jobtitle" type="string">Manager</attribute>
61         <relationship name="department" type="1/1" destination="DEPARTMENT"
               idrefs="z105"></relationship>
62     </object>
63 </database>
```

This is divided roughly into two parts. The first part, from lines 5–32, defines the database format. This is very important, since it means that Core Data will prevent you from loading a file with a different data model. Often this is helpful, but sometimes it can be very inconvenient. If you want to modify the model later, you will change the file format. In future versions of your application, you will need to include both versions of the model description and provide some means of translating between them. This is typically done by finding some entry point into the data store and visiting every node, creating a managed object in an in-memory store for the other data model, and then closing the first one.

Since the data store is defined entirely by the model description, you can use it in different applications as long as they both include a copy of the description to initialize their managed object instances with.

The metadata section, from line 9–31, contains a simple XML property list. You can load this without having to load the entire store, like this:

```
// 10.4 and earlier:
NSDictionary *metadata = [NSPersistentStoreCoordinator
    metadataForPersistentStoreWithURL: aURL
                                error: nil];
// 10.5 and later:
NSDictionary *metadata = [NSPersistentStore
    metadataForPersistentStoreWithURL: aURL
                                error: nil];
```

The rest of the file is used to store the entities and their relations. Each entity is stored in object tags, with an attribute tag for each attribute and a relationship tag for each relationship. Attributes store their value in XML character data, which is interpreted according to the type of the attribute.

Relationships have a `type` attribute, indicating the minimum and maximum number of destinations it must have. Lines 35–37 show three different types. A 0 as a minimum or maximum is used to indicate no limit in that direction. The destination is the type of entity at the other end of this relationship, not a specific instance. Instances are stored in the `idrefs` attribute, which stores unique object IDs, matching those in the `id` attribute of an object.

10.5 Choosing a Persistent Store

Core Data encapsulates a persistent store in a subclass of the `NSPersistentStore` class. Prior to 10.5 there was no public interface for interacting with persistent stores and so this hierarchy did not exist, although the underlying features did. There are four of these provided by default, each with different strengths and weaknesses.

10.5.1 In-Memory Stores

The simplest form of a 'persistent' store is Core Data's in-memory store. This is not really a persistent store. When the application terminates the store's contents will be lost unless it has been saved elsewhere. This is most commonly used for temporary storage. For example, when you create a new document you might use an in-memory store until the document is saved. Alternatively you might create a real persistent store somewhere in a temporary location, so a crash or power failure doesn't lose any data.

In-memory stores are sometimes used for temporary models that you want to use Core Data to manage. This allows you to get all of the free stuff that Core Data provides, such as automatic undo, without creating a real document.

10.5.2 XML Stores

Conceptually, one of the simplest stores is the XML data store. This is defined by the doctype definition in /System/Library/DTDs/CoreData.dtd. It contains some metadata in the XML property list format defining the store, and then a load of `<object>` tags. Each of these defines attributes and relationships.

Attributes in the store are the same as attributes in a real object; some exposed state that can be set via a standard mechanism. Relationships define links between objects. They effectively correspond to pointers in Objective-C.

The XML store is very verbose and slow to use. It also doesn't support partial loading, so the entire contents of the document must be resident in memory.

With these disadvantages it is difficult to see why you would use the XML store. It has one very significant advantage that counters them: It is very easy to read. This makes it ideal to use while building your application. When you have problems that need debugging, having a persistent data format that is easy to read is very useful. We saw an example of this earlier. There was a huge amount of redundant information, for example the type of every attribute and relation was stored once per object, in spite of it being a global property of the model. This makes it unsuitable for real-world use, but perfect for human inspection.

10.5.3 Binary Stores

As with property lists, there is a binary format designed for speed. The Core Data binary format is fast, but totally opaque. The format is not documented and so you cannot use it with anything other than the Core Data. This is not as much of a disadvantage as you might imagine, since the structure defined by Core Data in other formats does not really lend itself to being processed by other tools either.

As with the XML store, the binary store requires the entire object graph to be loaded into memory at once. Writing it back out again is very fast, however. It supports atomic operations, as the name suggests. The XML store is also atomic. They use the standard Foundation mechanism for writing to files atomically: writing a temporary file and then renaming it.

The terms binary store and atomic store are used interchangeably in the Cocoa documentation.

10.5.4 SQLite Stores

SQLite is a public domain SQL database backed by a single file. It is not a relational database server, but it does provide concurrent access to databases by processes on the same system. It is best known for being very fast and ACID[1]-compliant.

When you use an SQLite store, Core Data is performing an OR mapping just as EOF used to. Objects will be stored in SQLite tables. This has a few advantages. You can very easily sort and search objects in an SQLite database. This kind of access is exactly what relational databases are good at.

When you use an `NSPredicate` to sort Core Data objects, it can only rely on comparison selectors that map directly to the data in the database. These will be compiled down to SQL and executed in the database. For some more complex sorting options, this is not sufficient. This is not a total disaster, since you can migrate the document to an in-memory store, run the sort, and then migrate it back to the SQLite store for persistence. This is not ideal, since it loses the big advantage of SQLite stores: that they allow loading partial object graphs.

Core Data provides something like a high-level version of swapping. When you are low on memory, the operating system will store some pages of memory on disk and load them back when they are needed. This is known as *demand paging* or *faulting*. Core Data provides a mechanism for faulting on objects. You can load a root object in a document from an SQLite store and then transparently load the objects it references when you try to access them. This is very convenient for large documents and works very well with the data source models used by the Cocoa view objects. These request only the objects that can be displayed in the

[1] Atomicity, Consistency, Isolation, Durability.

currently visible portion of the view. Core Data allows the rest to be stored on the disk and only loaded when they are needed.

Although the objects will be loaded on demand, they will remain in memory permanently. You can avoid this by using the following line:

```
[managedObjectContext refreshObject: anObject mergeChanges: NO];
```

This instructs the managed object context that it can free the attributes of the object and disconnect its relationships. Any managed objects that this object references will then be deallocated unless other things have retained them. This allows you to free up memory used by Core Data if you have a large document and are only using a small portion of it at once.

10.5.5 Custom Stores

Starting with 10.5, Core Data gained the ability to support new stores. These can currently only be atomic stores—stores that read the entire model into memory at once—but they provide a simple mechanism for supporting *foreign file formats*.

In the outliner example in the last chapter, we defined a foreign file format using a translator. This works on the same principle but performs the mapping between a data model and a foreign format, rather than between an Objective-C representation and the data model. This is not quite such a clear-cut distinction when compared to the outliner example, since it used KVC to heavily abstract the implementation details of the object.

Creating a new kind of atomic object store is not a trivial endeavor, but can be a good way of migrating an existing application to use Core Data without needing to change the file format.

10.6 Storing Metadata

Every store type supports storing an `NSDictionary` of metadata. This may only contain types that can be stored in a property list, but can be loaded without needing to load the entire document.

A word processor might use this to store word counts, key words, author, and title information. An image editor might store a source image in a bundle, a load of modifications in a Core Data store, and the image size, type, and other similar information in the metadata dictionary.

The most common use for this is when writing metadata importers for Spotlight, since it allows the importer to run without knowing about anything other than the metadata dictionary. You can use it for a variety of other purposes, however, such as providing your own preview mode. Lots of image editors provide a directory view mode, where each image is displayed as a thumbnail with its properties written underneath. You could support something similar for your Core Data documents, quickly reading the metadata for each document to populate your display.

Alternatively, metadata can be used within the application for properties that are not directly part of the document. In theory, you could store everything in the metadata, although doing so would relegate Core Data to being an incredibly heavy implementation of `NSPropertyListSerialization`. More commonly, you will store some rarely modified or calculated properties of the document in this way.

The metadata of an object store is set using this method on `NSPersistentStore`:

```
+        (BOOL)setMetadata: (NSDictionary*)metadata
forPersistentStoreWithURL: (NSURL*)url
                    error: (NSError**)error;
```

You must be careful when using this not to overwrite the store type and UUID keys, since these are needed by Core Data. Before setting the metadata for a store, you should load it using:

```
+ (NSDictionary*)metadataForPersistentStoreWithURL: (NSURL*)url
                                             error: (NSError**)error;
```

This will return an immutable dictionary, so you need to send it a `-mutableCopy` message first; then you can modify the properties and save it out again. Note that these are class methods on the store. They work without loading the store. If you have an instance of the store, then you can just send it `-metadata` and `-setMetadata:` messages. Listing 10.4 shows a category on `NSPersistentStore` that adds a method for setting a metadata key. You could use a similar implementation to set metadata in an instance of this class. If you set metadata often then you might want to use something like this, or keep a mutable metadata dictionary cached in your application and periodically push it back into the store. Remember that metadata set on open stores will not be committed to disk until the file is written.

Listing 10.4: A category for setting individual keys on a store. [from: examples/CoreDataMetadata/NSPersistentStore+SetMetadata.m]

```
#import <Foundation/Foundation.h>
#import <CoreData/CoreData.h>

@interface NSPersistentStore (EditMetadata)
+ (BOOL) setMetadataValue:(id)aValue
               forKeyPath:(NSString*)keyPath
   inPersistentStoreAtURL:(NSURL*)anURL;
@end
```

```

@implementation NSPersistentStore (EditMetadata)
+ (BOOL) setMetadataValue:(id)aValue
               forKeyPath:(NSString*)keyPath
   inPersistentStoreAtURL:(NSURL*)anURL
{
    NSMutableDictionary *dict =
        [[self metadataForPersistentStoreWithURL: anURL
                                           error: NULL] mutableCopy];
    if (nil == dict)
    {
        return NO;
    }
    [dict setValue: aValue forKeyPath: keyPath];
    return  [self setMetadata: dict
    forPersistentStoreWithURL: anURL
                        error: NULL];

}
@end
```

10.7 Automatic Undo

One of the main selling points of Core Data is that it provides undo functionality for free. We saw in the last chapter how to handle undo operations manually. While this wasn't particularly difficult, it was time consuming and potentially error prone. Core Data goes a long way toward eliminating this work.

Try running the payroll example. Add some employees, and hit command-z. They should disappear. Now try deleting some and hitting command-z. They should come back. So far, so good. Now try adding a new department and hit command-z. If you are on Leopard, then the application should crash. You can reproduce this behavior with Apple's own OutlineEdit and Abstract Tree examples.

This is a known bug and is caused by the interaction between `NSOutlineView` and `NSTreeController`. The former has several other bugs related to retaining references to objects for too long that Apple seems unable to fix. This is not entirely surprising; this class has the highest concentration of bugs in every implementation of OpenStep I've seen. It is very complex to get right, and there is a strong temptation to optimize it before it is completely working.

If you are not using outline views, however, Core Data works well. The biggest disadvantage is that it doesn't set custom menu text for the undo operation. This is quite a nice UI detail, but largely irrelevant since most people use the keyboard shortcut for undo.

It is possible to implement your own undo system for Core Data; you are not required to use the built-in one. If you are migrating an existing application to use Core Data, then this might be beneficial, since the existing undo code is likely to be better tailored to the user interface than Core Data's generic code.

10.8 Core Data, Spotlight, and Time Machine

One of the disadvantages of Core Data is that it doesn't integrate well with *Time Machine*. Time Machine uses hard links to avoid the need to duplicate files that have not changed. This works very well with bundles. A Keynote presentation, for example, contains a single file for each image, which typically doesn't change, and a compressed property list representing the presentation. When Time Machine runs a backup, it will increment the link count for the image resource files and make a new copy of the plist. For the average presentation, this is only a small amount of the total data, and so Time Machine is very efficient.

Core Data, in contrast, stores the entire object graph in a single file. This means that any changes to it will result in a complete new copy being produced for every change. This can quickly fill up the backup volume and also degrades the user experience slightly as Time Machine monopolizes the disk and slows down other disk accesses during the backup period.

The other technology that doesn't always play nicely with Core Data is Spotlight. Every time you modify a file, Spotlight will run the metadata importer for that file and load the data. We'll look more at how to implement support for these in Chapter 17. Each importer needs to load the file and extract the metadata from it.

The suggested way of doing this is to store the metadata in a header when you save the file and then extract it quickly later. You can do this with Core Data quite easily by using its built-in metadata storage facilities, but these have some limitations, particularly with respect to the size of the data that can be stored. If you are using the atomic store types (XML or binary), then you have to load the entire document into memory in your metadata importer if this is not enough. Using the SQLite store does not have this problem, since it allows you to just load the part you need.

Both of these problems come from the big-blob-of-data approach that is the default with Core Data. This is not the only way you can use the framework, however. It is perfectly possible to have a document split across different stores for different parts of the data, and to have objects reference other resources outside of the managed object hierarchy.

If your documents contain a lot of data that doesn't change very often, it is worth considering using a bundle structure with Core Data (or without it) rather than the standard single-file version. You can use value transformers to do this, by storing references to external files in the Core Data store and loading them yourself using `NSBundle`.

10.9 Summary

In this chapter we've looked at the Core Data framework, a persistent object-oriented database designed for desktop applications and included with OS X 10.4 and later. We saw how Core Data builds on top of KVC, and therefore integrates cleanly with Cocoa Bindings. With bindings providing the controllers, Core Data providing the models, and AppKit providing the view objects, we can produce applications with almost no code.

Core Data does not totally eliminate the need to write code, however. We saw a simple example of a data-driven application; however, this did not actually do anything with the data that it stored. You still need to provide the operations on the data, but the storage is totally abstracted from you.

Using Core Data and Cocoa Bindings can dramatically simplify the task of writing a document-driven application, although neither technology depends on the other, or even on being used in document-driven applications. Sadly, Core Data is limited to desktop OS X—there is currently no implementation of it for the iPhone (unless you want to port the GNUstep version), and so you cannot share model objects easily between desktop and iPhone versions of an app if you use Core Data.

Part IV

Complex User Interfaces

Chapter 11

Working with Structured Data

Cocoa contains two view classes for displaying hierarchical data. We looked at `NSOutlineView` briefly already. The other is `NSBrowser`. These are used all over OS X, but most obviously in the Finder. If you want to display hierarchical data in your application, then these provide ready-made interfaces for doing so easily. We looked briefly at using an outline view in Chapter 9.

The outline view is a subclass of `NSTableView`. This class displays two-dimensional data, indexed by row. A good example of this is iTunes, which uses a table view to display the music library. Each track is a row and the columns represent the various metadata fields associated with it, such as the name, duration, rating, and so on.

OS X 10.5 added another view that follows a similar pattern. `NSCollectionView` is designed to display a grid composed of copies of a template view bound to their own data source. This allows views like iPhoto's image view to be easily constructed.

Most of these classes work with bindings, which we looked at in Chapter 6. In this chapter we will look in more detail at the lower-level mechanisms that they support. These are more flexible than bindings, but require writing more code. Either, or some combination of both, may be more appropriate for any given application.

11.1 Data Sources and Delegates

The data views provided by Cocoa typically have two *delegates*. One is a general-purpose delegate and is used for handling events; the other is a *data source*. The data source is the controller object in the *model-view-controller* (*MVC*) pattern. It is responsible for getting data from the model and formatting it in a way understandable by the view. In editable views, the data source is also responsible for sending modifications made by the view back to the model.

This abstraction makes it possible for the same model to be used for different views. We saw an example of this with text views in Chapter 8. This is most commonly done by having a separate data source instance for each view, but in some cases you can use the same data source but different delegates.

All of the views we will look at in this chapter are designed to integrate with scroll views. This means that they are written with the assumption that they may be connected to a data source that contains a lot more data than the view is currently displaying. When I go to iTunes, for example, I can see around 1% of my music library in the window. If the view fetched all of these from the data source and drew them all for every update, it would be very slow.

To make things faster, the table view only requests the items from the data source that are needed to draw the region it requests. When you scroll, new requests will be issued to the data source asking for the items in the next row. These will then be cached for a while. The exact algorithm used for maintaining the cache is not documented and may change between versions of OS X, but in practice it only caches a limited number of items to prevent the view from using all of your memory.

Because the view can cache items from the data source, the data source is responsible for manually invalidating this cache when the model changes. Doing this will often cause the view to redisplay its contents.

Data source messages tend to be relatively expensive when compared to accessing data from the cache. To avoid calling them unnecessarily, you can often reload only a subset of the data. In an outline view, you can indicate that only a specific tree node, or a tree node and its children, has changed. In a table view you can indicate that new rows have been added at the end and avoid reloading existing ones.

11.2 Tables

`NSTableView` is a relatively simple class for displaying two-dimensional structured data in the form of records. Data in the table is indexed first by row and then by column. Rows are identified by a numerical index and are implicitly ordered in the model. Columns are identified by `NSTableColumn` index and are not.

Columns in a table view can be reordered without any interaction with the model. The table view supports dragging them around to rearrange them. The data source is completely unaware of the order of columns in the model. Data for a specific row-column intersection is requested from the data source using this method:

```
-            (id)tableView: (NSTableView*)aTableView
objectValueForTableColumn: (NSTableColumn*)aTableColumn
                      row: (NSInteger)rowIndex;
```

The data source should map from table columns to some value in the model. This is usually done by sending a `-identifier` message to the column object. This returns an arbitrary object associated with the column when it was created. If you create the table column in Interface Builder, then this will be a string. This helps with *localization* since the identifier is separate from the column heading. The column can display any language in the header but still have the same identifier.

If you are using bindings to provide the data, rather than a data source, this is done for you automatically. You will create your binding from a specific table column, rather than the table view object, to some key path in the model.

11.2.1 Table View Drawing

Each value in a table view is drawn using a cell. The table view itself delegates this drawing to the columns. Each column contains a single cell that it uses for drawing. Recall that cells behave like rubber stamps, presenting a consistent image of an associated object. When drawing a column, the same cell will have its `-setObjectValue:` and `-drawWithFrame:inView:` methods called repeatedly, once for each column.

This means that every row in a table must provide the same sort of data for each column. If you have two columns in a table, one can contain an image and one text, but they must contain the same for every row, if you use the standard behavior. You could work around this limitation by defining your own cell type.

When a table column is created, a specific type of cell is associated with it. This can be one of the standard cells, or one of your own. The objects returned by the data source (or bindings) must be displayable by this kind of cell.

The drawing of columns in a table view is largely independent from each other. Figure 11.1 shows the relationship between the objects used to display a table view. The ellipses represent objects that are part of the view system. The controller and model objects—the ones typically provided by the user—are only a small part of this.

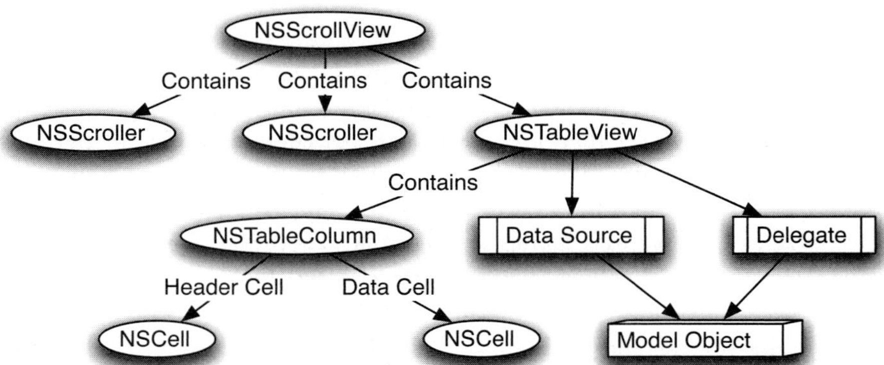

Figure 11.1: The relationships between objects in a table view.

The table view serves as a collection of columns and handles fetching data from the data source and drawing it using the columns' cells. Note that, although they are displayed in the view hierarchy in Interface Builder, `NSTableColumns` are not views. They inherit from `NSObject`, not `NSView`, and do not provide any methods for drawing themselves. The table view uses table column objects to encapsulate information about a column, but handles the drawing itself.

As well as the two cells used for drawing, the column contains a selection of flags for controlling its behavior. These indicate whether the column is editable, resizable, and so on. These are read by the table view when it renders cells in the column to control their size.

Prior to 10.4, the height of rows in the table was fixed. Every row had to be exactly the same height, although column widths were flexible. In more recent versions, it is possible to control the height of individual rows. This allows some complex layouts. As with column widths, the row height can now be set dynamically. You can use this, for example, to permit multi-line text cells a table row, with the height being defined by the size needed to display the text.

11.2.2 Using Sort Descriptors

When you click on a table column in OS X, the view typically sorts the data according to the values in that column. Prior to OS X 10.3, this required handling the click action message from the table header and rearranging the data. This required a lot of code, most of which was almost the same in every application, but not quite close enough to actually be reusable.

10.3 introduced *sort descriptors* as part of the *key-value coding* (*KVC*) mechanism. These are conceptually quite simple. Sorting in Cocoa is usually done by sending a `-compare:` or similar message to an object, with another object as an argument. This takes an object as an argument and returns an `NSComparisonResult`, an enumerated type with three values for the three possible comparison results.

A sort descriptor is a simple wrapper around this. Comparisons between arbitrary objects are performed by comparing some attribute of that object using some method. The attribute is identified by a key and the method by a selector. The sort descriptor is created like this:

```
descriptor = [[NSSortDescriptor alloc]
    initWithKey: @"aKeyName"
      ascending: YES
       selector: @selector(compareInSomeWay:)];
```

This is then used to compare two objects by sending it a `-compareObject:toObject:` message with the two objects as arguments. It will first get the values for the specified key in both and then send the first a message with the selector passed in when it was constructed and the second object as the argument.

Using sort descriptors eliminates the need to have a large number of `-sortUsingSomeAttribute:` methods, as was the case on earlier versions of Cocoa. Objects can now be ordered without supporting any comparison methods themselves, as long as they contain an attribute that does support comparisons and have provided KVC-compliant accessors for it.

The ordered collection types in Cocoa allow sorting on an array of sort descriptors. The first descriptor in the array will be used on each pair of objects initially. If this returns `NSOrderedSame`, then the second one will be used, and so on until all of the sort descriptors have been tried or an order for the two items has been determined.

If you click on one column in a table view and then click on another, the sort descriptors associated with both columns will be used in this way. The most-recently clicked column's sort descriptor will be used first, then the second-most-recent, and so on.

If you are using bindings, then the sort descriptors will be applied automatically. If you are using a data source, then you need to implement this method:

```
-         (void)tableView: (NSTableView*)aTableView
sortDescriptorsDidChange: (NSArray*)oldDescriptors;
```

This takes the old set of sort descriptors as an argument. The new set is found by sending a `-sortDescriptors` message to the table view. The data source should sort the data according to the new set of descriptors and then send the table a -reloadData message. Alternatively you can use the pre-10.3 mechanism by implementing this method in your delegate:

```
-             (void)tableView: (NSTableView*)tableView
mouseDownInHeaderOfTableColumn: (NSTableColumn*)tableColumn;
```

This lets you manually handle mouse events on the table column and handle your own creation and tracking of sort descriptors. You can also use this to provide other, custom, behavior to the column headers. This might include using a different header or data cell on the clicked column or anything else you can think of.

11.2.3 Customizing a Table View

The delegate mechanism provides a number of ways of customizing the behavior of a table view. Although you can subclass the view, the delegate mechanism is designed to avoid the need to in most cases.

Each version of OS X has added some new delegate methods, extending the amount of customization possible. With 10.5, the constraint regarding homogeneous columns was removed. A new delegate method allows every column and row intersection in the table view to use a different cell for drawing:

```
-   (NSCell*)tableView: (NSTableView*)tableView
dataCellForTableColumn: (NSTableColumn*)tableColumn
                   row: (NSInteger)row;
```

This will initially be called with a nil value for the second argument. If the method returns a non-nil value in response to this, then that cell will be used to draw the entire row. Alternatively, a different cell can be specified for individual columns. Returning nil will cause the row's default cell to be used. This builds on top of the method added in 10.4 for altering the height of a table row:

```
- (CGFloat)tableView: (NSTableView*)tableView
        heightOfRow: (NSInteger)row;
```

This returns the height of the specified row. You can use these two methods in combination to turn a table view into an arbitrary data list view. Each row can now be any size and drawn using any cell. This lets you draw completely unrelated things in a table view and just use it as a layout container, as shown in Figure 11.2.

This is implemented by the combined data source and delegate shown in Listing 11.1. This class uses the standard table view handling for even numbered rows, and its own version for odd ones. When reading this code, be aware that it is an incredibly inefficient version; if you were writing something like this for real use, you would cache the image and cell objects, rather than creating them on every

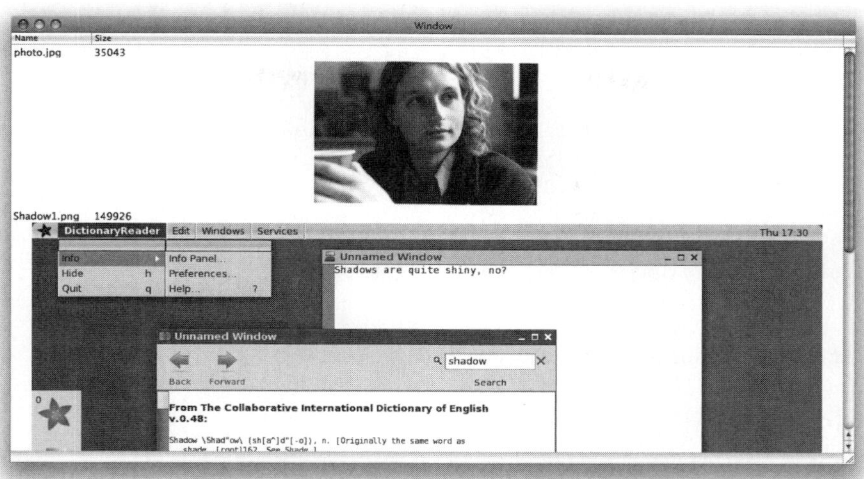

Figure 11.2: Displaying an irregular table layout.

invocation. If you try scrolling in this example, you will get a good demonstration of why data source methods should be efficient.

Listing 11.1: Abusing a table view for an irregular layout. [from: examples/TableViewAbuse/Delegate.m]

```
@implementation Delegate
-              (id)tableView: (NSTableView*)aTableView
objectValueForTableColumn: (NSTableColumn*)aTableColumn
                      row: (NSInteger)row
{
    NSInteger index = row / 2;
    NSString *path = [images objectAtIndex: index];
    if (row % 2 == 0)
    {
        if ([[aTableColumn identifier] isEqualToString: @"name"])
        {
            return [path lastPathComponent];
        }
        NSFileManager *fm = [NSFileManager defaultManager];
        NSDictionary *attributes = [fm fileAttributesAtPath: path
                                               traverseLink: YES];
```

```
        return [attributes objectForKey: NSFileSize];
    }
    return [[[NSImage alloc] initWithContentsOfFile: path] autorelease];
}
- (NSInteger)numberOfRowsInTableView: (NSTableView*)aTableView
{
    return [images count] * 2;
}
-   (NSCell*)tableView: (NSTableView*)tableView
dataCellForTableColumn: (NSTableColumn*)tableColumn
                   row: (NSInteger)row
{
    if ((tableColumn == nil) && ((row % 2) == 1))
    {
        return [[[NSImageCell alloc] init] autorelease];
    }
    return nil;
}
- (CGFloat)tableView: (NSTableView*)tableView
         heightOfRow: (NSInteger)row
{
    if (row % 2 == 0)
    {
        return 16;
    }
    NSImage *image = [self tableView: tableView
          objectValueForTableColumn: nil
                                row: row];
    return [image size].height;
}
- (IBAction)openImages: (id)sender
{
    NSOpenPanel *panel = [NSOpenPanel openPanel];
    [panel setAllowsMultipleSelection: YES];
    NSArray *types = [NSArray arrayWithObjects: @"png", @"gif", @"tiff", @"
        jpg", nil];
    if ([panel runModalForTypes: types] == NSOKButton)
    {
        [images release];
        images = [[panel filenames] retain];
        [view reloadData];
    }
}
@end
```

The last method in this class is connected to the Open menu item's action so that we can populate the table. This runs an open panel and sets an instance variable to the list of files returned. This method doesn't really belong in a view delegate, but it's here to simplify the example.

The first method that will be called by the view is on line 23. This returns the number of rows we want to display, two for each image. The other methods are then called to determine how to display each row.

The object to display is found by calling the first method. This is allowed to return any object, as long as the matching cell can display it. On line 10, we determine whether the data source is being asked for an object for an odd or even row. If it's an odd row, we return an image for both columns. If it's even, we return the filename for the name row and the file size for the other column.

The height of the row is given by the method that starts on line 37. This returns the height of the image for odd numbered rows and a constant for even numbered ones. Even numbered rows just contain the textual description of the image. This is a very inefficient method. It causes the image to be loaded from disk at least twice when the row is displayed. Try optimizing it so that images are lazily loaded into a cache and freed when a new set is opened.

The cell used to draw the object is defined on lines 33 and 35. For odd rows, we return a single cell for the entire row. This allows the image to span both columns. The end result is shown in Figure 11.2. This does not look much like a normal table. You could customize it further by hiding the table headers and formatting the text in a more friendly way.

There are a number of other ways in which you can customize a table. One of the simplest is to add tooltips. These are the little floating captions that appear when you leave the mouse pointer over a user interface element. Remember that these will not work with all pointing devices—most touch screens, for example, have no concept of hovering—and so should only be used as hints, not to display complex information.

In early versions of OS X, adding tooltips was a very complicated procedure. You needed to compute a set of bounding regions for the individual cells and register these to receive mouse events, and then display the tips yourself. This was dramatically simplified with OS X 10.4, and now you just need to implement this delegate method:

```
-(NSString*)tableView: (NSTableView*)aTableView
       toolTipForCell: (NSCell*)aCell
                 rect: (NSRectPointer)rect
          tableColumn: (NSTableColumn*)aTableColumn
                  row: (NSInteger)row
        mouseLocation: (NSPoint)mouseLocation;
```

This should return a string that will be used in the tooltip. As with all other delegate methods, this takes the view as the first argument. The row and column allow you to work out which item in the model corresponds to the cell. Often you will want to display something computed from the cell as a tooltip, and so the cell is also provided as the second argument to avoid the need for calling the data source to calculate it.

The rectangle is passed into this method by pointer to allow it to be modified. This defines the region for which the tooltip is valid. If you don't modify it, then the tooltip will apply to the whole cell. You can modify it to use different tooltips for different parts of a cell, or the same tooltip for more than one cell. If you want to show different tips for different parts of the cell, then you can use the mouse location to work out which one you should be using.

11.3 Outline Views

The `NSOutlineView` class is a subclass of `NSTableView`. Much of the behavior is similar, but it is designed to support hierarchical, rather than flat, data. As with the table view, the data is arranged in columns. Unlike the table view, the columns are indexed by an arbitrary object.

Fetching data from an outline view is done in several stages. For each node in the outline, the data source will be asked:

1. How many children that item has.
2. The child at each index.
3. The object to display for that child for each table column.

This process then starts again at step one with each child. To start this process, the outline view passes `nil` as the item for the first two requests. If you want to implement a single-rooted hierarchy, then you should return a single child here. If you want to implement a multi-rooted hierarchy, then you should return the number of top-level nodes.

For efficient reloading, the outline view allows you to invalidate some arbitrary subtree by calling this method:

```
- (void)reloadItem: (id)item
    reloadChildren: (BOOL)reloadChildren;
```

This reloads the specific item—and therefore the objects for that item at every column—and optionally reloads the children. This can be a lot more efficient than reloading the entire tree. In a very large hierarchy the root node may not be visible and neither may many of the children between the root and the currently visible part. Reloading all of these is not needed for updating the current display and will cause more reloading to be needed when you scroll. If possible, you should always prefer to call this method than `-reloadData`.

11.3.1 Extending the Outliner

To demonstrate some of the more advanced features of an outline view, we will take the outliner example from Chapter 9 and extend it to support multiple columns. To simplify the example, we will not bother supporting undo and not bother saving the column structure when we save and load files. You could try extending this example to provide these features.

The final version will have an inspector like the one in Figure 11.3. This will display the columns for the current document and allow them to be renamed and their types found dynamically.

In this example, we won't use bindings. Although it is possible to set bindings dynamically in code, a dynamic layout like the one we are defining here is easier to do using a static data source.

To begin with, we'll look at the code for the inspector. This will be a new panel in the main application nib with a window controller attached to it. The code for this controller is shown in Listing 11.2.

Listing 11.2: The column inspector controller implementation. [from: examples/MulticolumnOutliner/ColumnInspectorController.m]

```
@implementation ColumnInspectorController
- (void)awakeFromNib
{
    NSNotificationCenter *center = [NSNotificationCenter defaultCenter];
    [center addObserver: self
               selector: @selector(documentChanged:)
                   name: NSWindowDidBecomeKeyNotification
                 object: nil];
    [center addObserver: self
               selector: @selector(documentChanged:)
                   name: NSOutlineViewColumnDidMoveNotification
                 object: nil];
}
- (void) dealloc
{
    NSNotificationCenter *center = [NSNotificationCenter defaultCenter];
    [center removeObserver: self];
    [super dealloc];
}
- (void)documentChanged: (NSNotification*)aNotification
```

```
{
    if ([[NSDocumentController sharedDocumentController] currentDocument]
        != nil)
    {
        [table reloadData];
    }
}
- (NSInteger)numberOfRowsInTableView: (NSTableView*)aTableView
{
    OutlineDocument *doc = [[NSDocumentController sharedDocumentController]
         currentDocument];
    return [[doc viewController] numberOfColumns];
}
-            (id)tableView: (NSTableView*)aTableView
objectValueForTableColumn: (NSTableColumn*)aTableColumn
                      row: (NSInteger)rowIndex
{
    OutlineDocument *doc = [[NSDocumentController sharedDocumentController]
         currentDocument];
    if (aTableColumn == titleColumn)
    {
        return [[doc viewController] titleForColumnAtIndex: rowIndex];
    }
    return [[doc viewController] typeForColumnAtIndex: rowIndex];
}
- (void)tableView: (NSTableView*)aTableView
   setObjectValue: (id)anObject
   forTableColumn: (NSTableColumn*)aTableColumn
              row: (NSInteger)rowIndex
{
    OutlineDocument *doc = [[NSDocumentController sharedDocumentController]
         currentDocument];
    if (aTableColumn == titleColumn)
    {
        [[doc viewController] setTitle: anObject
              forColumnAtIndex: rowIndex];
    }
    [[doc viewController] setType: anObject
          forColumnAtIndex: rowIndex];
}
- (IBAction) addColumn: (id) sender
{
    OutlineDocument *doc = [[NSDocumentController sharedDocumentController]
         currentDocument];
```

```
60     [[doc viewController] addColumn];
61     [table reloadData];
62 }
63 - (IBAction) removeColumn: (id) sender
64 {
65     OutlineDocument *doc = [[NSDocumentController sharedDocumentController]
           currentDocument];
66     [[doc viewController] removeColumnAtIndex: [table selectedRow]];
67     [table reloadData];
68 }
69 @end
```

This is responsible for keeping the table in the inspector window in sync with the document. To make sure this happens, it registers for two notifications when it awakes. Whenever the key window changes or an outline view's columns are reordered, it will refresh. This is a fairly broad condition but will catch all document changes easily, at the expense of a little extra work refreshing the columns. Both of these notifications are connected to the method on line 23, which reloads the data in the table if there is a currently active document.

The three methods after this are datasource methods for the table view. These return the information about the columns in the active document. The table has two columns, one for the name of the outline column and one for the type. The name column object is attached to this controller via an outlet. This enables it to detect which column a data source request relates to using a pointer comparison. All three of these methods simply fetch or set the corresponding information in the view controller, which we will look at a bit later.

The last two methods, again, simply call view controller methods. They are action methods connected to the buttons in the inspector. The first adds a new column and the second removes an existing one. They both then reload the data.

Note that this controller triggers reloads very often. This is quite common for inspectors. Each inspector typically only displays a small amount of information. Reloading it all is not very expensive. In this view's case, the number of rows will very rarely be more than half a dozen, so we can afford to not bother optimizing this controller.

The outline item class is somewhat simplified and generalized from the last version. The code is shown in Listing 11.3. This no longer has an explicit "title" property. Instead, it stores the values in a dictionary.

The methods for getting and setting the title have been removed, and replaced with the two methods on lines 20 and 24. These are KVC methods called whenever the normal search operations fail. All of the old code that accessed the title via KVC will still work, but now the title will be stored in the dictionary instead of an instance variable. Using this mechanism allows us to store arbitrary objects in a dictionary.

This is a very common pattern in Cocoa, especially when prototyping. If you implement these two methods and make sure all accesses to attributes of the object go via KVC, then you can begin with a very simple object and then decide exactly how it should be storing its attributes later.

Listing 11.3: The multicolumn outline item. [from: examples/MulticolumnOutliner/OutlineItem.m]

```
#import "OutlineItem.h"


@implementation OutlineItem
@synthesize children;
- (NSArray*) allProperties
{
    return [values allKeys];
}
- (id)init
{
    if (nil == (self = [super init]))
    {
        return nil;
    }
    children = [NSMutableArray new];
    values = [NSMutableDictionary new];
    return self;
}
- (void) setValue: (id)aValue forUndefinedKey: (id)aKey
{
    [values setValue: aValue forKey: aKey];
}
- (id)valueForUndefinedKey: (NSString *)key
{
    return [values valueForKey: key];
}
- (id) initWithCoder: (NSCoder*)coder
{
    if (nil == (self = [super init]))
    {
        return nil;
    }
    if ([coder allowsKeyedCoding])
    {
```

```
        children = [coder decodeObjectForKey: @"children"];
        values = [coder decodeObjectForKey: @"values"];
        if (values == nil)
        {
            values = [NSMutableDictionary dictionary];
            [values setObject: [coder decodeObjectForKey:@"title"]
                       forKey: @"title"];
        }
    }
    else
    {
        children = [coder decodeObject];
        values = [coder decodeObject];
    }
    [children retain];
    [values retain];
    return self;
}
- (void) encodeWithCoder:(NSCoder*)coder
{
    if ([coder allowsKeyedCoding])
    {
        [coder encodeObject: children forKey:@"children"];
        [coder encodeObject: values forKey:@"values"];
    }
    else
    {
        [coder encodeObject: children];
        [coder encodeObject: values];
    }
}
- (void) insertObject: (OutlineItem*)item inChildrenAtIndex: (NSUInteger)
    index
{
    [children insertObject: item atIndex: index];
}
- (void) removeObjectFromChildren: (OutlineItem*)child;
{
    [children removeObjectIdenticalTo: child];
}
- (void) dealloc
{
    [children release];
    [values release];
```

```
79     [super dealloc];
80 }
81 @end
```

The NSCoding methods are similarly updated. These now store the dictionary, rather than the title. On lines 38–43 you can see a special case designed for backward compatibility. If you try to decode an older version of this object, then there will be a title, but not a values, property. This correctly moves the title into the dictionary.

The final change is the method on line 71, for removing objects. This is now changed to work better with a data source than with bindings. The old version could have been used, but this simplifies things slightly.

The next class is the outline view controller. This object is where most of the

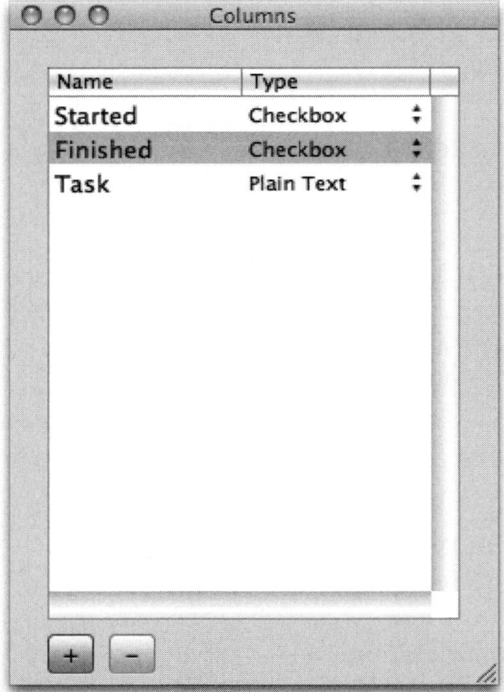

Figure 11.3: The columns inspector for the multicolumn outliner.

work happens, so we'll look at it a bit at a time. The initialization happens in Listing 11.4

Listing 11.4: Initializing the multicolumn outline view controller. [from: examples/-MulticolumnOutliner/OutlineViewController.m]

```
1 - (void) awakeFromNib
2 {
3     columns = [[NSMutableArray alloc] initWithObjects:
4                [NSMutableDictionary dictionaryWithObjectsAndKeys:
5                 @"title", @"title",
6                 @"0", @"type",
7                 nil], nil];
8     cells = [NSMutableArray new];
9     NSTextFieldCell *textCell = [[NSTextFieldCell alloc] init];
10    [textCell setAllowsEditingTextAttributes: NO];
11    [textCell setEditable: YES];
12    [cells addObject: textCell];
13    [textCell release];
14    NSButtonCell *buttonCell = [[NSButtonCell alloc] init];
15    [buttonCell setButtonType: NSSwitchButton];
16    [buttonCell setTitle: @""];
17    [buttonCell setEditable: YES];
18    [cells addObject: buttonCell];
19    [buttonCell release];
20 }
```

This class has two instance variables. The `columns` array stores dictionaries containing the name and type of each column. The type is just an integer, representing an index in the `cells` array. This array contains prototype cells for each type that the outliner supports. We create these cells on lines 12–23.

The first cell is a simple plain-text editing cell. The second is a check box. We can extend this program in the future by providing more cells, for example, images or sliders.

This example is only meant to demonstrate some of the aspects of using an outline view, and so some of the parts of a good document-driven application are omitted. The array created on lines 7–11 contains a single default column. This should really be either loaded from the document or initialized in the document object to these values.

Note that on line 10 the index is stored as a string. The only things we can store in Cocoa collections are objects, but most commonly we would use an `NSNumber` to represent a value like this, not a string. Doing this is an example of using the dynamic capabilities of Objective-C to be a little bit lazy. Whatever type the object has, we only care that it implements an `-integerValue` method, returning an `NSInteger`. Both `NSString` and `NSNumber` do, so we can use either here. Using a constant string simplifies the code.

The next part of this controller is shown in Listing 11.5. This shows the methods that are called by the column inspector controller that we saw earlier.

Listing 11.5: Titles and types in the outline view controller. [from: examples/MulticolumnOutliner/OutlineViewController.m]

```
1  - (id)typeForColumnAtIndex: (NSUInteger)index
2  {
3      return [[columns objectAtIndex: index] objectForKey: @"type"];
4  }
5  - (NSString*)titleForColumnAtIndex: (NSUInteger)index
6  {
7      return [[columns objectAtIndex: index] objectForKey: @"title"];
8  }
9  - (void)setType: (id)aType forColumnAtIndex: (NSUInteger)index
10 {
11     NSMutableDictionary *column = [columns objectAtIndex: index];
12     [column setObject: aType forKey: @"type"];
13     NSCell *cell = [cells objectAtIndex: [aType integerValue]];
14     [[[view tableColumns] objectAtIndex: index] setDataCell: [cell copy]];
15     [view reloadData];
16 }
17 - (void)setTitle: (NSString*)aTitle forColumnAtIndex: (NSUInteger)index
18 {
19     NSMutableDictionary *column = [columns objectAtIndex: index];
20     [column setObject: aTitle forKey: @"title"];
21     NSTableColumn *tableColumn = [[view tableColumns] objectAtIndex: index
           ];
22     [[tableColumn headerCell] setStringValue: aTitle];
23     [tableColumn setIdentifier: aTitle];
24 }
25 - (NSUInteger)numberOfColumns
26 {
27     return [columns count];
28 }
```

The last of these simply returns the number of columns available in the outline view. This is called first when populating the table in the inspector, to give the number of rows. The other four methods are used to set and get the values for each row in the inspector table. The get methods are very simple—they just return a value from the array—but the set methods are more complex.

The method for setting the type is shown on line 33. The first two lines update the information in the column and the last part updates the view. Line 37 gets the cell prototype corresponding to the selected type from the array. In the current implementation, this is either going to be a text field cell or a check box cell. The table column object corresponding to this index is then looked up from the view and its data cell is set to a copy of the prototype. Note that this has to be a copy—views may store some state in the cell, and setting the same cell for two columns may result in some very strange behavior.

Once the new cell has been set, the view is told to reload its contents. This is quite expensive, but unfortunately there's nothing we can do to make it faster. The cell has changed and so every single row needs that column updating, and the outline view lacks a method for updating a single column. Fortunately, changing the type of a column should be something that happens relatively rarely.

Setting the title is similar. Again, the first two lines update the values in the array. The last two modify the table column. We set both the header cell's value and the column's identifier to the new string. You can see in Listing 11.6 how this identifier is used when getting information for the outline view.

Note that using the identifier in this way has an unfortunate side effect. When you rename a column, with the current version, all of the data in that column will disappear. If you change the name back, it will reappear. Try adding a method to `OutlineItem` that recursively updates the data for a renamed column. This should get the value for the old key and set it as the value for the new one.

Listing 11.6: Multicolumn outline view controller datasource methods. [from: examples/MulticolumnOutliner/OutlineViewController.m]

```
- (id)outlineView: (NSOutlineView *)outlineView
            child: (NSInteger)index
           ofItem: (OutlineItem*)item
{
    if (item == nil)
    {
        return [document root];
    }
    return [item.children objectAtIndex: index];
}
- (NSInteger)outlineView: (NSOutlineView*)outlineView
  numberOfChildrenOfItem: (OutlineItem*)item
{
    if (item == nil)
    {
        return 1;
    }
    return [item.children count];
}
- (BOOL)outlineView: (NSOutlineView*)outlineView
```

```
21     isItemExpandable: (OutlineItem*)item
22 {
23     return [item.children count] > 0;
24 }
25 -          (id)outlineView: (NSOutlineView*)outlineView
26 objectValueForTableColumn: (NSTableColumn*)tableColumn
27                    byItem: (id)item
28 {
29     return [item valueForKey: [tableColumn identifier]];
30 }
31 - (void)outlineView: (NSOutlineView*)outlineView
32      setObjectValue: (id)object
33      forTableColumn: (NSTableColumn*)tableColumn
34             byItem: (id)item
35 {
36     [item setValue: object forKey: [tableColumn identifier]];
37 }
```

The data source methods are very simple, due to our use of KVC in the model object. Note how getting a displayable object from an item is a single line of code, on line 81. This uses the column identifier as a key and the KVC accessor to get the corresponding object. The corresponding set method is similarly simple, on line 88. Both of these methods have prototypes longer than their implementation.

The other methods just return the number of children of an item and whether it can be expanded. These are trivial, just returning the count of the array and whether it is greater than zero respectively.

Because we are no longer using bindings, we need a mechanism for adding and removing children manually. These two action methods are shown in Listing 11.7.

Listing 11.7: Multicolumn outline view controller action methods. [from: examples/-MulticolumnOutliner/OutlineViewController.m]

```
- (IBAction)insertChild: (id)sender
{
    OutlineItem *selected = [view itemAtRow: [view selectedRow]];
    if (selected == nil)
    {
        selected = [document root];
    }
    [selected insertObject: [[OutlineItem new] autorelease]
         inChildrenAtIndex: [selected.children count]];
    [view reloadItem: selected reloadChildren: YES];
    [view expandItem: selected];
}
- (IBAction)removeChild: (id)sender
```

```
{
    NSUInteger row = [view selectedRow];
    OutlineItem *selected = [view itemAtRow: row];
    OutlineItem *parent = [view parentForItem: selected];
    [parent removeObjectFromChildren: selected];
    [view reloadItem: parent reloadChildren: YES];
}
```

Line 91 looks up the currently selected item. When we insert an item, we want to add it as a child of this item. If no items are selected, then we default to adding a new child at the end.

On line 100, we reload the children of the item that we've just added a child to. This should be a lot faster than reloading all of the outline view. Because we are not using bindings, we are not limited to just adding the item here. We can also display it. Line 101 tells the outline view to expand the parent of the new item so that we can make sure that the new item is visible. Note that this line has to be after the reload. Putting them in the opposite order would not expand the item when you inserted the first child, since the outline view would have a cached copy of the selected item indicating that it had no children, and so would silently ignore the expand instruction.

The remove method is slightly more complicated. The outline item doesn't keep track of its parents and so you have to find it yourself. Rather than doing a tree traversal to find it, we simply ask the outline view. The outline view will maintain this information in a cache internally for all visible objects, and we are only deleting visible objects so this is very simple. Once the parent has been found, it is told to delete the child, and then the table view is instructed to update all of the children of the object that has just had a child removed.

The next two methods, shown in Listing 11.8, are for adding and removing table columns. Recall that these are called from the inspector's controller.

Listing 11.8: Adding and removing outline view columns. [from: examples/MulticolumnOutliner/OutlineViewController.m]

```
- (void) addColumn
{
    [columns addObject: [NSMutableDictionary dictionaryWithObjectsAndKeys:
                          @"newColumn", @"title",
                          @"0", @"type",
                          nil]];
    NSTableColumn *newColumn = [[NSTableColumn alloc] initWithIdentifier: @
        "newColumn"];
    [newColumn setDataCell: [[cells objectAtIndex: 0] copy]];
    [view addTableColumn: newColumn];
    [view reloadData];
```

```
}
- (void) removeColumnAtIndex: (NSUInteger) index
{
    NSTableColumn *column = [[view tableColumns] objectAtIndex: index];
    [columns removeObjectAtIndex: index];
    [view removeTableColumn: column];
    [view reloadData];
}
```

When we add a new table column, we give it some default values in the metadata stored by this object and then create the `NSTableColumn` instance. Note that if you create two table columns with the same name, they will display the same data, because we use the identifier to look up the table value. This might be desired behavior in some cases—you can have an outline that uses two types of cell to display different representations of the same value—but it can be confusing.

Removing is much simpler; the column object and metadata are deleted and the table is reloaded. Note that this doesn't delete any of the data in the items. You might choose to only save the values that are currently displayed, or save everything but provide an option for deleting values that are not displayed.

The final method, shown in Listing 11.9, is an outline view delegate method. This will be called whenever the user rearranges the table columns.

Listing 11.9: Rearranging table columns. [from: examples/MulticolumnOutliner/OutlineViewController.m]

```
- (void)outlineViewColumnDidMove: (NSNotification*)notification
{
    NSDictionary *userInfo = [notification userInfo];
    NSInteger oldIndex = [[userInfo objectForKey: @"NSOldColumn"]
         integerValue];
    NSInteger newIndex = [[userInfo objectForKey: @"NSNewColumn"]
         integerValue];
    id column = [[columns objectAtIndex: oldIndex] retain];
    [columns removeObjectAtIndex: oldIndex];
    [columns insertObject: column atIndex: newIndex];
    [column release];
}
```

Remember that we also listened for this notification in the inspector. The handler in the inspector required this object to have been updated already. This is a safe assumption, because the delegate method will always be called before the notification is posted. It is not safe, however, to make assumptions about the order in which other notification listeners will be invoked.

When the table columns are moved, we update the metadata in the controller. In theory we don't need this metadata array at all; we could store the data entirely in the view's state. This is generally considered to be a bad idea. If you wanted to turn this example into a real application, you should move this array into the document model object and have it saved along with the attributes of the items.

You can see the final version in Figure 11.4. This instance is displaying three columns, one of which contains text and the other two contain check boxes.

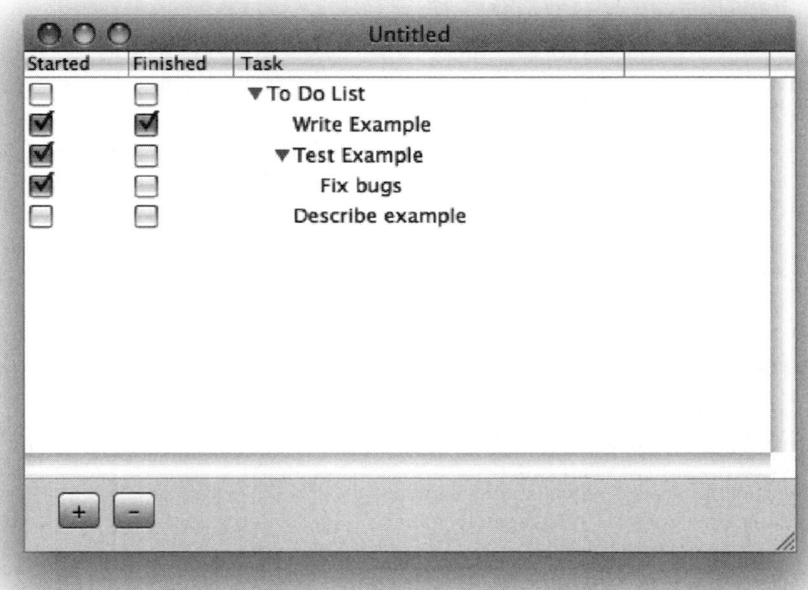

Figure 11.4: The multicolumn outliner.

All of the values for these will be stored as objects, typically `NSNumber` instances for the checkboxes and strings for the text fields. You might try adding support for rich text, too. This won't work with the standard encoder; you will need to store attributed strings as `NSData` instances by converting them to RTF first.

You can easily extend this framework to support arbitrary kinds of cell. You could also try supporting different cells for items with children and those without, for example, to display a computed summary in the items with children.

11.4 Browsers

The other kind of view designed for hierarchical data is NSBrowser. This is not a subclass of NSTableView and so is somewhat different from the first two compound views we've looked at.

The biggest difference is that the browser does not have a data source and delegate as separate objects; it just has a delegate that fulfills both rôles. This is not really a limitation, since most of the time developers tend to implement the delegate and data sources for the table view classes as a single object. Where the separate behavior really is required, it is possible to make your delegate object delegate the data source methods to another object, but this is very unusual.

Like the outline view, a browser displays a hierarchy, but unlike the outline view it only displays a single entry for each element. You can compare the two views in the Finder easily. In browser mode, the Finder displays an icon and label for each file. In outline mode it displays various other metadata fields. The browser can display more data than a single field in each entry. Each column contains an NSMatrix that can display an arbitrary selection of cells.

11.4.1 Browser Delegates

There are two ways of providing data to a browser. The simpler is to use a *passive browser delegate*. A passive delegate must implement this method:

```
- (NSInteger)browser: (NSBrowser*)sender
numberOfRowsInColumn: (NSInteger)column;
```

This is called by the browser when it creates a new column to let it know how many objects there are in this column. The browser will then populate the column with cells, calling this method for each row:

```
- (void)browser: (NSBrowser*)sender
willDisplayCell: (id)cell
          atRow: (NSInteger)row
         column: (NSInteger)column;
```

The cell used to draw the row is defined when the browser is created, or by calling -setCellClass: or -setCellPrototype: with either a cell class or instance as an argument. This cell—or a copy of it—will be passed back to the delegate via the above method. The delegate should then set the value of the cell and any other attributes that are needed for display. This allows a significant amount of customization, but does not expose all of the power of the browser.

The other kind of delegate is an *active browser delegate*. Instead of -browser:numberOfRowsInColumn:, an active delegate implements this method:

```
-     (void)browser: (NSBrowser*)sender
createRowsForColumn: (NSInteger)column
          inMatrix: (NSMatrix*)matrix;
```

This method is responsible for creating all of the cells manually. The matrix can be modified to contain different cells in any location. Unfortunately, any attempt to add a column to this matrix will cause an exception to be raised. This is a shame, since a lot of browsers want to display more than one kind of data in the cell.

All cells displayed by the browser must be subclasses of `NSBrowserCell`. This class provides some browser-specific behavior, such as indicating whether an item is a leaf node in the hierarchy.

11.4.2 Creating a Browser

To demonstrate how to control a browser from the delegate, we will create a very simple file browser. This will be a simplified version of the Finder's file browser view, as shown in Figure 11.5.

This will use an active delegate. Each column will be populated in a single call. The delegate is shown in Listing 11.10.

Listing 11.10: The simple filesystem browser delegate. [from: examples/FileBrowser/FileBrowserDelegate.m]

```
#import "FileBrowserDelegate.h"

@implementation FileBrowserDelegate
- (void) awakeFromNib
{
    [browser setTakesTitleFromPreviousColumn: YES];
    [browser setTitled: YES];
    [browser setTitle: @"/" ofColumn: 0];
    [browser setColumnResizingType: NSBrowserUserColumnResizing];
    [browser setDoubleAction: @selector(openFile:)];
    [browser setTarget: self];
}
-     (void)browser: (NSBrowser*)sender
createRowsForColumn: (NSInteger)column
          inMatrix: (NSMatrix*)matrix
{
    NSSize iconSize = [matrix cellSize];
    iconSize.width = iconSize.height;
    NSFileManager *fm = [NSFileManager defaultManager];
    NSString *path = [@"/" stringByAppendingPathComponent: [sender path]];
```

```
21      NSArray *files = [fm directoryContentsAtPath: path];
22      for (NSString *file in files)
23      {
24          NSString *filePath = [path stringByAppendingPathComponent: file];
25          BOOL isDir = NO;
26          NSBrowserCell *cell = [[NSBrowserCell alloc] init];
27          if (([fm fileExistsAtPath: filePath isDirectory: &isDir] && !isDir)
28              || [[filePath pathExtension] isEqualToString: @"app"])
29          {
30              NSImage *icon = [[NSWorkspace sharedWorkspace] iconForFile:
                    filePath];
31              [icon setSize: iconSize];
32              [cell setImage: icon];
33              [cell setLeaf: YES];
34          }
35          [cell setTitle: file];
36          [matrix addRowWithCells: [NSArray arrayWithObject: cell]];
37          [cell release];
38      }
39  }
40  - (void) openFile: (id) sender
41  {
42      [[NSWorkspace sharedWorkspace] openFile: [browser path]];
43  }
44  @end
```

The NSBrowser inspector in Interface Builder doesn't have nearly as many of its configurable options exposed as most of the other views, so we begin by setting some attributes of the browser when the nib is loaded.

The first three lines here set the behavior of the title. We want this to display the path to the current directory. The first call instructs the browser that the title of each column should be the value from the one to the left. This means that when we click on a directory in one column, the directory name will be used as the title of the next column without any extra code.

The last two lines define an action message to be sent when the user double-clicks on an item. We don't want to use the standard single-click action because this is used to open children, although we could use it to display some extra information about the file. When an item is double-clicked, the method on line 40 is called. This uses NSWorkspace to open the item with the default application. This allows the simple file browser to act as a launcher as well as simply displaying tasks.

The columns are all populated by the browser calling the method on line 13. This begins by calculating the size for the icon. This is done by asking the matrix

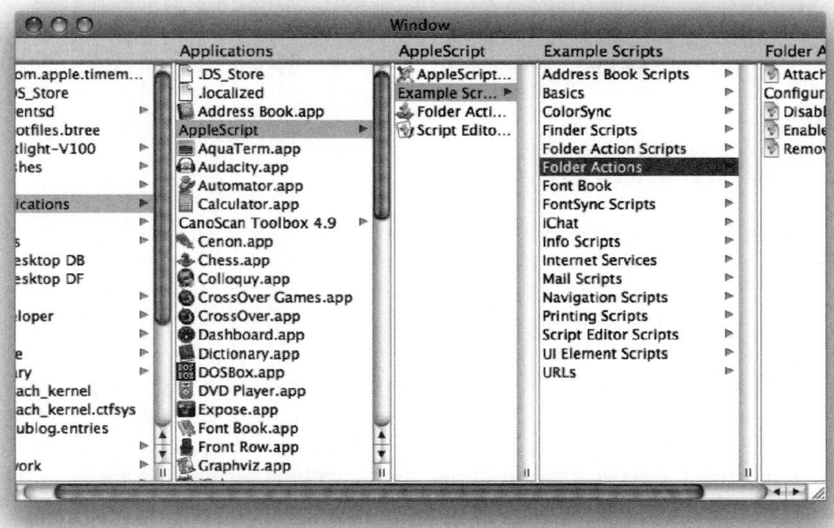

Figure 11.5: A simple filesystem browser.

being used for this column how big its cells should be and then constructing a square from the height. This is used later to scale the icon down to fit in the view.

Perhaps the most interesting part of this is line 20. Unlike outline views, which can display lots of branches in a tree, browsers only display one path from the root. You can access this by sending it a `-path` message. This returns a string with each selection item separated by the assigned path separator. This is a slash by default—so it works for file paths without modification—but it can be modified by calling `-setPathSeparator:` with a string argument. You might set this to a dot and use the path as a KVC key path, for example.

When we have the path to the current column, we get an array of all of the files in this directory from the file manager and iterate over all of them, adding them to the matrix.

The test on lines 27 and 28 determines whether the current file is a directory, and whether it has the `.app` extension. We use this to only display an icon for files, not for directories. This is a simple example of cell customization. You can do something like this to display entirely different browser cell subclasses for different types of files.

Because this is an active delegate, we set all of the rows in the matrix at the same time. This is a good way of quickly populating a column, since it avoids the need to repeatedly call the delegate. It can be much slower on big columns, however, since all of the cells are created even if they do not need to be displayed.

11.5 Collection Views

Collection views are a new addition with Leopard. They are conceptually similar to the older `NSMatrix` view. `NSMatrix` is a lightweight view for displaying a collection of cells in a regular grid. This is often useful for creating simple forms dynamically, by inserting cells for the label and value in two columns, and for other regular arrangements.

The `NSCollectionView` class displays a similar regular arrangement, but of views rather than cells. These views are generated by copying a prototype. This can be a simple view instance, but most often it will be an `NSView` created in Interface Builder containing a selection of different views to handle the various components.

The reason classes like `NSMatrix` exist is that implementing something like `NSCollectionView` on the systems where OpenStep originally ran—where a 33MHz CPU and 8MB of RAM was a high-end workstation—would not have been possible. Now, although cells are still much leaner than separate views, the additional RAM and CPU cost is no longer a massive problem. Even the iPhone is significantly more powerful than most of the NeXT workstations.

`NSCollectionView` is somewhat better than the naive approach at a view containing lots of different subviews arranged in a grid. It does not keep copies of the view that are no longer being displayed, it just maintains the ones that are within the currently visible bounds in the view hierarchy. This allows it to be used for very large collections without slowing down too much.

The individual grid item views in a collection view are managed by `NSCollectionViewItem` instances. This class maintains pointers to the view and the represented object. This enables the view to be easily constructed as a prototype in Interface Builder.

When you construct the template for an item view, you can set bindings pointing to the `NSCollectionViewItem` prototype in your nib. When copies of the item are made, these connections will be preserved.

If the prototype system is not enough for you—for example, if you want different item views for different kinds of item—you can create a custom subclass. This should override the following method:

```
- (NSCollectionViewItem*)newItemForRepresentedObject: (id)object;
```

You can use this to construct any kind of view to display the argument, and associate it with a new `NSCollectionViewItem`.

Newton Heritage

The Collection view, with its prototype-based design owes a lot to an Apple product that was killed by Steve Jobs as soon as he returned as CEO, the *Apple Newton*. The designers of this system were proponents of class-based object-oriented languages for designing models and prototype-based languages for designing user interfaces. You will see elements of this in a few places in Cocoa, but none more strongly than the collection view.

11.5.1 Displaying Files in a Collection View

To demonstrate the collection view, we will modify the filesystem browser to use the browser for directories and then display the files in a collection view underneath, as shown in Figure 11.7.

Although you would probably not want to implement your own file manager, you might consider using this kind of user interface for managing user-created collections in your own applications.

The code for the new delegate is shown in Listing 11.11. The collection view, as a new addition to Cocoa, depends heavily on bindings. As such, a lot of the complexity of this example lives in the nib file, shown in Figure 11.6. Two of the objects shown here are created automatically when the collection view is created.

The collection view item is a placeholder for collection view items. This contains pointers to both the view and the represented item. We don't modify this directly in the nib, but any bindings we make to it will be automatically updated to point to the real collection view item when one is created.

The view outside of the window is the prototype view for items in the collection view. We insert an image view and a text field in here and bind them to attributes of the `representedObject` property of the collection view item.

The array controller is bound to an instance variable in our delegate that is automatically updated when we populate a new column in the view. The collection view is then bound to this array controller. When the array is updated the array controller updates the contents view, and the contents view creates a new item for each object in the array. These items are instances of `NSCollectionViewItem` with their `representedObject` property set to object fetched from the array and their `view` set to a copy of the view in the nib.

The delegate is quite similar to the last version. Since we use the file and workspace manager singletons a lot in this class, we grab pointers to them in file **`static`** variables when the class receives its message. This saves a few lookups and, more importantly, some typing. The `fm` and `ws` variables are pointers to the shared file and workspace manager objects, respectively.

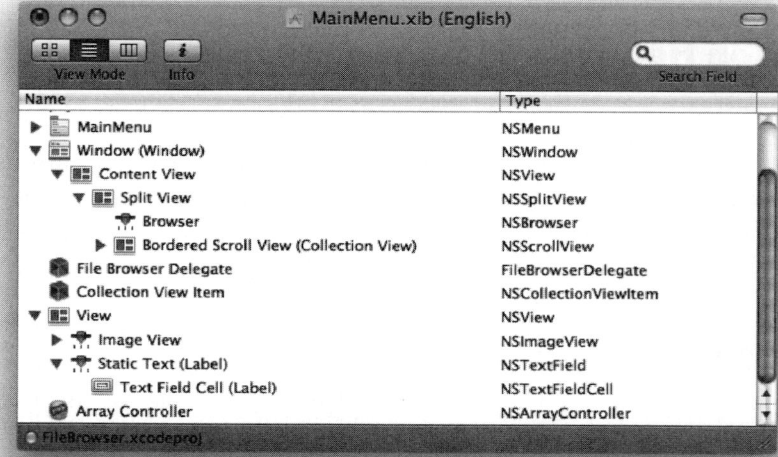

Figure 11.6: Objects in the nib file for the collection view.

Figure 11.7: A file browser with an icon view.

Listing 11.11: A browser delegate providing filesystem entries. [from: examples/FileBrowser2/FileBrowserDelegate.m]

```
21 -      (void)browser: (NSBrowser*)sender
22 createRowsForColumn: (NSInteger)column
23            inMatrix: (NSMatrix*)matrix
24 {
25     NSSize iconSize = [matrix cellSize];
26     iconSize.width = iconSize.height;
27     NSString *path = [@"/" stringByAppendingPathComponent: [sender path]];
28     NSArray *files = [fm directoryContentsAtPath: path];
29     NSMutableArray *fileImages = [NSMutableArray new];
30     for (NSString *file in files)
31     {
32         NSString *filePath = [path stringByAppendingPathComponent: file];
33         BOOL isDir = NO;
34         if (([fm fileExistsAtPath: filePath isDirectory: &isDir] && isDir)
35             && ![[filePath pathExtension] isEqualToString: @"app"])
36         {
37             NSBrowserCell *cell = [[NSBrowserCell alloc] init];
38             [cell setTitle: file];
39             [matrix addRowWithCells: [NSArray arrayWithObject: cell]];
40             [cell release];
41         }
42         else
43         {
44             NSDictionary *icon = [NSDictionary dictionaryWithObjectsAndKeys
                   :
45                 [ws iconForFile: filePath], @"icon",
46                 file, @"name",
47                 nil];
48             [fileImages addObject: icon];
49         }
50     }
51     [self willChangeValueForKey: @"directoryContents"];
52     [directoryContents release];
53     directoryContents = [fileImages retain];
54     [self didChangeValueForKey: @"directoryContents"];
55 }
```

The main differences occur after line 34. In this version, we are only populating the browser with directories. Files are no longer shown in this view. Instead, all of the files are added to an array. This array contains a dictionary for each file, with one entry for the icon and one for the name.

Once this array has been constructed, it replaces the existing one. The icon view is then updated automatically as a result of receiving the KVO notification. This is a somewhat round-about way of setting it. We could just as easily call `-setContent:` on the collection view. The advantage of this approach is that it does not tightly couple the two views together. We could easily create some other view for displaying the icons and have it update automatically without modifying this code.

11.6 Customizing Views with New Cells

We've seen how to customize the layout of the view that uses cells for drawing in a number of ways. With the newer interfaces, we can display an arbitrary cell for each slot in a table view and for the entire row, but one thing that we can't do is make a cell span two columns.

If you want to present this kind of user interface, the best thing to do is design a new cell that can draw the contents of two other cells. The simplest way of synthesizing this kind of interface is to join the two columns together as a single real column and then define a split cell.

This is relatively easy. The split cell just wraps two cells and draws the provided object using both of them. Figure 11.8 shows a simple demo where a single-column table view is showing two cells in each row.

The code to implement this cell is shown in Listing 11.12. This is initialized with two cells as arguments, one to draw on the left and one to draw on the right. It also declares three properties. Two of these are keys, used to access attributes of the object that it is supposed to draw, via KVC. The remaining one allows the user to decide what proportion of the split cell should be drawn by the left cell and what proportion by the right.

Listing 11.12: A simple split cell. [from: examples/SplitCell/SplitCell.m]

```
@implementation SplitCell
@synthesize leftKey;
@synthesize rightKey;
@synthesize split;
- (id) initWithLeftCell: (NSCell*)aCell rightCell: (NSCell*)aCell2
{
    if (nil == (self = [self init])) { return nil; }
    left = [aCell retain];
    right = [aCell2 retain];
    split = 0.5;
    return self;
}
- (void)drawWithFrame:(NSRect)cellFrame inView:(NSView *)controlView
```

```
{
    NSRect leftFrame = cellFrame;
    leftFrame.size.width *= split;
    NSRect rightFrame = cellFrame;
    rightFrame.size.width = cellFrame.size.width - leftFrame.size.width;
    rightFrame.origin.x = leftFrame.size.width;
    id obj = [self objectValue];
    if (nil != leftKey)
    {
        [left setObjectValue: [obj valueForKey: leftKey]];
    }
    else
    {
        [left setObjectValue: obj];
    }
    [left drawWithFrame: leftFrame
                 inView: controlView];
    if (nil != rightKey)
    {
        [right setObjectValue: [obj valueForKey: rightKey]];
    }
    else
    {
        [right setObjectValue: obj];
    }
    [right drawWithFrame: rightFrame
                  inView: controlView];
}
@end
```

When the cell is instructed to draw itself, it is given a rectangle and a view. The first thing it needs to do is split this rectangle into two pieces. The `split` instance variable stores what proportion of the total area should be drawn by the left cell. This is multiplied by the width of the rectangle to give the width of the left cell. The width of the right cell is the remaining space.

The code for drawing each cell is almost identical. First, the object value for the cell is obtained. This might have been set with `-setObjectValue:` or with one of the other set methods on `NSCell`. If a key is defined for either cell then the object is sent a `-valueForKey:` method with that key as the argument. If not, we simply assign the object to the cell. Note that this must be done every time the split cell is drawn. A common way of using cells—one employed by the data views we are looking at in this chapter—involves repeatedly drawing the same cell with different objects.

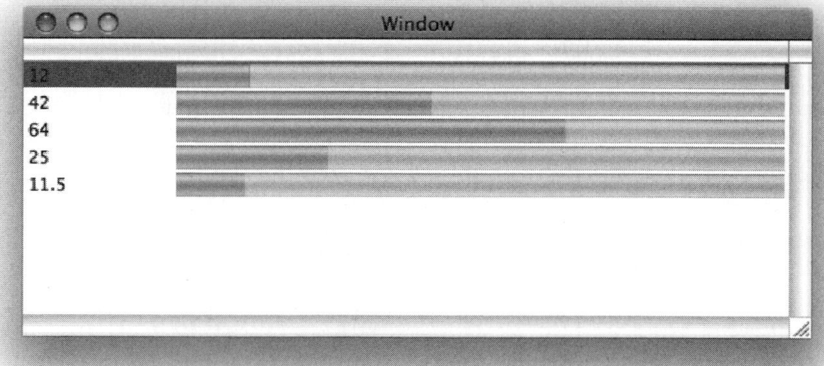

Figure 11.8: Displaying two cells in a single column.

The individual cells are then told to draw in the rectangles that have been calculated for them. To test this, we use the code in Listing 11.13.

Listing 11.13: Using the simple split cell. [from: examples/SplitCell/SplitCellDemo.m]

```
@implementation SplitCellDemo
- (void) awakeFromNib
{
    [self willChangeValueForKey: @"objects"];
    objects = [[NSArray alloc] initWithObjects:
                @"12", @"42", @"64",
                @"25", @"11.5", nil];
    [self didChangeValueForKey: @"objects"];
    NSLevelIndicatorCell *right = [[NSLevelIndicatorCell alloc] init];
    [right setMaxValue: 100];
    [right setLevelIndicatorStyle: NSContinuousCapacityLevelIndicatorStyle
        ];
    NSCell *left = [[NSTextFieldCell alloc] init];
    SplitCell *cell = [[SplitCell alloc] initWithLeftCell: left
                                                rightCell: right];
    cell.split = 0.2;
    [column setDataCell: cell];
}
@end
```

This class contains an array that is bound to the table column using an array controller. The array is just a constant set of string objects. To use the split cell, we define new cells for the left and the right. The left cell displays the text value of the string. The right cell is a level indicator. This will display a bar representing the numerical value of the object on a scale of 1 to 100.

For this simple demo we don't bother using keys for the objects. We will draw the same value in both cells. The split is set to 0.2 so that 20% of the width of the table column should be used to display the text cell and the remainder used for the level indicator. This compound cell is then set to the data cell for the column.

This version has one significant disadvantage over other cells; it does not handle events at all. You should try extending it by implementing this method:

```
- (BOOL)trackMouse: (NSEvent*)theEvent
            inRect: (NSRect)cellFrame
            ofView: (NSView*)controlView
      untilMouseUp: (BOOL)untilMouseUp;
```

This method is not usually overridden by `NSCell` subclasses as it is used to fire lots of other event-handling methods. In this case, however, we do want to override it. The replacement method should follow the same general pattern as the drawing method, calling the corresponding version in either the left or the right cell depending on which one the mouse began in. This will allow you to have text fields or buttons inside split cells.

You can extend the split cell concept even further by having more than two cells drawn by a single cell. This can be useful when you implement a `-tableView:dataCellForTableColumn:row:` method for the `nil` column. This allows you to replace the entire row with a single column. By combining this with a split cell, you can draw the normal values for most columns, but a combined value for some arbitrary pair.

You would do this by getting the table columns array and then sending each one a `-dataCell` message to get the cell that they expect to draw with and a `-width` message to get the width of that column. These can then be combined to produce a cell that will draw the normal appearance of the table. You can then modify it to replace any subset of the cells with something more interesting.

11.7 Creating Master-Detail Views

One very common pattern in Cocoa user interfaces is the *master-detail view.* This is a user interface with two components, one providing an overview of a large collection of data and the other providing detailed information about an individual element.

You can find examples of this all over OS X. The Finder, in browser mode, displays a list of file names and icons in a directory and some detailed information about the selected file. iTunes displays a list of tracks and shows the cover art for the selected one. iCal gives an overview of events in the calendar, and a detailed description of one.

On OPENSTEP, a great many applications made heavy use of a specialized form of detail view called an *inspector*. This provided a very detailed description of some aspect of the current selection. Applications that have been ported from, or inspired by, OPENSTEP applications continue this trend on OS X. The shortcut Command-i typically displays an inspector, although many applications add another modifier to it.

We saw a simple inspector in the multicolumn outliner example. The outline view was inspected to show the name and type of the columns. This wasn't really a master-detail view, merely a different presentation of the same information, but many of the same principles apply.

The only relatively complex part of implementing a master-detail view is keeping the detail part synchronized with the master. When you change the selection in the master view, you need to update the detail view. In general, there are three ways you can do this in Cocoa:

- Manually, by having the master view send a message to the detail view when its selection changes. This is easy for simple views, but is quite fragile, and difficult to extend to other detail views.

- Using a notification. This is how we kept the inspector updated in the example earlier in this chapter. This works fairly well, but requires the master view or its controller to post a useful notification when the selection has changed.

- Using KVO and bindings. This eliminates most of the difficulty in writing a master-detail view. You just bind a controller to the view's selection and it will automatically update the contents.

Bindings provide the easiest mechanism when you are watching a single view. If you press Command-Option-i in the Finder, you get a more complex kind of detail view. This is an inspector that shows information about the current selection. The important thing to notice is that this works even when you select something in a different Finder window. You can implement something similar in your own programs using a combination of the second two approaches.

Recall that you can set up bindings in code as well as using Interface Builder. First, you get a notification when the main window in your application has changed. This tells the detail view that the controller it is using may now be bound to the wrong master view. In the notification handler, you detach the controller from the selected object and bind it to the correct view in the new window. We will examine how to do this by adding an inspector to the simple file browser we wrote in the last section.

11.7.1 Inspectors as Detail Views

The second file manager implemented a simple master-detail view. The master view showed directories and the detail view showed the files. This was kept up to date using KVO.

We will extend this to provide an inspector that automatically tracks the currently selected item even if it is in a different window. The end result is shown in Figure 11.9. This shows two file browser windows and a floating inspector panel that inspects the selected file in either.

The first change required to do this is to move the views we defined in the last example into a separate nib and turn the browser view delegate into an `NSDocument` subclass. This isn't, strictly speaking, required, but it's the easiest way of getting support for multiple, identical, windows. After this change, we only need to press Command-n to get a new file browser window. This lets us easily test whether the inspector is really tracking the changes.

This requires some other small changes to the existing delegate class. These changes are all visible in the class interface, shown in Listing 11.14. This class now has a reference to the array controller, which it exposes via a read-only property. It also has an accessor that returns the path to the file at the specified index in the current directory.

Listing 11.14: File browser interface. [from: examples/FileBrowserInspector/FileBrowser.h]

```
#import <Cocoa/Cocoa.h>

@interface FileBrowser : NSDocument {
    IBOutlet NSBrowser *browser;
    NSArray *directoryContents;
    IBOutlet NSArrayController *arrayController;
}
@property (nonatomic, readonly) NSArrayController *arrayController;
- (NSString*) fileAtIndex: (NSUInteger)anIndex;
@end
```

Listing 11.15 shows the interface to the inspector controller. An instance of this, and its accompanying window, are inserted into the main nib. The controller has outlets for all of the views in this inspector. An icon view at the top and three text fields at the bottom display the file's owner, size, and name.

Listing 11.15: The interface to the inspector controller. [from: examples/FileBrowserInspector/InspectorController.h]

```
#import <Cocoa/Cocoa.h>

@class FileBrowser;

@interface InspectorController : NSObject {
    IBOutlet NSImageView *icon;
    IBOutlet NSTextField *size;
    IBOutlet NSTextField *owner;
    IBOutlet NSTextField *filename;
    FileBrowser *currentDocument;
}
@end
```

The inspector also keeps a reference to the current document. You will see why when we look at the implementation, shown in Listing 11.16.

This begins by registering to receive a notification whenever the main window changes. Recall that there are two important windows in Cocoa, the key window and the main window. The key window is the one that receives key events, while the main window is the active document. We only need to update the inspector if the main window changes, since the inspector should not inspect things in other inspectors or itself.

Listing 11.16: The implementation of the inspector controller. [from: examples/FileBrowserInspector/InspectorController.m]

```
#import "InspectorController.h"
#import "FileBrowser.h"

@implementation InspectorController
- (void) awakeFromNib
{
    NSNotificationCenter *center = [NSNotificationCenter defaultCenter];
    [center addObserver: self
               selector: @selector(windowChanged:)
                   name: NSWindowDidBecomeMainNotification
                 object: nil];
}
- (void) windowChanged: (NSNotification*)notification
{
    NSWindow *window = [notification object];
    FileBrowser *doc = [[window windowController] document];
    if (currentDocument != doc)
    {
```

```
        [currentDocument.arrayController removeObserver: self
                                            forKeyPath: @"selectionIndex"];
        [doc.arrayController addObserver: self
                              forKeyPath: @"selectionIndex"
                                 options: NSKeyValueObservingOptionNew
                                 context: NULL];
        currentDocument = doc;
    }
}
- (void)observeValueForKeyPath: (NSString*)keyPath
                      ofObject: (id)object
                        change: (NSDictionary*)change
                       context: (void *)context
{
    NSInteger index = [currentDocument.arrayController selectionIndex];
    if (index == NSNotFound) { return; }

    NSString *file = [currentDocument fileAtIndex: index];

    [icon setImage: [[NSWorkspace sharedWorkspace] iconForFile: file]];

    NSFileManager *fm = [NSFileManager defaultManager];
    NSDictionary *attributes =
        [fm attributesOfItemAtPath: file error: nil];
    [size setStringValue:
        [attributes objectForKey: NSFileSize]];
    [owner setStringValue:
        [attributes objectForKey: NSFileOwnerAccountName]];

    [filename setStringValue: [file lastPathComponent]];
}
@end
```

When the main window changes, the `-windowChanged:` method will be called. The first thing this does is get the current document. The object for the main window change notification is the new main window. Since we are using the document infrastructure, we can ask this for its controller, and then ask the controller for its document. This is set automatically by `NSDocument` when it loads the nib file. If we were using a little bit more of the document infrastructure, we could get this by sending a `-currentDocument` message to the shared `NSDocumentController` instance instead.

If the current document has changed, then the inspector needs updating. It doesn't just depend on the main window, however, it depends on the selection within that window. This is monitored using KVO.

Figure 11.9: A simple inspector.

The controller registers to receive a KVO notification for the "selectionIndex" key in the array controller. Note that we can watch the controllers supplied for use in bindings just as we can ask them to watch our objects. The same KVC/KVO mechanism is used on both sides of the controller.

If the inspector was already registered for a notification on one object, it relinquishes this before registering the new one. Now, when the user clicks on an item in the icon view, the view will update the array controller's selection binding. This will trigger a KVO notification, which will call the method on line 28 in the inspector.

This looks up the index of the selected object from the array controller and then gets the corresponding path from the document. The rest of this method simply sets the contents of the user interface.

This simple application demonstrated the double-notification system that is common for floating inspectors. First, you use an `NSNotification` to get a coarse-grained collection of objects to monitor and then KVO to get monitor the one you really need. This pattern is very useful when writing inspectors.

11.8 Summary

In this chapter, we've looked at the Cocoa views used to display structured data. Each of these uses a data source and a delegate to provide the data for display and handle user actions.

We saw how to use Cocoa Bindings, which are built on top of key-value coding and key-value observing to connect model objects to views without needing custom controller classes.

Cocoa makes heavy use of the model-view-controller pattern. We saw in this chapter how you can use this pattern with the standard Cocoa views to provide different views on the same data.

Chapter 12

Dynamic Views

The view hierarchy is a tree of view objects that exists at run time. A typical program will have a fairly static layout of views defined in Interface Builder, but you don't have to restrict yourself to this.

The view hierarchy is a dynamic structure and, just like the rest of a Cocoa program, can be introspected and modified while a program runs. Interface Builder allows you to create `NSView` objects in a nib file that have their own view hierarchy not connected to any window. This allows views to be created at design time, but not inserted into a window until run time. You can use this to implement a variety of dynamic behaviors.

12.1 Tabbed Views

The most commonly used dynamic view is the tab view. The `NSTabView` class implements this model by dynamically rebuilding the view hierarchy when a new tab is selected.

Each entry in a tab view is an `NSTabViewItem` instance. This contains some attributes used for drawing the tab and a view. When a tab item is selected, the tab view will remove the current tab's view from the view hierarchy and insert the new one.

Most of the time, when you use a tab view, you can ignore this. Interface Builder allows you to draw views onto each tab in a tab view, and switching between them is handled automatically in response to mouse events.

The tab view class is designed to be generic. Although it defaults to displaying buttons for switching between the items, these are optional. You can use the tab view class to implement your own switcher by sending it

-selectTabViewItemAtIndex: messages to switch between views that you've drawn in your nib.

12.2 Inspecting the View Hierarchy

More interesting dynamic behavior happens when you directly interact with the view hierarchy. Every item in the view hierarchy is an instance of NSView. This class is responsible for maintaining the hierarchy and ensuring that drawing and event messages move up and down it automatically.

You can get the children of a given view by sending it a -subviews message. This returns an array of all of the direct child views of the receiver. You can then recursively send each of these views a -subviews message to get the entire view hierarchy.

Figure 12.1 is a very simple program that displays an inspector showing the view hierarchy in an associated window. This program contains only a single line of code. The root view in the window is connected to an outlet in a new class. The only code in this program is the declaration of that outlet; everything else is done via Interface Builder.

The inspection is handled via an NSTreeController. This is bound to the outlet's subviews key, and this key is used in turn to locate children.

The outline view column is bound to the className key of the tree controller's model. The entire hierarchy is then accessed using KVC by the generic controller object and displayed in the outline view.

This simple program demonstrates the power of run-time introspection. The view hierarchy shown here is similar to the one shown in Interface Builder.

Nothing that Interface Builder does is magic. This is an important design decision behind the Cocoa APIs. Interface Builder makes things easier for you—assuming you want to do something it was designed to do—but it is not the only way of creating a view hierarchy, and it doesn't use any special mechanisms that are not available to you.

If you decided that you didn't want to use nib files, then you could write your own code for creating the view hierarchy and would not be restricted in any way. This is not recommended—Interface Builder exists to make life easier—but it does remain possible.

In this outline, you can see a mode detailed hierarchy that is exposed by Interface Builder. In particular, the _NSCornerView class is not shown in Interface Builder. This is the square corner in the bottom-right of the table view, used to leave space for when this view is overlapping the resize indicator in the corner of a window. You should not create or modify this view yourself. The underscore at the start of its name means that it is a private Apple class, and may not be

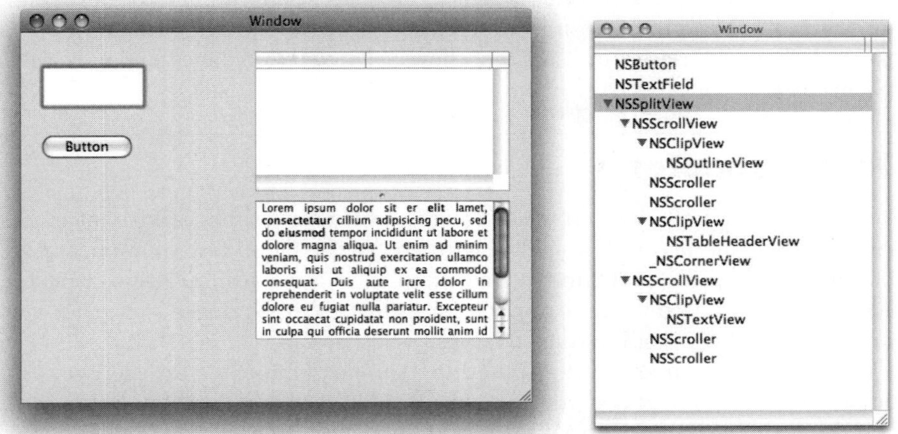

Figure 12.1: Inspecting the view hierarchy.

present in future versions of OS X, or may be present with an entirely different set of methods. You should, however, be aware that views like the table view may contain undocumented subviews for displaying parts of their user interface. Do not ever hard code indexes in a view hierarchy into your program, or you may find that a future version of a view has a different set of children and breaks your code.

More interestingly, you can expose some subset of the capabilities of Interface Builder to your users. Giving users the ability to modify the user interface to fit around their workflow can be very helpful. It is not a substitute for designing a user interface well (although it is often used as one) but it can help make working with a program a lot more enjoyable.

One of the big differences between Apple's consumer and professional creative suites is the amount of customization they allow in the user interface. Something like iMovie has a very rigid user interface, with a single, fixed, layout that has been designed to be easy to use for simple editing tasks. Final Cut, in contrast, is decomposed into simple elements that can be shown, hidden, or rearranged by the user to suit the task at hand.

You should remember this split when designing your own applications. In general, the more possible workflows an application can accommodate, the more likely it is to benefit from a dynamic user interface. Gratuitously allowing rearrangement of simple user interfaces will reduce the users' ability to quickly find standard tools. Not providing a flexible interface for a very complex program can make it difficult to use for unusual workflows. The exact balance depends on the application.

OmniInspector

Palettes provide a good way of generating flexible user interfaces without modifying the view hierarchy. If you have used any of the Omni Group applications, such as OmniGraffle or OmniOutliner, you may have admired the inspector palettes that are used in these applications. These can be docked together and can fold up to only display their headers.

You might try implementing something similar yourself as an exercise, but for use in real applications you can download the *OmniInspector framework*. This is available under an MIT-style license from `http://www.omnigroup.com/developer/`. Although it is undocumented, the code is quite readable, and you should have no problems adding your own connectible inspectors to a new application.

When you walk the view hierarchy, you can get any information you want from individual views. Every view in the hierarchy will respond to all of the messages that `NSView` understands. You can also send it `-isKindOfClass:` messages to identify the specific class and get information related to that kind of view.

12.3 Modifying the View Hierarchy

Once you can inspect the view hierarchy, the next step is to modify it dynamically. This has a variety of uses. You can rearrange controls in a window, move views into separate windows, or create user interface components at run time.

Many of the standard Cocoa views dynamically adjust parts of the view hierarchy dynamically. The most obvious example is `NSCollectionView`. This creates at least one new view object for every object it displays, and often more than one. In the example we saw in the last chapter, each object was represented by a text field and an image view contained in a parent view, giving a total of three new views for each item. This little cluster of views had its own hierarchy—an `NSView` as the parent of the other two views—which was inserted into the collection view.

12.3.1 Reparenting Views

There are two very important methods in NSView for manipulating the view hierarchy:

```
- (void)addSubview: (NSView*)aView;
- (void)removeFromSuperview;
```

The first of these inserts a view into the view hierarchy as a child of the receiver. There is no method for directly removing a child view from a view. You must first find the child view and then send it the second of these messages. Note that the view hierarchy and responder chain are closely related. Both of these methods will also update the responder chain. When you add a subview to a view, that view will be set as the new subview's next responder. This ensures that delegation up the responder chain continues to match the layout in the view hierarchy.

For non-overlapping views, these methods are sufficient. When views do overlap, you need to define their ordering. This is used for both drawing and event delivery. You can define this when you add a subview, using this method:

```
- (void)addSubview: (NSView*)aView
        positioned: (NSWindowOrderingMode)place
        relativeTo: (NSView*)otherView
```

This reuses an enumerated type from NSWindow. The place argument must be either NSWindowAbove or NSWindowBelow, indicating that the new subview is added either above or below the view given in the third argument. You can also use this method to add views above or below all other direct subviews of the receiver by passing nil as the third argument.

These methods alone are enough to rearrange objects in a view hierarchy. Listing 12.1 shows an action method for detaching a view from its current location in the view hierarchy and making it into a floating panel.

Listing 12.1: A method for reparenting a view. [from: examples/ReparentView/ReparentView.m]

```
#import "ReparentView.h"

@implementation ReparentView
- (IBAction) reparentView: (id)sender
{
    if (![sender isKindOfClass: [NSView class]]) { return; }

    NSUInteger style = NSTitledWindowMask | NSClosableWindowMask |
        NSUtilityWindowMask;
    NSPanel *panel =
        [[NSPanel alloc] initWithContentRect: [sender frame]
```

```
11                                    styleMask: style
12                                      backing: NSBackingStoreBuffered
13                                        defer: NO];
14      [sender retain];
15      [sender removeFromSuperview];
16      [panel setContentView: sender];
17      [sender release];
18
19      [panel makeKeyAndOrderFront: self];
20  }
21  @end
```

This method starts with a simple guard clause making sure that the sender really is a view. This will not work if the sender is a cell, since `NSCell` instances do not have their own space in the view hierarchy, although it could be modified to work on their containing view.

Lines 8–13 create a new floating panel. This is created with the same dimensions as the sender. This prevents any resizing when the view is moved. This happens on lines 14–17. Note that we need to retain the view before moving it and release it afterward. When a view is inserted into the view hierarchy, its superview will retain it. When it is removed, its superview will release it. After line 15, the view might be deallocated if we did not retain it first. The corresponding release message simply prevents a memory leak.

The view is set as the contents view of the new panel, replacing the `NSView` instance that is created by default. The final part of this method simply displays the new panel.

Figure 12.2 shows a simple window containing six buttons. Each of these is connected to this action message and, when clicked, pops out in a separate panel. To make this a bit more friendly, the panel's frame could be set so that the buttons did not move. You can do this by translating the sender's frame's origin into screen coordinates before you define the panel.

Having buttons jump to new windows whenever you click on them is not a very useful feature for applications not published on the first of April. A very small modification to this can be used to create panels from arbitrary views. You might use this with a set of views created as panes in a tab view, allowing each to be detached and shown as a floating panel.

The opposite transform can also be applied relatively easily, taking the contents view from a panel and inserting it back into a window. The only difficult part of this is deciding where in the target window to insert the view.

One way of avoiding this problem is to use something like a split view or a tab view as the container for the view that you insert back into the window. Split views, in particular, are very convenient for this kind of user interface.

A split view is a simple layout tool that can contain a set of other displays arranged either vertically or horizontally. They are most often created in Interface Builder containing a static set of views, but there is no reason why you can't use them in a more dynamic interface. The split view class overrides the `-addSubview:` method. A new view added to a split view with this method will automatically be assigned to a new pane in the view. The user can then resize it.

To demonstrate this, we will modify the last example so that detached buttons are reinserted in the original window in a horizontal split view when they are clicked a second time, as shown in Figure 12.3.

The code for accomplishing this is shown in Listing 12.2. When a view has been detached from the main window into a panel, its action is set to point to this method.

Listing 12.2: Detaching and reattaching buttons. [from: examples/ReparentView2/ReparentView.m]

```
- (IBAction) reattachView: (id)sender
{
    if (![sender isKindOfClass: [NSView class]]) { return; }

    NSWindow *win = [sender window];
    [sender retain];
    [sender removeFromSuperview];
    [win performClose: self];
    [win release];
    [splitView addSubview: sender];
    [sender release];

    [sender setAction: @selector(detachView:)];
}
```

When this method is called, it removes the view from the window and instructs the window to close itself. It then inserts the button as a new subview of the split view. As you can see in Figure 12.3, the buttons do not retain their old size when they are inserted into a split view. The split view will automatically resize any views that are added to it as children. This makes it inappropriate for some kinds of reparenting operations.

One alternative is to use a scroll view and manually position the new views. This takes a little bit more effort, since you need to track the location and size of existing views in the scroll view and often rearrange them.

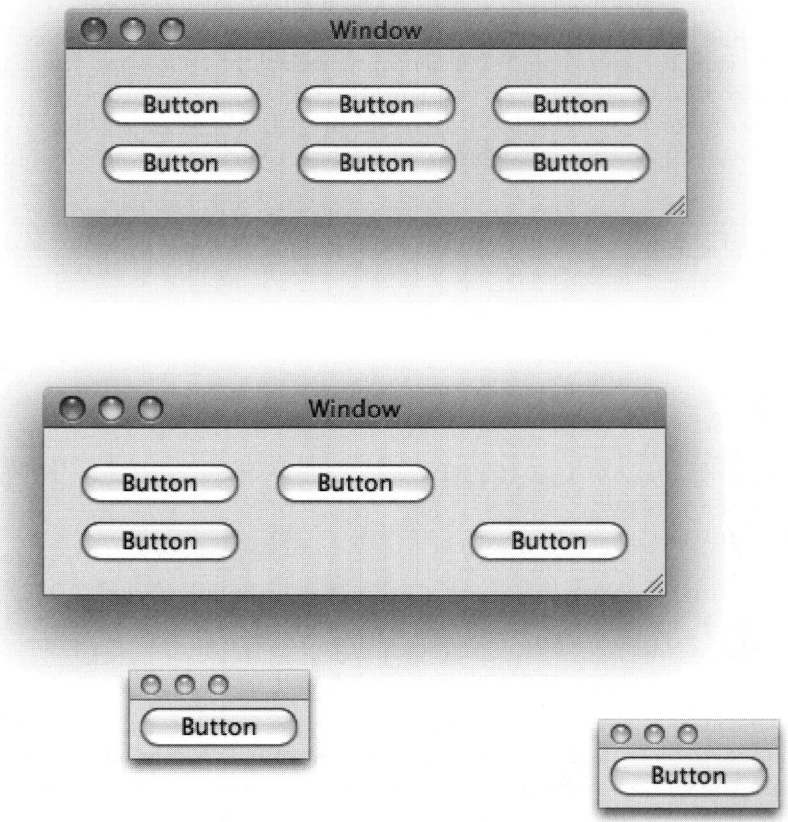

Figure 12.2: Before and after reparenting button views into a panel.

Two-Step Reparenting

In each of the examples in this section, we have performed the transition as a two-step process. First, the view is removed from its old superview and then inserted into the new one. This is not actually required. When you insert the view into a new place in the view hierarchy, it will automatically remove itself from its old parent; a view can only be in the view hierarchy in one place. Doing it in two stages is cleaner, since it gives an opportunity to modify the old parent before reinserting the view, but in most cases you can do it as a single operation. In Chapter 15 we will look at how to add effects to this kind of transformation. Performing the transfer as two distinct steps makes it easier to independently control the animations that occur with each part.

12.3.2 Rearranging Views

A scroll view, conceptually, is an infinite canvas for containing other views. At any given time, some subset of the scroll view is visible to the user. If you are defining a fixed layout for a user interface, you generally only use scroll views as containers for data views that may contain an arbitrary amount of data, for example, tables and text views. In a more dynamic user interface, scroll views are a convenient container for arbitrary views.

Unlike a split view, a scroll view will not adjust the size of any views contained inside it. It will also not arrange them in any sensible way. If you just insert subviews into a scroll view, you will get a mess.

We can implement some more friendly behavior with a custom `NSView` subclass. Note that we don't need to subclass `NSScrollView`. When you create a scroll view in Interface Builder, you really get quite a complex view hierarchy. The top-level scroll view contains three direct subviews: the horizontal and vertical scrollers and a clip view. The clip view contains the document view, which in turn contains all of the other views being shown in the scroll area.

Note that Interface Builder's view hierarchy omits the clip view. This can be slightly confusing, since you might think that changing the class of the view contained inside the scroll view will replace the clip view with something else. This is not the case; you can only replace the clip view in code. Setting a view as the custom view in a scroll view in Interface Builder is the equivalent of passing it as the argument to a `-setDocumentView:` message sent to the clip view associated with the scroll view.

Listing 12.3 shows the code for an `NSView` subclass designed to be set as the document view for a scroll view.

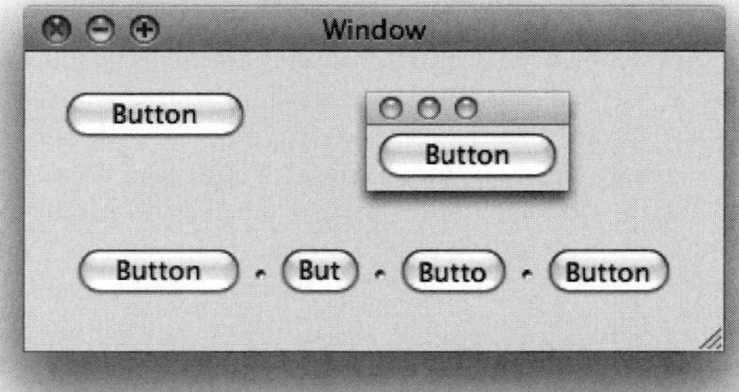

Figure 12.3: Reparenting the buttons back into the window.

Listing 12.3: A view that automatically arranges its contents. [from: examples/RearrangingScrollView/RearrangingScrollView.m]

```
#import "RearrangingScrollView.h"

@implementation RearrangingScrollView
- (BOOL)isFlipped
{
    return YES;
}
- (void)addSubview: (NSView*)aView
{
    [super addSubview: aView];

    NSRect frame = [aView frame];
    frame.origin.x = 0;
    frame.origin.y = (CGFloat)top;

    [aView setFrame: frame];

    top += frame.size.height;
}
- (void)willRemoveSubview: (NSView*)subview
{
    top -= [subview frame].size.height;
```

```
23      CGFloat y = 0;
24      for (NSView *view in [self subviews])
25      {
26          if (view != subview)
27          {
28              NSRect frame = [view frame];
29              frame.origin.y = y;
30              y += frame.size.height;
31              [view setFrame: frame];
32          }
33      }
34  }
35  - (void)setFrame: (NSRect)aFrame
36  {
37      CGFloat y = 0;
38      CGFloat width = aFrame.size.width;
39      for (NSView *view in [self subviews])
40      {
41          NSRect frame = [view frame];
42          frame.origin.y = y;
43          y += frame.size.height;
44          width = MAX(width, frame.size.width);
45          [view setFrame: frame];
46      }
47      aFrame.size.height = top;
48      aFrame.size.width = width;
49      [super setFrame: aFrame];
50  }
51  @end
```

This class overrides two methods related to modifying the view hierarchy. The `-addSubview:` method is one we have called before. The other, `-willRemoveSubview:` is called automatically just before a subview is removed from the receiver.

This class adds one instance variable, `top`, which keeps track of the top of the stack of views. Every view added to it will be added after this view. Since this is a flipped view, the top is actually the bottom of the view.

When a view is added, its height is added to this counter. The view is also moved. Line 14 sets the vertical location of the new subview to the end of the existing views. This is similar to the effect produced by the split view, but does not resize the subview or allow the user to do so.

When a subview is removed from this view, it rearranges all of the other views, setting their frames to have a new vertical offset closing the space left by the old view.

The final method is called whenever the view is either resized or moved. Views that are intended as document views in a clip view need to refuse to resize below the size of their contents. The scroll view uses the rectangle returned by sending a `-frame` message to the document view to determine the size of the scrollers. This frame is compared to the size of the clip view's frame and the difference determines how much scrolling in either direction is allowed.

When this view is resized, it refreshes the location of the subviews and calculates the minimum frame that it can have and still display all of them. If the clip view is shrunk to smaller than this size, the scrollers will be enabled. You can see this in Figure 12.4. In this screen shot, three of the buttons have been moved into the scroll view in a floating panel. The panel has been shrunk so that it no longer fits the buttons and the scroll bars have been enabled automatically.

This simple example program uses the class from Listing 12.3 as the contents view in the scroller in the panel and a set of six buttons in the other window. These buttons all have their actions connected to a simple action method that sends an `-addSubview:` message to the view in the panel with the sender as an argument.

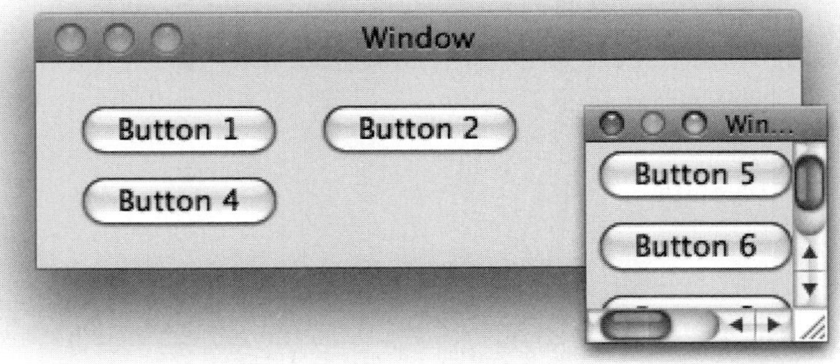

Figure 12.4: Moving views into a scroll view.

When you click on any of the buttons, it will be added to the end of the set already displayed in the floating panel. Because we don't modify the action for the buttons when doing this, clicking on the button a second time will move it to the end of the list. This enables you to trivially re-order views in the scroll view.

As before, we are just moving buttons around. This is not very useful. It would be nice to keep the action methods generic. We can do this very easily by using the sender's superview, rather than the sender itself, as the view we reparent.

Direct Manipulation

The examples in this chapter all use simple action messages to move views around. This approach is chosen to simplify the examples and highlight the view hierarchy manipulations, but does not provide the best kind of user interface.

Compare the detachable buttons in the earlier example with the detachable tabs in Terminal or Safari. There are two ways of detaching a tab in these applications. One is to select Move Tab to New Window from the Window menu. The other is to drag the tab into some free space. Very few users will choose the menu item.

After reading Chapter 19, which discusses how to support drag-and-drop, revisit this section and consider how you can implement this kind of direct manipulation, allowing views to be rearranged and reparented by dragging.

12.3.3 Detachable Tabs

One common reason for wanting to modify the view hierarchy is to implement detachable tabs. This simple user interface pattern is used by a number of applications. You begin with a window similar to the one in Figure 12.5. This contains two tabs, each containing a selection of views. When the user clicks on the Detach button, the tab will move itself to a separate window. Some applications use this for documents, but it is also a very nice way of implementing floating palettes. The tab view serves as a storage location for palettes that are only being used intermittently, but users can easily detach commonly used tabs and place them somewhere more convenient.

Ideally, we would not need to implement a separate detach method for every single button. Cocoa programming is all about implementing generic solutions that can be reused when required, and this is no exception. Listing 12.4 shows how this can be implemented. This class contains two action methods, one for detaching a tab and turning it into a panel, and another for turning a panel back into a tab.

Both of these methods act on the superview of the sender. This means that all you need to do to use them is place a button somewhere inside the view you want to move. In Figure 12.5 you can see that the Detach button is in the bottom of a pane inside a tab view. What you can't see in this screenshot is that there is an identical button, connected to the same action method, in the other tab.

Listing 12.4: Moving a view between a tab view and a panel. [from: examples/DetachTabs/TabDetacher.m]

```
#import "TabDetacher.h"

@implementation TabDetacher
- (IBAction)detachTab: (id)sender
{
    NSView *view = [sender superview];

    NSTabViewItem *containingItem = nil;
    for (NSTabViewItem *item in [tabview tabViewItems])
    {
        if ([item view] == view)
        {
            containingItem = item;
        }
    }

    NSRect frame = [view frame];
    frame.origin =
        [[[view window] contentView] convertPoint: frame.origin
                                         fromView: [view superview]];
    frame.origin = [[view window] convertBaseToScreen: frame.origin];

    [tabview removeTabViewItem: containingItem];

    NSUInteger style = NSTitledWindowMask | NSClosableWindowMask |
        NSUtilityWindowMask;
    NSPanel *panel =
        [[NSPanel alloc] initWithContentRect: frame
                                   styleMask: style
                                     backing: NSBackingStoreBuffered
                                       defer: NO];
    [panel setTitle: [containingItem label]];
    [panel setContentView: view];
    [panel makeKeyAndOrderFront: self];

    [sender setAction: @selector(reattachTab:)];
    [sender setTitle: @"Reattach"];
}
- (IBAction)reattachTab: (id)sender
{
    NSView *view = [sender superview];
    NSWindow *window = [view window];
```

```
42
43     NSTabViewItem *item = [NSTabViewItem new];
44     [item setView: view];
45     [view removeFromSuperview];
46     [item setLabel: [window title]];
47
48     [window performClose: self];
49
50     [tabview addTabViewItem: item];
51     [tabview selectTabViewItem: item];
52     [item release];
53
54     [sender setAction: @selector(detachTab:)];
55     [sender setTitle: @"Detach"];
56
57 }
58 @end
```

When you click on this button, the method has to find the tab view item representing this view. Unfortunately, tab views do not index their items by view, so we need to iterate over all of the items to find the correct one. Note that we are not inspecting the view hierarchy here. This will only work if the sender is a direct subview of the tab view pane. You could try extending this to compare every superview of the sender up to the window's content view against the tab views, allowing the button to be placed anywhere in the view hierarchy under the tab view.

On lines 17–21, we calculate a location for the new window. First, we translate the view's origin to the window's content view's coordinates, and then to the screen coordinates. Note that we have to use the superview as the second argument because the view's frame is in its superview's coordinate system.

This new frame is used to create a new panel, and the tab pane is assigned as its content view. Line 31 is a small user interface tweak. This sets the window's title from the tab's title.

When you click on the detach button, you should get a floating panel to appear almost in the same location as the original tab, containing all of the views from the tab. The final two lines in this method allow for the reverse transformation. They simply change the title and action of the button so that it now allows reattaching the floating view to the tab view.

The second method in this class performs the reattachment. This first creates a new tab view item from the sender's window. This takes its label from the window's title and its view from the window's content view. The window is then closed.

The tab view item is next added to the tab view and selected. The selection is

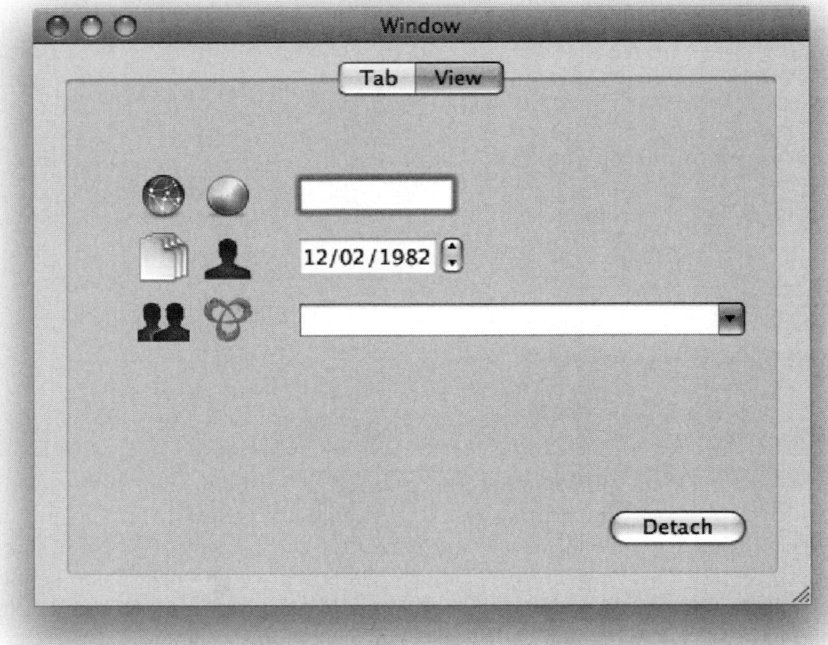

Figure 12.5: A window containing two tabs.

not required, but is done here so that the view that the user is looking at doesn't suddenly disappear into the background.

Finally, the button is updated to allow detachment again. Clicking on the detach button in both windows gives something like Figure 12.6.

This simple example just has a few random views in each tab. These are not connected to controllers and so don't do anything. The code for detaching the tabs, however, is completely generic. You can add this to any program using a tab view, irrespective of what you have inside the tabs. The other views inside the view that is moved will be completely unaware of the fact that they have moved, and will continue to work as normal.

In a real application, you probably wouldn't have a button in the tab pane for detaching it. Instead, you would implement a tabless tab view and draw the tab-switching user interface components yourself. Once you have read Chapter

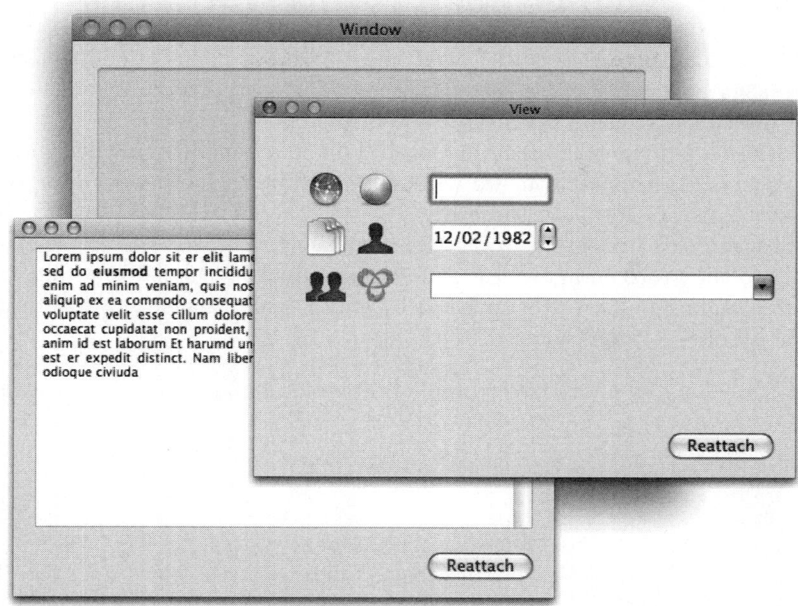

Figure 12.6: Detaching both tabs from the view.

19, try implementing a set of tab headers that allow the user to drag them around to reorder them and drag them into space to detach them.

The combination of tab, split, and scroll views provides a convenient set of building blocks for creating arbitrary, dynamic, layouts in your applications. Tab views allow you to stack views behind each other, split views allow you to create resizable views, and scroll views allow you to place views in fixed locations relative to each other without worrying about the amount of available space.

You can move views around within their superview by setting their frame, and move them to a different part of the view hierarchy—including a different window—easily. It is easy to create gratuitously dynamic user interfaces by applying all of the transformations we've looked at here, at the expense of usability. Used carefully, however, dynamic additions to your user interface can make it a lot more friendly.

12.4 Creating Dynamic Input Forms

Prior to OS X 10.5, there were two ways of creating input forms at run time. One was to use `NSMatrix` to lay out a set of cells in a regular pattern. The other was to do the same with a set of views.

OS X 10.5 added the `NSRuleEditor` class. This is a general class designed for displaying forms. In this section, we will examine how each of these approaches can be used to display forms to the user.

We will write three programs, one with each approach, which contain classes conforming to the protocol in Listing 12.5. This defines methods for adding text, Boolean, date, and number fields to the form, and a `-results` method that returns an array of all of the values entered by the user.

Listing 12.5: The dynamic form example protocol. [from: examples/FormMatrix/FormInterface.h]

```
@class NSString;
@class NSArray;
@protocol DynamicForm
- (void)addTextFieldWithLabel: (NSString*)aLabel;
- (void)addBoolFieldWithLabel: (NSString*)aLabel;
- (void)addDateFieldWithLabel: (NSString*)aLabel;
- (void)addNumberFieldWithLabel: (NSString*)aLabel;
- (NSArray*)result;
@end
```

To demonstrate each implementation, we will use the same simple test class, shown in Listing 12.6. This adds four fields to the form, one of each type. This doesn't demonstrate the dynamic behavior of the form to its fullest extent: You could easily create a form containing these four fields statically in Interface Builder. It is intended to provide a simple demonstration, rather than a proper use case.

Listing 12.6: Testing the dynamic form examples. [from: examples/FormMatrix/FormTest.m]

```
#import "FormTest.h"

@implementation FormTest
- (void)awakeFromNib
{
    [form addTextFieldWithLabel: @"Name:"];
    [form addBoolFieldWithLabel: @"Favourite Boolean:"];
    [form addNumberFieldWithLabel: @"Magic Number:"];
    [form addDateFieldWithLabel: @"Birthday:"];
}
@end
```

This kind of interface is very commonly needed for networked applications, where a server asks the client to provide a set of information and the client, in turn, asks the user. You cannot design a fixed-layout form easily for these cases, because you do not know at design time exactly what information the server will request.

12.4.1 Creating a Form with a Matrix

The simplest way of creating dynamic, regular, layouts is to use the `NSMatrix` class. This displays a rectangular grid of arbitrary dimensions containing `NSCell`s.

You can create the matrix in your nib file and then set the number and contents of its rows at run time. For an input form, we will use a two-column matrix. The left column will display a text label and the right column will contain an input cell of some kind. Interface Builder doesn't allow you to define an `NSMatrix` with no rows. This leaves two choices: either create the matrix entirely in code, or remove the first row when the program starts. The first approach is better, but the second is easier, and for a simple example easier is better. Listing 12.7 shows a controller for a matrix doing exactly this.

Listing 12.7: Setting up a form matrix. [from: examples/FormMatrix/MatrixFormController.m]

```
- (void)awakeFromNib
{
    results = [NSMutableArray new];
    [matrix removeRow: 0];
    [matrix setMode: NSTrackModeMatrix];
}
```

This method creates an array for storing the results and removes the row from the matrix that was added in Interface Builder. It also sets the mode of the matrix. This defines how the matrix tracks mouse events. In this mode, each cell is responsible individually for tracking mouse click-and-drag movements in its rectangle.

The next method, shown in Listing 12.8 is a helper method for adding cells to the matrix. This adds two cells, one provided by the first argument and another created from the label.

Listing 12.8: Adding form entries to a matrix. [from: examples/FormMatrix/MatrixFormController.m]

```
- (void)addCell: (NSCell*)aCell withLabel: (NSString*)aLabel
{
    NSCell *label = [[NSCell alloc] initTextCell: aLabel];
    [label setAlignment: NSRightTextAlignment];
```

```
14     CGFloat height = [label cellSize].height + 8;
15
16     [aCell setTarget: self];
17     [aCell setAction: @selector(cellValueChanged:)];
18
19     NSArray *cells = [NSArray arrayWithObjects:
20                       label, aCell, nil];
21     [matrix addRowWithCells: cells];
22     [label release]; [aCell release];
23
24     [results addObject: [NSNull null]];
25
26     NSRect frame = [matrix frame];
27     frame.origin.y += frame.size.height;
28     frame.size.height = [matrix numberOfRows] * height;
29     frame.origin.y -= frame.size.height;
30     [matrix setFrame: frame];
31 }
```

The label is a simple, non-editable, text cell. This is right-aligned, giving a label right next to the input cell. We use the height of this cell when calculating the new size of the matrix.

Lines 16–17 set up the cell's target and action so that they will call the method in Listing 12.10. A default value for this row is added to the array on line 24. This is an instance of `NSNull`, a singleton class used to represent `NULL` values in collections. Attempting to insert `nil` or `NULL` into a Cocoa collection will throw an exception. `NSNull` is the object equivalent, a valid value that has no meaning. Because `NSNull` is a singleton, you can test if an object is an instance of it by doing a pointer comparison against the return value from a `+null` message.

When you create a row in an `NSMatrix`, you have to set all of the cells that will populate it at the same time. This is done on lines 19–21 by creating an array for the label and input cells and then adding a new row containing these cells.

The matrix will not automatically be resized to contain these cells. Resizing the matrix is slightly tricky. Cells do not have a size in the same way that views do, just a minimum size at which they can display their contents. We can tell the matrix to resize the cells to fit its bounds with `-sizeToFit`, but that will look quite ugly. Alternatively, we could send it a `sizeToCells` message, which would shrink it to the smallest size that can contain all of the cells, but this would usually make it too small.

On lines 26–30, we manually define the size. The `height` variable was set back on line 14 from the minimum size of the label plus a small fudge factor. This is slightly larger than the intercell spacing and takes account of the fact that some of the input cells need to be taller. Try modifying this example to calculate the minimum height properly by sending a `-cellSize` message to each of the cells and an `-intercellSpacing` message to the matrix.

At first glance, lines 27 and 29 look slightly odd. These set the vertical location of the matrix. Recall that, by default, views have their origin in the bottom-left corner. This translation ensures that the top of the matrix is where it was before we resized it, in this kind of coordinate system. This is not needed if the matrix is contained in a *flipped view*. Adding the old height to the y coordinate sets it to the top of the view. Subtracting the new height sets it to the bottom for a view with the same top as the old view.

The individual cells are defined in Listing 12.9. This listing shows each of the methods declared in the protocol. All of these call the helper method to add the cells to the matrix; they just create the cell to add.

Listing 12.9: Defining cells for a form matrix. [from: examples/FormMatrix/MatrixFormController.m]

```
- (void)addTextFieldWithLabel: (NSString*)aLabel
{
    NSCell *cell = [[NSTextFieldCell alloc] init];
    [cell setEditable: YES];
    [cell setStringValue:@""];
    [cell setBezeled: YES];
    [self addCell: cell withLabel: aLabel];
}
- (void)addBoolFieldWithLabel: (NSString*)aLabel
{
    NSButtonCell *cell = [[NSButtonCell alloc] init];
    [cell setTitle: @""];
    [cell setButtonType: NSSwitchButton];
    [self addCell: cell withLabel: aLabel];
}
- (void)addDateFieldWithLabel: (NSString*)aLabel
{
    NSDatePickerCell *cell = [NSDatePickerCell new];
    [cell setBezeled: YES];
    [cell setBackgroundColor: [NSColor whiteColor]];
    [self addCell: cell withLabel: aLabel];
}
- (void)addNumberFieldWithLabel: (NSString*)aLabel
{
    NSTextFieldCell *cell = [[NSTextFieldCell alloc] init];
    [cell setFormatter: [[NSNumberFormatter new] autorelease]];
    [cell setEditable: YES];
    [cell setStringValue:@""];
```

```
    [cell setBezeled: YES];
    [self addCell: cell withLabel: aLabel];
}
```

One important thing to note is that we only set `-setEditable:` for text field cells. You might imagine from the name that this method defines whether the cell's contents can be edited. This is not quite correct; it defines whether the cells contents should be edited with the *field editor*. This is an `NSText` subclass (usually an `NSTextView`) that is associated with the window and is moved over the cell when it needs to be edited. The field editor can be used for any kind of cell, but you will get some very strange results when you use it with anything other than a text cell. Try configuring the `NSButtonCell` instance to use it. When you click on the check box, rather than toggling, it will be covered by a text view with the same dimensions. If you enter a value of '1' in this text box, the check box will be set. This is probably not what you want.

We use three kinds of cell for the four kinds of field. Numbers use the same kind as text, but with an extra attribute. The `NSNumberFormatter` instance is a subclass of `NSFormatter`. This is an abstract class that maps between strings and some arbitrary object value. Two concrete subclasses are provided with Cocoa, the other being `NSDateFormatter`. These allow text fields to edit `NSNumber` and `NSDate` instances, respectively. When the user enters a value in the text field, it will not be accepted unless the associated formatter can convert it into the required type.

We could use the same mechanism for dates, but the `NSDatePickerCell` is slightly more user friendly. This draws a stepper and allows each component of the date to be edited independently. Apart from that, it is very similar in behavior to the text field cell.

For Boolean values, we use a simple check box. This is an instance of `NSButtonCell` with the style set to `NSSwitchButton`. The object value of this will be an `NSNumber` representing a **`BOOL`**.

You can see all of these cells in Figure 12.7. This shows the running form with each of the fields requested by the test class. The only remaining part required to conform to the protocol is a mechanism for getting the values from the cells and storing them in the array. This is shown in Listing 12.10.

Recall that we set this method as the target for all of the cells. When it is called, it will be the matrix, rather than the individual cells, that is the sender. Before we can get the cell value, we need to work out which cell is in use. The result is then inserted into the array. This should always be a valid existing value, either the `NSNull` instance inserted at the start, or a value previously set with this method. The final line of this method logs the results array to the console, so you can see that the form is working.

This is all of the code you need to create forms dynamically using a matrix.

Listing 12.10: Collecting the form results. [from: examples/FormMatrix/MatrixFormController.m]

```
- (NSArray*)result
{
    return [results copy];
}
- (void)cellValueChanged: (id)sender
{
    NSCell *cell = [matrix selectedCell];
    [results replaceObjectAtIndex: [matrix selectedRow]
                       withObject: [cell objectValue]];
    NSLog(@"Results: %@", results);
}
```

Figure 12.7: A simple form in a matrix.

You might want to embed the matrix in a scroll view so that it has space to grow if more form elements are added than fit in a window, if you decide to use this model in an application.

Newer versions of OS X also allow you to use different cell types for individual rows in a table view. The `NSTableView` class is a wrapper around `NSMatrix` that does more efficient drawing and provides a data source interface. This is a fourth option for generating dynamic forms.

12.4.2 Creating a Form with a Custom View

A slightly more complex version of this involves using views, rather than cells, and laying them out yourself. We already did something similar once in this chapter, automatically adding views to a scroll view in a vertical column. Creating a form is almost identical to this, but requires two views per row, rather than the one we previously used.

We can work around this by embedding the label and input views in a parent `NSView` and then inserting this into a view that just needs to arrange all of its contents in a single column.

For this example, we will make use of a new class to appear with OS X 10.5. The `NSViewController` class is similar to `NSWindowController`, but is designed as the controller for a free-standing `NSView` in a nib, rather than a window.

We will populate our form by instantiating copies of prototype form elements laid out in nib files. Rather than using `NSViewController` directly, we create a subclass, `FormItemController`. This adds a `label` declared property. Each of the form item nibs has two subviews. A text field bound to this property and some other control bound to the `representedObject` property inherited from the view controller.

The class shown in Listing 12.11 is responsible for adding the form items to the view. As you can see, this is much simpler than the version that uses a matrix. All of the view configuration is done in Interface Builder. Each of the methods from our interface just calls the `-addViewNib:withLabel:` method that does the real work.

Listing 12.11: Adding views to a form. [from: examples/FormViews/FormViewLayout.m]

```
#import "FormViewLayout.h"
#import "FormItemController.h"

@implementation FormViewLayout
- (void)addViewNib: (NSString*)aNib withLabel: (NSString*)aLabel
{
    FormItemController *controller =
    [[FormItemController alloc] initWithNibName: aNib
                                         bundle: [NSBundle mainBundle]];
    controller.label = aLabel;
    NSView *subview = [controller view];
    [subview setAutoresizingMask: NSViewMinYMargin | NSViewWidthSizable];
    [view addSubview: subview];
    [controllers addObject: controller];
    [controller release];

}
```

```
18 - (void)addTextFieldWithLabel: (NSString*)aLabel
19 {
20     [self addViewNib: @"TextFormItem"
21            withLabel: aLabel];
22 }
23 - (void)addBoolFieldWithLabel: (NSString*)aLabel
24 {
25     [self addViewNib: @"BoolFormItem"
26            withLabel: aLabel];
27 }
28 - (void)addDateFieldWithLabel: (NSString*)aLabel
29 {
30     [self addViewNib: @"DateFormItem"
31            withLabel: aLabel];
32 }
33 - (void)addNumberFieldWithLabel: (NSString*)aLabel
34 {
35     [self addViewNib: @"NumberFormItem"
36            withLabel: aLabel];
37 }
38 - (NSArray*)result
39 {
40     NSMutableArray *results = [NSMutableArray array];
41     for (NSViewController *controller in controllers)
42     {
43         [results addObject: [controller representedObject]];
44     }
45     NSLog(@"results: %@", results);
46     return results;
47 }
48
49 @end
```

This method first instantiates a copy of the nib using the view controller. This loads the objects from the nib file and sets itself as the owner. Each of the views in the nib uses bindings to access and set values in this controller.

The standard view controller just has two attributes, the view and the represented object. The view is an outlet that must be connected to an `NSView` instance in Interface Builder, while the represented object is an arbitrary object that can be accessed via bindings. Everything in the nib can access the controller via the file's owner proxy, and the controller can access the view via its outlet.

Instantiating the controller loads the view, but does not insert it into the view hierarchy. You do this yourself on line 13. Before inserting the view, we set its resizing mask. This defines how it will be resized in the parent view. This set of options makes the view resize horizontally, but not vertically, when the superview is scaled.

We also add the controller to an array after instantiating it. This is used later to get the results array. Every time the user changes something in one of the editors in the form, the view's represented object will be updated via bindings. The `-result` method on this class collects all of the represented objects into a new array.

Each of the form elements is inserted into a container view on line 13. This view is an instance of the class shown in Listing 12.12. This view automatically lays out the form elements as they are inserted. For this simple version, there is no support for removing views. We assume that forms will be created, used, and destroyed, rather than recycled.

Listing 12.12: The form view class. [from: examples/FormViews/FormView.m]

```
#import "FormView.h"

@implementation FormView
- (BOOL)isFlipped
{
    return YES;
}
- (void)addSubview: (NSView*)aView
{
    [super addSubview: aView];

    NSRect frame = [aView frame];
    frame.origin.x = 0;
    frame.origin.y = (CGFloat)top;
    frame.size.width = [self frame].size.width;

    [aView setFrame: frame];

    top += frame.size.height;
}
- (void)setFrame: (NSRect)aFrame
{
    CGFloat y = 0;
    for (NSView *view in [self subviews])
    {
        NSRect frame = [view frame];
        frame.origin.y = y;
        frame.size.width = aFrame.size.width;
        y += frame.size.height;
```

```
        [view setFrame: frame];
    }
    aFrame.size.height = top;
    [super setFrame: aFrame];
}
@end
```

When a subview is added to this view, it is positioned after the existing form elements. It is also resized to match the width of the container view. The same resizing happens when the form view has its frame changed.

The form view lives inside a vertical scroll view. It resizes its subviews to match the new width, but does not adjust the vertical size. When using this kind of view, you should define a minimum size for the window that prevents it from shrinking too far horizontally.

The view doesn't do any vertical resizing. When the scroll view becomes smaller than the form elements, the scroller will be shown and the user can scroll the form.

Note that, unlike cells, views have an intrinsic size. This size is defined for our form elements when the nib is drawn. Figure 12.8 shows the form created from the test class. Unlike Figure 12.7, the rows in this layout are not all the same height. The date picker used here is the graphical version, which is much taller than the other form elements. Try rearranging the order in which these elements are created. You will see that the layout still works correctly.

You can add any arbitrary-sized form item with this approach. Unlike the matrix version, you could embed a full `NSTextView`, supporting multi-line editing of rich text in a larger area than a single line in the matrix. In contrast, every row in an `NSMatrix` must be the same size.

The big disadvantage of this approach, when compared to using cells in a matrix, is RAM usage. Each of the rows in the last example used two `NSCell` instances, with a total footprint of under a hundred bytes. This version uses two views nested inside a third view and a controller object, with a total size approaching a kilobyte.

Fortunately, we are not writing this code in the '80s, and so using a few tens of kilobytes for a single window is not considered too extravagant. You will notice that most of the newer Cocoa views do not make heavy use of cells and the cell abstraction is not present in the iPhone's UIKit. Using cells trades some ease of programming for efficiency, and on a modern system the efficiency gain won't be noticed by the user. Even if you waste a few megabytes of RAM in a view hierarchy, it's still only a fraction of a percent of the user's total RAM. On the iPhone the screen is smaller, so even though the views are more expensive, you tend to have fewer of them.

This approach was made a lot easier on 10.5, by the addition of

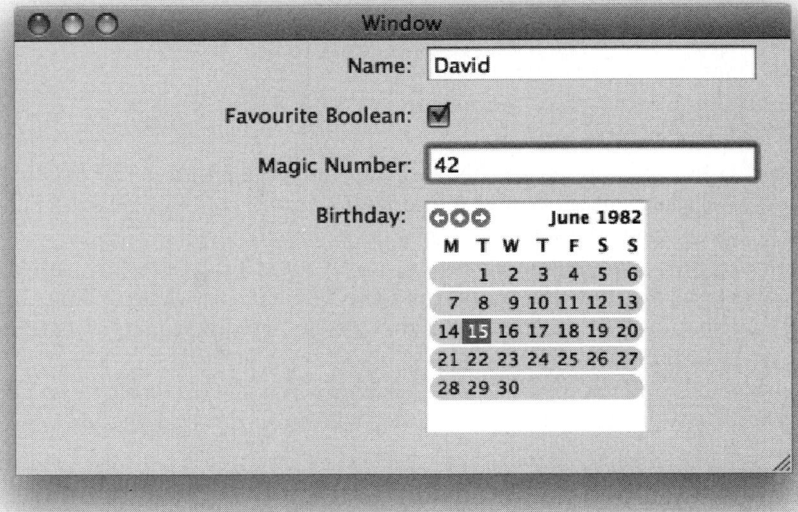

Figure 12.8: A form constructed from views in a nib file.

`NSViewController`. If you want to do the same thing on 10.4 and earlier, you need to instantiate the nibs yourself, using `NSNib`, and define your own class to act as the owner. None of this is particularly difficult, but it takes time to write and adds to the complexity of the code.

12.4.3 Creating a Form with a Rule Editor

The rule editor class, `NSRuleEditor`, was introduced with OS X 10.5. It is quite closely tied to its subclass, `NSPrediateEditor`, which we will look at in Chapter 17.

The aim of the rule editor is to make it easy to display dynamic forms containing a tree of simple elements. The rule editor is a lot more flexible than this simple task requires. It constructs its elements one at a time from a delegate and allows them to be re-ordered by the user. It also supports nested elements, so you can have a hierarchy of form elements.

As its name suggests, `NSRuleEditor` is designed for editing sets of rules. The subclass allows predicates to be created easily, but the rule editor itself is designed for editing of arbitrary rule sets.

We will provide a controller for the rule editor that will populate it with rows. The code for this is shown in Listing 12.13.

Listing 12.13: Initializing a rule editor with a form interface. [from: examples/FormRuleEditor/FormRuleEditorDelegate.m]

```
- (void)awakeFromNib
{
    [view setEditable: NO];
    items = [NSMutableArray new];
}
```

When this controller awakes, it disables editing of the rule editor. This does not prevent the items from being edited; it just stops the layout from being modified by the user. By default, the rule editor will display − and + buttons next to each rule, allowing the user to add and remove entries; this will then cause the rule editor to get a new rule from the delegate. For this example, we are just using the editor to lay out our own views, so we disable this behavior.

The delegate methods for the rule editor, shown in Listing 12.14, can be quite confusing. Each rule has one or more criteria associated with it, in a tree. A criterion is an object, roughly equivalent to the item in an outline view. The `-ruleEditor:numberOfChildrenForCriterion:withRowType:` delegate method is repeatedly called to find the structure of the tree of criteria for each row. Each nested criterion is found by calling `-ruleEditor:child:forCriterion:withRowType:`.

Listing 12.14: Rule editor delegate methods. [from: examples/FormRuleEditor/FormRuleEditorDelegate.m]

```
-        (NSInteger)ruleEditor: (NSRuleEditor*)editor
numberOfChildrenForCriterion: (id)criterion
                 withRowType: (NSRuleEditorRowType)rowType
{
    if (criterion == nil)
    {
        return 1;
    }
    return 0;
}
-          (id)ruleEditor: (NSRuleEditor*)editor
displayValueForCriterion: (id)criterion
                   inRow: (NSInteger)row
{
    return [[items objectAtIndex: row] view];
}
- (id)ruleEditor: (NSRuleEditor*)editor
```

```
27            child: (NSInteger)index
28     forCriterion: (id)criterion
29      withRowType: (NSRuleEditorRowType)rowType
30 {
31     return @"";
32 }
```

Our simple form editor just wants to display a single view for each row. It therefore only returns a single criterion for each row, and represents this with a constant object (an empty string). The method on line 20 is responsible for providing the contents of the row. This simple method hides a lot of complexity.

Each criterion can have a display value that is either a string, an `NSMenuItem`, or an `NSView`. If you allow more than one criterion as a child then each of the children will be presented as a pop-up button. Single criteria will be displayed as text labels. You can use this to easily create complex sets of choices, which is what the rule editor was designed to do.

For this example, we are just returning a different view for each entry. You should never return the same view for more than one row in a rule editor. The view will be used directly, not copied, and so you will get some undesirable results if you return the same one for two rows. A view can only be inserted into the view hierarchy in one place, so you will get gaps appearing in the form.

You don't have to use a delegate to provide the rules. You can also add new rows by sending the view a `-setCriteria:andDisplayValues:forRowAtIndex:` message. This takes arrays of criteria and display values as indexes, allowing you to directly configure a row.

The methods for adding fields to this form are shown in Listing 12.15. These reuse the same nib files from the last example, with the exception of the date field. Unlike our custom view, the rule editor requires fixed-size rows, as you can see in Figure 12.9, so we use a simple text-and-stepper date picker, instead of the graphical one.

Listing 12.15: Adding fields to the row editor form. [from: examples/FormRuleEditor/-FormRuleEditorDelegate.m]

```
33 - (void)addRuleWithViewNib: (NSString*)aNib label: (NSString*)aLabel
34 {
35     FormItemController *controller =
36         [[FormItemController alloc] initWithNibName: aNib
37                                              bundle: [NSBundle mainBundle
                                                   ]];
38     controller.label = aLabel;
39     [items addObject: controller];
40     [view addRow: self];
41 }
```

```
- (void)addTextFieldWithLabel: (NSString*)aLabel
{
    [self addRuleWithViewNib: @"TextFormItem"
                       label: aLabel];
}
- (void)addBoolFieldWithLabel: (NSString*)aLabel
{
    [self addRuleWithViewNib: @"BoolFormItem"
                       label: aLabel];
}
- (void)addDateFieldWithLabel: (NSString*)aLabel
{
    [self addRuleWithViewNib: @"DateFormItem"
                       label: aLabel];
}
- (void)addNumberFieldWithLabel: (NSString*)aLabel
{
    [self addRuleWithViewNib: @"NumberFormItem"
                       label: aLabel];
}
```

This code just loads the item controller and adds it to an array. It then sends the rule editor an `-addRule:` action message. This causes the rule editor to call back to the delegate to get the view to display in the row.

The final part, shown in Listing 12.16 is the same as the last example. This just collects the represented objects from the controllers and returns them.

Listing 12.16: Getting the results from the rule editor form. [from: examples/FormRuleEditor/FormRuleEditorDelegate.m]

```
- (NSArray*)result
{
    NSMutableArray *results = [NSMutableArray array];
    for (NSViewController *controller in items)
    {
        [results addObject: [controller representedObject]];
    }
    NSLog(@"results:␣%@", results);
    return results;
}
```

The rule editor provides a convenient way of laying out this kind of view. We are not using anything like the full power of the class in this example, nor are we using it quite as it is intended. The purpose of this example was to demonstrate that there are often container views in Cocoa that can be used to present the kind

Figure 12.9: Creating a form with the rule editor.

of use interface that you want, even if they weren't originally designed for that purpose.

There are lots of different ways of creating user interface layouts at run time with Cocoa. We have looked at three of them:

- Create a simple regular layout using cells.
- Create a custom layout in a new `NSView` subclass.
- Create a view hierarchy in an existing view.

These each have their strengths and weaknesses, in terms of flexibility, processor and memory footprint, and developer effort. The best choice for any given user interface may be any of these three, or even some combination.

12.5 Full-Screen Applications

Displaying a full-screen window is not a very common task, but it is one that applications occasionally need to support. Unfortunately, Cocoa does not provide a convenient way of doing this.

Displaying a window full screen requires some low-level interaction with the window server. This must be done using Core Graphics (Quartz) calls, rather than high-level Cocoa methods.

The `FullScreenWindow` class shown in Listing 12.17 is an `NSWindow` subclass that you can use to generate full-screen windows from `NSViews` stored in a nib file or created in code.

This class has a single constructor that takes a screen number and a view as arguments. Calling this method creates a new, full-screen, window that contains the specified view as its contents.

Listing 12.17: A full-screen window class. [from: examples/FullScreenWindow/FullScreenWindow.m]

```
#import "FullScreenWindow.h"

@implementation FullScreenWindow
+ (NSWindow*) fullScreenWindowOnScreen: (NSScreen*)screen
                          withContents: (NSView*)contents
{
    NSDictionary* screenInfo = [screen deviceDescription];
    NSNumber* screenID = [screenInfo objectForKey: @"NSScreenNumber"];
    // Capture the display.
    CGDisplayErr err = CGDisplayCapture([screenID longValue]);
    if (err != CGDisplayNoErr)
    {
        return nil;
    }

    // Create the window
    NSRect winRect = [screen frame];
    NSWindow *newWindow =
        [[FullScreenWindow alloc] initWithContentRect: winRect
                                            styleMask:
                                                NSBorderlessWindowMask
                                              backing:
                                                NSBackingStoreBuffered
                                                defer: NO
                                               screen: screen];
    [newWindow setContentView: contents];

    // Set it to above the shield window.
    int32_t shieldLevel = CGShieldingWindowLevel();
    [newWindow setLevel: shieldLevel];

    [newWindow makeKeyAndOrderFront:self];
    return newWindow;
}
- (BOOL) canBecomeKeyWindow
```

```
34 {
35     return YES;
36 }
37 @end
```

It would be nice to be able to create the view directly in Interface Builder. Unfortunately, current versions of Interface Builder are not capable of creating windows that do not have borders. A full-screen window is not terribly useful if it has a title bar just like any other window; the point of taking over the whole screen is to display a user interface that is separate from the usual Aqua windowed view.

The first thing that this method does is find the screen number of the requested display. The `-deviceDescription` message sent to the `NSScreen` instance returns a dictionary of attributes about this screen. This includes the color space, the resolution, and, most importantly for this use, the display number. Note that this is not necessarily the same as the index of the screen in the array returned by sending a `+screens` message to `NSScreen`.

Once the Quartz screen ID has been found, the method attempts to capture the display. Capturing the display prevents any other applications from drawing to it. This is not strictly required if all you want is a window taking up the entire screen, but it prevents graphics problems caused by overlays and other problems.

The next step is to create the window. Lines 17 defines the geometry of the window to create. It should be exactly the same size as the screen, and also in the same location. Note that we do not create the window at coordinates $(0, 0)$. Doing this would be correct for a window covering the first screen, but not for other screens. On OS X, screens do not have their own, independent, coordinate systems. Each screen displays a portion of the total available workspace. This is essential for supporting windows split over multiple devices. With per-screen coordinate systems, such a window would have different parts of it in different coordinate spaces, which would be very difficult to draw.

The window is created with a flag set indicating that it should not have any border. On line 24, the contents view is set. This is the root view in the window's view hierarchy and will be resized automatically to the window's dimensions.

The final step is to set the window level to the float above the shield window. The shield window is created automatically when we capture the display. This prevents things like the Classic environment that try to draw directly to the screen from interfering with the program that has captured the display.

Note that once you have a full-screen window created in this way, no key events will be passed to other windows. You should make absolutely certain that you have no breakpoints set. If the program reaches a breakpoint, it will jump to the debugger. Unfortunately, the debugger will be hidden under this window and will not be visible or able to receive events. The only way of getting out of this is to `ssh` in to your development machine from another computer on the network and kill the process.

This is not the only way of creating full-screen graphics. You can use the `CGDisplayGetDrawingContext()` function to get a graphics context that draws on a captured display and draw without using a window at all. Alternatively you can use OpenGL in the same way.

The most common use for full-screen windows is in gaming. Most of these use OpenGL, although you might implement a 2D game using Cocoa and Core Animation drawing routines. Games are not the only things that want to take over the screen, however. One of the most famous Mac applications with a full-screen mode is Keynote. This takes advantage of dual display to display the current slide on a projector and some information for the presenter on the other screen. You can use this class to implement similar interfaces by creating an instance of it for each screen.

One common misfeature that people implementing full-screen windows often add is to make the window return to its normal state when it stops being the key window. A number of video players on OS X do this. While it seems like an obvious feature, it has one serious flaw; it prevents the user from watching a video on one screen while doing something else on the other one. If you use full-screen windows in your application, make sure you consider possible uses like this.

12.6 Summary

In this chapter, we have seen how to manipulate the view hierarchy at run time to produce dynamic user interfaces.

We first saw how to inspect the view hierarchy at run time, creating an outline view of all of the views in a window. We then saw how to modify the hierarchy.

In this chapter, we saw several of the various container views in Cocoa and how to make use of them when constructing user interfaces. We moved views around between different containers in different windows, and discussed when this can be useful in various types of programs.

Next, we looked at how to construct input forms for a template, and how this can be used when creating custom dialogs at run time.

Finally, we looked at how to create full-screen windows, using the Quartz routines to take over the entire display.

Remember that we have only covered the mechanisms for designing dynamic interfaces. Good user interface design is a complex subject that is far beyond the scope of this book. Most of the things covered in this chapter can be easily abused to create completely unusable applications. Before you implement any of them, think about how they will be used and whether they are the best solution to the problem at hand. If you have any doubts, try to consult a usability expert, or read a book on human-computer interaction.

Part V

Advanced Graphics

Chapter 13

Custom Views

Cocoa's AppKit provides a lot of very flexible view objects. Some more are provided by additional frameworks on OS X, such as the people view from the Address Book framework. For a lot of applications, these are enough to define the user interface. Sometimes, however, you need to define new views.

A view has two main responsibilities, drawing and event handling. We created a simple new view in Chapter 8, although this glossed over most of the complicated aspects of defining a new view.

Cocoa uses a variant of the *PostScript drawing model.* Traditional PostScript drawing is based around the idea of a *path*, which is a sequence of curve and line segments. Text was rendered in PostScript by defining a path for each character in a particular font. This is extended in the *Portable Document Format* (*PDF*) to provide better support for raster images, including transparency, and for text. Cocoa uses something a lot closer to the PDF display model than PostScript, but the foundations of both are very similar. The basic components in Cocoa drawing are

Bezier paths represented by the `NSBezierPath` class contain open or closed paths constructed from lines and curves.

Text represented by a lot of different classes is drawn as a sequence of glyphs.

Raster Images typically represented by `NSImage` are bitmap images that cannot be decomposed into vector components.

From these it is possible to create complex visuals. Starting with 10.5, the Cocoa drawing system was extended by *Core Animation*, which we will look at in more detail in the next chapter. This was originally called *LayerKit* and began life on the iPhone. It was subsequently ported back to desktop OS X and is now used for a lot of visual effects in Cocoa.

> **iPhone**
>
> Custom views on the iPhone are created using UIKit, not AppKit. The AppKit drawing routines are unavailable on the iPhone; however, you can still use their Core Graphics counterparts. These provide a C API that is very similar to the Objective-C model described in this chapter.

13.1 The Graphics Context

A very important part of drawing on OS X, whether you use Core Graphics or AppKit drawing code, is the idea of a *graphics context.* This is an object that represents the current drawing state. Most drawing operations depend on the current context.

A graphics context of some kind is a core part of most 2D drawing APIs. Without one you would need functions like this:

```
DrawLine(Display * display, Drawable *d, Color *c, int LineWidth, LineStyle
    *style, Point *start, Point *end, ...);
```

Even simple drawing functions depend on a lot of surrounding state. If you wanted to draw a shape bordered by a set of straight lines, then you would need one of these calls for each side. This would be a huge amount of redundant data.

Most drawing APIs wrap this up in a graphics context type. In X11 this is a fairly simple structure containing a set of parameters. In Cocoa it is an object or an opaque type, depending on the API you use.

The context encapsulates the view in which you are currently drawing. This includes the top level window and the coordinate transform required to map to the view's local coordinate system. It also contains a set of drawing options, such as the foreground and background color.

One thing inherited directly from PostScript is the stack-based model. You can push the current graphics state on to a stack and pop it back off later, like this:

```
// AppKit:
[NSGraphicsContext saveGraphicsState];
// drawing code...
[NSGraphicsContext restoreGraphicsState];
// Quartz 2D:
```

```
CGContextSaveGState(context);
// drawing code...
CGContextRestoreGState(context);
```

This functionality is used a lot by the view hierarchy. After calling an `NSView`'s draw method, it will ensure that the graphics context is in the default state for that view, with coordinate transforms set accordingly.

You can also do this in cells. Cells always draw in a parent view. For a complex cell you are likely to want to do a lot of drawing operations inside the frame given by the view. Rather than calculate the transform manually each time, you may wish to save the graphics state when you begin drawing the cell, perform a coordinate transform to get the origin set to one corner of the cell, and then perform the drawing based on this origin; then finally pop the state back off the stack at the end.

For simple drawing, this can be done by saving and restoring individual components of the state. For more complex operations it is easier to just save the state at the start and restore it at the end.

13.2 Core Graphics

The *Quartz 2D*, or *Core Graphics*, APIs are the lowest level interface to the windowing system available to the programmer on OS X. They provide a C interface based (loosely) on PDF drawing commands.

You can use the Quartz APIs directly from Objective-C by using the `-graphicsPort` method on the `NSGraphicsContext` instance representing the current context. This returns a pointer to some platform-specific system. If you are using GNUstep or some other OpenStep implementation, then this will be defined by the implementation. With Cocoa, it is always a `CGContextRef` that can be used for Core Graphics drawing.

Figure 13.1 shows a simple view implemented using Core Graphics functions. This simply maintains a list of points and draws lines connecting them all together when its draw method is called.

Listing 13.1 shows the code needed to do this. The first thing you will notice about this is on line 2, where the Quartz headers are included in addition to the standard Cocoa ones.

This view implements both of the responsibilities of a view: drawing and event handling. The event handler is very simple; it just adds the current click location to an array. This is done by *boxing* it in an `NSValue` instance. We could define a more efficient way of storing these, but this is good enough for example code. For real code you should consider using a list of arrays of point structures, or similar.

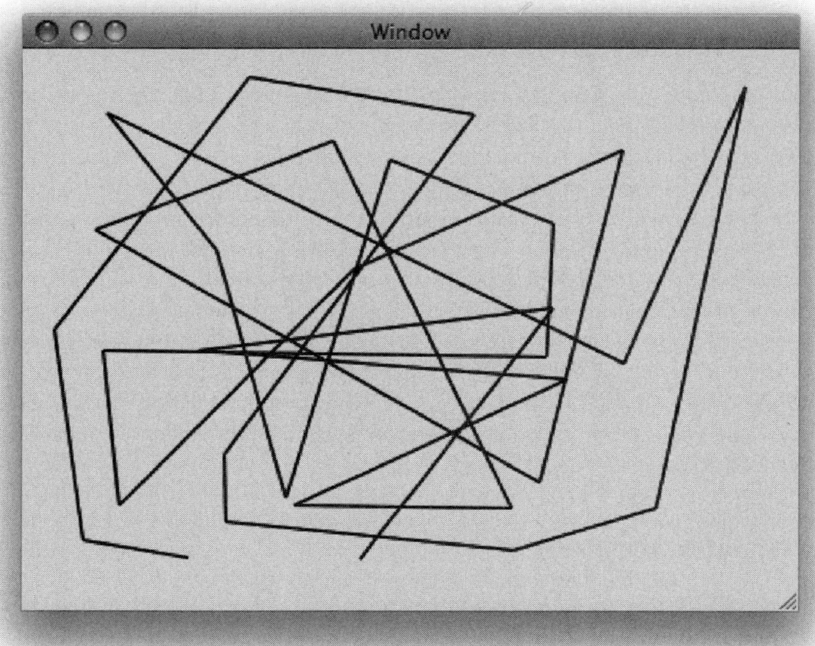

Figure 13.1: Scribbling on a window with Core Graphics.

Listing 13.1: A simple view using Core Graphics. [from: examples/CGTrackMouse/MouseTrackView.m]

```
#import "MouseTrackView.h"
#include <Quartz/Quartz.h>

@implementation MouseTrackView
- (void) awakeFromNib
{
    points = [NSMutableArray new];
}
- (void)drawRect:(NSRect)rect
{
    if ([points count] == 0)
```

```
12      {
13          return;
14      }
15      NSGraphicsContext *context = [NSGraphicsContext currentContext];
16      CGContextRef cgContext = [context graphicsPort];
17
18      CGContextSetLineWidth(cgContext, 2.0f);
19      CGContextSetStrokeColorWithColor(cgContext,
20          CGColorGetConstantColor(kCGColorBlack));
21
22      CGContextBeginPath(cgContext);
23      CGPoint firstPoint = NSPointToCGPoint([[points objectAtIndex:0]
            pointValue]);
24      CGContextMoveToPoint(cgContext, firstPoint.x, firstPoint.y);
25      for (NSValue *point in points)
26      {
27          CGPoint pt = NSPointToCGPoint([point pointValue]);
28          CGContextAddLineToPoint(cgContext, pt.x, pt.y);
29      }
30      CGContextDrawPath(cgContext,  kCGPathStroke);
31  }
32  - (void)mouseDown:(NSEvent *)theEvent
33  {
34      NSPoint click = [self convertPoint:[theEvent locationInWindow]
35                                fromView:nil];
36      [points addObject:[NSValue valueWithPoint:click]];
37      [self setNeedsDisplay:YES];
38  }
39  - (void) dealloc
40  {
41      [points release];
42      [super dealloc];
43  }
44  @end
```

The important code is inside the draw method that starts on line 9. This is the standard Cocoa drawing method, called by `NSView` in response to being notified that some regions need redrawing.

The method starts with a guard that avoids drawing if there are no points in the array. After this it extracts the Quartz graphics context from the AppKit context, on line 16. This is the last line to contain any AppKit code in this method.

The next two functions called set up some information about the graphics state. These define the line width and color. This information is stored in the current state in the graphics context and will remain there until it is explicitly replaced or the state is restored.

The block from lines 22–31 defines a path and draws it. Drawing lines is a two-stage process in Cocoa. The path of the line is defined and then the line is drawn. The same mechanism allows other things to be done with the path, such as filling it or using it for clipping.

Because this is a simple example, it uses the simplest mechanism for creating a path: repeatedly call a function to add a point to it. Note that this is a `CGPoint`, while our other code stored `NSPoints`. The `NSPointToCGPoint()` function is used to convert between the two. This is needed because C does not allow casting between two structure types with identical layouts. You can cast pointers to these types directly, since they have the same layout. This function is defined in Foundation's NSGeometry.h header, as shown in Listing 13.2. This does some ugly conversions via a union. When you use it in your code, the compiler will inline it and it will evaluate to no code.

Listing 13.2: Turning a Cocoa point into a Quartz point. [from: NSGeometry.h]

```
NS_INLINE CGPoint NSPointToCGPoint(NSPoint nspoint) {
    union _ {NSPoint ns; CGPoint cg;};
    return ((union _ *)&nspoint)->cg;
}
```

Once the path is defined, it is drawn as a stroked, but not filled, line using the context's current line style. We set this to be black, two points wide, and inherited all of the other attributes from whatever the parent view is set.

Core Graphics is very powerful. Anything you can do with Cocoa drawing routines can be done in Core Graphics, since it is implemented using these low-level functions. Quartz should generally only be used directly if you've first tried to use the AppKit drawing system and found it too slow. Quartz drawing functions map almost directly to PDF drawing commands, which is a much lower level of abstraction than you really want most of the time.

13.3 AppKit Drawing

In the original OpenStep specification, there were three major components: Foundation, AppKit, and Display PostScript. The final one of these was replaced with Quartz in OS X, but most code written for OpenStep can be run on OS X without modification. This was due to the rich drawing functionality in AppKit. Very few people needed to use DPS directly, and a similarly small number need to use Quartz directly. It is very easy to implement drawing code using just the classes in AppKit.

We've already seen one of these briefly in this chapter. The graphics context is represented by the `NSGraphicsContext` class. This wrapped a PostScript context on NeXT systems and wraps the Quartz context on OS X. Each thread that can perform drawing has an instance of this class. Using the same instance from two threads is not supported unless you handle synchronization yourself.

The graphics context doesn't always point to a window. When you print views the current context will be set to one that outputs a PDF. This will then be sent to a printer. Sometimes views will be drawn to off-screen buffers and composited later. You can implement this yourself by creating a new graphics context and setting the context for this thread to point to it, although most of the time you will let the standard frameworks do this for you.

The graphics context maintains a lot of state, but this is rarely set directly via the object from your code. In the last example, we saw how to set the line color using Core Graphics. This is done by calling a function directly on the context. With Cocoa, you use a different idiom. This is the equivalent AppKit code:

```
[[NSColor blackColor] setStroke];
```

A lot of the rest of Cocoa drawing works in the same way. You don't interact with the context directly; it is just assumed to be there. Instead, you work with objects that manipulate the current context. A lot of Cocoa drawing code will never directly hold a reference to the graphics context.

13.3.1 Drawing Shapes

The most important class for drawing in Cocoa is `NSBezierPath`. This encapsulates a PostScript path. You can store points in it and then draw them. This can be more efficient than drawing using the Quartz routines. In the last example, we constructed the path via a large number of calls, every time we drew it. Listing 13.3 shows an implementation of the same view using AppKit instead of CoreGraphics.

This is much simpler. Rather than maintaining an array, we simply append the drawing commands to the path. The efficiency of this is dependent on the implementation of the bezier path class. This is used for drawing all over OS X, so it is reasonable to assume that developers at Apple (and NeXT) have spent a lot of time ensuring that it is well optimized.

The drawing method in this class is an example of one that does not directly reference the context. It just has a single line, which tells the bezier path to draw a line along itself in the current graphics context. The shape and line style are all stored inside the bezier path object itself.

When the path is created, on line 14, it has the line width and the start location set. Every subsequent click just adds a new line segment to the path, using its

Listing 13.3: The AppKit version of the mouse tracking view. [from: examples/AppKitTrackMouse/MouseTrackView.m]

```
#import "MouseTrackView.h"

@implementation MouseTrackView
- (void)drawRect: (NSRect)rect
{
    [path stroke];
}
- (void)mouseDown: (NSEvent*)theEvent
{
    NSPoint click = [self convertPoint: [theEvent locationInWindow]
                              fromView: nil];
    if (nil == path)
    {
        path = [NSBezierPath new];
        [path moveToPoint: click];
        [path setLineWidth: 2];
    }
    else
    {
        [path lineToPoint: click];
    }
    [self setNeedsDisplay: YES];
}
- (void) dealloc
{
    [path release];
    [super dealloc];
}
@end
```

current style. This version is a lot simpler than the version that used the low-level code.

All of the operations on paths from Quartz are exposed via this class. Internally it will store a dense representation of the path that can be passed quickly to the display server. Each of the drawing methods will first send the path to the display server (or get a reference to it if it's already been cached there) and will then apply one of the drawing operations.

So far we've only tried drawing straight lines. The bezier path, as you might imagine from its name, can also draw bezier curves, using this method:

```
- (void)curveToPoint: (NSPoint)aPoint
      controlPoint1: (NSPoint)controlPoint1
      controlPoint2: (NSPoint)controlPoint2;
```

Bezier curves are a family of curves described by polynomial functions. The type supported here are *cubic bezier curves*. They are described by four points; the start and end points and two control points. To illustrate this, we'll write a short program that records four mouse clicks and draws a bezier between them.

The class just keeps four points and the count of the number of clicks as instance variables. The implementation is shown in Listing 13.4. Whenever it receives a mouse down event, it stores it. If this is the last of a sequence of four clicks, then it redisplays, giving an image like the one in Figure 13.2.

Listing 13.4: Drawing a bezier curve and its control points. [from: examples/Draw-Bezier/BezierTrack.m]

```
#import "BezierTrack.h"

@implementation BezierTrack
- (void)drawRect: (NSRect)rect
{
    NSBezierPath *control1 = [NSBezierPath bezierPath];
    [control1 moveToPoint: points[0]];
    [control1 lineToPoint: points[1]];
    [[NSColor redColor] setStroke];
    [control1 setLineWidth: 2];
    [control1 stroke];
    NSBezierPath *control2 = [NSBezierPath bezierPath];
    [control2 moveToPoint: points[2]];
    [control2 lineToPoint: points[3]];
    [[NSColor greenColor] setStroke];
    [control2 setLineWidth: 2];
    [control2 stroke];
    NSBezierPath *curve = [NSBezierPath bezierPath];
    [curve moveToPoint: points[0]];
    [curve curveToPoint: points[3]
          controlPoint1: points[1]
          controlPoint2: points[2]];
    [[NSColor grayColor] setFill];
    [[NSColor blackColor] setStroke];
    [curve fill];
    [curve stroke];
}
- (void)mouseDown: (NSEvent *)theEvent
{
```

```
    NSPoint click = [self convertPoint: [theEvent locationInWindow]
                              fromView: nil];
    points[pointCount++ % 4] = click;
    if (pointCount % 4 == 0)
    {
        [self setNeedsDisplay: YES];
    }
}
@end
```

The bulk of the program is in the draw method. This generates three temporary bezier paths, rather than reusing the same one each time. The first two are similar to ones we've seen already. This view could alternatively recycle a path by calling `-removeAllPoints` to reset its points. Often you will do this if you want to draw a new shape in the same style as an old one.

These will be used to demonstrate the locations of the control points. The first one draws a red line from the start to the first control point, while the second draws a green line between the second control point and the end point. The colors are set, as before, using `NSColor`. Note that the line width is an attribute of the bezier path, while the color is global. In practice, both will be set on the graphics context, but the bezier path will restore the state of the context after using it so the line width must be set for each one.

The last path is the most interesting one. This demonstrates the `-fill` method. This will fill everything enclosed by the path with the default fill color, which we set to gray with `NSColor`'s `-setFill` method. The definition of "enclosed" is configurable based on the *winding rule*, which defines how overlapping regions should be treated. For simple shapes where the path does not cross itself, the winding rules are irrelevant.

Try playing with this example to get an idea of how a bezier curve works. At each end, the gradient of the curve will be equal to the gradient of the straight line that this program has drawn: the line to the relevant control point. The curve gradually progresses between the two. We won't go into the mathematics behind it here (you can find it in any graphics textbook if you're interested), but you can get an intuitive feel for the shapes of the curves quite easily.

Bezier curves and straight line segments—which are really just a special case of a bezier curve where the control points are on the same line as the endpoints—can be joined together to make any shape. Some convenient ones can be created by convenience methods on the bezier path object. These include arcs and rectangles. Arcs are curves with a constant radius; segments form a circle.

The final type of data that can be stored in a bezier path is text. You can store glyphs associated with a specific font in a path. These will be drawn by the

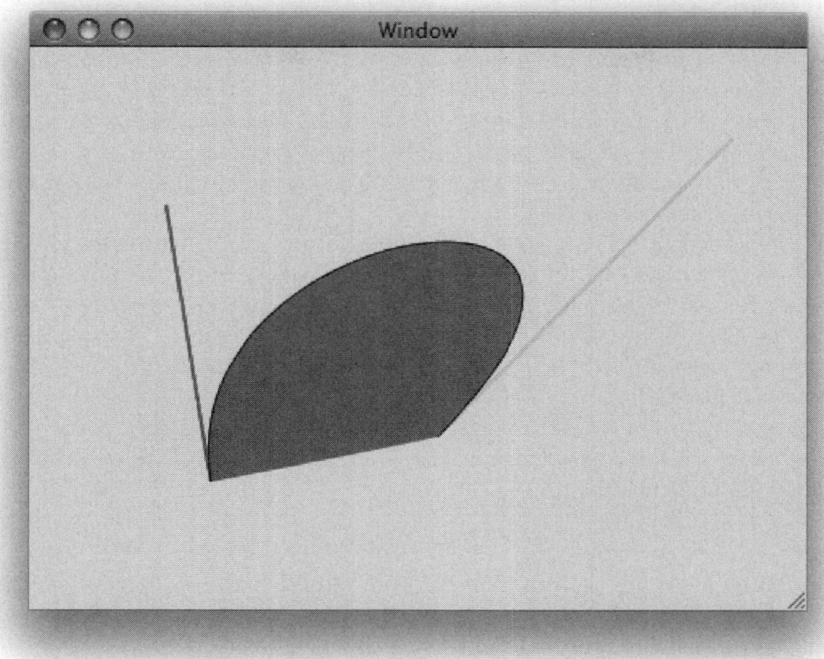

Figure 13.2: A bezier curve drawn by a bezier path.

path in order. If you put text in a complex path, it will not follow the shape of the path. That does not mean that curved text lines are impossible, however.

You can apply an affine transform (see Chapter 6) to a path or to the current graphics context. You can then use this to draw individual glyphs, either by drawing them with a bezier path or a layout manager. This is a lot harder than most other drawing tasks. We'll have a look at how to do this a bit later.

13.3.2 Drawing with Cells

Back in Chapter 8 we saw a simple example of using cells for drawing. A cell is best thought of as the programmatic equivalent of a rubber stamp. You carve it into a certain shape (by setting various flags) and then you can stamp it all over your view with minor variations.

State in Views

The decision of how much state to store in views is a very important part of their design. You can often make views faster by storing everything they need to draw in their instances, but this tends to make them inflexible. Cocoa encourages views to be nearly stateless. Simple controls store just a single value, and more complex views rely on a data source to supply the drawable subset of their state dynamically.

When you design a view, you need to decide how much to store in it. The correct balance between repeatedly fetching the same information—making the view very slow—and defining a fixed internal structure—making the view difficult to use in other situations—is a difficult one to reach. The Cocoa view objects have been refined over a period of about twenty years, so you can look to them for inspiration. A good rule of thumb is not to store more in a view than you can store in a cell; a single object pointer or primitive value. If the view needs more information than this, then give it a data source that can provide it dynamically.

One common use for cells is drawing text retrieved from a data source in to the current view. The Cocoa view classes that use a data source all render lots of different objects with roughly the same style. They use cells to do this. Something like a table column view will have a single cell that has its attributes set to match the style of the column's contents and will use this cell for every item it needs to draw.

The cell we saw already was a text cell. It simply drew a string of text in a specified rectangle. This is very useful if you are creating a new view that needs to display some text. It is not the only kind of cell available, however.

Most cells are used to display data of a specific type. The two core cell types each display images and text, respectively. You generally don't need to use image cells in your own view, since an `NSImage` can display itself directly, although sometimes the ability of the cell to draw borders, bezels, and so on can be useful.

Most of the simple user interface components in Cocoa are controls—views that wrap a cell—and the corresponding cell can be used in your own code. If you were implementing a spectrum analyzer view, for example, you might save yourself some work by using the `NSLevelIndicatorCell` to draw the levels at each discrete group. Most of the other cell types are difficult to work with, since they expect the enclosing view to handle events in a specific way. You can cheat slightly and use an `NSControl` subclass that wraps the cell as a subview if you want users to interact with the cells directly. This is slower, so if you have a lot of cells then you might consider using them directly.

Cells do not fit directly into the view hierarchy. You can reuse them for drawing all over your view, so attaching them to a fixed location in the hierarchy would be difficult. If you want a cell to provide event handling support as well as drawing, then you need to manually pass it the events using this method:

```
- (BOOL)trackMouse: (NSEvent*)theEvent
            inRect: (NSRect)cellFrame
            ofView: (NSView*)controlView
      untilMouseUp: (BOOL)untilMouseUp;
```

The first parameter of this method is the event object itself. The second two are needed because cells are stateless with respect to the view hierarchy. A given cell does not have a location; one is given to it whenever it is drawn. If you want a cell to handle mouse events, then it needs to have this information again so that it knows where the mouse events are relative to what the user is looking at. This information is also important for user feedback.

When you call this method, it may trigger an event that requires a redraw of the cell, so you should make sure you're not using a cell that you also use for drawing, unless you remember to reset its state at the end of the drawing method. The method will intercept subsequent mouse events sent to the view until a mouse up event occurs or until the mouse leaves the specified rectangle, depending on the value of the last parameter.

To demonstrate this, we'll implement a simple graphical equalizer view. This will show a few of the standard view concepts. It will use two cells, one for drawing and one for event handling. You can see the final result in Figure 13.3.

The first thing we need to do is define an interface. This is shown in Listing 13.5. Note that this header contains two interface definitions. One is an interface to a class—the equalizer view itself—and the other is an *informal protocol* for the data source.

The class declares an outlet for the data source. Note that the type of this is **id**. This is because we do not require the data source to be of any specific type, just that it implements some methods. We could alternatively require that the data source conform to a formal protocol. I personally prefer this, since it gives a little extra compile-time checking, but it's not common in Cocoa. This is largely due to older versions of Interface Builder not performing any type checking, making formal protocols useless for this case. It also decreases the tightness of the coupling somewhat, since you do not need anything in the interface declaration relating to the view.

Before we look at the view itself, we'll see how it will be used. Listing 13.6

Listing 13.5: The interface to the equalizer view. [from: examples/EqualizerView/EqualizerView.h]

```
#import <Cocoa/Cocoa.h>


@interface EqualizerView : NSView {
    IBOutlet id datasource;
    NSLevelIndicatorCell *cell;
    NSLevelIndicatorCell *editCell;
    NSUInteger trackingRow;
    NSRect trackingFrame;
}
@end

@interface NSObject (EqualizerDataSource)
- (NSUInteger) numberOfRowsInEqualizerView:(EqualizerView*)equalizer;
- (double) equalizerView:(EqualizerView*)equalizer
              valueAtRow:(NSUInteger)aRow;
// Optional:
- (void) equalizerView:(EqualizerView*)equalizer
              setValue:(double)aValue
                 atRow:(NSUInteger)aRow;
@end
```

shows a simple implementation of a data source for this view. It implements all of the methods in the informal protocol, even the optional one.

This data source is very simple, it has an array of ten floating point values as instance variables and just returns or sets them in response to messages from the view.

In previous examples, we've hard-coded something like this into the view. This is simple, but it breaks the separation between models and views. In good code, the view should be completely abstracted from the underlying data. Doing this makes it very easy to reuse objects. This equalizer, since it does not depend on any details of the storage, could be used for anything that wants to present a graphical equalizer to the user.

The view itself is quite complex. Quite a few bits of this are simple bookkeeping. These are shown in Listing 13.7. The initialization and awakening methods call `-createCells` that performs the real initialization, and the `-dealloc` method releases the cells if the view runs in a non-garbage-collected environment.

The real works starts on line 8. This creates the cell that is responsible for

Listing 13.6: A simple equalizer data source. [from: examples/EqualizerView/EqualizerDelegateExample.m]

```
#import "EqualizerDelegateExample.h"

@class EqualizerView;

@implementation EqualizerDelegateExample
- (id) init
{
    if (nil == (self = [super init]))
    {
        return nil;
    }
    for (unsigned i=0 ; i<10 ; i++)
    {
        values[i] = (double)i / 10;
    }
    return self;
}
- (NSUInteger) numberOfRowsInEqualizerView:(EqualizerView*)equalizer
{
    return 10;
}
- (double) equalizerView:(EqualizerView*)equalizer
              valueAtRow:(NSUInteger)aRow
{
    return values[aRow];
}
- (void) equalizerView:(EqualizerView*)equalizer
              setValue:(double)aValue
                 atRow:(NSUInteger)aRow
{
    values[aRow] = aValue;
}
@end
```

drawing. The next three lines set some attributes related to the visual appearance of the cell. The indicator cell used here displays a row of colored boxes representing a numerical value. It will display one box for each value between a minimum and a maximum. For this view we set the maximum to 10. As a simple extension,

Listing 13.7: Setting up the equalizer view. [from: examples/EqualizerView/EqualizerView.m]

```
5  static const double IndicatorBoxes = 10;
6  - (void) createCells
7  {
8      cell = [[NSLevelIndicatorCell alloc] initWithLevelIndicatorStyle:
           NSDiscreteCapacityLevelIndicatorStyle];
9      [cell setMaxValue:IndicatorBoxes];
10     [cell setWarningValue:IndicatorBoxes/2];
11     [cell setCriticalValue:IndicatorBoxes/4*3];
12     editCell = [cell copy];
13     [editCell setEditable:YES];
14     [editCell setContinuous:YES];
15     [editCell setTarget:self];
16     [editCell setAction:@selector(cellValueChanged:)];
17 }
18 - (void) awakeFromNib
19 {
20     [self createCells];
21 }
22 - (id)initWithFrame:(NSRect)frame
23 {
24     if (nil == (self = [super initWithFrame:frame]))
25     {
26         return nil;
27     }
28     [self createCells];
29     return self;
30 }
31 - (void) dealloc
32 {
33     [editCell release];
34     [cell release];
35     [super dealloc];
36 }
```

you could move the `IndicatorBoxes` constant into an ivar and let users of the view modify it.

Once we've set up the visual appearance of the cell, we also need to set up the cell we'll use for editing. This is created on line 12 by copying the display cell. This ensures that all of the properties of the cell are the same. Because we are going to use this cell for editing, we need to set the flag indicating that it is editable. Without this, it will ignore events sent to it.

The final three messages sent to the editing cell define its event handling behavior. The first indicates that it should keep sending action messages as long as the mouse is held down. Without this, it would only send one when the mouse was released, preventing the view from giving live feedback about the current value. Try disabling this and playing with the view. You can still set the values, but the display won't be updated until after you release the mouse.

The most important part of the view is the drawing method. This is the part that displays the view to the user, and is shown in Listing 13.8. This needs to get information from the data source and display it. Unlike previous views we've written, this one will only update the regions that actually need displaying.

Listing 13.8: Drawing the equalizer view. [from: examples/EqualizerView/EqualizerView.m]

```
- (void)drawRect:(NSRect)rect
{
    NSUInteger rows = [datasource numberOfRowsInEqualizerView:self];
    NSRect bounds = [self bounds];
    NSSize cellSize = {bounds.size.width, bounds.size.height / rows};
    CGFloat y= bounds.size.height - cellSize.height;
    for (NSUInteger row=0 ; row<rows ; row++)
    {
        NSRect cellLocation = { {0, y}, cellSize };
        y -= cellSize.height;
        if (NSIntersectsRect(cellLocation, rect))
        {
            double value = [datasource equalizerView:self
                                         valueAtRow:row];
            value *= IndicatorBoxes;
            [cell setDoubleValue:value];
            [cell drawWithFrame:cellLocation
                         inView:self];
        }
    }
}
```

This method starts by getting the number of rows from the data source. If this has changed and only a partial redisplay is requested, then the view will display incorrectly. To avoid this, the data source must send a `-setNeedsDisplay:` or a `-setNeedsDisplayInRect:` message with the visible bounds whenever it changes the number of columns. You could avoid needing this by caching the number of columns and testing here if it's changed. You can't just redraw everything here if you notice that the range has changed though, because the parent view will have set the clipping region for the current graphics context to the regions it thinks are dirty. You need to call `[self setNeedsDisplay: YES]` to make sure the draw method will be called again with the correct rectangle.

The next two lines get the bounds of the view and calculate the size of a single level indicator in the final display. These will be the full width of the view and will each take an equal proportion of the height.

Once these bounds are found, we loop over each of the rows. First, we calculate the rectangle for the indicator on this row, on line 45. Next we test whether it actually needs to be drawn. The test on line 47 returns `YES` if the two rows given as arguments overlap. If they don't, and we try drawing it, then the cell will make a lot of calls to the graphics context that will all be silently ignored due to the clipping region. This is a waste of CPU power, so we don't do it.

When a row does need drawing, we first get the value from the data source and scale it correctly for the number of indicator boxes we are displaying. Then we set this as the cell's value and update it. This is the bit that causes us to need two cells, since the value of the cell will be set to whatever the value of the last cell we draw was at the end of this process.

You can try modifying the code to only need one cell by caching the cell value before the drawing loop and resetting it later. This will make the class slightly lighter, but will require any future modifications to do the same resetting.

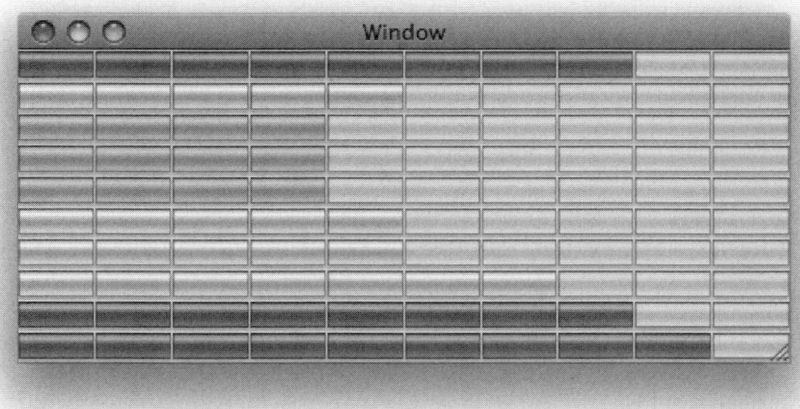

Figure 13.3: A simple graphical equalizer.

Once the cell's value has been set, it is told to draw itself in the location we've calculated for it. Note that on line 46 we subtract a value from the y-coordinate value. This is because our view is not flipped, so the origin will be in the bottom-left corner. We want the rows to be numbered from the top and so we need to either subtract here to get the location for the next cell.

Drawing is only half of a view's responsibility. The other half is handling events. The code for doing this is shown in Listing 13.9. The `-mouseDown:` method is similar to others we've seen. It extracts the location of the mouse event and does something with it.

Listing 13.9: Event handling in the equalizer view. [from: examples/EqualizerView/EqualizerView.m]

```
- (void)mouseDown:(NSEvent *)theEvent
{
    NSUInteger rows = [datasource numberOfRowsInEqualizerView:self];
    NSPoint click = [self convertPoint:[theEvent locationInWindow]
                              fromView:nil];
    NSRect bounds = [self bounds];
    NSSize cellSize = {bounds.size.width, bounds.size.height / rows};

    trackingRow = (bounds.size.height - click.y) / cellSize.height;

    trackingFrame.origin.x = 0;
    trackingFrame.origin.y = bounds.size.height - ((trackingRow + 1) *
        cellSize.height);
    trackingFrame.size = cellSize;

    [editCell trackMouse:theEvent
                  inRect:trackingFrame
                  ofView:self
            untilMouseUp:NO];

}
- (void) cellValueChanged: (id)sender
{
    if ([datasource respondsToSelector:@selector(equalizerView:setValue:
        atRow:)])
    {
        [datasource equalizerView:self
                         setValue:[editCell doubleValue] / IndicatorBoxes
                            atRow:trackingRow];
    }
    [self setNeedsDisplayInRect:trackingFrame];
}
```

Much of the code in this method is similar to code in the drawing method; it calculates the size and location of rows so that we can tell which row the mouse was clicked on. Both the frame and the number of this row are stored in instance variables.

Calculating the cell for the data here is quite easy because this view has a regular layout. For irregular views you might want to implement something like a binary space partitioning tree or just use `NSPointInRect()` on each rectangle you know about to find the correct one.

The final line in this method tells the cell to start tracking the mouse. The cell will track the mouse in the rectangle we've just calculated and will continuously send action messages to the view. Only mouse actions inside the rectangle will cause the cell to change its value. Note that this cell is not drawing itself; it is just tracking events. The drawing is all done by the view.

While the mouse is held down, the cell will send a stream of `-cellValueChanged:` messages to the view. These are simple action messages—we set the selector back on line 16—and allow us to handle changes in the value.

We need to do two things if the value has changed. First, we need to update the data source. Because we specified that the set method in the data source informal protocol is optional, we need to test whether it is implemented. A more complete view implementation would test this in the `-setDatasource:` and `-awakeFromNib` methods and cache the result, but this simple implementation doesn't provide methods for setting the data source in code and just checks every time. The value is scaled back down to be in the 0 to 1 range and then passed to the data source. The value of `trackingRow` that we pass to the data source was set in the `-mouseDown:` method.

Once the data source has been updated, we need to update the display of the rectangle containing the cell. Note that we don't call `-drawRect:` directly. This would be an obvious thing to do, but it would cause some very strange behavior since the state of the graphics context is undefined when in the action method and needs to be set to the view's translation matrix and clipping region for `-drawRect:` to work correctly. Instead we call `-setNeedsDisplayInRect:` with the tracking rectangle as the argument. This adds the rectangle to the set of dirty regions in the view. At some point in the future, the superview will tell this view to display and it will call `-drawRect:` with a rectangle containing this rectangle and possibly others depending on what other regions have been marked as dirty.

When you run this code the cell will periodically call `-displayIfNeeded` in the window containing the view. This will cause the message to be sent down the view hierarchy. When it reaches this view, it will cause the `-drawRect:` method to be called if the view has been marked as containing dirty regions.

Concurrent Drawing

Traditionally, drawing in OpenStep applications has been the rôle of the main thread. Attempting to draw from other threads has had undefined behavior. Starting with OS X 10.6, views have been able to mark themselves as supporting drawing from secondary threads by returning `YES` from `-canDrawConcurrently`. This can also be set for existing views with the corresponding set method.

Concurrent drawing is trivial when combined with the buffered drawing model introduced with CoreAnimation, where each view may draw into its own buffer and have the final results composited on the GPU. The difficult bit comes from the fact that views, traditionally, display some information loaded from a model object. Drawing buttons concurrently, for example, is a lot easier than drawing an outline view concurrently. In the latter case, the view's data source must also be thread-safe.

13.3.3 Drawing Text

We looked at the text system in detail in Chapter 8. For drawing typeset text, this is all you need. This allows you to render paragraphs of text easily. You can also draw individual glyphs by appending them to a bezier path.

Drawing text along an arbitrary path requires you to make use of an *affine transform*. This is a transform matrix wrapped in an `NSAffineTransform` class. Prior to OS X 10.3, this was an AppKit class. Newer versions of OS X modified it to use the same sort of separation as `NSAttributedString`, with the core definition in Foundation and the drawing-related parts provided by categories in AppKit.

The most important method defined in AppKit is `-concat`, which appends the transform to the graphics context's existing transform. The two transform matrixes—the one in the context and the one in the object—are multiplied together so that the result has the same effect as applying the matrix from the context then the matrix from the object.

Typically you will apply a transform, perform some drawing, and undo the transform. You can do this by saving and restoring the context, but that is very expensive. A better option is to apply the inverse transform, reverting the matrix to the old state, like this:

```
[transform concat];
// Some drawing code in the new transform
[transform invert];
[transform concat];
```

Note that this will only apply to the current view. You can't use this to scale sub-views. Since cells inherit the current context, they can be drawn scaled like this. The same transform will work when drawing text with `NSBezierPath`.

This allows you to draw text that follows an arbitrary path. There are a number of ways of doing this. The most complicated involves creating your own layout manager. The simplest involves using an attributed string to do this for you.

Listing 13.10 shows a simple way of drawing text along a curve. This is a very simple example that hard-codes both the text to display and the curve, as shown in Figure 13.4.

Listing 13.10: Drawing text along a curve. [from: examples/CurveText/CurveTextView.m]

```
1  - (void)drawRect:(NSRect)rect
2  {
3      NSDictionary *attributes = [NSDictionary dictionaryWithObjectsAndKeys:
4          [NSFont fontWithName:@"Zapfino" size:32],
5          NSFontAttributeName,
6          nil];
7      NSAttributedString *str =
8          [[NSAttributedString alloc] initWithString: @"Hello␣world!"
9                                          attributes:attributes];
10
11     NSAffineTransform *transform = [NSAffineTransform transform];
12     [transform translateXBy:10 yBy:10];
13     [transform concat];
14
15     NSPoint point = {0,0};
16     for (unsigned i=0 ; i<[[str string] length] ; i++)
17     {
18         NSAttributedString *substr =
19             [str attributedSubstringFromRange:NSMakeRange(i, 1)];
20         [substr drawAtPoint:point];
21
22         transform = [NSAffineTransform transform];
23         [transform translateXBy:[substr size].width + 3
24                             yBy:0];
25         [transform rotateByDegrees:6];
26         [transform concat];
27     }
28 }
```

This first constructs an attributed string containing the text “Hello world!” in the Zapfino font. It then draws it along a curve. Lines 15–17 define a transform that translates the origin to (10,10). This is done, rather than specifying a constant offset, since we are going to apply more transforms to the graphics context while

Figure 13.4: Drawing text along a curve.

rendering the string. This translation means that we just need to worry about drawing each character relative to the starting point, rather than relative to the origin.

The loop that starts on line 20 iterates through every character in the string and draws it in turn. Note that this will only work for strings that do not contain composed characters; for more complex strings you should use an `NSLayoutManager` to get the glyphs directly.

For each character in the string, it gets an attributed string representing that character and draws it. It then applies a new transform to the context. This transform is constructed from two elements. The first is a translation, which moves the origin to the right in the current frame of reference, which in this case means along a tangent to the curve at the current point. This is done to avoid drawing all of the characters on top of each other. The size of the displacement is taken from the attributed string, which will return the width and height of the glyph.

The next part of the transform is a rotation. Note that we are applying a constant rotation, so at first glance it appears that the text will eventually loop around in a circle. This is not quite correct, however. If you ever played with Logo as a child, you will probably remember drawing approximations of circles by going forward a small distance and then right a small amount, and repeating this until you had gone all of the way around. This is almost what we are doing here, except that the distance we are advancing is not constant, since it is defined by the width of text in a proportional font.

If you change the font from Zapfino to Courier, you will get text drawing in a circle, but overlaps at the end if you make the string long enough. Listing 13.11 shows how to adjust this method to draw in a circle.

The setup here is almost the same. To make the display slightly cleaner, it sets the background color to white on lines 14 and 15, and since this is going to give a bigger curve, it moves it out from the edge a bit more. A better implementation would work out how big the text would need to be to fit correctly; we'll look at how to do that in the next section.

Listing 13.11: Drawing text in a circular path. [from: examples/CircleTextView/CircleTextView.m]

```
1  - (void)drawRect:(NSRect)rect
2  {
3      NSDictionary *attributes = [NSDictionary dictionaryWithObjectsAndKeys:
4                                  [NSFont fontWithName:@"Zapfino" size:32],
5                                  NSFontAttributeName,
6                                  nil];
7      NSAttributedString *str =
8      [[NSAttributedString alloc] initWithString: @"Hello␣world!␣This␣is␣a␣
           long␣string␣which␣might␣wrap␣all␣around."
9                                      attributes:attributes];
10
11     [[NSColor whiteColor] setFill];
12     [NSBezierPath fillRect:rect];
13     NSAffineTransform *transform = [NSAffineTransform transform];
14     [transform translateXBy:250 yBy:10];
15     [transform concat];
16
17
18     NSPoint point = {0,0};
19     NSUInteger stringLength = [[str string] length];
20     const CGFloat extraSpace = 5;
21     CGFloat angleScale = 360 / ([str size].width + (extraSpace *
           stringLength));
22     for (NSUInteger i=0 ; i<stringLength ; i++)
23     {
24         NSAttributedString *substr =
```

```
25            [str attributedSubstringFromRange:NSMakeRange(i, 1)];
26            [substr drawAtPoint:point];
27
28            transform = [NSAffineTransform transform];
29            CGFloat displacement = [substr size].width + extraSpace;
30            [transform translateXBy:displacement
31                                yBy:0];
32            [transform rotateByDegrees:angleScale * displacement];
33            [transform concat];
34        }
35
36    }
```

Before drawing the characters in the string, this version calculates the size of the entire string, on line 22. Line 24 then calculates the number of degrees you need to turn for every point you advance. If you draw a line the length of the string, plus the amount of extra padding we are inserting between characters, you need to go completely around (360°). Smaller distances are calculated as some fraction of this.

After drawing the character, we get the horizontal displacement, on line 32. This is the width of the character plus the padding. We then add a translation by that amount and a rotation by a factor based on that amount to the graphics context's transform matrix.

The end result is shown in Figure 13.5. The string is drawn all around a circle, irrespective of the length. The radius of the circle is determined by the amount of text being drawn. The diameter of the circle is the length of the string plus the extra padding we add, and the radius is this divided by 2π.

It is possible to make text follow any path using this mechanism. Unfortunately, there is no method on `NSBezierPath` for drawing text along a path. If you want to do this, then you will need to calculate the transform matrix for a distance along the path manually and draw the glyphs one at a time. Since a lot of people are implementing this kind of code manually, it seems possible that this will be added in a future version of OS X, so make sure you check the documentation before implementing it yourself.

13.3.4 Creating New Cells

We've seen how to create new views that use existing cells, but often creating a new type of cell is the correct solution. For a simple view, such as the circular text view seen in Figure 13.5, you can decompose it into a view and a cell and then use the cell in other projects, too.

Drawing in cells is almost the same as drawing in views. The biggest difference

Figure 13.5: Drawing text in a circle.

is that cells do not have their own graphics context. This means that they are responsible for undoing any changes that they make to the context. This can be done by either saving and restoring the state, or by performing the inverse action to everything that modifies the state. Since we will be collecting a lot of matrix transforms, we will opt for the first option in our cell, shown in Listing 13.12.

Listing 13.12: A cell class for drawing text in a circle. [from: examples/CircleTextCell/-CircleTextCell.m]

```
#import "CircleTextCell.h"

#define PI (3.141592653589793)

@implementation CircleTextCell
- (void) drawWithFrame:(NSRect)cellFrame inView:(NSView *)controlView
{
    NSAttributedString *str = [self attributedStringValue];
    NSSize stringSize = [str size];
    NSUInteger chars = [[str string] length];
    CGFloat radius = (stringSize.width + extraPadding * chars) / (2 * PI);
    CGFloat diameter = 2*radius;
    NSPoint scale = {1,1};
    if (diameter > cellFrame.size.width)
    {
        scale.x = cellFrame.size.width / diameter;
    }
    if (diameter > cellFrame.size.height)
    {
        scale.y = cellFrame.size.height / diameter;
    }
    NSAffineTransform * transform = [NSAffineTransform transform];
    NSAffineTransformStruct identity = [transform transformStruct];
    [transform scaleXBy:scale.x yBy:scale.y];
    [transform translateXBy:radius yBy:0];
    [NSGraphicsContext saveGraphicsState];
    [transform concat];

    NSPoint origin = {0,0};
    CGFloat angleScale = 360 / ([str size].width + (extraPadding * chars));
    for (NSUInteger i=0 ; i<chars ; i++)
    {
        NSAttributedString *substr =
            [str attributedSubstringFromRange:NSMakeRange(i, 1)];
        [substr drawAtPoint:origin];

        [transform setTransformStruct:identity];
        CGFloat displacement = [substr size].width + extraPadding;
        [transform translateXBy:displacement
                            yBy:0];
        [transform rotateByDegrees:angleScale * displacement];
        [transform concat];
```

```
43     }
44     [NSGraphicsContext restoreGraphicsState];
45 }
46 - (void) setPadding:(CGFloat) aFloat
47 {
48     extraPadding = aFloat;
49 }
50 - (CGFloat) padding
51 {
52     return extraPadding;
53 }
54 - (NSSize)cellSize
55 {
56     NSAttributedString *str = [self attributedStringValue];
57     NSSize stringSize = [str size];
58     NSUInteger chars = [[str string] length];
59     CGFloat radius = (stringSize.width + extraPadding * chars) / (2 * PI);
60     CGFloat diameter = 2*radius;
61     return NSMakeSize(diameter, diameter);
62 }
63 @end
```

This code is very similar to that shown in the last example. Since cells inherit a mechanism for storing their state, we just use that on line 8 to get the attributed string value to draw. This could have been created by any of the set methods on `NSCell`. You can see exactly how this works when we look at the source for the accompanying view class.

The code from lines 11–21 is all new. This first asks the attributed string to calculate the size that the text will be if drawn normally. This is added to the amount of padding space that we will insert to give a new diameter. This is then divided by 2π to give the radius, and multiplied by two to give the diameter. If the diameter is bigger than the rectangle that the cell has been asked to draw in, it produces a scale factor that will enable it to fit. On line 24, we create an affine transform that scales by this amount and apply it. After doing this, the cell can draw the text in a circle of its natural size and it will automatically fit. The result of drawing the circle in a rectangle scaled down vertically can be seen in Figure 13.6.

Before applying this transform, we do two things. First, we record the structure used to represent the affine transform. This is a simple structure containing the six values needed to generate the matrix. We cache these for a new transform (one with no permutations applied) so that we can reset the transform object cheaply later on (line 37), rather than creating a new object for each character.

The second thing we do is save the graphics state. Note we call the method

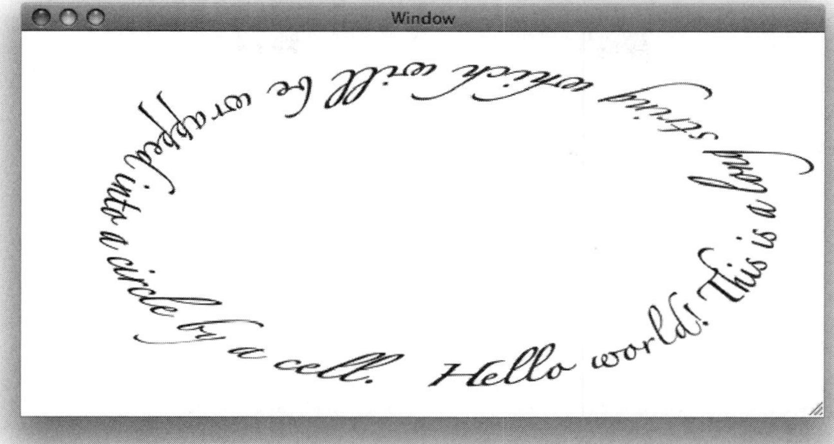

Figure 13.6: Text drawn in an ellipse by a cell.

on the graphics context class, rather than on an instance. This is because we just want to save the current state for this thread, we don't need an instance for anything else. We need to do this so that the cell can restore the context to the state that the view that asks it to draw expects.

The loop for drawing each character is similar to the version in the view. The main difference is that we reuse the same `NSAffineTransform` object, resetting it to the default state each loop, rather than creating a new one every iteration.

This class also contains some methods for setting and getting the amount of padding between characters. A view using the cell can use these to control the appearance of the rendered text circle. The final method returns the optimal size for drawing the cell. This is not quite what the definition in `NSCell` says it should do—it should return the minimum size for the cell—but it's close since this kind of cell doesn't really have a minimum size.

The other part of this example is a view using the new cell type. This is shown in Listing 13.13. This is now much simpler, since it delegates the actual drawing to the cell.

The `-awakeFromNib` method creates the cell. This uses the `-setAttributedStringValue:` that our new cell inherits from `NSCell`. This stores the attributed string internally and allows its value to be accessed in a variety of formats. The new cell class calls a superclass method to get the attributed string back. The view also sets the spacing, since this is no longer hard-coded in the drawing loop.

The drawing code is now very simple. The cell handles most of the drawing; all the view does is clear the background. This particular view is opaque. You could easily clear the background with a translucent color to have the view composited over the ones underneath.

Listing 13.13: Drawing a circle of text using a cell. [from: examples/CircleTextCell/CircleTextView.m]

```
#import "CircleTextView.h"
#import "CircleTextCell.h"

@implementation CircleTextView
- (void) awakeFromNib
{
    NSDictionary *attributes = [NSDictionary dictionaryWithObjectsAndKeys:
                                [NSFont fontWithName:@"Zapfino" size:32],
                                NSFontAttributeName,
                                nil];
    NSAttributedString *str =
    [[NSAttributedString alloc] initWithString: @"Hello␣world!␣This␣is␣a␣
        long␣string␣which␣will␣be␣wrapped␣into␣a␣circle␣by␣a␣cell."
                                    attributes:attributes];

    cell = [[CircleTextCell alloc] init];
    [cell setAttributedStringValue:str];
    [cell setPadding:5];
}
- (void)drawRect:(NSRect)rect
{
    [[NSColor whiteColor] setFill];
    [NSBezierPath fillRect:rect];
    [cell drawWithFrame:[self bounds]
                 inView:self];
}
@end
```

This separation allows the same drawing code to be reused easily. You could, for example, write an `NSControl` subclass that used this cell for drawing but, when you clicked on it, used an `NSTextFieldCell` to allow the text to be edited, or you could allow this kind of editing in a complex view that contained other cells.

13.3.5 Drawing Bitmap Images

So far all of the drawing we've looked at has been vector based. We have drawn straight and curved lines, and text made up of glyphs composed of bezier curves. Cocoa can also draw *raster images*.

A raster image is one that is already a two-dimensional array of pixel values. The simplest thing to do with these is simply write them directly to video memory and have them appear on the screen. This is what happens at the final stage of display of all graphics on OS X (and all other operating systems running on similar hardware).

With *QuickDraw*, the old Mac OS display technology, you could do exactly this. To speed up drawing, it lets you get exclusive access to a region of the video memory and write data directly there. Quartz does not permit this. Every context you draw to is an off-screen buffer. The window server then *composites* these together.

Sometimes, such as when you invoke Exposé, the window server will perform transforms on these. The simplest kind of transform is scaling. For vector data this is very easy, you simply move the points further apart or closer together. When you do this, however, they may not quite line up on pixels exactly. Diagonal lines never will, even in the absence of scaling.

Quartz uses *antialiasing* to try to prevent you from noticing this. When drawing a line over a pixel, it sets them to a gray value indicating how much of the pixel is covered by the line. If you zoom in on a single letter you will see something like Figure 13.7. Try this by holding down control and scrolling with the mouse.[1] You may be surprised to realize that a black letter only has a small number of black pixels.

This is because pixel boundaries are quite arbitrary. You do not really have color pixels on a TFT or CRT monitor. You have red pixels, green pixels, and blue pixels. By convention, we group a cluster of three together and regard them as being in the same place, but this is not quite true. If you set one pixel to blue and the next pixel to yellow, then this is equivalent to setting a pixel to white that is one-third of a pixel width to the left of the right pixel.

This allows the windowing system to get a bit more horizontal resolution when drawing vector images. Similar techniques are used when scaling raster images. When you expand these you will often get a set of rectangles that don't quite line up on pixels. If you render this to the screen directly, then you will get lots of jagged edges, just as you will when you draw a diagonal line without antialiasing.

Scaling and antialiasing are so closely related that a lot of graphics cards implemented the latter using the former, by a process called *oversampling*. This

[1] If this doesn't do anything, then you will need to enable it under the Universal Access settings in System Preferences.

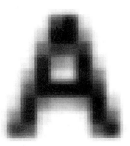

Figure 13.7: Text antialiasing in OS X.

involved drawing vector data to a frame buffer that was larger than the screen and then scaling it down to fit. The scaling algorithm used determines the quality of the result.

The simplest scaling algorithm is called *nearest-neighbor interpolation*, which simply picks the pixel in the source image that is closest to the center of the pixel in the new image. This was popular for a long time since it is very fast even on a slow CPU. A relatively modern (by which I mean less than a decade or so old) GPU can run much better interpolation algorithms fast enough for interactive use, so you will rarely find this in a modern system. More commonly you will find either *bilinear interpolation* or *bicubic interpolation*. These work by treating the pixel values as points on a line or a curve, working out the equation for that line and then evaluating it at the point where the new pixel needs to be displayed.

In general, you don't have to worry about the exact algorithm you use. Quartz provides three choices: default, good, or fast. Exactly what algorithm each corresponds to depends on the hardware available at the time. Most of the time, the default will be fast enough and good enough. If you want to change it, you can do so by sending a `-setImageInterpolation:` message to the graphics context. Note that this is not part of the state that is saved and restored, so you will need to manually reset it if you only want to change it temporarily.

Image Representations

There are two important classes for dealing with images in Cocoa. The one you will most commonly use is `NSImage`, a high-level wrapper around basic image functionality. This is an example of the *façade pattern* and does not really store the image itself. It manages one or more `NSImageRep` subclasses, which are the lower-level interface to the image. When you are dealing with an `NSImage` it may have several different representations of the same image, optimized for drawing to different devices.

An example of this happens when you load a vector image. The `NSImage` object will keep an image representation directly corresponding to the vector image, but drawing this to the screen is typically quite expensive. To help speed this up, it might also keep a bitmap image representation at the screen's DPI. When you display it, this just needs to be copied into video memory (if it isn't there already) and the GPU told to composite it in the correct place. This trick is used by Quartz 2D Extreme for rendering text; each glyph is rendered to a texture in the GPU and composited together. If you look at the last sentence, it contained 14 lower-case 'e' glyphs; not having to create each of these from a sequence of bezier curves and then copy the result to the GPU speeds up rendering a lot.

The low-level image representation class is quite simple. It has two important methods, one for creating it and one for drawing it. The first, `-initWithData:`, takes a representation of an image file and returns an object. The second, `-draw`, draws it in the current context.

You will rarely create an `NSImageRep` subclass directly, since the superclass has several convenience constructors that pick the correct subclass for the provided image source. These work by calling `-canInitWithData:` on subclasses to test for compatibility. You can call this on the superclass to find out if there is any representation class that understands a given format.

There is one important subclass of `NSImageRep` that provides some extra functionality. The `NSBitmapImageRep` class is a superclass of all of the image representations for raster image formats. This class adds methods for setting and getting the value at individual pixels, which is not possible for vector images without first rasterizing them.

Creating Images

All of the drawing code we have looked at so far uses the default graphics context. This has always been implicitly created by the caller, so far. When a `-drawRect:` method is called, a graphics context has already been created and the view just draws into it. This context has always been the context created by the window representing a buffer in the window server, but this is not the only option.

You can very easily create a new graphics context of your own and tell a view to draw there. There are three possible output devices supported when creating a graphics context. One is a window, which we have already seen. The next is a *graphics port*, which on OS X is always a `CGContextRef` and can write to anything that Core Graphics knows how to write to. The final option is a bitmap, as represented by an `NSBitmapImageRep`. Listing 13.14 shows how to create a context backed by a bitmap.

Listing 13.14: Writing a view to a tiff file. [from: examples/CircleTextCell2/CircleTextView.m]

```
- (void) writeViewToTiffFile:(NSString*)aFile resolution:(NSSize)aSize
{
    NSGraphicsContext * context = [NSGraphicsContext currentContext];
    NSBitmapImageRep *bitmap =
        [[NSBitmapImageRep alloc] initWithBitmapDataPlanes:NULL
                                                pixelsWide:aSize.width
                                                pixelsHigh:aSize.height
                                             bitsPerSample:8
                                           samplesPerPixel:4
                                                  hasAlpha:YES
                                                  isPlanar:NO
                                            colorSpaceName:
                                                NSCalibratedRGBColorSpace
                                               bytesPerRow:0
                                              bitsPerPixel:0];
    NSGraphicsContext *bitmapContext = [NSGraphicsContext
        graphicsContextWithBitmapImageRep:bitmap];
    [NSGraphicsContext setCurrentContext:bitmapContext];
    NSRect drawRect = { {0,0}, aSize};
    NSRect bounds = [self bounds];
    [self setBounds:drawRect];
    [self drawRect:drawRect];
    [self setBounds:bounds];
    [[bitmap TIFFRepresentation] writeToFile:aFile
                                  atomically:NO];
    [bitmap release];
    [NSGraphicsContext setCurrentContext:context];
}
```

This listing shows a new method added to the `CircleTextView` class from the last example. The same method could easily be added to any view, including `NSView` via a category. When it is called, it creates an image and writes it out to the specified file, with the given size. Since the drawing is all vector based, we can create arbitrary-sized images easily. Figure 13.8 shows the running view (left) and the saved .tiff file opened in Preview (right).

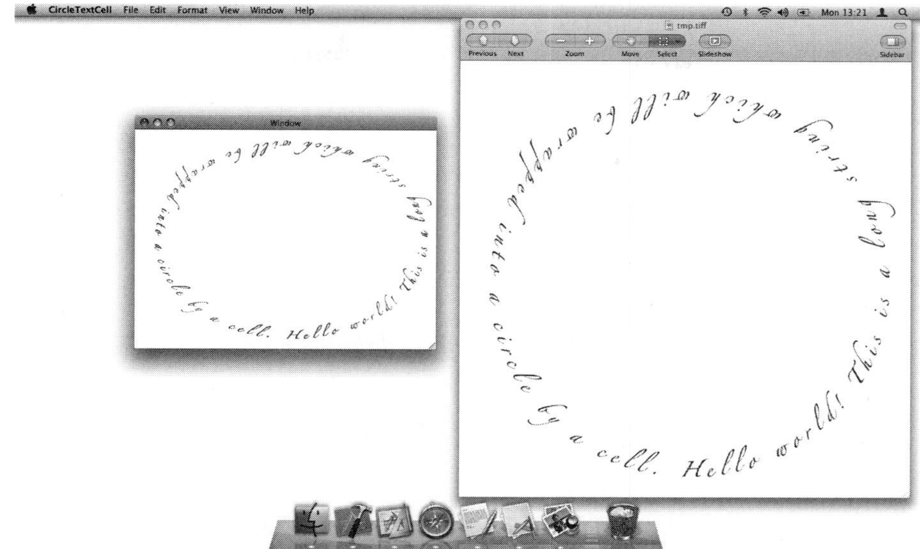

Figure 13.8: A saved image and the view that created it.

The first and last thing this method does is save and restore the old graphics context. Note that the context itself, rather than the state, is stored. The next step is to create a new bitmap object. The `NSBitmapImageRep` class probably has the longest initialization method you will ever see. The first argument is a pointer to the data for the image. Since we are creating a new image, we pass `NULL` here, which makes the object allocate its own backing store.

The next few arguments define the number and type of pixels. We get the size of the image from the argument, and simply hard-code eight bits per channel, four channels with alpha, giving a 32-bit image format. The `isPlanar:` argument is used to decide whether the pixels are all stored together, or stored in separate locations for each channel. For our purposes it doesn't matter, since we never touch the pixel data directly. We also pick a standard color space and set the last two arguments to zero so that the object will fill them in with sensible values itself.

Once the bitmap is created, we create a graphics context pointing to it and set this as the current context. This is very simple and means that all subsequent drawing commands will modify the bitmap object, rather than the screen.

Lines 21–25 draw the view. The drawing itself is done on line 24, where

-drawRect: is passed a rectangle of the same dimensions as the image. Doing this by itself will draw the view in the corner of the rectangle. This is because the view won't draw outside the bounds specified by its superview. We need to change these and restore them afterward so that we don't accidentally move and resize the view in its parent.

Once the view is drawn, the remaining step is to get a TIFF representation of it and write that out to a file. To make this all work, we add this line to the end of the -awakeFromNib method:

```
[self writeViewToTiffFile: [@"~/Desktop/tmp.tiff"
    stringByExpandingTildeInPath]
              resolution: NSMakeSize(1024,1024)];
```

This dumps a 1024×1024 bitmap of the view to the desktop when the view is loaded. This can then be opened by anything that can read TIFF files, including Apple's Preview application or any application that uses Cocoa's image loading capabilities.

13.3.6 Compositing Images

Drawing to an image is useful, but not the main thing an application will do with images. Most commonly you will want to load an image from a file or some other source and draw it in your user interface. Both NSImage and NSImageRep support this. Typically you will use an NSImage and make use of the caching it provides.

For displaying individual images, the NSImageView class is very simple to use. You can create one in Interface Builder and position it as you would any other view. Since it is a NSControl subclass, it uses a cell for most of the real drawing work. This is an instance of the NSImageCell class. You usually create these by sending a -initImageCell: message to an NSCell.

Image cells are really only useful for providing a generic interface to compound views that know how to draw cells. For your own views you can typically draw images directly. The drawing of an image representation is done by sending it a -draw message after setting up the graphics state. NSImage provides a number of convenience method for setting up the state and drawing. The most general of these is

```
- (void)drawInRect: (NSRect)dstRect
          fromRect: (NSRect)srcRect
         operation: (NSCompositingOperation)op
          fraction: (CGFloat)delta;
```

This draws some of the receiver in the current graphics context. The part of the image to draw is specified with the second argument and the destination is specified with the first. The last argument lets you set the opacity of an image. A value of zero draws the image as totally transparent, while a value of one makes it opaque. If the image has an alpha channel, then this is used as well.

The most powerful argument here is the third parameter. This defines the compositing operation to use. Figure 13.9 shows the result of compositing the OS X logo on top of the Mona Lisa using each operation. This is done using the code shown in Listing 13.15.

Listing 13.15: Compositing two images with all of the compositing operations.

[from: examples/CompositeDemo/CompositeView.m]

```
- (void)drawRect:(NSRect)rect
{
    NSCompositingOperation op = NSCompositeClear;
    NSRect bounds = [self bounds];
    NSSize imageSize = bounds.size;
    imageSize.width /= 7;
    imageSize.height /= 2;
    NSRect srcRect = { {0,0}, [src size] };
    NSRect dstRect = { {0,0}, [dst size] };
    for (unsigned y=0 ; y<2 ; y++)
    {
        for (unsigned x=0 ; x<7 ; x++)
        {
            NSRect drawRect;
            drawRect.origin.x = x*imageSize.width;
            drawRect.origin.y = y*imageSize.height;
            drawRect.size = imageSize;
            [src drawInRect:drawRect
                   fromRect:srcRect
                  operation:NSCompositeCopy
                   fraction:1];
            [dst drawInRect:drawRect
                   fromRect:dstRect
                  operation:op++
                   fraction:0.5];
        }
    }
}
```

The demo program has three views in the window. Two are `NSImageViews` with the editable attribute set. This allows them to have images dragged onto them. When this happens they fire their action message. This is connected to a simple controller that passes the two `NSImages` to our the custom view, which stores pointers to them in `src` for the left image and `dst` for the right image, and then marks the view as needing redisplay.

Figure 13.9: Compositing the OS X logo over the Mona Lisa.

When the view is drawn, it divides its area into fourteen segments, since there are fourteen compositing operations, and loops over each one first rendering the source image directly into the rectangle and then rendering the destination image over it at 50% opacity. You can use this simple application to experiment with different compositing operations. You could try extending it by providing a slider that lets you set the opacity of the destination image.

This is a fairly simple example of image drawing. You should remember that images use the same drawing context as every other drawing operation. This means that any affine transform you apply to the graphics context before drawing an image will be applied when drawing the image. This allows you to skew, scale, rotate, and translate images. You can, of course, apply any combination of these operations.

13.4 Printing and Paginating Views

We saw earlier how to draw into an image. This is almost what happens when you print. For simple consumer printers, rendering a bitmap is required before printing and this is then sent to the printer one line at a time. More expensive printers have their own CPU that understands a vector drawing language, often HP's *Printer Control Language* (*PCL*) or PostScript. If you are drawing a lot of text or vector art, then you can send the vector representation to the printer a lot faster than a raster representation.

The front end of the Mac printing system accepts PDFs. When you print, you send a PDF to the print subsystem and it then converts it to a format that the printer can understand. Sometimes the "printer" isn't a piece of hardware at all, it can be a PDF file or an *Automator* workflow. This is how every OS X application that can print has the ability to save and email PDF files directly from the print dialog.

Generating PDFs from a view is trivial. You simply send the view a `-dataWithPDFInsideRect:` message. This will call the draw method with a new Quartz context. Since Quartz uses the PDF drawing model internally, it can create PDFs easily by serializing the command stream.

Some views need to be displayed differently on screen to how they are printed. A simple example is a text field, which should not display its highlight or the insertion point when printing. A view can test whether it is being drawn to the screen by sending a `+currentContextDrawingToScreen` message to `NSGraphicsContext`. If you are creating a view that has some screen-only or printer-only elements, then you should perform this test at the start of your drawing method.

Printed and on-screen displays have one big difference; paper doesn't properly support arbitrary scrolling. If your view doesn't fit in a window, you can embed it in a scroll view and see only a subset of it at a time. You can do something similar with paper by splitting the view across several pages. Each page will be generated by a separate call to the draw method. Exactly where the pages are split depends on the view.

13.4.1 Print Info

When a view is drawing into a surface for printing, there is an associated `NSPrintInfo` object that provides information about the page layout. This contains a large number of flags that are used to determine how the view should be displayed.

The most important ones for implementing custom behavior are those related to the printing rectangle. When `drawRect:` is called, it will be passed a rectangle. This doesn't tell you anything about the page other than that you have been asked to draw into some part of it. If your view is embedded in another view, then the rectangle will be smaller than the printable region of the page. You can get the current print info with this line:

```
[[NSPrintOperation currentOperation] printInfo];
```

The returned object has a large number of attributes about the page, including the size of the margins on each side and the size of the whole page. It also contains the pagination settings and the printer in use.

> **Printing Raster Images**
>
> You should remember when printing raster images that the printer will typically be higher resolution than the screen. Screen and printer DPI can't be compared exactly, since the printer can usually only print one of three colors on a dot, while a screen can typically display a 24-bit value there. In a printed page, you will typically want to provide higher-resolution images than you would for the screen. In general, if you are being asked to output a raster image for printing, you should provide the highest-quality version you have access to.
>
> If you use `NSImage` for drawing raster images, then you don't need to worry about this. It will automatically give the representation that most closely matches the devices capabilities. If you are generating a bitmap and then printing it, then you might consider either passing the commands used to generate it to the printing context directly or, if this is impossible, generating a higher-resolution image and then printing this.

13.4.2 Creating Print Operations

Printing operations encapsulated in an `NSPrintOperation` object. This handles the mapping from a view to a printed document and every step in between. Typically this will include displaying the print dialog box and allowing the user to customize the print job.

By default, the Print menu item will send a `-print:` message to the first responder. This is implemented in `NSView` with a line like this:

```
[[NSPrintOperation printOperationWithView: self] runOperation];
```

This creates a new print operation with the default settings and runs it. You can customize the default page info by sending a `+setSharedPrintInfo:` message to the `NSPrintInfo` class. The print info you pass to this method will be used as the default for future printing operations.

The print operation object ties together the view, the target, and the print info. There are a few things you are likely to want to customize about this. The most obvious one is to suppress the print dialog. This is done by sending a `-setShowsPrintPanel:` message to the operation.

Most of the time you wouldn't want to do this for printing, but it can be useful if you want to implement your own export as PDF functionality. You can create a print operation that writes PDF or *Encapsulated PostScript* (*EPS*) data easily using one of the constructors like this:

```
+ (NSPrintOperation*)PDFOperationWithView: (NSView*)aView
                               insideRect: (NSRect)rect
                                   toData: (NSMutableData*)data
                                printInfo: (NSPrintInfo*)aPrintInfo;
```

This creates a print job that will generate PDF data directly using the specified page layout and the rectangle in the view. You can use this, for example, to export some specified region in a drawing application as a PDF.

Typically, you will provide your own dialog box for this kind of export, rather than going via the normal print dialog. Once you get the data back from this, you could use the `PDFDocument` class, part of the *PDFKit framework* to set PDF metadata. This lets you implement PDF saving very easily. You can also do some other tricks, such as embed some editable representation of your document in the PDF.

More commonly, rather than suppressing the print dialog, you will want to modify it. The simplest, and most common, change to make is to attach the dialog as a sheet to the window being printed, rather than run it modally. This is done by substituting the `-runOperation` message with a call to this method:

```
- (void)runOperationModalForWindow: (NSWindow*)docWindow
                          delegate: (id)delegate
                    didRunSelector: (SEL)didRunSelector
                       contextInfo: (void*)contextInfo;
```

When the operation completes, it will send a message to the delegate with the specified selector. This should expect arguments like this:

```
- (void)printOperationDidRun: (NSPrintOperation*)printOperation
                     success: (BOOL)success
                 contextInfo: (void*)contextInfo;
```

The first argument will be the print operation that just ran. The second will indicate whether it actually printed, or if some error occurred. The final parameter is the same `contextInfo` pointer passed in at the start.

Using this variant, only the window being printed will be blocked during printing, the rest of the application's windows will continue to receive and process events as normal.

For extra customization, you can create a separate view that will be attached to the print panel. This is done by sending a `-setPrintPanel:` message to the operation. This replaces the `NSPrintPanel` class that the operation will use for prompting the user.

Prior to 10.5, you customized this object by sending it a `-setAccessoryView:` message. This took an `NSView` instance as an argument. When the print panel was displayed, it would attach this view to the display. This mechanism is still used in other common panels, but is now deprecated for print panels.

10.5 introduced the `NSViewController` class. This is analogous to `NSWindowController`, but manages a view that is not bound to a window. It is used to load a view from a nib and then freeing it at the end. The class keeps a represented object, accessed by the `-representedObject` method, although subclasses may have other attributes. For print panel accessory views, the represented object will be the print info object.

A view controller passed used as an accessory view for a print dialog must conform to the `NSPrintPanelAccessorizing` protocol. This specifies two methods:

```
- (NSSet*)keyPathsForValuesAffectingPreview;
- (NSArray*)localizedSummaryItems;
```

The first returns a set of KVO-compliant key paths that defines keys that may affect the print preview. When you change one of these, the print panel will be notified and will update the preview. The second returns an array of dictionaries containing names and descriptions used to display the summary pane of the print dialog.

Starting with OS X 10.5, a print panel can have an arbitrary number of accessory views. These will each be displayed separately, with their titles displayed as items in the pop-up list in the print dialog. You can use this to group related customization settings together.

This change means that each accessory panel should now have its view in its own nib, just like a window, but with the file's owner set to an `NSViewController` subclass instead of an `NSWindowController`. The nib is then loaded with a snipped like this:

```
controller = [[NSViewController alloc]
    initWithNibName: @"MyView"
             bundle: [NSBundle mainBundle]];
[controller loadView];
```

This is strongly reminiscent of the `-initWithWindowNibName:` method on `NSWindowController`, the class on which this is modeled. Unlike the window controller, the bundle containing the nib must also be specified. This is done to make it easier to store views like this in frameworks and plugins. A common use for a view wrapped in this kind of controller is to provide a set of options to an existing panel, and so you might want to use it in your own code to allow third-party plugins to extend the UI in well-defined ways. A view controller supplied in a plugin would be instantiated in almost the same way, but the bundle would be created with +bundleForClass: or +bundleForTag: from within the plugin, or with the bundle object created when the plugin was loaded if the controller is being created outside the plugin.

13.4.3 Paginating a View

There are a number of methods declared in NSView to allow you to manually handle pagination. For simple views, this is not very important, but for more complex ones it can be vital to producing good output. The text view, for example, makes use of these to ensure that page breaks are between lines. Common spreadsheet views alter the size of the page slightly to align it on a cell boundary.

To demonstrate these we'll modify the simple compositing example from earlier so that it lets the user decide how many images to print. Since the view we want to print in this example doesn't accept first responder, we need to tweak the main nib so that the Print menu item's target is the view, instead of the first responder proxy.

The first thing we need to do is draw the accessory view. We do this by creating a new xib file in XCode that contains just an NSView and add a slider to it. Figure 13.10 shows what this should look like. The slider is connected up to the file's owner via the action and outlet shown in Listing 13.16.

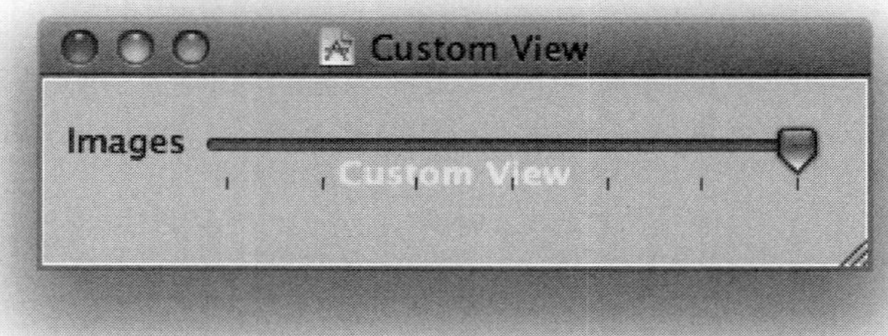

Figure 13.10: The print panel accessory view.

This class inherits from the view controller class and conforms to the extra protocol that the print panel requires. The implementation is shown in Listing 13.17.

This file begins defining two constant strings. These are not exported, but defining the keys as constants here lets the compiler check for typos when you use them in multiple locations.

Listing 13.16: The interface to the view controller for the print panel. [from: examples/CompositeDemoPrinting/PrintPanelController.h]

```
#import <Cocoa/Cocoa.h>

@interface PrintPanelController : NSViewController
        <NSPrintPanelAccessorizing> {
    IBOutlet NSSlider *slider;
}
- (IBAction) setPagesFromSlider:(id)sender;
@end
```

Listing 13.17: The implementation of the view controller for the print panel. [from: examples/CompositeDemoPrinting/PrintPanelController.m]

```
#import "PrintPanelController.h"

static NSString *kImagesPerPagePath = @"representedObject.dictionary.imagesPerPage";
static NSString *kImagesPerPage = @"imagesPerPage";
@implementation PrintPanelController
- (NSSet *)keyPathsForValuesAffectingPreview
{
    [self setPagesFromSlider:slider];
    return [NSSet setWithObject: kImagesPerPagePath];
}
- (NSArray *)localizedSummaryItems
{
    return nil;
}
- (IBAction) setPagesFromSlider:(id)sender

{
    NSMutableDictionary *dict = [[self representedObject] dictionary];
    [dict willChangeValueForKey:kImagesPerPage];
    [dict setObject:[sender objectValue]
            forKey:kImagesPerPage];
    [dict didChangeValueForKey:kImagesPerPage];
}
@end
```

The first two methods are required by the protocol. The second one is not needed by this example, since our pane doesn't display any summary information, so it just returns `nil`. You could try extending the controller by implementing this method to provide a line in the summary view.

The first method is very important. It provides the key path to the live preview in the print dialog. This panel only adjusts one value, but that value should modify the preview image, so it is flagged here. Before returning this, we set the value to the default.

The final method handles the action message from the slider. This updates the key containing the number of images per page. This is stored in the `NSPrintInfo`'s `dictionary` attribute. This is a mutable dictionary provided for exactly this purpose: specifying extra information related to this print job.

Note that we need to manually wrap this in the KVO notifications, since the dictionary does not send them automatically. Hopefully this will be fixed in future versions of OS X.

Rather than adding more methods directly to our view, this time we will separate out the concerns and put the printing code in a separate category, shown in Listing 13.18. All of these methods will be automatically added to the view class when it is loaded.

Splitting the class into separate categories like this makes it easier for someone unfamiliar with the code to navigate it. All of the printing-related functionality is in this definition, while all of the drawing code is in the main file.

Listing 13.18: The printing category for the composite view. [from: examples/CompositeDemoPrinting/CompositeViewPrinting.m]

```
#import <Cocoa/Cocoa.h>
#import "PrintPanelController.h"
#import "CompositeView.h"

static int imagesPerPage(void)
{
    NSPrintInfo *info = [[NSPrintOperation currentOperation] printInfo];
    NSDictionary *dict = [info dictionary];
    return [[dict objectForKey:@"imagesPerPage"] intValue];
}


@implementation CompositeView (Printing)
- (void) print:(id)sender
{
    PrintPanelController *controller =
        [[PrintPanelController alloc] initWithNibName: @"PrintView"
                                               bundle: [NSBundle mainBundle
                                                     ]];
```

```
    [controller setTitle:@"Images Per Page"];
    NSPrintPanel *panel = [NSPrintPanel printPanel];
    [panel setOptions:NSPrintPanelShowsPreview];
    [panel addAccessoryController:controller];
    [controller release];

    NSPrintOperation *op = [NSPrintOperation printOperationWithView:self];
    [op setPrintPanel:panel];
    SEL completeSel =
        @selector(printOperationDidRun:success:contextInfo:);
    [op runOperationModalForWindow:[self window]
                          delegate:nil
                    didRunSelector:completeSel
                       contextInfo:NULL];
}

- (BOOL)knowsPageRange:(NSRangePointer)range
{
    range->location = 1;
    int images = imagesPerPage();
    range->length = 14 / images;
    if (14 % images)
    {
        range->length++;
    }
    return YES;
}

- (NSRect)rectForPage:(int)page
{
    NSRect bounds = [self bounds];
    bounds.size.width /= 7;
    int images = imagesPerPage();
    int columns = images / 2;
    bounds.size.width *= columns;
    bounds.origin.x = bounds.size.width * (page-1);
    return NSIntersectionRect(bounds, [self bounds]);
}
@end
```

This file begins with a static function. This is a simple convenience function that gets the number of images per page from the current operation. We need to do this in two places, so it's separated out into a function. We could have made this a method, but since it is unlikely to be modified by a subclass and doesn't touch the object state it makes more sense for it to be a function. Remember that there is nothing unclean about using C functions in Objective-C programs; sometimes they make more sense than methods. The advantage of using a C function here is that it is very small and so likely to be inlined by the compiler in both cases where it is used.

The first method added by this category is the `-print:` action method. This will be called in response to the user clicking on the Print menu item. This needs to set up the print panel and then run it.

The first step is to create the controller with the nib we created at the start. This is part of the application, so we can find it in the main bundle. The title attribute on this controller is set to a human-readable value that will be shown in the print panel. You can see this in Figure 13.11 as the title of the pop-up button.

Since we have implemented support for the live preview, we tell the view to show it on line 21 and then add the accessory view. Once the panel is set up, we can create the print operation. We aren't customizing the page info here, so we just use a simple constructor to create a print job for the current view.

Rather than running it as an application-modal panel, we attach it to the current view's window. This doesn't make a huge amount of difference for this application, since it only has a single window, but for more complex applications it is cleaner. Since we don't need to do anything special once printing is completed, we set the delegate to `nil`. The printing-completed message will be ignored.

The remaining methods in this category are the important ones for pagination. We let the user modify the number of images to show per page, and this defines how the view should be paginated. To make this simpler, we configured the slider in the custom view to only allow values that are multiples of two, so we will always be displaying the full height of the image.

The `-knowsPageRange:` method asks the view if it knows the number of pages that it supports. This is called by the live preview in the print panel as soon as it loads, which is why we set the default value for the number of images per page early on; if we hadn't, then this method would not be able to access it.

The number of pages is simply the number of images (14) divided by the number of images per page. We need the code on lines 40–43 because we do integer division, which will round down. If we had eight images per page, then this would give one as the result, when in fact we need two pages: one complete page and one with the left-over images. Note that we set the location to one on line 37. This is because page ranges are indexed from one, unlike almost everything else in Cocoa, which is indexed from zero.

The final method, `-rectForPage:`, gets the rectangle in the view's coordinate system for a given page. The return value from this will be passed to `-drawRect:` to draw the page. Calculating this rectangle in our view is quite simple. First, we get the bounds of the entire view and divide the width by seven to get the bounds

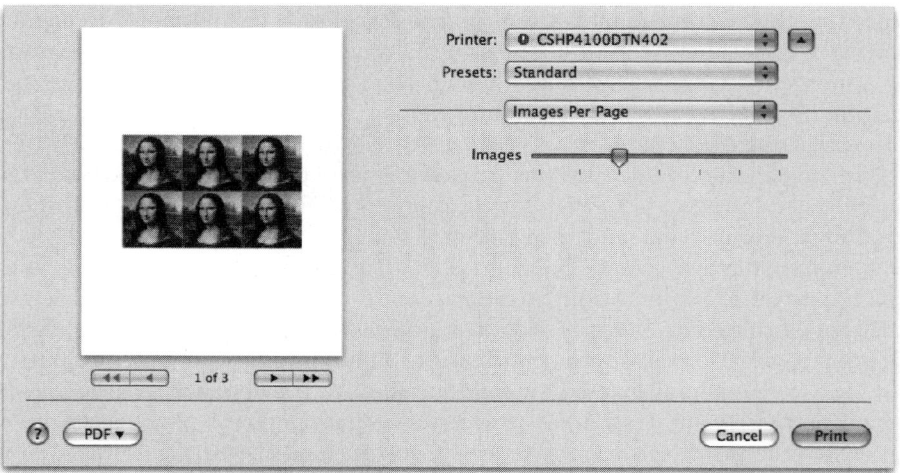

Figure 13.11: The custom print panel.

of a single column. Then we extend it to cover the number of columns that we are meant to draw per page. Finally, we displace it along the x axis by the correct amount for the current page.

The last line in this method is not strictly required. This crops back our rectangle to make sure it is in the view's bounds. For the last page, in cases where this will have a smaller number of pictures to the other page, this will crop the result. If you don't do this, then it won't make a difference—the range will be cropped before drawing anyway—it is just done here for clarity.

If you print to a PDF and open the result in Preview, you should see something like Figure 13.12. This contains all of the pages, correctly printed. You can use any of the printing output devices supported by OS X here, including fax machines, PDFs, and Automator workflows as well as real printers.

Note that the view is quite small here. Ideally, you would resize the view's bounds to the height of the page before printing and then restore them afterward. You can do this using the call-back in the print operation that we currently ignore. Try doing this to make the images fill up the entire page.

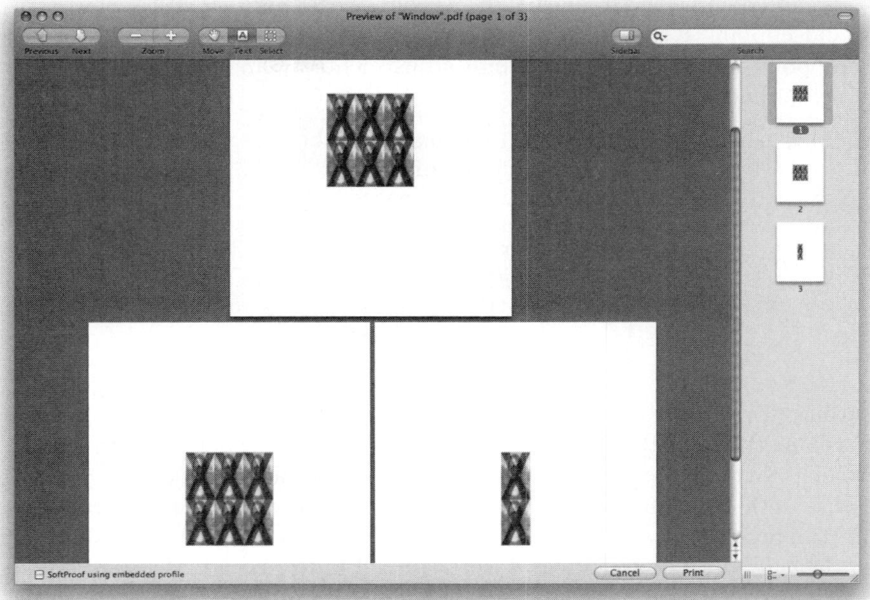

Figure 13.12: The output from printing, shown in Preview.

13.4.4 Automatic Pagination

If you don't want to manually create pagination rectangles, you can use the `-setVerticalPagination:` and `-setHorizontalPagination:` methods on `NSPrintInfo`. These each take one of the following values as an argument:

- `NSAutoPagination` divides the image into equal-sized rectangles.
- `NSFitPagination` scales the view to fit into a single row or column.
- `NSClipPagination` clips the view to fit into a single row or column of pages.

You can combine these in arbitrary ways, for example, scaling a view horizontally and clipping it vertically. You can also use these automatic methods as a starting point and then perform minor adjustments by implementing one or both of these methods:

```
- (void)adjustPageWidthNew: (CGFloat*)newRight
                      left: (CGFloat)left
                     right: (CGFloat)proposedRight
                     limit: (CGFloat)rightLimit
- (void)adjustPageHeightNew: (CGFloat*)newBottom
                        top: (CGFloat)top
                     bottom: (CGFloat)proposedBottom
                      limit: (CGFloat)bottomLimit
```

These are used to move the right and bottom edges of the printing rectangle. Something like a text view can use this to tweak the bottom so that it lines up with a line of text, without needing to completely define pagination manually.

Which of these mechanisms makes more sense depends largely on your view. The automatic mechanism works particularly well for data views where the total size of the printed data is not known at the start. The manual pagination mechanism is generally better for views with a fixed layout or which have very strict pagination requirements.

13.5 Extending Interface Builder with Palettes

Once you've defined a new view, you often want to use it in more than one application. The standard way of reusing Cocoa code is to package it in a framework. This is a bundle containing a library, a set of headers, and any resources that it might need. You can create frameworks for your view objects just as you would for any other objects. When you want to use them, just create a custom view in Interface Builder and set the class to your class.

This is not a perfect solution. Creating the standard Cocoa views is a lot easier; you just drag them from the palette. Ideally, creating your view would be this easy, too. This is possible if you create a new *Interface Builder Palette* for your view. XCode has a skeleton project for doing exactly this. It has two targets: an Interface Builder plugin and a framework. Figure 13.13 shows a project of this form. Note that the executable is Interface Builder, rather than any product of the project. This makes it very easy to test the plugin, since launching the executable in XCode will start a new copy of Interface Builder in the debugger.

To see how this all fits together, we will create an Interface Builder plugin for a view containing the `CircleTextCell` from earlier. The cell itself is unmodified, but we add a new, simple, view, shown in Listing 13.19.

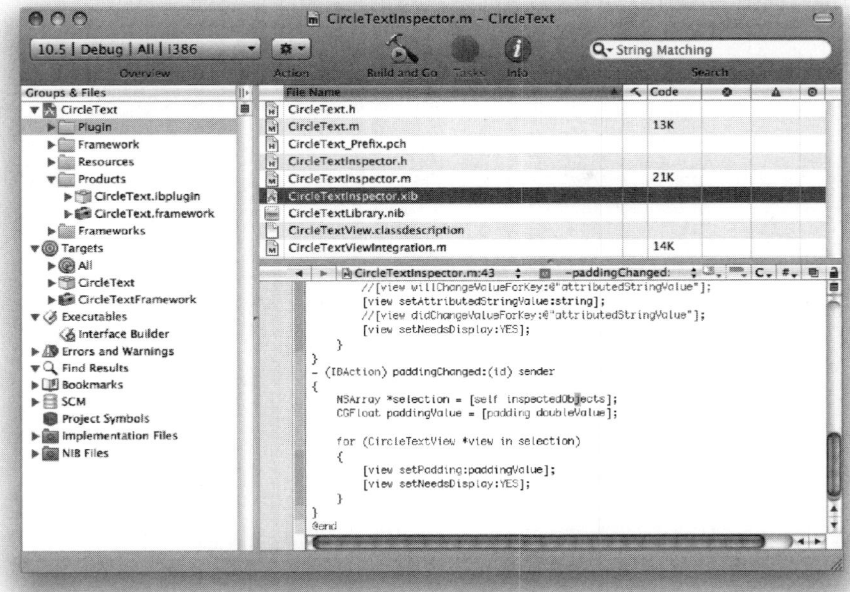

Figure 13.13: Creating an IB plugin in XCode.

Listing 13.19: The circle text view that will go in the framework. [from: examples/-CircleTextFramework/CircleTextView.m]

```
#import "CircleTextView.h"
#import "CircleTextCell.h"

@implementation CircleTextView
- (void) createCell
{
    [cell release];
    cell = [[CircleTextCell alloc] init];
}
- (void) dealloc
{
    [cell release];
    [super dealloc];
}
```

```
- (void) awakeFromNib
{
    [self createCell];
}
- (id)initWithFrame:(NSRect)frame
{
    if (nil == (self = [super initWithFrame:frame]))
    {
        return nil;
    }
    [self createCell];
    return self;
}
- (void) setAttributedStringValue:(NSAttributedString*)aString
{
    [cell setAttributedStringValue:aString];
}
- (NSAttributedString*) attributedStringValue
{
    return [cell attributedStringValue];
}
- (void) setPadding:(CGFloat)padding
{
    [cell setPadding:padding];
}
- (CGFloat) padding
{
    return [cell padding];
}
- (void)encodeWithCoder:(NSCoder *)encoder
{
    [super encodeWithCoder:encoder];
    [encoder encodeObject:[cell attributedStringValue] forKey:@"AttributedString"];
    [encoder encodeDouble:(double)[cell padding] forKey:@"Padding"];
}
- (id)initWithCoder:(NSCoder *)decoder
{
    if (nil == (self = [super initWithCoder:decoder]))
    {
        return nil;
    }
    [self createCell];
    [cell setAttributedStringValue:
```

```
58            [decoder decodeObjectForKey:@"AttributedString"]];
59     [cell setPadding:(CGFloat)[decoder decodeDoubleForKey:@"Padding"]];
60     return self;
61 }
62 - (void)drawRect:(NSRect)rect
63 {
64     [[NSColor whiteColor] setFill];
65     [NSBezierPath fillRect:rect];
66     [cell drawWithFrame:[self bounds]
67                  inView:self];
68 }
69 @end
```

This class does very little other than wrap the cell. There are two attributes exposed, on lines 28–43, which are just passed directly to the cell. A lot of the rest of the code relates to initialization. There are now three ways in which this class can be initialized:

- `-initWithCoder:` will be called to load it from a nib file.
- `-initWithRect:` will be called when it is created in code.
- `-awakeFromNib` will be called when this is created in a nib by specifying a custom class for a view, rather than using the palette.

We need to create the cell in all of these cases. We release the old one first (on line 7) because there are some cases where two or more of these methods will be called.

The two `NSCoding` methods, on lines 44 and 50, save and load the state of the two attributes we expose. This allows them to be set in Interface Builder and loaded from a nib later.

The final draw method, lines 62–68, is a tiny part of the actual code. This is mainly because all of the drawing is done by the cell. A lot of views look like this, with very little specific code and a lot of boilerplate.

This class and the cell are the only two that go in the framework. Everything else goes in the plugin. This also includes part of the view class. There are some methods that are only required for Interface Builder compatibility, and these live in a category in the plugin, shown in Listing 13.20.

This category provides two methods. The first provides support for Interface Builder's "lift-and-stamp" feature. It provides an array of key paths that Interface Builder should watch.

The second method is used to create the inspector. When you instantiate the view, this method will be called to collect the list of inspectors. Figure 13.14

Listing 13.20: Interface Builder support for the circle text view. [from: examples/CircleTextFramework/CircleTextViewIntegration.m]

```
#import <InterfaceBuilderKit/InterfaceBuilderKit.h>
#import <CircleText/CircleTextView.h>
#import "CircleTextInspector.h"


@implementation CircleTextView ( CircleTextView )

- (void)ibPopulateKeyPaths:(NSMutableDictionary *)keyPaths
{
    [super ibPopulateKeyPaths:keyPaths];

    [[keyPaths objectForKey:IBAttributeKeyPaths] addObject:@"attributedStringValue"];
}

- (void)ibPopulateAttributeInspectorClasses:(NSMutableArray *)classes
{
    [super ibPopulateAttributeInspectorClasses:classes];
    [classes addObject:[CircleTextInspector class]];
}

@end
```

shows the inspectors that will be shown for this view. Each class in the hierarchy can provide inspectors. This window shows one for the circle text view and one that is provided by `NSView`. Some views with a deep class hierarchy will have a lot. You should make sure that you call the superclass implementation first to collect all of these.

The inspector class returned here is shown in Listing 13.21. This is a subclass of `IBInspector` and defines two outlets and two actions. Both of these are connected to the two text fields in the inspector. One controls the padding and one controls the text. The top box in the inspector supports rich text editing, so you can set an attributed string directly.

The first method in this class is very important. It is used to find the nib file containing the inspector. The template project creates a skeleton nib that we can edit to contain all of the views we need for the inspector. Ours just contains two text fields and labels.

Listing 13.21: The inspector for the circle text view. [from: examples/CircleTextFramework/CircleTextInspector.m]

```
#import "CircleTextInspector.h"
#import "CircleTextView.h"

@implementation CircleTextInspector

- (NSString *)viewNibName
{
    return @"CircleTextInspector";
}

- (void)refresh
{
    [super refresh];
    NSArray *selection = [self inspectedObjects];
    if ([selection count] > 1)
    {
        [text setStringValue:@""];
    }
    else
    {
        NSAttributedString *str = [[selection objectAtIndex:0]
            attributedStringValue];
        if (nil != str)
        {
            [text setAttributedStringValue:str];
        }
    }
}

- (IBAction) textChanged:(id) sender
{
    NSArray *selection = [self inspectedObjects];
    NSAttributedString *string = [[text attributedStringValue] copy];
    for (CircleTextView *view in selection)
    {
        [view setAttributedStringValue:string];
        [view setNeedsDisplay:YES];
    }
}
- (IBAction) paddingChanged:(id) sender
{
    NSArray *selection = [self inspectedObjects];
```

```
    CGFloat paddingValue = [padding doubleValue];

    for (CircleTextView *view in selection)
    {
        [view setPadding:paddingValue];
        [view setNeedsDisplay:YES];
    }
}
@end
```

The rest of the code in this class is for synchronizing the view and the inspector. The `-refresh` method is called whenever the view changes—typically as a result of the selection changing—and the two `IBAction` methods are called by objects in the inspector nib.

The two actions are both similar in structure; they both iterate over all of the selected objects and set their properties. Note that more than one object can be selected at once in Interface Builder, and the inspector must update all of them.

There is one remaining class, shown in Listing 13.22. This is a subclass of `IBPlugin` and is the principal class for the plugin bundle. When the plugin is loaded, this is the class that will be instantiated.

There are only two methods implemented here, both of which are called by the superclass. The first returns all of the nib files containing palettes. We only

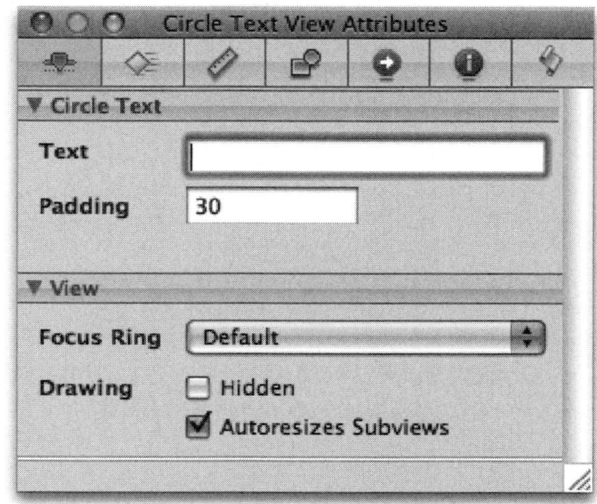

Figure 13.14: The inspectors for the circle view.

Listing 13.22: The circle text plugin class. [from: examples/CircleTextFramework/CircleText.m]

```
#import "CircleText.h"
#import "CircleTextView.h"

@implementation CircleText
- (NSArray *)libraryNibNames
{
    return [NSArray arrayWithObject:@"CircleTextLibrary"];
}

- (NSArray *)requiredFrameworks
{
    return [NSArray arrayWithObject:[NSBundle bundleForClass:[
        CircleTextView class]]];
}

@end
```

implemented one, with a single `CircleTextView` on it, but a more complex plugin might define lots of palettes.

The second returns bundles for frameworks needed. This is used by the interface simulator. When you simulate a user interface in Interface Builder, it spawns a new process, which loads the nib and connects it to a simple event loop. The bundles returned here will be loaded by the simulator before instantiating the nib. Since the plugin bundle is linked against the framework, we can just get the bundle that contains the view class here.

Beyond Palettes

Interface Builder plugins can be used to extend IB in interesting ways beyond simply providing new views. Nicolas Roard wrote a plugin for GORM, the GNUstep IB equivalent, which embedded a Smalltalk interpreter in a palette and lets you write controllers and models in the inspectors. More recently, *F-Script*, a Smalltalk dialect for Cocoa, has provided a similar panel, allowing you to write and run Smalltalk code communicating with Cocoa objects directly in Interface Builder.

With all of these classes finished, the view can be created in Interface Builder and its properties set. Figure 13.15 shows an instance of the circle view in a

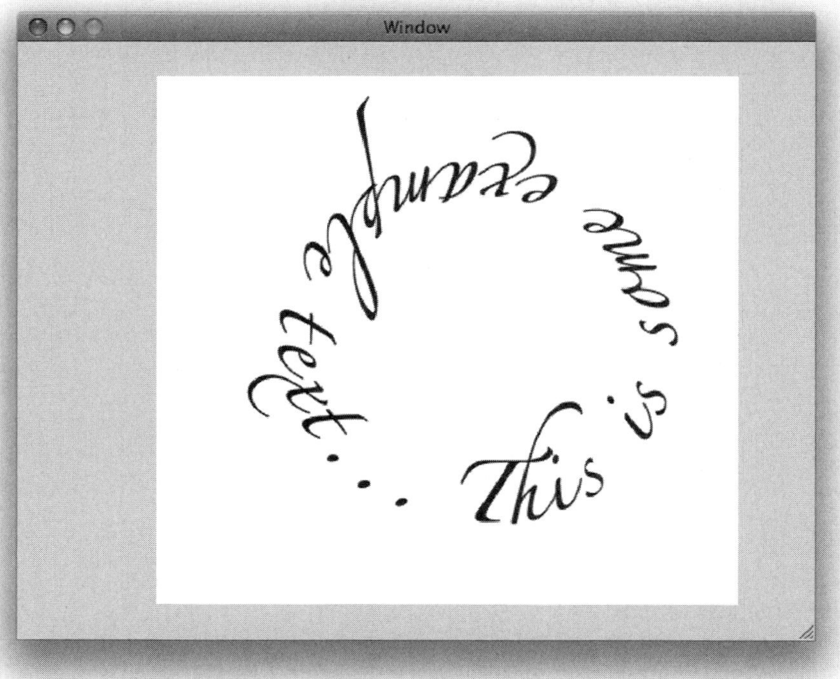

Figure 13.15: Creating a circle view in Interface Builder.

window, running in Interface Builder. Both the string and the padding have been set in the inspector.

This is not the most polished implementation of an Interface Builder palette. Generally this is not something you will bother doing for your own view objects. The only time it really makes sense to create an IB palette is if you plan on distributing a framework containing a selection of view objects. The amount of effort required to produce a working plugin is quite significant, and if you are only using a view a few times, then you will be doing more work than you will be saving by being able to create your views in the nib.

13.6 Summary

In this chapter, we've looked at how to create new view objects. We covered the basic drawing model in Cocoa, and how it inherits from PostScript and PDF. We saw how to use Core Graphics primitives with Cocoa drawing, and how Cocoa used them internally.

We looked at how to create bezier paths, the basic primitive of drawing in Cocoa, and how to draw lines along them and fill them. We saw how to use existing cells to simplify drawing complex shapes and how to composite images.

Aside from drawing, views also have to handle events, and we saw how to implement event handling code in a view and how to delegate it to a cell.

Moving away from the screen, we saw how views can be drawn to other graphics contexts, such as bitmap images and printers. We looked at manual and automatic pagination when printing a view and how to implement both.

Finally, we packaged up a view for distribution and created an Interface Builder plugin to accompany it.

Chapter 14

Sound and Video

Most user interfaces make some use of sounds. Even if this isn't done explicitly, several views will beep if you try to do something invalid. Judicious use of sound is one of the hallmarks of a polished user interface.

There are a number of APIs that you can use for playing sounds, depending on how complex your requirements are. These range from simple beeps to complex multichannel sound playback with real-time mixing.

Some of the more advanced Cocoa APIs for playing back music are also able to play back video and even edit audio and video files. In this chapter, we will take a look at some of the options for multimedia in Cocoa.

14.1 Beeping

The simplest way of making a sound is to use the `NSBeep()` AppKit function. This function returns immediately and plays the system's default beep in the background. Listing 14.1 shows how it is used.

Listing 14.1: A program that goes beep. [from: examples/Beep/beep.m]

```
#import <Cocoa/Cocoa.h>

int main(void)
{
    NSBeep();
    sleep(1);
    return 0;
}
```

This program, when compiled and run, plays the system beep and exits. Note the `sleep()` call after `NSBeep()`. Without this, the program would appear not to work. The beep function spawns a new thread that plays the sound in the background. Without sleeping, the program would exit before the beep was actually played.

In most cases, this is the desired behavior. You can start the beep and not worry about it. As long as your application doesn't exit immediately after, it will work as expected. The sound played by this function depends on the user's sound settings.

14.2 Playing Simple Sounds

The `NSBeep()` function is a simple wrapper around the `NSSound` class. This is the standard Cocoa way of playing sounds. The `NSBeep()` function creates an `NSSound` object for the default system beep and instructs it to play.

Traditionally, you could only create `NSSound` objects from simple, uncompressed, audio formats. With OS X, MP3 and MPEG-4 audio files are also supported directly by the class. More interestingly, it will make use of *filter services* to import other kinds of sound. This means that any audio format understood by either QuickTime or by Core Audio can be read and played by `NSSound`.

There are several ways of creating sound objects. As with many other Cocoa classes, it provides initializers for loading data from a pasteboard, a file, a URL, or an `NSData` instance. As well as these, there is a `+soundNamed:` method. This is particularly useful because it provides an easy way of loading sounds without knowing exactly where they are.

In Interface Builder 2 and earlier, every nib file appeared to contain a set of standard sounds. These are the common sounds that have been present on Mac OS since System 7. The Sosumi sound was the second to be added to Mac OS and its name is a reference to the trademark infringement lawsuit filed against Apple Computer by Apple Corps, the Beatles' music label. The settlement prevented Apple Computer from entering the music business. Prior to System 7, there was only one system beep. The new sounds were introduced with this version of the operating system, and Sosumi (pronounced "so sue me") was named in response to the threat of legal action if playing different sounds counted as entering the music business.

All of the sounds that appeared to be in the nib files were really present on the system in /System/Library/Sounds. If you look there on an OS X system, you will find copies of the standard system beeps. Most applications that make alert and warning beeps allow the user to select among these.

You can assign a name to a specific sound loaded by some other mechanism by sending it a -setName: message. When you create a sound object by name, the class will first try to find a sound you have named in this way. If one doesn't exist, it will look for the sound with that name set in System Preferences. If there is no named sound provided either by the application or globally, it will treat the sound as a file name (without an extension) and look for it in the application's main bundle and then in all of the Library/Sounds directories on the system, in the standard search order. You would typically create a sound object like this:

```
[NSSound soundNamed: @"Sosumi"];
```

This will usually return /System/Library/Sounds/Sosumi.aiff. If the user has altered the sound file for the Sosumi sound in System Preferences or installed a file called Sosumi in ~/Library/Sounds, for example, it will return the user's version instead.

Once you have a sound object, you can play it by sending it a -play message. As with NSBeep(), this will create a new thread to play the sound and play it in the background. You should make sure that the sound object is not deallocated before it has finished playing, or playback will be abruptly interrupted.

There are two ways of doing this. You can send the sound -isPlaying messages periodically and then release it when it has finished. This is not particularly elegant. A better solution is to register a *delegate* for the sound. When a sound stops, it will send its delegate this message:

```
- (void)sound: (NSSound*)sound didFinishPlaying: (BOOL)finishedPlaying;
```

If the second argument is NO then it means the sound was interrupted, typically by sending it a -stop message. You can use this method to release the sound. Note that sound playback is one of the things that *garbage collection* makes harder. If you are not using garbage collection, then you can send the sound a -retain message when it is created and assign it a simple singleton delegate that frees all sounds when they finish playing. In a garbage collected environment, the system will notice that nothing holds a reference to the sound object and will free it for you. You need to keep a (strong) pointer to the object around until after it has finished in a garbage collected environment. Typically you would do this by adding it to an array in the delegate and making sure you remove it when the delegate method is called.

To illustrate how this class works, we will assemble a very simple sound player, shown in Figure 14.1. This plays back a single sound file, optionally looping it, with the slider indicating the position within the file. The code for controlling this is shown in Listing 14.2.

The first method in this class is connected to the Open menu item. This runs a modal open dialog box to select a file to play—a bad user interface, but sufficient for a simple example—from some of the types that the NSSound class knows how to open. The second parameter when creating the sound object can be ignored most of the time. `NSSound` conforms to the `NSCoding` protocol. When you serialize a sound object representing a file, it can either store the file data or the name of the file, depending on the value of this flag.

Listing 14.2: A simple sound player. [from: examples/SoundPlayer/SoundPlayer.m]

```
#import "SoundPlayer.h"

@implementation SoundPlayer
- (IBAction)open: (id)sender
{
    NSOpenPanel *openPanel = [NSOpenPanel openPanel];
    [openPanel runModalForTypes: [NSArray arrayWithObjects: @"aiff", @"mp3"
        , @"m4a", nil]];
    [sound release];
    sound = [[NSSound alloc] initWithContentsOfFile: [openPanel filename]
                                        byReference: YES];
    [sound setLoops: loop];
    [window setTitle: [[openPanel filename] lastPathComponent]];
}
- (IBAction)setLoop: (id)sender;
{
    loop = [sender state] == NSOnState;
    [sound setLoops: loop];
}
- (IBAction)play: (id)sender
{
    [progress setMaxValue: [sound duration]];
    [NSTimer scheduledTimerWithTimeInterval: 0.1
                                     target: self
                                   selector: @selector(updateIndicator:)
                                   userInfo: sound
                                    repeats: YES];
    [sound play];
}
- (void)updateIndicator: (NSTimer*)aTimer
{
    NSSound *playingSound = [aTimer userInfo];
    if (!(sound == playingSound && [playingSound isPlaying]))
    {
        [aTimer invalidate];
        return;
    }
    [progress setDoubleValue: [sound currentTime]];
```

```
38 }
39 - (IBAction)takeCurrentTimeFrom: (id)sender
40 {
41     [sound setCurrentTime: [sender doubleValue]];
42 }
43 - (IBAction)stop: (id)sender
44 {
45     [sound stop];
46 }
47 @end
```

The check box is connected to the second method. This sets an instance variable flag indicating whether the sound should loop. This is then passed to the sound object, which handles looping. The variable was also used back on line 11, to make sure that newly loaded sounds loop if the check box is ticked.

The third method is called by the play button. On line 27, this starts playing the sound. Before doing this, it does two things to configure the user interface. Line 21 gets the duration of the current sound clip from the object and sets the progress indicator to count from zero to this value. The remainder of this method then schedules a timer to fire periodically calling the `-updateIndicator:` method.

The timer is used to update the slider to indicate how far into the clip the player has gone. The `-updateIndicator:` method automatically frees the timer once the sound has stopped playing. This may happen in response to a `stop` message, such as the one sent on line 46 when the user presses the stop button, or because the sound has played to the end and is not looping.

Users expect to be able to move sliders, and so the slider in our UI is connected to the `-takeCurrentTimeFrom:` method. This sets the `NSSound` instance's current time to the value read from the slider, allowing the user to skip around the sound by simply moving the slider.

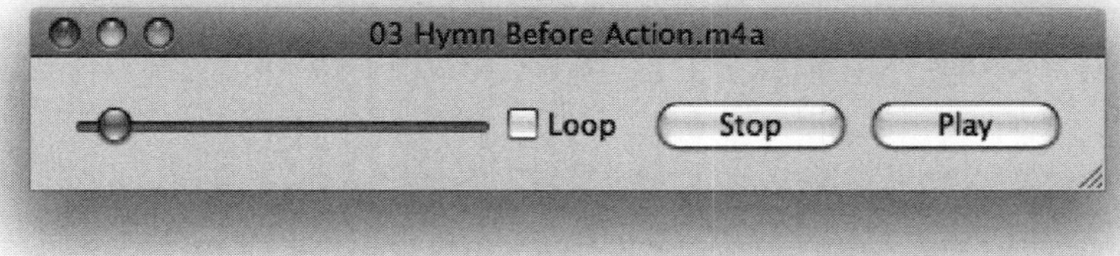

Figure 14.1: A simple sound player.

This shows the basic use of `NSSound` objects. You can create them encapsulating sound files and play them. Traditionally, you could only have one `NSSound` instance playing at once, but that limitation no longer applies on OS X. You can play as many sounds as you want, and the system will mix them together for playback.

For most applications, this is enough. You can play any audio file or files, with reasonably low latency. This lets you add audio notifications of events and feedback for user actions.

14.3 Understanding Cocoa Movie Objects

OS X 10.0 introduced the `NSMovie` and `NSMovieView` classes, representing models and view for multimedia content. The former was very simple, providing little more than a means of creating the object and getting a handle that could be used with the procedural *QuickTime* APIs. The latter played a movie in a window, displaying user interface components and so on.

When QuickTime 7 was introduced, it was accompanied by the *QTKit framework*, a more complete Objective-C wrapper around QuickTime. Using this framework, it is possible to create rich multimedia applications without needing to use the procedural API.

QTKit Introduction Date

The documentation for the QTKit classes is quite confusing. The `QTMovie` class says prominently at the top that it was introduced with Mac OS X 10.4, while many of the methods claim that they are "available in Mac OS X v10.3 and later." Both of these are true.

The framework was introduced with QuickTime 7, which was shipped with OS X 10.4 but available as a separate download for OS X 10.3. Something similar happened with the URL loading system and WebKit. These are available in OS X 10.2.7 or later if Safari is installed, but didn't become standard parts of OS X until the 10.3 release.

QuickTime was originally created back in 1991 and designed to run on Apple System 6. It was later ported to Windows and now runs on both platforms. The underlying API matches the style of programming that was common at the time, although it has evolved considerably since then. Unless you are writing a full-featured professional video editing suite, you probably don't need to use this API, and can restrict yourself to the Objective-C wrapper.

The `QTMovie` API is designed to be similar to both `NSSound` and the now-deprecated `NSMovie`. If you started off using `NSSound`, it is easy to adopt QTKit later. You can see the similarity by looking at Listing 14.3. This the last example, with a minimal set of modifications to use `QTMovie` instead of `NSSound`. The `sound` instance variable for this class has been changed to a `QTMovie`, but there were no other alterations to the interface or the contents of the nib file.

Listing 14.3: A sound player using QTKit. [from: examples/SoundPlayerQTKit/SoundPlayer.m]

```
#import "SoundPlayer.h"

@implementation SoundPlayer
- (IBAction)open: (id)sender
{
    NSOpenPanel *openPanel = [NSOpenPanel openPanel];
    [openPanel runModalForTypes: [NSArray arrayWithObjects: @"aiff", @"mp3"
        , @"m4a", nil]];
    [sound release];
    sound = [[QTMovie movieWithFile: [openPanel filename]
                              error: NULL] retain];
    [sound setAttribute: [NSNumber numberWithBool: loop]
                 forKey: QTMovieLoopsAttribute];
    [window setTitle: [[openPanel filename] lastPathComponent]];
}
- (IBAction)setLoop: (id)sender;
{
    loop = [sender state] == NSOnState;
    [sound setAttribute: [NSNumber numberWithBool: loop]
                 forKey: QTMovieLoopsAttribute];
}
- (IBAction)play: (id)sender
{
    NSTimeInterval duration;
    QTGetTimeInterval([sound duration], &duration);
    [progress setMaxValue: duration];
    [NSTimer scheduledTimerWithTimeInterval: 0.1
                                     target: self
                                   selector: @selector(updateIndicator:)
                                   userInfo: sound
                                    repeats: YES];
    [sound play];
}
- (void)updateIndicator: (NSTimer*)aTimer
{
    NSSound *playingSound = [aTimer userInfo];
    if (!(sound == playingSound && [playingSound isPlaying]))
    {
```

```
38         [aTimer release];
39         return;
40     }
41     NSTimeInterval currentTime;
42     QTGetTimeInterval([sound currentTime], &currentTime);
43     [progress setDoubleValue: currentTime];
44 }
45 - (IBAction)takeCurrentTimeFrom: (id)sender
46 {
47     [sound setCurrentTime:
48         QTMakeTimeWithTimeInterval([sender doubleValue])];
49 }
50 - (IBAction)stop: (id)sender
51 {
52     [sound stop];
53 }
54 @end
```

The first difference to notice is the initializer. The movie is constructed on lines 9–10. This does exactly the same thing as the `-initWithContentsOfFile:byReference:` method in the last example. Note that QTKit uses the newer convention adopted by most frameworks that were introduced after the first release of Safari of returning an `NSError` via a pointer in the final argument. For this simple example, we pass `NULL`, which will cause the method to fail silently if it doesn't work.

The next change is perhaps the most significant. Lines 11–12 and 18–19 replace `-setLoops:` calls on `NSSound`. There is no direct analogue to this method. Looping, in QuickTime, is an attribute of the movie. Every move has a dictionary of attributes associated with it. You can either set these one at a time, as shown here, or all in one go.

There are a lot of other attributes that you can't see here. One, related, setting is the looping mode. Our `NSSound` could only loop by playing to the end and then going back to the start. QuickTime also supports looping by reaching the end and then playing backward. You can also alter the volume, the playback speed, and a number of other attributes in this way.

The remaining change is related to the time. The `NSSound` object used `NSTimeIntervals` for its time. These are **`double`**s representing a number of seconds. QuickTime movies use the `QTTime` structure. This contains a 64-bit time value and a scale. The scale indicates how long an individual tick is. Typically, you will use time structures where the frame scale is defined as the number of frames per second for the movie and the values then give the number of frames. For example, a 48KHz audio file might have the scale set to 48,000, and the time interval count the number of samples.

This kind of structure for representing time is common in media frameworks. It avoids accumulating floating-point rounding errors when performing calculations with time. Each value is, effectively, a floating point value, but with two major differences from the traditional IEEE types. First, the precision is bigger. The `QTTime` structure uses a 64-bit mantissa, while even a **`double`** only needs to be 64 bits in total. The other important difference is that the equivalent is a divisor, rather than a multiplier. This allows you to represent any rational number, within the obvious size limitations.

A common problem with floating point values is that they are unable to represent some fractions sensibly. You cannot represent $\frac{1}{10}$ in any finite binary floating-point value. Similarly, you cannot represent $\frac{1}{3}$ as a decimal floating-point value. This is a problem in financial circles, and has lead to the creating of *binary-coded decimals*, which you can use in Cocoa via the `NSDecimalNumber` class. For movies, this is even more important. Film frame rates and audio sample rates are typically defined in terms of a number per second. This may be 24 frames per second for cinema, 29.97 frames per second for NTSC, 44,100 audio samples per second for CD audio, or any other similar number.

The time for each frame or sample is formed by a reciprocal. Each frame is one divided by the number of frames or samples per second. A large number of these give values that cannot be represented by finite binary floating point values without approximation, and approximation is something you want to avoid in this kind of application. You may remember that having the audio and video gradually become desynchronized was a common failing in computer movie playback systems as recently as a decade ago. These systems would often use floating point values for the duration of each sample of audio and each frame of video.

When you have a 44.1KHz audio track and a 30 frames per second video track, the accumulated error in the audio will only be 0.000036 seconds and the accumulated error in the video will be 0.033333 seconds after one hour, if you use double-precision floating-point values. If you use single-precision values, then the error in the video will be over four seconds, more than enough for the user to notice.

If, instead, you use a structure like `QTTime` for storing values, then incrementing the frame or sample counter just requires adding one to the value and ignoring the divisor. The only minor problem is the possibility of overflow.

Comparing `QTTimes` is harder. Before you can compare them, you need to normalize them. This is usually done by using Euclid's algorithm to find the greatest common divisor and then scaling both values to the same divisor. For 30 frame per second video and 41KHz audio, the common factor of ten would be extracted and the divisor set to 123,000, with the values in each scaled appropriately. At this granularity, the `QTTime` structure can represent around two million years—actually double this, but half of the values are negative—which is probably enough for most recordings.

Converting in and out of these times is complex, but because it's something you want to do relatively often there are functions defined in QTKit to do it for you. This example showed two of them. We used one on line 49 when setting the current offset in the clip. The `QTMakeTimeWithTimeInterval()` function takes an `NSTimeInterval` and returns a `QTTime`.

You can see the inverse operation on lines 25 and 43, when retrieving the duration and current time and turning them into time intervals for passing to the slider. These lines use the `QTGetTimeInterval()` function. This takes a `QTTime` as the first argument and a pointer to a `NSTimeInterval` as the second, returning a boolean value indicating whether the conversion succeeded.

14.4 Adding Video

So far, although we have been using QuickTime, which is a powerful multimedia editing and playback framework, we have not done anything with it that we couldn't already do with `NSSound`. The most obvious thing to add to our music player is support for video.

At the moment, we are using the model object to play directly. This is something of a violation of the *model-view-controller* (*MVC*) pattern. Ideally, we would have a "view" object representing the speakers and connect this to the model object representing the movie. In practice, there is little point. The most common case for playing a sound is to send it directly to the speakers, and so putting support for this directly into the model makes everyone's life easier. For more complex view analogs, we might have various filters performing dynamic modifications to the audio waveform, or stream the audio over the network, but these are far less common cases.

For video, a separate view object makes more sense. Videos, by definition, have a visual component that must be displayed on the screen somehow. Whether this is in its own window, embedded in another window, or taking over the entire screen, depends on the application. Separating these out into a separate concern makes more sense.

There are lots of displaying a movie object. You can send it through *Core Video*, get an OpenGL texture, and then render this on the side of a complex 3D mesh. Doing this requires an in-depth understanding of Core Video and OpenGL, both of which have had several books written about them. If you want to create this kind of complex visual application, then you should read more about these two frameworks.

Fortunately, there are simpler ways of playing a movie. You could try calling

-currentFrameImage periodically and setting the return value as the model for an NSImageView. This may work, but if it doesn't drop frames it is likely to be incredibly CPU intensive. The simplest way of displaying a QTMovie is to use a QTMovieView instance. This replaces the deprecated NSMovieView class as a standard way of showing movies in Cocoa.

To demonstrate this, we will extend the simple sound player application to display sound or video files, using a NSMovieView for playback. This class provides a number of action methods that will simplify our controller. The play and pause buttons in the user interface can be connected directly to the movie view, rather than needing to go through the controller.

We also no longer need to update the progress slider. The movie view object provides its own progress indicator, which we will use instead of the NSSlider instance in the earlier example.

The code for this example, shown in Listing 14.4 is even simpler than the last example, in spite of doing more. The playing and pausing of the movie are controlled by the movie view object directly, using the controls shown in Figure 14.2.

Listing 14.4: A movie player using QuickTime. [from: examples/MoviePlayer/MoviePlayer.m]

```
#import "MoviePlayer.h"

@implementation MoviePlayer
@synthesize movie;
- (IBAction)open: (id)sender
{
    NSOpenPanel *panel = [[NSOpenPanel alloc] init];
    [panel setAllowedFileTypes:
        [QTMovie movieFileTypes: QTIncludeAllTypes]];
    [panel beginSheetForDirectory: nil
                             file: nil
                   modalForWindow: window
                    modalDelegate: self
                   didEndSelector: @selector(openPanelDidEnd:returnCode:
                         contextInfo:)
                      contextInfo: NULL];
}
- (void)openPanelDidEnd: (NSOpenPanel*)panel
             returnCode: (int)returnCode
            contextInfo: (void *)contextInfo
{
    self.movie = [QTMovie movieWithFile: [panel filename]
                                  error: NULL];
    [movie setAttribute: [NSNumber numberWithBool: loop]
```

```
24                   forKey: QTMovieLoopsAttribute];
25      [window setTitle: [[panel filename] lastPathComponent]];
26      [panel release];
27  }
28  - (IBAction)setLoop: (id)sender
29  {
30      loop = [sender state] == NSOnState;
31      [movie setAttribute: [NSNumber numberWithBool: loop]
32                   forKey: QTMovieLoopsAttribute];
33  }
34
35  @end
```

Rather than hard-coding a set of file types, as we did previously, we ask the `QTMovie` class what kinds of file it knows about. This is done on line 9 by calling the `+movieFileTypes:` class method. The argument here is a mask indicating the types of movie we are interested in. By passing `QTIncludeAllTypes` we ask for every file type that QuickTime can open. This includes some that may not actually be playable and a number that you might not think of as movies. You can use this player to open PDF files, for example, and "play" them by showing each page for a short time.

Unlike the last example, this displays a non-modal open dialog connected to the window as a sheet. This is not hugely different from the previous version, but it separates out the code for loading the movie from the code for displaying the open panel. Try extending this further by moving it into an `NSDocument` subclass and allowing the user to open multiple windows.

The movie view's Movie binding is connected to the `movie` property in this class. This means it will automatically track the current movie, without needing any extra code. All of the code for setting up and controlling the slider is now gone. We can still play sound files, as shown in Figure 14.3, with the movie view displaying a slider indicating the current position and controls for playing and pausing the clip.

The looping state is not exposed via the movie view. Because the view is still using the same kind of model object as our last example, the same code for controlling this can be used. The `-setLoop:` method is unmodified from the last example. Try adding other controls that modify properties of the movie.

You may recognize the appearance of this player from earlier versions of QuickTime. You are not required to use the set of controls presented by the movie view. It implements action messages like `-play:` and `-stop:` that can be attached to other user interface components.

Figure 14.2: Playing a movie file.

Figure 14.3: Playing a sound file in the movie player.

14.5 Editing Media

Playing back sound and videos is only part of what a framework like QuickTime can do. It is somewhat surprising that Apple charges for QuickTime Pro, when all of the features it exposes are part of the standard QuickTime frameworks. The only thing you get from the Pro version is a few user interface components being enabled; all of the underlying functionality is there whether you pay extra or not.

The basic editing functionality is exposed via `QTMovieView`. If you make the movie view editable, either by sending it a `-setEditable:` message or by selecting Editable in the inspector in Interface Builder, it will support basic, destructive, copy-and-paste operations. You can select a region, copy it, and insert it into another movie. You can also trim a movie, deleting everything other than the selector, and save the movie back to a file.

Advanced movie editors typically have two features that are not exposed via the movie view. First, they support multi-track editing. The `QTMovie` class provides a `-tracks` method that returns an array of `QTTrack` objects. You can edit each of these individually if you write a user interface for doing so. They respond to messages like `-deleteSegment:` for removing the segment in a given time interval, and also allow segments from other tracks to be inserted easily. None of this is exposed via the movie view, but if you are willing to write your own view objects, then you can add it yourself easily.

The second feature is nondestructive editing. An application like Final Cut does not modify the source material. It stores a set of operations needed to construct the final product, and renders it only before exporting or playing back the current edit. This is not directly supported by QTKit, but is relatively easy to add in your own code. This method in `QTTrack` provides the core functionality you need to implement nondestructive editing:

```
- (void)insertSegmentOfTrack: (QTTrack*)track
                  fromRange: (QTTimeRange)srcRange
              scaledToRange: (QTTimeRange)dstRange;
```

This inserts a segment from one track into another. An editing package using this would have a set of source files, each containing one or more tracks, and a small selection of final tracks. You would store a simple set of mappings from regions in source tracks to times in the final output and then send a sequence of messages like this to construct the final version for playback.

Note that this does not provide a means of generating effects. The `-addImage:forDuration:withAttributes:` method can be used to insert visual effects that you have generated using other drawing mechanisms, but this requires you to handle things like blending frames from different tracks together yourself.

The other option is to use *Core Video*, which was introduced at the same time as QuickTime 7.

Core Video provides a generic mechanism for moving video frames around. The central concept in Core Video is the *display link*. This is an abstract interface for providing and consuming video frames. It introduces the `CVBuffer` Core Foundation type, which encapsulates a block of memory. There are various different subclasses of this for storing frames in main memory or on the graphics hardware's private RAM.

Core Video is quite a complex API, and a detailed discussion of it is beyond the scope of this book. QuickTime X, introduced with Snow Leopard, provides even closer integration with Core Video, allowing you to send compressed frames to the GPU and have them decompressed with shader programs or dedicated decoding hardware and made available as OpenGL textures for rendering. This offloads the entire video decoding and presentation process to the GPU, freeing up the CPU to do other things.

14.6 Low-Level Sound APIs

The sound stack on OS X has a number of layers, each providing increasing levels of abstraction. At the very bottom of the stack is the sound hardware. This may be a simple digital to analog converter—or even just a signal generator sending digital signals to an external decoder and amplifier—or it may be a complex signal processor. You will never interact with the hardware directly from an application; this requires privileged instructions that are only permitted in the kernel.

Each sound device is wrapped in a subclass of `IOAudioDevice` and a subclass of `IOAudioEngine`, Embedded C++ classes provided by the *IOKit framework*. These provide a uniform interface to sound hardware, handling creating streams and playing or recording from them. The IOKit interfaces provide something similar to the traditional UNIX model of a sound device as a source or sync for audio streams. This is a much lower-level interface than most application software needs.

The *Audio HAL* sits between the kernel's device drivers and userspace applications, providing an extensible interface for exposing device functions to programmers. This is used by the bottom level of the *Core Audio framework*. Core Audio is a filter-graph API. The discrete components are known as *audio units*. Each audio unit encapsulates a source, sync, or transform for audio data.

Some advanced sound chips, which do effects processing in the hardware, expose their functionality as a set of audio units. Each of these audio units can be inserted into a filter graph just as any other units can that are implemented in software. At the end of processing, you typically want to send the sound to the speakers. This is done using a playback device, which is either the default system output device or an `AUHAL` audio unit representing the output device. The `AUHAL` unit is a Core Audio wrapper around the Audio HAL, and is the closest a userspace developer is likely to come to the hardware.

The Cocoa sound functions are implemented on top of Core Audio. This is what allows `NSSound` instances to play different sounds, at different sample rates, at the same time.

The main reason to use Core Audio directly is to support some kind of processing on the sound being played. Core Audio provides a large number of filters that can transform an audio sequence. You can assemble very complex filter graphs with Core Audio, applying large numbers of effects and filters. If you want to implement audio processing and editing in your application, then you should spend some time familiarizing yourself with the Core Audio documentation.

Core Audio is a complex, low-level, API. It is not really part of Cocoa, rather it is one of the frameworks used to implement Cocoa. This does not mean you shouldn't use it in your applications, but you should be aware that it is a lot harder to use than the standard Cocoa classes. This extra complexity buys a lot of extra features, but you should generally avoid Core Audio unless you need this increased functionality. You can often use `NSSound` or QTKit to do the same thing in a lot less code.

The *Musical Instrument Digital Interface* (*MIDI*) standard defines a way of controlling digital musical instruments. A MIDI instrument produces a stream of MIDI events, short binary sequences encapsulating a note and its duration. These are then processed and passed to a synthesizer that generates waveforms from the notes. Early computer MIDI systems used FM synthesis, where each note was represented by a fixed frequency note. This technique largely gave way to sample-based synthesis, which uses a set of recorded samples and modulates them to produce the requested note. The Garage Band Jam Packs contain some very large sets of samples, which are used when playing music recorded from MIDI instruments.

The *Core MIDI framework* is part of Core Audio and provides a way of inserting MIDI samples into a Core Audio playback graph and recording MIDI events from digital instruments.

14.7 Sound and Video Recording

QTKit supports recording, as well as playback. Every device that can generate an audio or video stream is represented by a `QTCaptureDevice` instance. This includes things like microphones and cameras.

To capture sound and video using QTKit, you need to set up a *capture session*. This has one or more inputs and a set of outputs. The outputs can currently either be files or preview sessions. If you want to record video, you will typically use a `QTCaptureView` instance in a window to provide the user with a view of what is being recorded.

The class shown in Listing 14.5 is the controller for a very simple video recorder application, shown in Figure 14.4. This displays a preview as soon as the application is launched and, while the record button is down dumps the video to a VideoRecorder.mov file on the hard disk. This does not use any compression, so for an iSight camera it will generate around 10MB of data per second.

Listing 14.5: A simple video recorder. [from: examples/VideoRecorder/VideoRecorder.m]

```
#import "VideoRecorder.h"

@implementation VideoRecorder
- (void)awakeFromNib
{
    session = [QTCaptureSession new];
    QTCaptureDevice *camera =
        [QTCaptureDevice defaultInputDeviceWithMediaType:
            QTMediaTypeVideo];
    [camera open: NULL];
    QTCaptureInput *input =
        [[QTCaptureDeviceInput alloc] initWithDevice: camera];
    [session addInput: input
                error: NULL];
    [input release];
    file = [QTCaptureMovieFileOutput new];
    [session addOutput: file
                 error: NULL];
    [view setCaptureSession: session];
    [session startRunning];
}
- (void)startRecording
{
    NSString *path =
        [@"~/Desktop/VideoRecorder.mov" stringByExpandingTildeInPath];
    [file recordToOutputFileURL: [NSURL fileURLWithPath: path]];
}
- (void)stopRecording
{
    [file recordToOutputFileURL: nil];
}
- (IBAction)record: (id)sender
{
    if ([sender state] == NSOnState)
```

```
35      {
36          [self startRecording];
37      }
38      else
39      {
40          [self stopRecording];
41      }
42  }
43  @end
```

When the instance of this object is awoken, it creates a new recording session. Note that this example emits all error checking, for the sake of clarity. There are many ways in which this can silently fail. A real application should not pass `NULL` to any of the error parameters.

Once the session is created, it needs input and output devices assigned to it. The input comes from some video source. This is typically a camera; on a modern Mac it is likely to be the built-in iSight. Lines 7–9 get the default video capture device. This is then opened on line 10. Opening a device gains exclusive access to it; you can't record from the same camera or line in with two different programs at the same time. This will fail and return an `NSError` via the pointer argument if the object is already opened. You can try sending a device an `-isInUseByAnotherApplication` message to see if another process has opened the device. There is not much point doing this before sending an `-open:` message, because another program can still open the device between the two messages, but it's useful if you are displaying an interface allowing the user to select capture devices.

Once the device is open, it is configured as an input. The `input` object, created on line 12, is a QuickTime input stream connected to the camera. The recording session will read data from this and write it to all of the outputs.

For this application, we configure two outputs. One goes to the screen, and the other goes to a file. The file output is created on line 16. This writes a .mov file. The other output is created implicitly on line 19, when the `QTCaptureView` in the window is connected to the session.

Finally, on line 20, the session is started. The file output that we assigned to the session did not have a file name set, so it will silently drop all of the frames that are passed to it. When the record button is clicked, the `-record:` method is called and, if the button is now in the on state, will call the `-startRecording` method. This defines a new file for storing the output. Note that this file will be silently overwritten if it already exists, so don't run this example if you have a file called VideoRecorder.mov on your desktop already.

When the user stops recording, the output file name is set to `nil`. This stops recording, but doesn't remove the file output from the session. If the record button

Figure 14.4: Recording video with QTKit.

is pressed for a third time, then recording will start again, overwriting the file. This means that we don't have to create a new session every time the user starts and stops recording.

Note that this example, as well as omitting error checking, fails to close the camera. Every call to `-open:` on a capture device should have a matching call to `-close`. You are allowed to open a device more than once in a program, but once the number of calls to `-close` equals the number of calls to `-open` the device will be released for other applications to use. This simple example doesn't need to bother relinquishing the device because it always displays the output while the program runs. When the program exits, the operating system will reclaim the device.

Audio recording is accomplished in exactly the same way. Try modifying the sound player example to also support sound recording. This will not require a preview view, just a recording session that writes data to a file. Select the output file with a save panel, rather than hard-coding it as we did here.

As mentioned earlier, this example writes uncompressed video to the disk. This is almost never what you want. You can add compression by using this method on the file output object:

```
- (void)setCompressionOptions: (QTCompressionOptions*)compressionOptions
               forConnection: (QTCaptureConnection*)connection;
```

The `QTCompressionOptions` object is a simple identifier representing a set of compression options. These are created from a small set of constant strings for common compression options. For this kind of application, we would usually use

```
[QTCompressionOptions compressionOptionsWithIdentifier:
    QTCompressionOptionsSD480SizeH264Video]
```

This returns a set of compression options for H.264 (MPEG-4 AVC) for standard definition video. There are a number of other preset configurations, for audio and video. Note that you have separate compression options for audio and video, rather than a set of options saying "128Kb/s AAC and medium quality H.264" or similar. That is what the second parameter is for when you set the configuration options.

Each output object in a session has a number of connections. These encapsulate properties of a single audio or video stream in `QTCaptureConnection` objects. You can enumerate the connections that a given output has by sending it a `-connections` message, and assign different compression settings to each one.

14.8 Supporting Speech

While various sound effects can help enhance a user interface, you can often make it even better by adding support for speech synthesis and recognition. OS X uses speech synthesis automatically if you enable the Voice Over accessibility option. This functionality is also exposed to programmers.

Even shell scripts can make use of speech synthesis. The POSIX specification requires shells to implement an `echo` utility, which displays a string in the terminal. OS X has an analog of this that speaks the string. You can use this in the terminal to speak warnings:

```
$ say Hello world
```

14.9 Cocoa Speech Synthesis

There are two Cocoa interfaces to the speech synthesis subsystem. One is via the *system services* mechanism, discussed in Chapter 20. There is a Start Speaking Text service exposed to all Cocoa applications that will speak the selected text in any text view or field. This is typically a user-driven mechanism. You can call the service in code, but it is more common to have the user invoke it from the services menu.

More convenient is the `NSSpeechSynthesizer` class. This can be used for speaking simple text strings in a very small amount of code. Listing 14.6 shows a twist on the classical Hello World application. This says "hello world" rather than displaying it on the screen.

Listing 14.6: An aural Hello World. [from: examples/SayHelloWorld/hello.m]

```
1  #import <Cocoa/Cocoa.h>
2
3  int main(void)
4  {
5      [NSAutoreleasePool new];
6      NSSpeechSynthesizer *speaker = [NSSpeechSynthesizer new];
7      [speaker startSpeakingString: @"Hello world"];
8      while ([speaker isSpeaking])
9      {
10         usleep(100);
11     }
12     return 0;
13 }
```

Only two lines in this program are required for the speech generation. The synthesizer object is generated on line 6 and then told to say the string on line 7. The remainder of the program is a simple loop that prevents it from exiting before it has finished speaking. As with `NSSound` and `NSBeep()`, the speech synthesizer works asynchronously, returning immediately from the `-startSpeakingString:` call and speaking in the background. The condition for the loop tests whether the object is still speaking, and if it is, then it waits for a little while and then checks again.

The speech synthesizer can do a lot more than this. You can adjust the rate, volume, and voice used for generating speech. (This version used the system defaults.) The voices available with Mac OS didn't change much between System 7 and OS X 10.4. Leopard introduced a new voice, named Alex, which is a significant improvement on the older ones.

A common use for speech synthesis is reading out messages as they appear. If you tell the speech synthesizer to start speaking a new string before it has finished the old one, however, it will clip the first string. Try adding this line immediately after line 7 in the last example:

```
[speaker startSpeakingString: @"Goodbye␣world"];
```

When you run the program, it will just say "Goodbye world." The best way of queuing text to be spoken is to create a delegate. When the synthesizer has finished speaking, it will send this message to its delegate:

```
- (void)speechSynthesizer: (NSSpeechSynthesizer*)sender
        didFinishSpeaking: (BOOL)success;
```

You can maintain a queue of strings in the delegate and have it automatically play the next one when it is ready. Depending on the application, you may provide the option to discard some messages when the queue is too full. For example, a chat application might not want to discard messages that a person has said, but might discard notifications of people entering and leaving the room if they are not required.

14.10 Conversing with Users

Speech synthesis by itself is largely a gimmick. When combined with speech recognition, it becomes a powerful tool. There are two kinds of speech recognition:

- Dictation, also known as speech-to-text, where a stream of text is converted into a text string.
- Command recognition, where a small set of key words or phrases are recognized.

The `NSSpeechRecognizer` implements the latter. This allows you to define a small vocabulary of commands that the system will attempt to recognize when spoken. This can be combined with speech synthesis to allow your program to carry out simple dialogs with users. You can define the set of commands that the user may speak. These can be words or short phrases.

The speech recognizer is very easy to use. Listing 14.7 shows a simple class that does for the speech system the same thing that `NSAlert` does for the windowing system. Users of this class send it query strings and possible responses and then wait for a callback.

When this class is initialized, it creates an instance of the speech recognizer and the synthesizer and registers itself as the delegate for the recognizer. The feedback window, which line 10 instructs the synthesizer to use, is shown in Figure 14.5. This window is part of the speech system. The same window is used when you globally enable speech commands. The commands spoken by the user are displayed above the window, and the phrases spoken by the computer are shown below.

Listing 14.7: A verbal dialog object. [from: examples/Dialog/Dialog.m]

```
#import "Dialog.h"

@implementation Dialog
@synthesize delegate;
- (id)init
{
    if (nil == (self = [super init])) { return nil; }

    speaker = [NSSpeechSynthesizer new];
    [speaker setUsesFeedbackWindow: YES];
    listener = [NSSpeechRecognizer new];
    [listener setDelegate: self];

    return self;
}
- (void)sayString: (NSString*)outString
{
    while ([speaker isSpeaking]) { usleep(100); }
    [speaker startSpeakingString: outString];
}
- (void) sayString: (NSString*)outString
          listenFor: (NSArray*)commands
           delegate: (id)aDelegate
{
    [self sayString: outString];
    [listener setCommands: commands];
    [listener startListening];
    self.delegate = aDelegate;
}
- (void)speechRecognizer: (NSSpeechRecognizer *)sender
     didRecognizeCommand: (id)command
{
    NSString *selString = [@"speechCommand" stringByAppendingString:
         command];
    selString = [selString stringByReplacingOccurrencesOfString: @" "
                                                      withString: @""];
    SEL sel = NSSelectorFromString(selString);
    if ([delegate respondsToSelector: sel])
    {
```

```
39            [delegate performSelector: sel];
40        }
41        else if ([delegate respondsToSelector: @selector(speechCommand:)])
42        {
43            [delegate speechCommand: command];
44        }
45        self.delegate = nil;
46        [listener stopListening];
47        [listener setCommands: nil];
48    }
49    - (void)dealloc
50    {
51        [speaker release];
52        [listener release];
53        [delegate release];
54        [super dealloc];
55    }
56    @end
```

This class exposes two methods. The first, `-sayString:`, waits until it has finished speaking and says the string given as an argument. This is also called by `-sayString:listenFor:delegate`, the method responsible for implementing conversations. When this method is called, it says the first argument and listens for one of the strings in the array given as the second argument. When the user says one of the suggested phrases, the delegate provided as the third argument will be notified.

The method starting on line 30 is the speech recognizer delegate method. This is called by the recognizer when the user speaks one of the suggested phrases. The recognizer will be the first argument and the spoken word the second. This method constructs a new string from the spoken phrase by prepending "speechCommand" and removing spaces. On line 36, it converts this string to a selector and then, if the delegate responds to that selector, calls it.

This uses some of the dynamic features of Objective-C. The ability to call methods by name is very convenient for dynamic code. All you need to do to handle a specific command speech is implement a corresponding speech command method in the object you pass as the delegate. If the delegate doesn't implement a specific method, then this will call a fall-back, enabling both static and dynamic lists of command phrases to be used.

The class in Listing 14.8 shows how this is used to have a short dialog with the user.

An instance of this class is placed in the application's nib file and loads when the application starts. It greets the user by saying "hello" when the application launches. The call on lines 9–11 tells the dialog object that it should expect either

Listing 14.8: Greeting the user when the program starts. [from: examples/Dialog/Greeting.m]

```
#import "Greeting.h"

@implementation Greeting
- (void)awakeFromNib
{
    dialog = [Dialog new];
    NSArray *replies =
        [NSArray arrayWithObjects: @"Hello", @"Goodbye", nil];
    [dialog sayString: @"Hello"
            listenFor: replies
             delegate: self];
}
- (void)dealloc
{
    [dialog release];
    [super dealloc];
}
- (void)speechCommandHello
{
    [dialog sayString: @"Welcome"];
}
- (void)speechCommandGoodbye
{
    [dialog sayString: @"Goodbye"];
    [NSApp terminate: self];
}
@end
```

“Hello,” or “Goodbye,” as responses. When the user says one of these words, one of the last two methods in this class will be invoked.

If the user said “Hello” then the program simply replies “Welcome.” Alternatively, in response to the user saying “Goodbye,” it will reply and exit. This is a very basic example of using the speech system, but you can imagine easily extending it. For example, you could use it to control a music player, first expecting a command like “play album” or “play artist” and then asking which album or artist and providing a dynamically generated list from the music library as a set of expected commands. You could also incorporate simple commands like “pause” and “shuffle” that would not need a second question and response.

Figure 14.5: The speech feedback window.

You would typically implement this kind of user interface as a state machine. This example program is a very simple state machine with only one state. Each of the speech command methods provides a place for inserting a state transition. By calling `-sayString:listenFor:delegate` again, with a different object as the delegate, you enter a new state. Each delegate represents a single state and each command a transition between states. You can create complex command flows like this; a lot of callcenters around the world use exactly this model for interactions, but with a human, rather than a computer, tracking the states.

Speech synthesis and recognition can be very useful technologies for applications. Speech synthesis can be used very effectively for applications that are designed to run in the background most of the time. A chat application, for example, could announce the new status message for the user's contacts when it changes. A system monitoring application could speak alerts. A good example of this is the Temperature Monitor application, which announces the CPU temperature if it passes above a certain threshold. This is particularly useful because this is most likely to happen when running something both CPU- and GPU-intensive, such as a full-screen game, where on-screen alerts might not be seen.

Spoken alerts have the same advantage over sound effects as text labels do over icons. A user is able to very quickly distinguish between a small number of distinct icons, but this capability drops off as the number increases. The same is true of sound effects. OS X comes with fourteen standard sound effects. On a typical system, several applications will be using each of these. A pop or beep noise is very easy to recognize for common events, but if you use the same sound effect for an uncommon effect that another application uses for a common one, then it is likely to be ignored. On my system, for example, Mail is configured to play the Glass sound when mail arrives. This typically happens several times an hour and I don't always read the new messages immediately. This means that I tend to ignore any other application that uses this sound.

An application using a spoken alert may still be ignored, but only if the user intends to ignore it. It will not be confused with an alert from another application. You can use this most effectively for unusual events; speaking to the user all of the time is more likely to cause irritation than provide an effective user interface.

Speech recognition is more difficult to use effectively. The main reason it exists is to support visually impaired users, who find clicking on parts of the screen difficult. If you use the standard Cocoa widgets, then these users will automatically be able to use your application via the standard accessibility APIs, but this is not always ideal. Just as small-screen devices like the iPhone often want different user interfaces to desktop computers, an audio interface may have a different structure to a visual one.

You can use the speech synthesizer directly to provide a replacement user interface for people who find using the screen difficult. This does not always mean visually impaired users. Some or all of your application's user interface may be hidden for various reasons. If you are displaying a full-screen movie, then you might want to enable voice recognition for commands like "pause movie" and "resume movie" or even more complex things such as chapter navigation. These can be used to control playback without having to bring the user interface into view.

OS X has supported Bluetooth headsets since 10.4. This adds a number of opportunities for effective voice control because they provide a cheap way for users to use a microphone when not sitting directly in front of the computer. Think about use cases like this when designing unusual user interfaces. Your user might have the computer connected to a projector and be on the other side of the room using a Bluetooth headset to control your application.

14.11 Summary

In this chapter we have looked at the various multimedia options in OS X. At the bottom layer for audio support is Core Audio, a powerful audio processing framework. Cocoa provides both simple and feature-rich interfaces to this in the form of sound objects and the QuickTime APIs.

We saw how to add simple sound effects using the `NSSound` object and the simpler `NSAlert()` function. This provides a very simple way of adding support for basic audio feedback to an application.

Next, we looked at how to play back and record both sound and video using the QuickTime APIs exposed through QTKit. These provide a simplified interface to a rich multimedia framework without requiring the developer to understand all of the underlying complexity.

Finally, we saw how to add support for speech recognition and synthesis to applications. This provides an alternative to the traditional graphical user interface on OS X and can be used to extend an application's usability both to users who can't easily see the screen, either due to a disability or simply because they are not sitting in front of the computer.

Chapter 15

Advanced Visual Effects

Most of the drawing routines we've looked at so far have been relatively simple. They have resulted in a static rasterized image that is then composited to the screen.

In this chapter we will look at extending this to produce richer visual effects.

15.1 Simple Animation

An animation is nothing more than a sequence of still images. Anything that allows you to produce still images can be used for animation, as long as you can do it fast enough. The human brain will create the illusion of movement when shown two similar images in quick succession. If you draw an image by a small distance from where it was last drawn, the viewer will perceive it as having moved.

The key here is the speed at which you update. Twenty-four updates per second is generally considered the minimum for giving the appearance of fluid motion. This is the frame rate that you get from a cinema. You may have heard people who play computer games give something closer to 60 frames per second as a minimum. This wide difference is due to the different way in which computer games and cinemas produce their frames.

If you look at a cinema projector, you will see a relatively simple mechanism that runs at a fixed rate and always displays a new frame every $\frac{1}{24}$ seconds. In contrast, a computer game can take much longer to generate a frame when you are looking at a complex, dynamic scene than when you look at a wall. The 60 frames per second rule of thumb comes from this range. If you can render 60 frames per second on average, then you are likely not taking more than $\frac{1}{24}$ seconds to produce any one of them.

Drawing something periodically in Cocoa is easy. We've seen how to trigger periodic events before, using `NSTimer`. We can use this to trigger some dynamic visual behavior. Listing 15.1 shows a simple window controller that causes its window to bounce around the screen.

Listing 15.1: Making a window bounce around the screen. [from: examples/Bouncing-Window/BouncingWindowController.m]

```
@implementation BouncingWindowController
- (void)awakeFromNib
{
    [NSTimer scheduledTimerWithTimeInterval: 0.01
                                     target: self
                                   selector: @selector(animate:)
                                   userInfo: nil
                                    repeats: YES];
    dy = 1;
    dx = 1;
}
- (void)animate: (id)sender
{
    NSWindow *w = [self window];
    NSRect frame = [w frame];
    NSRect screen = [[w screen] visibleFrame];
    frame.origin.x += dx;
    frame.origin.y += dy;
    if (frame.origin.x + frame.size.width >= (screen.size.width + screen.
        origin.x)
        ||
        frame.origin.x < screen.origin.x)
    {
        dx = -dx;
    }
    if (frame.origin.y + frame.size.height >= (screen.size.height + screen.
        origin.y)
        ||
        frame.origin.y < screen.origin.y)
    {
        dy = -dy;
    }
    [w setFrame: frame
        display: NO
        animate: NO];
}
@end
```

When this controller awakes, it schedules a timer to run 100 times per second, sending it an `-animate:` message. It also initializes two instance variables to one. These are the displacement values for the window's x and y coordinates.

When the animation runs, it gets the window's frame and then translates it by the two displacement values. The tests on lines 21–32 determine if the frame has moved out of the visible region of the screen. This region is returned by the `NSScreen` associated with the window and excludes the dock and menu bars. If the window has moved out of this region in either direction, we invert the displacement in that direction, meaning that the window will move in the opposite direction at the next animation.

Finally, on lines 33–35, we tell the window that it's moved. This method both moves and resizes windows. The second parameter will cause the window's contents to be redisplayed, but this is not needed for translations, only for resizing. The final parameter indicates whether the window should be resized as a smooth animation. This is ignored, since we are not resizing.

When you run this, you will see the window bouncing around the screen. You will also notice that the CPU load is quite high, and that the window is not moving 100 points per second (unless you're reading this in a few years time and testing it with a computer much faster than mine).

`NSTimer` is far from ideal for animations. Each timer will only run once per run loop and will be interleaved with all of the other timer events you have scheduled. Updating the coordinates like this is also quite slow. The arithmetic involved was a tiny fraction of the total CPU time spent sending messages between the various objects involved.

15.2 Core Animation Overview

The *Core Animation* framework began life on the iPhone, where it was called *LayerKit*. It extends the Cocoa drawing model with a set of layers for the view hierarchy.

Conceptually, this is not a large change. Each view in Cocoa draws in something that looks like its own graphics context. This can be the screen, a PDF ready to be sent to the printer, or a bitmap image. The layer model provides a hierarchy of layers that is equivalent to the view hierarchy.

Using Core Animation in a simple way, you can assign a direct mapping from views to layers. Each view has a single layer and is responsible for compositing its sub-layers when drawing into the window.

Layers and views do not have to have such a simple mapping. A view may contain several layers, or it may not have any layers at all. You can use multiple

> **iPhone**
>
> The relationship between views and layers on the iPhone is more direct. The iPhone graphical environment is built using Core Animation for compositing. Every `UIView`—the iPhone equivalent of `NSView`—has an associated layer automatically. On the desktop, layers are optional, and a view can exist without its own layer. On both platforms you may have more than one layer in a view.

layers in a single view to create complex visual effects by modifying only a portion of the contents.

Every layer in Core Animation is represented by a `CALayer` instance. This class encapsulates the layer's geometry and provides a delegate for drawing the contents of the layer. The delegate can alter two aspects of the layer's behavior: the drawing and the event handling.

15.2.1 Drawing in a Layer

When a layer is displayed, it will call this method in the delegate:

```
- (void)drawLayer: (CALayer*)layer inContext: (CGContextRef)ctx;
```

This is similar to the `-drawWithFrame:inView:` method implemented by `NSCell` subclasses. On the iPhone, layer delegates fulfill a similar rôle to cells on OS X. A layer delegate is a very simple, lightweight, drawing object. It can be even smaller than a cell, since it doesn't have to maintain any internal state, and is very simple to implement. Unlike cells, however, layer delegates do not handle events.

Because Core Animation began on the iPhone, which does not include AppKit, it does not provide an AppKit `NSGraphicsContext` to draw on. Instead, it uses the lower-level CoreGraphics context. As we saw in Chapter 13, it is possible to convert between these two easily. On the desktop, you are likely to want to use Cocoa drawing routines to fill your layer. You can do this by creating a new `NSGraphicsContext` from the `ctx` argument and drawing to this as you would any other Cocoa graphics context.

To demonstrate this, we'll take the drawing code from the circle text view and turn it into a layer delegate. This is shown in Listing 15.2. Figure 15.1 shows the result of drawing in a layer in a view.

When this delegate is loaded, it constructs an attributed string to draw and attaches itself to the view's layer. This view was configured as needing a layer in Interface Builder. The delegate then flags the view as needing a redisplay.

Cells and Layers

The decision not to implement the cell abstraction on the iPhone's UIKit surprised a lot of people. Cells were originally created so that views could draw a lot of similar things in a cheap way. They were an optimization for the kind of machine that NeXTSTEP ran on, where memory was very tight.

The layer model is a similar abstraction for more modern hardware. On a modern system—even a mobile device—RAM is relatively cheap and compositing comes for free, but drawing complex shapes can still be relatively slow. An example of this is rendering text, where drawing the antialiased gylphs is still very CPU intensive and so the results are cached in texture memory and composited as they are needed. Core Animation provides a way of doing the same optimization in the more general case. You can reuse the same image, scaled, rotated, or transformed in any arbitrary way, without having to redraw it.

Listing 15.2: A layer delegate based on the circle text view. [from: examples/CircleTextLayer/CircleTextLayer.m]

```
#import "CircleTextLayer.h"


@implementation CircleTextLayer
- (void) awakeFromNib
{
    NSDictionary *attributes = [NSDictionary dictionaryWithObjectsAndKeys:
                                [NSFont fontWithName:@"Zapfino" size:32],
                                NSFontAttributeName,
                                nil];
    str = [[NSAttributedString alloc]
           initWithString: @"Hello world! This is a long string."
               attributes:attributes];
    [[view layer] setDelegate: self];
    NSLog(@"Layer: %@", [view layer]);
    [[view layer] setNeedsDisplay];
}
- (void)drawLayer: (CALayer*)layer inContext: (CGContextRef)ctx
{
    NSGraphicsContext *context =
        [NSGraphicsContext graphicsContextWithGraphicsPort: ctx
                                                   flipped: NO];
    [NSGraphicsContext saveGraphicsState];
    [NSGraphicsContext setCurrentContext: context];
```

```
25
26      NSAffineTransform *transform = [NSAffineTransform transform];
27      [transform translateXBy:150 yBy:10];
28      [transform concat];
29
30      NSPoint point = {0,0};
31      NSUInteger stringLength = [[str string] length];
32      const CGFloat extraSpace = 5;
33      CGFloat angleScale = 360 / ([str size].width + (extraSpace *
            stringLength));
34      for (NSUInteger i=0 ; i<stringLength ; i++)
35      {
36          NSAttributedString *substr =
37          [str attributedSubstringFromRange:NSMakeRange(i, 1)];
38          [substr drawAtPoint:point];
39
40          transform = [NSAffineTransform transform];
41          CGFloat displacement = [substr size].width + extraSpace;
42          [transform translateXBy:displacement
43                              yBy:0];
44          [transform rotateByDegrees:angleScale * displacement];
45          [transform concat];
46      }
47
48      [NSGraphicsContext restoreGraphicsState];
49  }
50  @end
```

Note that redisplay of views and layers is entirely independent. A view might not redraw layers when it draws itself, and a layer can be redrawn without redrawing the entire view. This latter capability is what makes Core Animation so powerful. Redrawing an entire complex view can be expensive. Redrawing a single layer is likely to be much cheaper. Each layer will be stored as a rasterized image and composited together by the GPU. Even the GPU on the iPhone is able to do this very fast, and so you can produce complex animations without much processing load.

With enough video memory, all of the Core Animation layers will be stored in a separate texture. A modern graphics card is designed to be able to render several million textured polygons per second, so compositing the few hundred that you might get in a moderately complex Core Animation application is trivial.

The drawing code in this example, from lines 26–46, is almost identical to the version that draws in the view. Only the parts before and after this are changed. The first part creates a new graphics context object for the CoreGraphics

Figure 15.1: A circle of text drawn by Core Animation.

context, and sets it as the current thread's context. The end part restores the old context. You can even reuse an `NSView`'s drawing code directly by setting up the graphics context and then calling `-drawRect:` with the layer's `frame` property as the argument.

If you run the application and then make the window bigger, you will see something like Figure 15.1. Notice how the edges of the text are jagged, while the version that drew into the view was smooth. You can see the reason for this by putting a breakpoint around line 20 and running the program in the debugger. The `-drawLayer:inContext:` method is called once, when the program launches, but is not called again when the view resizes. In contrast, the view's `-drawRect:` method would have been called periodically all through the resize operation.

If we were using a new `NSView` subclass for this, rather than a simple generic view object, then the `-drawRect:` method should instruct the layers to redisplay.

The automatic scaling you get with Core Animation layers is very cheap. It just uses the GPU's scaling ability when compositing the layer. Redrawing the layer is likely to be much more expensive. As such, you might want to defer actually redrawing while a view is being resized. A simple way of doing this is to keep a timer, reset it every time you are asked to draw, and only draw after the timer has been invalidated. This allows Core Animation to scale the contents of the layer automatically when it is stretched and then redraw with a nicer version afterward.

15.2.2 Setting a Layer's Content

There is another way of providing the contents of a given layer. Rather than drawing into the layer's graphics context, you can just set an image that represents the layer. You typically do this by implementing this delegate method:

```
- (void)displayLayer: (CALayer*)layer;
```

This should set the `contents` property on the layer. This property is a `CGImageRef`. You can get one of these from an `NSBitmapImageRep` by sending it a `-CGImage` message.

A complex view may contain both static and dynamic layers. The mechanism described in the last section is best for producing dynamic layers. This mechanism is best for layers whose contents does not change very often.

When you set the `contents` property, you are effectively loading a bitmap into texture memory on the GPU. This is a very cheap operation when compared to sending a load of operations to `NSBezierPath` and friends.

Note that Core Animation can scale images down very fast. If you have an image that is used for drawing every instance of a commonly used view, then you should consider creating a single constant `CGImageRef` at a relatively high resolution and storing it in a file-static variable, and then setting this as the contents for every layer rendering it. Core Animation should keep a single copy of the image in texture memory and use the GPU's compositing functions to render it in each layer that needs it.

15.3 Understanding Animation Concepts

So far, the bits of Core Animation that we've looked at fit better with the LayerKit name. They provide a mechanism for drawing parts of a view to off-screen layers and then compositing them in one go. Although this is useful when constructing animations, it does not provide much help.

In traditional animation, you draw each frame individually. When working with pen and paper, this was the only option. The next step in the evolution of animation was to use transparent sheets for drawing parts of the scene. This technique was made popular by Disney, who used it to produce a pseudo-3D effect in animated films. If you draw the background, the near scenery, and each of the characters on a separate sheet of transparency, then you can give the illusion of perspective by moving them at different speeds.

Hopefully, you will see the parallel between this, traditional analog, method and the Core Animation layer system. Each Core Animation layer is equivalent to one of these transparent sheets. This approach made things a lot easier for the animators. It reduced the amount of drawing that they needed to do, since they could reuse parts of a scene that had not changed and only draw new animation frames for the parts that had. It also allowed them to do simple animations by just moving some of the layers, rather than changing their images.

The archetypal demonstration of this kind of animation is a character walking along a forest path, with the near and back trees moving at different speeds. In an animation like this, only the front layer—the one containing the character—needs to change. The back two layers are just moved.

Readers who grew up with games consoles in the 1980s may find this approach familiar. Most side-scrolling platform games used it, and the consoles at the time supported it in hardware for a very limited number of layers (typically fewer than eight). Core Animation, in contrast, can scale easily to hundreds of layers.

Animations that just involve some permutation of a layer are made easy to support by the fact that the layer class supports KVC for all of its properties. The location and orientation of a layer are all exposed as KVC-compliant properties. If you want to move a layer, all you need to do is alter the `position` property. This is a `CGPoint` that represents the layer's origin.

It you adjust this value, then the layer will move. You could take the timer example from earlier and animate the property like this. The first example we looked at manually updated the position every time. Implementing this kind of loop for every property change would be very tedious and contain a lot of copy and pasted code.

Most of the time, modern animation is done by *keyframe animation*. Rather than defining the position of an object for every frame, you define it for two key frames and let some software automatically generate the intermediate steps.

This can be done quite easily using *linear interpolation*. If you have an object at (x, y) at frame 0 and (x_1, y_1) at frame n, then it's easy to work out the coordinates for any intervening frame. The horizontal displacement for each frame is given by

$$\Delta x \; per \; frame = \frac{(x_1 - x)}{n}$$

The vertical displacement for each frame can be calculated in a similar way. This makes life easier for the animator, who now only needs to specify the start and endpoints for the movement and the time the movement should take.

Linear interpolation isn't the only way you can do this, just the simplest. More complex animation programs allow you to use arbitrary polynomials for interpolation. While linear interpolation uses the equation for a straight line to work out where an object should be for each frame, polynomial interpolation uses the equation for a curve.[1] This allows the user to specify lots of intermediate points on a path and have the animation follow it automatically.

Core Animation provides a generic implementation of interpolation for arbitrary properties. The `CABasicAnimation` class allows you to specify the start and end values for an animation. This is then attached to a specific property in a layer and run.

The interpolation mechanism used by Core Animation is somewhat complex. The interpolation is linear, but the time values are not. Each animation has an associated *media timing function*. The timing function takes a real time value and maps it to a range from 0 to 1. This is then used to find the interpolated value for the property being animated.

The timing function is defined in terms of a bezier curve. The two end points of the curve are fixed at $(0, 0)$ and $(1, 1)$ respectively. The two control points can be specified when you create an instance of `CAMediaTimingFunction`. There are four standard instances of this defined:

- `kCAMediaTimingFunctionLinear` defines the identity function. Time proceeds at a constant rate, with the input being mapped to the output with no transformation.

- `kCAMediaTimingFunctionEaseIn` is linear for the second part of the animation but runs slowly at the start. The movement will gradually speed up at the start and then run at a constant speed until the end.

- `kCAMediaTimingFunctionEaseOut` is similar, but starts at a fixed speed and then slows down near the end.

- `kCAMediaTimingFunctionEaseInEaseOut` starts slowly, accelerates, and then slows down again near the end.

These are enough for a lot of animations. You may want to define your own ones for more complex animations. These will typically use the `CAKeyframeAnimation` class. This is equivalent to a sequence of `CABasicAnimations`. You specify arrays of values and timing functions when creating a keyframe animation. It will then interpolate between each sequence of values, using the matching timing function. You can use this to define complex paths for an object.

[1]Technically, linear interpolation is first-order polynomial interpolation.

15.4 Adding Simple Animations

Much of the power of Core Animation comes from the fact that you often don't have to use it explicitly. The method in Listing 15.3 will cause the sender of the action to move to a random location in the parent view.

Listing 15.3: The delegate for a self-hiding button. [from: examples/HidingButton/ButtonAnimator.m]

```
1  #import "ButtonAnimator.h"
2  #import <QuartzCore/CoreAnimation.h>
3  
4  @implementation ButtonAnimator
5  - (IBAction)hideButton: (id)sender
6  {
7      CALayer *layer = [sender layer];
8      CGSize destination = NSSizeToCGSize([[sender superview] bounds].size);
9      destination.width *= (((float)random()) / ((float)LONG_MAX));
10     destination.height *= (((float)random()) / ((float)LONG_MAX));
11     layer.position = *(CGPoint*)&destination;
12     NSRect frame = [sender frame];
13     frame.origin.x = destination.width;
14     frame.origin.y = destination.height;
15     [sender setFrame: frame];
16 }
17 @end
```

If you connect this to a button with its own layer, and set the parent view to have its own layer, then you get a simple button that moves away from the mouse to a random location in the window whenever it is clicked. This is not particularly useful, but it demonstrates several important aspects of Core Animation.

The first thing to notice is that we didn't define an animation. Setting properties on a layer in this way creates an *implicit animation*. The new value is set as the destination value and all of the intermediate steps are animated. This example contained no animation-related code, but still produces an animation of the button moving when it is clicked.

The other important point is that lines 12–15 look redundant. We've just moved the layer, why do we need to move the view too? The answer is that the layer and the view's frame are independent. When a view is being used in this way, the layer is used for drawing and the frame is used for event handling. Try commenting out line 15 and running this example again. The button will appear to move, but when you go to click on it in its new location, you will find that it doesn't work. If you keep clicking where it used to be, it will still receive the events and move again.

This disconnect is sometimes useful. It allows you to handle events in one region and draw in another. You might use this, for example, for something like the dock zooming animation. Each entry in the dock appears to expand when you move the mouse over it, but the region that accepts mouse events remains in the same place. You could implement something similar by putting each icon on a different layer and expanding them when the mouse moves over the view that accepts clicks for them.

A lot of the standard Cocoa views now have Core Animation support built in. The `NSView` and `NSWindow` classes both now conform to the `NSAnimatablePropertyContainer` protocol. This protocol defines four methods, but the most important one is `-animator`.

If you send an `-animator` message to an object that implements this protocol, you will get an *animator proxy* back. This proxy can be used as if it were the original receiver. Any property set via the proxy will create an implicit animation.

Using this facility, we can rewrite the last example without explicitly using layers at all. Listing 15.4 shows the new version. This calculates a new position for the button and sets it via the standard `NSView` method.

Listing 15.4: A self-hiding button without explicit layer use. [from: examples/Hiding-Button2/ButtonAnimator.m]

```
#import "ButtonAnimator.h"
#import <QuartzCore/CoreAnimation.h>

@implementation ButtonAnimator
- (IBAction)hideButton: (id)sender
{
    CGSize destination = NSSizeToCGSize([[sender superview] bounds].size);
    destination.width *= (((float)random()) / ((float)LONG_MAX));
    destination.height *= (((float)random()) / ((float)LONG_MAX));
    NSRect frame = [sender frame];
    frame.origin.x = destination.width;
    frame.origin.y = destination.height;
    [[sender animator] setFrame: frame];
}
@end
```

If you removed the `-animator` call from this, you would have a pure-AppKit method that would run on any OpenStep platform. This shows how easy it is to add Core Animation support to legacy code. You might have written methods like this that perform some modification to the properties of a view already. If you have, you can turn them into smooth transitions using Core Animation just by using the animator proxy.

This also works with windows. If you set a property on a window with the animator proxy, then the window will be animated, rather than abruptly change. So far we've only really looked at doing this with positions. This is an obvious property to animate, but a lot of the common effects adjust other properties, such as opacity. You can make a view (or a window) fade away like this:

```
[[view animator] setOpacity: 0];
```

This will create an implicit animation gradually making the view more transparent until it is invisible. You can animate any visual property of a view or window in this way.

Lots of simple transition effects can be created with concurrent animations. One of the transitions employed by Spaces, the virtual desktop manager on OS X, involves expanding a view and making it fade away at the same time. This gives the user the impression of flying through the view. You can do something like that easily by combining two simple animations. One will resize a window until it is the size of the screen. The other will fade it until it is transparent. Running these at the same time will give the fly-through effect. Implementing this in an action method is just two calls:

```
NSWindow *win = [sender window]
NSWindow *animator = [win animator];
[animator setFrame: [[win screen] visibleFrame] display: NO];
[animator setAlphaValue: 0];
```

The two animations are set at the same time and so run concurrently. If you connect this as the action to a button or some other view, then clicking it will cause the window to appear to fly toward the user. You can combine arbitrary effects like this to produce complex animations with very little code.

15.5 Image Filters

OS X 10.4 introduced a framework called *Core Image*. This is a nondestructive image manipulation framework designed for producing dynamic effects. Core Image is designed for highly accurate filtering. It uses a 128-bit color space, with four 32-bit floating point channels per pixel.

The use of floating point values for colors is relatively new to mainstream computing, although it has been common in high-end image processing for a while. The number of discrete colors that the human eye can see is not much more than you can represent with a 24-bit color space. As an experiment, try drawing two regions of the same color next to each other in an image editor. Next, increase the red component in one of the patches slowly until you can distinguish the two. Then reset them and try again with green and blue. You should find that for some

Animation and Bad UIs

Adding animations with Core Animation is very easy. This makes it very easy to overuse. Remember when you add an animation always to think about what information you are trying to convey to the user with it. If you can't think of anything, then avoid using animations.

Animated user interfaces can enhance usability a lot if designed carefully. Any time a user interface component is changing state you have the potential for a helpful animation. If some component is moving, in particular, it is a lot easier to follow a gradual animation than a teleport effect. The minimize effect in OS X is a good example of this. Seeing the window shrink down to the dock shows the user where it has gone.

Animations can also have the opposite effect. The human brain is much better at noticing abrupt changes than gradual ones. If you gradually fade a user interface component away, then the user will not notice it disappearing. This is sometimes intentional—you can use slow fades to remove components without distracting the user—but more often it will be confusing.

Be careful not to animate too many things at once. If there are several things all moving around in your user interface, then it becomes confusing. Try to restrict animations to important areas of the user interface and use them to provide helpful visual clues. Using them for gratuitous eye candy makes for nice demos but an unusable application.

colors a single bit change lets you distinguish the two, while for others you can increase a channel value by ten or more without being able to tell the difference.

This is where floating point values help a lot. Floating point color channels allow you to create calibrated color curves so that the precision of the floating point value at any given point corresponds to the precision of the human eye. For regions where the human viewer can't easily distinguish colors, you can use less precision.

In practice, 16-bit floating point values give enough depth without calibration that they can be used. Core Image does not use 16-bit floating point values for two reasons. The first is that they are not well supported. The so-called *half-precision floating point* is not a standard and is not supported on any CPUs. GPUs did for a while, but modern ones tend to extend them to 32 bit for computation so you get no speed benefit when using them. The other reason for using 32-bit values is to reduce the loss of precision from floating-point rounding errors.

A number of RAW image file formats use 16-bit floating point values internally. These are extended to 32-bit values when they are loaded.

Core Image allows you to apply filters to images. These are nondestructive. When you apply a filter, you get a new image; you don't modify the old one. Each filter is implemented as an *image unit*. This contains a kernel program written in a subset of *OpenGL Shader Language* (*GLSL*), which transforms the image, and an Objective-C wrapper.

The GLSL program is either run on the GPU or on the CPU of older machines. It will use SSE or AltiVec on the CPU or the native GPU functions. This allows the filters to run very quickly. There are also optimizations applied when combining filters so that redundant operations are eliminated.

Core Animation provides a simple interface for using Core Image filters. The `filters` property on `CALayer` contains an array of `CIFilter` objects. All of these filters will be applied to both the layer and its sublayers.

Core Image on the iPhone

At the time of writing, the iPhone does not support Core Image filters through Core Animation. The filters property will be ignored if you try to run code that uses it on the iPhone.

There are also two other properties that define special-purpose filters for use with Core Animation:

- `compositingFilter` defines a filter used for compositing a layer with its background. If this is not defined, then source-over compositing is used.
- `backgroundfilters` defines an array of filters that will be applied to the background layer underneath a given layer. You can use this to blur or emphasize the background under a view.

These properties can be set directly in Interface Builder using the inspector shown in Figure 15.2. This allows you to define static filters, for example, blurring a view or adding a shadow. These will be automatically applied to the layer and all of its sublayers.

You can also define these filters in code by setting the correct properties. Listing 15.5 shows how to extend the animated button example so that a motion blur is also applied to the button as it moves.

This works by creating an instance of one of the default Core Animation filters and applying it to the layer. Each Core Image filter is identified by a name. In this case we are loading the standard motion blur filter, on line 11. Line 12 sets the default values for all of the filter's attributes. You must either call this method or set the values manually when you create a filter.

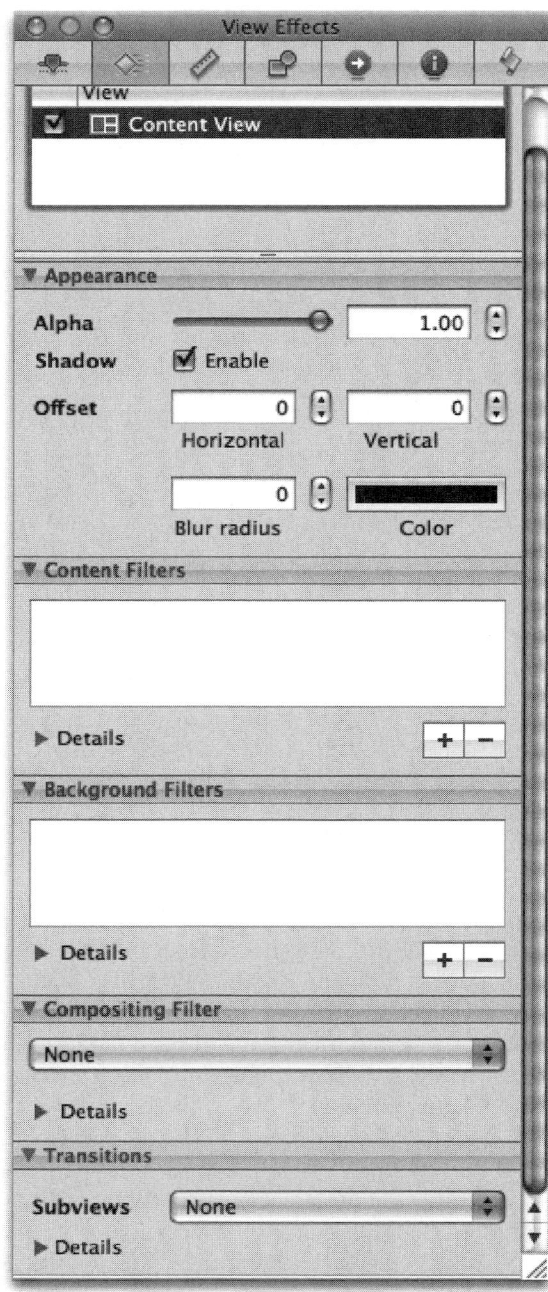

Figure 15.2: Setting Core Animation properties in Interface Builder.

Listing 15.5: Moving and blurring a button. [from: examples/HidingButton3/ButtonAnimator.m]

```
#import "ButtonAnimator.h"
#import <QuartzCore/QuartzCore.h>

@implementation ButtonAnimator
- (IBAction)hideButton: (id)sender
{
    CGSize destination = NSSizeToCGSize([[sender superview] bounds].size);
    destination.width *= (((float)random()) / ((float)LONG_MAX));
    destination.height *= (((float)random()) / ((float)LONG_MAX));
    [[sender animator] setFrameOrigin: *(NSPoint*)&destination];
    CIFilter *blur = [CIFilter filterWithName: @"CIMotionBlur"];
    [blur setDefaults];
    [sender layer].filters = [NSArray arrayWithObject: blur];
}
@end
```

Note that this example does not remove the blur when the animation is finished. We will look at how to do that in the next section. For now, the button will remain blurred after you click on it. Figure 15.3 shows the window before and after this action is run. In the left image you can see the button just as it was created in Interface Builder. The right image shows the button having moved and with the blur applied.

You can use image filters for a variety of effects. Some of the most dramatic come from changing the filter as it moves across the window. Figure 15.4 shows an example of this. This window contains a copy of the standard OS X network icon in an `NSImageView` subclass that applies a Core Image filter depending on the location of the mouse.

The view class implementation is shown in Listing 15.6. This registers to receive mouse movement events when it is loaded from the nib file. Then, whenever the user moves the mouse, the method on line 12 will be called.

Listing 15.6: An image view that deforms the contents. [from: examples/MouseDeform/DistortImageView.m]

```
4 @implementation DistortImageView
5 - (void) awakeFromNib
6 {
7     [[self window] setAcceptsMouseMovedEvents:YES];
8     [[self window] makeFirstResponder:self];
```

```
    [self setWantsLayer: YES];
}
- (BOOL)acceptsFirstResponder { return YES; }
- (void)mouseMoved: (NSEvent*)theEvent
{
    NSPoint mouse = [self convertPoint:[theEvent locationInWindow]
                              fromView:nil];
    CIFilter *distort = [CIFilter filterWithName: @"CIPinchDistortion"];
    [distort setDefaults];
    [distort setValue: [CIVector vectorWithX: mouse.x Y: mouse.y]
               forKey: @"inputCenter"];
    [self layer].filters = [NSArray arrayWithObject: distort];
}
@end
```

This creates a new Core Image filter instance. In this case it is a pinch distortion, which warps the image as though it had been pinched at the designated point.

As with most other Core Image filters, this distortion has a number of configurable parameters that are exposed via KVC. In this case we only care about one: the center of the distortion. This is set to the location of the mouse click.

Using this view, the filter will be updated whenever the mouse moves. Because the filters run on the GPU, they are very fast. Try running this example and moving the mouse over the window. The shape will deform in real time as you move the mouse.

Something very similar to this is used for the dynamic search effect in System

Figure 15.3: Before and after images of the blurred button.

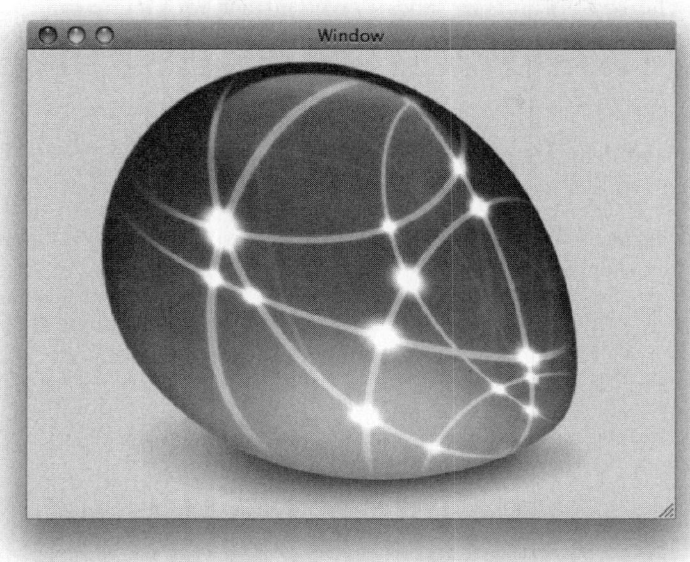

Figure 15.4: Deforming a view with Core Animation and Core Image.

Preference. This effect uses the "CISpotLight" filter. Try applying this to a view's layer. It will be highlighted as if a flashlight is shining on it. You can implement this kind of highlighted searching by adding this filter to all of the views that correspond to something matching your result and applying a darken filter to all of the others.

Core Animation provides a specific kind of animation object for use with Core Image filters. The `CATransition` class is used to define transitions that use Core Image filters. These transitions are most often used when layers are added to or removed from their parent layer, or when one layer replaces another.

Most commonly these are assigned as *Core Animation actions*. Classes that can be triggered in response to Core Animation events must conform to the `CAAction` protocol. This protocol defines one method:

```
- (void)runActionForKey: (NSString*)key
                 object: (id)anObject
              arguments: (NSDictionary*)dict;
```

The action receiving this message will run on the layer passed as the second argument. The `key` parameter defines an identifier for the action, and the dictionary gives some optional extra parameters. This protocol is implemented by `CAAnimation`. You can define an animation that will run in response to three action identifiers:

- `kCAOnOrderIn` indicates that a layer has just been inserted into the layer hierarchy or has just become visible.
- `kCAOnOrderOut` is used for layers becoming invisible, either as a result of being hidden or removed from the tree.
- `kCATransition` identifies an action where one layer is replacing another.

Actions can also be associated with properties. When you set a property via an animator proxy, or on a layer directly, it will look up the animation for the specified key and run it. This is how implicit animations work. They are registered with the class for that each property.

15.6 Defining Transitions

You can use this same mechanism to define transitions of your own. A transition will be run whenever a property in a layer changes. As with other animations, you can also run a transition explicitly.

Most of the time, you will want to set up transitions in Interface Builder using the layer inspector. This lets you define the transitions that a view will use whenever sublayers are added or removed. If you are writing a new view, then you may choose to define transitions for various layer actions explicitly in code.

The simple class in Listing 15.7 shows how to define transition animations and how to run them explicitly. Figure 15.5 shows this example program in the middle of running a transition.

Listing 15.7: Running Core Animation transitions. [from: examples/CoreAnimationTransitions/TransitionController.m]

```
static NSArray *transitionTypes;
static NSArray *transitionSubtypes;
@implementation TransitionController
+ (void)initialize
{
    transitionTypes = [[NSArray arrayWithObjects:
        kCATransitionFade,
        kCATransitionMoveIn,
        kCATransitionPush,
```

```
        kCATransitionReveal,
        nil] retain];
    transitionSubtypes = [[NSArray arrayWithObjects:
        kCATransitionFromRight,
        kCATransitionFromLeft,
        kCATransitionFromTop,
        kCATransitionFromBottom,
        nil] retain];
}
- (void)awakeFromNib
{
    layer = [[view layer] retain];
    hiddenLayer = [[hiddenView layer] retain];
    [hiddenLayer removeFromSuperlayer];
    [layer removeFromSuperlayer];
    [[windowView layer] addSublayer: layer];
    transition = [CATransition new];
    transition.type = kCATransitionMoveIn;
    transition.subtype = kCATransitionFromTop;
    transition.duration = 2;
}
- (IBAction)setTransitionType: (id)sender;
{
    transition.type =
        [transitionTypes objectAtIndex: [[sender selectedItem] tag]];
}
- (IBAction)setTransitionSubtype: (id)sender;
{
    transition.subtype =
        [transitionSubtypes objectAtIndex: [[sender selectedItem] tag]];
}
- (IBAction)runTransition: (id)sender
{
    CALayer *windowLayer = [windowView layer];
    [windowLayer setActions:
        [NSDictionary dictionaryWithObject: transition
                                    forKey: @"sublayers"]];
    [windowLayer replaceSublayer: layer
                            with: hiddenLayer];
    CALayer *tmp = layer;
    layer = hiddenLayer;
    hiddenLayer = tmp;
}
@end
```

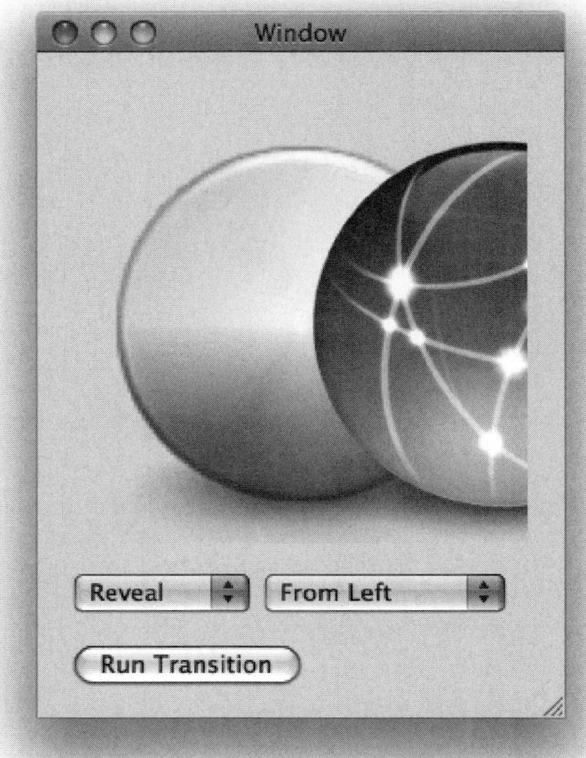

Figure 15.5: A Core Animation transition effect.

This example defines a single transition object and allows the user to modify it by selecting attributes from two `NSPopUpButtons`. These are connected to the first two action methods. Both of these use the tag of the selected menu item to find a constant string in an array and set this as either the type or the subtype of the transition. The two arrays are defined in the `+initialize` method. They contain the constants that are allowed for use in defining a simple transition.

We use a simple hierarchy of two layers in this example. The two images are created in `NSImageViews` with their own layers and these are placed inside a generic

`NSView`. When the class awakes, it removes the layers and then reinserts one into the `NSView`'s layer. The two image views are not used at all in the rest of this example; they are just a convenient way of creating layers containing images.

When the button is pressed, the third action method runs the transition layer. This first defines a new transition for the sublayers property on the `NSView`'s layer. This transition will be invoked any time something modifies the layer's children in the layer hierarchy, which is exactly what we do on the next line. The `-replaceSublayer:with:` call replaces the current image layer with the other one. This looks up the action for modifying the sublayers property and runs the associated animation.

You can use this same pattern when creating custom views that make use of layers for drawing. Things like the `NSCollectionView` class do this internally. This class uses a separate layer for each collection item and defines Core Animation transitions that are implicitly invoked when the layers are moved around. As well as looking nice, this provides useful visual feedback, allowing the user to easily track how the objects are rearranged when the view is resized or the contents changes.

15.7 Creating Complex Animations

Implicit animations provide a simple way of adding dynamic behavior to your application's user interface, but they don't expose the full richness of the Core Animation system.

To really produce interesting effects, you will want to explicitly create complex animation objects. We looked briefly at the classes used to do this earlier. Individual animations are either basic animations or keyframe animations. The first of these performs a single manipulation of a property, from one value to another. The second is equivalent to a sequence of the first.

The other way of grouping animations is in parallel. It doesn't make sense to have two animations modifying the same property in parallel—they would interfere with each other—but modifying different properties at the same time is often useful. You could, for example, modify the size and opacity of an object while moving it.

You group animations in parallel using a `CAAnimationGroup`. This is a trivial class that exposes a single property: `animations`. This is an array of all of the animations that should be run in parallel. Each of the animations associated with an animation group will run using the same time curve. Try replacing some of the individual animations in the examples in this chapter with animation groups.

15.8 3D Core Animation Transforms

The affine transform used for AppKit drawing are represented by a 3×3 matrix. This is enough to define transforms between 2D coordinate spaces. With Core Animation, we get a new kind of affine transform. The `CATransform3D` structure contains a 4×4 matrix. This can represent arbitrary transforms in 3D space.

Although transforms are structures, they can be manipulated using KVC key paths. For example, you can set the z-axis rotation in a layer like this:

```
[[self layer] setValue: [NSNumber numberWithInt: 2]
             forKeyPath: @"transform.rotation.z"];
```

This attribute can be animated, so you can define `CAAnimation` instances that will modify the rotation in 3D space. Listing 15.8 shows a simple action method that sets an animation for rotating the sender around the y axis. Figure 15.6 shows the result of attaching this to a button.

Remember that the axes specified for a rotation are the axes around which the object will be rotated, not the axes *in* which it will be rotated. When you rotate around the y axis, you are rotating in the x and z axes. The x and z coordinates of the layer will change as a result of the rotation.

Listing 15.8: Rotating a layer in 3D space. [from: examples/Rotate3D/RotateController.m]

```
#import "RotateController.h"
#import <QuartzCore/QuartzCore.h>

@implementation RotateController
- (IBAction)runRotate: (id)sender
{
    CAKeyframeAnimation *animation =
        [CAKeyframeAnimation animationWithKeyPath:@"transform.rotation.y"];
    animation.values = [NSArray arrayWithObjects:
                        [NSNumber numberWithFloat: (60 * M_PI / 180)],
                        [NSNumber numberWithFloat: (120 * M_PI / 180)],
                        [NSNumber numberWithFloat: (180 * M_PI / 180)],
                        [NSNumber numberWithFloat: (240 * M_PI / 180)],
                        [NSNumber numberWithFloat: (300 * M_PI / 180)],
                        [NSNumber numberWithFloat: (360 * M_PI / 180)],
                        nil];
    animation.duration = 5;
    [[sender layer] addAnimation: animation
                          forKey: @"spin"];
}
@end
```

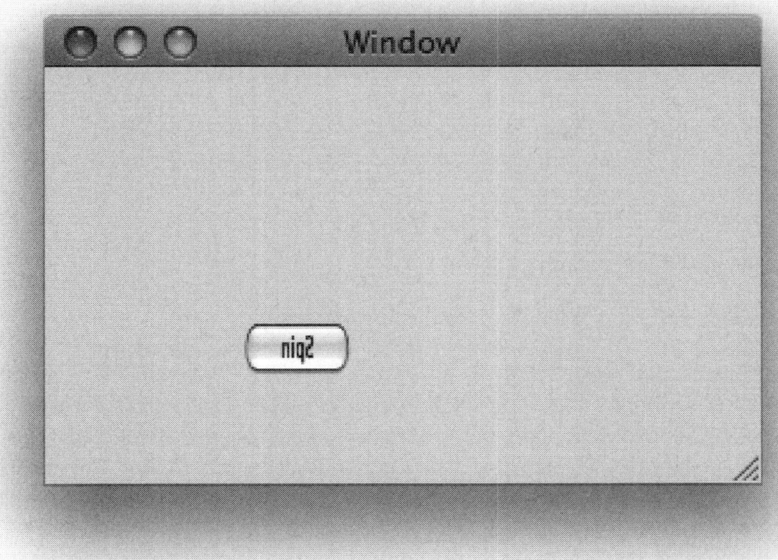

Figure 15.6: Rotating a button around the y axis.

This example sets up an explicit animation object. The animation is controlling the y-axis rotation via the key path exposed from the layer. The rotation is defined by six points around the edge of the circle. Note that we need to close it with a 360° rotation. If you miss the last step, then it will get to the end and then rotate all of the way back. We could get away with fewer rotation steps—only three are needed to describe a circular rotation—but these serve as an example.

We also set the duration to be a little longer than the standard animation length. Doing a complete 360° rotation in the standard time is too quick for the user to see exactly what is going on. When you click on this button, it will spin away from you and then spin back to where it started, in a complete circle.

This kind of animation can be used to create complex views, like the *CoverFlow* animation in iTunes and the Finder. For more complex transforms, you will need to define the affine transform structure manually.

As with 2D transforms, 3D transforms are just matrices that can be combined by multiplication. The result of applying one transform then another is the same as the result of applying the cross product of the two. A concatenation function is provided for doing exactly this:

```
CATransform3D CATransform3DConcat(CATransform3D a, CATransform3D b);
```

This multiplies the two matrices together and returns a transform that has the same result as applying both. We can use this to modify the animation described above so that it will spin the object around its center. This involves three steps:

1. Translate the layer so that its center is along the y axis.
2. Rotate the layer around the y axis.
3. Translate the layer back to its starting position.

If you have done any 3D graphics programming, then this idea should be familiar. This sequence must be done for each of the steps in the rotation and this is where the problems appear. Interpolating between two arbitrary affine transforms is beyond the ability of the animation classes. They can interpolate between rotation values or translation values, but the combination required for arbitrary rotations is too difficult.

Fortunately, the designers of Core Animation thought of this. Every layer has an *anchor point* that defines its location. The frame of a layer is actually defined implicitly from the anchor point, the size, and the position. Any rotations that are applied to the layer rotate it around the anchor point.

In the last example, the anchor point was at $(0, 0)$ and so the button rotated around the left edge. Listing 15.9 shows how to rewrite this so that it rotates around the horizontal center. You can see the result of using this action on a button containing some text and an image in Figure 15.7.

Anchor points are defined in an abstract coordinate space with values from zero to one, representing the corners of the layer. These will be transformed into coordinates in the enclosing layer when the frame is calculated. To rotate a button around its center, we need to move it from $(0, 0)$ to $(0.5, 0)$. We don't need any vertical movement, since we are rotating around the vertical axis, but we do need to move the anchor point horizontally.

The first thing this has to do is set the anchor point to the right place. Note that we assume here that the anchor point will either be where we want it, or at the origin. Lines 12–14 calculate the new location for the anchor point, and the origin after moving the anchor point.

If we just set these properties to their new values, we would create two new implicit animations. This would cause the button to jump slightly as it set the two new values with an animated effect. To avoid this, we use a *transaction.*

Listing 15.9: Rotating around a layer's center. [from: examples/Rotate3DInPlace/RotateController.m]

```
5  @implementation RotateController
6  - (IBAction)runRotate: (id)sender
7  {
8      CALayer *layer = [sender layer];
9      CGPoint point = {0.5, 0};
10     if (!CGPointEqualToPoint(point, layer.anchorPoint))
11     {
12         CGFloat displace = layer.frame.size.width / 2;
13         CGPoint origin = layer.position;
14         origin.x += displace;
15         [CATransaction begin];
16         [CATransaction setValue: [NSNumber numberWithInt: 0]
17                          forKey: kCATransactionAnimationDuration];
18         layer.anchorPoint = point;
19         layer.position = origin;
20         [CATransaction commit];
21     }
22     NSMutableArray *steps = [NSMutableArray arrayWithObjects:
23                             [NSNumber numberWithFloat: 1.0/3.0*M_PI],
24                             [NSNumber numberWithFloat: 4.0/3.0*M_PI],
25                             [NSNumber numberWithFloat: 2*M_PI],
26                             nil];
27     CAKeyframeAnimation *animation =
28         [CAKeyframeAnimation animationWithKeyPath:@"transform.rotation.y"];
29     animation.values = steps;
30     animation.duration = 5;
31     [[sender layer] addAnimation: animation
32                           forKey: @"spin"];
33 }
34 @end
```

Transactions are groups of Core Animation operations that are grouped together and treated atomically. Everything that happens between the `-begin` and `-commit` messages on lines 15 and 20 is part of the transaction.

The call on lines 16–17 sets the duration for this transaction. By setting the duration to 0 we ensure that the movement of the anchor point will not trigger an animation.

This pattern is needed anywhere where you want to set layer properties without

Figure 15.7: Rotating a button around its center.

triggering an animation. You must copy this block and replace lines 18 and 19 with the code to set whatever properties you are changing.

Lines 22–26 show another way of describing the angles that are combined to make a circular animation. The remaining parts of this method are the same as before, creating the animation from these steps and setting it to run.

Setting the anchor point is very important for rotations. It lets you rotate the layer around any arbitrary point on the screen. If you watch the CoverFlow animation carefully, you can see that it always rotates the flowed images around their center, just like we have done with the button. It then translates them to the side and back. You can implement this yourself using a combination of the rotation that we've just seen and a horizontal and depth displacement.

Objects are moved forward and backward by setting their `zPosition` property.

15.9 OpenGL and Cocoa Views

If you want more advanced effects, then Cocoa lets you embed an *OpenGL* graphics context in a window and use this for drawing. OpenGL is a cross-platform API for 3D drawing. It provides a low-level interface to the display hardware and is used by most 3D games that work on OS X and on a number of other platforms. Most modern mobile devices, including the iPhone, use OpenGL ES. This is not quite the same as the desktop version, but the two have a large common subset and it is relatively easy to port code between the two.

If you want to use OpenGL in Cocoa, the most common way is to create an `NSOpenGLView` in a window somewhere. This uses a slightly modified version of the standard Cocoa drawing mechanism. Prior to calling the `-drawRect:` method, it will set up the OpenGL context for drawing. You can then put OpenGL drawing commands directly into this method in a custom subclass, like the one shown in Listing 15.10. This draws a shaded triangle, like the one shown in Figure 15.8. This has a red, a green, and a blue corner and blends the color between them across its face.

Listing 15.10: Drawing a triangle in an OpenGL view. [from: examples/OpenGLTriangle/-TriangleGLView.m]

```
#import "TriangleGLView.h"

@implementation TriangleGLView
- (void)drawRect: (NSRect)rect
{
    glClearColor(1, 1, 1, 0);
    glClear(GL_COLOR_BUFFER_BIT);
    glBegin(GL_TRIANGLES);
    {
        glColor3f(1, 0, 0);
        glVertex3f(0.0,  0.6, 0.0);
        glColor3f(0, 1, 0);
        glVertex3f(-0.6, -0.6, 0.0);
        glColor3f(0, 0, 1);
        glVertex3f(0.6, -0.6,0.0);
    }
    glEnd();
    glFlush();
}

@end
```

Note that this example uses the old style of OpenGL calls, which are very

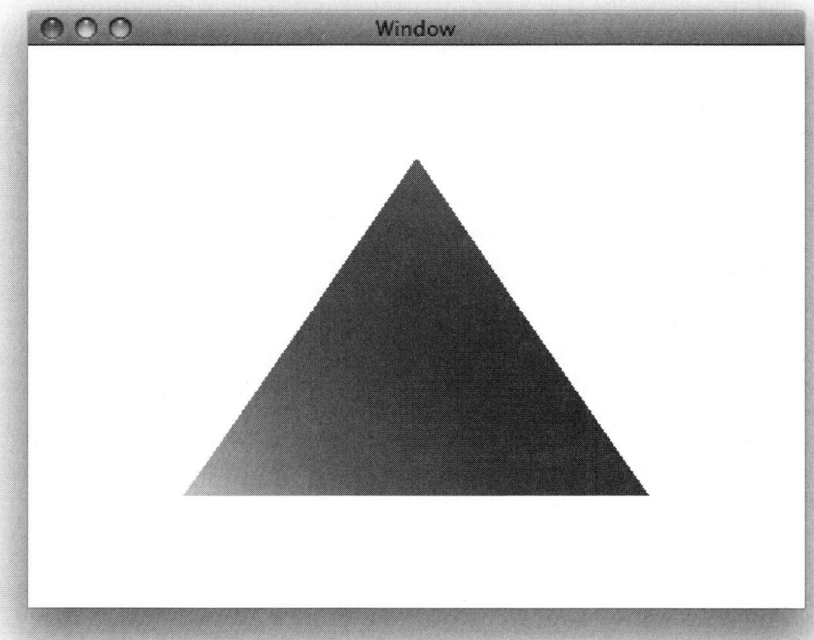

Figure 15.8: A triangle drawn using OpenGL.

inefficient on a modern GPU. This doesn't matter here, because drawing a single triangle isn't going to tax even the slowest GPU shipped with a modern computer, but for more complex programs, it will. For more information, consult a reference on the latest versions of the OpenGL specification.

You can draw using OpenGL in any other view by creating an `NSOpenGLContext` instance. This object controls an OpenGL drawing context and provides a number of options. You can use it for rendering to an off-screen buffer by sending it this message:

```
- (void)setOffScreen: (void*)baseaddr
               width: (GLsizei)width
              height: (GLsizei)height
            rowbytes: (GLint)rowbytes;
```

This instructs the context to output to the region of memory specified in the first argument, rather than to the screen. You can then save the result, which can be useful for printing, or you can apply additional transforms to it. Note that this will be very slow on most AGP graphics cards, and may not be supported at all with older ones.

If you want to render to the screen, then you can send the context a `-setView:` message. It will then draw into the region of the screen covered by the view. This is useful if you already have separate OpenGL drawing code that you don't want to move into an `NSOpenGLView` subclass. Alternatively you can send it a `-setFullScreen` message, which makes it cover the entire display.

Occasionally, it is useful to combine Cocoa and OpenGL from the other direction, drawing Cocoa views into an OpenGL context. You can do this in two steps. The first is to draw the view into a buffer in memory. The simplest way of doing this is to lock focus on the view and initialize an `NSBitmapImageRep` from it, like this:

```
[view lockFocus];
NSBitmapImageRep *texture =
    [[NSBitmapImageRep alloc] initWithFocusedViewRect: [view bounds]];
[view unlockFocus];
```

You can then send this object a `-bitmapData` message to get a pointer to the raw data. This can be used to initialize an OpenGL texture, which you can then map to the surface of any OpenGL shapes. Note that this does not work in the other direction; mouse-click events on the texture will not be passed back to the original view. You can simulate this by capturing the click location, discovering the coordinates in the displayed texture, and then injecting an `NSEvent` into the responder chain at the correct point. This requires a detailed understanding of both Cocoa and OpenGL.

This kind of drawing is much less useful now than it used to be. Core Animation makes a lot of the kind of simple animations that used to require OpenGL very easy. If you want to go beyond the capabilities of Core Animation, then OpenGL is still the best choice. You will find a lot of third-party libraries for working with OpenGL, as well as the standard support in Cocoa, which may make life easier.

One of the big advantages of OpenGL is that it directly exposes the GPU to the programmer. You can write short programs that run as OpenGL shaders and run them on the GPU (or, more slowly, on the GPU if the GPU does not support shaders). This makes it possible to create some very complex visual effects without taxing the CPU at all on a modern computer.

You can use a subset of the OpenGL shader language with Core Image, but using an OpenGL view gives you access to all of it. In particular, you get access to vertex shaders, as well as pixel shaders. If you are frustrated by the inability of Core Animation to implement the effect you want, take a look at OpenGL.

You can also integrate OpenGL with CoreAnimation very easily. The `CAOpenGLLayer` class provides a layer containing an OpenGL context. Any drawing that you do into this context from OpenGL is redirected to a buffer, which is then composited using CoreAnimation. If you set the `asynchronous` property, then you can draw into this layer in OpenGL without waiting for a notification that the layer needs redrawing. 10.6 introduced a new subclass of this, `NSOpenGLLayer`, which uses pure-AppKit interfaces, making it very easy to port code originally intended for an `NSOpenGLView` to draw into a layer.

15.10 Quartz Composer

Another alternative for visual effects on OS X is *Quartz Composer*. This provides a graphics way of connecting various visual filter effects and transitions together. You can then instantiate these and provide them with input from within a Cocoa application.

Quartz Composer is a complex visualization tool based on the same filter-graph approach as a lot of other packages. Each filter—or "patch" in Quartz Composer terminology—has a set of inputs and outputs that can be connected together in the visual editor shown in Figure 15.9. These have a small number of types, including the simple value types familiar to most programmers and some more complex ones, such as colors and images.

A Quartz Composer composition is a rendering pipeline. The simplest ones take no inputs and generate some static images. The more complex ones use internal data sources, such as the frame counter, to produce animations and take additional input from the outside world.

You can embed compositions in a Cocoa application using the `QCRenderer` class. This renders a composition using an OpenGL context. Alternatively you can use a `QCView` to render it directly to a view. The composition itself is wrapped in a `QCComposition` instance.

Although you can produce stand-alone animations with Quartz Composer, its real power comes from integration with Cocoa bindings. Every composition has a (possibly empty) set of input and output keys. You can enumerate these at run time by sending `-inputKeys` and `-outputKeys` messages to the composition object.

Combining Quartz Composer with bindings provides a very easy way of visualizing data in an application. Your Cocoa code only needs to expose the data via KVO-compliant properties, and the Quartz Composer composition can render it using a complex visualization pipeline.

You can integrate Quartz Composer with other Core Animation effects using

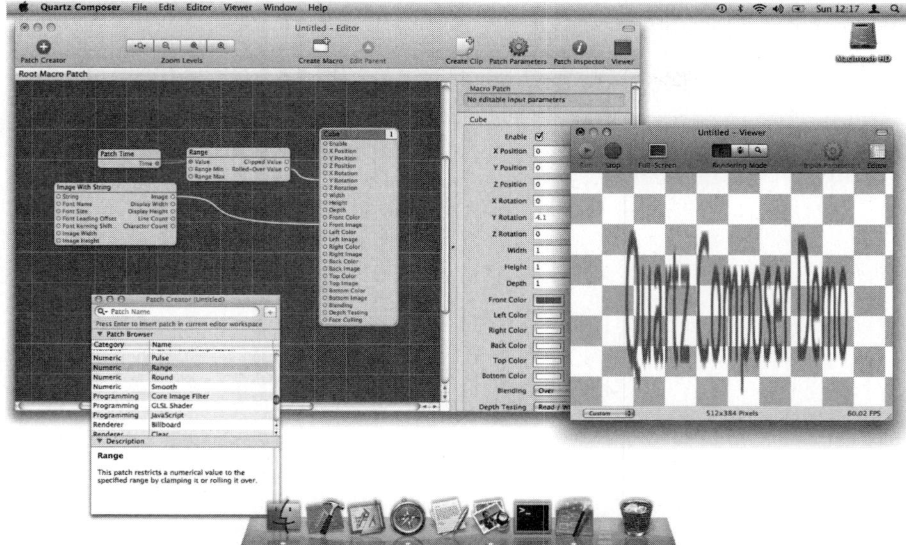

Figure 15.9: The Quartz Composer application.

QCCompositionLayer, which renders a composition into a Core Animation layer. This lets you combine compositions with any other Cocoa drawing mechanisms.

15.11 Summary

In this chapter we have looked at the various technologies in OS X that can be used for advanced visual effects. The more common of these is the Core Animation framework, which provides a very easy way of animating various visual properties of Cocoa views and windows.

We looked at the layer model employed by Core Animation and how it provides a drawing model that allows efficient use of modern GPUs. We saw how the layer hierarchy is similar to the view hierarchy and explored the differences.

Core Animation interacts quite closely with Core Image, a system for performing transforms on raster images very quickly, typically offloading the processing to the GPU. We saw how to use Core Image filters to define transition effects for Core Animation layers.

Finally, we looked at OpenGL, a cross-platform 3D graphics API that is well supported by Cocoa. If you are familiar with OpenGL, then you can use it in conjunction with Cocoa to produce complex 3D programs.

Chapter 16

Supporting PDF and HTML

Open standards are becoming increasingly important. Governments around the world are starting to require applications that they purchase to support standard file types for interoperability and to prevent long-term vendor lock in.

Two of the most common formats found on the Internet at the moment are *Portable Document Format* (*PDF*) and *Hypertext Markup Language* (*HTML*) documents. These have similar, but distinct, capabilities and uses. Both are typically used for documents that contain text and images, and in newer versions can include video and audio data as well.

PDF is intended as an electronic replacement for paper. The most common way of creating PDF documents is via a printer-like interface. On OS X, when you print a document you do so by first creating a PDF file and then sending it to the print spooler, which turns it into a set of commands that the printer understands. Some newer printers even understand PDF directly.

HTML, while often being used for the same sort of data, has a very different philosophy. An HTML document is intended to convey the semantics of a document, for example, indicating which parts are headings, which are body text, which are ordered lists, and so on. The formatting is supplied by a set of style sheets, allowing the same document to be rendered in different ways for different output devices.

PDF is generally considered a write-only format, one which can't be used for editing. It is possible to edit PDF files—there are some APIs provided by Cocoa for doing this—but a PDF file typically does not contain all of the information that the source document contained, and so editing it is not always a good idea. Most PDF editing falls into the category of *annotation*, adding extra information on top of the PDF, such as highlights and notes.

There is a very simple way of displaying HTML and PDF documents with Cocoa, using the `NSWorkspace` class. This just requires a single call:

```
[[NSWorkspace sharedWorkspace] openFile: HTMLorPDFfile];
```

This will launch the user's default PDF or HTML viewer, typically Preview or Safari, and open the specified file. In this chapter, we will look at ways of handling PDF and HTML documents that are more closely integrated with the application.

16.1 HTML in AppKit

The Application Kit provides a category on Foundation's `NSAttributedString` that adds support for a number of file formats. In particular, it provides methods for reading HTML data into an attributed string.

Attributed strings, in theory, can accurately represent any HTML document. HTML documents and attributed strings are very similar in terms of underlying model. HTML files contain markup that looks like this:

```
<h1>This is a Heading</h1>
```

You can think of this as the string "This is a Heading" with the heading level attribute set to one. Everything in HTML is defined like this, as an attribute with a particular range. Loading an HTML file into an attributed string and preserving the tag structure would be very easy. Unfortunately, it would not be very useful. Attributed strings can contain any aribitrary attributes that the user wants to define, but they cannot display them. Only the syntactic attributes defined by AppKit will be used when an attributed string is drawn on the screen.

Listing 16.1 shows one way to load an HTML document into an attributed string. This method is used to implement a very simple web browser that loads the page at the URL entered into a text field. You can see this working in Figure 16.1.

This simple program fetches the contents of the URL into an `NSData` object using a simple interface to the URL loading system. This is described in more detail in Chapter 22. It then creates a new attributed string object from the HTML data. The base URL allows the attributed string to fetch attachments. You will notice in Figure 16.1 that the loaded page contains a number of images. These are all specified in the HTML file as references to other files. The attributed string object turns these into attributed string attachments, resolving relative paths with the base URL.

As you can see from the screenshot, this is only a very rough approximation of the original HTML source. There is no support for tables, forms, or many of the more recent features of HTML, and certainly no support for scripting.

Listing 16.1: Loading an HTML document into an attributed string. [from: examples/ToyBrowser/PageLoader.m]

```
#import "PageLoader.h"

@implementation PageLoader
- (IBAction)loadPage: (id)sender
{
    NSURL *url = [NSURL URLWithString: [sender stringValue]];
    NSData *html = [NSData dataWithContentsOfURL: url];
    NSAttributedString *page =
        [[NSAttributedString alloc] initWithHTML: html
                                         baseURL: [url baseURL]
                              documentAttributes: nil];
    [[view textStorage] setAttributedString: page];
}
@end
```

Loading HTML in this way is simple and easy, but only really good for very simple documents.

You can use this very basic support if you create HTML documents specifically with this kind of viewing in mind. This might be useful for generating documentation or templates that can be viewed either in the application or in a web browser, but for most uses it is not sufficient.

16.2 Advanced HTML Support

Early versions of OS X shipped with Microsoft's Internet Explorer as the default browser. This was included as a result of a lawsuit settlement agreement with Microsoft, where Apple agreed to ship Internet Explorer and Microsoft agreed to continue to maintain the Mac port of Office. Mac IE used a different rendering engine to its Windows counterpart, and so was not generally well supported by web sites. Microsoft did not release any updates after 2000.

In 2003, Apple introduced the Safari web browser. This was an optional download for OS X 10.2 and was later shipped as a standard part of 10.3. Safari installed a number of frameworks, including some additions to AppKit that later became standard. The `NSError` class, in particular, began life as part of Safari.

The rendering engine used by Safari is *WebKit*. This began as a fork of two KDE projects, KHTML and KJS, for HTML rendering and JavaScript support respectively. The code diverged a lot over the first few years. Apple employed

Figure 16.1: The Apple web page as an attributed string.

a team of people to work on its fork full time, while KHTML was maintained by a small group of volunteers. To make matters worse, Apple was reluctant to pre-announce features, and so they kept its changes private until they released a new version of Safari, providing massive patch dumps to the KHTML team with each release. This made merging very difficult.

In 2005, Apple opened WebKit development. It is now developed in public at `http://webkit.org`, with nightly snapshot builds for OS X available, including a copy of Safari that uses an internal version of WebKit, rather than the system one.

Since being fully open-sourced, WebKit has been ported to the GTK and Qt, to Nokia's Series 60, and to Windows. Apple continues to provide a lot of the development work for WebKit, but other contributors also submit changes and have them incorporated into the engine used by Safari. This development model is followed by Apple with a few other projects that are not core to its business, such as the LLVM compiler infrastructure. Apple is not in the business of selling compilers or web browsers and the open source model allows the company to share development costs with others that benefit from a high-quality HTML rendering engine, including Nokia, Google, Adobe, and others.

Since 10.3, the WebKit framework has been shopped with OS X. As well as providing the rendering engine for Safari, this framework can be used by any third-party developers that need some or all of the functionality of a web browser.

16.2.1 WebKit Overview

KHTML was a C++ framework, and the rendering engine is still written in this language. WebKit was originally used to describe the Objective-C wrapper around WebCode, the Apple fork of KHTML. Somewhat confusingly, WebKit is now used to describe the whole framework. You will hear Google's Chrome described as using WebKit, even though it doesn't contain any Objective-C code.

All of the classes in WebKit use the `Web` prefix. The most important class provided by the framework is `WebView`. This is an `NSView` subclass encapsulating a web browser view. You can create a simple web browser by just dragging one of these into your window in Interface Builder and connecting up some actions. Figure 16.2 shows a simple web browser using this framework.

You can't see the code for this example, because there isn't any. The text field's action is connected to the web view's `-takeStringURLFrom:` method and the two buttons are connected to its `-goBack:` and `-goForward:` methods, respectively. Running this example gives a simple, single-window, web browser.

If all you want to do is display an HTML document, then the web view is all you need. You can embed it anywhere in your user interface and send it messages to load pages and navigate backward and forward.

Hopefully by this stage in the book you will have spent some time in XCode and will have used the API viewer. This uses a web view in the bottom pane. The forward and back buttons work exactly like they do in Safari, but there is no URL bar. The help browser uses *SearchKit* (see Chapter 17) to index help documents on the hard disk and loads them directly. The user is never exposed to the fact that they are stored in HTML documents. You can do this yourself using the `-loadRequest:` method on the web view, which loads a document described by a `NSURLRequest` object. We'll look at this class in more detail in Chapter 22, but for now just remember that you can create one from a URL object by sending a `+requestWithURL` message.

Note the difference in the rendering quality between the web view and the text view using an attributed string created from an HTML file. The layout is correct, respects the style sheet, runs scripts, and all links work as expected.

The `WebView` does not display the contents itself. It contains one or more `WebFrameView` instances. These each display a single frame. Frames have become less popular in recent years. They were originally designed to save reloading unmodified parts of a document when clicking on a link, but have largely given way to JavaScript methods. Inline frames are still used quite often, where a web

Figure 16.2: A very simple web browser using WebKit.

page contains an inline segment from another server. Each of these is represented by a separate frame view.

WebKit follows the same *model-view-controller* (*MVC*) pattern as the rest of Cocoa. Each frame view is backed by a `WebFrame` object, which encapsulates the data that is displayed in the frame. In more recent versions of WebKit, this exposes the frame's *Document Object Model* (*DOM*) tree. This tree is exposed to scripts running in the frame, and allows them to modify the document dynamically.

The frame model is provided by a data source, which provides a document representation. The data source model is complicated, because it is designed for loading documents from potentially slow remote sources. A typical web page may have tens of images and other inline objects. Each of these is fetched by a data source object over a separate connection. If one of the remote servers is very busy or one of these files is large (for example, an inline movie clip), then it can take a minute or more to load the file. Waiting until everything has been loaded before rendering the page would not be acceptable; the user would easily get bored waiting. Instead, the data source must be able to deliver partial documents and allow progressive rendering.

16.2.2 WebView Delegates

The WebView class delegates a lot of the standard behavior of a web browser to other objects. Each web view supports several, each described by an informal protocol and controlling some aspect of the browser's behavior. A single object may be used for as many of these rôles as you want. Each of these protocols describes a set of methods that one of the delegates may implement:

- WebFrameLoadDelegate defines methods that are called when a frame is loaded. This includes loading a page and handling redirections.
- WebResourceLoadDelegate methods are called when individual resources within a frame, such as inline images, are loaded. This can be used to show a loading status display or for more complex user interfaces like the timeline in Safari, which displays the time taken for each part of the page to load.
- WebUIDelegate is the most complex of the delegate protocols. This provides hooks for handling specific user interface events. It also handles a number of events that can be triggered by JavaScript.
- WebPolicyDelegate defines the policy for handling various kinds of resources. Whenever the view tries to spawn a new window, download a file, and so on. This is used to define security policies for the browser.
- WebEditingDelegate provides support for controlling the editing capabilities of a web view. This will receive notifications when the user changes anything in the view, and also provides hooks that can be used to disable or modify individual editing operations.

The most common delegate to provide is the UI delegate. Although this has a number of methods, they are not all needed. Most WebKit users will want to implement at least this method:

```
      (WebView*)webView: (WebView*)sender
createWebViewWithRequest: (NSURLRequest*)request;
```

This is called whenever the user clicks on a link that wants to be opened in a new window. It is expected to create a new WebView object to contain the target of the link. This can be in another window, another tab, or some other collection of views.

There are lots of browsers available for OS X, including a selection of open source and commercial ones that use WebKit. If you want to write a new browser, take a look at the MiniBrowser included as part of the XCode distribution. This includes all of the basic functions for a web browser and can be extended in any way you can imagine.

16.2.3 Editing HTML

Writing yet another simple web browser is not the most interesting thing we could do with WebKit. The version included with Leopard, and some of the later 10.4 updates, includes support for editing HTML documents.

If you import an HTML document into an attributed string and edit it, you lose all of the underlying HTML structure. This is not the case with WebKit. Every `WebFrame` object keeps track of its contents as a structured tree. You can enable basic HTML editing support by just sending the view a `-setEnabled:` message. Listing 16.2 shows a simple `NSDocument` subclass for editing HTML. This is connected to a web view object in the document nib. The result is shown in Figure 16.3, editing one of the HTML files that is included with the Apple developer documentation.

Listing 16.2: A simple HTML editor document. [from: examples/HTMLEditor/MyDocument.m]

```
#import "MyDocument.h"

@implementation MyDocument
- (NSString *)windowNibName
{
    return @"MyDocument";
}

- (void)windowControllerDidLoadNib: (NSWindowController*)aController
{
    [super windowControllerDidLoadNib: aController];
    [[view mainFrame] loadHTMLString: loadedDoc
                             baseURL: nil];
    [view setEditable: YES];
    [loadedDoc release];
    loadedDoc = nil;
}

- (NSData *)dataOfType: (NSString*)typeName
                 error: (NSError**)outError
{
    NSString *doc =
        [(id)[[[view mainFrame] DOMDocument] documentElement] outerHTML];
    return [doc dataUsingEncoding: NSUTF8StringEncoding];
}

- (BOOL)readFromData: (NSData*)data
              ofType: (NSString*)typeName
```

```
                error: (NSError**)outError
{
    loadedDoc = [[NSString alloc] initWithData: data
                                     encoding: NSUTF8StringEncoding];
    return YES;
}

@end
```

Note that this doesn't do any checking to see whether the file is of a valid type. When you try to load a document, it simply creates a string version of that file. This assumes all HTML documents are UTF8. This is not a good assumption in the general case. There used to be a private `WebCoreEncodings` method for automatically detecting the encoding of a file, but this has since been removed.

Note that the load method is called before the document nib file is loaded. To work around this, we store the loaded string in an instance variable. When the window controller has loaded the nib file, we tell the main frame of the web view to load and display the document, mark it as editable, and then dispose of the string.

Exporting the edited HTML as a string involves using some DOM methods. The `-documentElement` method is a standard part of the DOM, returning the root object of the tree. The `-outerHTML` attribute is a WebKit extension in the Objective-C DOM code. This returns a string containing the HTML representing the receiver and every DOM tree node that it contains. Calling this on the root element returns the entire DOM tree.

This example only supports very basic HTML editing. We can edit text and set fonts on it, just like in an `NSTextView`, but not edit the structure of the document or any of the HTML-specific attributes. If you have used the web inspector in Safari, then you will know that WebKit provides some much more advanced features for document editing and introspection.

You can navigate the DOM tree and replace individual elements yourself quite easily. This is made even more convenient by a number of `WebView` methods that allow you to map from a point on the screen to a DOM node. There are two of these that of particular interest:

```
- (DOMRange*)editableDOMRangeForPoint: (NSPoint)point;
- (DOMRange*)selectedDOMRange;
```

The first allows you to get the DOM elements at a specific point in the view's frame. The second allows you to get the DOM elements that the user has selected.

The DOM is a *World Wide Web Consortium* (*W3C*) standard defining set of object-oriented interfaces to a structured document. When an HTML, *Scalable Vector Graphics* (*SVG*), or any other XML or SGML file is parsed by WebKit,

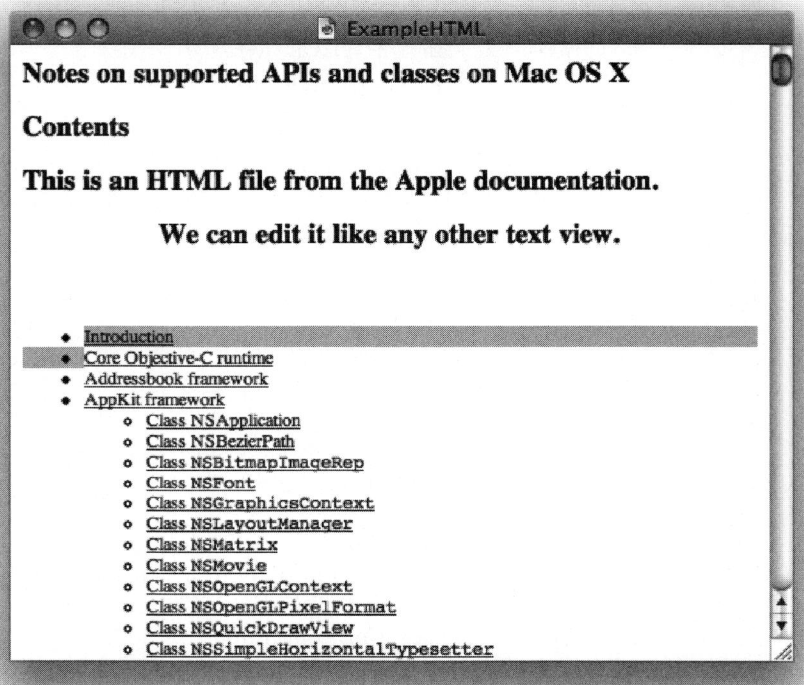

Figure 16.3: Editing an HTML document.

it constructs a DOM tree. This tree has one node for each tag in the source document.

The DOM standard is intended to be language-neutral. The objects for each of the tree nodes are all described in an interface definition language. This is very convenient for most languages, but is a problem for Objective-C. The IDL contains definitions like this:

```
Node                insertBefore(in Node newChild,
                                 in Node refChild)
                                    raises(DOMException);
```

This defines a method on the `Node` object for inserting a new child before an existing child. This takes two parameters, but only the first has a name. Trying to map this to Objective-C is nontrivial. The first versions of WebKit mapped it to this method:

```
- (DOMNode *)insertBefore: (DOMNode*)newChild
                         : (DOMNode*)refChild;
```

You may not have seen methods like this before. Although they are allowed by Objective-C, they are generally considered very bad style. This takes two parameters, but only provides a name for the first one. You would call it like this:

```
[aNode insertBefore: newChild : oldChild];
```

If you glanced at this, it would not be immediately obvious that this was sending an `-insertBefore::` message. Fortunately, this kind of method is no longer generated for DOM entries. As of 10.5, methods of this form were deprecated, although you may still find them in older code. The newer form generates a selector component from the parameter names, like this:

```
- (DOMNode*)insertBefore: (DOMNode*)newChild
                refChild: (DOMNode*)refChild;
```

This is a lot more readable to Objective-C programmers. It's not quite as friendly as it could be, but it has the advantage that it is still very close to the standard definition and so can be easily understood by someone familiar with DOM but not as familiar with Objective-C.

Note that the IDL defines a `DOMException`. In Objective-C, this will be mapped to an `NSException` with `@"DOMException"` set as its name. In other languages it may be a specific kind of exception object, or completely ignored if the language doesn't support exceptions.

If you have programmed using DOM in some other language, perhaps Java or JavaScript, then you should find it very easy to use DOM in Objective-C with WebKit. You can use this to dynamically modify documents in web views, either for editing or for displaying dynamic data.

16.3 Dynamic Interfaces with WebKit

Back in Chapter 12, we looked at some of the ways you can lay out views dynamically using AppKit. In many ways, this was reinventing the wheel. When you load a web page in Safari, every form element is an AppKit view, laid out by a very complex set of algorithms implementing the *Cascading Style Sheets* (*CSS*) box model.

The layout model for HTML is designed with no assumptions about the screen or window dimensions. If you resize a web view, the contents will automatically reflow to fit the new frame, or scroll if they won't fit. To demonstrate this, we'll create a simple example application that generates a form using DOM methods and handles the submitted result. You can see the form in Figure 16.4. This shows the same window with two different sizes. Note how the captions are moved above the input fields when the window is no longer wide enough to display them side by side. If you shrink the window even more, scroll bars will automatically appear.

If you need to construct forms at run time, then WebKit can make this very easy for you. There are two parts to doing this: creating the form and handling its submission. When you click on a Submit button in a form, the web view will call a policy delegate method to see if it should proceed. Listing 16.3 shows an implementation of this delegate method.

Listing 16.3: A web form policy delegate. [from: examples/WebKitForm/FormPolicyDelegate.m]

```
#import "FormPolicyDelegate.h"
#import <WebKit/WebKit.h>

@implementation FormPolicyDelegate
-                   (void)webView: (WebView*)sender
decidePolicyForNavigationAction: (NSDictionary*)actionInformation
                          request: (NSURLRequest*)request
                            frame: (WebFrame*)frame
               decisionListener: (id<WebPolicyDecisionListener>)listener
{
    int action =
        [[actionInformation objectForKey: WebActionNavigationTypeKey]
            intValue];
    if (action == WebNavigationTypeOther)
    {
        [listener use];
        return;
    }
    if (WebNavigationTypeFormSubmitted == action)
    {
        [delegate formSubmitted];
    }
    [listener ignore];
}
@end
```

This method is required to send either a `-use`, a `-download`, or an `-ignore` message to the `listener` argument indicating what the web view should do. This implementation handles two cases. If the action is a form submission, then it sends a message to its delegate, set in this example via an outlet in Interface Builder, and tells the web view to ignore the action. This allows the delegate to handle the form itself, rather than having the web view load the URL in the form's action attribute.

The other case, when the action is of type `WebNavigationTypeOther`, is allowed to proceed. This action type will occur when the view navigates to a page as the result of something other than user action, in this case because we have set the contents of the view by calling a method on the web frame. We automatically allow this. A more robust version might tell the view to ignore this kind of navigation as well, and only set the policy delegate after we have initialized the form.

Rather than create the entire form in code, we start with the template shown in Listing 16.4. This was created in XCode as an empty file and placed in the Resources folder. When you build the project, this will be automatically copied into the application bundle. Although this version was created by hand, it is possible to use any HTML editor you like and add CSS and other stylistic elements, including JavaScript field validation. The only important part is the `div` on line 7, with an `id` attribute that allows it to be found from the DOM. Note that we define a fake URL schema for submitting the form, to ensure that WebKit can't handle the form even if there is a bug in our policy delegate.

Listing 16.4: A HTML form template. [from: examples/WebKitForm/template.html]

```
1  <?xml version="1.0" encoding="UTF-8"?>
2  <!DOCTYPE html PUBLIC
3      "-//W3C//DTD␣XHTML␣1.0␣Transitional//EN"
4      "http://www.w3.org/TR/xhtml1/DTD/xhtml1-transitional.dtd">
5  <html xmlns="http://www.w3.org/1999/xhtml" xml:lang="en" lang="en">
6      <form action="fake://submit">
7          <div id="WebKitFormExample">
8          </div>
9  
10         <input type="submit" value="Submit">
11     </form>
12 </html>
```

Creating the form is handled by the class shown in Listing 16.5. Because this is just an example, we are hard-coding a lot of things that you would make into parameters in real code, including the form elements and the action on completion. This class will display three text fields in the form, and when it is submitted use them to construct an alert box like the one shown in Figure 16.5.

When the object awakes, it tells the web view to load the template. Lines 8–12 get the template HTML from the bundle as a string. This is then passed in to the web view's frame. As with most of the other WebKit loading methods, this is asynchronous. Displaying an HTML page requires several steps:

1. The source is parsed into a DOM tree corresponding to the structure of the HTML.
2. A layout tree is generated from the DOM, incorporating CSS information to position visual elements of the page.
3. The views used to display the page are created and inserted into the view hierarchy.

Listing 16.5: Creating an HTML form in Objective-C. [from: examples/WebKitForm/-FormController.m]

```
#import "FormController.h"


@implementation FormController
@synthesize formRoot;
- (void)awakeFromNib
{
    NSString *templatePath =
        [[NSBundle mainBundle] pathForResource: @"template"
                                        ofType: @"html"];
    NSString *template =
        [[NSString alloc] initWithContentsOfFile: templatePath];
    [[view mainFrame] loadHTMLString: template
                 baseURL: nil];
    [view setDrawsBackground: NO];
    [view setFrameLoadDelegate: self];
    formElements = [NSMutableArray new];
}
- (void)addTextField: (NSString*)title
{
    DOMDocument *doc = [[view mainFrame] DOMDocument];

    DOMHTMLInputElement *textField = (DOMHTMLInputElement*)
        [doc createElement: @"input"];
    [textField setAttribute: @"type" value: @"text"];
    [formElements addObject: textField];

    DOMElement *paragraph = [doc createElement: @"p"];
    [paragraph setTextContent: title];
    [paragraph appendChild: textField];

    [formRoot appendChild: paragraph];
}
```

```
34 - (void)webView:(WebView *)sender didFinishLoadForFrame:(WebFrame *)frame
35 {
36     self.formRoot = [[[view mainFrame] DOMDocument]
37         getElementById: @"WebKitFormExample"];
38     [self addTextField: @"Default␣Button"];
39     [self addTextField: @"Alternate␣Button"];
40     [self addTextField: @"Other␣Button"];
41 }
42 - (NSString*)textAtIndex: (NSInteger)index
43 {
44     DOMHTMLInputElement *textField = [formElements objectAtIndex: index];
45     return textField.value;
46 }
47 - (void)formSubmitted
48 {
49     NSAlert *alert =
50         [NSAlert alertWithMessageText: @"Form␣completed"
51                         defaultButton: [self textAtIndex: 0]
52                       alternateButton: [self textAtIndex: 1]
53                           otherButton: [self textAtIndex: 2]
54             informativeTextWithFormat: @"Buttons␣created␣from␣form␣elements
                 "];
55     [alert runModal];
56 }
57 @end
```

The standard interfaces to WebKit do all of these steps in the background. These steps can take time to complete, which should not block the user interface, and the view may perform them incrementally, displaying the top of a large page before the whole thing has loaded.

When the entire page has been loaded, the delegate method on line 34 will be called. This will be called because this class registered itself as the frame load delegate on line 16. After the page is loaded, the DOM tree will have been completely created, and so we can get the DOM element for the **<div>** in the template. This is done using a standard DOM method. If you have written any client-side JavaScript, then you will almost certainly have used the `getElementById()` method on the DOM document object before. The Objective-C version does exactly the same thing, returning the DOM element with the specified unique ID. The **id** attribute is required to be unique in the document and so this always returns zero or one elements.

After fetching the placeholder DOM element where the form entries will be inserted, we create three text field form elements by calling the `-addTextField:`

method three times. This method, beginning on line 19, shows how to construct simple DOM elements in Objective-C.

The DOM bindings are not very well documented. The documentation included with XCode and on the Apple site just contains the IDL, not the Objective-C interfaces. You can find out what each of these methods are meant to do by reading the W3C documentation at `http://www.w3.org/DOM/`. Don't try to create DOM objects as you would other Objective-C objects; they will throw an exception if sent an `-init` message. You must create them in the context of a DOM document. The `-createElement:` method on the DOM document creates a new element of the specified type. This is called twice, once on line 24 and again on line 28, to create **<p>** and **<input>** elements. This will create instances of the correct `DOMElement` subclass for the specified element type. Note that the return type is declared as `DOMElement`, so you need an explicit cast to get the expected kind. This is quite fragile—if you made a typo in the parameter name, it will break at run time but be undetected at compile time—so make sure you test every method that uses this call.

The text field DOM object is added to the `formElements` collection on line 26 so that we can retrieve it later. This is not strictly required. We could give it a unique ID and use the standard DOM methods to get it later. For a more complex implementation, you could add a KVC-compliant accessor that would automatically get the value corresponding to a named form element. For this simple version, we just provide the method on line 42, which returns the value for a text field at a specific index.

This simple form just puts the caption directly in a paragraph followed by the text field. This is quite poor HTML, and results in the kind of uneven layout shown in Figure 16.4. You can improve these by using nested **<div>** tags or even a table. Try extending this example to wrap the form elements in **<div>** tags and provide some CSS in the template to style them correctly.

The DOM tree is a hierarchy, and so nodes are inserted by adding them as children of existing entries. We use the same method, `-appendChild:`, to first add the text field to the paragraph and then to add the paragraph to the template **<div>**.

When the user clicks on the Submit button, the view's policy delegate will be called, and will, in turn, call the `-formSubmitted` method in this class. This is just a simple example, so we construct and show an `NSAlert` from the three fields to demonstrate that the values were correctly accessed.

You can access the form's values at any point, not just when the user hits submit. This can be used to validate entries. The web view's delegates are also able to handle any JavaScript events, so you can trigger validation in Objective-C by sending these events to the view from your code, or you can validate entirely in JavaScript.

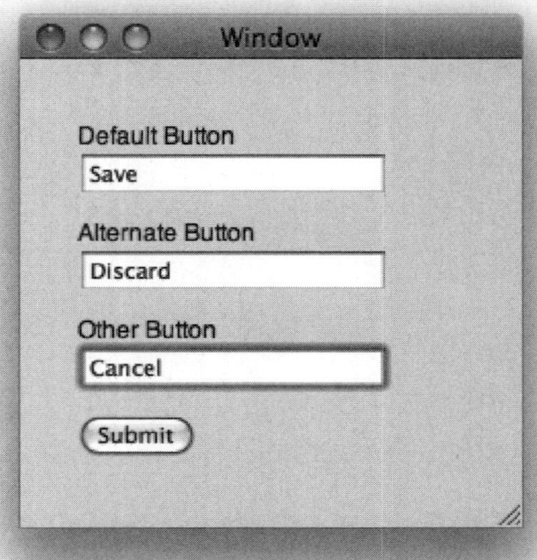

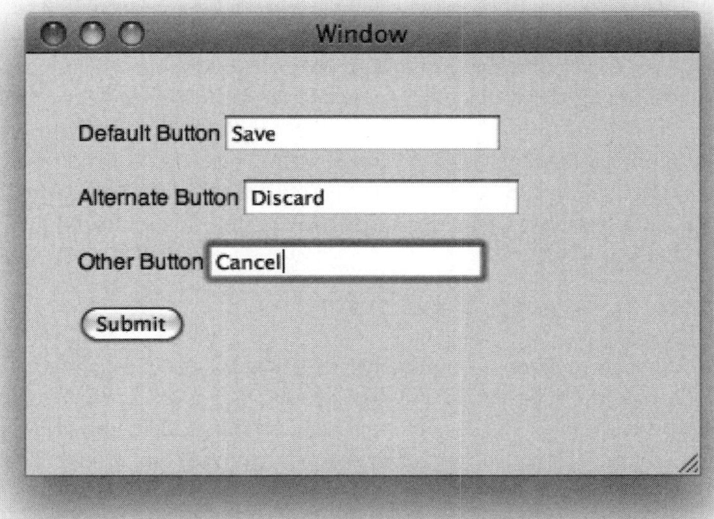

Figure 16.4: Resizing a form rendered with WebKit.

Figure 16.5: Submitting the form.

The easiest way of calling Objective-C from this kind of form is to use the exact same mechanism that we are already using to submit it. When the form is submitted, the policy delegate is called to decide what should be done. Our current implementation ignored the `request` parameter. This responds to a `-URL` message, returning the URL of the submitted form. You can use this to trigger different actions. Alternatively, you can export Objective-C objects as JavaScript global objects and call them directly; check the WebKit documentation to see how to do this.

You may have noticed that this form uses the Helvetica font used as the standard system typeface on OS X, rather than the Times font that is the default for web views. This is configured in Interface Builder for this example.

16.4 PDF and Quartz

PDF files have been mentioned before in several places in this book. The Quartz display system on OS X uses a PDF-like rendering model, which makes it very easy to load and display PDF files. PDF is used as the format for serialized Quartz display lists; you can trivially map everything displayed on screen to a PDF file and back again.

You have always been able to load, display, and create PDFs in OS X using `NSView` and `NSImage`. You can generate a PDF from any view by sending it a `-drawRect:` message with the current graphics context drawing to a PDF. We saw how to do this in Chapter 13. You can then load the resulting image back by

> **Reinventing Display PostScript**
>
> Anyone who wrote code for the early NeXT machines, or used Sun's NeWS system will find this eerily familiar. On these systems, the display server was sent short PostScript programs, which implemented view objects and sent events back to the controllers. The interface described in this section uses exactly the same idea. The display server, in this case, is a web view, and it uses HTML and CSS for layout and JavaScript for event handling, which is a lot easier to write by hand than PostScript, but the underlying idea is the same.
>
> One interesting thing about providing user interfaces in this way is that it makes it very easy to extend your application into a simple web app. Consider a music player that used this kind of view to display the playlist view. As well as displaying the page in a web view, it could dump it to a file that was shared by the OS X web server, and install a simple CGI program to handle form submissions by passing them back to the main program using distributed objects or some other mechanism. You could then control the application from a handheld device with a web browser.

sending an `NSImage` an `-initWithContentsOfFile:` and display it in an `NSImageView` or similar.

OS X 10.4 added the *PDFKit framework* to provide better support for PDFs. This is part of the Quartz framework, but extends the standard drawing functions to provide support for inspecting PDF documents.

The front end to PDFKit is the `PDFView` class, which displays a PDF document in a standard Cocoa view. Unlike an image view, this retains the structure of the underlying PDF and draws it as a structured document. It also understands the notion of a PDF page and allows the user to navigate around a document by jumping to pages or by searching for text strings.

As with WebKit, the PDFKit framework provides both model and view classes. A PDF view typically has a `PDFDocument` instance associated with it. This class encapsulates a complete PDF document, providing access to its global properties and allowing searching.

A PDF document has, generally speaking, two kinds of contents. Pages, containing PDF drawing commands that are rendered to give a raster image for screen display or printing, and metadata. Pages are represented by the `PDFPage` class.

Although most of the underlying drawing model is the same, PDF pages are very different to PostScript pages. With PostScript, you generated pages by issuing a set of drawing commands that drew into a raster buffer and then sending an end page command. Because PostScript contained loops and other complex flow-control structures, the only way of getting to a specific page was to start running the program at the beginning and discard every page before the one you wanted, which could be very slow. A PDF document, in contrast, has a page structure embedded directly in it. Each page is a separate section in the document, allowing you to jump directly to a given page.

Another major difference between PDF and PostScript is how text is rendered. In PostScript, the generating program would create short routines for drawing each glyph and just call them when drawing the page. PDF documents include the text directly, along with the font outlines used to draw the glyphs in the output. If the PDF file is created from something that makes use of this, rather than using the old PostScript technique, the text is searchable.

You can access the contents of a PDF page as a string or attributed string. This doesn't let you edit the text, but can be useful for importing PDF data into other applications.

16.5 Displaying PDFs

To demonstrate the basic support for PDFs in Cocoa, we'll write a simple PDF inspector. Note that, although the documentation refers to linking against PDFKit.framework in a number of places, you won't find this file in the system frameworks directory. It is an inner framework of Quartz.framework. The simplest option for applications wanting to use PDFKit is to link against the Quartz framework and get the PDFKit framework indirectly.

This example will display a four-pane user interface, as shown in Figure 16.6. The middle view is a `PDFView` containing the document. The left pane is another view provided by PDFKit, a `PDFThumbnailView`, which displays a thumbnail representation of the document. On the right, we create an `NSOutlineView` that will show the document outline. At the bottom, we will put a text view containing the attributed string representation of the current page.

Listing 16.6: A PDF viewer controller class. [from: examples/PDFInspector/PDFController.m]

```
#import "PDFController.h"

@implementation PDFController
@synthesize document;
- (void)awakeFromNib
{
    NSNotificationCenter *center =
        [NSNotificationCenter defaultCenter];
    [center addObserver: self
               selector: @selector(pageChanged:)
```

```
                 name: PDFViewPageChangedNotification
               object: view];
    [center addObserver: self
               selector: @selector(pageChanged:)
                   name: PDFViewDocumentChangedNotification
                 object: view];
}
- (IBAction)open: (id)sender
{
    NSOpenPanel *panel = [NSOpenPanel openPanel];
    [panel runModalForTypes: [NSArray arrayWithObject: @"pdf"]];
    NSURL *url = [NSURL fileURLWithPath: [panel filename]];
    self.document = [[[PDFDocument alloc] initWithURL: url] autorelease];
    [view setDocument: document];
    [outline reloadData];
}
- (id)outlineView: (NSOutlineView*)outlineView
            child: (NSInteger)index
           ofItem: (PDFOutline*)item
{
    if (nil == item)
    {
        item = [document outlineRoot];
    }
    return [item childAtIndex: index];
}
- (BOOL)outlineView: (NSOutlineView *)outlineView
   isItemExpandable: (PDFOutline*)item
{
    if (item == nil)
    {
        return YES;
    }
    return [item numberOfChildren] > 0;
}
- (NSInteger)outlineView: (NSOutlineView *)outlineView
  numberOfChildrenOfItem: (PDFOutline*)item
{
    if (item == nil)
    {
        item = [document outlineRoot];
    }
    return [item numberOfChildren];
}
```

```
55 -          (id)outlineView: (NSOutlineView*)outlineView
56 objectValueForTableColumn: (NSTableColumn*)tableColumn
57                     byItem: (PDFOutline*)item
58 {
59     return [item label];
60 }
61 - (void)pageChanged: (NSNotification*)aNotification
62 {
63     NSAttributedString *text = [[view currentPage] attributedString];
64     [[textView textStorage] setAttributedString: text];
65 }
66 - (void)outlineViewSelectionDidChange: (NSNotification*)notification
67 {
68     PDFOutline *item = [outline itemAtRow: [outline selectedRow]];
69     [view goToPage: [[item destination] page]];
70 }
71 @end
```

When this object awakes, it registers for two notifications from the PDF view. These both cause the same method to be called. One is triggered when the page changes, and the other when the document changes. One of these will be caused by our own code, loading a new PDF file, while the other is triggered by the user, scrolling or jumping around the displayed document.

These notifications call the method on line 61, which updates the text view. This gets the current page of the document and asks it for an attributed string representation. The current page is a slightly fuzzy term in a PDF view. If you have configured the view to display a single page at once, there is a well-defined current page; the one currently on the screen. When the view is in continuous-scrolling mode, it will display the entire document with a short gap between pages. The current page in this case will be the page that is taking up more than half of the screen, biased slightly to account for scrolling direction.

The action method on line 18 is connected to the Open menu item. This shows a modal open panel and creates a PDF document object from the selected file. When a new document is loaded, we need to update all of the views. We update the center view manually by setting its document. The thumbnail view has its `PDFView` outlet connected to the main view in Interface Builder, so it will update itself automatically. Something similar happens with the text view. The controller class will receive the notification that the document has changed and update the text view, as mentioned earlier. The final view that needs updating is the outline view. We send this a `-reloadData` message, causing it to call the data source methods, shown on line 27–60, to get the new outline.

The outline is generated by inspecting the hierarchy of `PDFOutline` objects associated with the document. A lot of PDFs include a tree of outline items in

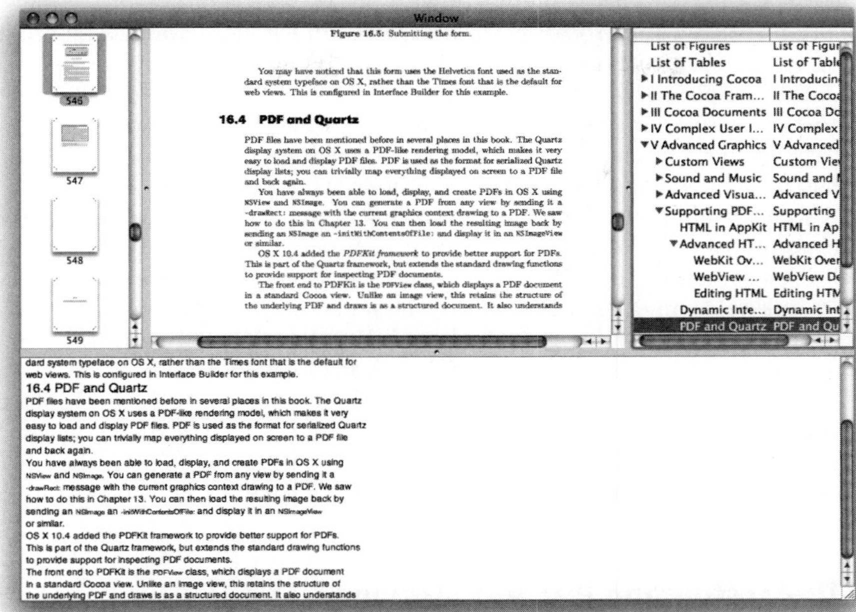

Figure 16.6: A simple PDF-viewing application.

the metadata representing the table of contents. Typically, typesetting programs will generate these automatically from sections and subsections. These allow the user to navigate the document easily by jumping to a particular section.

The outline document has a root outline node, and this contains a set of children. We use these to populate the outline view's structure. Each of these items has several properties associated with it. A PDF document can define the initial view state of the outline. You can retrieve this by sending `-isOpen` messages to the outline items and setting up the outline view's disclosure state depending on the result. This is often done to automatically expand chapters, but not sections and subsections, in a complex outline. Try extending the example to respect this setting.

As well as the title, each outline item has an action and a destination. We use the destination on line 69. When the selection in the outline view changes, we retrieve the newly selected PDF outline object and use its destination to jump to the correct page. This is only a rough approximation of the right thing. A destination is an accurate location within the document. It contains a point and a page. The page is a `PDFPage` object and the point is an `NSPoint` within that page.

A more complete PDF viewer, such as Preview on OS X, will scroll the PDF view to the destination. This is very easy to implement; you just need to call `-goToDestination:` on the view, instead of `-goToPage:`. This wasn't done for the example, to highlight the fact that destinations are not opaque pointers.

We aren't using the outline's action in this example. `PDFAction` is an abstract superclass representing a small family of actions that are allowed to happen when you click on something in a PDF document. This can be a link inside the document, a link to some other URL, or a command to control the viewer. You can send the action a `-type` message to find out which subclass a given instance really is, which is faster than sending a set of `-isKindOfClass:` messages.

This viewer demonstrates most of the simple features of PDFKit. It shows a PDF document and allows the user to navigate around it by scrolling within the document, clicking on thumbnails, or by selecting outline items from the table of contents. This is more than you need for just displaying PDF documents in a Cocoa application.

16.5.1 Understanding PDF Annotations

PDF was intended to provide a file format that represented electronic paper. You typically use PDFs in workflows that would have used paper previously. For example, if you want to send someone a copy of a document to read, you can either print it and post it, or create a PDF and email it. Adobe, the format's creators, quickly discovered that one of the main reasons that people printed things was to doodle on them.

PDF allows a number of different types of annotation. The most familiar is the sticky note type. This is displayed in different ways by different editors. They are traditionally shown as some kind of icon and then pop up to display a sticky note where the user clicked. Newer versions of Adobe's PDF reader show them in a separate section at the bottom of the display, and Preview on OS X 10.5 displays them in a panel to the side. PDFKit did not originally provide a standard mechanism for displaying this kind of annotation, but with Leopard it added support for automatically displaying pop-up annotations in a sidebar as used by Preview.

Each annotation in a PDF document is described by a subclass of `PDFAnnotation`. This class contains a number of attributes defining the annotation. This includes where it is drawn, what kind of annotation it represents, and the text contents.

The typical sticky note annotation is represented by two objects. The icon on the page is an instance of PDFAnnotationText. This defines the icon type and the location on the page where the icon should be displayed. The icon is not stored in the file as an image, just as a type. Different PDF viewers may render different icons for each type of sticky-note annotation.

Getting the PDF Specification

The more advanced features of PDFKit require you to understand the PDF document model and some of the more intricate parts of the specification. You can download a copy of the specification from Adobe (http://www.adobe.com/devnet/pdf/pdf_reference.html). This document gets longer with every version of the specification and is currently heading toward 2,000 pages. Unless you have a deep love of electronic formats, you probably don't want to read all of it. Fortunately, it is well structured and it is generally quite easy to find the relevant part of the specification when they are mentioned by the PDFKit documentation.

You can change the way annotations are displayed by instructing a page not to display annotations itself, and then handling the drawing yourself. The example shown in Listing 16.7 displays annotations in a text box under the page view, as shown in Figure 16.7.

Listing 16.7: Overriding annotation display. [from: examples/PDFAnnotationViewer/AnnotationController.m]

```
#import "AnnotationController.h"

@implementation AnnotationController
- (void)awakeFromNib
{
    NSNotificationCenter *center =
    [NSNotificationCenter defaultCenter];
    [center addObserver: self
               selector: @selector(pageChanged:)
                   name: PDFViewPageChangedNotification
                 object: view];
}
- (IBAction)open: (id)sender
{
    NSOpenPanel *panel = [NSOpenPanel openPanel];
    [panel runModalForTypes: [NSArray arrayWithObject: @"pdf"]];
    NSURL *url = [NSURL fileURLWithPath: [panel filename]];
    [document release];
```

```
    document = [[PDFDocument alloc] initWithURL: url];
    for (NSUInteger i=0 ; i<[document pageCount] ; i++)
    {
        PDFPage *page = [document pageAtIndex: i];
        [page setDisplaysAnnotations: NO];
        for (PDFAnnotation *note in [page annotations])
        {
            PDFAnnotationPopup *popup = [note popup];
            if ([popup isOpen])
            {
                [popup setIsOpen: NO];
            }
        }
    }
    [view setDocument: document];
    [self pageChanged: nil];
}
- (void)pageChanged: (NSNotification*)aNotification
{
    PDFPage *page = [view currentPage];
    NSMutableString *notes = [NSMutableString string];
    for (PDFAnnotation *note in [page annotations])
    {
        NSString *contents = [note contents];
        if (contents != nil)
        {
            [notes appendString: [note contents]];
        }
    }
    NSRange range = NSMakeRange(0, [[noteBox textStorage] length]);
    [[noteBox textStorage] replaceCharactersInRange: range
                                         withString: notes];
}
@end
```

When the file is opened, but before it is displayed, we have to do two things. First, turn off annotation display for every page. This prevents the pages from drawing their annotations when the view asks them to draw themselves to the screen. The second thing is close any open pop-up annotations. Without the second step, the view would not display the annotations, but would still reserve space in the sidebar for them, so the PDF would suddenly jump to the right when you got to a page containing an annotation.

As with the last example, this registers for a notification when the page changes. The notification handler simply iterates over all of the annotations in

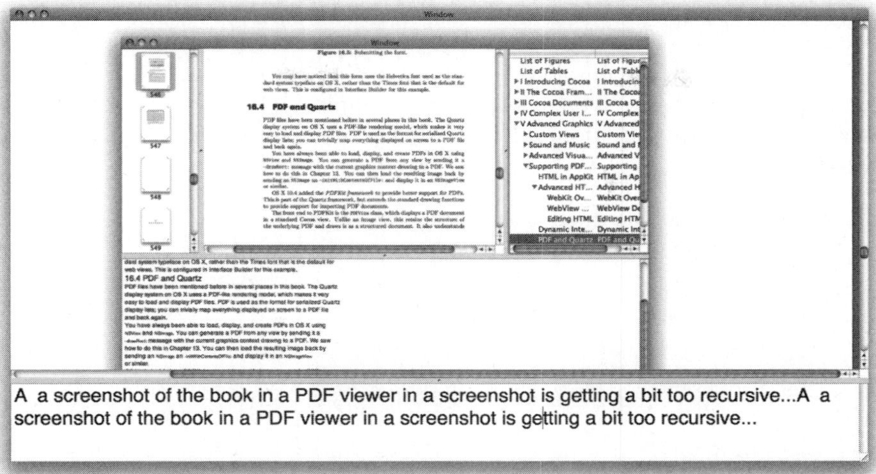

A a screenshot of the book in a PDF viewer in a screenshot is getting a bit too recursive...A a
screenshot of the book in a PDF viewer in a screenshot is getting a bit too recursive...

Figure 16.7: Displaying PDF annotations.

the new page. Note that in Figure 16.7 you can see what appears to be the same annotation twice. This is because pop-up annotations have the same text as the text annotation that launches them. You can explicitly exclude the pop-up annotations from the list to avoid this.

Note that, at the time of writing, there is no way to disable a particular type of annotation, and so this will disable things like lines and boxes that have been added as annotations, as well as text annotations. If this is not the desired behavior, you have two options. You can either add support for drawing all of the different types of annotation yourself, or you can individually disable the annotations you don't want to show.

Annotations respond to a `-setShouldDisplay:` message, which indicates whether they should be drawn. Try modifying the loop that runs when a document loads to use this method to only disable some kinds of annotation. You can create annotations in Preview for testing this.

16.5.2 Setting Document Metadata

Every PDF document contains a set of metadata fields describing how the document was created, and by whom. These are stored by the `PDFDocument` object as a dictionary. You can access them by sending a `-documentAttributes` message to the document and set them with a `-setDocumentAttributes:` method.

Listing 16.8 shows a simple command-line tool that extracts these fields and prints any that are set. This contains two simple functions. The first prints a key-value pair from a dictionary, if it exists. The second loads the document attributes.

Listing 16.8: Print document metadata for a PDF file. [from: examples/PDFInfo/PrintInfo.m]

```
#import <Cocoa/Cocoa.h>
#import <Quartz/Quartz.h>

void printAttribute(NSDictionary *attributes,
                    const char *title,
                    id key)
{
    id attribute = [attributes objectForKey: key];
    if (nil != attribute)
    {
        printf("%s:␣%s\n", title,
            [[attribute description] UTF8String]);
    }
}

int main(int argc, char **argv)
{
    if (argc != 2) { return 1; };
    [NSAutoreleasePool new];
    NSString *path = [NSString stringWithUTF8String: argv[1]];
    NSURL *url = [NSURL fileURLWithPath: path];
    PDFDocument *doc = [[PDFDocument alloc] initWithURL: url];
    NSDictionary *attributes = [doc documentAttributes];
    printAttribute(attributes, "Title", PDFDocumentTitleAttribute);
    printAttribute(attributes, "Author", PDFDocumentAuthorAttribute);
    printAttribute(attributes, "Creator", PDFDocumentCreatorAttribute);
    printAttribute(attributes, "Subject", PDFDocumentSubjectAttribute);
    printAttribute(attributes, "Producer", PDFDocumentProducerAttribute);
    printAttribute(attributes, "Creation␣Date",
        PDFDocumentCreationDateAttribute);
    printAttribute(attributes, "Modification␣Date",
        PDFDocumentModificationDateAttribute);
    printAttribute(attributes, "Keywords", PDFDocumentKeywordsAttribute);
    return 0;
}
```

You can try running this on PDF various documents and see what they have set, like this:

```
$ gcc -framework Quartz -framework Cocoa PrintInfo.m
$ ./a.out /Applications/Mail.app/Contents/Resources/Mailbox_Alert.pdf
Title: URLButton_down
Creator: Adobe Illustrator CS2
Producer: Mac OS X 10.5 Quartz PDFContext
Creation Date: 2007-07-13 00:29:26 +0100
Modification Date: 2007-07-13 00:29:26 +0100
```

The inspector in Preview displays the same information. This will be automatically indexed by Spotlight (see Chapter 17). If you are creating PDF files from your application, then setting the relevant fields will make it easier for the user to find the PDF in the future. In particular, you should set the title attribute to something meaningful.

To set the metadata, just populate a dictionary with the same keys used here and pass it as the argument to `-setDocumentAttributes:`. Most of these properties are strings. The two exceptions are the dates, which should be `NSDate` instances, and the keywords attribute, which is an array of strings.

You may wish to allow the user to modify these when you export a document as a PDF, or provide similar metadata fields in your document type and use these when exporting.

16.5.3 Editing PDFs

PDFKit does not currently provide direct support for editing PDF documents beyond adding annotations. The format is not really designed for editing—it loses a lot of the information that the source format typically uses for editing—but it can sometimes be useful to draw over a page.

You can create new `PDFPage` instances from images. You can also create images from individual pages. This allows you to do some basic editing, although it can lose some of the information from the original PDF. You can also use the standard Cocoa printing system to generate PDF data.

To show how all of these fit together, we will write a simple application for watermarking PDF pages. Technically, a watermark should go behind the other details on the page, and this version will draw it on top. Doing the opposite is slightly harder—you need to create the view hierarchy the other way around—and is left as an exercise to the reader.

The code for doing this is shown in Listing 16.9. As before, this opens a single PDF file and displays it in a PDF view. It also provides an image well (an editable

`NSImageView` instance) that the user can drop any kind of image onto. When you hit the export button, it writes out the displayed page to the desktop with the image drawn over it. Figure 16.9 shows the resulting PDF opened in Preview. Note that the text is highlighted; the export process has not destroyed any of the information in the original PDF. This PDF was generated from one of the informative PDF files included with OS X and a bitmap image that is included with the Apple developer tools, as shown in Figure 16.8.

This simple example only works on a single page. Doing the same thing to multiple pages is not conceptually harder, it just requires a bit more code. This was omitted intentionally to keep the example simple.

Listing 16.9: Watermarking a PDF page. [from: examples/PDFWatermark/PDFWatermark.m]

```
@implementation PDFWatermark
- (IBAction)open: (id)sender
{
    NSOpenPanel *panel = [NSOpenPanel openPanel];
    [panel runModalForTypes: [NSArray arrayWithObject: @"pdf"]];
    NSURL *url = [NSURL fileURLWithPath: [panel filename]];
    PDFDocument *doc = [[PDFDocument alloc] initWithURL: url];
    [pdf setDisplaysPageBreaks: NO];
    [pdf setDocument: doc];
    [doc release];
    [self applyWatermark: self];
}
- (IBAction)applyWatermark: (id)sender
{
    [waterMark removeFromSuperview];
    NSView *pdfDocView = [pdf documentView];
    waterMark = [[NSImageView alloc] initWithFrame: [pdfDocView bounds]];
    [pdfDocView addSubview: waterMark];
    [waterMark setImage: [waterMarkWell image]];
    [waterMark release];
}
- (IBAction)export: (id)sender
{
    NSView *pdfDocView = [pdf documentView];
    NSData *pdfData =
        [pdfDocView dataWithPDFInsideRect: [pdfDocView bounds]];
    NSString *savePath =
        [@"~/Desktop/WatermarkedPDFPage.pdf" stringByExpandingTildeInPath];
    [pdfData writeToFile: savePath
              atomically: NO];
}
@end
```

Most of the -open: method will look familiar. Note the -setDisplaysPageBreaks: message on line 11. This is important because without it the view would draw a border around the page, even when exporting its contents as a PDF. The exported PDF would contain a page containing the original page with a gray border, which is not what we want.

The interesting code starts in the -applyWatermark: method on line 16. The waterMark instance variable is an NSImageView instance that is created at run time and inserted into the view hierarchy. The -documentView message, sent to the PDF view, returns the view that is responsible for drawing the PDF data. The PDF view, like the text view, hides a small view hierarchy, including a scroll view and various other subviews. We need to insert the watermark view into this subview directly to have it drawn correctly.

This method is triggered explicitly when a new document is loaded, and as a result of an action message sent from the image well when the user drags an image into it. This implementation just inserts a single image view on top of the PDF, but you can create any views in this hierarchy. If you want to draw some text over a PDF, try creating an NSTextField or NSTextView. The only thing you need to remember is that the views you insert should be told not to draw an opaque background, unless you want white rectangles all over the resulting PDF.

We export the page from the final method in this class. This dumps the resulting PDF into a file on the user's desktop. Not the most elegant solution, but sufficient for a simple example. Note that we don't use anything specific to PDFKit in this method beyond the first line, which gets the correct view to draw. The -dataWithPDFInsideRect: method comes from NSView and is part of the printing system, and the resulting PDF is written to the disk using a standard NSData method.

There are several limitations to this approach. The most obvious is that it will only work on a single page. We can work around that by creating a new PDF page object from the PDF data stream, rather than writing it directly to the disk. Unfortunately, the only way of creating a PDF page directly is from an NSImage. You might think that you could create an image object from an NSPDFImageRep and then get a new PDF page from this image. This works, but it rasterizes the PDF data and generates a new page containing a bitmap image representation of the page. This makes the file size much larger and destroys the ability to extract text from the PDF, as well as losing the resolution-independence of the original.

Fortunately, there is a simple indirect way of generating a PDF page. The PDF data is a complete PDF document and so we can create a new PDFDocument and then extract the page, like this:

```
PDFDocument *newDoc =
    [[[PDFDocument alloc] initWithData: pdfData] autorelease];
PDFPage *newPage = [newDoc pageAtIndex: 0];
```

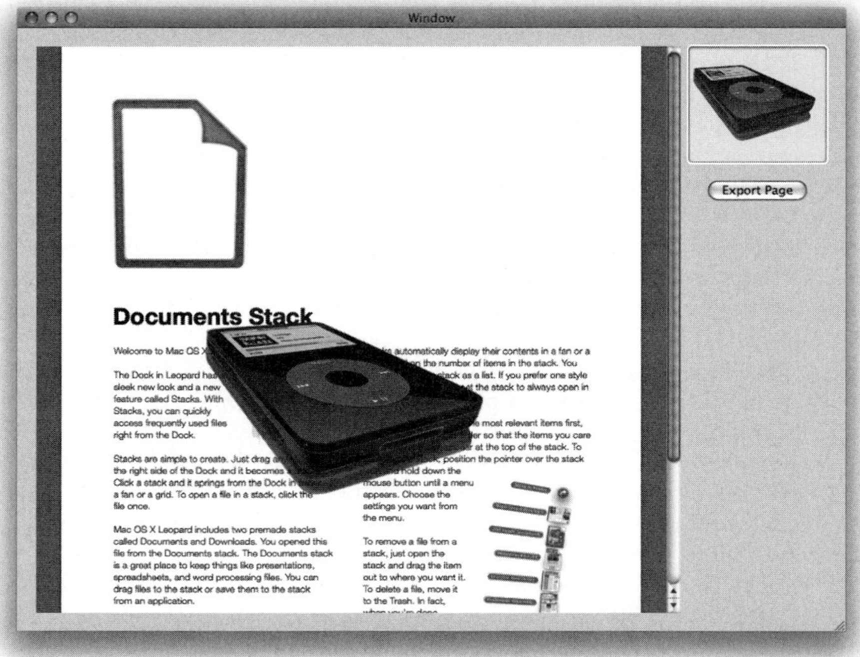

Figure 16.8: Adding an image to a PDF.

Note that the page will no longer be retained by the document once we have destroyed the document. By autoreleasing the document, rather than releasing it, we defer this destruction until after we have finished with the page.

This new page can then be inserted into the old document by sending it an `-insertPage:atIndex:` message. This still isn't a perfect solution. Try using this example with a PDF containing annotations and then open the exported page in Preview. You will see that it has flattened the annotations. If the original contained pop-up notes, the new version will display them in their open position and turn them into part of the PDF data, rather than the metadata.

We can avoid this behavior easily by turning off annotation display, as we did in an earlier example. This lets us modify the PDF data correctly, but now loses annotations. The final step in a complete solution is to move the annotations across from the old page. We saw earlier how to iterate over the annotations in a

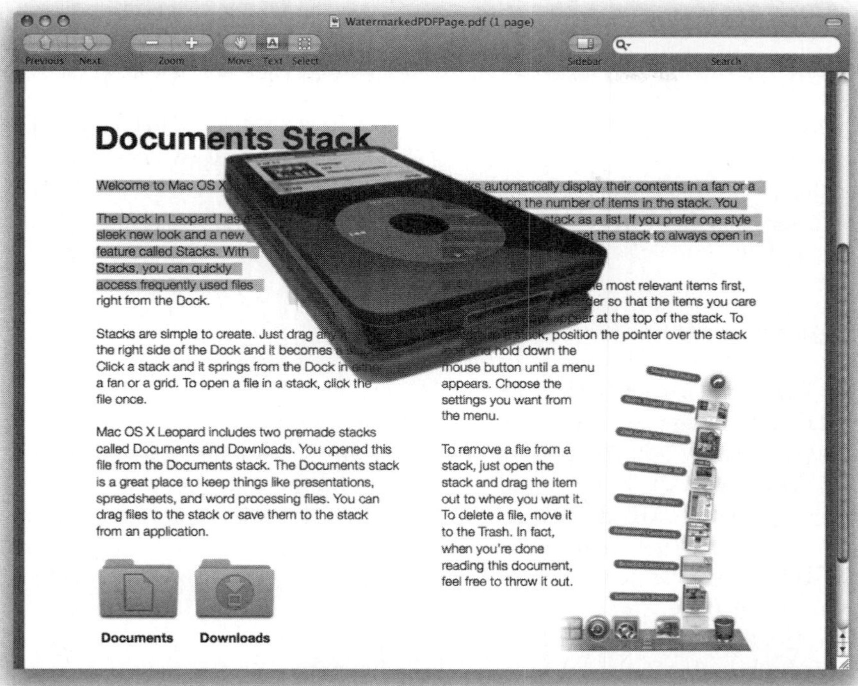

Figure 16.9: Opening the watermarked PDF in Preview.

page. You need to do this with the annotations on the original `PDFPage` and send the new one an `-addAnnotation:` message for each one. The full implementation would contain these steps:

1. Create a PDF data stream by sending a `-dataWithPDFInsideRect:` message to the view.
2. Create a new PDF page object by loading this data into a `PDFDocument` and getting the first page.
3. Copy the annotations over from the original page.
4. Remove the original page from the document by sending it a `-removePageAtIndex:` message.

5. Insert the new page into the document, replacing the original.

If you follow all of these steps, you can replace an existing page in a PDF document with a new page that contains a modified version of the old one. Note that this doesn't let you edit the structures in the original page, but it does let you draw over them. There was a case a few years ago with government departments using this technique to censor documents before release, drawing black boxes over the sensitive words. This appeared to work on screen, but the original data was still present in the PDFs and could be extracted relatively easily.

16.6 Summary

In this chapter we have looked at two important frameworks in OS X, WebKit and PDFKit. These provide support for HTML and PDF documents in Cocoa programs, allowing you to open, display, edit, and export files of these types.

We first looked at WebKit and saw how to implement a trivial web browser. WebKit exposes HTML documents as structured documents and we saw how to examine this structure using the DOM interfaces and modify it. We created a simple HTML editor using WebKit and a class for generating forms using the WebKit layout code.

Finally, we looked at PDFKit, part of the Quartz umbrella framework. This provides high-level manipulation of PDF documents. We saw how to inspect and modify PDF metadata, as well as how to generate and modify PDF files.

You should now be able to create Cocoa applications that incorporate support for PDF and HTML data, both as simple readers and as generators.

Part VI

User Interface Integration

Chapter 17

Searching and Filtering

Searching is an important part of any data-driven application. Often you will begin writing an application with no search support. At some point, you will realize that users expect it, and implement something that iterates over all of the objects in a document and compares. Finally, you will discover that this is too slow on large documents and implement proper indexing.

With 10.3, Apple introduced the *Search Kit framework*. This framework is designed to make it easy for you to create indexes and integrate them into your search. If you have used Apache Lucene on other platforms, you will be familiar with most of the concepts behind Search Kit.

The main use of Search Kit and Spotlight is to perform mappings from queries to documents. A common example of this would be finding the email that contains a specific keyword or phrase. If you've been using Macs for a few years, you may remember that starting Mail for the first time in OS X 10.4 was very slow. Apple switched the way it stored mail from the older mbox format to the maildir format, where there is one file per email. This translation took a while, and using Spotlight to build indexes of the new structure took even longer. Once it was done, however, searching was a lot faster than it had been previously. Search Kit was not the only reason for this switch—deleting from maildir is a lot easier than from mbox mail stores—but it was one of them.

Search Kit creates mappings to document URLs. By putting each email message in a separate file, the application guaranteed that each one had a different URL. Often you may wish to provide slightly more fine-grained indexing, for example, by encoding a page number in the URL, too.

Search Kit is designed to be fast and not use too much space for its indexes. The more fine-grained you allow its search to become, the slower it will get overall. In general, you are better off using the Search Kit index as a quick first pass, and then using a more primitive search mechanism for narrow searching. You might generate an index for a PDF file when it is loaded, mapping to page numbers. A single page of text can then be searched very quickly, so you can easily find the instance of the search string within the page when you need to jump to it.

With OS X 10.4, Apple introduced *Spotlight*. This is built on top of Search Kit and indexes all of the files on your hard disk. Spotlight and Search Kit can work together. If you have written an import plugin for Spotlight, you can use this for Search Kit.

Both APIs are built on top of Core Foundation. They are not Objective-C frameworks, but they make use of the Core Foundation types that are toll-free bridged with Cocoa, and so can be easily used from Objective-C code.

17.1 Maintaining Document Indexes

If you want to use Search Kit in your application, you need to maintain a set of indexes. The most common type of index you will create is an *inverted index*, which maps from terms to documents. Documents, as mentioned earlier, are uniquely identified by URL. Terms are simple text strings.

For efficient storage, both terms and document URLs are stored in a normalized form. Each term is given a unique integer identifier in an index, and so is each URL. The index is then a very long list of pairs of integers. Starting with a term, you first look up the unique identifier for that term, then look up the values for it in the index, and then get the resulting URLs.

There are two ways of importing text from a document into an index. You can either do it all yourself, or you can delegate it to Search Kit. Prior to 10.4, Search Kit exposed an API for registering text importers. These were simple plugins that allowed a document to be translated into a text representation. Starting with OS X 10.4, the Spotlight metadata import plugin subsumed this rôle. If Spotlight knows how to handle a particular kind of file, you do not need to extract the text yourself.

17.1.1 Creating an Index

The first step when using Search Kit is typically to create an index. There are two kinds of indexes supported by Search Kit: in-memory and on-disk. These are created using either a URL or a mutable data object as a store location. The mutable data versions are typically used for temporary indexes. You might use a three-tier approach to searching:

- Spotlight or Search Kit to find one or more documents

- Search Kit with a temporary index to find a section in a document
- Linear searching to find the exact location of the term

You can also create in-memory indexes for transient data. A web browser might create a temporary index for all of the pages that a user visits in a single session, for example, to allow jumping back to relevant sections easily. This might be combined with a much larger index for searching every page the user has ever visited. Searching the small index will be faster, so it can be used to return search results immediately in response to a search, while waiting for the longer search to complete.

Both kinds of index have similar constructors. You can create an on-disk index with this function:

```
SKIndexRef SKIndexCreateWithURL(
    CFURLRef          inURL,                    // NSURL*
    CFStringRef       inIndexName,              // NSString*
    SKIndexType       inIndexType,
    CFDictionaryRef inAnalysisProperties); // NSDictionary*
```

The Cocoa types corresponding to the Core Foundation types are shown in comments at the end of the lines. The `SKIndexCreateWithMutableData()` function is almost identical, but takes a `CFMutableDataRef` (`NSMutableData*`) as the first argument.

The index name should be a unique name for this index. This is not currently used for anything, but should be unique. The third argument is the type of the index. There are three possible types. The most common kind is the inverted index, identified by `kSKIndexInverted`, which maps from terms to documents. You can go the other way with a vector index (`kSKIndexVector`). These are most often used for similarity searching, getting a list of documents that are like an example document, in terms of textual contents. The final kind, inverted-vector indexes (`kSKIndexInvertedVector`), combine the capabilities of both but take up more space. You can perform any kind of search on these, but unless you want to do similarity matching you can save a lot of space by using an inverted index.

The dictionary contains a number of properties describing how words are mapped to terms. You can use this to specify the minimum size for terms, words to ignore, words that have equivalent meanings, and various other things.

When you have finished with an index, you need to close it. This is done with the `SKIndexClose()` function, which takes an `SKIndexRef` as an argument.

While you may want to create in-memory indexes every time they are used, you probably won't do this with on-disk indexes. These are created once and then loaded later. Indexes are loaded from files using this function:

```
SKIndexRef SKIndexOpenWithURL(
    CFURLRef    inURL,          // NSURL*
    CFStringRef inIndexName,    // NSString*
    Boolean     inWriteAccess); // BOOL
```

This takes the URL where an index was originally created as the first argument and a name as the second. The flag indicates whether the index should be opened for writing. You can reopen an in-memory index using similar functions that take either mutable or immutable data objects as arguments. These do not take an equivalent to the `inWriteAccess` parameter since the amount of access permitted is defined by the type of the data object.

> **Concurrent Indexing**
>
> Search Kit indexes are thread safe. A thread updating an index will not prevent others from searching it. Only one thread may write to an index, however. This is especially important when you have an index shared over multiple processes. You should use an `NSDistributedLock` or similar to ensure that only one process has it open for writing at any given time.

17.1.2 Indexing Documents

Once you have created your index, the next step is to add documents to it. A document is conceptually stored as a pair containing the URL and the full text of the document. When you add a document to the index, you need to provide both of these.

The first thing you need to do, before indexing the document, is create a unique reference for it. If your index is just mapping to files (or URLs), then you can use this simple function:

```
SKDocumentRef SKDocumentCreateWithURL(CFURLRef inURL);
```

This takes a URL object and returns a unique identifier representing it. For more complex indexes you can specify a little more information, using this function:

```
SKDocumentRef SKDocumentCreate(
    CFStringRef   inScheme, // NSString*
    SKDocumentRef inParent,
    CFStringRef   inName);  // NSString*
```

This will construct a URL for you from the provided information. The scheme is used as the URL scheme. This function is designed to allow you to easily index hierarchical information. The parent should be the name provided for some other document you have already indexed, and the name a unique identifier for this document. You could, for example, use the parent to identify a file and the name to be the title of a chapter, or a page number, within that file. Whichever of these functions you use, you must free the returned object later with `CFRelease()`.

There are two ways of adding a document to the index, depending on whether Spotlight already knows how to read this file type. This is the case for plain text, RTF, MS Word documents, and a number of other formats by default, and for any other formats where you have installed an import plugin. If this is the case, you can just tell Search Kit to index the file directly:

```
Boolean SKIndexAddDocument(
    SKIndexRef    inIndex,
    SKDocumentRef inDocument,
    CFStringRef   inMIMETypeHint, // NSString*
    Boolean       inCanReplace);  // BOOL
```

The MIME type hint provided here is your guess at the type of this file. Note that MIME types are bing phased out in OS X in favor of UTIs, so this function may be deprecated soon in favor of one that takes a UTI hint. The final flag indicates whether this operation is allowed to replace an existing index entry for this file. If the file is not understood by Spotlight, or is not on the local filesystem, you should call this function instead:

```
Boolean SKIndexAddDocumentWithText(
    SKIndexRef    inIndex,
    SKDocumentRef inDocument,
    CFStringRef   inDocumentText, // NSString*
    Boolean       inCanReplace);  // BOOL
```

This has a similar prototype, but requires you to provide the text contents yourself. This is the only way of providing index data for things that are not part of the filesystem.

After calling one or both of these functions on your index, it will be ready for searching.

17.1.3 Searching an Index

As of 10.4, Search Kit provides a completely asynchronous API for implementing searches. The older, synchronous, API is still available, but is now deprecated. When the user enters a search term, you should start the search running and periodically check for new results, adding them to the user interface as they are found. You can create a query using this function:

```
SKSearchRef SKSearchCreate(
    SKIndexRef      inIndex,
    CFStringRef     inQuery,
    SKSearchOptions inSearchOptions);
```

The first two arguments are the index to search and the query string. Note that you can have lots of different indexes in an application. A mail client, for example, has a different index for each header field and one for the body of the email.

When you call this function, Search Kit will spawn a new thread that will scan the index. This will continue to run until you call `SKSearchCancel()` to stop the search, or until it has scanned the entire index.

The search options are a set of flags from an enumerated type. By default, searches treat spaces in the query string as a Boolean AND operation and compute relevance scores for each of the results. You can alter this behavior by specifying one or more of these constants in the search options:

- `kSKSearchOptionNoRelevanceScores` tells the query not to compute relevance scores. This makes the search quicker and so should be used for any query where the user interface is not displaying scores.
- `kSKSearchOptionSpaceMeansOR` treats spaces as Boolean OR operations instead of ANDs. This causes the query to return results containing any of the words in the query, rather than all of them. The user can override this by putting "AND" between terms in the query string.
- `kSKSearchOptionFindSimilar` tells the query to perform similarity matching. This will treat the query string as a source document and try to find similar ones. This will be very slow if you create an inverted index. If you plan on making this kind of query, generate a vector index, or an inverted-vector index.

The query will buffer the results as it accumulates them. You should periodically fetch them by calling this function:

```
Boolean SKSearchFindMatches (
    SKSearchRef    inSearch,
    CFIndex        inMaximumCount,        // NSInteger
    SKDocumentID   *outDocumentIDsArray,
    float          *outScoresArray,
    CFTimeInterval maximumTime,           // NSTimeInterval
    CFIndex        *outFoundCount);       // NSInteger*
```

This function returns true if the search is still running. When it returns false, you can call `CFRelease()` on the `SKSearchRef` to free the search.

The `outDocumentIDsArray` and `outScoresArray` parameters should point to arrays of at least `inMaximumCount` elements. They will be populated with the documents and the scores for each result. The number of results found will be returned in the variable pointed to by `outFoundCount`.

Flushing the Index

Before you run a search, it is typically a good idea to flush the index. This is done by calling `SKIndexFlush()` with the index pointer as the argument. This will ensure that any changes made to the index have been committed. You should also consider doing this after indexing documents, to avoid the changes getting lost.

17.2 Displaying Search Boxes

Search Kit provides a mechanism for creating indexes and running searches, but does not provide any support for displaying a user interface. This is intentional. Search Kit is a low-level Core Foundation API that can be used by command-line tools and dæmons, as well as by Cocoa applications.

At the same time Search Kit was introduced, the `NSSearchField` and `NSSearchFieldCell` classes were added to AppKit. These two are extensions of `NSTextField` and `NSTextFieldCell`, respectively. They provide a simple user interface for search boxes, as shown in Figure 17.1.

For the most part, these boxes behave as if they were normal text fields. They provide a user interface tailored to searching, but still act like a normal text field. The biggest change is that they can send an action after every key press, rather than after the user presses Enter or the field stops being first responder.

The other main difference is the ability of the search field to maintain and display a menu of recent searches. This is done almost automatically for you. The menu used by the search field can be customized in Interface Builder, as shown in Figure 17.2.

To do this, you should create a new, free-standing, menu and add items to it. Each of the items in this menu should have their tag value set in the inspector. This menu has two items. The selected one, with the tag value of 1001 (`NSSearchFieldRecentsMenuItemTag`) is used as a placeholder. All of the recent searches will appear wherever this item is in the menu. The other item has its tag set to 1002 (`NSSearchFieldClearRecentsMenuItemTag`) and will clear the recent menu.

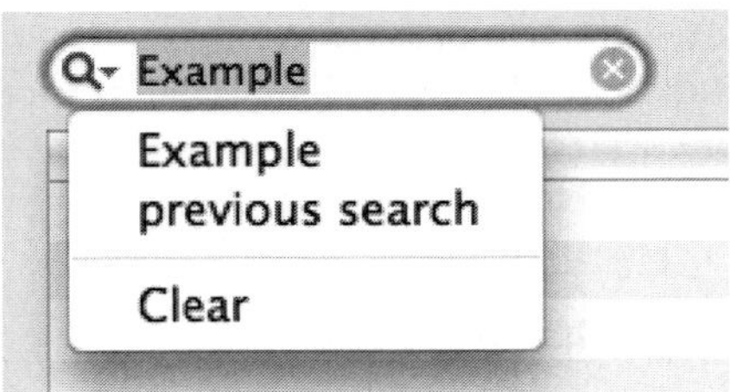

Figure 17.1: A search field showing a recent searches menu.

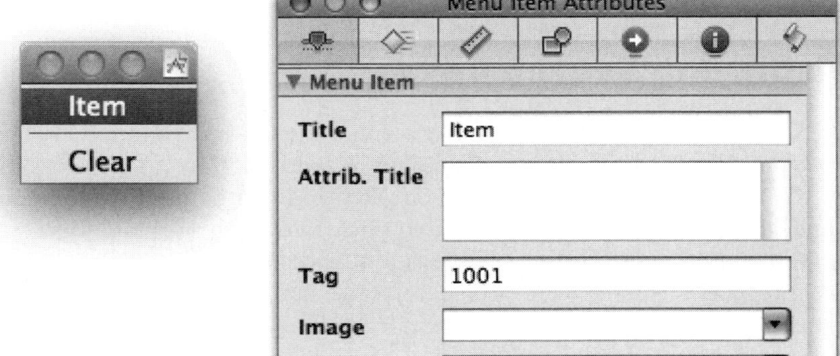

Figure 17.2: Defining a search menu template in Interface Builder.

This menu does not have items with tags set to `NSSearchFieldRecentsTitleMenuItemTag` or `NSSearchFieldNoRecentsMenuItemTag`. The first of these will only appear if there are recent searches, and can be used to present a title for the search items. The second will be used as a placeholder when there are no items in the menu. If you don't specify this, then you will just get a disabled menu item saying "Empty" when there are no recent searches.

When the menu is defined, you can connect it up to the cell's `searchMenuTemplate` outlet. Note that this outlet is supplied by the `NSSearchFieldCell`, not the view. You will need to click twice in Interface Builder to get at the cell before you can connect the outlet.

17.3 Searching for Documents

To demonstrate how all of these pieces fit together, we will write a simple UNIX manual viewer. The UNIX manual pages (man pages) are all stored in /usr/share/man on an OS X system as troff source code. You can turn them into plain text or HTML using the groff utility that ships with OS X.

This example will display a window like the one in Figure 17.3, with a search box at the top and a list of results underneath. The bottom part of the window will display the page currently selected from the results.

For our simple example, we will index them all as plain text, and display them in the same way. You might consider extending this example using a WebKit view to display them in a formatted way.

This example will use a helper class, shown in Listing 17.1. This is responsible for getting a string representation of a UNIX manual page.

Listing 17.1: Loading UNIX manual pages. [from: examples/ManSearch/ManPage.m]

```
#import "ManPage.h"

@implementation ManPage
- (id) initWithPath: (NSString*)aPath
{
    if (nil == (self = [self init])) { return nil; }
    path = [aPath retain];
    return self;
}
+ (ManPage*)manPageWithPath: (NSString*)aPath
{
    return [[[self alloc] initWithPath: aPath] autorelease];
}
- (void)dealloc
{
    [path release];
    [contents release];
    [super dealloc];
}
- (NSURL*)URL
{
    return [[[NSURL alloc] initFileURLWithPath: path] autorelease];
}
- (NSString*)stringValue
{
    if (contents == nil)
    {
```

```
28          id file = [NSFileHandle fileHandleForReadingAtPath: path];
29          if ([[path pathExtension] isEqualToString:@"gz"])
30          {
31              NSPipe *decompressed = [NSPipe pipe];
32              NSTask *gzcat = [[NSTask alloc] init];
33              [gzcat setLaunchPath: @"/usr/bin/gzcat"];
34              [gzcat setStandardInput: file];
35              [gzcat setStandardOutput: decompressed];
36              file = decompressed;
37              [gzcat launch];
38              [gzcat autorelease];
39          }
40          NSPipe *formatted = [NSPipe pipe];
41          NSTask *groff = [[NSTask alloc] init];
42          [groff setLaunchPath: @"/usr/bin/groff"];
43          [groff setCurrentDirectoryPath: [path
                stringByDeletingLastPathComponent]];
44          [groff setStandardInput: file];
45          [groff setStandardError: [NSFileHandle fileHandleWithNullDevice]];
46          [groff setStandardOutput: formatted];
47          [groff setArguments: [NSArray arrayWithObjects:
48              @"-Tutf8", @"-man", @"-P", @"-b", @"-P", @"-c",
49              @"-P", @"-d", @"-P", @"-u", nil]];
50          [groff launch];
51          NSData *pageData = [[formatted fileHandleForReading]
                readDataToEndOfFile];
52          [groff waitUntilExit];
53          [groff release];
54          contents = [[NSString alloc] initWithData: pageData
55                                           encoding: NSUTF8StringEncoding];
56      }
57      return contents;
58  }
59  @end
```

Most of the -stringValue method is responsible for typesetting the man page, and caching the result. This is done by running an instance of the groff program on the input file, with a set of command-line options defined to set the formatting options. These are defined on line 47–49. If you are interested in what these mean, consult the groff man page, but otherwise you can ignore them. We will look in more detail at how NSTask is used in Chapter 23. This method simply uses NSTask to invoke an instance of groff as a filter. The input source is passed through groff and a typeset UTF-8 string is created as output.

Man pages are often stored in a format compressed with gzip. These files need to be decompressed before they can be typeset. The code on lines 31–38 creates an instance of gzcat to handle the decompression, if it is required. This is connected to the groff process's standard input instead of the compressed file. This entire method is the equivalent of running one of these two commands in a terminal:

```
$ groff -Tutf8 -man -P -b -P -b -P -d -P -u < manpage
$ gzcat < manpage.gz| groff -Tutf8 -man -P -b -P -b -P -d -P -u
```

Now that we have a way of extracting text from a man page, we can begin building an index. This is done by the ManPageIndex class, shown in Listing 17.2.

Listing 17.2: Building an index of man pages. [from: examples/ManSearch/ManPageIndex.m]

```
@implementation ManPageIndex
- (void) awakeFromNib
{
    NSSet *stopWords = [NSSet setWithObjects:
        @"NAME", @"SYNOPSIS", @"DESCRIPTION",
        @"EXAMPLES", @"DIAGNOSTICS", @"ENVIRONMENT",
        @"COMPATIBILITY", @"STANDARDS", @"HISTORY",
        @"BUGS", nil];
    NSDictionary *attributes = [NSDictionary dictionaryWithObjectsAndKeys:
        [NSNumber numberWithInt: 4], kSKMinTermLength,
        stopWords, kSKStopWords,
        [NSNumber numberWithBool: YES], kSKProximityIndexing,
        nil];
    index = SKIndexCreateWithMutableData((CFMutableDataRef)[NSMutableData
        data],
                                  (CFStringRef)@"Man page index",
                                  kSKIndexInverted,
                                  (CFDictionaryRef)attributes);
    [self buildIndex];
}
- (SKIndexRef) searchIndex
{
    return index;
}
- (void) dealloc
{
    CFRelease(index);
    [super dealloc];
}
@end
```

The first part of this defines a set of stop words. These are words that will be excluded from the index. All of the words here are common section headings in man pages, and so we don't bother indexing them. If we did, then they would be found on almost every page and so would not help provide good results.

The other attributes we set, on lines 64 and 66, define the minimum word length and whether this index supports proximity indexing. Proximity indexing gives a higher score to documents that contain search words near each other than ones that have them far apart.

Once the attributes are defined, the object creates the index and then sends itself a `-buildIndex` message. This is implemented in the category shown in Listing 17.3. This takes advantage of the thread safety of the Search Kit framework to build the index in a background thread without blocking the user interface.

Note that we are creating a new index every time the program starts. This is not a good idea; it is done in this example to demonstrate the relative speeds of creating and searching the index. If you leave it running for long enough, then line 38 will be reached and it will tell you how long building the index took. This is likely to be several minutes, even on a fast computer. On a 2.16GHz MacBook Pro, it took almost a quarter of an hour, much longer than you'd want to wait for a program to become usable. In contrast, searching happens very quickly.

Listing 17.3: Adding man pages to the index. [from: examples/ManSearch/ManPageIndex.m]

```
4  @interface ManPageIndex (IndexingThread)
5  - (void)buildIndex;
6  - (void)indexManAtPath: (NSString*)path;
7  @end
8  
9  @implementation ManPageIndex (IndexingThread)
10 - (void)buildIndex
11 {
12     [self retain];
13     [NSThread detachNewThreadSelector: @selector(buildIndexInThread)
14                              toTarget: self
15                            withObject: nil];
16 }
17 - (void)buildIndexInThread
18 {
19     NSAutoreleasePool *pool = [NSAutoreleasePool new];
20     NSDate *start = [NSDate date];
21     NSFileManager *fm = [NSFileManager defaultManager];
22     for (NSString *dir in [fm directoryContentsAtPath: @"/usr/share/man"])
23     {
24         BOOL isDir = NO;
25         NSString *manPath = [@"/usr/share/man"
               stringByAppendingPathComponent: dir];
26         if ([fm fileExistsAtPath: manPath isDirectory: &isDir] && isDir)
```

```
27         {
28             for (NSString *file in [fm directoryContentsAtPath: manPath])
29             {
30                 NSString *manFile = [manPath stringByAppendingPathComponent: file];
31                 if ([fm fileExistsAtPath: manFile isDirectory: &isDir] && !isDir)
32                 {
33                     [self indexManAtPath: manFile];
34                 }
35             }
36         }
37     }
38     NSLog(@"Indexing took %d seconds", 0-(int)[start timeIntervalSinceNow]);
39     [pool release];
40     [self release];
41 }
42 - (void)indexManAtPath: (NSString*)path
43 {
44     NSAutoreleasePool *pool = [NSAutoreleasePool new];
45     ManPage *page = [ManPage manPageWithPath: path];
46     CFURLRef url = (CFURLRef)[page URL];
47     CFStringRef text = (CFStringRef)[page stringValue];
48     SKDocumentRef doc = SKDocumentCreateWithURL(url);
49     SKIndexAddDocumentWithText(index, doc, text, YES);
50     [pool release];
51 }
52 @end
```

The methods in the category are separated out to show that they run in another thread. The only methods that should run in the main thread are the ones given in the main class definition.

The `-buildIndex` method spawns a new thread, running the `-buildIndexInThread` method. Note that this needs to create its own autorelease pool, since it does not have a run loop doing this for it. It first iterates over every directory in the /user/share/man folder and tests whether it is a directory. If it is, then the method iterates over each file in this directory and indexes it by calling the `-indexManAtPath:` method.

This method also creates an autorelease pool. This is not strictly required, but since the `ManPage` object uses a lot of autoreleased objects it is a good idea. The code on lines 48 and 49 is responsible for adding the page to the index. This first creates a document reference from the URL for the page—it's on-disk representation in the file:// URL scheme—and then associates this with the text representation of the page.

Note the -retain/-release pair on lines 12 and 40. This is to protect against the index being freed in the main thread while the indexing thread is still running. By retaining itself on line 12, the object guarantees that it will not be freed prematurely. The matching -release is needed to prevent this safeguard from becoming a memory leak. Note that it would be cleaner to provide some mechanism for freeing the object while the thread is running, for example, by setting a flag that would be tested for in the thread and cause it to terminate before it has finished indexing.

With the index constructed or, more accurately, in the course of construction, we can begin searching it. This is handled by a query controller. The interface to this class is shown in Listing 17.4. The action method defined here will be associated with the search box, and called whenever the user types something. The outlet is connected to the ManPageIndex instance created in the nib file.

Listing 17.4: The interface to the query controller. [from: examples/ManSearch/QueryController.h]

```
#import <Cocoa/Cocoa.h>

@interface QueryController : NSObject {
    SKSearchRef query;
    NSTimer *poll;
    IBOutlet id index;
    float maxScore;
    NSMutableArray *results;
}
- (void)runQuery: (NSString*)queryString;
- (IBAction)runQueryFrom: (id)sender;
@end
```

We use bindings to display the results in a table view. The array controller is bound to the results instance variable. The maxScore value is also used via bindings. The right-hand table column contains an NSLevelIndicatorCell with its maximum value bound to this variable. This enables the relevancy scores to be properly scaled automatically.

The implementation of this class begins in Listing 17.5. This shows the setup code for the controller. When it awakes, it creates a new, empty, array. We don't bother firing off KVO notifications here, since the array controller doesn't care about the difference between no array and an empty array.

When the object is deallocated, we need to do several cleanup operations. This code could be omitted, since the object won't be deallocated before the program exits in this particular example, but they are all needed in the more general case. If a query is running, then it must be aborted and released, and the timer must be invalidated and released. The run loop may still have a reference to the timer, so releasing it may still not prevent it from firing again after this object has been freed. If this happens then you will get a segmentation fault as you try to send a message to an invalid object.

Listing 17.5: Setting up the query controller. [from: examples/ManSearch/QueryController.m]

```
- (void)awakeFromNib
{
    results = [NSMutableArray new];
}
- (void)dealloc
{
    if (NULL != query)
    {
        SKSearchCancel(query);
        CFRelease(query);
    }
    [results release];
    [poll invalidate];
    [poll release];
    [super dealloc];
}
- (IBAction)runQueryFrom: (id)sender;
{
    [self runQuery: [sender stringValue]];
}
```

The action message is very simple. It just calls the `-runQuery:` method with the string value of the sender. This action is connected to the search field in the nib and so this will be called whenever the user types something in the search box.

The real work is done by the `-runQuery:` method, shown in Listing 17.6. This begins by cleaning up after any existing search.

If a search is already underway, then lines 29 and 30 stop it and free the resources allocated to it. Lines 32–34 remove all of the existing search result and trigger the KVO notifications required to update the display. This will cause the table view to empty itself of old results as soon as a new search starts.

Before we can start the search, we flush the index, on line 37. This ensures that all of the documents we have added to the index will actually be searched. We then create a background search with the default search options. Recall that the default options are to return a relevancy score for each item and to treat spaces as Boolean AND operations.

Listing 17.6: Beginning a search with the query controller. [from: examples/ManSearch/-QueryController.m]

```
- (IBAction)runQuery: (NSString*)queryString;
{
    if (NULL != query)
    {
        SKSearchCancel(query);
        CFRelease(query);
    }
    [self willChangeValueForKey: @"results"];
    [results removeAllObjects];
    [self didChangeValueForKey: @"results"];

    SKIndexRef idx = [index searchIndex];
    SKIndexFlush(idx);
    query = SKSearchCreate(idx,
                           (CFStringRef)queryString,
                           kSKSearchOptionDefault);
    [poll release];
    maxScore = 0;
    poll = [[NSTimer scheduledTimerWithTimeInterval: 1
                                             target: self
                                           selector: @selector(
                                               updateResults:)
                                           userInfo: nil
                                            repeats: YES] retain];
}
```

The `maxScore` is reset to zero, but again we don't bother firing off KVO notifications. At the moment, there are no results, so the maximum value isn't being used by anything. The final operation in this method is to set up a timer that will be used to poll for results later. The method called by the timer is shown in Listing 17.7.

The search runs in the background and enqueues results. The `-updateResults:` method is called periodically by a timer to fetch them. The function to get the results from the query is called on line 54. This populates the arrays declared on lines 51 and 52 with a set of document IDs and scores.

If this function returns `false`, then we have just retrieved the last of the results. Lines 57–61 clean up the objects that were used to run the search, invalidating the timer and freeing both it and the search object.

Listing 17.7: Fetching search results. [from: examples/ManSearch/QueryController.m]

```
- (void) updateResults: (id)sender
{
    SKDocumentID ids[20];
    float scores[20];
    CFIndex found = 0;
    Boolean more = SKSearchFindMatches(query, 20, ids, scores, 0, &found);
    if (!more)
    {
        [poll invalidate];
        [poll release];
        poll = nil;
        CFRelease(query);
        query = NULL;
    }
    if (found > 0)
    {
        [self willChangeValueForKey: @"results"];
        for (NSUInteger i=0 ; i<found ; i++)
        {
            SKDocumentRef ref = SKIndexCopyDocumentForDocumentID(
                [index searchIndex], ids[i]);
            NSURL *url = (NSURL*)SKDocumentCopyURL(ref);
            CFRelease(ref);
            NSDictionary *result = [NSDictionary
                dictionaryWithObjectsAndKeys:
                [NSNumber numberWithFloat: scores[i]], @"score",
                [url autorelease], @"URL",
                [[url path] lastPathComponent], @"name",
                nil];
            [results addObject: result];
            if (scores[i] > maxScore)
            {
                [self willChangeValueForKey: @"maxScore"];
                maxScore = scores[i];
                [self didChangeValueForKey: @"maxScore"];
            }
        }
        [self didChangeValueForKey: @"results"];
    }
}
```

The `SKSearchFindMatches()` call will store the number of results that are being returned in the `found` variable. We need to iterate over each of these and update the results array.

The results are returned as an array of document IDs. These are just numbers, indicating the index in a table of document URLs stored with the index. We can't do anything particularly useful with these. The call on line 69 retrieves an object corresponding to this identifier in the specified index. From this, we can then get the URL that was stored along with the document. This is done on line 70.

Note that we use the toll-free bridging mechanism in the opposite direction here, casting a Core Foundation object to a Cocoa object. Both `NSURL` and `CFURLRef` objects can be used interchangeably, and for Cocoa code it is more convenient to deal with one as if it were an Objective-C object.

The next step constructs a dictionary representing this result, containing the name of the file, the score, and the URL. The name is not particularly human-readable. You could improve this by getting the fourth line from the man page, which is always a one-line description, but this is good enough for a simple example.

Finally, if this result has a higher score than we've found so far, we update the maximum score. Note that the KVO notification calls are outside the loop for the `results` array, so that we don't trigger twenty notifications every time this method is called. We expect the maximum score to change a lot less frequently, so we can update this every time we find a new value rather than complicate the code.

The final piece of this program is the `PageViewer` class, shown in Listing 17.8. This is responsible for displaying the man page in the user interface when it is selected.

Listing 17.8: Displaying man pages in the user interface. [from: examples/ManSearch/-PageViewer.m]

```
#import "PageViewer.h"
#import "ManPage.h"

@implementation PageViewer
- (void)awakeFromNib
{
    [view setString:@""];
    [view setFont: [NSFont fontWithName: @"Monaco" size: 12]];
    [pages addObserver: self
            forKeyPath: @"selection"
               options: NSKeyValueObservingOptionNew
               context: NULL];
}
```

```
- (void)observeValueForKeyPath: (NSString*)keyPath
                      ofObject: (id)object
                        change: (NSDictionary*)change
                       context: (void*)context
{
    if ([pages selectionIndex] == NSNotFound) { return; }
    NSURL *selectedURL = [[pages selection] valueForKey: @"URL"];
    ManPage *page = [ManPage manPageWithPath: [selectedURL path]];
    [view setString: [page stringValue]];
}
@end
```

When this object is loaded, it sets the font in the text view to a readable monospaced font and registers to receive a KVO notification whenever the selection changes. The fixed-width font is needed because man pages are typeset for reading on a terminal.

When the selection changes, this simply gets the text value of the man page and sets it in the view. As you can see in Figure 17.3, this is very readable in spite of being plain text in a monospaced font.

A simple extension to this example would pass `@"-Thtml"` and `@"-man"` to groff to generate HTML output and then use `NSAttributedString`'s `-initWithHTML:documentAttributes:` method to construct an attributed string version for display. Note that if you do this, you will still need to typeset the page in plain text form for indexing.

The most obvious extension to this example is to save the index on disk. The second time that the program runs, you should open the existing index, rather than generating a new one every run. This is a relatively simple modification. The problem is made slightly harder by the need to handle partial updates.

You would need to keep a log of the dates at which you indexed every file and then, the next time the program runs, scan over each file and check whether it has been modified since its last indexing date. This is a lot less demanding on both the disk and the processor than decompressing, typesetting, and indexing every page when the program starts. You might also consider moving the index maintenance to a separate process that runs in the background. This is the approach taken by the apropos utility, which does more basic searches of man pages from the command line. The companion makewhatis program is run periodically to build a database of the short descriptions from man pages, and can be easily searched.

Keeping an index synchronized with the filesystem is still a difficult task, however, and this is where Spotlight helps a lot.

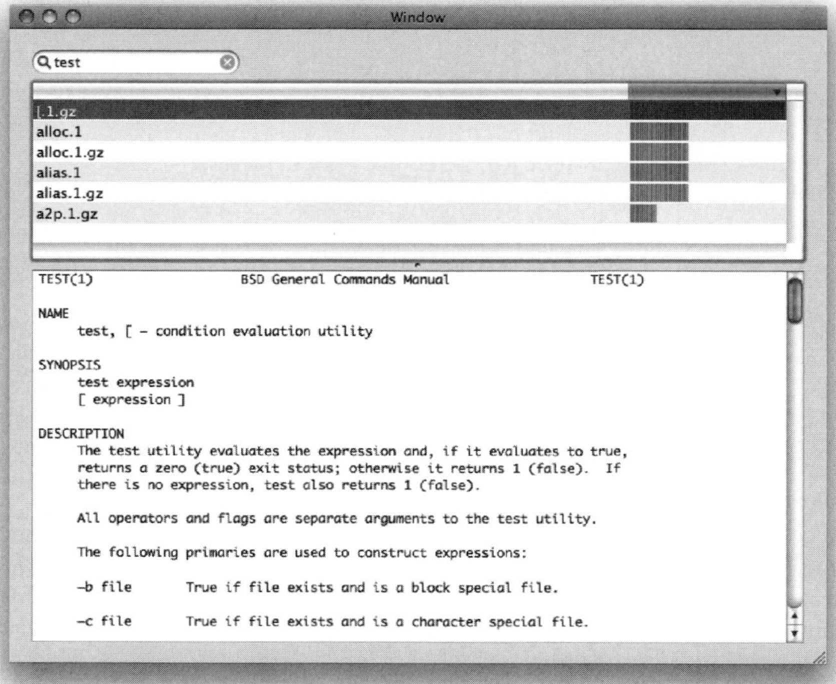

Figure 17.3: Searching the UNIX manual.

17.4 Spotlight

Spotlight was introduced with OS X 10.4 as a system-wide search interface. It builds on top of Search Kit by providing a set of indexes that are automatically kept up-to-date with the state of the filesystem.

Spotlight runs in the background and creates indexes for all of the files it understands. You can search these indexes in your application and display information about them. This frees you from the difficult task that we saw in the last example: making sure that your index is up to date. With Spotlight, indexing and searching are entirely separate tasks. The mdimport tool runs to import metadata related to any files on the system in the background.

17.4.1 Monitoring Filesystem Events

The key feature of Spotlight is the fact that it is constantly updated. The key to this is the *fsevents* device and dæmon. Every filesystem write triggers an event that can be read from the /dev/fsevents device. This must be done very quickly because the kernel will not buffer an unlimited number. A lightweight userspace process, fseventsd, monitors this device and logs all of the changed files to a store that can easily be played back later. Spotlight also watches this device.

Every time a file is written to, Spotlight will run the associated metadata importer to update its indexes.

17.4.2 Metadata Indexing

The key word that is used whenever discussing Spotlight is *metadata*. Metadata means "data about data," a description of what the data really is. Any filesystem stores some forms of metadata. At an absolute minimum, it will contain the name and size of every file in it.

Many of the concepts in Spotlight will be familiar to former BeOS users. This is not a coincidence. Dominic Giampaolo, creator of the *Be Filesystem* (*BFS*), has been working on filesystems and Spotlight at Apple since 2002.

Metadata indexing was a key feature of BFS. Every file could have an arbitrary set of key-value pairs associated with it, stored in the filesystem, and indexed if required. The main limitation of this approach was that it only worked with BFS volumes. As soon as you started storing data on FAT disks or CIFS shares, you lost all of the metadata support. Spotlight moves the metadata to a separate index, which allows it to work across all filesystem types.

You can see what information Spotlight has stored about a specific file using the mdls command-line tool. This is analogous to the ls utility, which lists filesystem entries. Running it on a file will give some output like this:

```
$ mdls photo.jpg
kMDItemBitsPerSample           = 32
kMDItemColorSpace              = "RGB"
kMDItemContentCreationDate     = 2005-02-08 15:11:27 +0000
kMDItemContentModificationDate = 2005-02-08 15:11:27 +0000
kMDItemContentType             = "public.jpeg"
kMDItemContentTypeTree         = (
    "public.jpeg",
    "public.image",
    "public.data",
    "public.item",
    "public.content"
```

```
)
kMDItemDisplayName               = "photo.jpg"
kMDItemFSContentChangeDate       = 2005-02-08 15:11:27 +0000
kMDItemFSCreationDate            = 2005-02-08 15:11:27 +0000
kMDItemFSCreatorCode             = "GKON"
kMDItemFSName                    = "photo.jpg"
kMDItemFSOwnerGroupID            = 501
kMDItemFSOwnerUserID             = 501
kMDItemFSSize                    = 34842
kMDItemFSTypeCode                = "JPEG"
kMDItemHasAlphaChannel           = 0
kMDItemKind                      = "JPEG image"
kMDItemLastUsedDate              = 2005-02-08 15:11:27 +0000
kMDItemOrientation               = 1
kMDItemPixelHeight               = 257
kMDItemPixelWidth                = 256
kMDItemResolutionHeightDPI       = 400
kMDItemResolutionWidthDPI        = 400
kMDItemUsedDates                 = (
    2005-02-08 08:00:00 +0000
)
```

A lot of these are standard filesystem metadata, which is also indexed by spotlight. Examples of this include the file name, size, and owner. Some of these are standard fields that are found on any item in the Spotlight indexes. These include the UTI type and tree.

The more interesting keys are the ones that are specific to this kind of file. The color space used, for example, is only applicable to images, as are the keys related to the resolution. Looking at other files will give you a different set of metadata.

One of the problems that frequently occurred on BeOS was that it was difficult to tell what was data and what was metadata. The BeOS address book, for example, created files with no contents and stored all of the information about people in the filesystem metadata. This is not a problem with Spotlight, since it only provides metadata indexing, not storage. You cannot store anything in Spotlight that is not either stored in, or computed from, your documents.

The question of exactly what should be indexed, however, remains. In principle, you want to store as much as possible in Spotlight. Any information that a user might conceivably ever want to search for should go in. Unfortunately, doing this effectively results in duplicating your file in the metadata index, which slows down searching and wastes a lot of space.

Some compromises are required. The metadata on an image is a good example.

In theory, you could add color curves, pixel distributions, and a whole raft of other attributes to Spotlight. In practice, people are most likely to search for images by name, size, color depth, and resolution, so these are the most important attributes to store. These can be quickly extracted from an image header and so will remain up-to-date in the index.

17.4.3 Building a Metadata Import Plugin

The mdimport program is run on every directory that Spotlight notices has changed. This loads plugin bundles and then invokes them on every file that needs reindexing.

Spotlight ships with a number of standard plugins. You will probably already have several in two locations. The ones that are shipped as part of OS X are in /System/Library/Spotlight/ while installed third-party ones live in /Library/Spotlight/. If your Mac came with the iWork demo, you will have importers for each of the iWork applications in the latter location.

Some of the system-provided import plugins are very general. The rich text importer, for example, works on RTF, HTML, ODF, OXML, and plain text files. All of these can be read using AppKit methods and so the importer itself is very small.

A Spotlight plugin contains three components:

- The standard Info.plist file must contain keys describing the UTIs that the plugin understands and the UUID of the importer.
- Optionally, a schema.xml and accompanying strings file defining new metadata keys.
- The executable code for the plugin.

Spotlight plugins use the `CFPlugin` interface. This is based around Microsoft's *Component Object Model* (*COM*), which specifies a binary interface for representing something like the C++ (Simula) object model in any language. Plugins are defined in terms of interfaces: named structures containing function pointers. Interfaces follow a simple inheritance model, each inheriting from IUnknown interface. This defines three function pointers, conceptually roughly equivalent to the Objective-C `+new`, `-retain`, and `-release` methods.

When you instantiate an object from a plugin, you do so via a specific interface. Although an object can have multiple interfaces, you must get a separate pointer for each one you want to use. This allows multiple inheritance to work correctly. Implementing these is not at all fun. The COM interfaces were designed to work with C++, and using them from C requires a lot of very verbose code. Fortunately, the interface defined by Spotlight only defines one method. If you create a new Spotlight Plugin project in XCode, all of the CFPlugin code will be generated for you in a separate file. The only thing you need to implement is this function:

```
Boolean GetMetadataForFile(void* thisInterface,
    CFMutableDictionaryRef attributes,
    CFStringRef contentTypeUTI,
    CFStringRef pathToFile);
```

The first argument is a pointer to the COM interface and is usually ignored. The second is a dictionary you need to populate with metadata. The third and fourth are the type and path of the file. You can use the UTI to implement different methods for each type that your importer implements.

To demonstrate how this all works, we'll write a simple import plugin for the Outliner example from Chapter 9. When we wrote this example originally, we didn't use UTIs. This, unfortunately, makes it impossible for Spotlight to index the files it creates. We need to add a new UTI declaration to the outliner's Info.plist, as shown in Figure 17.4, and modify it to expect the UTI, rather than the string "Outliner" when saving and opening in this format.

Note that we change the extension to .exampleOutline when doing this. The .outline extension is already associated with a UTI for OmniOutliner documents.

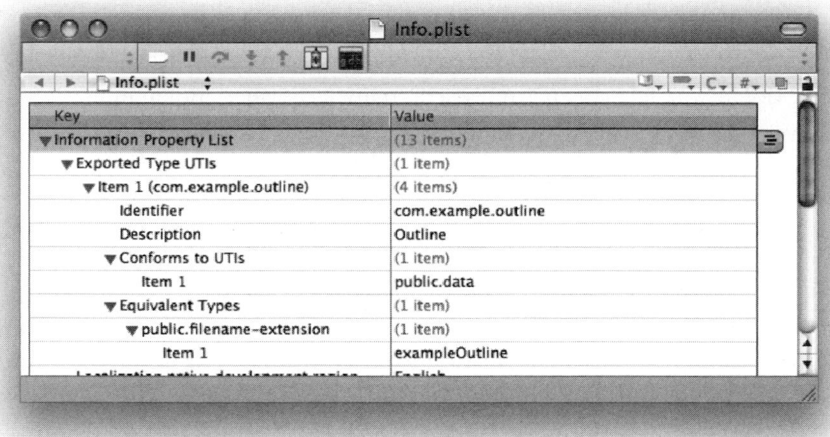

Figure 17.4: Declaring a UTI for the outline file format.

To create the skeleton of the project, we start with a Spotlight Import plug-in and make two small changes. First, we add Cocoa.framework to the list of frameworks the plugin links again. Then we rename the automatically created GetMetadataForFile.c to GetMetadataForFile.m.

The function declared in this file will be called automatically by the plugin. If you want to see exactly how this works, look in main.c, which contains the CFPlugin structures and functions. Don't worry if you don't fully understand these declarations; you shouldn't need to modify them ever.

We want to write our plugin in Objective-C, not C, so we implement the import function as a simple trampoline that instantiates an object and sends it a message, as shown in Listing 17.9.

Listing 17.9: The metadata import function. [from: examples/MetadataImport/GetMetadataForFile.m]

```
#include <CoreFoundation/CoreFoundation.h>
#include <CoreServices/CoreServices.h>

#import "MDImporter.h"

Boolean GetMetadataForFile(void* thisInterface,
               CFMutableDictionaryRef attributes,
               CFStringRef contentTypeUTI,
               CFStringRef pathToFile)
{
    id pool = [NSAutoreleasePool new];
    MDImporter *import = [[MDImporter alloc] init];
    Boolean success = [import getAttributes: (id)attributes
                         forFileWithUTI: (id)contentTypeUTI
                                atPath: (id)pathToFile];
    [import release];
    [pool release];
    return success;
}
```

This is called from C code, so there may well not be an autorelease pool in place. We create one at the start of this function and destroy it at the end to clean up any temporary objects created by our import object. You can reuse this simple stub in any Spotlight plugin that you write.

The real implementation is shown in Listing 17.10. This contains two methods, one for collecting the text from the outline and the other for setting the metadata. This makes use of the `OutlineItem` class, which is copied over from the examples/UndoOutliner directory.

Ideally, any classes that are used by both the metadata plugin and the application should be stored in a framework and linked to both, rather than being copied, but for a class this small the wasted space is minimal.

Listing 17.10: A metadata importer for the example outliner. [from: examples/MetadataImport/MDImporter.m]

```
#import "MDImporter.h"
#import "OutlineItem.h"

@implementation MDImporter
- (NSString*)collectText: (OutlineItem*)item
              inBuffer: (NSMutableString*)buffer
{
    [buffer appendString: @" "];
    [buffer appendString: item.title];
    for (OutlineItem *child in item.children)
    {
        [self collectText: child
                 inBuffer: buffer];
    }
    return buffer;
}
- (BOOL)getAttributes: (NSMutableDictionary*)attributes
       forFileWithUTI: (NSString*)aUTI
               atPath: (NSString*)aPath
{
    OutlineItem *root =
        [NSKeyedUnarchiver unarchiveObjectWithData: [NSData
            dataWithContentsOfFile: aPath]];
    if (nil == root) { return NO; }

    [attributes setObject: root.title
                   forKey: (id)kMDItemTitle];
    NSMutableString *text = [NSMutableString string];
    [self collectText: root inBuffer: text];
    [attributes setObject: text
                   forKey: (id)kMDItemTextContent];
    return YES;
}
@end
```

The first method in this class recursively visits every item in the tree in turn and generates a plain text representation of the entire outline. This is used to support full-text indexing.

The second method is the one called from the trampoline function. This first tries to deserialize the outline. If this fails, then it returns immediately. If not, it adds two metadata attributes to the dictionary.

The first attribute is the item title, which is taken from the root item in this outline. For the current version of the outliner, this will always be "New Item," but a future version might store something more useful here. The second attribute is the text representation of the item.

The `kMDItemTextContent` attribute is slightly unusual. Unlike most other Spotlight attributes, it cannot be read back again. This attribute is used to generate an index similar to the ones created by Search Kit. You can search for a document using this key, but only the mappings from words to documents are stored, not the text itself.

To test that this all works, we can invoke mdimport from a terminal. First, we create a document, as shown in Figure 17.5, and then run the importer. To avoid having to install the plugin every time we test it, we use the -g flag to tell mdimport to load it explicitly. We also add the -d flag to set the amount of debugging output that the importer should emit. A value of 2 here tells it to dump all of the keys it generates to the terminal:

```
$ mdimport -g /build/Debug/MetadataImport.mdimporter -d 2\
Demo.exampleOutline

(Info) Import: Import  /Users/book/Desktop/Demo.exampleoutline  type
 com.example.outline  using
 /Users/book/Desktop/MetadataImport/build/Debug/MetadataImport.mdimporter
(Debug) Import: Attributes for file /Users/book/Desktop/Demo.exampleoutline:
{
    "_kMDItemFinderLabel" = <null>;
    "com_apple_metadata_modtime" = 256230595;
    kMDItemContentCreationDate = 2009-02-13 15:09:55 +0000;
    kMDItemContentModificationDate = 2009-02-13 15:09:55 +0000;
    kMDItemContentType = "com.example.outline";
    kMDItemContentTypeTree =     (
        "com.example.outline",
        "public.data",
        "public.item"
    );
    kMDItemDisplayName =     {
        "" = Demo;
    };
    kMDItemKind =     {
        "" = Outline;
        en = "Outline File";
```

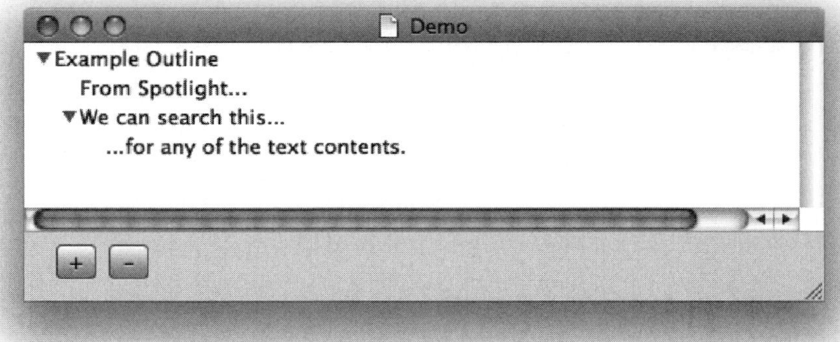

Figure 17.5: A simple outline document to index.

```
    };
    kMDItemTextContent = "New Item A example outline We can search this...
...from Spotlight. Featuring: Full text indexing.";
    kMDItemTitle = "New Item";
}
```

As you can see, the last two lines were set by our new plugin. The item's text contents is visible here, because this is a simple dump of the dictionary, before it is imported into Spotlight. To test whether the import actually worked, we can check these two keys with mdls:

```
$ mdls -name kMDItemTitle Demo.exampleoutline
 kMDItemTitle = "New Item"
$ mdls -name kMDItemTextContent Demo.exampleoutline
 kMDItemTextContent = (null)
```

As expected, the text content cannot be read back. We didn't create this attribute for reading back; we created it for searching. The test is whether Spotlight can find the correct document using it. Figure 17.6 shows the result of searching for outline documents containing the word "spotlight." This finds one file: the one we just indexed.

That's all it takes to create a metadata importer for Spotlight. Users of the outline application can now find outlines by their title and text. You can add any other kinds of standard metadata in this way. If you want to define new metadata fields, then you need to create a schema.xml file.

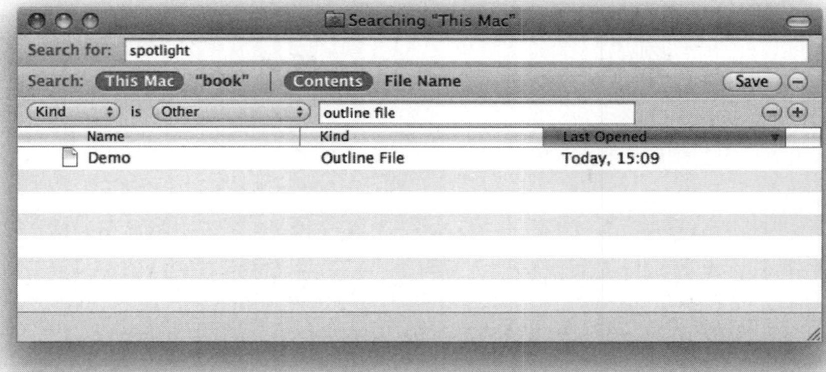

Figure 17.6: Finding the outline with Spotlight.

17.4.4 Searching with Spotlight

You can run Spotlight queries from the Spotlight menu, the finder, or the mdfind command-line tool. All of these use the same underlying mechanism, and you can add this to your own code easily.

There are two ways of invoking Spotlight searches. Spotlight is exposed to programmers via the *Core Services framework*, which is built on top of Core Foundation and provides a set of C APIs. You can use these directly via the `MDQuery` interface.

As a Cocoa programmer, you are more likely to want to use the Objective-C interface provided by Foundation. The NSMetadata.h header appeared with OS X 10.4, and provides a small set of classes for interfacing with Spotlight.

If you want to create a Spotlight search query, you need to use the `NSMetadataQuery` class. This encapsulates a Spotlight search. Using it is very simple. Listing 17.11 shows all of the code that you need to enable Spotlight searching in your application. This is connected as the action method for the search box in the window shown in Figure 17.7. The nib also contains an array controller bound to the results key in the query. The table column is bound to this with the kMDItemDisplayName model key.

This class just contains a single method, which searches for a word entered in the search box. All that you need to do to begin a Spotlight search is set a predicate that defines the search terms and send it a `-startQuery` message.

Listing 17.11: A simple spotlight search program. [from: examples/SimpleSpotlightSearch/SearchDelegate.m]

```
#import "SearchDelegate.h"

@implementation SearchDelegate
- (IBAction)runQuery: (id)sender
{
    if (nil == query)
    {
        [self willChangeValueForKey: @"query"];
        query = [NSMetadataQuery new];
        [self didChangeValueForKey: @"query"];
    }
    else
    {
        [query stopQuery];
    }
    NSPredicate *predicate =
        [NSPredicate predicateWithFormat: @"kMDItemTextContent LIKE %@",
            [sender stringValue]];
    [query setPredicate: predicate];
    [query startQuery];
}
@end
```

The `results` array is KVO-compliant and will contain an array of `NSMetadataItem` instances. This class is KVC-compliant for the metadata properties exposed by the item. The results are automatically updated via bindings.

To make this a little bit more user-friendly, you may want to register a set of sort descriptors with the query, allowing the results to be sorted according to any of the visible keys.

This is a very general kind of search. It will find any document, irrespective of type, containing the search word. Most of the time you will want to restrict it further. You can do this in two ways. For fine-grained restrictions, you can add extra conditionals to the search predicate. You can also restrict the search to one of three *search scopes*:

- `NSMetadataQueryUserHomeScope` restricts the search to the user's home directory. Files that the user cannot access will not be returned, but this prevents files in other users' home directories that are publicly readable from being returned.

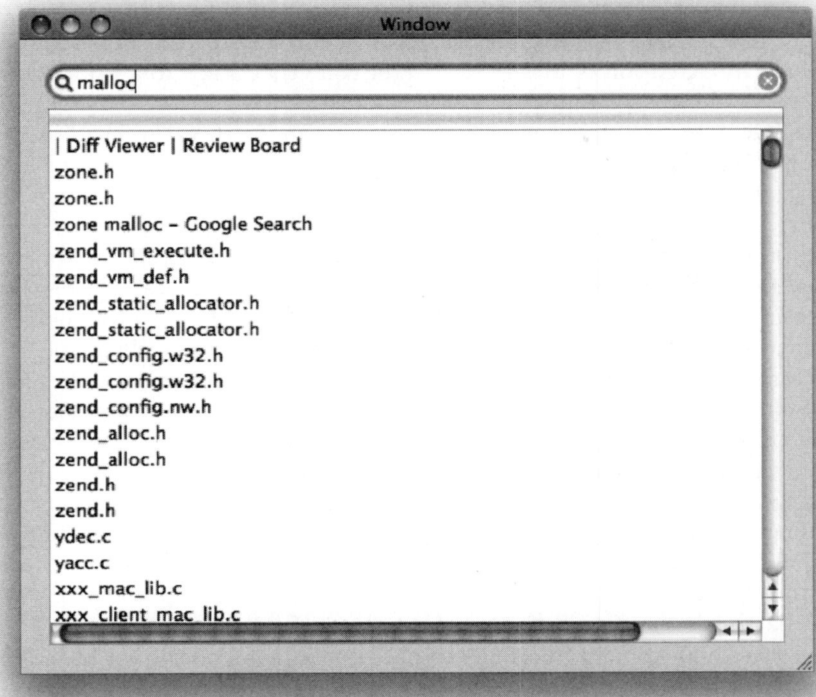

Figure 17.7: Running simple searches with Spotlight.

- `NSMetadataQueryLocalComputerScope` searches all local disks and the user's home directory, whether it is local or mounted over the network.
- `NSMetadataQueryNetworkScope` searches every mounted network volume.

The array returned by `-results` is a proxy object. Using it is relatively slow. It is intended solely for use by bindings. If you want to access query results manually, then you should use the `-resultCount` and `-resultAtIndex:` methods instead.

17.4.5 Spotlight Limitations

Spotlight indexes files by selecting an importer for their UTIs. This requires the file to have an extension or an HFS+ creator code that maps to a UTI. Files with no extension will not be indexed.

Spotlight also only indexes files. This is an unfortunate reduction in functionality when compared to Search Kit, which worked on arbitrary URLs. An application like Stickies, which stores all of its contents in a single database, can't make much use of Spotlight. The most it can do is have Spotlight index that one file and tell the user that some text is in a sticky note; it can't tell you which note.

You can work around this limitation by creating symbolic links. The stickies application would need to create one link for every note and give them all an extension like .sticky that was associated with the application. When one of these was selected, it would then display the real note corresponding to it. In contrast, using Search Kit allows it to store URLs like file://path/to/database#noteID.

You might have noticed that things from your browsing history sometimes show up in the Spotlight search results. This is because Safari creates a file for every page you visit. This may contain a cached copy of the page, or just a link, depending on your settings. In either case, it can be indexed by Spotlight. You can use this trick to index arbitrary URLs for remote resources; create a short file containing the URL and have Spotlight index that file using a metadata import plugin that reads the data from the remote location, or a local cache.

The other limitation of Spotlight is that it only indexes a subset of the filesystem. By default, it will not index removable volumes. You can use the `mdutil` tool to list the status of every mounted volume. Disk images and remote drives will not be indexed, by default, and neither will system directories.

It would have been nice to be able to rewrite the man page index using Spotlight. This is not easy, because the /usr/share/man directory is ignored by Spotlight and you cannot override this. You could create a symbolic link to this directory inside ~/Library or similar, but this is not ideal.

Although Spotlight replaces a lot of Search Kit uses, there are still a number of cases where Search Kit makes more sense. If you are only creating indexes to search from your application, rather than from the system-wide search facility, then Search Kit can make more sense. It is also generally better to use Search Kit for indexes that are updated while the application runs. Search Kit makes it trivial to update individual index entries, while Spotlight requires an entire file to be reindexed and all metadata entries replaced.

17.5 Predicates

A *predicate* is a logical expression that evaluates to either true or false. In set theory, predicates are used to define sets; a set contains all of the elements from some greater set for which the predicate is true.

The `NSPredicate` class was added to Cocoa at the same time as Spotlight. It is used when searching metadata in the Spotlight database, but can also be used in a variety of other places. Each `NSPredicate` instance represents a single predicate expression.

Predicates implement a simple *domain-specific language* (*DSL*) for describing queries. Spotlight only supports a subset of the more general query language. The query language is similar to SQL. If you have experience with SQL, then you will find the predicate language easy to pick up.

Predicates in Cocoa are built on top of the KVC mechanism. They are designed to search and filter key-value combinations. You use a predicate by sending it an `-evaluateWithObject:` message. This returns a Boolean value, indicating whether the object matches the predicate. The predicate will perform tests on the values associated with some of the object's keys to decide whether this is the case.

17.5.1 The Predicate Language

The most common way of creating predicates is to use the `+predicateWithFormat:` method. This constructs a predicate from a format string by parsing it as an expression in the predicate query language.

In general, most predicates are composed of expressions defining a relationship between a key and a value. You might define predicates for matching someone's name and age like this:

```
[NSPredicate predicateWithFormat: @"name␣==␣ Charles "];
[NSPredicate predicateWithFormat: @"age␣>=␣21"];
```

Note that you need to escape the value in the first of these. This is difficult to get right and so it is more common to write this using a format string with the value as a separate argument, like this:

```
[NSPredicate predicateWithFormat: @"name␣==␣%@", @"Charles"];
```

This works almost exactly like the `NSString` equivalent, but escapes the argument. You can use this safely with user-supplied data, like this:

```
[NSPredicate predicateWithFormat: @"name␣==␣%@", aValue];
```

Often you want to create both the key and value using variables. The obvious thing to do here is to use this same kind of format string for both, like this:

```
[NSPredicate predicateWithFormat: @"%@␣==␣%@", aKey, aValue];
```

Unfortunately, this will not work. It will check whether the literal values provided by both arguments are equal, rather than treating one as a key. The format strings supported by `NSPredicate` provide another escape sequence for inserting key names:

```
[NSPredicate predicateWithFormat: @"%K␣==␣%@", aKey, aValue];
```

Note that `aValue` does not have to be a string here. If you want to compare it as a string, you may want to quote it, like this:

```
[NSPredicate predicateWithFormat: @"%K␣==␣ %@ ", aKey, aValue];
```

Without the quotes, the predicate will test for object equality between the value for the key and the specified object.

Most of the examples we've seen so far have tested for equality. For string comparisons, you are more likely to want to use the `LIKE` operator instead. You might alternatively use `MATCHES`, which uses regular expression matching.

A variety of other comparison operations are available, including the standard ones you would expect from C and several inspired by SQL. You can use either the SQL or C forms of the Boolean logical operations, for example, both `AND` and `&&` are valid for a Boolean AND operation.

Several operations apply to collections. You can test, for example, whether an array attribute contains a given value like this:

```
[NSPredicate predicateWithFormat: @"%@␣IN␣values", aValue];
```

Constructing a predicate from a format string every time is slightly unwieldy. It requires the predicate to be parsed every time it is used, and defers syntax checking right up until the last moment. Quite often, you will have a class that only needs to perform a certain sort of query, with different values. You can do this by constructing *template predicates*. These contain placeholders where values will go. You construct them like this:

```
template = [NSPredicate predicateWithFormat: @"$VALUE␣IN␣values"];
```

This can be created in a class's `+initialize` method and stored in a file-static variable. The template will not be modified. It will be used as a prototype when constructing real predicates, like this:

```
predicate = [template predicateWithSubstitutionVariables:
    [NSDictionary dictionaryWithObject: aValue forKey: @"VALUE"];
```

This only performs the parsing once, and so it is slightly quicker, but the main advantage is that you can create the template early on in your program's life cycle, allowing you to catch parsing errors more easily. This won't catch all errors. If you make a mistake in a key name, for example, then it will not be caught until you try to use the predicate and get an exception caused by an unrecognized key path. You should try to use static constant strings, rather than string literals, as keys when you construct predicates, to avoid this.

17.5.2 Creating Predicates Directly

Although the format string constructor is very convenient, it is not the only way of creating predicates. You can create them directly, without invoking the parser, from three building blocks:

- `NSExpression` represents an expression in a predicate. This can be a single value—a key name or a literal value—or a simple expression.
- `NSComparisonPredicate` defines a predicate comparing two expressions.
- `NSCompoundPredicate` assembles a predicate from other predicates using a Boolean logical operator.

A simple predicate is typically constructed from two `NSExpressions` and a `NSCompoundPredicate`. The predicates we looked at in the last section were all comparing a single key path against a constant value. This kind of predicate is relatively easy to construct in code. The first step is to construct the expressions for the key and value:

```
NSExpression *key = [NSExpression expressionForKeyPath: @"name"];
NSExpression *value = [NSExpression expressionForConstantValue: @"Charles"
    ];
```

The next step is to construct the compound predicate comparing these two. For string objects, we might decide to use a custom comparison selector, like this:

```
SEL sel = @selector(isEqualToString:);
NSPredicate *predicate =
    [NSComparisonPredicate predicateWithLeftExpression: key
                                       rightExpression: value
                                        customSelector: sel];
```

This predicate can then be used on an object to test whether its `name` key is equal to `@"charles"`. The following conditionals are equivalent:

```
if ([predicate evaluateWithObject: obj]) ...
if ([[object valueForKeyPath: @"name"] isEqualToString: @"charles"]) ...
```

This mechanism allows arbitrary expressions that compare objects to be constructed and passed around. The other way of constructing comparison predicates is less generic, but more abstract:

```
+ (NSPredicate *)predicateWithLeftExpression: (NSExpression*)lhs
                             rightExpression: (NSExpression*)rhs
                            modifier: (NSComparisonPredicateModifier)
                                modifier
                                        type: (NSPredicateOperatorType)type
                                     options: (NSUInteger)options;
```

This constructs a predicate using one of the comparison operations defined in the predicate language. The first two arguments are the left and right sides of the expression. The `modifier` argument is a used to construct predicates using the `ALL` or `ANY` modifiers. These are used for comparing elements against collections, to indicate that either at least one, or all of the elements in the collection should match the relation.

The `type` parameter defines the comparison operation. Any of the comparison operations supported by the predicate language are exposed here as values in an enumerated type.

The final argument lets you specify some flags for string comparisons. These allow case-insensitive and diacritic-insensitive comparisons. Spotlight's full-text searching always uses both of these. Content provided for full-text indexing will be converted to lowercase and have accents stripped before being stored.

Exporting Predicates

Spotlight and Core Data can both make use of predicates, but they don't evaluate them directly. Each of these frameworks uses the `NSPredicate` class to represent general predicate expressions but decomposes it into some other format for comparisons. Core Data, for example, will turn predicates into SQL expressions for evaluation in an SQLite data store.

This translation means that arbitrary predicates are not supported. Both Spotlight and Core Data support a subset of the predicate language. Core Data can support the whole language for in-memory stores, but others can have different limitations.

In particular, predicates constructed from arbitrary selectors are not likely to be supported by external frameworks that make use of predicates. These expressions only make sense when the executing environment is an Objective-C program; they do not necessarily have a mapping that makes sense in other data representations.

Most of the power of predicates comes from being able to combine them in arbitrary ways. You might want to say something like "all rock music from the

1960s except The Beatles." This is expressed in a compound predicate with three components combined with an AND operation:

- The genre is rock.
- The date is between 1960 and 1970.
- The artist is not The Beatles.

In Cocoa, this kind of condition is represented with an `NSCompoundPredicate`. You would create it with `+andPredicateWithSubpredicates:` with predicates representing each of the individual components as arguments. Additional constructors are available for disjunctions and negations.

Compound predicates are predicates themselves, and so can be used to construct very complex, nested, compound predicates. For example, you might want all music that is from the 1960s and is in the rock genre, or which is by The Beatles. You would do this by making a predicate ANDing the first two subpredicates together and then making an OR predicate combining this with the third one.

Normal Forms

It is possible to express any predicate logic expression in terms of expressions combined with either AND and OR. Predicates defined in this way are said to be in *conjunctive normal form* if all of the terms are combined with AND operations or *disjunctive normal form* if they are combined with OR operations.

Translating into a normal form requires an application of *De Morgan's laws*, which say that A AND B is equivalent to A OR (NOT B).

Although this is a mathematical possibility, it makes for some very bad user interfaces. The predicate editor in iTunes used to require predicates used to construct Smart Playlists to be in either conjunctive or disjunctive normal form. Although this is expressive enough for describing any subset of a user's music library, it forces users to create very long and complex predicates where simpler ones with nested subexpressions would do.

17.5.3 Using Predicates

Predicates can be used by Spotlight and Core Data to generate search results. They can also be used on an individual object to see if it matches. Much of their power, however, comes from their integration with the standard Foundation collection classes.

The most obvious use for predicates is to create subsets. You can use an NSPredicate to filter NSSet and NSArray instances, creating a new set or array containing only the elements that the predicate matches.

This can be a very quick way of searching some arbitrary data in your application. If you are using an NSArrayController bound to a table view to display your data, you can implement a search box that filters this very easily. When the user enters something in a search box, you would run an action method containing something like this:

```
NSPredicate *searchPredicate =
    [NSPredicate predicateWithFormat: @"attribute == %@", [sender
        stringValue]];
self.results = [allObjects filteredArrayUsingPredicate: searchPredicate];
```

The first line constructs a predicate that compares an attribute of the objects in the array to the string provided in the search box. In a slightly more advanced case, you would allow the user to select this field. The results property is then set to a filtered array of all of the objects that this object knows about. If your array controller is bound to the results property, then it will automatically be updated when the search results change.

This mechanism is used by applications like iTunes to quickly filter the list of all of the songs in a user's music library.

17.5.4 Displaying a Predicate Editor

Most of the time that you use predicates, you will want the user to have some input into how they are created. Sometimes this will be very simple, such as providing the value that is searched for in a fixed field. Other times it will be much more structured.

OS X 10.5 added a new view, the NSPredicateView class, for constructing predicates. This inherits from another new view class, NSRuleEditor. The rule editor is a general interface for creating sets of rules. The predicate view is a specialized version of this designed for creating NSPredicate instances.

The predicate view is controlled by an array of predicate row templates, instances of NSPredicateRowTemplate, which describe the predicates that it can create. These can be created in code, or with Interface Builder. The simplest form is given a set of left and right expressions and operations using this method:

```
- (id)initWithLeftExpressions: (NSArray*)leftExpressions
             rightExpressions: (NSArray*)rightExpressions
                     modifier: (NSComparisonPredicateModifier)modifier
                    operators: (NSArray*)operators
                      options: (NSUInteger)options;
```

This is very similar in structure to NSComparisonPredicate's constructor. A row initialized in this way will create comparison predicates with the values given as arguments. Each of the arrays is displayed in the predicate view as a pop-up box. A slightly more flexible row can be created with this method:

```
- (id)initWithLeftExpressions: (NSArray*)leftExpressions
 rightExpressionAttributeType: (NSAttributeType)attributeType
                     modifier: (NSComparisonPredicateModifier)modifier
                    operators: (NSArray*)operators
                      options: (NSUInteger)options;
```

This presents an editing box for the right expression, allowing the user to enter an arbitrary value. The kind of editor displayed depends on the type specified with the second argument.

The final kind of predicate row template is for compound predicates. This produces a nested user interface where all of the subpredicates are indented and combined to give a compound predicate matching any, all, or none of the children.

Most of the time, it is easier to create predicates row templates in Interface Builder than in code. Figure 17.8 shows the inspector for setting their options. This is enough to specify a large number of predicate types.

Using the predicate editor is very easy. It supports bindings and so can be connected directly to a predicate. When the user modifies the predicate, it can send an action message. Listing 17.12 shows a simple user of this view that displays the predicate's textual representation in a text field. You can see this in operation in Figure 17.9.

Listing 17.12: The predicate editor controller. [from: examples/PredicateViewer/PredicateViewController.m]

```
#import "PredicateViewController.h"

@implementation PredicateViewController
- (IBAction)predicateChanged: (id)sender
{
    [textField setStringValue: [predicate predicateFormat]];
}
- (IBAction)addCompoundRule: (id)sender
{
    [predicateEditor insertRowAtIndex: 0
                             withType: NSRuleEditorRowTypeCompound
                        asSubrowOfRow: -1
                              animate: YES];
}
@end
```

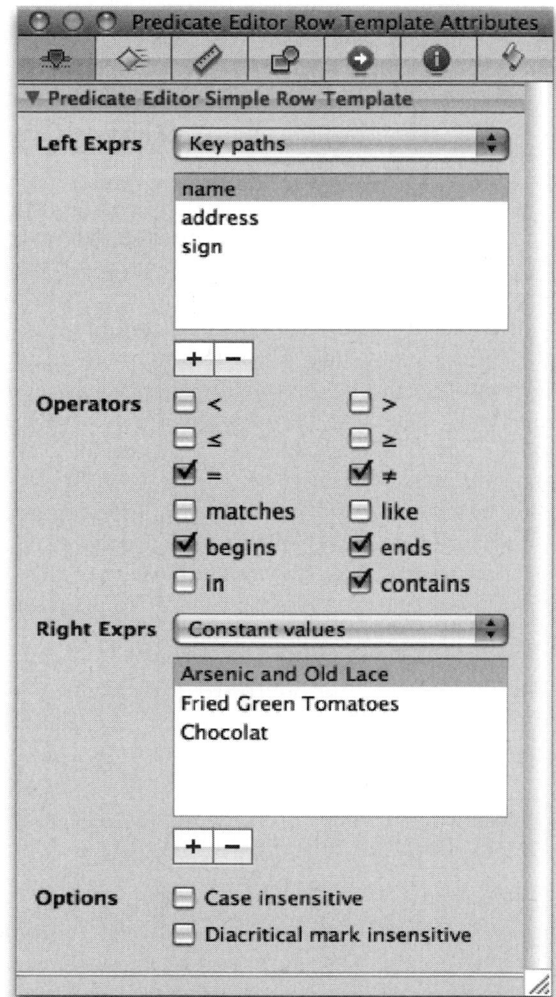

Figure 17.8: Configuring a predicate row template in Interface Builder.

This class is very simple. It uses bindings to keep its `predicate` instance variable synchronized with the display in the predicate editor. Whenever it receives an action message from the predicate editor, the predicate has already updated the instance variable via bindings. Line 7 extracts the format string from the predicate and assigns it to the text field.

The second method is more interesting. Each row in the predicate editor has two buttons next to it: one for removing the row, and one for adding a new child. For rows that do not represent compound rules, the add button will add a new sibling rule. There is no way, with the standard user interface, to add a new compound rule. The `-addCompoundRule:` action method in this class fixes this limitation.

This action is connected to a button outside of the predicate editor. When it is pressed, it inserts a new compound predicate row at the top of the editor. The method called here is declared in the `NSRuleEditor` class. The first argument is the index at which to insert the row and the third is the index of the parent row. The combination of these allows the row and the indent level to be specified. The -1 used as the parent is a special value, indicating that this should be a new root rule.

As long as the predicate editor has a compound predicate template row associated with it, then this will insert a new compound predicate at the top. You can see these at rows zero, two, and four in Figure 17.9.

The final argument controls whether the predicate editor should animate. As with all of the new views introduced with and after OS X 10.5, the predicate editor is designed with Core Animation in mind. Every transition is animated. It supports drag and drop using these animations, so once you have a compound predicate created you can move it to anywhere in the tree and create complex, nested predicates.

This example shows all of the code you need to set up a complex predicate using the predicate editor. Inserting compound predicates is not currently done in a very user-friendly way. You might try modifying this example so that it inserts the predicate under the current row, rather than at the top. You can do this by sending a `-selectedRowIndexes` message to the editor to get the current selection and then a `-parentRowForRow:` message to find the parent that you should pass as an argument when creating the new row.

In a real program, you probably wouldn't want to just display the predicate in a text field. Most often, you would want to filter an array based on it, or use it as input to a Spotlight search. You can do this by replacing the code in the `-predicateChanged:` method of this controller.

If you use bindings to connect your filtered array to a text view, then you don't need any code to keep the display in sync with the predicate. `NSArrayController` has a Filter Predicate binding. If the target of this binding is also the target of

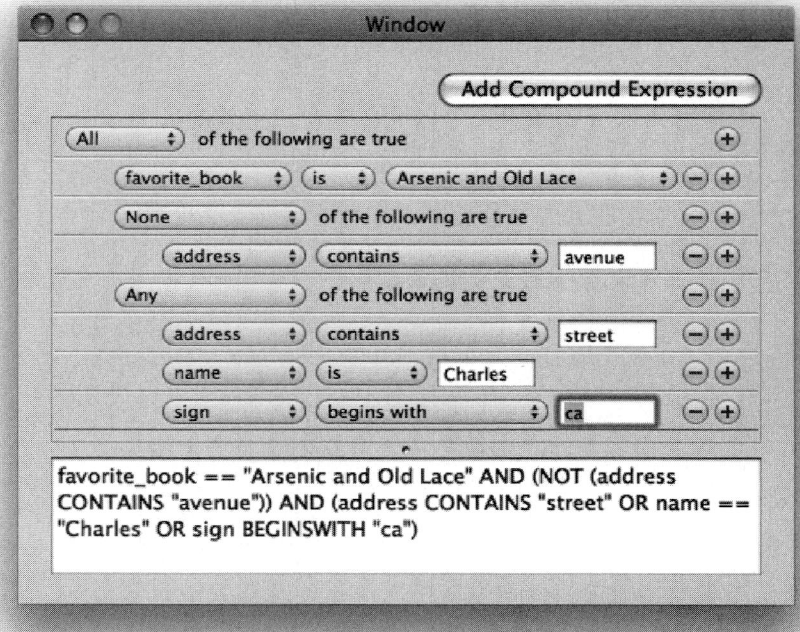

Figure 17.9: Creating predicates with the predicate editor.

predicate editor's binding, then anything bound to the array controller will only see the subset of the array that is generated by filtering it using the predicate.

17.6 Quick Look

The main benefit of adding support for Spotlight to your application is that it enables the user to quickly find documents from outside of your application. OS X 10.5 added a technology that complements this, allowing the user to quickly glance through documents and find the one that they wish to open.

A lot of Mac applications store a preview representation of a document in the resource fork, as the icon image, allowing the Finder to display a simple version of it in folder windows. This mechanism is not very well defined, and has the problem that it doesn't work well with filesystems that do not support resource forks.

The Quick Look architecture provides a better mechanism for implementing this kind of support. As with Spotlight, it uses a plugin architecture, where each application provides importers for the file types that it understands. When the Finder—or any other application providing a graphical view of a folder—inspects the file, the plugin is used to generate a thumbnail representation for display.

Often, a thumbnail is not quite enough to decide whether a selected file is the correct one. Quick Look also provides the opportunity to display preview windows for various file types. These pop up as floating windows and allow the user to quickly inspect the contents of a document. Ideally, this should be much quicker than launching the full application.

17.6.1 Previewing Bundles

If your application uses bundles to save documents, then you can support Quick Look with almost no additional code. In the top level of your bundle, create a folder called QuickLook. Note that this is the top level, not inside the Contents folder where everything else lives.

The QuickLook folder should contain two files, one for the preview and one for the thumbnail. These must be named Preview and Thumbnail, respectively and should be either .tiff, .png, or .jpg files, whichever is most appropriate to your contents. You can create these easily from a view in your application when you save by sending a `-dataWithPDFInsideRect:` message to the view and then converting the result, or by creating a new graphics context backed by an `NSBitmapImageRep` and saving the result.

You can test this support without writing any code, by creating a directory structure like this, either in the Finder or from the terminal:

```
$ ls -R example.bundle/
QuickLook

example.bundle//QuickLook:
Preview.png   Thumbnail.png
```

When you open the folder containing the example bundle in the Finder, you will see Preview.png as the icon for the bundle and Thumbnail.png will be shown when you click on the Quick Look icon.

17.6.2 Implementing Quick Look Plugins

As with Spotlight, Quick Look plugins use COM interfaces via the CFPlugin mechanism. When you create a Quick Look plugin in XCode, you are hidden from all of the messy details of this and just have to provide an implementation of one function for generating thumbnails:

```
OSStatus GenerateThumbnailForURL(void *thisInterface,
                                 QLThumbnailRequestRef thumbnail,
                                 CFURLRef url,
                                 CFStringRef contentTypeUTI,
                                 CFDictionaryRef options,
                                 CGSize maxSize);
```

As with other COM functions, this returns an error code and sends the real return data back via a parameter. In this case, the `thumbnail` parameter, which is a pointer to a mutable object that encapsulates the thumbnail that the plugin is expected to provide.

The `maxSize` parameter is important. This contains the maximum size for the returned image. Thumbnails can be displayed in a variety of different ways, and the maximum size may differ between them. This allows your plugin to handle different uses easily.

A similar function is required for supporting previews:

```
OSStatus GeneratePreviewForURL(void *thisInterface,
                               QLPreviewRequestRef preview,
                               CFURLRef url,
                               CFStringRef contentTypeUTI,
                               CFDictionaryRef options);
```

Both of these functions take the URL and UTI of the requested file as arguments and are expected to return some data for display. There are three ways of providing this data:

- Get a bitmap graphics context and draw into it.
- Get a multipage PDF graphics context and draw onto it.
- Write the preview as data in a format understood by Quick Look.

The first of these is rarely useful. It does not let you do anything that you can't do by creating a QuickLook folder in the bundle. The only time you would do this is when you want to provide Quick Look support for a document format that does not use a bundle. This is only advisable when your format is defined by some external standard. Formats designed for OS X generally benefit from being implemented as bundles.

The second provides a simple way of creating multipage documents. To create a multipage context for rendering a preview, you call this function:

```
QL_EXPORT CGContextRef QLPreviewRequestCreatePDFContext(
    QLPreviewRequestRef preview,
    const CGRect * mediaBox,
    CFDictionaryRef auxiliaryInfo,
    CFDictionaryRef properties);
```

There is no equivalent to this for thumbnails; they are always single-page documents, provided by one of the other two mechanisms. The returned graphics context can be used by Core Graphics drawing functions or attached to an `NSGraphicsContext` for use with AppKit drawing code. You should bracket each page with calls to `CGPDFContextBeginPage()` and `CGPDFContextEndPage()`.

Remember that Quick Look previews are meant to be quick. Generating the preview should be a lot faster than loading the application and the document. If possible, you should save the preview version inside the document bundle and have a very simple QuickLook plugin that just loads the preview and passes it to this function:

```
QL_EXPORT void QLPreviewRequestSetDataRepresentation(
    QLPreviewRequest preview,
    CFDataRef data,
    CFStringRef contentTypeUTI,
    CFDictionary properties);
```

`QLThumbnailRequestSetImageWithData()` is a variant of this that takes an image file for use as a thumbnail. Previews generated in this way are very flexible. They can be rich text, audio, video, or image data. This exposes all of the standard preview facilities, allowing the user to click on audio and video data to play it in the Finder.

Implementing a simple plugin can be done very quickly, especially if you do most of the work when you save the document and store the data in the bundle. Many of the same techniques that are useful for Spotlight importers apply to Quick Look plugins. You should make sure that both run as fast as possible. If you are dynamically providing data, then you may want to separate your model objects into a framework that can be linked against your application and both plugins. This should only contain the subset of the code required to load and index or preview the document. You should separate code that is required to modify the document out into categories or classes that are only in the application.

17.7 Summary

Searching is an important task in any application that handles a lot of data. In this chapter we looked at some of the technologies provided by OS X to make implementing these features easier.

Search Kit provides a simple way of creating for finding documents. You can use this to index any metadata, including long texts, and provide a mapping to document URLs.

For system-wide searching, OS X provides Spotlight. We saw how to create an import plugin that allowed Spotlight to index metadata from a new application. We also saw how to use Spotlight to search from within an application.

Next we looked at the `NSPredicate` system, used by Spotlight and other parts of OS X. This allows arbitrary conditions to be defined and used to filter array and other collections. We saw how to create predicates both in code and with a graphical editor.

We saw how bindings can be used to provide a display of a subset of a large array, filtered using a predicate, with no additional code.

Finally we looked at Quick Look, the preview infrastructure introduced in OS X 10.5 that makes it easy for users to find documents in large folders. These technologies all work together to allow the user to quickly find the correct document and the correct place within that document.

If you implement support for all of the features discussed in this chapter, then the documents created by your application will integrate well with the rest of the system and be easy for the user to locate. These features should not be the highest priority in a new application, but they go a long way toward making an application feel like an integrated part of the system.

Chapter 18

Contacts, Calendars, and Secrets

Mac OS X 10.2 introduced two new features for managing user information. The first is the *system-wide address book*. The original front end to this was the Address Book application, which allows the user to create and modify *vCards*. When Apple introduced Dashboard in 10.4, it also provided a simplified version of this application as an example widget. Since the interfaces are published and concurrency-safe, any application can use them to access information about the user's contacts.

The other addition is related but very different. While the Address Book is a shared, open, store of public information, the *Keychain* is a store of private information with strict access control. You can use the two in combination to store information about the user. For example, an instant messaging client might store the user's public address in his or her own vCard and his or her login details in the keychain.

During the 10.2 series, Apple introduced the *iCal* application as a free download and began bundling it with OS X. Leopard included a number of improvements to iCal. It became a CalDAV client, making it possible to edit shared calendars easily. Most importantly to developers, the *Calendar Store Framework* was introduced. This provides generic access to calendars from any application.

18.1 Address Book Overview

The Address Book is accessed via the AddressBook framework. This is modeled loosely after the *user defaults* system. While user defaults stores a set of generalized dictionary entries, the Address Book stores a set of people and has specific classes for handling each one.

The address book is designed as a central store of information about people. It is used throughout OS X. As well as the Address Book application, shown in Figure 18.1, a number of other Apple applications use it. Mail will use it as a source of email addresses, and Safari automatically populates a bookmarks menu from homepage entries. Even iCal uses it, to automatically generate a calendar from birthday entries. An RSS reader might do something similar, either automatically fetching RSS URLs from contacts' homepages or adding a news feed property.

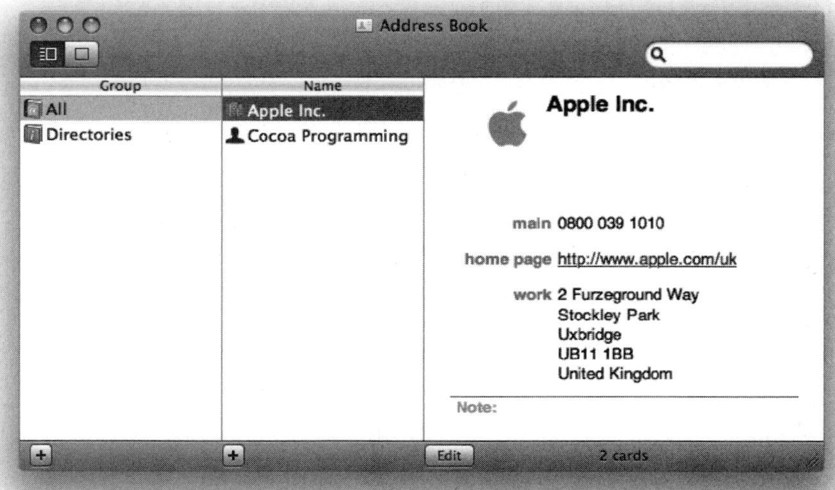

Figure 18.1: The OS X Address Book.

18.1.1 General Concepts

The basic unit of data in an address book is a person. This is represented by the `ABPerson` class, a subclass of `ABRecord`. The other subclass is `ABGroup`, which represents an arbitrary group of people.

The purpose of an address book is to store a set of metadata about people. Each person object has a set of properties that can have one or more values set for them. The framework introduces some new collection types—in a sense the

> **vCards**
>
> Entries in the Address Book are often referred to as vCards. This is standard file format for exchanging personal information, analogous to a business card or a calling card, in electronic form. The format is very simple, with one entry per line, each entry containing a record name and its data, separated by a colon (:). The Address Book can export and import entries in this format and its internal model corresponds quite closely to the vCard format.

entire framework is a set of new collection types—specifically tailored to the kind of data that an address book contains.

One person in the address book has special significance. The "me" vCard is the one identified as the user. This is the one that applications will often use even if they don't care about the user's contacts, since it stores a lot of information that can be used to populate a user interface. For example, you might want to get the user's address to provide local information in an application.

As with user defaults, there are two copies of the address book, the one committed to disk and the one in memory. If you make changes to the address book, you need to manually flush them back to disk. If another process modifies the address book, then you will receive a notification describing the changes. You can then either merge the changes manually, or (starting with 10.5) close the address book and open a new copy.

18.1.2 Collection Classes

There are two important collection classes in the Address Book framework. The first is `ABRecord`. This is the superclass for top-level entries in the address book. All people and groups are subclasses of this general interface. This provides a KVC-like mechanism for accessing properties of the entry.

Each property has a type. This is set when the property is created. Properties are divided into two broad categories: single and multiple values. Single values are strings, numbers, dates, arrays, dictionaries, or data. These may look familiar; they are the types that can be stored in property lists. This is not a coincidence; the first version of the Address Book stored its data in a property list.

Multi-value properties are an instance of the `ABMultiValue` class. This is a special kind of array, which behaves slightly like a dictionary (and doesn't inherit from `NSArray` or `NSDictionary`) for storing homogeneous lists of key-value pairs.

Each entry in a multivalue is uniquely identified by an index, just like an array. At each index, there is a label, which must be a string, and a value. All of the values must have the same type in a multivalue. You can store differently typed values in an `NSMutableMultiValue` but attempting to access them will cause an error. This is done to allow you to insert values immediately and then clean up the collection later.

Fast Enumeration

The `ABMultiValue` class is the only one of the Address Book classes that supports fast enumeration directly. If you want to enumerate all of the people in a group, then you first need to get an array. Enumerating properties in a record is a bit more complicated.

The type of a multivalue is an `ABPropertyType`, an enumerated type. This same enumerated type is used to identify the types of properties in records. There is a value in this enumeration for each of the single-value types, and a corresponding multivalue version. The types for multivalues are defined by values like this:

```
kABMultiStringProperty = kABMultiValueMask | kABStringProperty,
```

This means that you can independently test whether a property is a string and whether it is a multivalue by performing a bitwise AND (`&`) on one of the components and the value. For example, you could write a function that would print all string values, including those in multivalues. Listing 18.1 iterates over every person in the address book, then every property, and prints all that are strings.

Listing 18.1: Printing all strings in an address book. [from: examples/AddressBookList-Strings/main.m]

```
#import <Foundation/Foundation.h>
#import <AddressBook/AddressBook.h>

static void printPropertyIfString(NSString *key, id value, ABPropertyType
    type)
{
    if (type & kABStringProperty)
    {
        if ((type & kABMultiValueMask))
        {
            for (id subvalue in value)
            {
                printPropertyIfString(key, subvalue, type ^
                    kABMultiValueMask);
            }
        }
```

```
15          else
16          {
17              printf("%s: %s\n", [key UTF8String], [value UTF8String]);
18          }
19      }
20  }
21
22  int main(void)
23  {
24      [NSAutoreleasePool new];
25      ABAddressBook *book = [ABAddressBook sharedAddressBook];
26      for (ABPerson *person in [book people])
27      {
28          for (NSString *property in [ABPerson properties])
29          {
30              ABPropertyType type = [ABPerson typeOfProperty:property];
31              id value = [person valueForProperty:property];
32              if (value != nil)
33              {
34                  printPropertyIfString(property, value, type);
35              }
36          }
37      }
38  }
```

The function at the top of this listing takes the name of a property, the value, and the type as arguments. First, it checks if the type is a string. This uses a bitwise AND, rather than a comparison, and so will catch both single and multi-value properties. It then tests the type against the multivalue mask to determine whether this entry is a multivalue. If it is, then it recursively calls itself on each entry in the multivalue after clearing the multivalue flag. This is done on line 12. The multivalue mask is XORed with the type, which clears the bits that are set in the mask. When it reaches a single-valued string, it prints the key and the value.

The `main()` function shows how to enumerate all of the people and properties. These cannot be directly enumerated, unlike entries in a multivalue. To enumerate all of the people in an address book, you first need to get an array containing pointers to all of them and enumerate this. Enumerating properties is slightly harder.

Each `ABRecord` subclass—people and groups—has a set of properties defined at the class level. Every group has the same properties and every person has the same properties. Individual instances may implement a subset of these, so you might wonder why they are defined for the class. The reason is the type. If one person has a property with a given type, then every other person that implements that property also has to use the same type. This means you can create a user interface for a given property and not have to worry about handling different types in a particular component.

The test for `nil` is important. We can't enumerate the properties that a particular person object has; we can only get the total set that it might have and ask it if it has a value for each one in turn.

18.2 Getting Information About People

The Address Book framework makes it very easy to provide part of an address book user interface. The `ABPeoplePickerView` class was added with OS X 10.3 and provides a standard way of selecting people. This is a two-column view, with the left column showing all of the groups and the right showing all of the people in the selected group.

The Address Book application, shown in Figure 18.1, uses this view on the left side of its user interface. Unfortunately, the right view, which shows the properties of the person, is not provided for reuse.

This view is highly dynamic. Apart from the top component, the layout of the rest is configured based on the available properties. Creating a view like this yourself is quite a lot of work, but this is rarely required. Most of the time that you use the Address Book framework, you won't be trying to re-implement an address book application—there is a perfectly serviceable one supplied with OS X—you will be trying to use the contained information in your application.

Most often, you will want to get some subset of the data available for a given person. A common example is the user's image. OS X sets this to the avatar you choose for login for your own vCard. For other people it may be provided by you, or set automatically by your IM client.

As a simple example of using the address book, we will write an application that displays the avatars for everyone in your address book.

The first thing you need to do when writing any application that uses the address book is include AddressBook.framework in your project. You will find this in /System/Library/Frameworks. Drag it into your project, under Linked Frameworks, as shown in Figure 18.2. This allows the compiler to find the headers and the linker to find the library, both of which are contained in the framework bundle.

To display the avatars, we will just use a simple `NSTableView` with a single column containing `NSImageCells` and bind its contents to an array controller. The array will be loaded by a simple controller class, shown in Listing 18.2.

The image for each person is accessed by the `-imageData` method. This returns an `NSData` representation of the image, which can be turned into an `NSImage` or `NSImageRep` easily for drawing, or written out to disk.

Listing 18.2: Loading avatars from the address book. [from: examples/AvatarView/AddressBookImageLoader.m]

```
1 #import "AddressBookImageLoader.h"
2 #import <AddressBook/AddressBook.h>
3 
4 @implementation AddressBookImageLoader
5 - (void) awakeFromNib
6 {
7     [view setRowHeight:128];
8     [self willChangeValueForKey:@"images"];
9     images = [NSMutableArray array];
10     for (ABPerson *person in [[ABAddressBook sharedAddressBook] people])
11     {
12         NSData *imageData = [person imageData];
13         if (nil != imageData)
14         {
15             [images addObject:imageData];
16         }
17     }
18     [self didChangeValueForKey:@"images"];
19 }
20 - (NSMutableArray*)images
21 {
22     return images;
23 }
24 @end
```

In this case, we simply add each image to an array, which is accessed via bindings. Note how we make the KVO notification calls on lines 13 and 23, wrapping the entire operation rather than a single manipulation.

Exactly the same pattern can be used to load any other kind of data from the address book. If you wanted to implement mail merge in your application, you could use this same kind of loop to iterate over all of the people, or all of the people in a group, and get their addresses.

18.3 Searching the Address Book

Running this simple application just gives a table of images, as shown in Figure 18.3. Most of the time that you want to fetch an image, you will want to find the

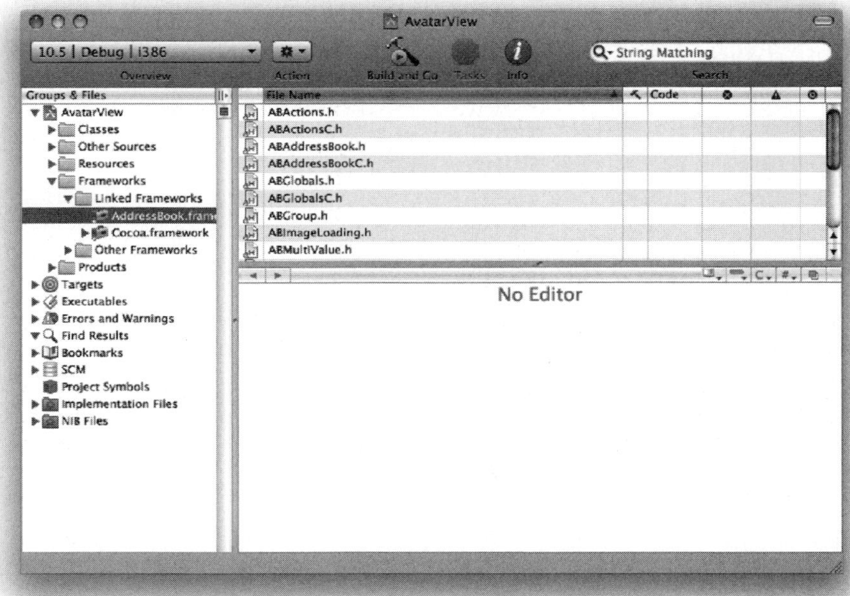

Figure 18.2: Linking the Address Book framework.

image for a specific user. For example, you might have received a message from a specific user and want to put his or her face (or avatar) next to it.

The obvious way of doing this is simply to iterate over each person and compare the property you were looking for (for example, his or her email address). This is not ideal, since it requires a linear search. For a property like the email address, you also have to make sure you properly handle multivalues, which can be quite complex.

Fortunately, the Address Book framework has some functionality for searching built in. Unfortunately, this doesn't use the standard `NSPredicate` mechanism that every other part of Cocoa uses. Instead, you search using the instances of the `ABSearchElement` class.

This class is constructed by sending a message to either the `ABPerson` or `ABGroup` class. To find the person with a specific email address, you would do this:

```
ABSearchElement *search =
    [ABPerson searchElementForProperty: kABEmailProperty
                                 label: nil
                                   key: nil
                                 value: emailAddress
                            comparison: kABEqual];
NSArray *people =
    [addressBook recordsMatchingSearchElement: search];
```

The first message here creates the search element. Note that you don't create search elements directly; you create them by sending a message to the type of record you want to find. The first parameter defines the property being matched, in this case the email address. This is a multivalue, and so you could specify something in the second argument if you wanted to restrict the search results to only home or work emails, for example.

The third argument only applies to dictionaries. The postal address is stored as a dictionary, by default. If you want to search for a postal code, or street name, then you would specify a key here. You might do this in a mapping application, for example, to find all of the people living near the visible region and automatically populate the display with their addresses.

The last two parameters specify the desired value and the kind of search to perform. In this case, we want a specified email address and it must be exactly equal to the one in the property.

When we search the address book, we get an array of `ABPerson` instances matching the search. For a search like this one, we would expect at most one result, since you rarely get two people with the same email address. Information about the person could then be displayed. This is exactly what Apple's Mail application does when it displays an email from someone with both an email address and an image in the address book.

You can combine search elements by sending a `+searchElementForConjunction:children:` message to the class. This takes an array of search elements as the second argument and returns a new search element matching any or all of them depending on the value of the first argument.

18.4 Populating the "Me" vCard

The "me" vCard is supposed to contain information about the current user. When you create an account on OS X, this card will be created with your login picture and your full name. You can fill in other information, and sometimes applications will do this for you.

If you create a new kind of property that is related to the user, then you might consider adding it. If you were writing a SIP client, for example, then you might want to store the user's SIP account in his or her vCard.

The first thing you would need to do is get a pointer to this card. This is one of the easiest things to do with the address book:

```
ABPerson *me = [[ABAddressBook sharedAddressBook] me];
```

A SIP address is like a telephone number or an email address, in that you can have more than one for different rôles. It makes sense therefore that it should be

Figure 18.3: Displaying avatars in a table view.

a multivalue. You can't just add a new property to the card; you first need to register it as a known type of property for people to have.

```
const kSIPAddress = @"com.example.sip-address";
NSDictionary *property =
    [NSDictionary dictionaryWithObject: kABMultiStringProperty
                                forKey: kSIPAddress];
[ABPerson addPropertiesAndTypes: property];
```

If this succeeds, the last line will return one—the number of properties successfully added—and we can begin adding the property. Note that the key is written in reverse-DNS notation. This helps to avoid collisions, but harms interoperability. If possible, you should try to collaborate with other people wanting to store the same kind of information. If every SIP client uses the same key to identify the address then this is much more convenient for the user.

Properties on Groups

We have only looked at properties on people so far. These are the only kind that the Address Book application can display, so it is easy to imagine that they are the only kind that exists. Since groups are a kind of record, just like people, they have the same ability to have properties added to them. You might want to do this, for example, to define the address of a mailing list that contains all of the people in a group. You could then expose this via a mail client to allow groups as recipients as well as individuals.

The final step is to set the property. The type we set is a multivalue, so we need to define a new multivalue for this entry and store a value in it and then add it. It would be nice if the address book provided convenience functions for setting the value of a label in a multivalue property, but since it doesn't you might consider writing categories that do if you use the framework a lot.

```
ABMutableMultiValue *value = [[ABMutableMultiValue alloc] init];
[value addValue: mySIPaddress
      withLabel: kABAddressHomeLabel];
[value setPrimaryIdentifier:  kABAddressHomeLabel];
[me setValue: value
 forProperty: kSIPAddress];
```

This will create a "home" SIP address. You should ideally prompt the user to select the kind of address that he or she is creating. This is a slight simplification of the general case, where you will want to add a label to an existing property. We know that at this point that there is no SIP address associated with any vCard, since we only just created the property. If this isn't the case, then you should get the original first and then add the new label. Remember that labels don't have to be unique, so inserting a value like this will not replace an old one; you need to find the old version and remove it with `-replaceLabelAtIndex:withLabel:` if you are changing a property.

Once you've gone to the trouble of adding a property to the "me" card, it would be a shame not to use it elsewhere. The address book is a good place to store information about any of the user's other contacts, too.

18.5 Adding People to the Address Book

One of the more common tasks with the address book is to add new vCards. You might want to do this in a communication application, for example, to automatically add people when they send you messages or when they publish their contact details in a protocol-specific way.

Creating a new person in the address book is quite simple. You need to generate the `ABPerson` object, set its various properties, and then insert it. Most of the work happens in the middle step, where you add properties to the new person. The general skeleton for creating a new person will look something like this:

```
ABPerson *person = [ABPerson new];
// Set properties of the person
[[ABAddressBook sharedAddressBook] addRecord: person];
```

Often, you will want to insert new records in a group, rather than in the top level of the address book. You may want to generate a new group for all of the people automatically inserted by your program, so the user can easily delete them later if they are not required. If you do this, then you will send an `-addMember:` message to an `ABGroup` instance instead.

The real work happens in the comment. A person is a subclass of a record and most of the properties are set by calling `-setValue:forProperty:` for each of the properties that you wish to set. A number of these are likely to be multivalues. This includes things like email addresses, where a person may have one address for work, one for home, and so on. We saw how to create multivalues in the last section.

The one value that is not set via a property is the photo, or avatar, property for the person. You set this by sending a `-setImageData:` message to the person. This takes an `NSData` representation of the image as an argument.

18.6 Storing Secrets

The Keychain API, unlike Address Book, is purely procedural C. There are Objective-C wrappers around it provided by third parties[1] but none are shipped by Apple.

The keychain API is massive, and wraps the *Common Data Security Architecture* (*CDSA*), which is even more complicated. The API description for CDSA is as long as this entire book and is quite dense. A full description of the power and flexibility of this system is far beyond the scope of this book—the Keychain itself is not technically part of Cocoa since it is a pure C API—but we will look at a few common keychain tasks, since they are important for providing a good user experience.

One of the most common complaints leveled at the Firefox web browser on OS X is that it uses its own password manager, rather than the keychain. This is bad for two reasons:

- Users are used to the Keychain and so trust it. If you provide your own password manager, then users will only trust it as much as they trust you, which is generally less than they trust Apple.
- Users can't access the passwords from outside of your application. Safari and Opera, for example, will share web login details since they both use the Keychain, and you can edit the passwords they see with the *Keychain Access* application.

Keychain items are locked to a small set of programs. The keychain will prompt the user if a program that tries to access a keychain item does not have permission or if it does have permission but has been modified since that permission was granted.

The most common use for the keychain is as a password store. The keychain understands two kinds of password: Internet and generic. Generic passwords are simply identified by a service and account name. Internet passwords have a lot more information, related to the server and protocol used. Exactly which is appropriate depends on the kind of application that you are writing.

Most applications use the login keychain. This is created by default and automatically unlocked when the object is created. For especially sensitive data you might want to create a new keychain. Since this will not be unlocked automatically, it is likely to irritate the user slightly if you do this for passwords that are not vitally important. The keychain implements its own access control, so passwords

[1]For example, the BSD-licensed Keychain framework (`http://sourceforge.net/projects/keychain/`).

stored in the login keychain should not leak to other processes without the user's permission.

You can create new keychains with the `SecKeychainCreate()` function. This stores a keychain in a specific location and sets a default password. The prototype for the function looks like this:

```
OSStatus SecKeychainCreate(
    const char *pathName,
    UInt32 passwordLength,
    const void *password,
    Boolean promptUser,
    SecAccessRef initialAccess,
    SecKeychainRef *keychain);
```

The first three parameters should be self-explanatory. The fourth one is fairly common in keychain functions. If it is true, then the user will be prompted to enter a password and the `password/passwordLength` parameters will be ignored. Lots of keychain functions provide the option of prompting the user like this, as a simple way of providing a consistent user interface. The `initialAccess` parameter indicates the access control for the keychain. Creating this requires several steps, and is one of the reasons why you should avoid creating keychains yourself.

The final parameter is a pointer into which the resulting keychain will be written. This is a `CFType` and so the usual `CFRetain()` mechanism applies. You need to `CFRelease()` it when you are finished with it.

Keychain History

The keychain grew out of a discontinued email application for Classic MacOS. Some of the coding conventions used are inherited from the Pascal-like conventions from early MacOS, some come via the CDSA specification, and some come from Carbon. This mesh of ideas makes the keychain one of the least friendly APIs on OS X. A simple example of this is the API for creating keychains, which expects a C-like `NULL`-terminated string to represent the path, but requires Pascal-like explicit lengths on the other strings. It then returns a Core Foundation reference via a pointer argument and an error code as its return value.

It is very unlikely that you will ever want to create a new keychain like this. Most programs can confine themselves to four functions in the Keychain API: those for setting and retrieving generic and Internet passwords.

Since generic passwords are simpler, we'll look at them first. Generic passwords are set with this function:

```
OSStatus SecKeychainAddGenericPassword(
    SecKeychainRef keychain,
    UInt32 serviceNameLength, const char *serviceName,
    UInt32 accountNameLength, const char *accountName,
    UInt32 passwordLength, const void *passwordData,
    SecKeychainItemRef *itemRef);
```

As when creating a keychain, the return value is simply a result code. The keychain item is returned via a pointer-to-a-pointer in the final argument. This function is slightly more consistent in its string arguments, requiring a length for all of them. All of these should be UTF-8 strings, and will typically be generated from `NSString`'s `-UTF8String` method.

The first argument is the keychain to use. Most of the time you will pass `NULL` here, which uses the generic keychain. The only time you need the keychain item opaque pointer is when you are manually modifying the access settings for the item, and so it is usually safe to pass `NULL` as the last parameter, too.

It is tempting to call this function with a simple Objective-C wrapper like this:

```
// DON T DO THIS!
OSStatus result = SecKeychainAddGenericPassword(
    NULL,
    [service length], [service UTF8String],
    [account length], [account UTF8String],
    [password length], [password UTF8String],
    NULL);
```

This contains a subtle bug that will probably pass most casual testing. The length parameters are meant to contain the number of bytes of the string, while `-length` returns the number of characters in the string. For ASCII and similar encodings, these will be the same. For UTF-8, they will be the same for common characters used in English, but not for all strings. This will cause silent truncation, which may cause a security hole. The following version would be correct:

```
OSStatus result = SecKeychainAddGenericPassword(
    NULL,
    [service lengthOfBytesUsingEncoding: NSUTF8StringEncoding],
    [service UTF8String],
    [account lengthOfBytesUsingEncoding: NSUTF8StringEncoding],
    [account UTF8String],
    [password lengthOfBytesUsingEncoding: NSUTF8StringEncoding],
    [password UTF8String],
    NULL);
```

To demonstrate the correct use of the keychain, we'll write a simple application for storing and retrieving passwords. This will be written in two parts: a generic

Objective-C wrapper around the most common parts of the keychain and a simple UI for using it. The first part is shown in Listing 18.3.

Listing 18.3: Bookkeeping for the Objective-C wrapper around the keychain. [from: examples/Keychain/Keychain.m]

```
1 + (void) initialize
2 {
3     if (self == [Keychain class])
4     {
5         defaultKeychain = [[Keychain alloc] init];
6     }
7 }
8 + (Keychain*) standardKeychain
9 {
10     return defaultKeychain;
11 }
12 - (Keychain*) initWithKeychainRef: (SecKeychainRef)aKeychain
13 {
14     if (nil == (self = [self init])) { return nil; }
15     keychain = (SecKeychainRef)CFRetain(aKeychain);
16     return self;
17 }
18 + (Keychain*) keychainWithKeychainRef: (SecKeychainRef)aKeychain
19 {
20     return [[[self alloc] initWithKeychainRef:aKeychain] autorelease];
21 }
22 - (void) finalize
23 {
24     CFRelease(keychain);
25 }
26 - (void) dealloc
27 {
28     CFRelease(keychain);
29     [super dealloc];
30 }
```

This class implements the *singleton pattern* for the default keychain. All calls to `+standardKeychain` will return the same instance, which is created on line 11 when the class receives its first message. For general use, we provide constructors that allow a specific keychain to be used, on lines 18–27, but these won't be used by the example UI.

Note that we need to release the keychain object using the Core Foundation release function. Since this needs to be called even in a garbage-collected environment, it is done in both the `-dealloc` and `-finalize` methods.

The code for setting a generic password is shown in Listing 18.4. This is a two-step process since the Keychain API does not include functions for doing this directly. We have to have different cases for changing a password and adding a new one.

Listing 18.4: Setting a generic password. [from: examples/Keychain/Keychain.m]

```
1  - (BOOL) setGenericPassword: (NSString*)aPassword
2                  forAccount: (NSString*)anAccount
3                     service: (NSString*)aService
4  {
5      SecKeychainItemRef item = NULL;
6      SecKeychainFindGenericPassword(keychain,
7          [aService lengthOfBytesUsingEncoding: NSUTF8StringEncoding],
8          [aService UTF8String],
9          [anAccount lengthOfBytesUsingEncoding: NSUTF8StringEncoding],
10         [anAccount UTF8String],
11         NULL,
12         NULL,
13         &item);
14     OSStatus result;
15     if (item != NULL)
16     {
17         result = SecKeychainItemModifyAttributesAndData(
18             item,
19             NULL,
20             [aPassword lengthOfBytesUsingEncoding: NSUTF8StringEncoding],
21             [aPassword UTF8String]);
22         CFRelease(item);
23     }
24     else
25     {
26         result = SecKeychainAddGenericPassword(keychain,
27             [aService lengthOfBytesUsingEncoding: NSUTF8StringEncoding],
28             [aService UTF8String],
29             [anAccount lengthOfBytesUsingEncoding: NSUTF8StringEncoding],
30             [anAccount UTF8String],
31             [aPassword lengthOfBytesUsingEncoding: NSUTF8StringEncoding],
32             [aPassword UTF8String],
33             NULL);
34     }
35     return (result == noErr);
36 }
```

The first step, from lines 41–49, is to see if there is an existing password entry for this account. If there is, then `item` will be set to reference it. If there is already a keychain entry, then we need to modify it, as shown on lines 53–57. This is done via a very general function that allows arbitrary attributes on the keychain item to be modified. Since we are not using this functionality, we just pass `NULL` to the second argument and set the password with the last two. We then need to remember to release the item before continuing.

The other code path, lines 62–69, is for the case when the item isn't already in the keychain. This adds it, using the information provided. The result of both of these calls is an `OSStatus` code, a type inherited from Classic MacOS. This can contain a number of error values, but we just return a Boolean indicating whether the operation succeeded.

The inverse operation, getting a generic password from the keychain, is shown in Listing 18.5. This is much simpler. We use the same call as before to find the existing password, but with slightly different values. This time we don't want the keychain item; we just want the password data, so we pass `NULL` as the last argument and pointers to an integer and a pointer as the preceding two arguments.

Listing 18.5: Retrieving a generic password. [from: examples/Keychain/Keychain.m]

```
1  - (NSString*) genericPasswordForAccount: (NSString*)anAccount
2                                   Service:(NSString*)aService
3  {
4      UInt32 length;
5      void *password;
6      OSStatus result = SecKeychainFindGenericPassword(keychain,
7              [aService lengthOfBytesUsingEncoding: NSUTF8StringEncoding],
8              [aService UTF8String],
9              [anAccount lengthOfBytesUsingEncoding: NSUTF8StringEncoding],
10             [anAccount UTF8String],
11             &length,
12             &password,
13             NULL);
14     if (result != noErr) { return nil; }
15     NSString *passwordString =
16         [[NSString alloc] initWithBytes: password
17                                  length: length
18                                encoding: NSUTF8StringEncoding];
19     SecKeychainItemFreeContent(NULL, password);
20     return [passwordString autorelease];
21 }
```

If this fails for any reason, then we just abort and return `nil`, with the guard on line 86. Lines 87–90 construct and return an Objective-C string from the returned data.

Note that the returned string will not be `NULL`-terminated. If you passed it as an argument to `+stringWithUTF8String:`, then you would either get back a string containing the password followed by some random data, or your application would crash. Since the returned data is not reference counted or garbage collected, we need to manually free it after constructing the string. This is done on line 91.

Listing 18.6 shows the corresponding operations on Internet passwords. These are conceptually similar to generic passwords, but have more fields for uniquely identifying them.

Listing 18.6: Operations on Internet passwords. [from: examples/Keychain/Keychain.m]

```
- (BOOL) setInternetPassword: (NSString*)aPassword
                  forAccount: (NSString*)anAccount
            inSecurityDomain: (NSString*)aDomain
                    onServer: (NSString*)aServer
                        port: (UInt16)aPort
                    protocol: (SecProtocolType) aProtocol
                        path: (NSString*)aPath
{
    SecKeychainItemRef item = NULL;
    SecKeychainFindInternetPassword(keychain,
        [aServer lengthOfBytesUsingEncoding: NSUTF8StringEncoding],
        [aServer UTF8String],
        [aDomain lengthOfBytesUsingEncoding: NSUTF8StringEncoding],
        [aDomain UTF8String],
        [anAccount lengthOfBytesUsingEncoding: NSUTF8StringEncoding],
        [anAccount UTF8String],
        [aPath lengthOfBytesUsingEncoding: NSUTF8StringEncoding],
        [aPath UTF8String],
        aPort,
        aProtocol,
        kSecAuthenticationTypeDefault,
        NULL,
        NULL,
        &item);
    OSStatus result;
    if (item != NULL)
    {
        result = SecKeychainItemModifyAttributesAndData(
            item,
            NULL,
            [aPassword lengthOfBytesUsingEncoding: NSUTF8StringEncoding],
            [aPassword UTF8String]);
        CFRelease(item);
    }
    else
```

```
    {
        result = SecKeychainAddInternetPassword(keychain,
            [aServer lengthOfBytesUsingEncoding: NSUTF8StringEncoding],
            [aServer UTF8String],
            [aDomain lengthOfBytesUsingEncoding: NSUTF8StringEncoding],
            [aDomain UTF8String],
            [anAccount lengthOfBytesUsingEncoding: NSUTF8StringEncoding],
            [anAccount UTF8String],
            [aPath lengthOfBytesUsingEncoding: NSUTF8StringEncoding],
            [aPath UTF8String],
            aPort,
            aProtocol,
            kSecAuthenticationTypeDefault,
            [aPassword lengthOfBytesUsingEncoding: NSUTF8StringEncoding],
            [aPassword UTF8String],
            NULL);
    }
    return (result == noErr);
}
- (NSString*) internetPasswordForAccount: (NSString*)anAccount
                        inSecurityDomain: (NSString*)aDomain
                                onServer: (NSString*)aServer
                                    port: (UInt16)aPort
                                protocol: (SecProtocolType) aProtocol
                                    path: (NSString*)aPath
{
    UInt32 length;
    void *password;
    OSStatus result = SecKeychainFindInternetPassword(keychain,
            [aServer lengthOfBytesUsingEncoding: NSUTF8StringEncoding],
            [aServer UTF8String],
            [aDomain lengthOfBytesUsingEncoding: NSUTF8StringEncoding],
            [aDomain UTF8String],
            [anAccount lengthOfBytesUsingEncoding: NSUTF8StringEncoding],
            [anAccount UTF8String],
            [aPath lengthOfBytesUsingEncoding: NSUTF8StringEncoding],
            [aPath UTF8String],
            aPort,
            aProtocol,
            kSecAuthenticationTypeDefault,
            &length,
            &password,
            NULL);
    if (result != noErr) { return nil; }
```

```
    NSString *passwordString =
        [[NSString alloc] initWithBytes: password
                                 length: length
                               encoding: NSUTF8StringEncoding];
    SecKeychainItemFreeContent(NULL, password);
    return [passwordString autorelease];
}
```

To see how this works, we create a simple window with three text fields, for the service, account, and password data in a generic password, and two buttons, one for setting and one for fetching the password. The resulting Window is shown in Figure 18.4. The controller for this window is shown in Listing 18.7.

Listing 18.7: The password controller implementation. [from: examples/Keychain/GenericPasswordController.m]

```
#import "GenericPasswordController.h"
#import "Keychain.h"

@implementation GenericPasswordController
- (IBAction) storePassword: (id)sender
{
    Keychain *keychain = [Keychain standardKeychain];
    [keychain setGenericPassword: [password stringValue]
                      forAccount: [account stringValue]
                         service: [service stringValue]];
}
- (IBAction) findPassword: (id)sender
{
    Keychain *keychain = [Keychain standardKeychain];
    NSString *pass =
        [keychain genericPasswordForAccount: [account stringValue]
                                    Service: [service stringValue]];
    [password setStringValue: pass];
}
@end
```

This simply defines two action methods, one for each button. The first sets the password and the second retrieves it, both using the singleton default keychain.

If you set a password using this application and then try to look at the password from the Keychain Access application, you will get a dialog box like the one in Figure 18.5. This is because the password was created by the new application, and any other application that wants to access it must acquire permission from the user to do so.

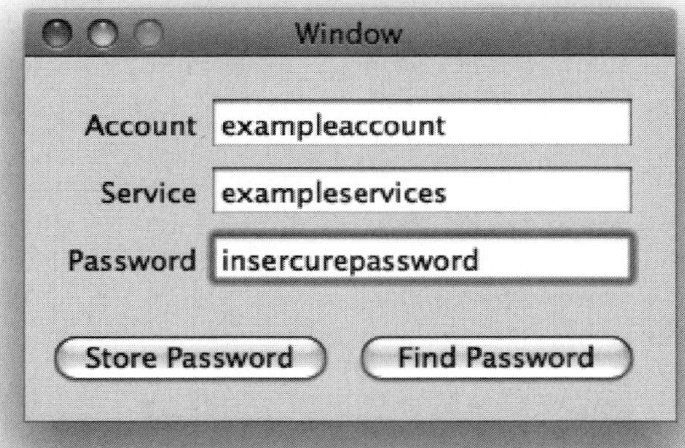

Figure 18.4: A simple keychain-using application.

Figure 18.5: Requesting access to a keychain item.

Once this permission is granted, the item can be inspected, as shown in Figure 18.6. This shows one of the big advantages of using the keychain: Passwords are stored in a secure, application-independent, way.

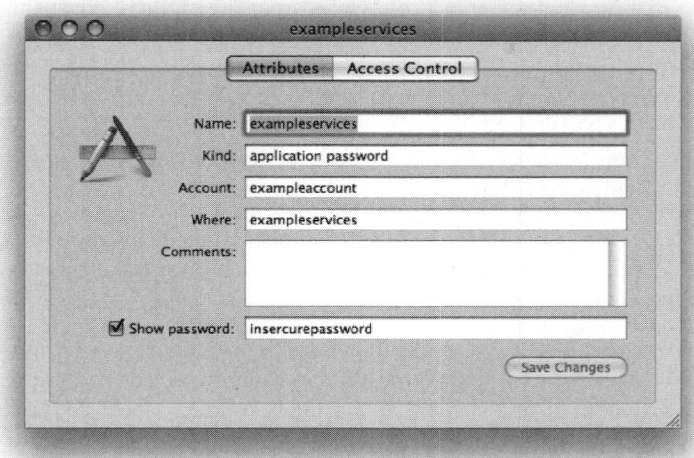

Figure 18.6: Accessing the keychain.

18.7 Calendars

Calendars are closely related to contact information. The combination of contacts, calendaring, and email is often referred to as *groupware*. If you are familiar with the iCal application, then you will find the calendar model provided by the Calendar Store Framework to be very easy to grasp.

The basic idea of a calendar is a set of events associated with dates. In iCal and the calendar framework, calendars can also store tasks. These are items on a to-do list. They fit with the calendar model since they have a due date.

18.7.1 Calendar Store Concepts

The top level in the Calendar Store Framework is the `CalCalendarStore` class. This represents an abstract location where calendars are stored. It is another example of the *singleton pattern*, since each user has a single calendar store.

iCalendar

Just as the standard for storing and exchanging address book information was the vCard, the standard for calendar information was the *vCalendar*. In newer versions, this was renamed *iCalendar*, which can be slightly confusing for Mac users. The iCalendar format is not specific to iCal, or even to Apple. It is an open, IETF-approved, standard with a similar format to vCards.

Inside the calendar store, there can be a variety of different calendars. There are six kinds of calendars that are currently supported:

- Local calendars are the simplest, stored on the local machine in a file somewhere (abstracted from the user and the developer and subject to change in future versions).
- CalDAV calendars are stored on a remote server, but can be modified. The CalDAV protocol extends WebDAV to provide a set of well-defined properties on calendar objects that can be independently modified. A number of CalDAV servers exist, including an open source one developed by Apple and bundled with OS X Server.
- IMAP calendars are similar to CalDAV, but are accessed via the IMAP protocol. The permissions on the server define what changes you can make to these calendars.
- Exchange calendars are stored on a Microsoft Exchange server. OS X 10.6 added integration with Exchange at the system level, so any application running on this version of the system can connect to Microsoft Exchange calendars.
- Subscription calendars are stored remotely and are read-only. They are periodically fetched from the server and cached locally.
- The final kind is the special birthday calendar, maintained by the address book.

Each of these calendars stores items, which are either events or tasks. Somewhat confusingly, you do not access the items via their calendar. Items have a pointer to the calendar that contains them, but you cannot ask a calendar to enumerate all of the items that it contains.

Calendar objects are actually very simple. They just have six properties, defining the basic attributes of the calendar. To get at items, you need to go via the calendar store.

Calendars and Properties

The Calendar Store Framework uses declared properties everywhere. They are not used in much of the rest of Cocoa, since they only work on OS X 10.5 and newer, but since this framework doesn't work on older versions of OS X either it is free from backward-compatibility constraints.

Unlike the address book, the calendar store is searched using `NSPredicate` instances. There are some helpful methods on the `CalCalendarStore` class for constructing predicates specific to the calendar properties. You can use these to quickly construct a predicate for a set of calendars. Future versions of this will probably support arbitrary predicates, but the version shipped with Leopard can only handle predicates created by the class.

The inability to easily access all of the events in a particular calendar is a design choice. Calendars stored on a remote server can be very large and there might not be an up-to-date local cache of all of their data. Fetching all of this and then iterating over it will be incredibly slow.

By forcing all access to calendar items to go via predicates, the framework ensures that access is efficient. Both CalDAV and IMAP have server-side search facilities. Predicates that will search over remote calendars will be translated into requests for server-side searches, reducing the bandwidth usage required. Typically the server will have an index that allows these searches to run quickly. The predicates isolate you from needing to create server-specific requests.

18.7.2 Accessing Events

To see how the calendar and address book interact, we will create a simple meeting viewer. This will use a people picker view to let the user select people and then display all events that they are attending.

The final version will display a window like the one shown in Figure 18.8. This is a simple split view with a people picker on the left and a table view on the right. The controller will create an array of events, bound to an array controller, with each table column to be bound to one of the properties of the event.

This highlights the main difference between the calendar and address book frameworks. The calendar classes are all designed with a modern Cocoa environment in mind. Since the address book predates predicates and bindings, it is not designed to be usable with either, making it feel very clunky to use.

The controller for this interface is shown in Listing 18.8. When it is loaded, it registers for two notifications, one from the people picker and one from the calendar store. The user interface needs to be updated when one of two things happens, either the user selects a different set of people or the calendar events change. These two notifications are requested and directed to the same method.

Listing 18.8: The meeting viewer controller. [from: examples/MeetingViewer/MeetingController.m]

```
#import "MeetingController.h"
#import <CalendarStore/CalendarStore.h>
#import <AddressBook/AddressBook.h>

@implementation MeetingController
- (void) awakeFromNib
{
    NSNotificationCenter *center = [NSNotificationCenter defaultCenter];
    [center addObserver:self
               selector: @selector(selectionChanged:)
                   name: ABPeoplePickerNameSelectionDidChangeNotification
                 object: peopleView];
    [center addObserver: self
               selector: @selector(selectionChanged:)
                   name: CalEventsChangedExternallyNotification
                 object: [CalCalendarStore defaultCalendarStore]];
}
- (void) dealloc
{
    [[NSNotificationCenter defaultCenter] removeObserver:self];
    [super dealloc];
}
- (void) selectionChanged:(NSNotification*)notification
{
    CalCalendarStore *store = [CalCalendarStore defaultCalendarStore];
    NSArray *people = [peopleView selectedRecords];
    NSArray *events = nil;
    if ([people count] > 0)
    {
        NSPredicate *predicate =
            [CalCalendarStore eventPredicateWithStartDate: [NSDate date]
                                                  endDate: [NSDate
                                                      distantFuture]
                                                calendars: [store calendars
                                                     ]];
        NSArray *events = [store eventsWithPredicate: predicate];
        names = [NSMutableArray array];
        for (ABPerson *person in people)
        {
```

```
38            NSString *name = [NSString stringWithFormat:@"%@ %@",
39                                  [person valueForProperty:kABFirstNameProperty
                                      ],
40                                  [person valueForProperty:kABLastNameProperty
                                      ]];
41            [names addObject:name];
42        }
43        predicate = [NSPredicate predicateWithFormat:
44            @"ANY attendees.commonName IN %@", names];
45        events = [events filteredArrayUsingPredicate:predicate];
46    }
47    [self willChangeValueForKey:@"meetings"];
48    [meetings release];
49    meetings = [events retain];
50    [self didChangeValueForKey:@"meetings"];
51 }
52 @end
```

The user interface is updated by the method that begins on line 23. On lines 30-34, this gets an array of all calendar events that are still in the future. It would be nice to be able to pass the predicate for creating the final array in here, but unfortunately this is not possible in the current version. This means that we get a potentially large array on line 34 and then filter it later.

Unfortunately, there is no easy way of getting the common names of all of the people in an array of `ABPerson` instances. The code on lines 38–40 writes their names in the common order for English names. By interrogating the flags for the person, you can find out what the correct order for displaying them is, but for this simple example we just create an array of names in this order.

On lines 43–44 we create a new predicate for filtering the array. This matches all events that have an attendee in the list. Once we've got this array, we set it to the meeting attribute and call the KVO notification methods so that the UI will be updated.

You can test this by creating events in iCal, as shown in Figure 18.7 and marking them as having one or more attendees. When you select some of the attendees, the date and name of the event should show up in this application, as shown in Figure 18.8.

You can filter events by any similar set of criteria. The only predicates supported directly are those that are based on date ranges and calendars, but you can filter the returned array by any predicate you can construct. A simple example might be anything with "meeting" or "party" in the event title.

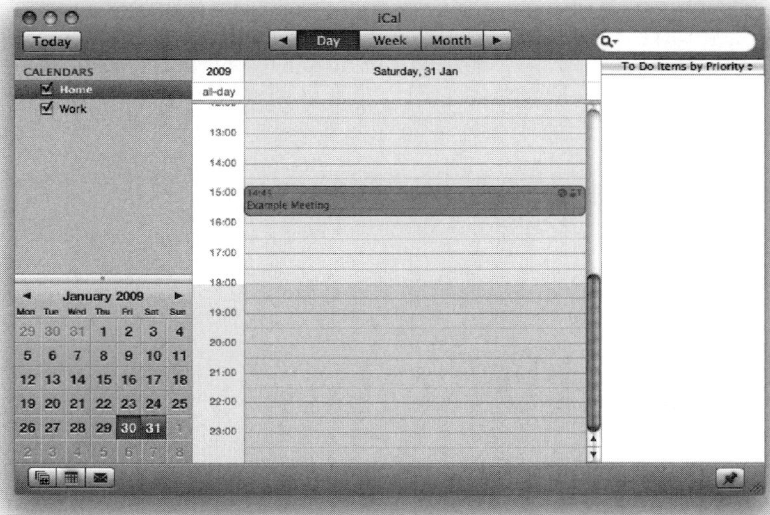

Figure 18.7: Creating a meeting in iCal.

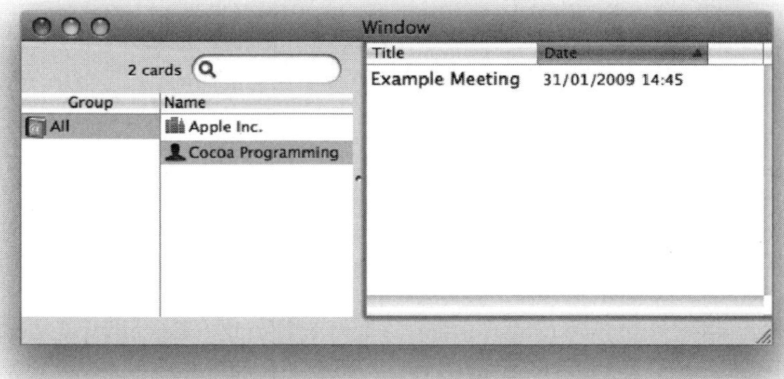

Figure 18.8: Displaying meetings from the calendar.

18.7.3 Creating Calendars

Accessing calendars and events is often useful, but it is a long way from exercising the full power of the calendar system. One calendar that a typical OS X user has is generated and maintained entirely outside of iCal: the birthdays calendar, maintained by the address book. It is sometimes convenient for a new application to add a new calendar for a similar purpose.

Creating a new calendar is trivial. All you need to do is create a new instance of the `CalCalendar` class, like this:

```
CalCalendar *cal = [CalCalendar calendar];
```

This will create a new local calendar, but will not commit it to the store. After you have set properties on the calendar you can save it like this:

```
[store saveCalendar:cal error:&err];
```

This will return **YES** if the save succeeds. Creating a new calendar is not a very common occurrence. A project management tool might create one for each new project, with milestones and meetings added as tasks and events, but most other applications that interact with the calendar store will just create new entries in an existing calendar.

All entries in a calendar are instances of a subclass of `CalCalendarItem`. This class has a set of declared properties that are common to all calendar items, such as the set of associated alarms and the calendar holding the item.

The two concrete subclasses are `CalEvent` and `CalTask`, for events and tasks, respectively. Neither of these declares any methods; both simply add a set of properties that represent the information specific to the item type.

Creating either of these is a three-step process. First, you create an instance of the object, then you set properties on it, and finally commit it to the store. In both cases there is one property that you must set—the calendar that contains the item—with all of the others being optional. In most cases, however, you will also set the title, at the very least. The three steps are shown here:

```
CalTask *task = [CalTask task];
task.calendar = cal;
task.title = @"New␣task";
[store saveTask:task error:&err];
```

The heavy use of declared properties in the framework makes setting the attributes of the new item very easy. If you wanted to write a simple to-do list manager, you could do so with almost no code by just binding some or all of the properties declared by `CalCalendarItem` and `CalTask` to columns in a table view. The only code you'd need would be for flushing the changes back to the disk and for getting the array of tasks from the calendar.

Bindings and Calendar Items

You can use bindings on calendar items to edit them in something like a table view, but this will not automatically flush them back to the store. If you bind an array of calendar items to an array controller, then the data view bound to the controller will modify the items, but only in the local copy. You should register as an observer on the items yourself, or use the data source's notification that it has performed an editing operation, and use this as a signal to flush changes back to disk.

18.8 Synchronizing Data

Although you can use the address book and calendar stores directly, a lot of the time all that you want to do is make sure that they are kept in sync with some other store. This might be some online service, a peripheral device, or even locally generated data.

With 10.4, Apple added the *Sync Services* API. This exposed a lot of the functionality that was previously private to the *iSync* application. Using this API you can keep your own data store synchronized with ones provided by other clients.

Sync services presents a client-server API to the user. The server is provided by the system and maintains a *truth database*, a store of dictionaries containing the current state of various supported models. Clients try to synchronize their states with some subset of this database. This is typically a two-step process. First, the client pushes any changes that have happened locally to the server; then it pulls down any changes that have been created by other clients.

The client interface is very general. A client can be any producer or consumer of data that follows a published schema. There are four standard types:

- Application clients are programs like iCal or Address Book. These maintain an internal store and present some kind of user interface for modifying it. They use sync services to share their data with other clients.

- Device clients are sync drivers for external hardware. Something like a mobile phone or an iPod can store some data from various other sync clients. Some allow the data to be edited; some just display it.

- Server clients encapsulate some server-side store. Apple provides one of these for their Mobile*Me* service. This allows data from any client to be pushed to the server.

- Peers are similar to server clients, except that they represent a machine that may change the data directly, rather than just storing data that other clients will update.

You can use these to represent almost any producer or consumer of data. Most applications will fall into the application client category. These are single programs that may both produce and consume data via sync services.

You can use sync services both to access the standard Apple data stores and to provide your own for other developers to use. When you publish a schema for use with Sync Services, you make it possible for any other developer to write applications that modify the data that your application manages, without invoking your application directly. This is very useful for any program which, like the Address Book or iCal, manages an internal store of user data.

18.8.1 Using Apple Schemas

The data to be synchronized is defined by a *schema*. This is an *entity-relationship* model similar to the kind used by Core Data. Schemas have a slightly richer set of data types that they can store that Core Data, permitting URLs, colors, and dates as well as the standard property list types.

You can define a new schema in XCode. This is very similar to creating a new data model. Creating a new schema lets you synchronize different instances of your application easily, but the more interesting use of sync services is to sync with other applications.

Using sync services is more flexible than using the calendar and address book frameworks directly. You can easily store data that other applications don't understand and only sync the subset that they do. There are four schemas shipped with Leopard:

- Safari bookmarks are stored in folders and contain the name, URL, and position in the folder for each bookmark. You could write a client that kept these synced with some online bookmark store, for example.
- iCal calendars are accessible via sync services instead of the calendar store framework.
- Address book contacts are also shared with sync services. You can use this to keep an application's internal address book, or a remote server or device's address book synchronized with the system-wide address book.
- Mail notes are stored on IMAP servers or locally by Mail and can also be synchronized with any sync services client.

You can use any of these to get access to existing data stores provided by OS X. To demonstrate how to use the sync services API, we'll take one of the simpler Apple-provided schemas and write a program that will fetch a subset of its contents and display it.

Mixing Access

If you are using sync services to communicate with the address book or the calendar, then you should not use the native frameworks as well. Doing so will confuse the sync server, since it will receive updates from your client and updates from the framework separately. In general you should use the native APIs when you want to access and modify the data and sync services if you want to keep your own store and allow other applications to access and modify part of it.

If you want to use the sync services API, then you will need to create a client description. The simplest way of doing this is to create a property list, from the template provided in XCode. Listing 18.9 shows the simple version that we will use.

Listing 18.9: Describing the sync client. [from: examples/NotesViewer/ClientDescription.plist]

```
<?xml version="1.0" encoding="UTF-8"?>
<!DOCTYPE plist PUBLIC "-//Apple//DTD PLIST 1.0//EN" "http://www.apple.com/DTDs/PropertyList-1.0.dtd">
<plist version="1.0">
<dict>
    <key>DisplayName</key>
    <string>NotesViewer</string>
    <key>Entities</key>
    <dict>
        <key>com.apple.notes.Note</key>
        <array>
            <string>com.apple.notes.Note</string>
            <string>content</string>
            <string>subject</string>
        </array>
    </dict>
    <key>Type</key>
    <string>app</string>
</dict>
</plist>
```

This defines a very simple client that is interested in two of the properties of the `com.apple.notes.Note` entity, specifically the content and subject properties. We'll divide the rest of the code up into two classes. The first one, shown in Listing 18.10, is the interface to the application that creates a sync session and then monitors the client for changes using KVO. The other class, shown in Listing 18.11, is the data source for the sync session driver.

Listing 18.10: Running a sync session. [from: examples/NotesViewer/NoteSync.m]

```
1  #import "NoteSync.h"
2  
3  @implementation NoteSync
4  @synthesize notes;
5  - (void)awakeFromNib
6  {
7      client = [SyncClient new];
8      driver =
9          [ISyncSessionDriver sessionDriverWithDataSource: client];
10     [driver sync];
11     [client addObserver: self
12              forKeyPath: @"notes"
13                 options: NSKeyValueObservingOptionNew
14                 context: NULL];
15     self.notes = [client.notes allValues];
16 }
17 - (void)observeValueForKeyPath: (NSString*)keyPath
18                       ofObject: (id)object
19                         change: (NSDictionary*)change
20                        context: (void*)context
21 {
22     self.notes = [client.notes allValues];
23 }
24 @end
```

The sync session driver is created on line 9 of Listing 18.10. This class was introduced with OS X 10.5, and dramatically simplifies the task of implementing sync services support. This is the only code in this class specific to sync services. The rest of it relates to creating the `SyncClient` instance and monitoring its `notes` property for changes. The `notes` property in this class is bound to an array controller, which is bound to the table columns shown in Figure 18.9.

The `SyncClient` class implements the `ISyncSessionDriverDataSource` protocol, which defines a set of methods that a data source for use with the session driver must implement.

Remember that this API is for synchronization and not just remote access. We must make sure that we keep track of a local copy of the data so we can apply any changes since the last run. This is done by storing the dictionary in user defaults. On line 9, we load the saved version from defaults when the class is loaded. If there is no existing version, then we just create an empty dictionary.

Listing 18.11: A sync session driver data source. [from: examples/NotesViewer/SyncClient.m]

```
1 #import "SyncClient.h"
2 
3 @implementation SyncClient
4 @synthesize notes;
5 - (id)init
6 {
7     if (nil == (self = [super init])) { return nil; }
8     NSUserDefaults *defaults = [NSUserDefaults standardUserDefaults];
9     notes = [[defaults dictionaryForKey: @"CachedNotes"] mutableCopy];
10     if (nil == notes)
11     {
12         notes = [NSMutableDictionary new];
13     }
14     return self;
15 }
16 - (NSString*)clientIdentifier
17 {
18     return @"com.example.NoteViewer";
19 }
20 - (NSURL*)clientDescriptionURL
21 {
22     NSString *path =
23         [[NSBundle mainBundle] pathForResource:@"ClientDescription"
24                                         ofType:@"plist"];
25     return [NSURL fileURLWithPath: path];
26 }
27 - (NSArray*)schemaBundleURLs
28 {
29     return [NSArray arrayWithObject: [NSURL fileURLWithPath:
30         @"/System/Library/SyncServices/Schemas/Notes.syncschema"]];
31 }
32 - (NSArray*)entityNamesToSync
33 {
34     return [NSArray arrayWithObject: @"com.apple.notes.Note"];
35 }
36 - (ISyncSessionDriverChangeResult)applyChange: (ISyncChange*)change
37                                 forEntityName: (NSString*)entityName
38                    remappedRecordIdentifier: (NSString**)
                           outRecordIdentifier
```

```
39                                               formattedRecord: (NSDictionary**)outRecord
40                                                         error: (NSError**)outError
41 {
42     [self willChangeValueForKey: @"notes"];
43     if ([change type] == ISyncChangeTypeDelete)
44     {
45         [notes removeObjectForKey: [change recordIdentifier]];
46     }
47     else
48     {
49         [notes setObject: [change record]
50                   forKey: [change recordIdentifier]];
51     }
52     NSUserDefaults *defaults = [NSUserDefaults standardUserDefaults];
53     [defaults setObject: notes
54                  forKey: @"CachedNotes"];
55     [self didChangeValueForKey: @"notes"];
56     return ISyncSessionDriverChangeAccepted;
57 
58 }
59 - (BOOL)deleteAllRecordsForEntityName:(NSString *)entityName error:(NSError
       **)outError
60 {
61     return NO;
62 }
63 - (NSDictionary*)recordsForEntityName: (NSString*)entityName
64                            moreComing: (BOOL*)moreComing
65                                 error: (NSError**)outError
66 {
67     *moreComing = NO;
68     return notes;
69 }
70 - (ISyncSessionDriverMode)preferredSyncModeForEntityName: (NSString*)entity
71 {
72     return ISyncSessionDriverModeSlow;
73 }
74 @end
```

The methods from line 16–35 will all be called at the start of the sync session and provide information about this client. The URL returned by `-clientDescriptionURL` points to the property list for the client. This is stored in the bundle, but for a network service could equally be stored online. The schema for this session is supplied by the `-schemaBundleURLs` method. Because we are using an Apple schema for this example, we don't need to include our own copy. This method just returns a path to a standard location on the filesystem where the schema should exist.

The method on line 32 is options, and in this simple example is superfluous. It is included to show that you can introduce dynamic variations into the sync client behavior. In this case we are only synchronizing one entity anyway, but it is possible to restrict the set that you want to sync for any given session. This can be very useful for a network sync service, which might be used over expensive and slow mobile connections or cheap and fast broadband links. You could give the user the option of only syncing a subset of the entities, giving an overview of the available changes, rather than everything at once.

The `-preferredSyncModeForEntityName:` method is called next and returns the desired sync mode. In this case, we always request slow syncing, which asks for all of the records by calling the method on line 63. This returns the notes that we've just loaded from the user defaults system. It is important that this returns all of the entities that the client has previously been passed. Any that are omitted will be assumed to have been deleted and will be removed from the truth database.

Finally, the session driver will call the method on line 36 for each change. There are three kinds of change: addition, deletion, and modification. In this simple example, we handle modification and addition in the same way and just get the other record. For more complex programs, you can just read the changed properties and merge them with the data structure that you are using for your own data store.

Note that it is very important to retain the record identifier for each record. This is a UUID that uniquely identifies the record. The dictionary returned on line 68 must be indexed by this identifier. Each of the values is a dictionary representing the entity with that identifier. This dictionary stores the properties of that entity as well as the entity name as the value for the `ISyncRecordEntityNameKey` key.

This is a very simple example of sync services. For one thing, it doesn't make any local changes. Try modifying the example to allow modifications to the notes. All you need to do is ensure that the changed versions are stored in user defaults and are returned by `-recordsForEntityName:moreComing:error:`.

At the moment, the sync only runs once, when the application starts. Try adding a timer so that it runs periodically until the application exists. The best way of synchronizing like this is to do a slow sync initially and then a fast sync. With a fast sync, only the changed records are sent. Try implementing this, tracking changes on the client side and pushing the changes, rather than the whole model, back. This is not really important for something that manages as little data as this, but can be for bigger projects.

To make sure that you fully understand sync services, try merging this code with Apple's Stickies example. This is found in /Developer/Examples/CoreData/-

Figure 18.9: Syncing with the notes published by Mail.

Stickies and displays sticky notes on the screen. Try modifying that example to sync the sticky notes with the notes exposed via Sync Services. If you do this, then Mail will automatically store your sticky notes on IMAP mail servers, and you can get at them from any computer that you use.

18.9 Summary

The Address Book, Calendar Store, and Keychain provide three systemwide stores of user information. These store, respectively, contact information, events, and secrets. A lot of different categories of application can benefit from integrating with these stores.

Using these stores has several advantages over rolling your own. In the case of the keychain, it is likely to be more secure than anything you create for yourself. All of them benefit from having a set of standard tools for editing and viewing outside of your application. This makes things more convenient and familiar for your users, but also makes life easier for you while you are testing.

We also looked at Sync Services, which provides an alternate system for accessing some of these stores. Sync Services allows a user to define data models and share them among computers using a standard mechanism. You should use this for any kind of application that a user might want to install on several computers and share data between, or any application that provides data that the user may wish to access while mobile.

Chapter 19

Pasteboards

If you've used OS X for more than a few minutes, you've probably interacted with the pasteboard system many times. This system dates back to the early NeXTSTEP days and is the primary means of moving data between running applications.

They are used to implement copy-and-paste, drag-and-drop, system services, and a few other systems. On OpenStep, it was also used by `NSDataLink`, which allowed an application to embed a selection that was automatically updated by another app. This is not supported on OS X, although there are third-party extensions that provide similar functionality.

19.1 Pasteboard Overview

A pasteboard is basically a dictionary containing a mapping from types to data. You can store data of any arbitrary type on a pasteboard, although a number of standard types are also defined.

Each pasteboard is owned by a single process. This process can write data to it, but others are allowed to read it. This is managed by the *pasteboard server*, a central repository for pasteboard data.

In general, there are two kinds of transfer between applications. Something like drag and drop or X11's select buffer copies data to another application while the sending application still has a copy of it. Others, like the copy-and-paste mechanism, can allow a lot of time to elapse between one application making some data available and another requesting it. For this kind of transfer, the pasteboard server maintains a copy of the shared data that lasts until another process replaces the data on the pasteboard.

An application can use an arbitrary number of pasteboards. The `NSPasteboard` class provides the Cocoa interface to the pasteboard system. Each pasteboard is reference counted in the pasteboard server and destroyed when no processes have references to it.

Pasteboards are uniquely identified by name. If you want to create a new pasteboard, there are two methods that you can use. The `+pasteboardWithUniqueName` method will create a new pasteboard with a name that is not already in use. The `+pasteboardWithName:` method creates a new pasteboard object that may or may not reference an existing pasteboard depending on whether a pasteboard with that name has already been created.

There are several pasteboards that are guaranteed to exist. These are used for common operations between processes:

- `NSGeneralPboard` is used for copy-and-paste operations. The pasteboard server will maintain a copy of all data placed on this pasteboard so a paste operation will work even if the application that performed the copy has been exited.

- `NSFontPboard` is used for storing `NSFont` instances. This implements the Copy Style and Paste Style operations that `NSTextView` implements (Command-Option-C/V in applications that support it).

- `NSRulerPboard` is a similar pasteboard used for Copy Ruler and Paste Ruler operations. These allow rulers and styles to be copied and applied separately to normal pasteboard operations, so you don't lose the current copied item when you use either of these special copy-and-paste systems.

- `NSFindPboard` is used to share the text in find dialog boxes. You may have noticed that if you search for something in one application and then switch to another the find box contains the same text. This is done by sharing the find text via the `NSFindPboard` pasteboard.

- `NSDragPboard` stores drag and drop data. Data on this pasteboard is short-lived.

You can also define a new name if you want to share a particular kind of data. Most commonly you will use the `NSApplicationDidBecomeActiveNotification` notification to get data from it. This is how the find pasteboard works; the contents can only be changed externally when another application has been active. Unfortunately, there is no notification that is automatically sent when a pasteboard's contents changes. This means that you have to poll the pasteboard periodically.

You can test whether a pasteboard has changed since you last polled it by sending it a `-changeCount` message and testing this against the last version. Listing

19.1 shows a simple application that monitors the general pasteboard—the one used for copy and paste—to see if it has changed and logs the current version after each change.

Listing 19.1: Showing the version of the general pasteboard. [from: examples/PasteboardVersion/pbversion.m]

```
#import <Cocoa/Cocoa.h>

int main(void)
{
    [NSAutoreleasePool new];
    NSPasteboard *pboard = [NSPasteboard generalPasteboard];
    NSInteger version  = [pboard changeCount];
    while (1)
    {
        id pool = [NSAutoreleasePool new];
        NSInteger newversion = [pboard changeCount];
        if (newversion != version)
        {
            printf("Version %lld\n", (long long)newversion);
            version = newversion;
        }
        [pool release];
        sleep(1);
    }
}
```

This program is just a simple loop that runs and polls for the pasteboard version every second. If it has changed, it logs the new version. Running this on an OS X session that has been active for about three weeks gives this output:

```
$ gcc -framework Cocoa pbversion.m && ./a.out
Version 1874
Version 1875
Version 1876
```

Each time I copy something while the program is running, it prints a new line. You can use this mechanism (probably called from a timer, rather than a loop using `sleep()`) to monitor any pasteboard that you are interested in.

19.2 Pasteboard Types

Each pasteboard has a set of types associated with it. When you write data to a pasteboard you must first declare the types and then set the data for each type.

Listing 19.2 shows a simple tool that reads data from the standard input and copies it to the pasteboard. You can run it like this:

```
$ gcc -framework Cocoa topasteboard.m -o pboard
$ ls | pboard
```

The general pasteboard will now contain a listing of the files in the current directory.

Listing 19.2: Writing a string to the pasteboard. [from: examples/PasteboardTool/topasteboard.m]

```
1  #import <Cocoa/Cocoa.h>
2  
3  int main(void)
4  {
5      [NSAutoreleasePool new];
6      NSData *data = [[NSFileHandle fileHandleWithStandardInput]
           readDataToEndOfFile];
7      NSPasteboard *pboard = [NSPasteboard generalPasteboard];
8      [pboard declareTypes: [NSArray arrayWithObject: NSStringPboardType]
9                     owner: nil];
10     [pboard setData: data forType: NSStringPboardType];
11     return 0;
12 }
```

This is a very simple program. Line 6 reads all of the data on the standard input. Lines 8 and 9 then declare that the pasteboard should expect some string data. The string data is then written on line 10 and the program exits. The pasteboard server now contains a copy of the data and it can be pasted later.

There are two things to note about how types are declared. The first is that it takes an array of types as an argument. You can define an arbitrary number of different representations of the same data. You might, for example, include a rich text and a plain text representation of the data. You might also add a PDF or TIFF rendering of the text that could be pasted into graphical editors. Most often, you will only want to have one authoritative version and then some lossily converted forms. When you copy a region of a PDF, for example, you might get rich and plain text versions of the selected text as well as a raw PDF, or you might get some bitmap image representations.

It is worth noting that recent versions of OS X use UTI strings as well as the string constants listed in the documentation. This is currently only documented in the Carbon section of the pasteboard programming documentation, but it is likely to become more important in the future. If you are adding new, application-specific, pasteboard types, then you should consider using UTIs to handle this.

The second notable thing about registering types is the second parameter, which is ignored in this example. This is used to implement *lazy copying.* When you declare types on a pasteboard, you do not need to provide the accompanying data immediately (although you should for the general pasteboard). The owner set when you call `-declareTypes:owner:` must implement this method:

```
- (void)pasteboard: (NSPasteboard*)sender
provideDataForType: (NSString*)type;
```

When another process requests data from the pasteboard of a specific type, the owner will be sent this message. It must then call `-setData:forType:` or one of the equivalent methods on the pasteboard to set the data.

This is very important for large data being copied to the pasteboard. If you copy an image, you may want to provide two or three representations of it. Imagine dragging a RAW image. This might be a 40MB image with a 1MB JPEG representation that takes ten seconds of CPU time to generate. The user begins the drag, and the system freezes for a few seconds while copying the data and creating the JPEG representation. Then the user gives up before dropping it anywhere, and the entire operation was done for no reason. Using lazy copying, the drag starts immediately. When the drop occurs, the destination requests a single type of data and this is then copied. This gives a much better user experience.

Pasteboards Contain Data

It is worth remembering that pasteboards contain data, not objects. You can store objects on it if they conform to the `NSCoding` protocol or similar, but you can't store arbitrary objects. This makes sense, since you commonly use pasteboards to copy data between applications. Often, however, you use pasteboards for drag and drop between views in your own application. In this case, you may not want to go to the trouble of serializing and deserializing your data. You can work around this by defining a private pasteboard type and storing a pointer in the data.

Getting data from a pasteboard is equally simple. To demonstrate this, we will write a companion tool to the one previously shown. This one will read the current pasteboard contents and write it to the standard output, allowing you to use pasteboards in shell scripts. The code is shown in Listing 19.3.

This first tries to get string data from the pasteboard, on line 7. If this works, then it writes it to the standard output and exits. If it fails, then it will log the types that are in the pasteboard to the standard error and exit with an error status. You can use this in conjunction with the first tool like this:

Listing 19.3: A tool for getting the pasteboard contents. [from: examples/Pasteboard-Tool/frompasteboard.m]

```
#import <Cocoa/Cocoa.h>

int main(void)
{
    [NSAutoreleasePool new];
    NSPasteboard *pboard = [NSPasteboard generalPasteboard];
    NSData *data = [pboard dataForType: NSStringPboardType];
    if (data == nil)
    {
        NSLog(@"Unable␣to␣get␣string␣from␣pasteboard.␣␣Types␣are:␣%@",
                [pboard types]);
        return 1;
    }
    NSFileHandle *standardout = [NSFileHandle fileHandleWithStandardOutput
        ];
    [standardout writeData: data];
    return 0;
}
```

```
$ gcc -framework Cocoa frompasteboard.m -o frompasteboard
$ frompasteboard | sort | pboard
```

This will get the contents of the pasteboard, sort it, and then return it to the pasteboard.

19.3 Filtered Types

There are a large number of potential types that you might want to put on the pasteboard. Getting agreement between two programs about the kind of data that they want to use for interchange is difficult. You can work around this by advertising and accepting a large variety of formats, but this quickly gets unwieldy. An image editor might support several dozen file formats. Should it export the current selection in all of them to the clipboard when the user hits Copy?

A better solution is available in OS X through the use of *filter services*. These are special kinds of *system services* (see Chapter 20) that transform data from one type to another. You can find out what types can be filtered to a specific type by sending a `+typesFilterableTo:` message to `NSPasteboard`. This takes a pasteboard type string as an argument and returns an array of types that can be filtered to produce this type.

You can use these filters in your own code by putting data on a pasteboard and then getting it off in a different format, like this:

```
pboard = [NSPasteboard pasteboardByFilteringData: data
                                          ofType: SomeType];
newdata = [pboard dataForType: FilteredType];
```

This creates a new pasteboard containing the original data and a new entry for every filter that takes that type as input and returns something different. This doesn't actually run the filters; it uses the lazy copying mechanism described earlier to defer their execution until you try to access the data.

19.4 Property List Data

It is often useful to store structured data on a pasteboard. Cocoa already defines a set of representations for this in the form of *property lists*. These are files that can contain strings, numbers, and arbitrary data in dictionaries and array.

You can generate them easily using `NSPropertyListSerialization` and store them in a pasteboard using the standard `-setData:ofType:` method. Because this is such a common operation, there are two convenience methods provided on `NSPasteboard` to help with this:

```
- (BOOL)setPropertyList: (id)propertyList
                forType: (NSString*)dataType;
- (id)propertyListForType: (NSString*)dataType;
```

When you want to store a property list in a pasteboard, you use the first of these. The argument can be any object that `NSPropertyListSerialization` can encode into a property list. Note that there is no default property list pasteboard type. Lots of different types use property list data; the type defines both the fact that plist data is used and the layout of this data.

Getting the encoded object back is even simpler; just specify the type you want and you will get a decoded property list back. This eliminates the need to worry about which property list encoding to use, or to manually handle the encoding.

If you are defining a new pasteboard type for copying and pasting your own data, then you might consider using this—at least for prototyping—rather than defining a complex serialization strategy.

If you are just storing individual strings, there are two, similar, helper methods you can use:

```
- (BOOL)setString: (NSString*)string
          forType: (NSString*)dataType;
```

```
- (NSString*)stringForType: (NSString*)dataType;
```

These convenience methods are all implemented in terms of `-setData:forType:` and `-dataForType:`. You might consider defining similar convenience methods in a category on `NSPasteboard` if you are constantly converting a specific kind of object into data and back again for storage on a pasteboard.

19.5 Self-Encoding Objects

Starting with OS X 10.6, Apple introduced a mechanism that makes it easy to incorporate the encoding and decoding of the pasteboard representation of an object into the object itself. The two new protocols, `NSPasteboardWriting` and `NSPasteboardReading`, define methods for transforming between a pasteboard representation of an object and an instance.

Several Cocoa types now implement these protocols. Rather than calling a dedicated method for adding a string to a pasteboard for a given type, for example, you can just call the `-writeObjects:` method, which takes an array of objects conforming to the `NSPasteboardWriting` protocol.

When you add an object to a pasteboard in this way, it will first be sent a `-writableTypesForPasteboard:` message. The object should then return an array of pasteboard types that it can write. For `NSString`, this is quite a large selection, containing the various historical pasteboard types representing strings. The object will then receive a `-pasteboardPropertyListForType:` message for each of these types. It should return one of the objects that are valid in property lists, such as `NSData` or `NSString`.

In the opposite direction, `NSPasteboard` now responds to `-readObjectsForClasses:options:` messages for reading objects. The first argument to this method is an array of classes conforming to the `NSPasteboardReading` protocol. Classes that conform to this protocol must be capable of constructing themselves from pasteboard data. The pasteboard will try each of these classes in turn to find one that can read the pasteboard data, sending it an `+readableTypesForPasteboard:` message to get an array of types that the class can decode and then matching these to the types stored on the pasteboard.

Once the pasteboard has found a class that can be used to create objects representing the pasteboard contents, it will send it an `+alloc` message and then send the returned instance a `-initWithPasteboardPropertyList:ofType:` message. The first argument to this will be the same as the return value of the `-pasteboardPropertyListForType:` method called when the pasteboard was instantiated.

Adopting these two protocols in your model objects—or via categories on your model objects—can simplify your controllers and custom views a lot because you now only have a single place for transforming objects of that type into property list data for the pasteboard. This doesn't allow you to do anything that you couldn't do before, but it does make it easier to write maintainable code.

This new system for encoding and decoding pasteboard data is a lot cleaner than the older system, but unfortunately it is limited to OS X 10.6 and later. If you need to support 10.5 or earlier, then you need to use the older mechanisms; there is little point supporting both, because the older approach still works on newer systems. Mac OS X 10.5 was the last version to support PowerPC platforms, so not supporting it also means not supporting PowerPC Macs.

19.6 Files and Pasteboards

If you look at any running document-driven app, you will notice a document proxy icon in the title bar. When you drag this, a file reference is stored on the drag pasteboard. Files are often used as data sources with the pasteboard and so there is a lot of special-case behavior for handling them.

There are four different ways that you can put file data in a pasteboard. The first two are conceptually very simple, and similar. The `NSFilenamesPboardType` pasteboard type contains an array of file paths. These are stored in a property list, so you should use `-propertyListForType:` to retrieve them. The related form is `NSURLPboardType`. This takes a single string representing a URL. If you drag an image or a link out of Safari, then this will be one of the supported pasteboard types.

The `NSFilesPromisePboardType` pasteboard type is more interesting. This can be used to represent files that don't really exist. You can use this to implement a RiscOS-style save function, where you drag an icon into the Finder and then save the document at the drop location.

The data for *file promises* is an array of the types of the files that will be created. This must contain all of the top-level files, but if you include a bundle type, then you don't have to specify the types of any of the files inside it. The drop location will then pass a URL back representing the drop location and the sender will create the files at this location. We'll look at this in more detail toward the end of the chapter, when we see how to implement drag and drop.

The final way of using files with the pasteboard is to simply copy the file contents directly into the pasteboard. There are two convenience methods for doing this:

```
- (BOOL)writeFileContents: (NSString )filename;
- (BOOL)writeFileWrapper: (NSFileWrapper*)wrapper;
```

These both set the data for the `NSFileContentsPboardType` type. This can be accessed at the far end as data, or by using these helpers:

```
- (NSString*)readFileContentsType: (NSString*)type
                           toFile: (NSString*)filename;
- (NSFileWrapper*)readFileWrapper;
```

The first writes the contents of the pasteboard directly to a file. You can use this for any data type that you want to write to a file, but if the type you specify is not found, then `NSFileContentsPboardType` will be used instead.

The second returns a file wrapper for the file contents. This can often avoid copying the file into memory.

19.7 Copy and Paste

Implementing copy and paste is very simple. We've already seen how to write data to the general pasteboard and read it back. You can use these methods to implement copy and paste in any view.

If you are using the standard view objects, then you don't need to do anything to support copy and paste in your applications. It will work automatically. If you are creating your own view, then there are three methods that you should implement:

```
- (IBAction)copy: (id)sender;
- (IBAction)cut: (id)sender;
- (IBAction)paste: (id)sender;
```

The standard Edit menu will send each of these to the first responder. When your view is first responder, it will receive each of these in response to user actions. You should also implement the `NSMenuValidation` protocol. This defines a single method:

```
- (BOOL)validateMenuItem: (NSMenuItem*)menuItem;
```

You should use this to enable and disable the copy and cut menu items depending on whether anything is selected, and possibly disable pasting if your view is sometimes read-only.

Each of the methods interacts with the current selection and the general pasteboard. A general copy method would look something like this:

```
- (IBAction) copy: (id)sender
{
    NSPasteboard *pboard = [NSPasteboard generalPasteboard];
    NSArray *types = [self copyTypes];
    [pboard declareTypes: types
                   owner: nil];
    for (id type in types)
    {
```

```
        [pboard setData: [self dataForSelectionAsType: type]
                forType: type];
    }
}
```

This depends on you implementing a -copyTypes method that returns all of the types that your view supports and a -dataForSelectionAsType: method that returns the current selection as the specified type. The cut method should be similar, but should also delete the current selection.

You can also implement copying in a lazy fashion. This is easy for drag and drop, but much harder with copy and paste. To do this, you start by just declaring the types in the -copy: method; you don't copy the data in and set **self** instead of nil as the owner.

The copied data may not be requested for a long time, so you must first make sure that you have a cache of the data so that editing does not overwrite it. You must make sure that you write the data to the pasteboard if the view is destroyed or the application exits. Most applications don't bother sending every object a -dealloc message when they exist, since the operating system will reclaim any memory used by the process anyway, so you need to register to receive NSApplicationWillTerminateNotification notifications from NSApp.

You don't want to do this if something else has been copied and overwritten whatever you put on the pasteboard. To prevent this, you should implement this delegate method:

```
- (void)pasteboardChangedOwner:(NSPasteboard *)sender;
```

This is called when some other object claims ownership of the pasteboard. You should free your cached data in this method and unregister for the notification from NSApp.

Implementing paste in your view is similar. You will generally have an action method looking like this:

```
- (IBAction) paste: (id)sender
{
    NSPasteboard *pboard = [NSPasteboard generalPasteboard];
    NSArray *types = [self types];
    if ([types containsObject: favoriteType])
    {
        [self setSelectionFromData: [pboard dataForType: favoriteType]];
    }
    else if ([types containsObject: secondFavoriteType])
    ...
}
```

This iterates over all of the types that it knows how to handle, in the order in which it prefers them. A rich text view, for example, would prefer RTF data but would accept plain strings if RTF is not available. Remember that the `sender` parameter here is the sender of the action message—typically the Paste menu item—and not the pasteboard or object providing the data.

> **Copying Fonts**
>
> If you want to implement Copy Style functionality in your application, then you need to use the `NSFontPboard` pasteboard. You might be wondering how you copy a font onto this pasteboard, since it does not support the `NSCoding` protocol and cannot give a data representation of itself.
>
> The solution to this is to create a one-character `NSAttributedString` and set the font on this. You then create an RTF representation of the attributed string and store it in the pasteboard. When you want to get a font back, you create an attributed string from the data and then read the font attribute.

19.8 Drag and Drop

Drag and drop is a bit more complicated. The basic mechanism is the same; you write data to a pasteboard when the drag operation starts and retrieve it at the end. This is complicated by the fact that drag operations are live—there is no intermediate storage—allowing a much greater interaction between the sender and the receiver. To further complicate matters, there are several possible operations that can be created by the user dragging an object:

- `NSDragOperationMove` is the most obvious kind of drag operation. This moves the object from the origin of the drag to the destination of the drop.
- `NSDragOperationCopy` is similar, but the source does not remove the object. This distinction is mainly important in intraprocess drag operations. If the source and destination are in different processes, then a copy occurs for both copy and move operations, but the sender deletes its copy after the drop. If they are in the same process, then they can just pass an object reference for a move, but not for a copy. OS X displays a + symbol next to the cursor while performing this kind of operation.
- `NSDragOperationLink` is used for operations where the source and destination should share the object. This is most often done for drag operations between

windows in the same application, but can be used across applications when the object is a file.

- `NSDragOperationDelete` is used for items that can be dragged to the trash can. This kind of operation is ignored by the destination but should cause the source to delete the object. This is equivalent to a move operation with no destination.

19.8.1 Drag Operations

If you want to support drag operations, then you must implement this method:

```
- (NSDragOperation)draggingSourceOperationMaskForLocal: (BOOL)isLocal;
```

The argument to this is set to **YES** if the drop target is in the same processes and **NO** if it isn't. You can use this to support different drag operation in and outside your application. The return should be a mask formed by bitwise-ORing (|) the constants above together. There are a few other values that can be used here. `NSDragOperationGeneric` indicates that the destination is allowed to pick the kind of operation that occurs from the other values OR'd together in the mask. `NSDragOperationEvery`[1] indicates that any operation is allowed.

If you want to bypass the normal negotiation mechanism, you can return `NSDragOperationPrivate` here. This indicates that the source and destination will use some out-of-band mechanism to negotiate the drag operation. Typically this is done through some data placed on the drag pasteboard.

Drag and Drop Terminology

The Cocoa documentation is quite confusing on the subject of dragging and dropping. It uses "drag" to describe both ends of the operation. To help reduce this confusion, I will use "drag" to describe the source operation and "drop" to describe the destination. When you press the mouse button down, you begin a drag operation, and when you release it you complete a drop operation. Hopefully this is more clear.

Although this is the only method you need to implement to support dragging, there are several others that can improve the user interface. These are described in the `NSDraggingSource` informal protocol. Many of these relate to the display of the image used while dragging. If you select some text in OS X and then drag, you will see a copy of this text drawn on a transparent background follow the mouse

[1] Previously known as `NSDragOperationAll`.

around. If you drag an image, a scaled copy of image will do the same thing. This image is set when you start the drag operation, which is done by calling a method present in both NSView and NSWindow from your subclass of either of these:

```
- (void)dragImage: (NSImage*)anImage
               at: (NSPoint)imageLoc
           offset: (NSSize)mouseOffset
            event: (NSEvent*)theEvent
       pasteboard: (NSPasteboard*)pboard
           source: (id)sourceObject
        slideBack: (BOOL)slideBack;
```

This method is quite complicated. The first argument is the image to be displayed by the mouse when you perform the drag. This will be passed back to most of the delegate methods. The second tells the view where it should start drawing the image. This is the coordinate of the bottom-left corner of the image. This allows you to center the image on the mouse or place it in any position relative to the mouse. The relative distance from the mouse cursor will be calculated from the location in the event object and maintained throughout the drag operation.

In modern OS X applications the offset can be any value. It has been ignored since OS X 10.4 and it is unlikely that you will need to support versions older than this.

The pasteboard object supplied here is the one used for the drag operation. You will usually get this pasteboard like this:

```
NSPasteboard *pboard = [NSPasteboard pasteboardWithName:NSDragPboard];
```

There is no requirement to use this pasteboard for drag operations, however. You are free to use any other pasteboard. There aren't many reasons why you'd want to, but there are a few. If the user has just copied the same data that will be dragged, then you might want to check the result of -changeCount and pass the general pasteboard if it hasn't increased. This saves some copying. You might want to create a new pasteboard for the drag operation and keep it around for a while in case the user performs a drag in the future on the same object. These techniques are only important if the cost of filling the pasteboard is high.

The source object is the object that conforms to the NSDraggingSource informal protocol and will receive the drag operations. Typically this will be **self**. The final argument indicates whether the drag image should slide back to where it started if the drag is rejected.

If you are implementing move or delete drag operations, you need some notification that the drag operation has finished. This will happen automatically if you implement the following method:

```
- (void)draggedImage: (NSImage*)anImage
             endedAt: (NSPoint)aPoint
           operation: (NSDragOperation)operation;
```

This is called when the object has been dropped on a target. The `operation` argument tells you what kind of operation has just completed. A number of views on OS X—including the Dock—treat a drag into empty space as a delete operation. You can implement this behavior by passing `NO` as the `slideBack` parameter when creating the drag operation and then implementing this method. If the drop operation fails, you can implement the evaporating animation and delete the object.

19.8.2 Drop Operations

The methods that should be implemented at the drop end are defined in the `NSDraggingDestination` protocol. Before any view will be treated as a potential drop target, it must send a `-registerForDraggedTypes:` message to itself, with an array of pasteboard types as arguments. When a drag moves over a view, the set of registered types will be compared to the types in the attached pasteboard, and if there is any overlap, the view will be considered a potential drop target.

When the drag moves over a potential drop target, the target begins receiving messages. The protocol for receiving drops is a lot more complicated than the one for acting as a drag source. The first message received will be `-draggingEntered:`.

```
- (NSDragOperation)draggingEntered: (id<NSDraggingInfo>)sender;
```

This looks like an action message, but it isn't. The sender is an object encapsulating the drag operation. Typically you will send this a `-draggingSourceOperationMask` message to get the dragging operations permitted, compare these with the ones your view accepts, and select one to use.

You may wish to change this behavior based on what is being dragged. You can find this out by sending a `-draggingPasteboard` message to the sender to get the pasteboard and then finding its types. You may also alter the behavior based on where in the view the object is being dragged. This is especially true for compound views. If you send the sender a `-draggingLocation` message, then you will get a point in the destination window's coordinate system representing the location. You will typically have to translate this into the view's coordinate system by sending a `-convertPoint:fromView:` message to the view.

As the mouse moves across the view, it is given the opportunity to alter the drag operations that it supports. This method will be called when the mouse moves, and periodically if it doesn't in case something in the view has changed:

```
- (NSDragOperation)draggingUpdated: (id<NSDraggingInfo>)sender;
```

This should do exactly the same thing as `-draggingEntered:`. If your view is static, you do not need to receive the periodic updates. You can turn them off by implementing this method:

```
- (BOOL)wantsPeriodicDraggingUpdates
{
    return NO;
}
```

This means that the view will receive messages when the mouse moves, but not at other times. If the mouse then moves off the view, it will be sent a `-draggingExited:` message with the same signature. This can usually be ignored, but you can use it to clear any state that was generated when the mouse entered the view. If the cursor moves back over the view, it will get another `draggingEntered:` message.

When the user finally decides where to drop the dragged item, three methods will be called, in order, on the target. These are

```
- (BOOL)prepareForDragOperation: (id<NSDraggingInfo>)sender;
- (BOOL)performDragOperation: (id<NSDraggingInfo>)sender;
- (void)concludeDragOperation: (id<NSDraggingInfo>)sender;
```

The first two of these allow the drop to be rejected at the last minute. The first is to perform last-minute checks that it is a valid operation. The real work should be done in the second method. This performs the equivalent of a paste operation, but with the pasteboard provided by the sender and at the point where the drop occurred, rather than the replacing the selection with the contents of the general pasteboard.

Only the middle one of these methods is required; without it the drag operation will always fail. The others are optional and simply provide extra hooks for performing preparation and cleanup operations.

19.8.3 Implementing Drag and Drop in a Custom View

To demonstrate how to implement drag-and-drop support in a custom view, we will extend the view we wrote in Chapter 13. As you will recall, this used a cell to draw an attributed string in a circle.

To extend this, we will add two categories, one for supporting drags and another for supporting drops. We also add the convenience method shown in Listing 19.4. This is connected to a slider's action message so that we can dynamically set the padding in a dropped string.

This method is very simple; it just takes the floating point value of the sender, passes it to the cell, and redraws the view. This is not strictly required for drag-

Listing 19.4: Dynamically setting the spacing. [from: examples/CircleTextDragAndDrop/CircleTextView.m]

```
- (IBAction)takePaddingValueFrom: (id)sender
{
    [cell setPadding: (CGFloat)[sender doubleValue]];
    [self setNeedsDisplay: YES];
}
```

and-drop, but since we are now drawing arbitrary it is convenient to be able to control the spacing without recompiling the program.

The category providing drag support is shown in Listing 19.5. This implements lazy copying to the pasteboard and implements the copy, move, and delete operations.

Listing 19.5: Drag support in the circle text view. [from: examples/CircleTextDragAndDrop/CircleTextView+DragAndDrop.m]

```
@implementation CircleTextView (Drag)
- (void)mouseDragged:(NSEvent *)theEvent
{
    NSPasteboard *pboard = [NSPasteboard pasteboardWithName: NSDragPboard];

    NSArray *types = [NSArray arrayWithObjects:
        NSPDFPboardType,
        NSRTFPboardType,
        NSStringPboardType,
        nil];

    [pboard declareTypes: types
                   owner: self];

    NSPoint click = [self convertPoint: [theEvent locationInWindow]
                              fromView: nil];

    NSData *imageData = [self dataWithPDFInsideRect: [self bounds]];
    NSImage *dragImage = [[NSImage alloc] initWithData: imageData];
    [dragImage setSize: NSMakeSize(40, 40)];

    [self dragImage: dragImage
                 at: click
             offset: NSZeroSize
              event: theEvent
```

```
           pasteboard: pboard
               source: self
            slideBack: YES];
    [dragImage release];
}
- (NSDragOperation)draggingSourceOperationMaskForLocal: (BOOL)isLocal
{
    return NSDragOperationCopy | NSDragOperationDelete |
        NSDragOperationMove;
}
- (void)pasteboard: (NSPasteboard*)pboard
provideDataForType: (NSString*)type
{
    if (type == NSStringPboardType)
    {
        [pboard setString: [cell stringValue]
                  forType: NSStringPboardType];
    }
    else if (type == NSRTFPboardType)
    {
        NSAttributedString *str = [cell attributedStringValue];
        NSData *rtf = [str RTFFromRange: NSMakeRange(0, [str length])
                     documentAttributes: nil];
        [pboard setData: rtf
                forType: NSRTFPboardType];
    }
    else if (type == NSPDFPboardType)
    {
        [self writePDFInsideRect: [self bounds]
                    toPasteboard: pboard];
    }
}
- (void)draggedImage: (NSImage*)anImage
             endedAt: (NSPoint)aPoint
           operation: (NSDragOperation)operation
{
    NSDragOperation deleteMask = NSDragOperationDelete |
        NSDragOperationMove;
    if ((deleteMask & operation) != 0)
    {
        [cell setStringValue: @""];
        [self setNeedsDisplay: YES];
    }
    if ((operation & NSDragOperationDelete) != 0)
```

```
71     {
72         NSShowAnimationEffect(NSAnimationEffectPoof,
73             aPoint, NSZeroSize, nil, 0, NULL);
74     }
75 }
```

The first method is the user drags the mouse anywhere in the view. This is not part of the drag and drop mechanism, it is just another event type. You will receive this message in any view where the user moves the mouse with the button held down, even if you don't support drag and drop. It is also used to define a selection and for drawing.

The first part of this method sets up the pasteboard. We aren't doing any clever caching here, so we just get the default drag pasteboard. The types we support are defined in the array declared on lines 9–13. These are specified in their order of richness. A drop target should favor the ones to the start of this array if it supports more than one. There is unfortunately a bug in Apple's `NSTextView` implementation that means that it will prefer RTF content to PDF irrespective of their order. To test dropping PDF data in TextEdit or some other application using a text view, comment out lines 11 and 12.

The pasteboard is set up on lines 15 and 16, but no data is provided. The owner is set to **`self`** so that this view will receive `-pasteboard:provideDataForType:` messages when the drop target needs the data.

The rest of the method sets up the drag operation. Lines 21–23 create an image to use when dragging. This is simply a scaled-down version of the view. We use `NSImage` to perform the scaling. The PDF generated will be resolution-independent, since it is generated entirely from glyphs composed of vectors so when we set the size we are just defining an affine transform to use when rasterizing the image.

With the image prepared, we call the superclass method that begins the drag. Note that the receiver here is **`self`** not **`super`**. At the moment, they are equivalent, but this means that we can later override this method in this class or a subclass without it breaking.

The arguments here are fairly self-explanatory. The image and pasteboard are the ones we have just prepared and the event is the argument. The offset, as mentioned earlier, is ignored. We use the location of the mouse click as the initial location for the image. This means that the drag image's bottom-left corner will follow the mouse corner. This isn't ideal, but it's simple. Try modifying this so that the mouse follows the top-left corner instead.

When a potential drop target is identified, the method on line 34 will be called. This is trivial, simply returning the three drag operations that we support. We don't distinguish between drops in this application and drops elsewhere, so this method just returns a constant expression in all cases.

When a drop operation completes, the target will (probably) request some data from the pasteboard. This will, indirectly, call the method that starts on line 38. This checks the requested type and provides the data. Note that we can use pointer comparison (==) rather than `-isEqual:` messages when comparing these strings, because we always set them to the global constants provided by AppKit, rather than a literal value.

For strings, we just set the string using the convenience method on `NSPasteboard`. We can do something similar with PDF data, this time using a convenience method on `NSView` that sets up a graphics context, renders a PDF, and then sets it in the pasteboard for the PDF pasteboard type.

Setting rich text is not quite so easy. We have to do this manually by getting an RTF representation from the attributed string object and then setting the data.

After the drag has completed, we will receive a `-draggedImage:endedAt:operation:` message. If the operation was a delete or move operation, we delete the current string. This is done on line 67 by setting the cell's string value to the empty string and redrawing the view. If you run this example and drag to the trash can, the text should now disappear. To make this a little bit more friendly, we use `NSShowAnimationEffect()` to display the "puff of smoke" animation when the contents of the view is deleted. This is available in OS X 10.3 and later. The animation is told to run at the current mouse location, and not bother notifying anything when it completes. Try dragging from the view to the trash can to see this work.

That's all we need for drag support. Figure 19.1 shows this having worked. This is the example running with lines 11 and 12 commented out so that it only supports PDFs. When the user drags from this view to TextEdit, the PDF representation is inserted.

The next step is to add drop support. A small part of this can't go in the category. We need to add the code in Listing 19.6 to the `-awakeFromNib` method, defined in the main class file. This indicates that this object may accept drags that contain either plain or rich text. Without this, none of the methods in the `Drop` category will be called.

Listing 19.6: Registering to receive drop events. [from: examples/CircleTextDragAndDrop/-CircleTextView.m]

```
	NSArray *types = [NSArray arrayWithObjects:
	                   NSRTFPboardType,
	                   NSStringPboardType,
	                   nil];
	[self registerForDraggedTypes: types];
```

Figure 19.1: Dragging a text circle to TextEdit.

The category itself is shown in Listing 19.7. This defines two methods. Although there are a lot of possible things you can do when implementing drop support, only a few of them are needed.

The first method, `-draggingEntered:` is called as soon as a drag containing one of the types we requested earlier moves over the view. This is responsible for determining whether the view would really accept this drag.

Listing 19.7: Drop support in the circle text view. [from: examples/CircleTextDragAndDrop/CircleTextView+DragAndDrop.m]

```
@implementation CircleTextView (Drop)
- (NSDragOperation)draggingEntered: (id<NSDraggingInfo>)sender
{
    NSDragOperation op = [sender draggingSourceOperationMask];
    if ((op & NSDragOperationCopy) != 0)
    {
        return NSDragOperationCopy;
    }
    if ((op & NSDragOperationMove) != 0)
    {
```

```
87            return NSDragOperationMove;
88        }
89        return NSDragOperationNone;
90    }
91    - (BOOL)performDragOperation: (id<NSDraggingInfo>)sender
92    {
93        NSPasteboard *pboard = [sender draggingPasteboard];
94        NSArray *types = [pboard types];
95        BOOL didDrop = NO;
96        if ([types containsObject: NSRTFPboardType])
97        {
98            NSData *data = [pboard dataForType: NSRTFPboardType];
99            NSAttributedString *str =
100               [[NSAttributedString alloc] initWithRTF: data
101                                   documentAttributes: nil];
102           [cell setAttributedStringValue: str];
103           didDrop = YES;
104       }
105       else if ([types containsObject: NSStringPboardType])
106       {
107           [cell setStringValue: [pboard stringForType: NSStringPboardType]];
108           didDrop = YES;
109       }
110       if (didDrop)
111       {
112           [self setNeedsDisplay: YES];
113           return YES;
114       }
115       return NO;
116   }
117   @end
```

This implementation always accepts any drop that is either a copy or a move operation, but no other types. The operations on lines 76 and 80 check whether the set of operations supported contains either a copy or a move and returns one of these options if it does. We favor copy operations over move if both are supported. This is a fairly arbitrary decision, but is more likely to be what the user expects from this kind of view. For other views move may be a more sensible default.

This view does not implement a `-draggingUpdated:` method. This is only needed for views where different parts may accept different kinds of drop. Since this method is not implemented, it is assumed that the same drag operations that were defined when the drag entered the view are supported everywhere.

The second method is the one where the real work happens. This sets the cell's value from the current pasteboard. Since we prefer rich text to plain text, we test for RTF first. It doesn't matter which order these were on the pasteboard since, unlike the PDF and RTF issue discussed earlier, RTF will always be a better representation of a pasteboard's contents than plain text.

Getting the data from the pasteboard and setting it in the cell uses the same mechanisms we used for the drag operation, but in reverse. We get a string from the pasteboard and set it in the cell, or we get some data, construct an attributed string and set that in the cell. In both cases we set a flag indicating that the drop operation worked.

If the drop operation worked, we flag the view as needing redrawing and return `YES`, otherwise we just return `NO`. Figure 19.2 shows some text in TextEdit that has been dropped on to the text view, and the text view itself.

This view now supports drag and drop, as both an origin and a destination. There are a few things that could be improved, which are left as exercise for the reader:

- Try moving the drag image so that it is centered over the mouse cursor as the drag proceeds.
- The drag image itself currently has a white background. Try modifying the view so that it draws a transparent background.
- The dragged image currently has the same proportions as the view. Try fixing this so that it is always square in the optimal size for drawing the string.
- Add support for TIFF (bitmap) images as well as PDFs in the drag.

19.9 Drag and Drop with Data Views

Most of the time you won't need to implement all of these complex operations yourself. These are only required when implementing your own view. Most of the existing views that might be used for drag and drop support it natively and allow their delegate to control it.

Most of the data views support a small selection of delegate methods that control drag-and-drop operations. These allow individual items to be dragged and locations in the view to act as drop targets.

These methods are always optional. Not implementing them simply means that the view will not support drag and drop. These are designed to be simple, but often hide some of the drag-and-drop system from the developer. To implement a table view that supports dragging, all you need to do is implement this method in the data source:

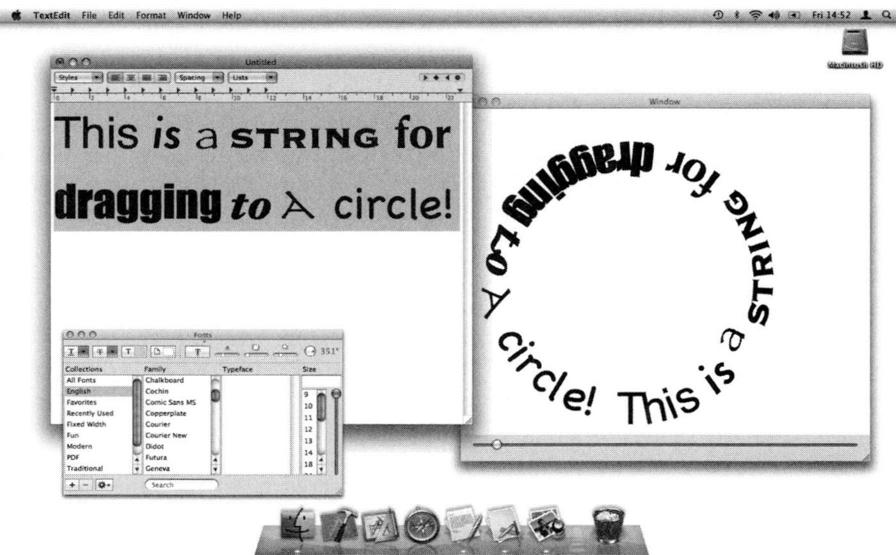

Figure 19.2: Dropping rich text on the circle view.

```
-    (BOOL)tableView: (NSTableView*)aTableView
writeRowsWithIndexes: (NSIndexSet*)rowIndexes
        toPasteboard: (NSPasteboard*)pboard;
```

This method should write the data corresponding to the specified rows into the table. If your table doesn't support multiple selection, then this will be a single index, otherwise it may be an arbitrary number.

If this method is implemented and returns **YES**, a drag operation will proceed. Note that although the name of this method implies that you should write the data to the pasteboard, you don't actually have to do so. You can simply set the types and set the data source of the owner and then provide the data using the lazy copying mechanism described earlier. If you set `NSFilesPromisePboardType` as one of the pasteboard types, then this method will be called when the destination wants to retrieve the promised files.

```
-                        (NSArray*)tableView: (NSTableView*)aTableView
namesOfPromisedFilesDroppedAtDestination: (NSURL*)dropDestination
               forDraggedRowsWithIndexes: (NSIndexSet*)indexSet;
```

When this method is called, the data source must create all of the promised files at the destination and return an array of their names.

Accepting drop operations in a table view begins in the same way as accepting drop operations in any view. You must call `-registerForDraggedTypes:` on the table view object. This is typically done by either the delegate or data source objects when they are awoken from the nib. The table view will then call this delegate method when it receives `-draggingEntered:` and `-draggingUpdated:` messages:

```
- (NSDragOperation)tableView: (NSTableView*)aTableView
              validateDrop: (id<NSDraggingInfo>)info
               proposedRow: (NSInteger)row
     proposedDropOperation: (NSTableViewDropOperation)operation
```

The table view will calculate the row corresponding to the current mouse location and pass this to the data source as the third argument. The fourth argument should not be confused with a dragging operation. It is either `NSTableViewDropOn` or `NSTableViewDropAbove` and indicates whether the target is on the specified row or above it. The latter is used when dragging between rows.

The data source should return the drop operation that it will support for this drag. If it does, and the drag is released over the table, then this method will be called:

```
- (BOOL)tableView: (NSTableView*)aTableView
       acceptDrop: (id<NSDraggingInfo>)info
              row: (NSInteger)row
    dropOperation: (NSTableViewDropOperation)operation;
```

This should insert the data into the table at the specified location. To demonstrate how this all works we will write a simple table data source that only works with a single column and uses an array of string objects to handle the operations. The end result is shown in Figure 19.3.

Listing 19.8 shows how the data source registers to receive drops. The `MultipleStringRows` is a new pasteboard string declared for this data source. It is used internally to support multiple-item drags. This table only supports dragging multiple items to this kind of table, not to arbitrary objects.

Listing 19.8: Registering a table view for drops. [from: examples/TableViewDragAndDrop/-DataSource.m]

```
NSString *MultipleStringRows = @"MultipleStringRows";

@implementation DataSource
- (void) awakeFromNib
{
    NSArray *types = [NSArray arrayWithObjects:
        NSStringPboardType,
        MultipleStringRows,
```

```
        nil];
    [view registerForDraggedTypes: types];
}
```

The code for supporting drag operations is shown in Listing 19.9. This is very simple, simply writing the desired values to the pasteboard. If multiple rows are selected, then this method stores them all on the pasteboard in property list form. If only one is selected, it just copies the string.

Listing 19.9: Handling drags from a table view. [from: examples/TableViewDragAndDrop/-DataSource.m]

```
-    (BOOL)tableView: (NSTableView*)aTableView
writeRowsWithIndexes: (NSIndexSet*)rowIndexes
        toPasteboard: (NSPasteboard*)pboard
{
    if ([rowIndexes count] == 1)
    {
        [pboard declareTypes: [NSArray arrayWithObject: NSStringPboardType]
                       owner: nil];
        [pboard setString: [array objectAtIndex: [rowIndexes firstIndex]]
                  forType: NSStringPboardType];
        return YES;
    }
    [pboard declareTypes: [NSArray arrayWithObject: MultipleStringRows]
                   owner: nil];
    [pboard setPropertyList: [array objectsAtIndexes: rowIndexes]
                    forType: MultipleStringRows];
    return YES;
}
```

This is a trivial example. A real implementation would provide several different pasteboard types, such as a string separated by newlines, for multiple row selections.

This doesn't do any lazy copying; it always puts the data on the pasteboard even if it is not going to be requested. This is not very efficient, as you will see when we look at the drop implementation, but is very simple. For a data source like this, the cost of copying the data to the pasteboard is so low that it is not worth optimizing unless people start using it to drag thousands of rows.

The code for handling the drop is much more complex and is shown in Listing 19.10. This requires two methods, one to determine the drop type and one to actually handle the drop.

The method that starts on line 61 determines the drag type. This data source performs some optimization and special behavior for the case where objects are dragged around in the same view. If the drag started in this view, then we perform a move operation; otherwise, we perform a copy.

Listing 19.10: Handling drops on a table view. [from: examples/TableViewDragAndDrop/-DataSource.m]

```
- (BOOL)tableView: (NSTableView*)aTableView
       acceptDrop: (id<NSDraggingInfo>)info
              row: (NSInteger)row
    dropOperation: (NSTableViewDropOperation)operation
{
    NSPasteboard *pboard = [info draggingPasteboard];

    if (operation = NSTableViewDropOn) { row--; }

    [self willChangeValueForKey: @"array"];

    if ([info draggingSource] == view)
    {
        NSIndexSet *rows = [view selectedRowIndexes];
        if (row == [array count]) { row--; }
        id placeholder = [array objectAtIndex: row];
        NSArray *moved = [array objectsAtIndexes: rows];
        [array removeObjectsAtIndexes: rows];
        row = [array indexOfObject: placeholder];
        if (row == NSNotFound) { row=0; }
        NSIndexSet *indexes = [NSIndexSet indexSetWithIndexesInRange:
                              NSMakeRange(row, [moved count])];
        [array insertObjects: moved
                   atIndexes: indexes];

    }
    else
    {
        if ([[pboard types] containsObject: MultipleStringRows])
        {
            NSArray *objects = [pboard propertyListForType:
                MultipleStringRows];
            NSIndexSet *indexes = [NSIndexSet indexSetWithIndexesInRange:
                                  NSMakeRange(row, [objects count])];
            [array insertObjects: objects
                       atIndexes: indexes];
        }
        else
        {
```

```
53             [array insertObject: [pboard stringForType: NSStringPboardType]
54                         atIndex: row];
55         }
56     }
57 
58     [self didChangeValueForKey: @"array"];
59     return YES;
60 }
61 - (NSDragOperation)tableView: (NSTableView*)aTableView
62                 validateDrop: (id<NSDraggingInfo>)info
63                  proposedRow: (NSInteger)row
64        proposedDropOperation: (NSTableViewDropOperation)operation
65 {
66     if ([info draggingSource] == view)
67     {
68         return NSDragOperationMove;
69     }
70     return NSDragOperationCopy;
71 }
```

The implementation of the drop, similarly, has a special case for drags inside the same view. This begins on line 28. Note that this doesn't reference the pasteboard at all. If the dragging source is the view, the current selection in the view will be the set of rows being dragged. This can be found without going via the pasteboard mechanism at all.

When moving rows around inside the view, the data source first creates a new array from the selected indexes then removes them all from the array. This implementation is not quite correct. There are a number of special cases that you need to think about when doing this. What happens if the drag destination was one of the selected rows? What happens if some of the selected rows are before and some after the insert point? This version assumes that the destination row is not selected and defaults to inserting at the start if this assumption is incorrect.

If the destination row is not one of the ones being moved, then the placeholder mechanism will work. This is implemented on lines 30 and 33. This first gets the object at the desired row and then gets the row for that object. In between these two operations a number of rows will have been removed, so the index is likely to change. Note that the `-indexOfObject:` call is an $\mathcal{O}(n)$ operation and so will become quite slow on large tables.

The removed rows are then reinserted on lines 37 and 38. This didn't copy any of the data; it just moved the resulting values around. You can use a similar mechanism to handle any moves between views in the same application. To support this in a more general case, you might store an array of pointers in the pasteboard. You can test whether the origin of the drag is in the same application by sending

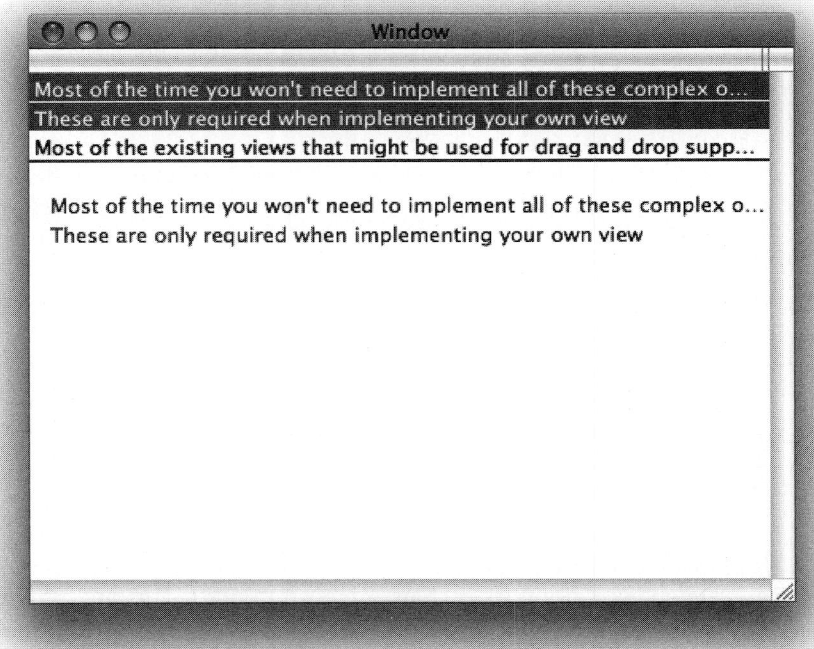

Figure 19.3: A simple table view supporting drag and drop.

a `-draggingSource` message to `info`. This will return `nil` for interprocess drags. Note that this is not specific to data views; it works with any drop operation.

The other case in this method is for handling drops that come from a different view. This is comparatively simple. It simply inserts the values into the array at the drop location. There are two cases here, one for multiple selections and one for individual strings.

Since there is no mechanism provided for inserting rows into the table other than drag and drop, it is important that drop works from any target. You can try this by selecting some text and dragging it to the view. It should be inserted into the table wherever you drop it.

You may have noticed that the drop method on this data source is bracketed by KVO change notification calls. This tells the array controller in the nib file that we have changed the layout of the data. This highlights one very important fact: data sources and bindings can be used together.

This data source provides drag-and-drop methods, but not accessors. The table's data source outlet is connected to this object, but the table column's value is bound to an array controller. In this configuration, the data source is expected to do everything that the bindings don't.

If you added another column to the table and didn't configure a binding for it, then the data source would be expected to provide data for it. Just because you want to do something that bindings don't support doesn't mean that you have to abandon them entirely.

`NSOutlineView` has a similar set of data source methods for supporting drag and drop. Items in an outline view are indexed by objects rather than integers, so the methods are slightly different, but the overall principle is the same. For supporting drags, you just need to implement this method:

```
- (BOOL)outlineView: (NSOutlineView*)outlineView
         writeItems: (NSArray*)items
     toPasteboard: (NSPasteboard*)pboard;
```

This is almost identical to the `-tableView:writeRowsWithIndexes:toPasteboard:` method. It serves exactly the same function but takes an array of objects uniquely identifying outline view rows, rather than an array of indexes, as an argument.

`NSBrowser` is slightly different. It does not make a distinction between its delegate and data source. It also provides a slightly lower-level interface for supporting drag and drop. This is the method to begin a drag from a browser:

```
-             (BOOL)browser: (NSBrowser*)sender
canDragRowsWithIndexes: (NSIndexSet*)rowIndexes
                 inColumn: (NSInteger)columnIndex
                withEvent: (NSEvent *)dragEvent;
```

This provides the drag event directly, and does little more than bounce the `-mouseDragged:` message to the delegate. The only help it provides is to give a column and row index for the event.

The browser also allows the delegate to set the drag image. This is most likely because browsers are most commonly used for things like viewing the filesystem, where individual objects will have different drag images.

The remaining methods are similar to those provided by the table and outline views. If you understand the table view and circle view examples from this chapter, you will have no problems implementing the delegate methods related to drag and drop for any of the Cocoa views.

19.10 Summary

This chapter has covered the pasteboard system that underlies both copy-and-paste and drag-and-drop behavior in Cocoa applications. We have looked at the structure of the pasteboard and how it is used to store typed data for transit between applications.

We saw that pasteboards are used both for moving data between views in the same application and across processes. Because of this, pasteboards can only store data, not arbitrary object graphs. We looked at some mechanisms for working around this and then saw how to bypass it when the source and destination are in the same application.

Copy and paste is implemented in views and we saw the *responder chain* is used to deliver messages to trigger these operations. We saw the methods that need to be implemented to support these and then looked briefly at the specialized copy-and-paste operations for rulers and fonts.

Finally, we took a detailed look at drag and drop. This mechanism is used all over OS X and, as a form of direct manipulation, is a very easy user interface to understand. The implementation is slightly more difficult. We saw how to implement drag-and-drop support in new views and how to use the integrated delegate support provided by existing Cocoa views.

You should now be able to support both the copy-and-paste and drag-and-drop operations in your application. This goes a long way toward making an application feel polished and an integrated part of the OS X desktop experience, rather than a foreign program, quickly hacked together and unfinished.

Chapter 20

Services

One of the most underrated parts of OS X is the *system services*. On OPENSTEP, every application had a top-level Services menu. On OS X, this was relegated to a submenu of the application menu. A large part of the reason for this was marketing. When OS X was launched, the majority of applications were ported from MacOS 9, using the Carbon API, and Carbon applications could not use Services. Making a user interface element prominent when most applications couldn't use it would not have been a good idea.

This limitation no longer applies. Services can now be used by any application that uses pasteboards. The *system-wide spell checker* is an example of a service that is pervasive throughout OS X. It does not expose itself via the Services menu; it is used directly by the text view.

20.1 Example Services

A lot of the standard OS X applications install services. Figure 20.1 shows an example services menu from OS X 10.5. In 10.6, the menu was improved to hide services that are not applicable to the current selection. This is more convenient for the user, but doesn't give such a good overview of the range of services available. Note that a lot of these have keyboard shortcuts.

You can use these from any Cocoa applications. For example, if you press Shift-Command-Y from any services-aware application while you have some text selected, you will get a new sticky note created from the selected text.

Services can be either producers or consumers of data, or both. The sticky note service takes some text from a pasteboard and creates a new sticky note from it. Another service like this is invaluable to anyone doing low-level programming:

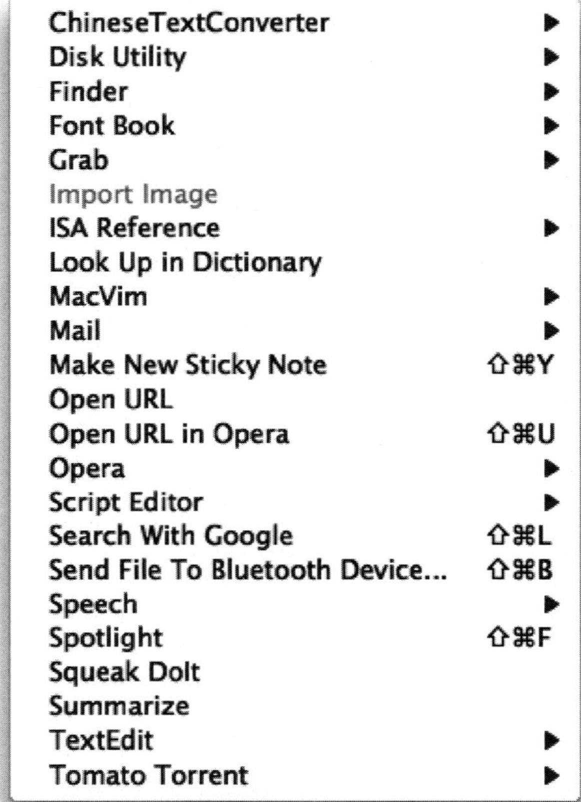

Figure 20.1: An example services menu.

The ISA Reference service looks up the selected text as a PowerPC, x86, or x86-64 instruction.[1] This makes it very easy to quickly jump to documentation. Spotlight also exposes a service like this.

At the opposite extreme, the Grab application provides a way of inserting a screenshot into any application via services. As long as the first responder can

[1]Unfortunately for Intel Mac owners, it uses the Intel assembly syntax, while gcc uses AT&T syntax.

accept image data insertions, this service can be used to get and insert a screenshot in a single operation.

One of my favorite services sadly never made the Intel switch. The Equation Service took selected text, ran it through pdflatex, and returned a PDF containing the typeset equation. This allowed you to insert beautifully typeset LaTeX equations into any OS X application. It also stored the LaTeX source in PDF metadata, allowing the transformation to be reversed. A few services work like this, taking some input and returning a result, but none are included with OS X. We'll show how to write a simple one of these later.

There are two ways of providing a service. Either an application or a special .service bundle. The canonical example of a services bundle is the AppleSpell service. This is used by all applications for spelling and grammar checking. The standard services are installed in /System/Library/Services/. You can look in this directory to find the ones that come with your version of OS X.

The other kind of service is provided by applications. These are registered when the application first runs. When they are used in the future, the application will be automatically started if it isn't already running. Service bundles have exactly the same capabilities as applications—they can display user interface elements—but they are not intended to be run as stand-alone programs.

20.2 An Evaluate Service

To demonstrate system services, we will write a simple "evaluate" service. This will take the current selection, pipe it through bc, the GNU arbitrary-precision calculator bundled with OS X, and return the result.

Unfortunately, at the time of writing, there is no template project for system services. The service itself should be a bundle with the .service extension. There are several ways of creating this. The easiest two are to start with a bundle project and add the missing bits, or start with an application project and remove the unneeded bits.

The important part is to make sure that you have a bundle target in your current project. There are two settings in the build tab of the bundle's inspector that will need changing. You must set the type to executable and the wrapper extension to service.

Once this is done you can start writing the real code. Unfortunately, for the system to detect the service it must be in Library/Services in one of the standard search locations. You will need to copy the bundle here yourself.

Listing 20.1 shows the skeleton for this example. This is the entry point for the application and is responsible for registering the service and getting ready to host it.

Listing 20.1: The service skeleton. [from: examples/EvaluateService/main.m]

```
1 #import <Cocoa/Cocoa.h>
2 #import "Evaluate.h"
3 
4 int main(int argc, char *argv[])
5 {
6     [NSAutoreleasePool new];
7     NSRegisterServicesProvider([Evaluate new], @"EvaluateService");
8     NSUpdateDynamicServices();
9     // Required on OS X 10.4 and below.
10     //[[NSRunLoop currentRunLoop] configureAsServer];
11     [[NSRunLoop currentRunLoop] runUntilDate:[NSDate
        dateWithTimeIntervalSinceNow:1]];
12 }
```

The important code is on Line 7, which registers the service. System services are built on top of distributed objects. This line will export the service via distributed objects in a standard location. Line 8 tells the system to enumerate the contents of all of the Library/Services directories and update the services menu. If you don't call this, then you will have to log out and log back in to get the menu updated. With this in place we just need to copy the bundle into /Library/Services and double click on it.

The call on line 10 sets the run loop into a special mode for handling service requests. This is not required as of OS X 10.5 and so is commented out. If you want your services to run on older versions, then add it back in.

Finally, we start the run loop. This only runs for one second and then the program exits. This should be long enough for the program to receive and reply to a request. The program will be launched on demand, so there is no reason to keep it running. If this were an application that also provided services, then it would need to keep running.

The next component is the Info.plist that describes the service. We need to add a new section to this to specify information about the services. The executable tells the services system which program to run. This is generally not required, since there is only one executable in the bundle, but it allows you to produce a single services bundle with multiple executables.

The menu key equivalent is the key that will be used, in combination with Command and Shift, as a shortcut for the service. Note that Command and Shift are always modifiers for invoking services. You should therefore avoid using them in your own application for shortcuts, or you are likely to introduce conflicts with services that the user runs later. The V shortcut was chosen here for nostalgic reasons. The Psion Series 3 palmtop used this as the shortcut for its system-wide evaluate function. This feature was incredibly useful and largely rendered the

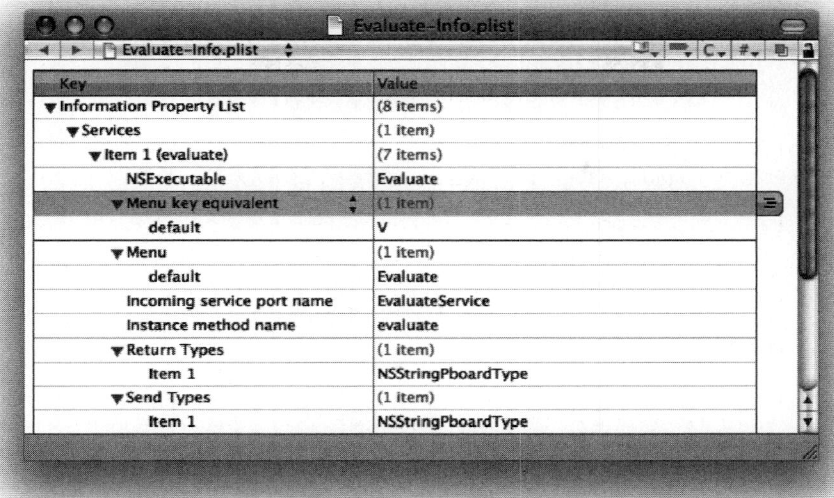

Figure 20.2: The Evaluate service info property list.

supplied calculator application obsolete, but is missing on most other platforms. Fortunately OS X provides a mechanism for replacing it.

The incoming service port name is the same name that we passed to `NSRegisterServicesProvider()`. This is used to let the services menu know what it should connect to. The other part of this is the instance method name that is used to identify the method to be called. This is not a full selector name, just the first component. The second two components are standard, as we will see later.

The send and return types are pasteboard types corresponding to the types that this service accepts and produces. The menu item will only be enabled if the first responder is able to accept one or more of the return types and the selection is one of the send types.

The service itself is implemented by the `Evaluate` class. This is shown in Listing 20.2. This class only contains a single method, `-evaluate:userData:error:`, which performs the evaluation. The first part of this selector is in the info property list. The argument provided here is a pasteboard containing the data to be processed. The second argument is unused in this example, and the third is a pointer to a string used to store an error. This API predates `NSError` by over a decade, but shows the programming pattern that led to the invention of this class.

Listing 20.2: A simple evaluate service. [from: examples/EvaluateService/Evaluate.m]

```
- (void)evaluate: (NSPasteboard*)pboard
        userData: (NSString*)userData
           error: (NSString**)error
{
    NSArray *types = [pboard types];
    if (![types containsObject: NSStringPboardType])
    {
        if (error != NULL)
        {
            *error = @"Invalid␣pasteboard␣type";
        }
        return;
    }
    NSString *equation = [pboard stringForType: NSStringPboardType];

    NSTask *bc = [NSTask new];
    [bc setLaunchPath: @"/usr/bin/bc"];
    [bc setArguments: [NSArray arrayWithObject: @"-q"]];
    NSPipe *input = [NSPipe pipe];
    NSPipe *result = [NSPipe pipe];
    [bc setStandardInput: input];
    [bc setStandardOutput: result];
    [bc launch];

    NSData *data = [[equation stringByAppendingString:@"\n"]
              dataUsingEncoding: NSUTF8StringEncoding];
    [[input fileHandleForWriting] writeData: data];
    [[input fileHandleForWriting] closeFile];
    data = [[result fileHandleForReading] readDataToEndOfFile];
    [bc release];

    types = [NSArray arrayWithObject: NSStringPboardType];
    [pboard declareTypes: types
                   owner: nil];

    NSString *equationResult =
        [[NSString alloc] initWithData: data
                              encoding: NSUTF8StringEncoding];
    [pboard setString: [NSString stringWithFormat:@"%@␣=␣%@",
                            equation, equationResult ]
              forType: NSStringPboardType];
    [equationResult release];
}
```

It should be impossible for this to be called with any pasteboard that doesn't contain string data, as this was the only type advertised in the property list, but just in case we add a guard clause at the top, in line 10. This sets the error string if it has been called incorrectly, and returns.

Assuming that we have a usable pasteboard, we get the string from it. This should contain a sum to be evaluated. We don't test this at the moment; there isn't much error checking in this code at all. Making it more robust is left as an exercise to the reader.

Lines 20–27 handle the launching of the `bc` program. We'll look in more detail at exactly what this is doing in Chapter 23. It is basically spawning a new process with its `stdin` redirected to the `input` pipe and its `stdout` redirected to `result`.

On lines 29–30 we prepare the data to send to the `bc` process. You can try running this in the terminal to see what it does. It is designed as an interactive process, so it reads a line from the standard input and then writes the result. We add a newline to the end of the selection so that it will be treated as a command and write it back.

Again, this is not very robust code. If the input is over multiple lines, this will be confusing. A better implementation would be to separate the string into substrings at line breaks and create an array of strings created by sending each in turn to `bc`.

Line 32 closes the standard input file descriptor for the child processes, which should cause it to exit. We then read the result on line 33 and turn it back into a string.

The rest of this method is responsible for writing the result back to the pasteboard. As always, this is a two-step process. We need to first set the types of the pasteboard and then the data. The types are set on lines 36–38. Since we are only writing back plain text, this is very simple.

On lines 43–45 we write back the string. This is the input string and the result separated by an equals sign. Compiling this and running it should insert an evaluate menu item, like the one shown in Figure 20.3.

Figure 20.4 shows what happens when you use this service from TextEdit. You can select text, hit Command-Shift-V, and have the result appended. This turns every application that contains a text view into a calculator.

This is a much better user interface than having a calculator application, since it removes a mode and makes it possible to evaluate sums in a consistent way all across the system. You could even build something like a spreadsheet on top of this by providing a table user interface that scanned cell values for references to other cells, replaced them, and then used the evaluate service to perform calculations.

The services system is the graphical equivalent of the UNIX philosophy of having small tools doing one thing and doing it well. It allows you to create simple programs that can easily be joined together to do complex things.

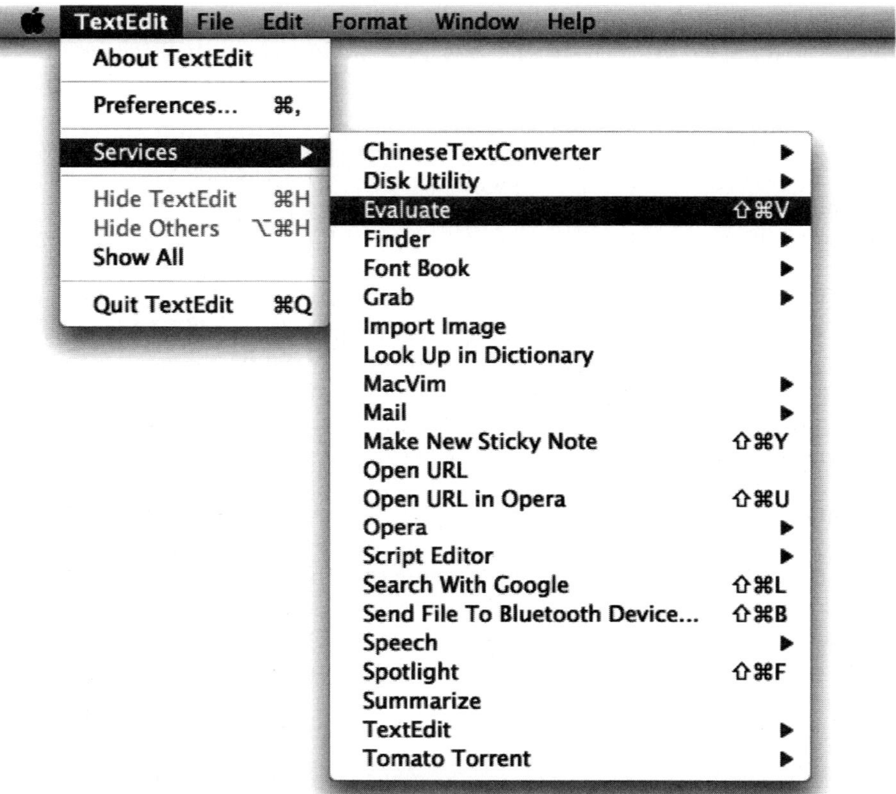

Figure 20.3: The Evaluate service in the Services menu.

20.3 Using Services

Creating services allows the user to manually use them, but sometimes you want to use services directly. The spell and grammar services are used in this way, but often there are other services that you might want to use directly.

The `NSPerformService()` function allows you to do this. This takes two arguments. The first is the name of the service in the services menu and the second is the pasteboard. You can write applications and even command-line tools that interact with services using this.

Background Services

Most of the time that you create a service, you will want it to run in the background, without displaying any user interface. Setting the `LSBackgroundOnly` key in the Info.plist file accompanying the service will ensure that it does not appear in the dock or show a menu.

This flag allows you to write dæmons that still make use of the standard `NSApplication` machinery. They are launched as applications and get all of the normal run loop and distributed objects' support that normal applications use, but do not display an interface to the user. This is often a better way of writing background tasks than writing them as simple tools.

Figure 20.4: Using the evaluate service from TextEdit.

One of the nicest things about OS X as a UNIX system is the open command. This uses `NSWorkspace` to open the specified file in whichever GUI application is registered to edit it. You can use this easily to jump from the terminal to the Finder by doing this:

```
$ open .
```

We can write a companion to this, an inspect command-line tool that uses the Finder's Show Info service on the specified file. The code for this is shown in Listing 20.3.

Listing 20.3: Launching a file inspector with a service. [from: examples/InspectWithService/inspect.m]

```
#import <Cocoa/Cocoa.h>

int main(int argc, char **argv)
{
    [NSAutoreleasePool new];
    NSFileManager *fm = [NSFileManager defaultManager];

    for (unsigned i=1 ; i<argc ; i++)
    {
        NSString *path = [fm currentDirectoryPath];
        NSString *file = [NSString stringWithUTF8String: argv[i]];
        path = [path stringByAppendingPathComponent: file];

        NSPasteboard *pboard = [NSPasteboard pasteboardWithUniqueName];

        [pboard declareTypes: [NSArray arrayWithObject: NSStringPboardType]
                       owner: nil];
        [pboard setString: path
                  forType: NSStringPboardType];

        NSPerformService(@"Finder/Show Info", pboard);
    }

    return 0;
}
```

The body of this simple program is a loop that iterates over all of the command-line arguments except the first one (the program name). For each one, it first constructs a string containing the absolute path. This is needed because the Finder does not have access to the current working directory of the application that invoked its service.

It then creates a new, unique, pasteboard and sets the contents to the name of the file to inspect. This is then passed to the Finder's service. Note that the service name is specified as a path. Each slash (/) shows a separation between a menu and a submenu. Try compiling and running this simple tool, like this:

```
$ gcc -framework Cocoa inspect.m -o inspect -std=c99
$ ./inspect *
```

You should get a Finder inspector opening for each file in the current directory. This is a very simple demonstration, but it's also a very useful tool. Any time you are in the terminal, you can now pop up a graphical view of a file and change any of the properties that the Finder knows about.

Note that you don't need to write a full application for this to work. Simple command-line tools like this can interact with applications easily. On a lot of UNIX-like systems, it's common to write graphical applications that are wrappers around command-line utilities. You might consider doing the reverse on OS X: writing a graphical application and then exposing aspects of its functionality to the command line via simple tools like this that use services.

20.4 Controlling the Services Menu

Most of the time, you don't need to do anything to make the services menu work. The instance of `NSApplication` associated with your app will make everything work as it should. Sometimes, however, you might wish to have a different services menu to the default. Each `NSResponder` subclass in your application will call this method on `NSApp`:

```
- (void)registerServicesMenuSendTypes: (NSArray*)sendTypes
                          returnTypes: (NSArray*)returnTypes;
```

This ensures that every services item that accepts one of the send types and returns one of the return types is shown. If your application only handles text, for example, it will not necessarily show services that only work with images or video.

Not all of the items in the services menu will be enabled at any given time. The following method is called to determine whether a menu can be active:

```
- (id)validRequestorForSendType: (NSString*)sendType
                     returnType: (NSString*)returnType;
```

Each item in the responder chain will receive one of these messages. If it returns `nil`, then the message will be sent to the next item in the chain until it reaches the application.

At any point, any object along the responder chain can return itself (or some other object) in response to this message. If it does, then it will be the focus for service interactions. It will be asked to produce a pasteboard from its current selection and then write the returned data back. If there is no valid requester, then the menu item will be disabled. You can see this behavior easily by selecting and deselecting text in TextEdit. When text is selected, a large selection of services will be available, but when there is no selection they will all be disabled.

The transfer of data between the responder and the service is handled by the `NSServicesRequests` informal protocol. This defines two methods:

```
- (BOOL)writeSelectionToPasteboard: (NSPasteboard*)pboard
                             types: (NSArray *)types;
- (BOOL)readSelectionFromPasteboard: (NSPasteboard*)pboard;
```

When the service runs the first of these will be called. The second argument specifies the types that the service understands. The responder may write data for any of these, and should write data for at least one. If it can, it returns **YES**; otherwise, it returns **NO**.

The service then runs. If it returns something, then the second method will be called. The receiver should replace the current selection with the data provided by the pasteboard. In our evaluate example earlier, we copied the data in the service so that replacing the old data did not destroy it.

It is, of course, up to the responder exactly what it does with data returned from a service. A responder might decide that it wants to be able to undo all operations involving services and keep the old selection around somewhere. You might even write the old selection in the attributes when you save the current document. If you are designing an application that integrates closely with services, then you might not save the output from some services at all, instead you would save the old selection and the service name, and reapply it when the document was loaded or printed.

You are also not required to put up with the default location of the services menu. You can send a `-setServicesMenu:` to `NSApp`. This takes an `NSMenu` as an argument. This menu will be populated with the available services. This allows you to move the services menu to a more prominent location if you are using services a lot. You can even add it to the context menu, or connect it to a pop-up button on your user interface.

20.5 Filter Services

OS X supports a special kind of service for handling transformations between types. These are called *filter services* and are slightly different from conventional services.

You don't have to use pasteboards to communicate with filter services. The system also supports a kind of service that communicates via standard UNIX pipes. Using this allows you to very easily wrap simple UNIX tools very easily. This is generally the best option for implementing filter services since there is a bug in OS X that prevents it from reading the result back from filter services that use the standard pasteboard mechanism.

Every filter service needs a section in its Info.plist describing the types and transport mechanisms that it supports, like this:

```
<key>NSServices</key>
<array>
    <dict>
        <key>NSFilter</key>
        <string></string>
        <key>NSSendTypes</key>
        <array>
            <string>NSStringPboardType</string>
        </array>
        <key>NSReturnTypes</key>
        <array>
            <string>public.aiff-audio</string>
        </array>
        <key>NSInputMechanism</key>
        <string>NSUnixStdio</string>
    </dict>
</array>
```

This defines a filter service that reads text and writes audio. The service will be invoked with a file name as its first argument and is expected to write the converted data to the standard output. A filter like this should declare a single return type, but may specify as many send types as you like, as long as you can distinguish between them by their data; a filter invoked like this will not receive a pasteboard and so can't use the pasteboard type to determine the input type.

Filter services are invoked automatically when you try to filter a pasteboard and can also be used implicitly when an application attempts to open a file. Filter services were very important on OPENSTEP because they provided a way of supporting lots of different file types without needing a single application to be linked against all of the possible importers. This helped reduce the memory usage, which was very important back then. Now, frameworks like QuickTime, Core Audio, and Core Graphics provide support for importing a large number of different file types and filter services are a lot less important.

20.6 Summary

In this chapter, we've looked at the System Services mechanism, which allows applications to modify the current selection in other applications. We saw how this special case for distributed objects allows you to extend all existing applications by adding simple functionality.

You don't have to export any of your application's functionality as a service. Many applications don't, and a lot that do publish services that don't make life any easier for the user. If you are thinking of writing a simple application, however, then you may find that it works better as a service, or as an application that exposes a service. This is true of any kind of application that is designed to produce data for embedding or which works as a filter.

We also saw how to interact with existing services from an application. This allows you to provide a convenient user interface for invoking services that work particularly well with your application.

Chapter 21

Adding Scripting

There are, generally speaking, two forms of scripting that an application can support. The first is *in-application scripting*, where the application provides a runtime environment for hosting scripts and runs them itself. The second is *cross-application scripting*, where scripts run outside the process and send it messages.

In-application scripting is very useful for automating repetitive tasks. It allows users to join together sequences of actions, and run them again easily. Macros in a text editor are one of the classic examples of this kind of scripting. They don't interact with anything outside of the editor, and they are generally "programmed" by turning on a recording mode and doing something, and then playing back the events that were generated.

Cross-application scripting is more powerful. It is the feature that makes the difference between stand-alone applications and an integrated environment. Scripts in an environment that supports cross-application scripting can turn simple applications into complex suites.

21.1 Scripting Overview

AppleScript provides support for both in-application and cross-application scripting. Technically, it implements the former in terms of the latter, allowing applications to invoke scripts that, in turn, send them messages.

The key concept behind scripting on OS X is `Apple Events`. These are structured messages that encapsulate some high-level event. AppleScript is a domain-specific language designed for generating Apple Events and sending them to applications.

This scripting mechanism dates back to Apple System 7—before the Mac OS

More UNIX than UNIX

A big part of the UNIX philosophy is that you should have small tools that do one thing and do it well, rather than large, monolithic, applications that try to do a lot of things. Traditional UNIX tools take some input, process it, and produce output, allowing them to be combined by shell scripts. This is a primitive form of cross-application scripting, but lacks some interactivity and the ability to join together more complex tools.

OS X takes this further with AppleScript. Using AppleScript, you can easily join together separate applications. Even if they weren't written with each other in mind, AppleScript provides a means of creating glue that joins them together into a cohesive workflow. Keep this in mind when you are defining scripting interfaces to your applications.

brand name was used for Apple's operating systems—and contains a lot of historical baggage as a result. A language like Objective-C is very well suited to scripting, because you can easily call methods on an object by name. AppleScript was originally designed to work with C and Pascal applications, however, and so was not able to take advantage of this dynamic behavior.

On Classic Mac OS, AppleScript was the only supported way of creating Apple Events. OS X introduced the *Open Scripting Architecture* (*OSA*). This provides a standard interface for providing language interpreters. The `osalang` tool can list all of the language modules you have installed:

```
$ osalang
AppleScript
Generic Scripting System
```

Although only AppleScript is provided as standard, other language modules are available. One of the most popular is a JavaScript implementation based on the Spidermonkey JavaScript interpreter from the Mozilla project. This allows users to write scripts in JavaScript that can control any application that supports Apple Events.

The events mechanism means that scripting languages do not have to use the OSA. Any language that can generate OSA events can be used for controlling scriptable applications on OS X. This includes Perl, Python, Ruby, and Objective-C.

Apple Events have a structure that should be familiar to anyone who has programmed in a Lisp dialect. The core type for events is the *descriptor*, a pair containing a type ID and a value. The type is always a 32-bit identifier, typically represented as a four-character string. The data can be anything. These are combined into *descriptor lists*, a special kind of descriptor whose data is a (potentially empty) list of other descriptors. These are combined to produce objects.

21.1.1 The AppleScript Object Model

The Apple Events object model is a very lightweight dynamic object system, similar to Smalltalk, Self, or JavaScript. It defines a single-inheritance model and a set of methods and properties for each object.

The AppleScript object model is designed for exposing models to scripting, and so attributes form a very important part of the description of a given model. In AppleScript, these are divided into properties and elements. A property in AppleScript is an attribute with a single value, while an element is an attribute pointing to a collection, for example, the pages of a book. The **of** keyword is used in AppleScript to access both, as in this line:

```
set p to page 1 of the current document
```

Both properties and elements are accessed in the same way in AppleScript, although they are implemented in different ways in the underlying event system.

When you implement scripting from Cocoa, both properties and elements are accessed via KVC. This allows you to define scripting objects that are similar, but not identical, to your Cocoa objects. You might only expose some of the KVC-compliant attributes of a given object to scripting, while keeping others for internal use.

You can also export a single object in more than one way, so that it appears to be two or more independent objects on the scripting side. These might have a different set of keys exposed, giving entirely separate views on the same object.

21.1.2 Scripting Vocabulary

Scripting is described in terms of dictionaries, in the natural language sense rather than the `NSDictionary` sense. Each dictionary contains a way of mapping natural-language expressions to scripting operations. AppleScript is designed to be close to English, and the dictionary contains a set of words that are made available to it by an application.

Each application supports a number of *scripting suites*. You can think of these as sections in a dictionary, or the equivalent to Cocoa frameworks. A scripting suite is a set of classes, data definitions, and other values that are associated with each other in some way. You can browse the dictionaries associated with each application in Script Editor. Figure 21.1 shows the dictionary supported by iTunes.

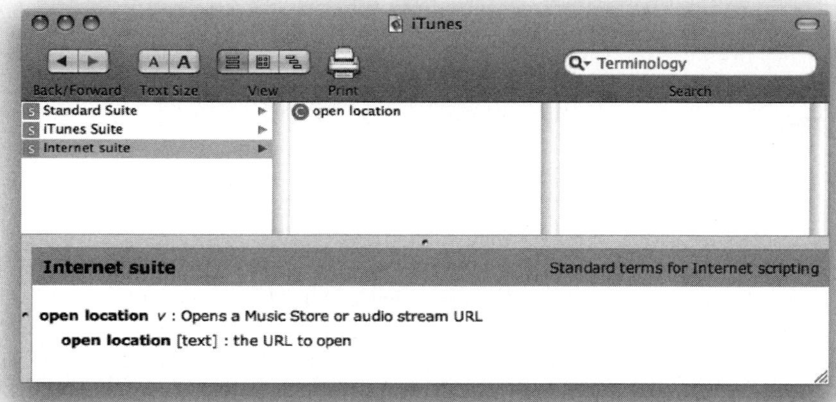

Figure 21.1: The scripting suites supported by iTunes.

The standard suite contains a basic set of commands that most applications should implement. Implementing these is usually very easy; in some cases they are supported automatically by Cocoa classes. The Internet suite is not specific to iTunes; it is shared among a few applications. iTunes implements the "open location" command in this for opening URLs. Supporting a command from an existing suite is usually better than defining a new command, since it allows users to write more generic scripts.

The final suite is the iTunes suite, where all of the iTunes-specific scripting information is defined. Each suite contains commands and classes. A command is equivalent to a function; it may require arguments, or it may be a single word. iTunes, for example, defines a "play" command that simply starts playing, and a "reveal" command that displays the item passed as a parameter as an argument.

Classes in the scripting suite are closer to Cocoa dictionaries than Objective-C classes. They contain elements and properties, as described earlier, but not methods. They are very similar, conceptually, to the data held by Core Data. This contains entities with attributes (similar to AppleScript elements) and relations (similar to AppleScript properties).

21.2 Making Objects Scriptable

If you want to support AppleScript in your applications, you need to select some objects and make them scriptable. You can expose either some or all of their attributes to the scripting system. Parsing and handling Apple Events is a complicated process that, fortunately, Cocoa programmers get to avoid.

The most important thing that you need to do to make an application scriptable is provide a *scripting definition* (*sdef*) file to accompany it. In this section, we will look at what this needs to contain, and how AppleScript maps to Objective-C.

21.2.1 Understanding AppleScript Objects

This describes the classes and commands exposed by your application. Objects exposed to scripting are arranged in a hierarchy. The top level object is always the application. The `NSApplication` class provides two properties that are designed for scripting, `-orderedDocuments` and `-orderedWindows`. These are exposed to AppleScript as elements of the application object. You can provide other top-level elements by implementing this delegate method in your application delegate:

```
- (BOOL)application: (NSApplication*)sender
 delegateHandlesKey: (NSString*)key;
```

This is called to look up keys when AppleScript sends an event to the application object. AppleScripts that interact with your application will have a block looking something like this:

```
tell application "MyApplication"
 -- do some things
end tell
```

This defines a scope in AppleScript. All of the code in the middle will be transformed into a set of Apple Events that are passed to your application. These will then be decoded according to the rules in your scripting definition and turned into Objective-C messages. For **set** and **get** statements, these will call the delegate method previously shown to determine if the delegate understands the key.

The **tell** command is at the core of AppleScript. It is used to navigate down the hierarchy of objects exposed by a given application to find the correct one for sending messages. You can think of a **tell** clause as equivalent to a message send operation. Although they are not directly comparable, the following two are roughly equivalent in AppleScript and Objective-C.

```
tell object to play
```

```
[object play];
```

All of the commands that occur in a **tell** block are handled by the object. They are therefore equivalent to Objective-C methods, and are typically implemented as methods. Because AppleScript originates on a platform where Pascal was the primary development language, they are not described in this way. Commands are defined independently of classes. In the standard suite, you will find a description of the close command, saying "**close** *v*: Close an object." The *v* is next to all commands in the scripting dictionary. It signifies that the word is a verb, reinforcing the dictionary metaphor. This is not attached to a class; it is supported by various objects. You can use it in scripts like this:

```
tell application "TextEdit"
    tell front window
        close
    end tell
end tell
```

This first looks up the window element of the application, returning an ordered collection of windows. The **front** specifier gets the first element in this collection. The window object is then the target for any messages inside the inner **tell** block. This is sent a close command. Whether the object understands this command is not defined until run time.

This is an example of the *command pattern*. You are unlikely to see this design pattern in Objective-C code. It is a way of implementing something like Objective-C's dynamic dispatch mechanism in languages that do not support it natively. The dispatch mechanism used by AppleScript is not quite the same as the one used in Objective-C. If an object does not know how to handle a given command, it will be passed up to its container and so on until a handler is found. If you replace close with quit in the last example and try running it, TextEdit will exit. The quit command is handled by the application, not the window, and the nested scope mechanism automatically finds the handler. This can be very confusing. If both the application and the window understand a command, then the user might copy something from outside the inner tell block inside and get very different results.

You should be aware of this scoping when defining commands that are supported by different objects. Make sure that users won't want to invoke these commands on the application while sending commands to a document or window, and that they won't want to invoke them on a document while sending commands to an interior object.

21.2.2 Providing Object Specifiers

When an AppleScript command is received by a Cocoa application, it is wrapped in an NSScriptCommand instance. This is conceptually similar to NSInvocation,

Exposing Models

It is often tempting to expose view objects to scripting. This is how a number of older scripting systems worked, including the Recorder application that shipped with Microsoft Window 3. This is generally a bad idea. When you are writing scripts for an application, you typically want to interact with models directly, rather than via an interface designed for humans.

If you are using the model-view-controller pattern, you should think of AppleScript as another view, using different controllers, for your models.

encapsulating an AppleScript, rather than an Objective-C, message send in an object. It is then passed as the parameter to a method that is associated with the object identified as the receiver.

The identification of the receiver can take several steps. Apple Events provide a distributed objects mechanism that is not tied to Objective-C. Every object returned by the application to a script is passed out as an *object specifier*. This is used in much the same way as an object pointer, but is implemented in a very different way. When an object specifier is passed back into a scripted application, it is wrapped in an instance of a subclass of `NSScriptObjectSpecifier`.

Object specifiers are used like pointers or references, but they contain a lot more structure. Every specifier encapsulates a path from the root object (typically the application) down to the specified object. You need to create object specifiers for all of your scriptable objects by implementing this method:

```
- (NSScriptObjectSpecifier*)objectSpecifier;
```

This returns an object specifier capable of finding your object its container. Typically the returned object will be either an `NSIndexSpecifier` or an `NSNameSpecifier`. These identify an object by its index in an ordered collection, or by a name, respectively. Initializing these two classes is quite complicated. Each contains an initializer like this:

```
- (id)initWithContainerClassDescription: (NSScriptClassDescription*)
    classDesc
                    containerSpecifier: (NSScriptObjectSpecifier*)
                        container
                                   key: (NSString*)property
                                  name: (NSString*)name;
```

The first two arguments to this method specify the container. The second argument is the object specifier for the parent object in the containment hierarchy, typically found by sending it an `-objectSpecifier` message. The first is the description of the AppleScript class for this object. This is defined in the application's scripting definition. You typically get this from the object specifier by sending it a `-keyClassDescription`, although you can also look it up by calling class methods on `NSScriptClassDescription`. These two parameters are the same for all of the `NSScriptObjectSpecifier` subclass initializers.

The remaining two parameters are used to identify the receiver in the parent container. The equivalent method on `NSIndexSpecifier` takes an index, rather than a name, for the property.

21.2.3 Providing a Scripting Definition

Before you can use any of your objects via scripting, you need to provide a script definition. This is an XML file with the .sdef extension. Unfortunately, XCode does not currently provide any support for writing this file; you have to create it as a plain text file.

The scripting definition is not compiled, and so there is no checking performed when you build the application. If you try to open it as a scripting definition, rather than a plain text file, you may get some errors reported. Others can appear when you try to use the script. A few errors, in particular missing elements, will just cause silent failures.

You can perform some checking on this file from the xmllint utility. This is a command-line tool that parses and attempts to validate an XML file against its *Doctype definition* (*DTD*). You typically use it with the −valid option, to enable DTD checking, when you want to check an sdef file. First, it will check that the file is really XML, and give an error like this if it isn't:

```
$ xmllint --valid example.sdef
example.sdef:32: parser error : Opening and ending tag mismatch:
cocoa line 19 and class
</class>
^
```

This shows that you have forgotten to close a tag. This is quite easy to do when you are creating AppleScript definitions, because there are several tags that are usually written in short-hand form and so omitting the closing tag is a one-character typo. After you fix this error, it will check that it is really a scripting definition by comparing the tags and their attributes with the ones specified in the DTD. If it fails, you will get errors like this:

```
$ xmllint --valid example.sdef
example.sdef:14: element parameter: validity error : Element
parameter does not carry attribute code
```

```
</parameter>
^
```

This points to the closing tag of a tag that is missing an attribute. Every parameter has to have an Apple Event code associated with it, but the one on line 14 of this file is missing it. The xmllint tool won't find everything that's wrong with an sdef file, but it will find the most obvious. Mismatched closing tags, in particular, are incredibly difficult to find without a tool like this.

To demonstrate the basics of exposing objects to scripting, we will write a very simple program that displays a table view. The only way of adding and removing items from this view is by scripting. The scripting definition for this example is shown in Listing 21.1.

Scripting definition files each define a single dictionary containing one or more suites. Each suite contains definitions of classes, commands, and data types. This example will only provide the first two.

The first part of any scripting definition file is the doctype definition. You should copy lines 1–3 of this tile into any new sdef file. You can also copy line 4 and the corresponding closing tag, because every definition file contains a dictionary. The XML namespace declaration here is for the *XInclude* standard, which defines a mechanism for including files from other files. Lines 6–7 include the definition of the standard suite. Prior to OS X 10.5, you were required to copy and paste these into your own file. Now you can simply reference them. This has the advantage that your application automatically benefits from any new parts of the standard suite added in future versions of OS X. These are typically implemented by `NSApplication` and so will be supported automatically if you link against a newer version of the framework.

Listing 21.1: The scripting definition from the ScriptTable example. [from: examples/ScriptTable/ScriptTable.sdef]

```
1  <?xml version="1.0" encoding="UTF-8"?>
2  <!DOCTYPE dictionary
3      SYSTEM "file://localhost/System/Library/DTDs/sdef.dtd">
4
5  <dictionary title="ScriptTable␣Terminology"
6      xmlns:xi="http://www.w3.org/2001/XInclude">
7
8      <xi:include href="file:///System/Library/ScriptingDefinitions/
           CocoaStandard.sdef"
9          xpointer="xpointer(/dictionary/suite)" />
10
11     <suite name="ScriptTable␣Suite" code="stbl" description="Classes␣for␣
           the␣ScriptTable␣example">
```

```

        <command name="clear rows" code="tablcler" description="Clear the rows in the table." >
            <direct-parameter type="specifier" description="the table to empty."/>
        </command>
        <command name="add row" code="tabladdr" description="Add a new row to the table." >
            <direct-parameter type="specifier" description="the table to modify."/>
            <parameter code="rtxt" name="displaying" description="The text of the row.">
                <type type="text" list="no"/>
                <cocoa key="entry" />
            </parameter>
        </command>

        <class name="document" code="docu" description="A ScriptTable document">
            <cocoa class="TableModel" />

            <element type="row">
                <cocoa key="items" />
            </element>

            <responds-to name="clear rows">
                <cocoa method="handleClearScriptCommand:" />
            </responds-to>
            <responds-to name="add row">
                <cocoa method="handleAddScriptCommand:" />
            </responds-to>

        </class>

        <class name="row" code="trow" description="An item in the table">
            <cocoa class="TableItem" />
            <property type="text" name="title" code="str ">
                <cocoa key="string" />
            </property>
        </class>

    </suite>
</dictionary>
```

This definition defines one new scripting suite, the ScriptTable Suite, for the example application. Figure 21.2 shows what the definitions in this file look like when you open the dictionary in Script Editor. It contains two commands and two classes. Many of these tags have a description attribute. This attribute is ignored by the system; it exists solely to provide the human-readable description that you can see in the documentation.

Scripting command definitions in this file are very similar to method prototypes in Objective-C. They define the name of the command, the number and types of arguments, and the names of these arguments. The first command is called `clear rows`. Note that this is similar to an Objective-C selector name, but is allowed to contain spaces. In Objective-C, you would typically use `-clearRows` instead. This command doesn't take any explicit arguments but has one implicit one. The direct parameter here and on line 17 is the equivalent of the receiver in Objective-C. This will be the target of the **`tell`** block containing the command.

The second command is more complicated. This defines the `add row` command, which takes a single explicit argument. This command will add a new row to the

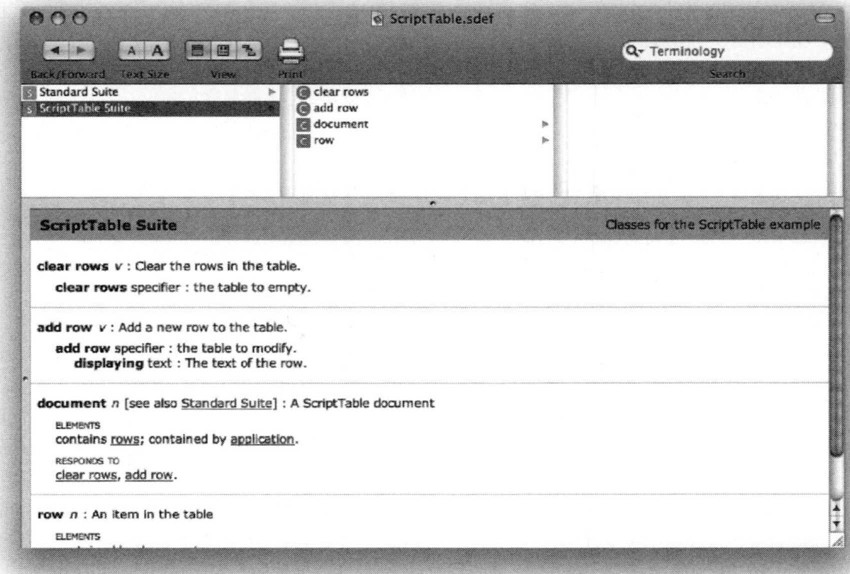

Figure 21.2: The ScriptTable example's scripting dictionary.

table, with the argument providing the text of the new row. The explicit parameter has a name that defines the equivalent of the selector component preceding the parameter. AppleScript parameters can be provided in any order. They are delivered to program in an object that supports KVC. The key is defined on line 20.

All of the commands and parameters have a code attribute, which defines a four- or eight-character sequence used to uniquely identify them. You can pick anything for these; it just has to be unique within that application. The purpose of the scripting dictionary is to look up these codes for each element of a script's syntax.

The second part of the file defines two classes. The first is the document class. Note that in a real application this should support the document functions from the standard suite, while this one doesn't. Each AppleScript class must have a Cocoa class associated with it. This is done on lines 25 and 41.

Typical classes have three components: elements, properties, and commands. Elements and properties are both handled via KVC when you implement a scriptable Cocoa object. Lines 28 and 43 define the key used to access a property and an element in the two classes. Note the difference between the two declarations. You do not need to specify a code or a description for elements; they always take these from their class. This means that you cannot expose two different elements with the same class. Recall that elements are to-many mappings, so you cannot have two relations of this form containing the same target. There are several ways of working around this. The easiest is to define a new subclass of a class that does not define any new properties, elements, or commands, and use this as the target for one, and the superclass for the other.

The commands that a class understands are defined by the responds to sections. These provide a mapping between the command and a selector. The command is defined earlier, and the selector must accept a single argument, an object encapsulating the command, so these sections are relatively simple. By convention, AppleScript methods are called `-handle<command name>ScriptCommand:`. This is not a requirement, as it is with KVC accessor methods, and so you can name them whatever you want.

Once you have written a scripting definition, you need to tell the scripting system what it is called and enable scripting. These are both done in the application's Info.plist. Listing 21.2 shows the two new entries required to support scripting.

Note that if you just want to support the standard suites, you only need to supply the first of these keys. You can also do this with other applications that don't support scripting out of the box, such as Preview. Adding this pair of lines will enable the basic AppleScript functionality provided by `NSApplication`, for example, allowing scripting to open documents, close windows, and so on.

Listing 21.2: Enabling scripting in the application's property list. [from: examples/ScriptTable/Info.plist]

```
	<key>NSAppleScriptEnabled</key>
	<true/>
	<key>OSAScriptingDefinition</key>
	<string>ScriptTable.sdef</string>
```

21.2.4 Handling Scripting Commands

Defining the scripting dictionary is only half of the solution. A dictionary translates between two languages, in this case between AppleScript and Objective-C. You also need to implement the Objective-C part. The first thing we want to be able to do is return a custom object for the document. This example application does not use the Cocoa document system; it just has a single document object, which is controlled entirely via scripting.

We define this using the application delegate shown in Listing 21.3. This is connected to the application's `delegate` outlet in Interface Builder. The application, as defined by the standard suite, has two elements. These are ordered collections of the windows and the documents in the application.

Listing 21.3: Manually providing documents for scripting. [from: examples/ScriptTable/AppDelegate.m]

```
#import "AppDelegate.h"

@implementation AppDelegate
- (BOOL)application: (NSApplication*)sender
 delegateHandlesKey: (NSString*)key
{
	if ([@"orderedDocuments" isEqualToString: key])
	{
		return YES;
	}
	return NO;
}
- (NSArray*) orderedDocuments
{
	return [NSArray arrayWithObject: model];
}
@end
```

When a script asks the application for its documents, it will first send the delegate an `-application:delegateHandlesKey:` message, with itself as the first argument and the string `@"orderedDocuments"` as the second. If this returns **YES**, then it will send a `-valueForKey:` method with the same last argument. In our implementation this returns a simple one-element array containing the model object. This object is instantiated in the nib file and connected to the application delegate's `model` outlet.

The model object is an instance of the `TableModel` class, shown in Listing 21.4. When this object wakes up, it initializes the array bound to the table column with a new table item containing a placeholder value. This is not required; it just lets us use all of the scripting properties and command immediately, rather than having to add some items first.

Listing 21.4: The scripted table model object. [from: examples/ScriptTable/TableModel.m]

```
@implementation TableModel
- (void)awakeFromNib
{
    items = [NSMutableArray new];
    TableItem *placeholder = [TableItem itemWithString: @"foo"];
    [placeholder setContainer: self];
    [self willChangeValueForKey: @"items"];
    [items addObject: placeholder];
    [self didChangeValueForKey: @"items"];
}
- (void)handleClearScriptCommand: (NSScriptCommand*)aCommand
{
    [self willChangeValueForKey: @"items"];
    [items removeAllObjects];
    [self didChangeValueForKey: @"items"];
}
- (void)handleAddScriptCommand: (NSScriptCommand*)aCommand
{
    NSString * newEntry =
        [[aCommand evaluatedArguments] objectForKey: @"entry"];
    TableItem *newItem = [TableItem itemWithString: newEntry];
    [newItem setContainer: self];
    [self willChangeValueForKey: @"items"];
    [items addObject: newItem];
    [self didChangeValueForKey: @"items"];
}
- (NSScriptObjectSpecifier*)objectSpecifier
{
    NSScriptClassDescription *parent =
```

```
74             [NSScriptClassDescription classDescriptionForClass: [NSApp class]];
75     return [[[NSIndexSpecifier alloc]
76         initWithContainerClassDescription: parent
77                         containerSpecifier: nil
78                                        key: @"orderedDocuments"
79                                      index: 0] autorelease];
80 }
81 @end
```

All of the remaining methods are directly related to scripting. The first two are the methods defined in the scripting definition as handlers when this class is sent a command. The first is simpler, simply deleting all of the rows. This ignores the script command object; it does exactly the same thing every time it is invoked.

The second adds a new row to the table. The parameter of this, you should recall, is the text of the item to add. Our table model doesn't use plain strings for the rows; it uses a class exposed to scripting that has the text as a property. A new instance of this class, shown in Listing 21.5, is created whenever this action is called. The `-evaluatedArguments` message sent to the command object returns a dictionary of the arguments passed along with this command. The "evaluated" part of this method name refers to the fact that it performs the mapping from object specifiers back to objects.

The object specifier is a path from the application to the reference object. When this model object is returned in response to the application being asked for its documents, the `-objectSpecifier` method will be called to create an object encapsulating this path. This has to provide a mechanism for finding the object from its parent in the containment hierarchy.

The model object is contained directly by the application. It is the only, and therefore first, document returned by the application when its `document` element is accessed. The class of the parent is therefore the application class, and so the first part of this method finds the class description for `NSApp`. The container specifier is `nil`, a special value indicating that this object is contained by the root element.

Note that both the key and the index, specified on lines 78 and 79, use Objective-C terminology. In AppleScript, the element is `document` and the index is 1. In Objective-C, we specify the name of the KVC member used to access the property, and the index in an Objective-C collection, which counts from zero.

The table item class is very simple. You could write an equivalent application without it, using an array of strings to populate the table. This class is provided to give another example of constructing and using object specifiers.

The object specifier for this class tells the system how to find it from the model object. In both cases where we created these objects, we sent them a `-setContainer:` message with the model as the argument. This ensures that the object has a reference to the parent, which it can use when creating specifiers.

Listing 21.5: The class encapsulating a scriptable table row. [from: examples/ScriptTable/TableModel.m]

```
@interface TableItem : NSObject {
    id container;
    NSString *string;
}
+ (TableItem*)itemWithString: (NSString*)aString;
- (void)setContainer: (id)aTable;
@end
@implementation TableItem
- (TableItem*)initWithString: (NSString*)aString
{
    if (nil == (self = [self init])) { return nil; }
    string = [aString retain];
    return self;
}
+ (TableItem*)itemWithString: (NSString*)aString
{
    return [[[self alloc] initWithString: aString] autorelease];
}
- (void)setContainer: (id)aTable
{
    container = aTable;
}
- (void)dealloc
{
    [string release];
    [super dealloc];
}
- (NSScriptObjectSpecifier*)objectSpecifier
{
    NSScriptObjectSpecifier *parent = [container objectSpecifier];
    NSUInteger index = [[container valueForKey: @"items"]
        indexOfObjectIdenticalTo: self];
    id a= [[[NSIndexSpecifier alloc]
         initWithContainerClassDescription: [parent keyClassDescription]
                        containerSpecifier: parent
                                       key: @"items"
                                     index: index] autorelease];
    return a;
}
@end
```

The specifier created here also identifies the child by index. This time, it is not a constant index, however. The item must look itself up in the collection that contains it to find the index. This pattern is very common when creating AppleScript object specifiers. Because we already have the object specifier for the parent, we can ask it directly for its class description.

Note that this method recursively computes the path from the root object down to the requested one. The method calls the container's implementation before returning. This, in turn, will call its implementation until the root element is reached. As each of these calls returns, it will pass a more complete path up the stack, until the original call returns the complete path.

21.2.5 Testing Scripting Support

We can test that this works by running some simple scripts. The easiest way of doing this is to open them in Script Editor and run them. You should be careful of the caching provided by Script Editor when you are testing application scripting. If you open the dictionary with Script Editor, by pointing it at the application bundle, then a window like the one shown in Figure 21.2 will appear. This will contain the current contents of the dictionary in a convenient, browsable, form. When you run a script, however, you may find that it is not doing the right thing. This is because Script Editor caches the scripting dictionaries when it launches and does not invalidate this cache until it exits. If you modify an application's sdef file, you must relaunch Script Editor for the changes to take effect. Alternatively, you can use the osascript command-line tool to run the script.

Some problems are easy to spot in Script Editor. The syntax highlighting will color variables green and command names blue. If you enter something like Listing 21.6 and find that `create row` is green, then you should try relaunching Script Editor. If it is still green, then this means that there is a bug in your scripting definition file. Try running it through xmllint, and if this doesn't indicate any errors, carefully check that each element has the correct values.

Listing 21.6: Create some rows in the table. [from: examples/ScriptTable/CreateRows.applescript]

```
tell application "ScriptTable"
    tell the front document
        clear rows
        add row displaying "wibble"
        add row displaying "fish"
        add row displaying "banana"
        add row displaying "aubergine"
    end tell
end tell
```

Listing 21.6 is a short script for creating some simple rows in this table. The outer structure contains two nested **tell**s. The outer one finds an object identifier for the application object. The second one gets the `document` element, which is the ordered collection of documents provided by this application. The **front** keyword is one of the many array accessing keywords provided by AppleScript. Saying **front** `document` is equivalent to saying `document 1`.

AppleScript Articles

AppleScript treats the definite article as a keyword with no meaning. This means that you can write **the** anywhere in AppleScript without changing the program semantics. The short examples in this section do this for readability. It is equivalent in AppleScript to say **front** `document` and **the front** `document`. You can also write things like **the** `any item`. AppleScript doesn't check the English grammar of your programs. Think of this as another way of commenting your code. Ideally, AppleScript programs should read like a plain English description of what is happening.

All of the commands inside the inner tell block are passed to the table model object. This short script uses both of the commands that we defined. You can see the result of running it in Figure 21.3. The script first removes all of the existing rows and then adds four new ones containing some random words.

This will call the `-handleClearScriptCommand:` method on the model object once and then the `-handleAddScriptCommand:` method four times. This demonstrates that both of the commands work. If, when you run this script, the table is populated with four rows, then everything worked correctly.

Listing 21.7 shows another short script that tests the other aspects of this example's scripting support. On line 3, this accesses the array of rows and assigns the result to a temporary variable.

Listing 21.7: Display a dialog containing the text of the first row. [from: examples/ScriptTable/DialogRow1.applescript]

```
1 tell application "ScriptTable"
2     set t to the front document
3     set r to the first row of t
4     display dialog ((title of r) as string)
5     -- quit
6 end tell
```

The next line uses a standard AppleScript command to display a dialog box containing the text of this row. You can see this in Figure 21.4. If you uncomment

Figure 21.3: Populating the table from a script.

the `quit` command, then the application will quit if you click OK. The script will abort if you click Cancel. This can be very useful for debugging scripting support. Typically, if a test script doesn't work as expected, you will want to quit the application, modify the scripting definition or command-handling methods, and restart.

One facility that can help a lot with debugging scripting support is the Event Log in Script Editor. This records the Apple Events that are generated when the script runs and translates them back into a human-readable form using the script dictionaries. This is the output from running the last script:

```
tell application "ScriptTable"
    get document 1
        document 1
    get row 1 of document 1
        row 1 of document 1
    get title of row 1 of document 1
        "wibble"
    display dialog "wibble"
    «event ascrgdut»
        {}
    display dialog "wibble"
        {button returned:"OK"}
    quit
end tell
```

Each command is followed by an indented line showing the result. You can see that most of the get commands don't actually return any more information than was originally sent. These **get** commands are really just asking whether a path from the application object actually represents an object or not. The third **get** command finally does return a value. Strings are passed back to AppleScript as primitive values.

This output lets you see exactly what commands are being sent to your application. If your scripting definition file contains errors, this will show how the script is really being interpreted and you can spot where this differs from how you think it should be interpreted. This is much easier when you define simple scripts than complex ones.

As with other code, defining a good set of tests is important when making a scriptable application. You should assemble a small collection of very short scripts for your application as you add scripting support. You can then use these to pinpoint problems with the scripting definition and implementation.

21.3 Scripting from Cocoa

If you are writing a suite of applications, you may want to provide support for integrating them. If your applications are scriptable, then it makes sense to reuse the scripting support to allow them to interact.

Prior to OS X 10.5, this was very difficult. You needed to construct the Apple Events by hand and send them to the scripted application. This required creating a lot of complex objects to achieve even simple scripting tasks. Most of the time, developers avoided this by embedding AppleScript in constant string objects directly in their applications. The `NSAppleScript` object allows you to

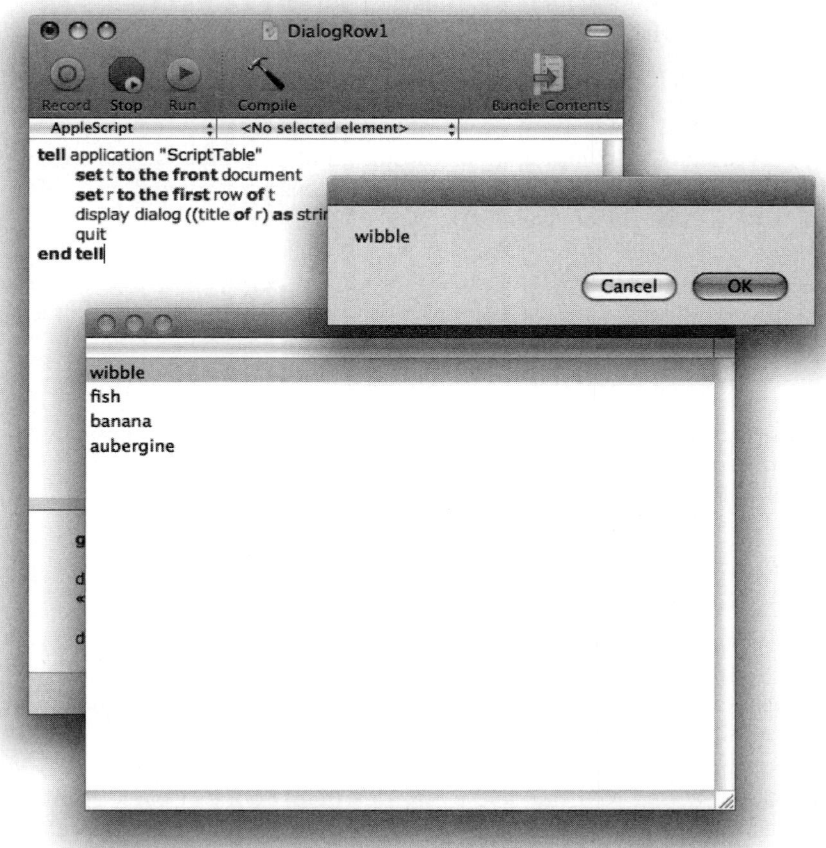

Figure 21.4: Displaying a dialog from the table.

create Apple Events by invoking the OSA framework's compiler from within your code, like this:

```
NSAppleScript *play = [[NSAppleScript alloc] initWithSource:
    @"tell application \"iTunes\" to play"];
NSDictionary *err;
[play executeAndReturnError: &err];
```

This short snippet creates an NSAppleScript object that encapsulates a script that will tell iTunes to play and then runs it. If an error occurs, the err dictionary will be populated with information about it. You might use something like this, with an accompanying pause script, in a conferencing application to stop the user's music during a call.

This works, but is far from an ideal way of integrating with the scripting system. Anything more complex than sending simple commands typically requires some complex and error-prone format strings to construct the program. This can very quickly become unmaintainable.

10.5 added the *Scripting Bridge*, which makes it easy to call remote AppleScript-exported objects from Objective-C. The Scripting Bridge dynamically creates Objective-C objects corresponding to OSA objects. As with AppleScript, you start interacting with bridged objects via an application.

The SBApplication class provides a wrapper for a remote application object. When you call one of the named constructors on this object, you get an instance of a dynamically created subclass exposing all of the commands that the receiver understands as methods. Using the scripting bridge, we can rewrite the last example like this:

```
id *iTunes =
    [SBApplication applicationWithBundleIdentifier: @"com.apple.iTunes"];
[iTunes play];
```

The first part of this gets an instance of the iTunesApplication class, a subclass of SBApplication. The identifier is the name specified in the application's Info.plist. You can also create a scripted application object by specifying the process ID of a running application or the URL of the application bundle.

If you compile code like this, you are likely to get warnings that the selectors are unknown. The sdp tool can help avoid this. This tool can parse sdef files and output their contents in a variety of formats. Most of these are for interaction with older versions of OS X. The sdef format was introduced with 10.3, but prior to 10.4 you had to create .scriptSuite and .scriptTerminology files, or the even old aete resources for the scripting system to read at run time. As of 10.5, this tool can also emit Objective-C header files, when used like this:

```
$ sdp ScriptTable.sdef -f h
```

The -f option is used to specify the output format, with h specifying an Objective-C header. This header defines a set of SBApplication and SBObject subclasses for the scriptable objects in the scripting definition. Listing 21.8 shows the model object from the example in the last section.

The definitions here come from the standard suite. Note the last two methods. These are the ones we defined as part of the ScriptTable suite, but because they

Listing 21.8: The ScriptTable model object from the standard suite. [from: examples/ScriptTableControl/ScriptTable.h]

```
// A document.
@interface ScriptTableDocument : SBObject

@property (copy, readonly) NSString *name;  // Its name.
@property (readonly) BOOL modified;  // Has it been modified since the last
     save?
@property (copy, readonly) NSURL *file;  // Its location on disk, if it has
     one.

- (void) closeSaving:(ScriptTableSaveOptions)saving savingIn:(NSURL *)
    savingIn;  // Close a document.
- (void) saveIn:(NSURL *)in_ as:(id)as;  // Save a document.
- (void) printWithProperties:(NSDictionary *)withProperties printDialog:(
    BOOL)printDialog;  // Print a document.
- (void) delete;  // Delete an object.
- (void) duplicateTo:(SBObject *)to withProperties:(NSDictionary *)
    withProperties;  // Copy an object.
- (void) moveTo:(SBObject *)to;  // Move an object to a new location.
- (void) clearRows;  // Clear the rows in the table.
- (void) addRowDisplaying:(NSString *)displaying;  // Add a new row to the
    table.

@end
```

are commands they are applied to every object in the application, whether it actually responds to them or not.

Most of the methods defined by this definition will not actually work. The header is intended to be conservative; it declares methods for every command that an object might respond to. This prevents compile-time errors from things that will work. You will still get run-time errors if you send a message to an object that it doesn't understand.

The definition maps scripting properties to Objective-C 2 declared properties. Elements are handled differently. You can see an example in the category for the ScriptTable suite shown in Listing 21.9. The `rows` element is exposed as a method that returns an `SBElementArray`.

This is a new collection class defined by the bridge. It is a subclass of `NSMutableArray`, and so most of the time you can just use it as a mutable array object. The main extension is the `-get` method. This corresponds to the **`get`**

Listing 21.9: The ScriptTable model object from the ScriptTable suite. [from: examples/ScriptTableControl/ScriptTable.h]

```
// A ScriptTable document
@interface ScriptTableDocument (ScriptTableSuite)

- (SBElementArray *) rows;

@end
```

keyword in AppleScript. It forces all of the objects specifiers in the array to be resolved. When you retrieve an element from an object, you will get an element specifier representing the array. Unless you send it a `-get` message, the specifiers for the individual elements will not be retrieved.

To demonstrate how this works, we'll write a simple application for controlling the ScriptTable example from the last section. This will display a simple window, allowing the user to clear the table, add a new row, or retrieve the contents of a single row. This is shown in Figure 21.5.

All of the actions from the user interface are connected to methods in an instance of the class shown in Listing 21.10. When this loads, it retrieves a proxy for the ScriptTable application. This will be a valid object as long as the system knows about the application. The application does not have to be running for this to work. The first time that you send a command to the application, it will be launched if it is not already running. If you want to only send a message to an application that is already running, you can first send an `-isRunning` message to the application object to test whether it is running.

The `table` instance variable is set in this object when it launches, but this does not cause ScriptTable to start. The value for this variable will be an `SBObject` subclass containing the path to the object, calculated on the client side. Unless you send a `-get` message or another command to this object, it will remain disconnected. The Scripting Bridge uses *lazy evaluation* to defer sending events for as long as possible. Sending events is quite expensive and it is often possible to completely avoid sending many of the events that a piece of code might appear to require. If you only access a single element in an array, for example, there is no reason to send events fetching all of them, and if you just send the array a `-count` message, then you don't need to fetch any.

The three action messages in this class are very simple. The last two just bounce the message to the table proxy. Note that the scripting commands have been automatically translated into camelCase to match the Cocoa coding style.

The `-clearRows:` action method sends a `-clearRows` message to the proxy rep-

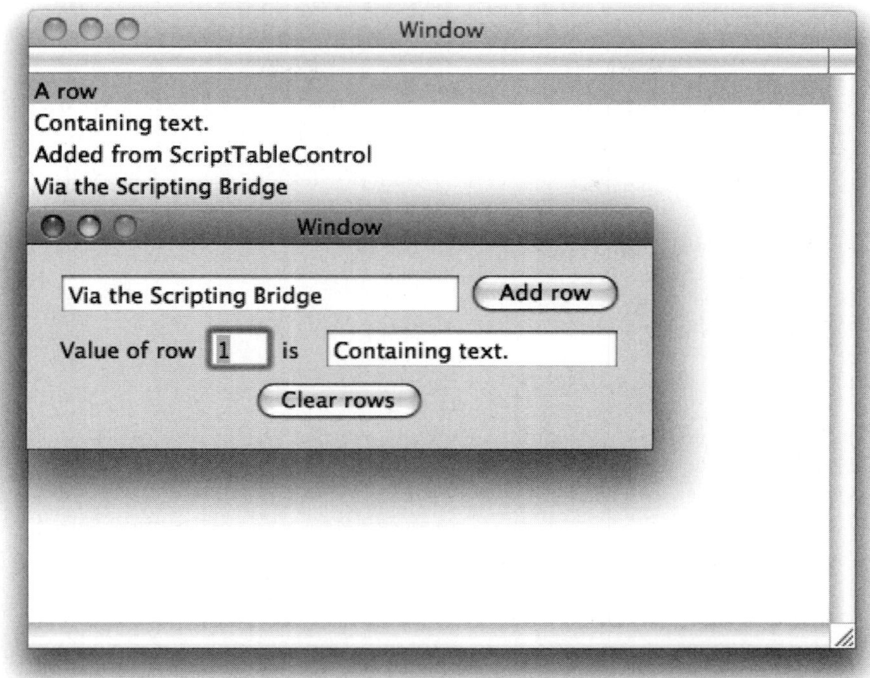

Figure 21.5: Controlling another application via the scripting bridge.

resenting the table. This is then translated into a `clear rows` Apple Event and sent to the other process. At the receiving end, this will be wrapped in an `NSScriptCommand` object and passed to the `-handleClearScriptCommand:` method in the table. Prior to 10.5, you had to implement most of these steps yourself to control scripted applications from Objective-C.

The `-fetchRowValue:` method sends the table proxy a `-rows` message to access the `rows` element. This is used just like any other array object. The fact that it is full of remote objects is not important at this stage. When the `title` property is accessed, this will be fetched from the remote application as an `NSString`. This is then passed back as the argument to the command.

Nothing in this application after line 8 looks like it interacts with a remote program. All of the code is standard Objective-C, sending messages to objects.

Listing 21.10: Controlling the ScriptTable application. [from: examples/ScriptTableControl/ScriptTableController.m]

```
#import "ScriptTableController.h"

@implementation ScriptTableController
- (void)awakeFromNib
{
    ScriptTableApplication *app =
        [SBApplication applicationWithBundleIdentifier:
            @"com.example.ScriptTable"];
    table = [[[app documents] objectAtIndex: 0] retain];
}
- (IBAction)fetchRowValue: (id)sender
{
    NSUInteger index = [sender integerValue];
    SBElementArray *rows = [table rows];
    if (index < [rows count])
    {
        ScriptTableRow *row = [rows objectAtIndex: index];
        [rowValue setStringValue: row.title];
    }
}
- (IBAction)addRow: (id)sender
{
    [table addRowDisplaying: [newRowText stringValue]];
}
- (IBAction)clearRows: (id)sender
{
    [table clearRows];
}
@end
```

The fact that the objects are really proxies that send events to a remote application is completely hidden.

You can use this as a general *interprocess communication* (*IPC*) mechanism. If the application that you want to communicate with already supports scripting, then this is very easy. If all you are doing is sending simple commands, then this may be a good choice. You should remember that going via the Apple Event system incurs a lot of overhead. Where good throughput is required, one of the mechanisms outlined in Part VII would be more appropriate.

Scripting and Concurrency

When scripts take a long time to execute, it is possible that the application state will change a lot in the middle. For example, we might get a reference to the third row in our table and then send it a `clear rows` command. The reference would then become invalid. This is not a huge problem for AppleScript. The extra layer of indirection means that it will always point at the third row of the table, irrespective of which object this is and whether it is a valid object or not. You should try to ensure that this kind of condition only happens when the user does something silly. Objects that are exposed to scripting should not be modified by anything that does not originate with a direct user action, either in the UI or via the scripting system. Users who modify a document while running scripts on it expect strange behavior, but no one expects a script to fail because a worker thread has chosen that moment to restructure some data.

21.4 Exposing Services to Automator

OS X 10.4 introduced a new way of scripting applications. The *Automator* application allows the user to define workflows. These are simpler than AppleScript scripts: They have no flow control. An Automator workflow is similar to a sequence of commands on a UNIX command-line. It is a sequence of filters, each taking the output of the last one as its input.

Automator is a lot less flexible than AppleScript, but a lot easier to use. If you have already exposed your application's functionality via AppleScript, then you can add Automator support very easily by wrapping some of the AppleScript commands in an Automator Action. XCode has a project type for AppleScript Automator Actions. Simply create one of these and write a script like this:

```
on run {input, parameters}
    -- do some processing
    return output
end run
```

The comment should be replaced with calls to the AppleScript commands invoking your application. Every Automator action takes some input and produces some output. Some actions ignore their input or produce empty output. These are intended to go at the start or end of a workflow. Because of their simple interface, Automator actions can be implemented by a single function or method. If you implement an action in Objective-C, then you just need to create an `AMBundleAction` subclass that implements this method:

```
- (id)runWithInput: (id)input
        fromAction: (AMAction*)anAction
             error: (NSDictionary**)errorInfo;
```

The input is usually an NSArray instance. The contents of this array depends on the parameters that you declare your action as supporting. This is defined in the Info.plist accompanying your bundle. As well as this class, your bundle needs to contain a nib with an NSView instance containing the user interface for your action. This configures the parameters for your action.

21.5 Other Scripting Technologies

The purpose of supporting scripting is to allow users of your program to control and automate it in ways you did not anticipate. You can do this via AppleScript, but there are a number of other scripting languages and systems available from third parties that may be more relevant. If your users are likely to be more familiar with a specific language, then you can always embed an interpreter in your program and use this for scripting. If you are writing a tool targeting web designers, for example, then you might consider linking against the WebKit framework and exporting some of your objects to the WebKit JavaScript engine for scripting.

You may even choose to write a domain-specific language, designed specifically for controlling your application. This is a common approach for highly specialized applications, but is less likely to be the right choice for programs intended for general use.

21.5.1 Distributed Objects

If you want to make your application scriptable from other Cocoa applications, rather than AppleScript, you can use the *distributed objects* (*DO*) system described in Chapter 22. This exposes objects to transparent access by other processes.

If AppleScript had been designed for OS X, rather than for Classic Mac OS and ported to OS X, it would probably have been built on top of DO. This would have dramatically simplified the task of making applications scriptable; you would just define a small set of Objective-C objects that you want to expose as scriptable objects and publish them in a well-known location.

You can use this to define your own, private, scripting mechanism to allow applications that you have written to control each other. If you do this, then you don't get the big advantage of AppleScript—that it is well supported by most OS X applications—but you do get something usable in some of the situations where AppleScript is useful, for a fraction of the effort.

Distributed objects are best used in addition to AppleScript. As we've seen, creating Apple Events in Cocoa is nontrivial. If you want to allow both compiled and scripted code to control your application, then implementing both mechanisms makes this easy.

21.5.2 F-Script

One third-party scripting system that has become popular in recent years is *F-Script*. This is a dialect of Smalltalk that is bridged with Objective-C. F-Script is very similar in both design and implementation to *StepTalk*, a scripting system that began life on GNUstep and has since been ported to OS X.

F-Script provides a lightweight Smalltalk runtime environment, which allows you to manipulate Objective-C objects from Smalltalk code. If you are familiar with Objective-C, then you will find Smalltalk a much easier language to learn than AppleScript. All of the bits of Objective-C that are not C are based on Smalltalk. Message send operations in Smalltalk are exactly the same in both Objective-C and Smalltalk.

The big advantage of using a system like F-Script or StepTalk for scripting your application is that you can reuse your Objective-C objects directly, without the need for a wrapper. This is perfect for rapid prototyping. Because Smalltalk syntax is so similar to Objective-C, it is very easy to write an initial implementation using Smalltalk and then, if it is too slow, rewrite it in Objective-C.

When using these frameworks, it is very easy to blur the line between script and application. The scripts interact directly with the application's objects and can be used to extend the application in arbitrary directions. You may find, if you start using either framework, that it becomes tempting to write large chunks of your application in a Smalltalk dialect.

This is not necessarily a bad thing. In general, Smalltalk will be slower than Objective-C, but the speed is not always important. The Mélodie music jukebox application for Étoilé, for example, is mostly written in Smalltalk but rarely uses more than a few percent of even a slow CPU. The really processor-intensive code is all provided by a decoding library that is written in a mixture of C and hand-optimized assembly code. Most applications are the same; 90% of the time is spent executing 10% of the code. If you write the 10% in Objective-C or even pure C and the remaining 90% in an even higher-level language, then you can save yourself time and effort without slowing down the user's perception of the program. In particular, most user interface code spends much more time waiting for I/O than it does executing on the CPU, and is an ideal choice for a scripting language.

F-Script and StepTalk do not provide a mechanism for cross-application scripting. Because they can both interact with Objective-C objects, however, they can make use of distributed objects and remotely control any application that exposes its model objects via DO. They can also make use of the Scripting Bridge, as can any other languages bridged with Objective-C.

21.6 Summary

In this chapter we have looked at how to add scripting support to a Cocoa application. The standard way of making applications scriptable on OS X is to expose their properties and methods via AppleScript. We saw how to do this in a simple example.

We also looked at some of the alternatives to AppleScript and how they can be used. The ability to control an application via a mechanism other than the standard GUI makes it a lot more flexible. AppleScript was one of the main reasons why Mac OS became so popular in the publishing and design world in the mid 1990s: It allowed complex workflows to be automated, even when they involved multiple applications.

The importance of AppleScript varies a lot between applications. If you are designing a program that is likely to be used in conjunction with a number of other systems, then you should consider AppleScript a priority, because it allows the user to easily tie your application into a workflow.

Part VII

System Programming

Chapter 22

Networking

Since the 1990s, it has become increasingly rare for computers to be regarded as stand-alone devices. Most will be connected to the Internet, and a lot will run as part of a *local-area network* (*LAN*) as well.

The NeXT systems were designed for networking from the start. The original NeXT workstation was one of the first to come with Ethernet as standard and most ran in a networked configuration. Since then, the support for networking in the operating system has evolved a great deal, and a modern OS X system provides a large number of network-related libraries for developers.

The UNIX underpinnings of OS X provide low-level code for connecting to other systems, and these are wrapped in progressively higher-level abstractions. In this chapter, we will look at the progressively higher-level abstractions available to the programmer.

22.1 Low-Level Socket Programming

The original *Berkeley socket* API was a fairly simple set of extensions to the original UNIX file handling mechanisms. It extended the UNIX "everything is a file" approach by allowing you to create new file handles corresponding to network connections.

The original idea of the socket API was to abstract away connection details of the underlying connection mechanism. In UNIX, everything is a file. A simple UNIX program starts with three files open, one for reading and two for writing. These are the standard input, output, and error streams. They are typically connected to the terminal, but can be redirected to point to files or anything that behaves like a file. On a traditional UNIX system, this even includes devices.

OS X exports a number of devices in this way. The `/dev/` directory lists a lot of devices that are exposed with file-like interfaces. You can read from these or write to them just as you would any other file, although typically access to them is restricted to the superuser.

The first form of interprocess communication on UNIX was the *pipe*, a very simple interface that looked like a file at both ends. One end was used for reading and the other for writing. Anything that could read from or write to a file could do the same with pipes. They were—and still are—most commonly used for connecting processes together via their standard streams.

The socket API was designed to keep this metaphor. Sockets are represented by integers, just as file handles are, and can be passed to any of the standard file I/O routines. If you have a library that works on files, then you can pass it a socket handle in place of a file handle and it will work as expected, as long as it doesn't try to seek in the file.

This is very convenient in OS X, where there are already a number of high-level APIs for interacting with files. Although using sockets in this way hides some of the more advanced features, it means that we can use them very easily with existing code. It is also possible to combine these approaches, for example, by using some of the Cocoa APIs to determine when a socket is ready for reading or writing and then use the low-level functions for sending or receiving data.

SRV Records

In recent years there has been a gradual trend away from using standard ports, caused by the shortage in IPv4 addresses. You can only run one server of a particular type on a single IP address if you use well-known ports. The alternative, standardized in 1996, is to use *DNS SRV records*. These contain a service name, such as HTTP or XMPP, as well as the domain to be looked up. This allows a single service-domain pair to map to any IP and port.

Starting with 10.5, the `getaddrinfo()` function on OS X will handle these transparently, so you don't need to write any custom code to handle the DNS queries.

Listing 22.1 shows how to open a connection to a remote server using the Berkeley socket API and then wrap the result in a Cocoa file handle. This allows you to mix Cocoa and BSD operations on the same socket easily. For example, you can send the returned object a `-waitForDataInBackgroundAndNotify` message to receive a notification when it has data waiting and then use BSD functions to read the data. Alternatively, you can use `select()` or `poll()` to wait for data and then read it with `NSFileHandle`'s methods.

Listing 22.1: Creating a BSD socket in a Cocoa file handle. [from: examples/Socket/NSFileHandle+Socket.m]

```
@implementation NSFileHandle (SocketAdditions)
+ (NSFileHandle*) fileHandleConnectedToRemoteHost:(NSString*)aHost
                                       forService:(NSString*)aService
{
    const char * server = [aHost UTF8String];
    const char * service = [aService UTF8String];
    struct addrinfo hints, *res0;
    int error;

    memset(&hints, 0, sizeof(hints));
    hints.ai_family = PF_UNSPEC;
    hints.ai_socktype = SOCK_STREAM;
    //Ask for a stream address.
    error = getaddrinfo(server, service, &hints, &res0);
    if (error)  { return nil; }

    int s = -1;
    for (struct addrinfo *res = res0;
        res != NULL && s < 0 ;
        res = res->ai_next)
    {
        s = socket(res->ai_family, res->ai_socktype,
            res->ai_protocol);
        //If the socket failed, try the next address
        if (s < 0)  { continue ; }

        //If the connection failed, try the next address
        if (connect(s, res->ai_addr, res->ai_addrlen) < 0)
        {
            close(s);
            s = -1;
            continue;
        }
    }
    freeaddrinfo(res0);
    if (s < 0) { return nil; }
    return [[[NSFileHandle alloc] initWithFileDescriptor:s
                                          closeOnDealloc:YES] autorelease];
}
@end
```

This example uses the `getaddrinfo()` function. This function was added to the POSIX specification in 2000 for better IPv6 support. Applications using this interface will get an array of potential addresses that can use different protocols. If a server supports both IPv4 and IPv6, then this function will return both and the client can try them all until it finds one that works. Other protocols, like AppleTalk, can also be used here.

The first thing to do is get the list of possible socket addresses. This is done on line 19, using information provided earlier. The two most important parts, the domain and service, are provided as arguments. The third parameter is a set of hints that indicate the kind of socket we would like. We set two hints here on lines 16 and 17. The first indicates that we don't care which protocol the address uses and the second indicates that we want a stream protocol of some kind (e.g., TCP).

The loop that starts on line 23 does the real work of constructing the socket. This tries each returned address in turn. It first tries to create the socket on line 27. This will usually succeed, since it has not tried to connect at this point. This will only fail if some kernel resources have been exhausted or if the network stack does not support the requested kind of socket (which shouldn't ever be the case with addresses generated in this way). If this fails, it skips to the next address to try.

If the socket has been created successfully the next step is to try to connect it. This can fail for a number of reasons. If you have an IPv6 local network, but the network between you and the remote host doesn't support IPv6, then you will potentially get IPv6 addresses returned, which will fail when you try to connect.

Well-Known Services

The file /etc/services contains a list of port numbers for well-known services. If the host does not provide SRV records for the named service, then this file will be consulted to provide the port number. If this does not exist, then the lookup will fail.

If the socket has been created and connected after trying some subset of the addresses returned, then it is wrapped in a file handle object on line 42 and returned. The socket will be closed when this object is deallocated. You'd use this method to create a socket like this:

```
id s = [NSFileHandle fileHandleConnectedToRemoteHost: @"apple.com"
                                          forService: @"http"];
```

This would give you a socket connected to Apple's web server. To demonstrate this, we'll write a simple implementation of the standard telnet utility, supporting

IPv6 and using BSD sockets via Cocoa objects. The code for this tool is shown in Listing 22.2.

Listing 22.2: A simple Cocoa telnet program. [from: examples/Socket/cocoatelnet.m]

```
#import "NSFileHandle+Socket.h"

@interface Telnet : NSObject {
    NSFileHandle *network;
    NSFileHandle *input;
    NSFileHandle *output;
}
- (id) initWithServer: (NSString*)server service: (NSString*)service;
@end

@implementation Telnet
- (id) initWithServer: (NSString*)server service: (NSString*)service
{
    if (nil == (self = [self init])) { return nil; }
    network = [NSFileHandle fileHandleConnectedToRemoteHost: server
                                                 forService: service];
    if (nil == network)
    {
        [self release];
        return nil;
    }
    input = [NSFileHandle fileHandleWithStandardInput];
    output = [NSFileHandle fileHandleWithStandardOutput];

    [network retain]; [input retain]; [output retain];

    NSNotificationCenter *center =
        [NSNotificationCenter defaultCenter];
    [center addObserver:self
               selector:@selector(printData:)
                   name:NSFileHandleDataAvailableNotification
                 object:network];
    [center addObserver:self
               selector:@selector(sendData:)
                   name:NSFileHandleDataAvailableNotification
                 object:input];

    [network waitForDataInBackgroundAndNotify];
    [input waitForDataInBackgroundAndNotify];

```

```
    return self;
}
- (void) printData:(NSNotification*)notification
{
    [output writeData:[network availableData]];
    [network waitForDataInBackgroundAndNotify];
}
- (void) sendData:(NSNotification*)notification
{
    [network writeData:[input availableData]];
    [input waitForDataInBackgroundAndNotify];
}
- (void) dealloc
{
    [network release];
    [input release];
    [output release];

    NSNotificationCenter *center =
        [NSNotificationCenter defaultCenter];
    [center removeObserver:self];

    [super dealloc];
}
@end

int main(int argc, char **argv)
{
    [NSAutoreleasePool new];
    if (argc != 3)
    {
        fprintf(stderr, "\tUsage: %s {server} {service}\n", argv[0]);
        return 1;
    }
    NSString *server = [NSString stringWithUTF8String:argv[1]];
    NSString *service = [NSString stringWithUTF8String:argv[2]];

    [[Telnet alloc] initWithServer: server service: service];

    [[NSRunLoop currentRunLoop] run];
    return 0;
}
```

The main() function for this program is very simple. It parses the arguments, creates an instance of the Telnet class and then starts the run loop. The real work is done by the class.

Most of the code in this class is in the initialization. The designated initializer takes two arguments—the same two that a socket requires—and tries to create a file handle with them on lines 15–16. If, for some reason, this fails it aborts. Note that it sends itself a -release message on line 19 before returning nil. This is a common idiom in Cocoa. Without it the caller would have to do something unwieldy like this:

```
id obj = [Example alloc];
realPointer = [obj init];
if (realPointer == nil) { [obj release]; }
```

If the network socket is created correctly, the class also grabs file handles corresponding to stdin and stdout. Finally, it registers for notifications when either the standard input or the network has any waiting data and tells both file handles to wait in the background and post a notification.

The rest of the program will be spent in one of the methods on lines 43 and 48. These are mirror images of each other, each reading data from one handle and writing it to the other. We can test this simple program like this:

```
$ gcc *.m -framework Foundation -std=c99
$ ./a.out apple.com http
GET /
HTTP/1.1 302 Object Moved
Location: http://www.apple.com/
Content-Type: text/html
Cache-Control: private
Connection: close

<head><body> This object may be found
<a HREF="http://www.apple.com/">here</a> </body>
```

This shows a simple HTTP session with the Apple web server. Recall that no port numbers or other pieces of protocol-specific information are specified manually. The socket is constructed from two pieces of information: the apple.com domain and the HTTP protocol.

22.2 Cocoa Streams

With OS X 10.3, Apple introduced a new class wrapping socket connections. The NSStream class is an abstract superclass for wrapping arbitrary streams. It has two subclasses, one for input and one for output streams.

Although this class has better run loop integration, it comes with a number of limitations. The biggest is the fact that it does not provide any mechanism for negotiating an SSL/TLS session after the connection has been opened. A large number of common Internet protocols require you to connect with an unencrypted connection and then negotiate an encrypted connection after the server has advertised the capability.

The other major limitation should be obvious after looking at the designated constructor:

```
+ (void)getStreamsToHost: (NSHost*)host
                    port: (NSInteger)port
             inputStream: (NSInputStream**)inputStream
            outputStream: (NSOutputStream**)outputStream;
```

As you can see, this takes a port number as the second argument. This means that port numbers must be hard-coded when using an `NSStream`, or they must be looked up separately before creating the stream. This makes the class unsuitable for a number of other protocols. The last two parameters here are pointers to the two streams that will be created, one for each direction.

You can also create input and output streams directly. In addition to the socket streams created by the superclass, both support memory and files as targets.

The run-loop integration provided by `NSStream` is slightly better than that provided by `NSFileHandle`. Rather than needing to go via the notification center, you simply call `-scheduleInRunLoop:forMode:` on the stream. When it is ready for use, it will send the delegate a message like this:

```
- (void)stream: (NSStream*)theStream
   handleEvent: (NSStreamEvent)streamEvent;
```

This will be sent when the open operation is finished, when a stream can be read from or written to, or when the stream reaches the end or an error.

22.3 URL Handling

If you only want unidirectional network communication, the *URL loading system* is very powerful. It provides a number of mechanisms for loading data from an *Uniform Resource Locator* (*URL*).

A URL is a uniform way of representing the location of some resource. The syntax is very simple; it is a protocol and an address separated by a colon (':'). The format of everything after this separator is defined by the specific protocol.

There are a huge number of *URL schemes*—ways of understanding the part after the separator—but only a few are really common. The most common in everyday use are HTTP URLs. These are so common that you are likely to see them written on the side of buildings. Others are less common. Fax numbers can be specified using the "fax:" URL scheme, where the colon is immediately followed by a telephone number.

> **Safari, WebKit, and Curl**
>
> The basic NSURL class was present in OpenStep. It had a simple companion, NSURLHandle, which provided a way of loading data from a URL. This was insufficient for Safari. When it was introduced, during the 10.2 series, the entire URL loading system was redesigned. Internally, *WebCode* used CFURL objects, which are toll-free bridged with NSURLs. These were implemented on top of libcurl, an MIT-licensed URL loading library. To make WebCore more portable, recent versions use libcurl directly, but the *WebKit* Objective-C wrapper still uses NSURL.

22.3.1 Creating URLs

URLs are encapsulated in NSURL objects all over Cocoa. The file:// URL scheme is used now in preference to file paths in most of the file handling functions. Some of these provide a back-door into the URL loading system. You can load a URL very easily from NSData, for example. To get the front page of Apple's website as a string, this is all the code you need:

```
NSURL *url = [NSURL URLWithString: @"http://apple.com"];
NSData *data = [NSData dataWithContentsOfURL: url];
NSString *page = [[NSString alloc] initWithData: data encoding:
    NSUTF8StringEncoding]);
```

Note that the string encoding here is not necessarily correct. HTTP will provide you with the encoding when you perform the download, but this simple wrapper does not expose this.

Constructing URLs from strings like this is very common. There are also convenience methods for constructing file URLs. The +fileURLWithPath:isDirectory: method creates a URL pointing to either a file or a directory, depending on the value of the second argument. This can then be converted back to a file path by sending it a -path message. Since file URLs are so common, the -isFileURL method is provided to test whether a URL is in the "file" scheme.

Note that the -path method will return a path for any URL scheme that complies with RFC 1808, but this will only be a local filesystem path for file URLs. RFC 1808 is mentioned a lot in the URL documentation. This is a standard that defines a way of constructing URLs out of a set of optional components. The format for URLs using this template is

```
scheme://user:password@host:port/path;parameterString?query#fragment
```

Each of the segments in braces here is a method on NSURL that will return this part of the URL string. For example, you can send a -host message to a URL object to get back the remote host name. You can think of an NSURL as a structured string. Not all URLs conform to this standard, however, so these methods cannot be guaranteed to return anything sensible for an arbitrary URL.

22.3.2 Loading URLs

We saw earlier how to load data easily from a URL, but this did not handle the encoding at all. If you want to load a string in the correct encoding then you need to use the NSURLResponse class. Loading data from a URL is a two-step process: sending the request and getting the response. When you issue an HTTP request, the response will be an NSHTTPURLResponse. When you send this an -allHeaderFields message,[1] you will get back a dictionary representing the headers. One of these will contain the encoding used, for text data.

The simplest way of fetching data is to create an NSURLRequest and tell NSURLConnection to load it synchronously. This snippet does the same thing as the last example, but also allows the encoding to be found from the Content-Type header. This is likely to be something like "text/html; charset=utf-8." The StringEncodingForContentType() function must be supplied to parse this.

```
NSURL *url = [NSURL URLWithString: @"http://apple.com"];
NSURLRequest *request = [NSURLRequest requestWithURL: url];
NSURLResponse *response;
NSData *data = [NSURLConnection sendSynchronousRequest: request
                                     returningResponse: &response
                                                 error: NULL];
if (nil != data)
{
    NSDictionary * headers = [response allHTTPHeaderFields];
    NSString *contentType = [headers objectForKey: @"Content-Type"]

    NSStringEncoding encoding = StringEncodingForContentType(contentType);
    NSString *page = [[NSString alloc] initWithData: data encoding:
        encoding];
}
```

[1]The HTTP response also adds a category on NSURLResponse that provides methods for accessing these properties on all responses, although they will not return anything for non-HTTP responses.

Note that there is no Cocoa function for trivially implementing `StringEncodingForContentType()`. One common way of implementing this is to send `NSString` an `+availableStringEncodings` message. This will then return a C array of encodings. You can then send `NSString` a `+localizedNameOfStringEncoding:` message for each one to get its name. This can be used to construct a dictionary of supported type names.

If you are willing to stray outside Cocoa, there are three ways of doing it. The WebKit framework includes a method on `WebCoreEncodings` for handling decoding. You can send it a `+decodeData:` message with data as an argument and get a string back. This does not parse the encoding at all; it infers it from the content.

The other option is to use Core Foundation functions. First, the `CFStringConvertIANACharSetNameToEncoding()` function parses the type encoding and returns a Core Foundation encoding. This is then converted to a Cocoa encoding using `CFStringConvertEncodingToNSStringEncoding()`.

The final option is to use the standard UNIX `iconv` functions. These take character set names as arguments so you can use them directly with the returned character set name.

This mechanism is not the best way of loading URLs. If the remote file is big, or if the network is slow, then this will block for a long time. The `NSURLConnection` class is also capable of operating in an asynchronous mode. This connects to the server in the background and periodically sends notifications to a delegate.

A normal URL loading session will get delegate methods called for the following events:

1. The first response was received. The same delegate method is called again for any redirections.

2. Some data has been received. The delegate method will be called periodically as more data arrives.

3. The download has finished.

You would more commonly use the URL loading system in this way so that the user interface can remain responsive while you fetch files. Note the point about redirections. When we pointed our simple telnet program at Apple's website earlier, we got an HTTP 302 error indicating that the page had moved. Loading the page using the URL loading system works transparently, because it automatically parses this response and handles the redirection.

When you use the simple synchronous interfaces, the redirections are totally hidden from you. With the asynchronous version you are notified of them. You can use this to update a user interface element to indicate that the redirection has taken place. Safari does this with the status bar at the bottom of the main window.

The connection delegate should implement these methods:

```
- (void)connection: (NSURLConnection*)connection
didReceiveResponse: (NSURLResponse*)response;
- (void)connection: (NSURLConnection*)connection
    didReceiveData: (NSData*)data;
- (void)connection: (NSURLConnection*)connection
  didFailWithError: (NSError*)error;
- (void)connectionDidFinishLoading: (NSURLConnection*)connection;
```

The first one will be called for each redirection and for the first response. The second is called each time that some data is received. The data passed here will only be the next part of the received document. The delegate is responsible for storing it. The last method is called when the file is fully downloaded. If something goes wrong during the downloading process, then the error method will be called.

`NSURLConnection` is not the only way of getting data from a URL. The other option is `NSURLDownload`. This is slightly simpler to use, and downloads data directly to a file. This is used to implement file downloaders with progress updates. The delegate is just notified periodically of how much data has been received.

22.3.3 Extending the URL Loading System

One of the more interesting parts of the URL loading system is that it is extendible by the user. The handling for each URL type is done by a `NSURLProtocol` subclass. If you want to introduce a new URL type, you can create your own subclass of this. There are a few cases where this is useful. The most obvious is to support the attachment URLs in some mail and IM protocols, which allow attachments to reference each other. By implementing a URL handler for these, you can load local and remote attachments in the same way.

The rest of the URL system interacts with the protocol handler in a very simple way. First, it calls `+canInitWithRequest:` on each handler to find the correct one for loading a request. It then calls `initWithRequest:cachedResponse:client:` to create a new instance of the class for handling a specific request.

This handler must implement the `-response` method to return a response and it must call the relevant delegate method declared in the `NSURLProtocolClient` protocol to pass this response back to the higher-level delegate.

It will then be sent a `-startLoading` message. It should then begin downloading the remote file and, again, calling the correct delegate methods. This should happen asynchronously, typically by registering the stream or file descriptor with the run loop.

To show how this all works, we'll define a new URL scheme that uses the "example:" scheme and loads data from a dictionary. This is shown in Listing 22.3.

Listing 22.3: Defining a new URL scheme. [from: examples/ExampleURLProtocol/ExampleURLProtocol.m]

```
#import "ExampleURLProtocol.h"

static NSMutableDictionary *urls;

@implementation ExampleURLProtocol
+ (void)load
{
    [self registerClass:self];
}
+ (void)initialize
{
    urls = [[NSMutableDictionary alloc] init];
}
+ (BOOL)canInitWithRequest: (NSURLRequest*)request
{
    NSURL *url = [request URL];
    return [[url scheme] isEqualToString:@"example"];
}
+ (NSURLRequest *)canonicalRequestForRequest:(NSURLRequest *)request
{
    return [NSURLRequest requestWithURL: [request URL]];
}
- (void)startLoading
{
    NSURL *url = [[self request] URL];
    NSString *key = [url absoluteString];
    NSData * data = [[urls objectForKey: key]
                      dataUsingEncoding: NSUTF8StringEncoding];

    id<NSURLProtocolClient> client = [self client];
    NSURLResponse *response = [[NSURLResponse alloc]
              initWithURL: url
                 MIMEType: @"text/plain"
    expectedContentLength: [data length]
         textEncodingName: @"utf-8"];

    [client URLProtocol: self
     didReceiveResponse: response
```

```
        cacheStoragePolicy: NSURLCacheStorageNotAllowed];

    [client URLProtocol: self didLoadData: data];

    [client URLProtocolDidFinishLoading: self];
}
- (void)stopLoading { /* Not implemented */ }
+ (BOOL) setString: (NSString*)aString forURL: (NSURL*)aURL
{
    if (![[aURL scheme] isEqualToString:@"example"])
    {
        return NO;
    }
    [urls setObject: aString
             forKey: [aURL absoluteString]];
}
@end
```

I said near the start of this book that you will rarely need to implement a `+load` method. This is one of the exceptions. The `+load` method here calls a superclass method to register this class. When this class is sent the `+load` message, it can guarantee that its superclass has already been loaded, but it can't guarantee anything else about the application state.

We can't guarantee that `NSMutableDictionary` will be loaded by the time this class is loaded, so we create the dictionary in `+initialize`. In practice, the Foundation framework will always be loaded before your code, but it is bad style to depend on this.

The first method that will be called in this class is `+canInitWithRequest:`. This will be passed the URL request object that is being downloaded. This class, being registered after all of the Foundation ones, is likely to have this method called for every URL that is loaded. Registered protocol loaders are called in the opposite order to the order that they were added. This means that you can add a new handler for existing URL schemes and have it replace the standard functionality.

This protocol handles all requests in the "example" URL scheme, and so the test to determine whether it can handle the URL is very simple; just compare the scheme.

The next method to be called is `+canonicalRequestForRequest:`. This is expected to turn a request into a canonical form. This is used mainly for URL schemes that support relative URLs. It should turn something like http://example.com/directory/../file into http://example.com/file. The URL caching mechanism uses this to identify cached resources. Canonical URL requests can be compared for equality to determine if they point to the same resource. For our simple scheme there is no aliasing—no two requests point to the same resource—so we just construct a simple request with no properties set and the same URL as the request that we are given.

The real work of "downloading" the URL is in the `-startLoading` method. This calls the `-client` and `-request` methods on **`self`** to get the client and request objects. These are set in the designated initializer, which we are not overriding.

First, we get the data for this URL from a dictionary. For this trivial example, we assume that the URL is always valid. This will crash on invalid URLs. A more complete implementation would send the client a `-URLProtocol:didFailWithError:` message and abort if `data` is `nil`.

The next step is to create a response object. We create a simple one on lines 31–35 that indicates that we are returning a UTF-8 string. This is then passed to the client. The size of the data does not have to be accurate; it is just a first approximation returned by the server. Typically the client will use this to allocate some space for receiving the data and later resize it if it is not sufficient.

Normally at this point we would create a connection to the remote server and add it to the run loop. We would then get a call back every time there was data ready to receive. We don't do that here since the data is stored in memory. Instead we pass the entire document to the client in one go on line 41.

Finally, we tell the client that the document has finished loading, on line 43. These last two lines would be split over at least two methods in a real implementation and would push fragments of the downloaded document to the client as they are received.

The `-stopLoading` method is a stub in this implementation. Since we load the entire document synchronously, there is never an opportunity for it to be called.

The final method in this example is a convenience method for setting data in an example URL. You wouldn't implement this for most URL handler types; it is just provided here so that you can use this class. This fragment demonstrates how it would be used:

```
NSURL *url = [NSURL URLWithString: @"example:exampledata"];
[ExampleURLProtocol setString: @"A simple document stored in RAM"
                       forURL: url];

NSURLRequest *request = [NSURLRequest requestWithURL: url];
NSURLResponse *response;
NSData *data = [NSURLConnection sendSynchronousRequest: request
                                     returningResponse: &response
                                                 error: NULL];
```

This sets a simple example document for a URL and then fetches it. At the end of this `data` will contain a UTF-8 representation of the string set at the start. Note that we don't need to use the `ExampleURLProtocol` class at all when loading the URL. Any of the standard URL loading mechanisms will work.

22.4 Bonjour

Making connections is only part of the problem. The other part is identifying remote servers. Some work using well-known addresses. If you want to connect to Apple's web server, the odds are that you know that the address is `http://apple.com`. If you don't, then you can go to a search engine, enter "apple." and browse the results.

If you went to a search engine and entered "iTunes shares on my local network," then you probably wouldn't get anything useful. These are located using a different mechanism, built in two layers. This was originally branded as *Rendezvous* with OS X 10.2, but a trademark lawsuit made Apple change the name to *Bonjour*. You may also see the protocol called *Zeroconf* after the IETF working group responsible for standardizing it.

22.4.1 Multicast DNS

The lowest level is *multicast DNS* (*mDNS*). The usual way of performing DNS lookups is to send a UDP packet containing the request to a known server address and wait for the reply. This is a simple and low-overhead way of getting domain names, but it requires the address to be known.

The idea behind mDNS is to remove this need. Rather than sending UDP packets to a specific address, you send them to the broadcast address. The top-level domain .local is reserved for link-local addresses. A computer appearing on a network can publish its own name as computername.local by responding to multicast DNS requests. The protocol also specifies a mechanism for caching and a few other cases, but you can think of it as a simple way of a machine on the local network publishing its own DNS entries.

Over the years, the number of types of DNS record has grown considerably. As well as the traditional A records for addresses, there are records for looking up port numbers, mail servers, and even more obscure ones for finding telephone numbers and geographical location. Any record type that can be published over DNS can be published over mDNS.

22.4.2 DNS Service Discovery

The other half of the Zeroconf protocol is *DNS Service Discovery* (*DNS-SD*). This defines some DNS record types for looking up services. The services that a particular system supports are published as a set of SRV, TXT, and PTR records. We saw SRV records already in this chapter. TXT records just contain arbitrary text, and PTR records are used for reverse lookups.

DNS was originally designed to find servers for particular services—that is what you want to do whenever you look up a given name—and so using it for local service discovery seems quite obvious. The combination of mDNS and DNS-SD means that you can easily advertise a set of services on the local network segment.

22.4.3 Browsing Services

The `NSNetServiceBrowser` class is the front end used to browse the network. Because this may take a while to retrieve all of the services, it has an asynchronous API. When you tell it to look for services, it will return immediately and then send delegate messages periodically until it has found all of them.

We will demonstrate this by writing a simple browser that will collect all of the services with a specific name. This is shown in Listing 22.4. An instance of this class is stored in a nib with a window containing a table view, a text field, and a progress indicator. The text field and progress indicator are connected to outlets in the object and the text field's action is connected to the `-searchForService:` action. When this runs it presents a window like the one in Figure 22.1, allowing the user to see the names of all of the services of a specific type.

Listing 22.4: Browsing for Bonjour services. [from: examples/BonjourBrowser/BrowserController.m]

```
#import "BrowserController.h"

@implementation BrowserController
- (IBAction) searchForService:(id)sender
{
    NSNetServiceBrowser *serviceBrowser;
    serviceBrowser = [[NSNetServiceBrowser alloc] init];
    [serviceBrowser setDelegate:self];
    [serviceBrowser searchForServicesOfType:[service stringValue]
                                   inDomain:@""];
    [service setEnabled:NO];
    [indicator startAnimation:self];
}

- (void)netServiceBrowser:(NSNetServiceBrowser *)netServiceBrowser
          didFindService:(NSNetService *)netService
              moreComing:(BOOL)moreServicesComing

{
    [self willChangeValueForKey:@"services"];
    [services addObject:[netService name]];
```

```
22      [self didChangeValueForKey:@"services"];
23      if (!moreServicesComing)
24      {
25          [service setEnabled:YES];
26          [indicator stopAnimation:self];
27          [netServiceBrowser release];
28      }
29  }
30  - (void)netServiceBrowserWillSearch:(NSNetServiceBrowser *)
        netServiceBrowser
31  {
32      [self willChangeValueForKey:@"services"];
33      if (nil == services)
34      {
35          services = [NSMutableArray new];
36      }
37      else
38      {
39          [services removeAllObjects];
40      }
41      [self didChangeValueForKey:@"services"];
42  }
43  - (void) dealloc
44  {
45      [services release];
46      [super dealloc];
47  }
48  @end
```

The action method is responsible for creating the service browser instance. It sets the delegate to itself on line 8 and then tells it to begin searching on line 9. The empty string as the search domain is used to indicate that the default domain should be used. You will almost always use this when browsing for services.

Lines 11 and 12 are purely cosmetic. They start the progress indicator running and disable the text box while the search is taking place.

The method on line 30 will be called by the browser as soon as it begins running. This lazily creates the array storing the results or removes all of the contained objects if it already exists.

The important method is the one that starts on line 15. This is called every time the service browser gets a DNS response. A `NSNetService` instance is constructed representing the service and passed to this method.

For now, we are just interested in providing a list of service names, so we just add the name to the array. You would be more likely to cache the service object and later use it to collect all of the information that you needed to connect.

Figure 22.1: The Bonjour browser looking for iTunes shares.

When the service browser has gotten the last item, it will set the `moreServicesComing` flag to `NO`. When this happens, we clean up by reenabling the text field, stopping the progress indicator, and releasing the service browser.

In Figure 22.1 you can see the result of searching for the "_daap._tcp." service in my house. DAAP is the protocol used by iTunes for sharing music, so this will return the names of all of the shared music collections on the local network.

Service names are arranged as {service name}.{transport name} for service discovery. The underscore prefix is used to distinguish service addresses from domain names.

These services are advertised by publishing an mDNS SRV record. This will be something like _daap._tcp.local. When you try to resolve this address, you will get responses from each service advertised in this way.

22.4.4 Advertising Services

Most of the time that you use Bonjour, you want to both advertise and browse services. If your application supports both browsing and advertising services, it can communicate with other instances of itself on the local network very easily. There are quite a few examples of applications bundled with OS X that do this:

Safari populates a bookmark list with web servers that advertise themselves with Bonjour.

iChat finds people to talk to on the local network using Bonjour.

iTunes shares your music collection with Bonjour.

There are also lots of third-party examples, such as SubEthaEdit that lets you collaboratively edit text files and uses Bonjour to find published documents.

If you are writing a client application, then you can use just the service discovery functionality, as Safari does, to find servers. If you are writing an application that has any collaborative features, you can use Bonjour to expose them. This is true even for applications that you might not think of as particularly networked. iTunes is commonly used for playing local files, but the addition of streaming mode is a more social application. The same is true of the other iLife applications, such as iPhoto.

Note that Bonjour is just a mechanism for advertising and discovering services. You still need to write some networking code to do the actual sharing, although we will look in the next section at a way of keeping this to a minimum.

Advertising a service is very simple. You just need to create an `NSNetService` object and then send it a `-publish` message. If you wanted to advertise an iTunes-compatible music share, you would do something like this:

```
NSNetService *service =
    [[NSNetService alloc] initWithDomain: @""
                                    type: @"_daap._tcp."
                                    name: @"My Playlist"
                                    port: 3689];
[service publish];
```

This creates a new service in the default domain advertising the DAAP protocol, on the protocol's default port. Of course, this doesn't actually run the DAAP server, you still need to do this yourself.

In the next section, we will write an example chat client that advertises itself using Bonjour and uses distributed objects for the network communication. This eliminates the need to write any low-level networking code.

22.5 Distributed Objects

One of the most powerful parts of the foundation framework is the *distributed objects* system. This allows objects in different processes, possibly on different computers, to be used almost transparently.

The distributed objects system in OS X is based on NeXT's *Portable Distributed Objects* (*PDO*) product. This provided bridges to Microsoft's COM and to CORBA. PDO was released before Microsoft's DCOM and was the only way of connecting together COM components on different computers for a while. As a historical curiosity, the keynote speech where Steve Jobs unveiled PDO can be found online.

The distributed objects system works via the second-chance dispatch mechanism provided by the Objective-C runtime. This process involves several stages.

When you send a message to an object, a runtime function is called that performs the lookup. If this doesn't find anything, then it will substitute a forwarding hook; a function that is called when no method is available.

This function is typically provided by the Foundation framework. It is responsible for inspecting the stack and creating an object from the arguments. This is not possible in the general case on OS X, because selectors are untyped. The forwarding function will send a `-methodSignatureForSelector:` message to **`self`** with **`_cmd`** as the argument. If the object knows how to handle the kind of message specified by **`_cmd`**, then it will return information about the stack frame; otherwise it will throw an exception.

When you send a message to a remote object, you are really sending it to an instance of a subclass of `NSProxy`. The object typically has a fairly complex implementation of `-methodSignatureForSelector:`, which either requests the types from the remote object or returns a cached copy.

Once the forwarding function has the types of the method, it can introspect the stack and get the arguments. This uses exactly the same mechanism that an implementation of the C standard `printf()` function uses when it prints the arguments after the format string.

The object constructed by the forwarding code is then passed to the object's `-forwardInvocation:` method. You can use this yourself to forward messages between objects in the same process easily. The proxy provided by distributed objects forwards the invocation via an `NSPort` subclass.

Before transmitting the invocation object over the network, the proxy must serialize it. This is done using an `NSPortCoder`. Unlike the `NSCoder` subclasses commonly used for local storage, this does not support keyed coding, so you need to implement support for non-keyed coding in every object that you want to send by copy over the network.

By default, however, objects are sent by reference. When you pass a pointer

DO versus RMI

DO might seem similar to Java's *Remote Method Invocation* (*RMI*) system. This is not a coincidence; RMI was heavily inspired by NeXT's work. The type system in Java required a new proxy to be created for each object that was vended using this mechanism until Java 1.3 when they introduced a second-chance dispatch mechanism. DO does not require specific stub classes for any vended objects.

to an object to a DO proxy, you will get a remote proxy for the object created in the remote process. This will then forward any messages sent to the new proxy back to the original.

This can result in a lot of proxies being created on both sides of the DO bridge. Eventually, you will get some messages sent that have their arguments passed by value. This is true for any primitive C types (integers and floating point values) and for some pointers.

It is also possible to specify that an argument should be passed by copy in the method declaration.

22.5.1 Publishing Objects

Connections between processes are encapsulated in an `NSConnection` object. This is used for both server and client processes, and is created in a variety of ways. By default, every thread has its own connection object. You can use this for communicating between threads, although it is a very heavy-weight mechanism for doing this and so is discouraged. You can also vend objects over this default connection and share them with other processes on the same computer. The most general way of creating a new connection is to use this method:

```
+ (id)connectionWithReceivePort: (NSPort*)receivePort
                       sendPort: (NSPort*)sendPort;
```

This creates a new connection with the specified ports. When you are serving objects it is common to use the same port for both rôles. There are three concrete subclasses of `NSPort` that you might want to use:

- `NSMachPort` is a wrapper around the fundamental IPC capabilities of the Mach kernel at the heart of OS X. This can be used for authenticated communication between two processes if you are willing to make Mach system calls to set the rights.

- `NSMessagePort` is a general port for local communication. This hides all of the details of the underlying IPC mechanism used.
- `NSSocketPort` uses a Berkeley socket for communication. Usually this means a TCP connection, but it can be any kind of socket. This can be used for local or remote communication.

It is quite rare to use Mach ports for DO. They are roughly equivalent in capability to message ports if you do not wish to do any low-level manipulation to the port.

> **Ports and Ports**
>
> The port terminology can be confusing in the context of `NSSocketPort`. A port is an endpoint in some communication system. With a socket port, there are two kinds of ports. The endpoint of the TCP connection is an TCP/IP port. The endpoint of the DO connection is a DO port. Both of these are commonly abbreviated to simply "port," but they should not be confused.

For communication across a network you have no options, you must use a socket port. Creating one of these with `+alloc` / `-init` will create a new TCP/IP port on an arbitrary TCP/IP port number. Since DO connections usually work via a *name server*, this is usually all you need.

Name servers are subclasses of `NSPortNameServer`. There is one provided for each kind of port. The socket port name server runs on a well-known TCP/IP port, allowing you to easily map from service name and hosts to ports usable for DO.

Serving an object with the distributed objects system usually involves these steps:

1. Create the port to use. This can be done implicitly for local communication.
2. Create a connection object from the ports.
3. Register a root object for the connection.
4. Advertise the connection with a name server.

Vending an object over the network is as simple as this:

```
NSPort *port = [[NSSocketPort alloc] init];
NSConnection *conn =
    [NSConnection connectionWithReceivePort: port
```

```
                                    sendPort: port];
[conn setRootObject: obj];
[conn registerName: @"ObjectName"];
```

To make this robust, you should also check whether the last line returns **NO** and handle this case. Any process on the network can now send messages to `obj`. Note that there is no security here; you are responsible for ensuring that no messages sent to `obj` are capable of compromising the system.

The `NSProtocolChecker` class is designed to make this easier for you. It is a simple `NSProxy` subclass that takes an object and a protocol as arguments when you create it. Any message sent to it that is not part of the protocol will be silently discarded. Any other message will be forwarded correctly. You can create the proxy like this:

```
id proxy = [NSProtocolChecker protocolCheckerWithTarget: obj protocol:
    @protocol(SafeRemoteProtocol)];
```

Remember that **`@protocol()`** will return a protocol with the requested name, but it will only contain methods if the protocol declaration is visible to the compiler where the protocol directive is used. Make sure that the definition of the protocol that you use for this is either in the same file where you use it, or in a header that this file includes, or all messages sent to the proxy will be removed.

22.5.2 Getting Remote Objects

Once an object has been shared, you commonly want to access it from another process and send it messages. The second part of this, sending it messages, is trivial; it works in exactly the same way as sending messages to any other object.

The slightly harder part is getting the object proxy in the first place. This is usually done via a single call to `NSConnection`, like this:

```
id remoteObj = [NSConnection rootProxyForConnectionWithRegisteredName:name
    host:host]
```

The returned object will be an `NSDistantObject`, an `NSProxy` subclass, wrapping the object advertised by the default name server on `host` with the specified name. If you pass `nil` for the host, then it will look up objects on the local machine.

You can then use this object exactly as if it were a local one. There are some limitations. In particular, sending C arrays is not supported. If you send a C array, then you will only get the first element arriving, since the DO mechanism has no way of distinguishing a pointer to a single element and a pointer to a part of an array.

22.5.3 A Simple Chat Program

To demonstrate how distributed objects work, we will write a simple chat room application. This will be a pure peer-to-peer application running a chat room on the local network. Everyone who runs the application will automatically be added to the room and will send every message that they type to every other user.

This will make use of both Bonjour and DO. When the application starts, it will create a server port exporting its own chat room object and then publicize this using the Bonjour. It will then request all other similar services and send all of them a copy of every message.

The user interface will be split into three sections. At the bottom we will have a text field for typing messages, and two table views at the top. The left one will contain sent messages and the right one a list of people currently in the chat.

Each peer will publish one object implementing the protocol shown in Listing 22.5. This has two methods, one for handling new messages and one for returning the name of the user.

Listing 22.5: The protocol for chat peers. [from: examples/LocalNetChat/ChatPeerProtocol.h]

```
@protocol ChatPeerProtocol
- (void) handleMessage:(NSString*)aMessage
                  from:(NSString*)aUser;
- (NSString*) name;
@end
```

When the application starts up, there are two classes loaded by the main nib. One handles receiving messages and the other handles sending. The receiver is shown in Listing 22.6.

Listing 22.6: The class for receiving messages via DO. [from: examples/LocalNetChat/MessageReceiver.m]

```
#import "MessageReceiver.h"

@implementation MessageReceiver
- (void) awakeFromNib
{
    messages = [[NSMutableArray alloc] init];
    name = [NSFullUserName() retain];
    NSString *servicename =
        [@"LocalNetChat/" stringByAppendingString:name];

    NSPort *port = [[NSSocketPort alloc] init];
    NSConnection *conn = [NSConnection connectionWithReceivePort:port
                                                         sendPort:nil];
```

```
14     [conn retain];
15     [conn setRootObject:self];
16     [conn registerName: servicename
17         withNameServer: [NSSocketPortNameServer sharedInstance]];
18     [port release];
19 
20     NSNetService *service =
21         [[NSNetService alloc] initWithDomain:@""
22                                         type:@"_localchat._tcp."
23                                         name:servicename
24                                         port:123];
25     [service publish];
26 }
27 - (void) handleMessage:(NSString*)aMessage
28                   from:(NSString*)aUser
29 {
30     NSDictionary *message = [NSDictionary dictionaryWithObjectsAndKeys:
31         aMessage, @"message",
32         aUser, @"sender",
33         nil];
34     [self willChangeValueForKey:@"messages"];
35     [messages addObject:message];
36     [self didChangeValueForKey:@"messages"];
37 }
38 - (NSString*) name
39 {
40     return name;
41 }
42 @end
```

Most of the important code here is in the `-awakeFromNib` method. This is run as soon as the application starts. It first does some basic initialization, creating an instance variable and setting a value for another one. The `NSFullUserName()` function returns the full name of the current user, as set when their account on the computer was created. The method then offers the object over distributed objects.

The first step in serving this object is to create a new connection. This is done on lines 11–14. First, a new socket port is created and then a new connection using that port. Note first that the send port is `nil`. This could alternatively be `port`, although `nil` is less to type.

Line 14 is very important. Even though we will never use this connection object again directly, we have to retain it here. If we don't, then it will still be offered for remote clients to connect to, but then their connection will point to a random bit of memory. This is most likely to cause them to pause for a long time while attempting to get the root object and then fail, but it can have other random and hard-to-debug results.

Once the connection is created, the receiver sets itself as the root object and registers the connection with the name server. Note that we have to explicitly specify the socket name server on line 17. Without this, it will only be advertised on the local machine and remote clients won't be able to find it. This is often useful, but not for something intended to communicate between processes on different computers.

With the object offered through DO, the next step is to use Bonjour to advertise it to the local network. This is done on lines 20–25. The port number on line 24 is chosen entirely at random; we don't actually use the port at the receiving end so it can be any number. The most obvious choice here would be 0, but since 0 is not a valid port number this will not work.

When we have created the `NSNetService` object, we send it a `-publish` message and it advertises the service on the network. Any other processes can then get the required information. Note that we are using the name here to specify the DO name. More usually, this contains a human-readable description of the shared resource, although in this case we could easily transform it back into something human-readable.

The last two methods are quite simple. The `-handleMessage:from:` method simply constructs a dictionary from the two parameters and adds it to the end of an array. We use an array controller in the nib to bind to this array and set the model path for the two columns in the chat window to the two keys. You can see the result in Figure 22.2.

The other class in this example is responsible for sending messages. This one is quite a bit more complicated, so we'll look at it a part at a time. The initialization code is in Listing 22.7.

Listing 22.7: Initializing the message sender. [from: examples/LocalNetChat/MessageSender.m]

```
- (void) awakeFromNib
{
    peers = [NSMutableArray new];

    NSNetServiceBrowser *serviceBrowser;
    serviceBrowser = [[NSNetServiceBrowser alloc] init];
    [serviceBrowser setDelegate:self];
    [serviceBrowser searchForServicesOfType:@"_localchat._tcp."
                                   inDomain:@""];
}
```

This first initializes the array of peers and then begins browsing for new peers to add to it. The service browsing here is very similar to the earlier example. The service browser is created, its delegate set, and then it is told to go and find as many instances of the service as it can. The delegate method is shown in Listing 22.8.

Listing 22.8: Handling a discovered service. [from: examples/LocalNetChat/MessageSender.m]

```
- (void)netServiceBrowser:(NSNetServiceBrowser *)netServiceBrowser
            didFindService:(NSNetService *)netService
                moreComing:(BOOL)moreServicesComing
{
    [netService setDelegate:self];
    [netService retain];
    [netService resolveWithTimeout:10];

}
```

This is called once for each service found. Since we are not killing the browser here, it will keep running in the background. This method will be called any time a new user appears on the network. This is very convenient, because the same code can be used for adding the people present at the start and for adding late arrivals. If you run this demo on a number of machines on a local network segment,[2] then you will see the new people appearing as the program starts.

For each system that the browser finds, it will call this method once with a new `NSNetService` instance. Note that this includes the local message receiver. For consistency and simplicity we are going to use the same distributed object system to communicate with the local receiver. This is slow and uses more memory than is needed, but it serves as a demonstration that "distributed" objects don't need to be in separate processes.

The returned net service is told to resolve itself. In 10.5 the `-resolve` method is deprecated; now you must specify a timeout for the resolution. We use ten seconds here, which should be far more than you need to resolve anything on the local network. When this completes, one of the two methods shown in Listing 22.9 will be called.

The second of these is the simpler. It will be called if resolution does not succeed before the timeout. This is very unlikely to happen, but if it does then we just log the error to the console and release the service that failed.

The interesting part is what happens when the lookup succeeds. This means that `-host` will now return a value. This is the first thing we do with the resolved net service. The second thing is to get the name, which is where we stored the DO name of the remote service. Remember that we can't use the port here, because we didn't set it to anything sensible.

[2] For testing, you can also run it in different accounts on the same machine using fast user switching.

Listing 22.9: Establishing a connection to a remote chat peer. [from: examples/LocalNetChat/MessageSender.m]

```
25 - (void)netServiceDidResolveAddress: (NSNetService *)netService
26 {
27     NSString *host = [netService hostName];
28     NSString *servicename = [netService name];
29 
30     NSSocketPortNameServer *nameserver =
31         [NSSocketPortNameServer sharedInstance];
32     id peer = [NSConnection
33         rootProxyForConnectionWithRegisteredName: servicename
34                                             host: host
35                                 usingNameServer: nameserver];
36 
37     if (nil != peer)
38     {
39         [peer setProtocolForProxy:@protocol(ChatPeerProtocol)];
40         [self willChangeValueForKey:@"peers"];
41         [peers addObject:[NSDictionary dictionaryWithObjectsAndKeys:
42             peer, @"peer",
43             [peer name], @"name",
44             nil]];
45         [self didChangeValueForKey:@"peers"];
46         [[peer connectionForProxy] setReplyTimeout:5];
47     }
48     [netService release];
49 }
50 - (void)netService:(NSNetService *)sender didNotResolve:(NSDictionary *)
       errorDict
51 {
52     NSLog(@"Resolving␣failed:␣%@", errorDict);
53     [sender release];
54 }
```

Given the name and host of the remote peer, we can now create the `NSDistantObject` proxy for the remote message receiver. This is done by sending a message to `NSConnection`, on line 32. This asks for the root object (which we set back on line 15 of MessageReceiver.m) of the connection corresponding to the named service on the specified host.

Hopefully, if everything worked, this will return something other than `nil`. If it does then we store the name and the proxy in a dictionary and add this to the array of peers.

On line 39, we set a protocol for the remote object. This is not required, but it does mean that messages in the protocol do not need to have their types looked up. This saves a network round-trip for each message.

The final part of this class is the method after which it is named; the one that actually sends the messages. This is shown in Listing 22.10.

Listing 22.10: Sending a message via DO. [from: examples/LocalNetChat/MessageSender.m]

```
55 - (IBAction) sendMessage:(id)sender
56 {
57     NSString *message = [sender stringValue];
58     if ([@"" isEqualToString: message]) { return; }
59     [sender setStringValue:@""];
60 
61     NSMutableIndexSet *failedPeers = [NSMutableIndexSet indexSet];
62     for (unsigned int i=0 ; i<[peers count] ; i++)
63     {
64         NSDictionary *dict = [peers objectAtIndex:i];
65         id<ChatPeerProtocol> peer = [dict objectForKey:@"peer"];
66         @try
67         {
68             [peer handleMessage:message from:NSFullUserName()];
69         }
70         @catch (NSException *e)
71         {
72             [failedPeers addIndex:i];
73         }
74     }
75     if ([failedPeers count] > 0)
76     {
77         [self willChangeValueForKey:@"peers"];
78         [peers removeObjectsAtIndexes:failedPeers];
79         [self didChangeValueForKey:@"peers"];
80     }
81 }
```

The first part of this gets the string from the text box and clears it. It returns if the string is empty, so we don't bother sending empty strings to people.

The loop on line 62 iterates over every object in the array. It would be nicer to use a **for...in** array here. One of the things that we need to do is find out if any of the connections have died, and collect the indexes that have. If we used fast enumeration, we would have to keep a separate counter.

We set the timeout back on line 46. If the message on line 68 takes longer than this to complete, then an exception will be thrown. This is used to detect that the remote peer has abruptly disconnected. Messages will no longer be sent to it in the future.

Note that we have to use an index set here. We can't just store the object and send the array a `-removeObject:` message. This method, and the related ones, are all implemented by sending `-isEqual:` messages to the object. We could send individual `-removeObjectIdenticalTo:` messages to the array, but sending a `-removeObjectsInArray:` message will result in `-isEqual:` messages being sent to the broken proxy, which will cause more exceptions. Collecting the indexes is both faster and easier.

The main limitation with this implementation is that it waits until you send a message before removing people from the "online" list. You could fix this relatively easily by copying the loop from this method out into a method called periodically by a timer. Rather than sending a `-handleMessage:from:` message, you could send a `-name` message, which will return very quickly if the peer is online or time out if it is not.

There are quite a lot of things to learn from this example. The most important is that it's possible to write distributed applications in Cocoa without writing any networking code. This program uses service discovery and remote messaging, but nowhere in the entire program is a network address, a port, or any information about any specific network protocol. No special code was used to encapsulate messages either. The sending and receiving parts of the code are totally unaware that they are in separate processes.

The other thing to note is that I cheated a lot here. The only objects retained are strings. These will always be passed by copy. If you used attributed strings, then even if you specified that they were passed **bycopy** then some of the values in their dictionary would be passed by reference.

This does not matter in the general case. The problem here is that we are keeping the chat log around for longer than the remote clients are likely to exist. If the chat log contained objects passed by proxy, then attempting to interact with them would cause exceptions to be thrown. Because the bindings read this array, you will get exceptions at random times during drawing, which will cause a broken user interface.

If you want to retain objects beyond the lifetime of the process owning them, then you need to take special care. You can do a *deep copy* of objects that implement the `NSCoding` protocol like this:

```
id copy = [NSUnarchiver unarchiveObjectWithData:
    [NSArchiver archivedDataWithRootObject: obj]];
```

This turns the object graph into an `NSData` instance and then restores it. Of

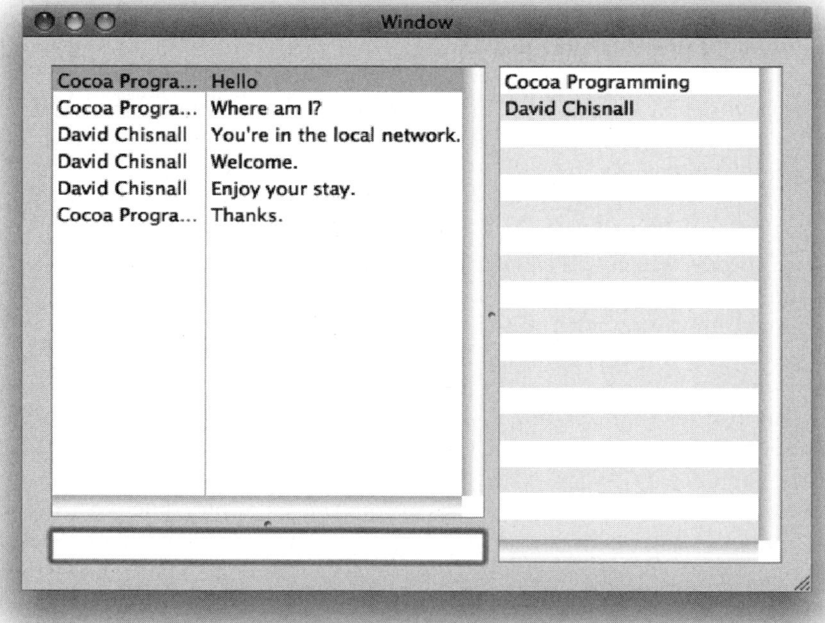

Figure 22.2: Running the simple chat program.

course, this requires every object in the graph to also support `NSCoding`. In general, it is better to design your APIs so that only simple data needs to be sent. Rather than sending an `NSAttributedString` directly, you could make use of one of its existing serialization methods, such as `-RTFFromRange:documentAttributes:`. This would give you an `NSData` representing the object, which could then be passed to `-initWithRTF:documentAttributes:` at the far end.

This, unfortunately, breaks some of the transparency of distributed objects, but it is still a lot simpler than writing network code yourself. Of course, this doesn't need to happen before sending. The sender in this case could pass the attributed string and the client, having decided that it wants to retain it, could get the RTF value and create a new string.

When you use distributed objects, you do need to be careful to design your APIs. Passing around pointers to arbitrary C data structures is likely to cause problems. Passing around simple primitive types and object pointers is likely to work exactly as expected. Most APIs are somewhere between these two extremes. You can generally wrap the methods that don't work quite correctly in versions that take `NSData` or `NSArray` arguments when you start exposing them via DO.

22.6 Summary

In this chapter we have looked at the various ways of writing distributed systems in Cocoa. At the lowest level, we have the BSD socket API, inherited from OS X's UNIX roots. This is very powerful, but not very friendly. It can be used directly or wrapped in Cocoa objects.

We then looked at the network stream classes in Cocoa and their integration with the run loop. The URL loading system provides a very flexible means of getting data from a variety of sources on the network, and we saw how it can be used.

Finally, we looked at two of the much higher-level network APIs provided by Cocoa. The first used multicast DNS to advertise services to the local network, giving a clean and simple API for service discovery. The second allowed objects to be transparently accessed from other processes. By combining these two, we wrote a simple chat program that didn't make use of any low-level networking code directly at all.

Chapter 23

Concurrency

For several decades, microprocessor development has followed *Moore's Law*. This is an observation by Gordon Moore that the number of transistors that you can fit on a chip, for a fixed cost, doubles roughly every 18 months.

There are a number of results of this. One is that the cost of chips goes down over time. Something like the iPhone has a faster CPU than the first desktop machines OS X ran on, but costs a fraction of the price. The second is that processors tend to get faster.

One of the ways that this benefited programmers was the addition of extra instructions. Early microprocessors couldn't do floating point operations in hardware. If you wanted to add two floating point numbers together you had to split them into a mantissa and an exponent, perform shifts on the mantissa to normalize the two values, add them, and then recombine the result with the new exponent. Multiplication was even more complex. When CPUs started coming with a floating-point coprocessor on chip, software like spreadsheets that did a lot of floating point calculations became much faster. Even existing operations can often be made faster by providing more transistors to them.

In recent years, the extra transistors have been used for two things: cache and extra cores. Cache is needed because main memory access speeds have not increased at the same rate as processor speeds. Adding some fast memory near the processor lets it spend less time waiting for data to be read from memory. Adding small amounts of cache gave huge performance improvements, but adding more quickly leads to diminishing returns. If an entire program and its data can fit in cache then adding more will not make the program faster. Most programs spend most of their time dealing with a small subset of their code and data, so even going from fitting 10% of it into cache to fitting 20% often provides only a tiny performance improvement.

Extra cores have provided an easy way of doubling the maximum throughput of a design; just put two copies of it on the same die. Next year, when process technology has improved, double the number of copies that you were including this year. Unfortunately, software needs more than a simple recompile to take advantage of this.

As with adding cache, adding small numbers of extra cores gives an immediate boost. The average user runs several programs at once. A second core allows you to run each of these on their own processor, or run background OS tasks on one and user applications on another. Very quickly, however, the number of cores exceeds the number of CPU-limited applications.

In order to take advantage of parallel processing, a program must be written to take advantage of it explicitly. Fortunately, OS X includes a wide selection of APIs that make this easier. In this chapter, we will look at some of them.

23.1 Distributed Objects

We looked at *distributed objects* in the last chapter in the context of communicating between programs on different computers. There is no reason why you can't use it for different processes on the same computer. This is a very simple way of writing concurrent code; simply run parallel components in different programs.

This is very easy to get right, since you have entirely separate processes for your parallel components and all interaction between them is via a message passing interface. If you have a big, processor-intensive, job to do, then you can spawn a new process for handling it and push data and commands to it via distributed objects.

If you are doing this, then you should declare your messages in a protocol like this:

```
- (oneway void) doSomethingWithObject:(bycopy id)anObject;
```

There are two DO-specific modifiers here. The parameter is marked **bycopy**, which means that it will be encoded using the port coder and the copy sent. The return value is marked **oneway**, meaning that the call will return immediately, rather than waiting for the method to complete.

This allows safe asynchronous communication. If all of the methods calling in to the second process have this kind of structure, then you do not need to worry about *deadlocks* or *race conditions*.

Deadlocks can occur in programs using distributed objects relatively easily with synchronous messages. When you pass an object as an argument to a method via DO, the receiver will get a proxy by default. Messages to this will be handled synchronously by the run loop waiting for the method to return. You can create deadlocks in this situation by making some of these methods depend—usually indirectly—on the result of the remote method. This is not usually a problem with DO since you typically design code that will work sequentially and then run it as if it were serial code, just distributed.

Doing this eliminates much of the benefit of DO, however. If the first process blocks while the second runs, you don't have any useful concurrency. The **oneway** designation on this method means that this will not happen. This provides another way for things to go wrong. If you pass an object to this method and then modify it, then the remote process will get the modified version. Worse, it might get different versions at different points. Imagine passing a mutable array. First, the remote side might send a `-count` message. Then you might remove some items. Now the remote side can easily try to access off the end of the array.

The solution here is simply to copy. Ideally, you would refine this and only copy immutable objects. Alternatively, you can send a `-copy` message to the parameter before you pass it.

Be careful with this; both mechanisms only perform a shallow copy. If you pass a copy of a collection, for example, you will not get copies of the contained objects. Modifications to these objects will still cause breakage.

Note that distributed objects don't have to be in separate processes. You can send a `-runInNewThread` message to an `NSConnection` instance and have it detach. The root object then lives in a separate thread and can have messages sent to it transparently.

You can add this method to your object to have it run in a separate thread:

```
- (id)detachThread
{
    NSConnection *conn = [NSConnection new];
    [conn setRootObject: self];
    [conn runInNewThread];
    return [conn rootProxy];
}
```

The returned object is a proxy for the receiver. All messages sent to this will be passed via DO to the new thread. If you mark a method as oneway, then it will complete asynchronously; otherwise, it will run synchronously. This is a very simple, although quite a heavy-weight, way of passing messages between objects.

23.2 Threading

The Mach operating system at the core of OS X was designed with concurrency in mind. The UNIX process model is built on top of *Mach tasks*. Each task has a set of memory rights associated with it, and a number of threads.

Although you can use Mach threads directly on OS X, this is generally discouraged. The BSD subsystem wraps Mach threads as *POSIX threads* (*pthreads*). This is a standard threading API that works on most UNIX-like systems and is the lowest-level that most developers will want to use.

23.2.1 Creating Threads

POSIX threads, in turn, are wrapped by Cocoa as `NSThread` objects. These provide a simple way of creating threads and a convenient way of handling thread-local storage.

> **Threads and Run Loops**
>
> By default, only one run loop is created per program. It is often convenient to use run loops in separate threads, however, and you can do this easily. Sending a `+currentRunLoop` message to the `NSRunLoop` class will create a run loop for the current thread if one doesn't already exist.
>
> You can then use this exactly as you would any other run loop, for example, by scheduling timers in it. Typically, a new thread will create an autorelease pool and then a run loop, although simpler threads may not need the run loop.

The lowest-level way of creating threads on OS X is to call `pthread_create()`. This spawns a new thread and calls a function on it. The constructor for `NSThread` is similar to this, but instead of calling a function with a `void*` parameter it sends a message with an `id` parameter. The normal way of creating a new thread in Cocoa is to send this message to `NSThread`:

```
+ (void)detachNewThreadSelector: (SEL)aSelector
                       toTarget: (id)aTarget
                     withObject: (id)anArgument;
```

This detaches a new thread and sends it a message. The thread will exit when the method completes.

23.2.2 Thread-Local Storage

On most operating systems supported by GCC, the `__thread` specifier can be added to static and global variables to indicate that you get one copy per thread, rather than the standard one copy per process. This requires support from the loader and the threading library, which is not present on OS X.

The standard way of storing per-thread information is to use `pthread_key_create()` function to define a key and a destructor function. Any thread can then set a value for this key and have it destroyed automatically when the thread exits. This is wrapped by `NSThread` to give the *thread dictionary*. This is an `NSMutableDictionary` instance in thread-local storage. You can acquire the thread dictionary by sending the current thread object a `-threadDictionary` message. This dictionary will be deallocated when the thread exits.

You can use the thread dictionary to store any objects. Some parts of Cocoa store values in the thread dictionary. Default exception handlers, AppleScript Events and various other things are stored in the thread dictionary by Cocoa. You can use it in your frameworks to store things that need to be available to every thread. An example would be something like the default typesetter used to draw strings and attributed strings. An instance of the typesetter would be stored in the thread dictionary and then any object that tried to draw itself would have one that it could use without having to worry about locking.

23.2.3 Synchronization

The most difficult part of programming with threads is locking. Locking is used to protect shared resources. In a multi-process environment, these are commonly things like files. In a threaded environment, every byte of memory is a potentially shared resource.

Consider the simple expression `a++`. This looks like something simple and safe to do. On an x86-64 system, this is compiled to the following three instructions:

```
movl    _a(%rip), %eax
incl    %eax
movl    %eax, _a(%rip)
```

The value is loaded into the first register, incremented, and then the register is written out. In a multithreaded environment, the thread could be preempted at any point between any pair of these instructions. Imagine if you had two threads doing this at once. You might get this sequence of events:

1. Thread 1 loads `a`.

2. Thread 2 preempts thread 1.

3. Thread 2 loads `a`.

4. Thread 2 increments the register.

5. Thread 2 stores the result in memory.

6. Thread 1 increments the register.

7. Thread 1 stores the result in memory.

The result will be that `a` will be incremented once, not twice. The simplest way of protecting this is to associate a lock with `a`. Before modifying it, you must acquire the lock, and afterward you must release it.

Locking

There are two kinds of locks provided by Cocoa, both wrapping their POSIX equivalents. These are `NSLock` and `NSRecursiveLock`. For this example, you would need to replace the single increment line with something like this:

```
[aLock lock];
a++;
[aLock unlock];
```

After calling `-lock` once, any subsequent calls to `-lock` will block until `-unlock` has been called. This is the easiest way of introducing deadlock into a program. Because locks enforce mutual exclusion, they can easily create situations where two threads are waiting for locks that the other thread has.

There are two methods on `NSLock` that help you work around this. The first is `-tryLock`. This never blocks, and so cannot cause deadlock, and returns **`YES`** if the lock has been acquired. A common strategy to avoid deadlocks is to try to acquire a lock, and if it fails to defer the operation until later. A slight variation of this is to call `-lockBeforeDate:`. This is similar to `-tryLock` but will block for a limited amount of time if it can't get the lock immediately.

Using the timeout is most commonly used as an example of `defensive programming`. Well-designed concurrent code will never reach the timeout, but if you have a deadlock, then you may. In this case, the thread that times out should release all of the locks it holds and then try again.

One problem with simple locks is that they block whenever they are already locked, even if the lock is held by the calling thread. The recursive lock avoids this problem. It must be unlocked the same number of times as it is locked, but locking it will only block if the lock is held by a *different* thread.

One of the big problems with locks in traditional OpenStep programming came from the exceptions. Consider this piece of code:

```
[lock lock];
doSomething();
[lock unlock];
```

If the `doSomething()` function throws an exception, then the lock will never be released. The next time you get to this bit of code, it will block forever. The solution to this is to wrap the code in exception handling blocks, like this:

```
[lock lock];
NS_DURING
    doSomething();
    [lock unlock];
NS_HANDLER
    [lock unlock];
    [localException raise];
NS_ENDHANDLER
```

This is now very expensive. Setting up the handler requires the register set to be saved. The lock itself is also expensive. By the time you've done this, you may well not be any faster than the non-threaded version of the code.

This was improved somewhat with OS X 10.3. This added some new syntax for exceptions so that you could just do this:

```
[lock lock];
@try {
    doSomething();
} @finally {
    [lock unlock];
}
```

If you are using the modern Objective-C runtime, then this will be cheaper since the zero-cost exception mechanism will be used. Now entering the **`@try`** block is free, only throwing the exception is expensive.

Because this is such a common idiom, a shorthand variant was added at the same time. This is based on similar syntax from Java:

```
@synchronized(anObject) {
    doSomething();
}
```

There are two differences between this and the previous version. The first is that `anObject` does not have to be a lock. You can lock on any object and a lock will be implicitly created. The second difference is that this is a recursive lock. Since recursive locks are more expensive than non-recursive locks, you trade some convenience for speed here.

Note also that while this looks like Java-style synchronization, it has very different trade-offs. In a modern Java VM, lock directives like this will be analyzed and removed if the VM can prove that the threads holding the lock are all bound to the same processor. Instead of a real lock, it will just avoid scheduling other threads that might acquire this lock while one thread has it. Objective-C, being statically compiled, does not have the option of doing this. A lock will always be acquired in this case.

Condition Variables

The other synchronization primitive provided by POSIX threads is the condition variable. This is associated with a lock, and the two are used as a pair. In Cocoa, the `NSCondition` class encapsulates both the lock and the condition variable.

Condition variables are used to avoid running code while a condition holds. You don't need them for expressiveness, but they help efficiency a lot. You could implement a naive condition lock like this:

```
while (!condition)
{
    [lock lock];
    if (condition)
    {
        doSomething();
        [lock unlock];
        break;
    }
    [lock unlock];
}
```

This is very inefficient, since it keeps locking and unlocking while the condition holds. Your CPU usage will jump to 100% and stay there while you are waiting for the condition. This is not ideal. What you most likely want is for your thread to sleep until it has something to do.

This is exactly what condition variables do. First, you acquire the lock, then you test the condition. If the condition still doesn't hold, you wait. Waiting on a condition variable is an atomic operation that releases the lock sleeps the thread and sets it to wake up when the condition variable is signaled.

When the condition variable is signaled, a sleeping thread will wake up and atomically reacquire the lock. You typically use them like this:

```
[conditionVariable lock];
while (!condition)
{
    [conditionVariable wait];
}
doSomething();
[conditionVariable unlock];
```

At the start, you acquire the lock associated with the condition variable. At this point no one else is allowed to modify `condition`, which is some Boolean value. The condition is then tested, and if it is not the value that this thread wants, then the thread sleeps on the condition variable by calling `-wait`. This method puts the thread to sleep and releases the lock.

When `conditionVariable` is signaled by another thread, this thread will wake up and atomically reacquire the lock. The **`while()`** loop will test the condition again and sleep if it doesn't hold yet.

If the condition is met then the real code can execute. When it has finished, it must release the lock. This will not automatically wake up any other sleeping threads. When a thread has called `-wait` it is in one of three states:

1. Waiting for the condition variable to be signaled.

2. Waiting for the lock to be released.

3. Acquiring the lock and continuing.

Each of these happens in order. You can wake up threads that are sleeping on a condition variable in two ways, either by sending a `-signal` or a `-broadcast` message to the `NSCondition` instance. These do almost the same thing. The first will signal one thread that is sleeping on the condition, chosen at random. The second signals all of them.

Both of these methods should only be called by the thread that has the lock. At this point, one or more other threads will be in condition 2 from the earlier list. When the signaling thread releases the lock, one thread will then enter the third state and continue. Any others that were moved to the second state will then wake up when the lock is released again; they will not need the condition variable to be signaled again.

This allows a simple mechanism for implementing relatively lightweight message queues. You would implement the sending part of the queue like this:

```
[conditionVariable lock];
[queue addMessages: messages];
[conditionVariable signal];
[conditionVariable unlock];
```

The receiving end would be implemented like this:

```
[conditionVariable lock];
while ([queue isEmpty])
{
    [conditionVariable wait];
}
```

```
NSArray *messages = [queue messages];
[queue empty];
[conditionVariable unlock];
[self processMessages: messages];
```

The implementation of `queue` is up to you. Ideally you would move the sending part inside of the class used to implement the queue so you just called `-addMessages:` and it automatically used the condition variable.

The receiving thread grabs all of the messages from the queue and empties it while it has the lock. It then processes the received messages without the lock. This means that the receiving thread is very rarely blocking the sending thread, since the receiving thread spends most of its time either waiting or processing messages.

Avoiding Locking

Locking is difficult to get right, and avoiding it is often a better option. You can avoid the need for most locking by enforcing a simple rule in your design:

No object may be aliased and mutable.

This means that the only objects that two threads may have access to are immutable. When you pass a mutable object to another thread, you must release all references you have to it.

This is the policy enforced by languages like *Erlang*, which are designed to be highly parallel. In Erlang, spawning new processes is very cheap. Messages passed between Erlang processes may only contain immutable data. The only mutable object in Erlang is the process dictionary, similar to the thread dictionary in Cocoa, which is, by definition, not aliased.

Read-Write Locks

There is another kind of lock that is provided by POSIX but not wrapped in Cocoa. The POSIX threading specification provides a *read/write lock* (*rwlock*) type. This is useful for a large number of situations where you have a *producer-consumer relationship* between two threads.

A rwlock can be held in two modes, reading and writing. Only one thread may hold the lock for writing, but any number can hold it for reading. Table 23.1 shows what happens when you try to acquire a lock and other threads have read or write locks.

Lock Requested	Locks held by other threads		
	Read	Write	None
Read	May Block	Blocks	Proceeds
Write	Blocks	Blocks	Proceeds

Table 23.1: The behavior of read/write locks.

If a write lock is requested by one thread, then it has a higher priority than read locks. Consider the case where there are three threads, one with a read lock, then one requesting a write lock, and finally one requesting a read lock. The fact that the first thread is reading prevents the second thread from getting a write lock. The fact that the second thread is waiting for a write lock prevents the third thread from getting a read lock.

When the first thread releases its read lock, the second one will get its write lock. When it releases this lock, the third thread will get its read lock. If the third thread requested the read lock before the second requested the write lock, then it would have proceeded immediately and the second thread would have had to wait for both readers to finish before it could write.

You can use a rwlock to protect something like an array easily. When you create the object, you need to initialize a lock in an instance variable, like this:

```
if (pthread_rwlock_init(&lock, NULL) != 0)
{
    [self release];
    return nil;
}
```

The lock is always passed by pointer. This is true for most of the POSIX threading objects, since they need to be modified in-place. Unlike Objective-C objects, you don't need to allocate them as pointers. The instance variable would be declared like this:

```
pthread_rwlock_t lock;
```

In the corresponding `-dealloc` or `-finalize` method you should destroy the lock. Note that you must do this even in a garbage-collected environment. The function does not release the memory used by the lock, but it may release kernel or library resources associated with it. Failing to do this may result in the inability to create locks in the future, or a memory leak.

```
pthread_rwlock_destroy(&lock);
```

With the creation and the destruction of the lock done, all that remains is to wrap the methods in lock operations. For an array, you would first wrap the accessing methods like this:

```
- (id) objectAtIndex: (NSUInteger)index
{
    if (pthread_rwlock_rdlock(&lock) != 0)
    {
        [NSException raise: ArrayLockException
                    format: @"Failed to acquire read lock"];
    }
    id ret = [[[super objectAtIndex: index] retain] autorelese];
    pthread_rwlock_unlock(&lock);
    return ret;
}
```

This first tries to acquire a read lock. If this succeeds, then it calls the superclass implementation. Note that you can't use this method in an `NSMutableArray` subclass since `NSMutableArray` doesn't implement this method, it relies on subclasses to do it, so this would have to be a locking subclass of a concrete mutable array subclass.

If acquiring the lock fails, then this throws an exception. This should never happen, and so an exception is a good fit. It generally means something very bad has happened and the array can't handle it itself.

After getting the value, it releases the lock and returns. Note the extra `-retain` and `-autorelease` messages that are sent to the object to return. This is important since, once the wrlock is released, another thread can remove the object from the array. If there are no other references to it then it will be deallocated.

Methods that modify the array look similar, but acquire write locks instead:

```
- (void)insertObject: (id)anObject atIndex: (NSUInteger)index
{
    if (pthread_rwlock_wrlock(&lock) != 0)
    {
        [NSException raise: ArrayLockException
                    format: @"Failed to acquire read lock"];
    }
    id ret = [super insertObject: anObject atIndex: index];
    pthread_rwlock_unlock(&lock);
    return ret;
}
```

You might think that you can simply implement wrappers around the primitive methods in the array classes and have it work. Unfortunately, this is not the case. A number of the other methods call several of these, and all need locking. If

Locking Granularity

The granularity of locking is always a trade. If you lock around small elements, then you need a lot of locks, which adds overhead. If you implement very coarse-grained locking, then threads hold locks for longer than they should and cause other threads to block, reducing the degree of concurrency.

The classic BSD multiprocessor kernel design held a single lock for the entire kernel. This meant that only one process could be making system calls at once. This was very simple and easy to get right, but meant that on more than 2 to 4 CPUs at least one would be idle waiting for the lock at any given time. Newer designs lock the subsystems individually, which allows more to run concurrently but means that more time is spent acquiring and releasing locks.

The best designs, like the Solaris network stack, divide code into completely independent parts and only put locks around the edges. This means that you only need to lock when passing messages between components, and sometimes not even then.

you tried to get a sub-array, for example, a number of calls to `-objectAtIndex:` would be made and, while each of these is individually thread-safe, the repeated calls might have modifications between them. You therefore also need to lock the high-level methods.

This starts to get very complicated and it's usually better to only share very simple objects between threads.

23.2.4 Atomic Operations

Locking, as I mentioned before, is quite expensive. For the example earlier where you wrapped `a++` in a lock you have three operations:

- The increment, which is one of the fastest thing a CPU can do.
- The message sends to the lock objects, which are quite slow.
- The locking operations, which are also slow.

There are two sources of overhead here. The first, the message send, can be avoided by using the POSIX primitives directly. This is usually better if you do not need to store the lock in a collection, since the object versions do not provide any real benefits aside from that, and do add some overhead.

The locking overhead itself can be avoided by using *atomic instructions*. These are the primitive CPU instructions used to construct things like locks. Simple operations on memory can be performed directly using the CPU's cache coherency circuits to ensure that they are atomic. These are implemented very differently on PowerPC and x86, but the basic idea is the same. They load a value from a memory location and set a flag with the memory controller. The memory controller then signals the CPU if that address is written to before it commits the operation.

There are three ways that you can use atomic operations on OS X. The libkern/OSAtomic.h header provides functions implementing atomic operations. Starting with version 4.2, GCC provides a set of built-in functions for atomic operations. These are specific to the current target and will be inlined, rather than being function calls. Finally, you can write some inline assembly for your target architecture.

Listing 23.1 shows a simple test program that runs a loop incrementing a variable a hundred million times. The variable is marked as **volatile** to make sure that the compiler doesn't optimize the additions away.

The timing is done by two macros defined at the top of the file. They use the `clock()` C standard library function that returns the amount of processor time used. For each version we print the total time taken and then the number of times longer than the unlocked version.

Listing 23.1: Timing different locking strategies. [from: examples/LockTime/LockTime.m]

```
#define TIME_START() a=0 ; c1 = clock(); \
    for (unsigned i=0 ; i<100000000 ; i++) {
#define TIME_END(message) \
    } c2 = clock();\
    difference = ((double)c2 - (double)c1) / (double)CLOCKS_PER_SEC;\
    printf(message "␣took␣%f␣seconds.␣(%d␣times␣longer)\n", difference, \
    (int)(difference / normal));

int main(void)
{
    [NSAutoreleasePool new];
    clock_t c1,c2;
    double difference;
    double normal = 1;
    TIME_START()
        a++;
    TIME_END("Lock␣free␣version");
    normal = difference;
    NSLock *lock = [NSLock new];
    TIME_START()
        [lock lock]; a++; [lock unlock];
    TIME_END("NSLock␣version");
    lock = [NSRecursiveLock new];
```

```
31     TIME_START()
32         [lock lock]; a++; [lock unlock];
33     TIME_END("NSRecursiveLock␣version");
34     pthread_mutex_t mutex;
35     pthread_mutex_init(&mutex, NULL);
36     TIME_START()
37         pthread_mutex_lock(&mutex); a++; pthread_mutex_unlock(&mutex);
38     TIME_END("POSIX␣mutex␣version");
39     TIME_START()
40         OSAtomicIncrement32(&a);
41     TIME_END("Atomic␣function␣version");
42     TIME_START()
43         __asm__ __volatile__ ("lock␣addl␣$1,␣%0"
44                                               :"=m" (a));
45     TIME_END("Atomic␣assembly␣version");
46     TIME_START()
47         __sync_fetch_and_add(&a, 1);
48     TIME_END("Atomic␣GCC␣version");
49 
50     return 0;
51 }
```

Lines 22–24 are the base version, with no locking. This is used to compare the time for the other runs. On line 28 we see a version with an `NSLock`. The next version, on line 32, is almost the same. The code here is identical, but the `lock` object is now an `NSRecursiveLock`.

After this, we start on the more primitive versions. On lines 34–35 we create a POSIX threads *mutual exclusion lock* (*mutex*). This is then used to protect the increment on line 37. This is likely to be exactly the same underlying code as the `NSLock`, but avoids the message send.

The remaining versions don't use locks; they all use atomic operations to increment the counter. The version on line 40 is the one from OSAtomic.h. On lines 43–44 you can see the inline assembly version. This is x86-only. The `addl` instruction means add a long (a 32-bit value). This is one of the slightly peculiar parts of the x86 architecture; it allows operations directly on memory. The constant value one is added to the value provided by the first argument. The argument list part here specifies that `a` is given as a memory address.

The final version, on line 47, is the GCC atomic builtin. This, like the version from OSAtomic.h, is not architecture dependent in the source. (The binary is, but binaries always are unless you run them in an emulator.) Each of these introduces slightly different dependencies into your code. The `OSAtomicIncrement32()` call makes the code depend on Darwin (OS X). The inline assembly makes the code depend on an x86 chip. The `__sync_fetch_and_add()` call makes the code depend on GCC 4.2 or later, or another compiler that implements the GCC extensions. Which of these is acceptable depends on your project.

Running this program is likely to give quite different output on different computers and on different versions of OS X. On a 2.16GHz Core 2 Duo running OS X 10.5, it gives the following output:

```
$ gcc-4.2 LockTime.m -framework Foundation -std=c99 && ./a.out
Lock free version took 0.281171 seconds. (0 times longer)
NSLock version took 8.526229 seconds. (30 times longer)
NSRecursiveLock version took 8.729425 seconds. (31 times longer)
POSIX mutex version took 3.956869 seconds. (14 times longer)
Atomic function version took 3.095634 seconds. (11 times longer)
Atomic assembly version took 1.986703 seconds. (7 times longer)
Atomic GCC version took 1.972773 seconds. (6 times longer)
```

This lets you see exactly how much overhead each of the different locking strategies has. Using `NSLock` is roughly twice as expensive as using the POSIX mutex directly. Using `NSRecursiveLock` has a very similar cost. The atomic increment function is not much faster than using a mutex. A lot of the cost here is the function call, rather than the atomic operation itself.

The mutex is probably implemented as an atomic test-and-increment. When it succeeds, it will be be very close to the atomic operation. The unlock operation just needs to decrement the mutex. It should only ever be incremented if it is zero, and when it is not zero, no other thread may decrement it, so no test is required when unlocking.

The inline assembly and GCC builtin versions are the fastest, only a factor of 6 to 7 slower than the non-atomic version. The difference in the speed of these is smaller than the error when you run this a number of times. This is not entirely surprising, since they ought to be generating the same code, but it is nice to confirm that they do.

With Objective-C 2, you have another way of telling the compiler to generate atomic operations. If you set the atomic attribute (or, rather, don't set the `nonatomic` attribute) when declaring properties, will make property accessors atomic. It ensures that one thread can always get a valid value for the property even if another thread sets the value in the middle.

This is very rarely useful, since it does not guarantee thread safety at the object level. It works by retaining and autoreleasing the object while holding a lock and then returning it. This is much more expensive than simply returning the value, so you should only use it when you expect your object to be thread safe. The two versions emitted, for atomic and nonatomic properties, will be roughly equivalent to these accessors:

```
- (id) atomicProperty
{
    @synchronized(self) {
        return [[property retain] autorelease];
    }
}
- (id) property
{
    return property;
}
```

The atomic version must acquire a lock and send two messages, while the nonatomic version simply returns immediately.

Atomic Is Not Thread Safe

Atomicity is a property of methods or functions. That they complete atomically with respect to each other means that they can be treated as indivisible operations. Thread-safety is a property of classes or APIs. This is much more difficult to get right. Imagine that you have to call two methods to get some information from an object. Both methods might be atomic but the class is not thread-safe because the value can be modified *between* the two calls.

Generally, thread-safety is only guaranteed at an instance level. No mutable object should be shared by more than one thread. If it is, then it will need to provide mechanisms for serializing requests into transactions.

23.2.5 Futures and Forwarding

When you implement your own threading code, you can make use of the forwarding mechanism in Objective-C to pass messages between them. The original paper on *higher-order messaging* (*HOM*) used this as an example.

The idea presented was to send a `-future` message to an object. This would return a proxy that would run messages sent to it in a separate thread and then get the result back when you sent a `-result` message. You would use it like this:

```
id future = [[object future] doSomethingThatTakesALongTime];
// Do other things
id result = [future result];
```

This would only block on the last line, and only then if the other thread had not completed by the time the `-result` message was sent. The *EtoileThread* framework, part of *EtoileFoundation*, provides a similar mechanism. This is used in the Étoilé music player application to move the decoder into a separate thread. Spawning the player in the second thread is as simple as sending it an `-inNewThread` message:

```
MKMusicPlayer *player = [[MKMusicPlayer alloc] initWithDefaultDevice];
// Move the player into a new thread.
player = [player inNewThread];
```

The `player` object is now a proxy and the real object is running in a separate thread. EtoileThread uses a hybrid ring buffer for forwarding messages, which switches between using a lockless mode and using a condition variable depending on whether the queue is full or not. The implementation of this buffer is beyond the scope of this book, but we can look at this class as an example of the problems that you are likely to encounter when forwarding invocations between threads.

In Objective-C, there are three categories of return type. Every method returns either nothing (**`void`**), an object, or a primitive C value. The first case is easy; these messages can complete asynchronously.

For object returns, we can use a proxy. This is returned immediately. When the message completes, the return value is written into the proxy. Any message sent to the proxy is forwarded to the proxy. You can see how this is implemented in Listing 23.2.

Listing 23.2: The future proxy object forwarding implementation. [from: ETThreadProxyReturn.m in the EtoileThread framework.]

```
- (void) setProxyObject: (id)anObject
{
    pthread_mutex_lock(&mutex);
    object = [anObject retain];
    pthread_cond_signal(&conditionVariable);
    pthread_mutex_unlock(&mutex);
    [self release];
}
- (id) value
{
    if (INVALID_OBJECT == object)
    {
        pthread_mutex_lock(&mutex);
        if (INVALID_OBJECT == object)
        {
            pthread_cond_wait(&conditionVariable, &mutex);
        }
        pthread_mutex_unlock(&mutex);
    }
    return object;
```

```
}
- (void) forwardInvocation: (NSInvocation *)anInvocation
{
    if (INVALID_OBJECT == object)
    {
        [self value];
    }
    [anInvocation invokeWithTarget:object];
}
```

The first two methods shown here are related to setting and getting the real object. When the proxy is created, its `object` instance variable is set to a constant value for an invalid object. When you try to get the real object by sending a `-value` message to the proxy, you get it returned immediately if it is not this value. If it is, then it means that the method has not yet finished. The accessor first acquires a lock and then tests it again. If it were not set between the first test and acquiring the lock, then it waits on the condition variable. Remember that this releases the mutex and makes the thread sleep.

Meanwhile, the other thread should complete executing the method and call `-setProxyObject:` on it. This first acquires the lock. The other thread only holds the lock very briefly, so this will rarely block. It then sets the `object` ivar and signals the condition variable. This will move the thread that is sleeping on the condition variable in the `-value` method into the state where it is now blocking on the mutex. Finally, the method unlocks the mutex allowing the `-value` thread to proceed and releases the reference to the proxy held in the worker thread.

The `-value` thread will then wake up and acquire the mutex. It must therefore release it before returning the object. The final method is the one that makes this all transparent to the user. This first tests if the object has already been returned. If it hasn't, it calls the `-value` method, which, as we just saw, blocks until the value is ready, and then forwards the invocation to the real target.

You can use this proxy as if it were the real object that will be returned by the method that you run in the other thread. Messages to the threaded object will return immediately if they return **`void`** or an object. Messages that return a primitive value will block, since these cannot safely be wrapped in proxies. If you then send a message to the object that is returned, the proxy will block until execution completes.

There are a few things to be careful of here. The first is that you must send `-retainArguments` to the invocation that you forward between threads. If you don't, then the calling thread may release the arguments and cause the other thread to send messages to an invalid pointer.

Although this mechanism is very powerful, you can't use it on arbitrary objects. The API of objects that you expose in this way should be defined so that the only arguments are either immutable objects, pointers to immutable data (e.g., constant C strings), or primitive values passed by copy. Any other values will need you to worry about manual locking.

The `MKMusicPlayer` class used in the preceding example only has a small number of methods that take arguments. One appends an URL to the current playlist, and another sets the playlist to contain the URLs from an immutable array. The others all take primitive values as arguments, for example, setting the volume level. This design means that the music player can run in a separate thread and interleave decoding of frames with messages from the UI. All of the synchronization between the two threads happens entirely implicitly and there is no threading code in the music player at all.

You can implement a similar mechanism very easily. If you are not worried about producing a general solution, then you don't have to go via `NSInvocation`, you can write a specific proxy and add lightweight commands to your message queue.

23.2.6 Stress Testing Threads

It is very common to write threaded code that works perfectly and then get bug reports claiming that it fails. The combination of C library, kernel, and CPU(s) on one computer may cause a deadlock or race condition never to occur, while the different combination of these factors on another computer causes it to appear all of the time.

When looking for a particularly difficult threading bug, I used this loop:

```
for (unsigned i =0; i<10000; i++)
{
    id pool = [NSAutoreleasePool new];
    ret = [object test];
    usleep(i % 500);
    [ret value];
    [pool release];
}
```

The `[object test]` and `[ret value]` messages both interacted with the same thread. The `usleep()` command sleeps for a number of microseconds. This loop repeats 10,000 times, sleeping for between zero and 500μs each time. For the bug I was hunting at the time, this caused the failure around 200 times on my computer, a bug that I couldn't reproduce at all in normal operation but which happened all of the time for someone else.

You might consider adding something similar to your test suite. It is not as good a solution as proving deadlock freedom in your code, but it is a lot easier.

23.3 Child Processes

The POSIX threading specification was released in 1995. This was over two decades since the initial release of UNIX and over a decade since UNIX had been regularly running on multiprocessor systems. A few of these had their own, incompatible, threading libraries, but threads were not seen as the normal way of creating concurrent code on UNIX. Instead, UNIX programs would create a small family of processes.

23.3.1 Creating Child Processes

The basic mechanism for creating new processes on UNIX is the `fork()` system call. This produces two identical copies of the same processes. On the machines where this design was invented, it made a lot of sense. Only one process could be running at a time and performing a context switch meant writing one process out and loading a new one in. When you created a new process, you wrote out the current process and if you didn't do anything you got a new copy for free. On modern processors this is a lot more expensive. The entire address space has to be marked as copy-on-write and then each page that one of them modifies needs to be copied.

On newer systems, including OS X, there is a cheaper mechanism for starting a new process that is not a copy of its parent. This is wrapped by Cocoa in the `NSTask` class. You can use this to run any process. The simplest way of using it is to send a `+launchedTaskWithLaunchPath:arguments:` message to `NSTask`. The first argument is a string giving the path to the executable and the second is an array of arguments to pass to the process. You can use this with `NSBundle` to launch a helper contained inside your application bundle. You can then communicate with the spawned process using distributed objects.

23.3.2 Communicating with Children

The more traditional way of communicating with child processes on UNIX-like systems is via pipes. A pipe is a simple *first-in first-out* (*FIFO*) buffered *interprocess communication* (*IPC*) mechanism. It looks like a file descriptor and so can be written to and read from just like a file.

This is the classical way of joining processes together in UNIX. You often use commands like this:

```
$ du | sort
```

This is a very simple example of parallel programming. The `du` and `sort` programs will run concurrently. Everything that `du` writes to `stdout` will be pushed into a pipe, buffered, and then read by sort when it reads from `stdin`. This even contains some primitive synchronization. When the pipe is full, the `write()` call will block allowing sort time to run and empty the buffer.

You can use tasks like this as simple filters. Each task has one input and two outputs, the standard input, output, and error streams. When you spawn a task with the constructor shown earlier, these are connected to the current process's standard streams. For command line tool this will be the current terminal; for a graphical application they will be connected to the system console.

If you create a task with `+alloc` and `-init` it will not be started immediately, and you can set various properties on it. Listing 23.3 shows a simple program that runs the equivalent of the simple redirection shown earlier. This spawns two child processes, instances of the du and sort programs and joins them together with a pipe.

Listing 23.3: A simple program connecting tasks with a pipe. [from: examples/DuSort/dusort.m]

```
1  #import <Foundation/Foundation.h>
2
3  int main(void)
4  {
5      [NSAutoreleasePool new];
6
7      NSTask *du = [[NSTask alloc] init];
8      [du setLaunchPath: @"/usr/bin/du"];
9
10     NSTask *sort = [[NSTask alloc] init];
11     [sort setLaunchPath: @"/usr/bin/sort"];
12
13     NSPipe *pipe = [NSPipe pipe];
14     [du setStandardOutput: pipe];
15     [sort setStandardInput: pipe];
16
17     [sort launch];
18     [du launch];
19     [sort waitUntilExit];
20     return 0;
21 }
```

These two tasks are created in the same way. The objects are created just like any other Objective-C object and then have the path to the executable set. They are joined together on lines 13–15. This is very simple. It first creates an `NSPipe` instance. This is a very simple class encapsulating a UNIX pipe. This has two file descriptors associated with it, one for reading and one for writing.

When the pipe is set as the standard output stream for the first task, the write end of the pipe is automatically closed in this process. This prevents both the current process and the child from writing to the pipe. The same is true of the read end of the pipe when it is connected to the standard input on the second task.

On lines 17 and 18 the two tasks are launched. The order doesn't really matter. We create the second task first here so that there will already be something waiting to read data when the first one starts writing it. If you don't do this, then the pipe will buffer some and then cause the first task to block. This isn't a problem, but it's slightly less elegant.

When this program exits, it will kill any running child processes automatically. To prevent this, we send the `sort` task a `-waitUntilExit` message. This will block until the process terminates. This will happen when it receives an end-of-file marker in its standard input, which will happen when the `du` task exits.

Although here we just connected two external processes together with a pipe, you can use them to communicate just as easily with the parent process. `NSPipe` provides two methods, `-fileHandleForReading` and `fileHandleForWriting`. Both return instances of `NSFileHandle` and so all of the standard methods that we've already seen for reading and writing data to file handles will work. You can send the file handle a `-waitForDataInBackgroundAndNotify` message and then be notified when the child process has some data for you. This can be useful for long-running tasks.

23.3.3 Sharing Memory

Pipes and distributed objects are both good ways of sending messages to other processes, but they involve a lot of copying. Pipes are buffered, and so when you write data to the pipe it is first copied into the kernel and then copied out again when the other process reads from the pipe.

For the most part, you will spawn external processes when you need to do a lot of processing in the background. Typically, the time spent processing will be a lot longer than the time spent copying data to the child process. In some cases, particularly those involving images or video, you may want the child to work on a large amount of data.

The most efficient way of sharing data between processes is to use *shared memory*. This was originally added to UNIX by System V, and was later standardized by POSIX. OS X supports both of these sets of APIs, but they are rarely used. Instead, the `mmap()` system call is preferred.

If you only want read-only access to shared memory, you can use `NSData`'s `+dataWithContentsOfMappedFile:` method rather than directly using `mmap()`. Write access requires a little bit more low-level programming.

Threads versus Processes

You can often use threads and processes for the same thing. The difference between a thread and a process is that a thread shares the address space with its parent, while a process does not. This means that you can pass pointers between threads, but not between processes. The down side of this is that every object in a threaded program is potentially shared.

The difficulty of debugging a concurrent program is proportional to the number of concurrent threads multiplied by the number of resources shared between them. If you use multiple processes then the number of shared resources is constrained to the number of proxies that you pass between them. In a multithreaded environment a bug with pointers can make every single byte of memory a shared resource. This makes threaded programs vastly more difficult to debug.

The most common way of programming with threads is to arrange them in a tree and treat them as processes. Each object is owned by one thread, and should not be referenced by others. Messages flow down and up the tree, but not between branches.

The `mmap()` call is used to establish a mapping between a region of memory and a file. When you try to access the memory, if it is not in RAM already it will be paged in on demand. When you write to the memory, the changes will be silently pushed back to the file.

You can use `mmap()` in two ways. Private mappings do not push changes back to the file, while shared mappings keep the memory and the file in sync. The virtual memory subsystem will optimize this. When any process needs a page from a file, it will be loaded. If more than one process wants the same page, they will get the same memory page mapped into their address space. If one process writes to it and they all have shared mappings, then the changes will be instantly visible to the other processes (since they are all using the same memory page). If any have private mappings, then the page will have been mapped read-only. The kernel will catch the trap that results and will copy the page. All of the processes with shared mappings will see the new version, but all of the processes with private mappings will keep their copy unmodified.

Listing 23.4 shows a subclass of `NSMutableData` that represents a shared memory segment using `mmap()`. You can use this with the same parameters in two processes and they will see identical objects. Any changes in one will be automatically reflected in the other.

This class describes two instance variables, `bytes` and `length`, representing a

Listing 23.4: A mutable shared data class. [from: examples/SharedMemory/SharedData.m]

```
#import "SharedData.h"
#include <sys/mman.h>

@implementation SharedData
- (id) initWithSharedFile: (NSString*) aFile size: (NSUInteger) aSize
{
    if (nil == (self = [self init])) { return nil; }
    int file = open([aFile UTF8String], O_RDWR | O_CREAT, 0600);
    lseek(file, (off_t) aSize+1, SEEK_SET);
    write(file, "\0", 1);
    bytes = mmap(NULL,
            aSize,
            PROT_READ | PROT_WRITE,
            MAP_FILE | MAP_SHARED,
            file,
            0);
    close(file);
    length = aSize;
    return self;
}
- (void) dealloc
{
    munmap(bytes, length);
    [super dealloc];
}
- (NSUInteger)length
{
    return length;
}
- (const void *)bytes
{
    return bytes;
}
- (void *)mutableBytes
{
    return bytes;
}
- (void)setLength:(NSUInteger)length
{
    if (length <= aSize) return;
    [NSException raise: @"SharedMemoryResizeException"
                format: @"You can not resize shared memory"];
}
@end
```

pointer to the memory and the size of the region. When the instance is initialized, it first opens the specified file. It then seeks just past the end and writes a 0. This is a quick way of ensuring that the file is big enough to store the desired amount of data. If opening the file caused it to be created, this will create a file completely full of zeros.

The file is then mapped. The `mmap()` call takes a lot of arguments. The first is a pointer to where we would like the memory to be mapped. Since we don't care, we pass `NULL`. The second is the size of the region to map. This is paired with the last argument, which indicates the offset from the start of the file to map. We went to map the entire file, from the start to the specified size.

The third and fourth arguments specify the kind of mapping. The permissions we want are read and write but not execute, and the type of mapping is a shared mapping pointing to a file. We then close the file descriptor. This does not unmap the memory; it just stops us from using `read()` and `write()` calls to access it.

The `-dealloc` method performs the inverse operation, unmapping the memory region. The remaining methods are the primitive methods in `NSData` and `NSMutableData`. All of the other methods in these classes are implemented in terms of these.

Most of these are quite simple. The only one that is nontrivial is the resizing method. Resizing a shared memory segment is complex. Shrinking it is simple, but expanding it generally requires resizing the file and often requires moving the mapped region. For this simple example, we don't implement this; we just silently ignore resizing requests that would shrink the data and throw an exception when asked to expand it.

Using shared memory introduces some of the same problems as using threads. Two processes can modify the shared memory region at any time. The same solution that was used for threads is provided for shared memory: locks. The `NSDistributedLock` class provides the companion to our `SharedMemory` class, a lock that uses an entry in a filesystem to work across processes. Unlike the other locks, which implement the `NSLocking` protocol, this does not have any mechanism for blocking if the lock cannot be acquired immediately. Typically you would use it like this:

```
while (![lock trylock])
{
    [NSThread sleepForTimeInterval: 0.2];
}
[self doSomethingWith: sharedData];
[lock unlock];
```

This will try to acquire the lock and, if it fails, then sleep for 200ms and try again. Note that this method is only available in 10.5. Earlier versions should use `+sleepUntilDate` or the `usleep()` function.

Once the lock has been acquired, you can safely modify the shared memory. Afterward, you release the lock and continue. This is somewhat safer than threads because you have a well-defined region of shared memory, rather than sharing everything.

You can combine this easily with distributed objects. If you begin using DO for your application and later find that there is a bottleneck, then you can change a method that takes a large value argument into one that takes the name of a shared memory region instead. This will eliminate the need to copy the data between the two processes. A common use for this is something like an image convolution. You would write the image to the shared region, run the convolution in the other process, and get the image back in the same location.

23.4 Operation Queues

OS X 10.5 added a new mechanism for managing background processing. In a lot of processor-intensive applications the work can be parceled up into smaller work units. To support this style of programming, the `NSOperation` class was added.

Each operation represents a single task, a combination of code and data that can execute independently of the rest of the program. By itself, it does nothing; it exists solely for subclassing. Each subclass must implement a small number of methods that actually perform the work.

The companion to `NSOperation` is `NSOperationQueue`, which is responsible for managing a set of operations. Operations have dependency relations between them, allowing you to make sure that they run in the right order.

You use a system like this when you build any piece of software using make, XCode, or something similar. A very simple project might be defined by a Makefile like this:

```
program: source1.o source2.o
gcc source1.o source2.o -o program

source1.o: source1.c header1.h programheader.h
gcc -c source1.c

source2.o: source2.c header2.h programheader.h
gcc -c -O3 source2.c
```

Each of these lines defines an operation, a result, and some dependencies. You could create an implementation of this amount of the make utility very easily using `NSOperation`. Each of these sections would be a simple wrapper around an `NSTask`, and would be implemented by a custom operation class. You would create an instance for each section in the file. The first pass through would create an operation from the target, dependencies, and command, and would store this in a dictionary. Each operation would then look up each of its dependencies in the dictionary and see if they had corresponding operations. If so, they should be added with `-addDependency:`. Finally, all of the operations would be added to an operation queue and run. This would simply create an `NSTask` for the specified command.

Operation queues manage one or more threads. By default, it will run all operations that are ready in parallel, although you can limit this. To demonstrate the simple use of operations, we will define a simple class that provides a naive implementation of the Fibonacci sequence, as shown in Listing 23.5.

Listing 23.5: A naive Fibonacci sequence implementation. [from: examples/Invocation-Operation/Fibonacci.m]

```
#import "Fibonacci.h"

@implementation Fibonacci
- (NSUInteger) fibonacci: (NSUInteger)i
{
    switch (i)
    {
        case 0:
        case 1:
            return 1;
        default:
            return [self fibonacci:i-1]
                 + [self fibonacci:i-2];
    }
}
@end
```

This runs in polynomial time and quickly grows to take a very long time. We can use this with operations as a placeholder for something that does real work. The simplest way of working with operations is to use an `NSInvocationOperation`. This turns an invocation into an operation.

Listing 23.6 shows a single invocation operation being constructed and run. This kind of operation is limited to running something that takes a single argument. Although it expects an object as an argument we can cheat slightly and pass an integer cast to an object. You can also construct an invocation operation by creating the invocation yourself. In this case, there are no constraints on the kind of parameters that you can pass to the invocation.

Listing 23.6: Running a single invocation operation. [from: examples/InvocationOperation/main.m]

```
1  #import "Fibonacci.h"
2
3  int main(void)
4  {
5      [NSAutoreleasePool new];
6      NSInvocationOperation* op =
7          [[NSInvocationOperation alloc] initWithTarget: [Fibonacci new]
8                                               selector: @selector(fibonacci
                                                    :)
9                                                 object: (id)40];
10     NSOperationQueue *q = [NSOperationQueue new];
11     [q addOperation: op];
12     sleep(1);
13     printf("op␣finished:␣%d␣running:␣%d\n", [op isFinished], [op
           isExecuting]);
14     [q waitUntilAllOperationsAreFinished];
15     printf("op␣result:␣%ld\n", (int)[op result]);
16     return 0;
17 }
```

On line 11 we add the operation to a new queue. This will start running in a new thread almost immediately. To make sure it has enough time to start, we sleep for a second and then log the state of the operation. On line 14 we tell the queue to wait until all of the operations are finished.

The `isFinished` method in `NSOperation` is KVO compliant. This means that you can register an object as an observer on the `finished` key for a given operation and be notified when it completes. Doing this allows you to start operations in the background and then handle their completion asynchronously. In this simple case, we just wait synchronously and then print the returned value. Running the program gives this output:

```
$ gcc -framework Foundation *.m && ./a.out
op finished: 0 running: 1
op result: 16815920
```

This demonstrates that the operation is running in the background and has successfully run to completion. Note that all of the usual constraints about threading apply. For this to work transparently, the operation object should not have pointers to any mutable objects outside of the operation.

The NSInvocationOperation here is very simple. One of the most important things that it doesn't define is any way of canceling the operation. If we add a statement saying [op cancel], then the operation still runs to completion, but then attempting to get the result throws an exception. This is very unlikely to be what you want.

We can extend this example by turning the Fibonacci class into an NSOperation subclass. The interface to this class is shown in Listing 23.7. We have to implement our own -result method (or some other way of getting the result) since this came from the invocation operation. We also need a new constructor and some state.

Listing 23.7: The interface to the Fibonacci operation. [from: examples/Operations/Fibonacci.h]

```
#import <Foundation/Foundation.h>

@interface Fibonacci : NSOperation {
    NSUInteger start;
}
- (id) initWithStart:(NSUInteger)i;
- (NSUInteger) result;
- (NSUInteger) fibonacci: (NSUInteger)i;
@end
```

The implementation of this class is shown in Listing 23.8. The initializer is very simple, it just assigns the argument to the instance variable. This is used when the operation runs as the value to pass to the method that actually does the work.

The -main method is where all of the real work happens. This is the method that will be called by -start to run the operation. The default implementation does nothing, so we don't need to call the superclass implementation here. This is true of most of the NSOperation methods that you might override. Some, like -start, must not be called from a subclass; others just don't need to be.

The important addition to the -main method is the exception handling block. This is used to detect that the operation was canceled. If the -fibonacci: method doesn't throw an exception, the result will be assigned to start. This is allowed because operations are one-shot objects; rerunning an operation is undefined behavior.

The -fibonacci: method now checks on each invocation whether the operation has been canceled. The -isCancelled method, like the other predicate methods in this class, is thread safe. If the operation is canceled in any thread, then this will return **YES**. If this happens then we throw an exception. This will cause the stack to be unwound all the way up to the -main method.

The final part of this operation class is to return the result. This should

Listing 23.8: The implementation of the Fibonacci operation. [from: examples/Operations/Fibonacci.m]

```
#import "Fibonacci.h"

@implementation Fibonacci
- (id) initWithStart:(NSUInteger)i
{
    if (nil == (self = [super init])) { return nil; }
    start = i;
    return self;
}
- (void)main
{
    @try
    {
        start = [self fibonacci: start];
    }
    @catch (id exception) {}
}
- (NSUInteger) result
{
    if (![self isCancelled] && [self isFinished])
    {
        return start;
    }
    return 0;
}
- (NSUInteger) fibonacci: (NSUInteger)i
{
    if ([self isCancelled])
    {
        [NSException raise: NSGenericException
                    format: @"Operation␣cancelled"];
    }
    switch (i)
    {
        case 0:
        case 1:
            return 1;
        default:
            return [self fibonacci:i-1]
                 + [self fibonacci:i-2];
    }
}
@end
```

only happen if the operation were not canceled and, since this can be called from another thread, should not happen until the operation has completed. Attempting to access the value of `start` may give an undefined result while the operation is running, but once the operation is finished it will not be modified by any thread and so is safe to access. We return 0 here if the result can't be accessed. Other operations may throw an exception.

The code in Listing 23.9 shows how this can be used. This version starts two copies of the operation at once and then cancels one.

Listing 23.9: Running the Fibonacci operation. [from: examples/Operations/main.m]

```
1  #import "Fibonacci.h"
2  
3  int main(void)
4  {
5      [NSAutoreleasePool new];
6      Fibonacci* op = [[Fibonacci alloc] initWithStart: 40];
7      Fibonacci* op2 = [[Fibonacci alloc] initWithStart: 40];
8      NSOperationQueue *q = [NSOperationQueue new];
9      [q addOperation: op];
10     [q addOperation: op2];
11     sleep(1);
12     printf("op␣finished:␣%d␣running:␣%d\n", [op isFinished], [op
           isExecuting]);
13     printf("op2␣finished:␣%d␣running:␣%d\n", [op2 isFinished], [op2
           isExecuting]);
14     [op2 cancel];
15     [q waitUntilAllOperationsAreFinished];
16     printf("op␣result:␣%ld\n", (int)[op result]);
17     printf("op2␣result:␣%ld\n", (int)[op2 result]);
18     return 0;
19 }
```

Since we did not specify a maximum number of operations to run at once, they should both start running as soon as they are added to the queue. We test this on lines 12 and 13 and then cancel one of the operations on line 14. After the other has run, we test the results from both. Running it gives this output:

```
$ gcc *.m -framework Foundation && ./a.out
op finished: 0 running: 1
op2 finished: 0 running: 1
op result: 165580141
op2 result: 0
```

The operation queue mechanism allows an easy way of creating parcels of background processing in a process. Conceptually, it is very close to spawning a set of new child processes, but has the advantage of being much cheaper and easily able to access immutable data from the rest of the program.

This simple example ran in three threads—the main thread and two operation threads—without any manual threading code being written. This doesn't absolve you of the responsibility to write thread-safe code, but it does make it easier if the work you want to do is a background task.

As part of the push to use blocks everywhere in Cocoa, Apple introduced the `NSBlockOperation` class. This is similar to `NSInvocationOperation`, but is constructed with a block rather than an invocation. You can use this to add a snippet of code to an operation queue easily if the operation isn't already encapsulated in a method.

23.5 Grand Central Dispatch

With OS X 10.6, Apple introduced *Grand Central Dispatch* (*GCD*) as a new way of interacting with threads. Quite often, a program has a little bit of processing that needs to be done in the background. The most common way of implementing this is to spawn a worker thread in the background. There are several problems with this model.

Thread creation is not cheap. At a minimum, every thread needs its own stack. On OS X, the kernel and C library provide a 1:1 threading model, so creating a thread requires a system call to create an entry in the process table for the thread.

After the thread has been created, it needs to be scheduled. Context switches between threads are faster than between processes on systems like x86, because you don't need to update the CPU's address mapping, but they still require every register to be stored and then reloaded, and can cause a lot of cache churn. If you have a lot of threads, then the overhead from the extra context switches can become large enough to offset the gain from using a second core.

Determining the optimum number of threads to create is difficult. To make the best use of a multicore computer, you want one thread to be running on every core. Note the word "running"; having one busy thread and three sleeping threads is far from ideal. In some situations, you may have more tasks than cores, but some will be higher priority than others. You don't want your high-priority tasks being starved of CPU time by the less-important ones, so you may spawn threads with different scheduling priorities. If two applications are doing processor-intensive things at the same time, then it may be more efficient for them each to have two threads, one on each core of a quad-core machine, than for each to have four threads and each core keep switching between them.

These decisions are difficult to make inside a process. Grand Central manages a set of threads for each process. Each of these threads has an associated queue and will run tasks in a given order. The exact number of threads is determined by both the hardware configuration and the current load. Because GCD is a system-wide feature, it will choose an optimal number of threads, taking into account both your code and the current system state.

The core units of work for GCD are *blocks* (see Chapter 3). A block is a closure: a function (optionally) incorporating to some external state. These can be created either as completely isolated work units, or incorporating some aspect of the containing state. Be careful when doing this. Imagine that you create a block like this:

```
void (^work)(void) =
^(void)
{
    [someObject doSomething];
};
```

The value `someObject` is a reference to an external variable. When you pass this block to GCD, it will execute it (eventually) in another thread. If you keep a reference to `someObject` around outside this block, then you need to ensure that the `-doSomething` method is thread safe. Ideally, when creating blocks for use with GCD, you should ensure that locking is not required until after the block has run. A simple way of achieving this is to process unaliased objects in the block and then add them to a collection at the end.

As with many of the newer features in OS X, Grand Central is built in layers. Blocks are a language extension and are available to C, Objective-C, and C++. Grand Central provides a set of C APIs at the lowest level of the system that make heavy use of blocks. These are built on top of the `kevent()` mechanism, inherited from FreeBSD, that provides a unified way of retrieving kernel events from a single call. The `kevent()` function is a generalized form of the traditional UNIX `select()` or `poll()` calls. Unlike these, it can retrieve any kind of kernel-generated event, including timers, signals, Mach events, and so on.

Grand Central introduces the notion of *dispatch queues*. These are simple to use for running blocks asynchronously relative to the caller but (optionally) synchronously relative to other blocks. The main thread of any Cocoa application has a dispatch queue associated with it and you can create more. Other queues are divided into two groups. Serial queues will execute the blocks that are added to them in the order that they are added. Concurrent queues will begin executing blocks in the order that they are added, but may start executing one block before the preceding one has finished.

Dispatch queues are connected to low-level events by *dispatch sources*, which typically wrap a `kevent()` call. These will insert a block into a specific dispatch queue whenever an event is received, for example, when a file descriptor has some data ready for reading. The block will then execute and can handle the event.

Grand Central is one of the low-level parts of Mac OS, sitting below Cocoa and even below Core Foundation. It is available to any OS X program, including those not using Cocoa. With 10.6, several parts of Cocoa itself use Grand Central. Most of the time, you will not need to use GCD directly, but if you are finding that your code is CPU-bound, then it provides a much more convenient programming model than using threads directly.

23.6 OpenCL

With OS X 10.6, Apple introduced a new technology called *OpenCL*. This is an open standard, certified by the Khronos Group, who are responsible for OpenGL, and backed by AMD, Intel, and nVidia among others. OpenCL was originally created by Apple, but is now a cross-platform language and API. AMD, for example, provides OpenCL development tools along with its drivers.

OpenCL is based on OpenGL and the *OpenGL Shader Language* (*GLSL*). It provides a way of writing short programs, called kernels, which execute on the GPU. These can take advantage of the GPU's parallel vector units and perform signal processing operations very quickly. They are best suited to massively parallel operations on arrays of data.

Using OpenCL is a two-step operation. You have to write the kernel in a C-like language designed to run on the GPU and then you have to load it into the CPU. This is similar to writing an OpenGL program involving shaders, where the shaders are written in GLSL and then uploaded to the card.

OpenCL programs operate on buffers that are similar to OpenGL textures. They are blobs of memory that can be read from or written to by the kernel. Typically these will be copied into the GPU's local memory when the program starts and copied back when it has finished.

OpenCL is a superset of C99, just as Objective-C is. Clang, one of the compilers supported by XCode, also supports most of the OpenCL extensions. This makes it possible to write OpenCL kernels that are compiled as functions and called directly by the rest of your program. This is not the fastest way of running OpenCL code. If you load it as a kernel, then it will be *just-in-time* (*JIT*) compiled for your native CPU or (ideally) GPU. If you compile it as if it were C, then you can benefit from cross-module optimizations and compatibility with versions of OS X that don't support OpenCL directly. This means that OpenCL code, with a few tweaks, can be used for both the heavily optimized GPU code path and for the fallback path.

A full explanation of OpenCL is far beyond the scope of this book. It is not part of Cocoa and is a massive topic by itself. If you are doing a lot of parallel floating point operations, then you should consider looking at it in more detail.

23.7 Summary

Writing concurrent programs is not always important. If your code runs fast enough on a single core, then the only reason to write concurrent code is if it is conceptually parallel. If this is the case, then writing a program that is split over multiple threads or processes will make development easier.

If your program is conceptually serial, or has interlocking components that make splitting it into parallel parts difficult, then try running it before you decide to make it parallel. While I am writing this, Activity Monitor tells me I have 454 threads running in 119 processes and yet my CPU load is only 5%. Splitting any of the running processes into more threads would make the load higher from the extra locking and context switching overhead; it wouldn't make anything faster.

In this chapter we've looked at a number of the ways in which you can write concurrent code on OS X. The distributed objects system makes it easy for you to send Objective-C messages between threads and processes on a single system, or between computers distributed over a network.

The threading primitives in OS X allow you to easily create threads and some of the dynamic dispatch system in Objective-C can be used to implement your own lightweight version of distributed objects. The new low-level mechanisms introduced with OS X 10.6 make writing parallel code with the work queue model very easy, but require some thought before you can start coding.

You can fall back to the traditional UNIX model and spawn child processes to run particular parts of a program and communicate with them in a variety of ways. We looked at how to use DO, shared memory, and UNIX pipes for this.

We saw how operation queues can be used to run background tasks in separate threads, with automatic dependency resolution between them.

OS X provides a host of technologies for writing parallel code. If you need to take full advantage of a modern multicore CPU, you have a number of options.

Part VIII

Appendixes

Chapter 24

Portable Cocoa

Although Cocoa is typically thought of as a proprietary Apple API, this is only partly true. The core is an implementation of the OpenStep specification. This core is enough to build some very rich applications, and is portable to a number of different systems.

24.1 NeXT and Sun

OpenStep was created in 1993 as a result of a collaboration between Sun and NeXT. The two companies each released an implementation of the specification for their own operating systems. For a while there were two competing OpenStep operating systems for Sun's SPARC workstations, Solaris with Sun's OpenStep layer, and NeXT's OPENSTEP/Mach for SPARC.

The Sun implementation used the *X Display PostScript* (*XDPS*) extension, which allowed OpenStep applications to use DPS drawing functions inside X windows. It also included a daemon that wrapped Mach port operations in Solaris IPC calls, allowing code that depended on Mach ports to work properly.

NeXT shipped their own operating system for a number of platforms in addition to SPARC. It ran on PA-RISC, SPARC, Motorola 68k (the CPU in NeXT's own workstations), and Intel 486 CPUs. This was an updated version of the older NeXTSTEP operating system, renamed OPENSTEP for Mach, or just OPENSTEP/Mach, to indicate that it complied with the OpenStep specification. This later evolved into Mac OS X.

If you can find a copy of the i486 port of OPENSTEP, then you can install it in a virtual machine on Intel Macs or an x86 emulator like VirtualPC on PowerPC. Since a 66MHz 486 was a fast computer when it was released, it runs incredibly quickly even in virtualization on a modern system. You will have difficulty installing it on real hardware due to the lack of drivers, but in a virtual machine it can give you a good impression of the solid foundation that Apple began with when they built OS X.

In addition to the OPENSTEP operating system, NeXT produced another implementation of OpenStep, *OPENSTEP Enterprise* (*OSE*). This was a port of OpenStep to Windows NT 4.0.

Applications from this era could run on OpenStep implementations on NeXT's own operating system, Windows NT, or Solaris.

24.2 Mobile OS X on the iPhone

The iPhone and iPod Touch both run a cut-down port of OS X to the ARM architecture. This does not include all of the libraries found on desktop OS X and does include a few not found on the desktop version.

The only supported development language for this platform is Objective-C. Unlike the desktop version, the iPhone does not allow the use of garbage collection. This was considered too big of an overhead for the small device.

Apple also took the opportunity to remove some legacy support from the mobile version. There is no Carbon, for example. Somewhat surprisingly, there is also no AppKit. Instead, there is UIKit. This is very similar to AppKit, and moving between the two is relatively easy; in many cases you just substitute `UI` for `NS` as a prefix in your code. The biggest change is that UIKit does not have an equivalent of `NSCell` as a lightweight alternative to creating views. This is surprising, since `NSCell` was created specifically to allow complex UIs on underpowered machines, which ought to make it a model that fits well with the iPhone.

A lot of the low-level parts of AppKit are not present at all on the iPhone; you use the Core Graphics functions directly. Every view in the iPhone is backed by a Core Animation layer. While using Core Animation on the desktop is typically done to add visual effects, on the iPhone it is also a mechanism for offloading drawing to the GPU and reducing battery consumption.

24.3 OpenStep and GNU

NeXT provided a lot of inspiration to the GNU project early on. Steve Jobs' aim at NeXT was to produce the perfect computer or, at least, the closest approximation possible with the current technology, a goal worth copying. Early hopes for the GNU project were to be able to persuade NeXT to donate their GUI code to run on top of GNU Mach. The resulting hypothetical system was called GnUStep.

NeXT initially implemented Objective-C support in the *GNU Compiler Collection* (*GCC*) and intervention from Richard Stallman forced them to release this to the public. A replacement for the NeXT Objective-C runtime library was written shortly after.

There was a lot of interest in Objective-C from the early GNU project after they gained their own compiler. This gradually diminished over the years as more and more people joined with experience of C and C++ toolkits.

The GNU Objective-C compiler is still developed, although it receives a lot less attention than C and C++, or even languages like Ada and Fortran. Most of the work was done by Apple, until recently, and since they are not working on any of the versions that will be released under GPLv3, Objective-C support is likely to languish. Fortunately, there is a replacement compiler that still does receive considerable support from Apple in development.

24.4 GNUstep

Work on the project that would eventually become GNUstep began in 1991. Andrew McMullen started working on an Objective-C toolkit known as libcoll, based on Smalltalk, the collections library (which also provided inspiration for OpenStep Foundation). At the same time Paul Kunz wrote libobjcX, which implemented the NeXTSTEP GUI classes that would later evolve into AppKit on top of X11.

In 1993, in response to the OpenStep specification being released, these were merged into a new project, informally named *GnuStep*. The libcoll library evolved slowly to implement a lot of Foundation and was renamed libobjects. In 1995, the *GNUstep* project was officially formed, with the aim of implementing the newly finalized OpenStep specification.

The Free Software Foundation paid for a DPS implementation to be developed, *Display GhostScript* (*DGS*), based on the open source PostScript interpreter GhostScript. This was eventually discontinued when it was realized that no one actually used the DPS functionality of OpenStep directly, since it was slower than implementing control structures in Objective-C and calling the AppKit functions. DGS was developed by Alladin, but was never able to support more than one graphics context in a window, which made it impossible to support nested `NSViews`. It was, therefore, largely useless and is not used in modern GNUstep versions. The GNUstep AppKit implementation uses an abstraction layer to talk to the windowing system. Early versions used first an XDPS extension and then direct calls to XLib functions.

More recently, a back end based on libart was implemented. This is a high-performance 2D graphics library supporting vector and compositing operations. This is slowly being phased out in favor of one based on *Cairo Graphics*. Cairo is a new graphics library from the X.org developers, which provides a PDF-like display model and is designed for supporting hardware acceleration through X.org. Semantically, Cairo and Core Graphics are very similar, although the APIs differ. There is a partial reimplementation of Core Graphics on top of Cairo called *Opal* in the Étoilé subversion repository.

There is also a back end supporting the Windows GDI, allowing GNUstep applications to run on Windows. Back ends are in two components, drawing and event handling. The drawing part of the windows back end is likely to be deprecated in the future, since Cairo is capable of drawing on Windows.

GNUstep initially aimed for compatibility with OpenStep. When OS X was released, this goal changed. Although OpenStep compatibility was still important, tracking changes introduced with OS X became a priority. The current version implements some functionality from all OS X releases, although the longer the class or method has existed the more likely it is to be in GNUstep. Most things are implemented when a GNUstep contributor uses them. A lot of the Foundation library implementation was contributed by developers working for Brainstorm, a company that provides SMS and related services. Their code uses GNUstep and contributing the code back reduces the amount that they need to implement.

The GNUstep project includes a quite large number of libraries. Some of the more interesting ones include

base is a Foundation implementation.

gui is an AppKit implementation.

back is the back end used by GNUstep-gui.

gscoredata implements the Core Data framework.

gsweb is a reimplementation of WebObjects 4.5, the last WebObjects release written in Objective-C. This can be used to write web applications that share model objects with GNUstep applications.

gdl2 is an implementation of the Enterprise Objects Framework, mapping relational databases to Objective-C objects. This is most commonly used with GNUstepWeb, but can be used with other applications.

sqlclient provides a database abstraction layer for SQL queries.

A few other frameworks are implemented by third parties, for example, AddressKit implementing the Address Book APIs from OS X. There are also language bridges to Java, Ruby, Guile (a Scheme dialect), and scripting support for Smalltalk through StepTalk.

The biggest limitation of GNUstep is that it only implements Cocoa. There is no support for any of the Core Foundation types, for example, and none of the Carbon APIs are available. Other things, like QuickTime, are similarly missing. In spite of this, a lot of Cocoa applications can be ported with only minor modifications. Recent versions of GNUstep have much improved support for reading nib files created with Interface builder, and the pbxbuild tool can be used to build XCode projects.

24.4.1 GORM

Figure 24.1 shows the GNUstep *Graphical Object Relationship Modeller* (*GORM*). This is the GNUstep replacement for Interface Builder. This screenshot is not the default appearance for GNUstep. The Mac-style menu bar at the top of the screen and the theme are both provided by Étoilé.

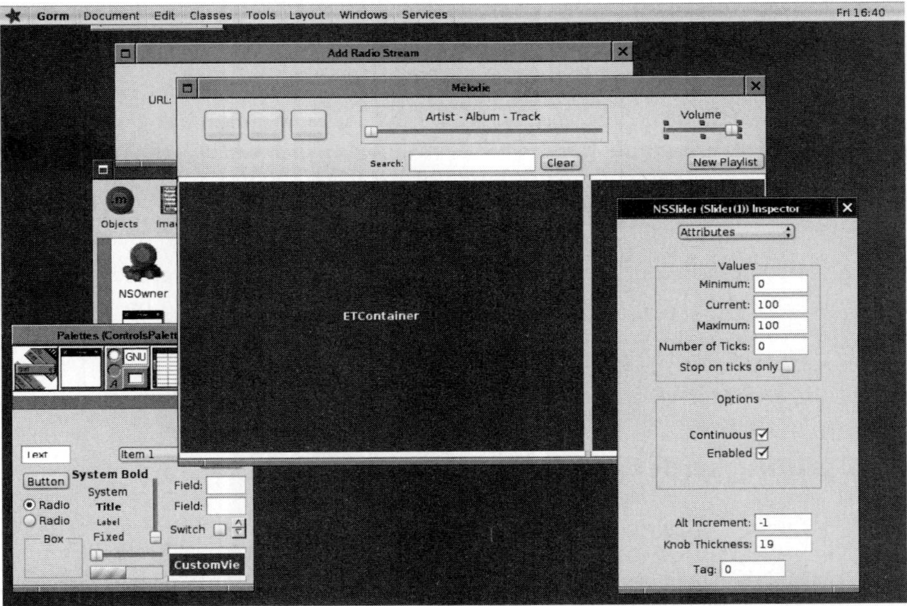

Figure 24.1: GORM, the GNUstep Interface Builder.

Gorm is less polished than Interface Builder, but is quite functional. It can be used to create both .gorm files and OS X-compatible .nib files. If you are porting an application from OS X, then you will likely already have a set of nib files that you don't want to have to re-create from scratch. Often, GNUstep will be able to use these directly. If not, then Gorm will probably be able to import them. You can then create a GNUstep version after some minor tweaks.

If you find that your nib files do not work out-of-the-box, please remember to file a bug report with GNUstep. Supporting Cocoa nib files is a priority for them, but they are only aware of problems when they personally encounter them or are sent a bug report.

As with Interface Builder, Gorm allows arbitrary groups of objects to be connected together using outlets and actions. It does not currently support Cocoa Bindings, although they are supported by the GNUstep code base, and so can be connected in code by implementing the `-awakeFromNib` method in a controller.

It is a lot more common for GNUstep applications to need to implement `-awakeFromNib` than it is with Cocoa. Interface Builder exposes a much richer set of options for configuration than Gorm. This means that a lot more need to be set in code. Somewhat ironically, you can often get better support by bringing a nib file from Cocoa than from creating it from scratch with the GNUstep tools.

In addition to Gorm, GNUstep provides Project Center, shown in Figure 24.2. This is a code editor and project manager, equivalent to the Project Builder application from NeXT. This is widely used by GNUstep, although a lot of developers prefer to work without an IDE. The GNUstep Make package provides skeleton make files for all of the supported kinds of projects. You can typically use this without Project Center.

Project Center is a rough equivalent to XCode, although it is more similar to the older Project Builder from the NeXT era. It only recently gained graphical debugging support, for example. It does provide quite a nice code browser, which allows you to browse from files to classes and then to methods. The code editor lacks most of the features of XCode. When developing for GNUstep, I tend to prefer to use vim for editing code and compile using GNUstep Make directly.

24.4.2 Building with GNUstep

GNUstep applications are built using GNUstep Make. This is a package of macros for GNU Make that greatly simplifies the process of writing a Makefile. OS X ships with GNU Make as standard, and it is a relatively simple process to install GNUstep Make. If you intend on deploying an application on multiple platforms, you can use GNUstep Make to build it on OS X as well, stopping you from having to maintain multiple build configurations.

There is also a utility called pbxbuild included with GNUstep that can create GNUstep Make files from XCode projects.

The GNUstep Make package is a collection of complex makefiles that contain rules for building different sorts of projects. By convention, GNUstep makefiles

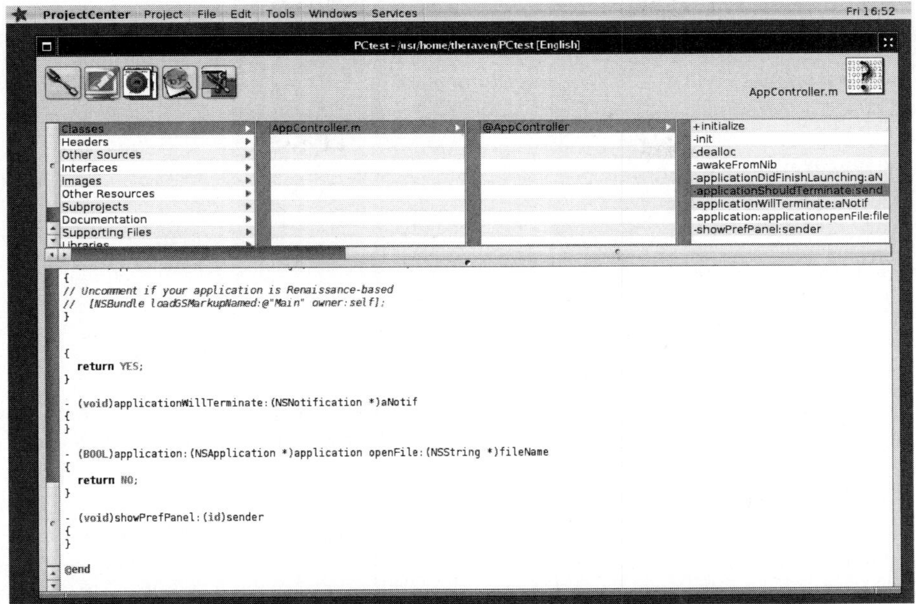

Figure 24.2: GNUstep Project Center.

are named GNUmakefile. GNU Make will use these as a source for build rules, but other Make implementations will not.

While GNUstep Make includes a very complicated set of Make rules, using them is comparatively simple. This is a simple GNUmakefile used to build a graphical application:

```
include $(GNUSTEP_MAKEFILES)/common.make

VERSION = 0.1
APP_NAME = SomeApp

SomeApp_LANGUAGES = English

ifeq ($(FOUNDATION_LIB), apple)
    SomeApp_LOCALIZED_RESOURCE_FILES = \
              MainMenu.nib
    SomeApp_MAIN_MODEL_FILE = MainMenu.nib
else
```

```
    SomeApp_LOCALIZED_RESOURCE_FILES = \
              MainMenu.gorm
    SomeApp_MAIN_MODEL_FILE = MainMenu.gorm
endif

SomeApp_OBJC_FILES = \
        SomeClass.m\
        main.m

ADDITIONAL_OBJCFLAGS = -std=c99 -g -Werror
ADDITIONAL_LDFLAGS += -g

include $(GNUSTEP_MAKEFILES)/application.make
```

This shows most of the important features of GNUstep Make. The first and last lines include the rules required to parse all of the declarations in the rest of the file and turn them into a set of build rules.

Lines three and four are a simple preamble that specify the name and version of the application. If you wanted to build a command-line tool (that doesn't link AppKit), you would replace `APP_NAME` here with `TOOL_NAME` and application.make with tool.make in the last line. Libraries and frameworks can also be built in the same way.

Note the conditional statement beginning on line eight. This allows different build rules to be used for OS X and GNUstep targets, in this case, using an Interface Builder .nib file on OS X and a GORM .gorm file on GNUstep. GNUstep can read a lot of .nib files, and each release adds more support, but since the format is unpublished it requires reverse engineering and can introduce bugs. You may find some of your interface definitions need to be rewritten, but not all.

24.4.3 Étoilé

The Étoilé project was founded in 2004 by a number of developers, including myself, who wanted to produce a desktop environment on top of GNUstep. Although built on some of the same technologies as OS X, it does not aim to duplicate the Mac experience. The project is still quite young, but has succeeded in producing a set of core tools on which the more user-visible features can be built.

The core frameworks in Étoilé are

EtoileFoundation, which implements a number of extensions to Foundation, and provides rich introspection features.

EtoileSerialize, which can serialize arbitrary object graphs using runtime introspection.

CoreObject, which presents a persistent model of objects with automatic, persistent, versioning, and branching.

EtoileUI provides a dynamic user interface that exposes the same interfaces as defined by CoreObject, allowing automatic views to inspect the view hierarchy as if it were a model.

The LanguageKit framework provides a generic abstract syntax tree for dynamic languages and a code generator. This can be used for both static and just-in-time compilation and maps objects defined in this AST directly to Objective-C objects. Parsers are loaded as bundles, with two currently implemented. These are a dialect of Smalltalk and a dialect of JavaScript (EScript).

Étoilé uses a feature of GNUstep called *AppKit user bundles*, which allows code containing categories on GNUstep classes and additional code to be loaded automatically by all GNUstep programs. A theme engine that updates the look of GNUstep called Camaelon is one example of such a bundle provided by Étoilé. Another is the EtoileBehavior bundle, which exposes applications to scripting and causes scripts written in any of the languages supported by LanguageKit to be loaded.

24.5 QuantumSTEP

There is a friendly fork of GNUstep called *mySTEP* that aims to provide an implementation of OpenStep tailored for mobile devices. This runs on a number of Linux-based handhelds. It was designed, unlike GNUstep, for cross-compiling from the Mac, and provides a set of tools for integrating closely with XCode.

The developer of mySTEP has signed a copyright assignment form with the Free Software Foundation, which allows any code from mySTEP to be allowed back into GNUstep. This is why the fork is friendly; code travels in both directions, but they remain distinct since they have different goals.

Most of the differences between GNUstep and mySTEP now relate to the fact that mySTEP aims to be very lightweight and so doesn't include all of the customization options in GNUstep. It also contains a number of modifications designed to make applications more usable on a tiny screen.

There is a commercial distribution built on top of mySTEP, and maintained by the same person, called QuantumSTEP. This includes the mySTEP libraries and a small selection of applications aimed mobile devices.

You can often port Cocoa apps to mobile Linux devices using mySTEP with just a recompile from in XCode, although for best results you will design a modified interface to support the small screen of your target devices.

24.6 Cocotron

A more recent attempt to implement the Cocoa APIs is *Cocotron*. This is a from-scratch implementation aiming for complete compatibility with Cocoa. It is much less mature than GNUstep at the time of writing, although it does have a few advantages. The biggest, from the point of view of Cocoa programmers, is that it is designed for porting Cocoa apps. This means that it integrates closely with XCode and provides a new target.

Currently, Cocotron only supports Windows, although most of the code should be portable to other platforms. GNUstep also supports Windows, but it was originally designed for UNIX platforms and so Windows support generally lags behind other platforms. Recent releases of GNUstep have improved support for Windows a lot, but it still requires installing a MinGW environment on a Windows machine to build Windows applications. In contrast, Cocotron can build Windows binaries just by clicking on a button in XCode.

The license is also more permissive than GNUstep. Cocotron is MIT-licensed, the same license as X.org, which means you can do anything you like with it except claim that you wrote it. This includes building it into embedded devices and bundling it binary-only. GNUstep is released under the GNU *Lesser General Public License* (*LGPL*), which means that you must release any changes you make to the library to anyone you distribute it to, and you must allow users to re-link your application against their own versions of GNUstep. For most uses, these obligations are trivial to comply with.

24.7 GNUstepWeb and SOPE

At the moment, web applications are becoming increasingly popular both as an alternative and an addition to traditional desktop applications. If you have written a complex Cocoa application, you might want to also provide a web application based on the same code ideas.

Cocoa encourages you to separate your code out into models, controllers, and views. While the view objects are highly specific to the desktop, and the controllers often are, the model objects generally are not. They would be easily reusable in a web application, if you had access to a good web application framework.

NeXT released a good web app framework in the mid 1990s, known as WebObjects, and it quickly spawned open source clones. The two most popular are GNUstepWeb and SOPE. These have been used by a number of web applications. The biggest user of SOPE is the OpenGroupware.org suite, which provides a complete groupware suite. Both of these frameworks reimplement the WebObjects 4.5 APIs, the last version of WebObjects to be written in Objective-C.

You can use either if you want to implement a web application based on Cocoa. If you are thinking of porting your application to the iPhone, then you will already have clean separation at the user interface layer, so you can use AppKit and UIKit for the desktop and mobile user interfaces. Adding another implementation providing a web UI is a relatively small amount of work.

Chapter 25

Advanced Tricks

Objective-C is a powerful dynamic language. It was designed as a simple Smalltalk-like extension to the C language to support object orientation. While there are some limitations in this approach, it generally conveys most of the power of both languages.

The C language is little more than a cross-platform assembly language. As with an assembly language, it is very good for writing code that is close to the hardware. C is a great language for people who love microoptimization, as it's often possible to control exactly what the processor is doing. This is especially true of GCC, which exposes a number of instructions directly to the programmer as built-in functions. These are compiled to single instructions, only using the C language for register allocation (and even this can be controlled if required).

Smalltalk is at the opposite extreme. Smalltalk is typically executed on a virtual machine, and so completely isolates the developer from everything to do with the host architecture. Instead, it focuses on making it easy for programmers to concentrate on high-level design and produce clean, neatly abstracted code.

Objective-C combines both of these, allowing developers to write flexible, dynamic, Smalltalk-like code, and then tune the slow parts as carefully as a C programmer would.

This amalgamation of two languages is very powerful, but sometimes tricky to master. People coming from a C or C++ background tend to forget that the dynamic nature of Objective-C's Smalltalk inheritance gives it a lot of expressiveness that they are not used to. In this chapter we will explore the strengths of the language, and see how to get the most from it.

25.1 The Preprocessor

Objective-C, being a pure superset of C, inherits the C preprocessor. While this is not very powerful next to something like the Lisp macro facility, it does allow some degree of metaprogramming and can, used wisely, significantly reduce the number of copy-and-paste errors in a piece of code.

C macros are applied at compile time and so, unlike function calls or message sends, have no overhead associated with their use.

25.1.1 Initializers

Any time the same pattern is repeated often, it is a good idea to define a macro. This prevents copy-and-paste errors; if you get it right in one place, then it will be right everywhere.

One common pattern comes in the `-init:` methods of new classes. In these, the superclass should be initialized first; if this succeeds, then continue with the initialization.

```
#define SUPERINIT if((self = [super init]) == nil)\
    {return nil;}
```

There are a few patterns that can be replaced with macros in this manner. For example, it is common to forget to include `[super dealloc]` at the end of a `-dealloc` method. Recent versions of GCC will, with the correct options, remind you when you've done this. A better alternative, however, is to define a macro that will include this automatically, like this:

```
#define DEALLOC(x) - (void) dealloc { x ; [super dealloc];}

DEALLOC(
    //Deallocation here:
    [anObject release];
)
```

A similar set of macros could be defined for other common methods that need to fulfill some obligations to their superclass. Try using the `__builtin_apply_args()` family of GCC built-in functions to write macros for generically calling the superclass implementation of a method by constructing the call to `objc_msgSendSuper()` in a macro.

25.1.2 For Each

Some languages provide a `foreach` construct. This iterates over every object in a collection and runs a block of code using it. With Cocoa and Objective-C 1.0, the following pattern is usually used instead:

```
NSEnumerator * enumerator = [collection objectEnumerator];
id object;
while((object = [enumerator nextObject]))
{
    //Do something
}
```

The collection in this can be anything that responds to `-objectEnumerator`, including `NSArray`, `NSDictionary`, and so on. Since this is used so often, it makes sense to package this up into a macro. This is an example of one way that you can do it:

```
#define FOREACHE(collection,object,type,enumerator)\
    NSEnumerator * enumerator = [collection objectEnumerator];\
    type object;\
    while((object = [enumerator nextObject]))
```

While this will work, we don't actually use the enumerator outside of the macro, so having to specify a unique name for it is a bit messy. Ideally, we could tell the preprocessor to create a new variable name. Unfortunately, this is not possible with the C preprocessor. We can, however, do something similar. The next version shows one way that we can do it. The ## operator instructs the preprocessor to concatenate the two tokens. In this case, it appends "enumerator" to the variable name that we choose for our object.

```
#define FOREACH(collection,object,type)\
 FOREACHE(collection,object,type,object ## enumerator)
```

The usage of this macro is quite simple. The line (or block) following it is executed once for each object in the collection, defined to have type. The following code shows how this macro could be used. This snippet defines a function that logs every string in an `NSArray`:

```
void logStrings(NSArray* strings)
{
    FOREACH(strings, string, NSString*)
    {
        NSLog(@"%@",string);
    }
}
```

With Objective-C 2.0, Apple introduced a "for each" construct into the language. If compiling with Objective-C 2.0, you can replace the `FOREACH` macro declaration with this:

```
#define FOREACH(collection,object,type)\
 for(type object in collection)
```

```
// Ignore the enumerator
#define FOREACHE(collection, object,type, enumerator)\
 for(type object in collection)
```

The Objective-C 2.0 version is faster, since it doesn't require the creation of an iterator, and returns several objects in response to every message. If you have used the FOREACH macro in your code, then you can get this speed boost trivially by changing the macro definition.

If you need your code to work with old and new versions of the language, you can use conditional compilation to replace it with either depending on the compiler. This highlights the advantage of meta-programming. You can use this same macro—or one like it—to do classical enumeration when targeting Tiger or earlier and fast enumeration when targeting Leopard or later. Modifying a single macro definition when switching between the two is a lot easier than modifying every single case of enumeration in your program.

25.1.3 Objective-C Constants

Objective-C does not have the concept of constant objects. The common replacement is to use the immutability pattern; an object is instantiated to be of a class that does not have any methods for modifying its value. In most cases, this is sufficient. An immutable object can be created in a class's +initialize method and stored in a file-static variable, and accessed via a class method.

There are times, however, when it is more convenient to be able to interact with a constant object in the same way that one would with a constant intrinsic value. This can be achieved by defining the immutable object with a macro.

The following snipped shows a definition of a constant FORTYTWO that is an NSNumber containing the numeric constant 42:

```
#define FORTYTWO [NSNumber numberWithInt:42]
```

The main reason why something of this nature would be useful is when you need to define constant values for mutable classes. A constant, by definition, should be immutable, but sometimes you want to define a mutable object with a constant value.

Below, you can see a simple example of how such a constant might be used. Note that constants declared in this way incur a creation and destruction cost with every use, and so are less efficient than pure immutable objects.

```
if([theAnswer isEqualTo:FORTYTWO)
{
    NSLog(@"Deep Thought run completed");
}
```

Don't forget to use a named constructor or explicitly autorelease objects created this way. In general, it is better to create constant instances by creating them as singletons. If you do this, you might consider overriding the -release method to ensure that the object is never deallocated. For debugging, you can implement -release so that it keeps track of the retain count using the standard Foundation functions and use an assertion if the retain count drops to zero, rather than deleting the object.

25.1.4 Simple Templates

Any Lisp programmer will tell you that the C preprocessor is barely worthy of the name, but used judiciously it can dramatically reduce the amount of code required to solve a particular problem. In the EtoileSerialise Framework, which provides a generic mechanism for serializing Objective-C objects, there are a number of classes that are over 50% preprocessor directives.

One common use for this is when you want different methods implementing the same behavior with different types. This is one of the few things that C++ does well, since it allows you to parameterize the type and produce a template. Objective-C doesn't have quite as nice of a mechanism, but you can do something similar with the preprocessor. Note that this is only needed for primitive types—with objects that you can use introspection to achieve generic behavior.

The key to this is the ## preprocessor command, which concatenates two tokens. This is a short snippet from the EtoileSerialise code showing this in real-world use:

```
#define LOAD_METHOD(name, type) - (void) load ## name:(type)aVal withName:(
    char*)aName LOAD_INTRINSIC(type, name)
LOAD_METHOD(Char, char)
LOAD_METHOD(UnsignedChar, unsigned char)
LOAD_METHOD(Short, short)
LOAD_METHOD(UnsignedShort, unsigned short)
```

The first line from this snippet defines a macro that takes a token and a type as arguments. The token is used to construct the method name, and the type is used in the method body. The second line will be expanded to

```
- (void) loadChar:(char) aVal withName:(char*)aName LOAD_INTRINSIC(char,
    Char)
```

In this example, LOAD_INTRINSIC is another preprocessor macro, which is expanded to the method body. When I was testing this code, I discovered a bug in the implementation of this macro. If I had copied and pasted the code, then I would have had to fix it in a dozen or so places, but the use of macros meant that a single fix removed a large number of instances of the bug. If you have some code that is reused in slightly modified form, you might find that parameterizing the modified bit and implementing it as a preprocessor macro dramatically simplifies your code.

Because preprocessor macros are expanded at compile time, they incur no performance penalty other than increased code size; the same penalty you would get if you wrote each of the versions by hand. You can generalize this mechanism even more by writing a generic implementation of some code in a separate file and using **#include** to insert it multiple times. If the code in the included file depends on the definition of some macros, then you can change these macro definitions between each inclusion and get different versions.

This technique is also useful if you have a small set of methods that you want to add to more than one class at different places in the class hierarchy. You can define the methods in a separate file and then include them in each class implementation file.

25.1.5 Friendly Debug Output

Whenever I am chasing a bug in Objective-C code, I find myself littering the source with endless `NSLog` statements to try to find it. Most of these are telling me what a variable's value was at a specific time. In a lot of cases, I find this easier than using an interactive debugger, since it means that I can quickly inspect values over a long program run, and then switch to using the debugger when I have narrowed down the error to a smallish segment of code.

Many of these debug statements are just telling me the value of a variable. Listing 25.1 shows a simple macro that dramatically simplifies this kind of statement.

Listing 25.1: Simplifying debugging statements. [from: examples/AdvancedTricks/debug.m]

```
#import <Foundation/Foundation.h>

#define LOG_INT(foo) NSLog(@"%s:%d %s = %d", __FILE__, __LINE__, #foo, foo);

int main(void)
{
    int foo = 5;
    LOG_INT(foo);
    return 0;
}
```

Running this code gives the following output:

```
$ gcc -framework Foundation debug.m
```

```
$ ./a.out
2009-02-26 13:40:41.923 a.out[25094] debug.m:8 foo = 5
```

There are three preprocessor functions being shown here. The first two are implicit macros, `__FILE__` and `__LINE__`, which expand to a C string containing the file name and an integer containing the current line, respectively. The other is the `#` command, which turns a token into a C string. This is used to print the name of the variable, as well as its name.

By using the `LOG_INT` macro in a number of places, you can quickly get an idea of how a variable's value changes over the course of a program run.

Using the preprocessor in this way can make your code a lot more readable, since your methods become a description of what the code is doing, rather than how it is doing it.

25.2 Control Structures

In Smalltalk, from which Objective-C inherits its object syntax, there are no control structures in the language. Instead, they are implemented by the library. A conditional, for example, is implemented by passing a block of code to a Boolean value's `ifTrue:` method.

In Objective-C, you do not have a direct equivalent of Smalltalk blocks, although Snow Leopard introduces something similar, but you can still implement some new control structures without modifying the language. This section will explore a few ways in which the dynamic features of the language can be used to alter flow control.

25.2.1 NSDictionary Abuse

It is quite common to want to create a large switch statement using strings. Unfortunately, the C case statement doesn't understand Objective-C objects. One solution to this is to make use of the `NSDictionary` class.

Objects stored in an `NSDictionary` are stored in buckets based on their hash and so can be looked up faster than by using a load of nested **`if`** statements using `-isEqualTo:`. This makes them a relatively efficient way of implementing code vectors.

An `NSDictionary` contains a set of key-value mappings. The keys can be any Objective-C class that implements a certain set of methods. The values can be any object. One thing to remember is that classes in Objective-C are also objects. This means that classes can be stored as the values in `NSDictionaries`.

This method shows an example of how you can use an `NSDictionary` as a replacement for nested **`if`** statements.

```
- (void) handleString:(NSString*)aString
{
    NSDictionary * vector =
        [NSDictionary dictionaryWithObjectsAndKeys:
        [fooHandler class], @"foo",
        [barHandler class], @"bar",
        nil];
    Class handlerClass = [vector objectForKey:aString];
    id handler = [handlerClass new];
    [handler handle:aString];
    [handler release];
}
```

In this example, we begin by populating our NSDictionary with pairs of strings and classes. In a real implementation, this population should be done once and stored, rather than being created every single time it is used. It might also be mutable, so that other objects can register handlers for different strings.

The value in the dictionary doesn't have to be a class. It would be nice to be able to store selectors in these, allowing a specific method to be called. Unfortunately selectors are scalar types and can't be inserted into an NSDictionary directly. There are a few ways around this. One is to store the selector name, rather than the selector itself. The NSSelectorFromString() function can then be used to generate the selector. Another is to use an NSMapTable, which supports primitive types as both keys and values. The final option is to encapsulate the selector in something like an NSInvocation.

Using NSInvocations as the values in the dictionary provides a lot of flexibility. An invocation object encapsulates a selector, a set of arguments, and a target. Once created, you can simply set the arguments and then send it an -invoke message.

25.2.2 Key-Value Coding

The Key-Value Coding (KVC) mechanism used in Cocoa is very flexible; it allows users of a class to get and set values without knowing how they are stored. You might wish to implement something similar in your code.

The mechanisms used to implement KVC can be useful for providing generic dispatch code. When you use KVC to set an instance variable via a set method, it inspects the current class and re-routes the message.

Consider the example of a class acting as a delegate in a streaming XML parser. The parser might send it messages of the form:

```
- (void) handleNode:(NSString*)aNode withAttributes:(NSDictionary*)
    attributes;
```

Implementing something that will handle this is likely to end up with some spaghetti code if you use a load of nested `isEqualToString:` calls to find special handlers for node types.

A cleaner solution is to have it automatically call a method that handles a particular node type. If you are parsing XHTML, and you encounter a **<body>** tag, it should call `-handlebodyWithAttributes:`, for example. It turns out, implementing this kind of mechanism is fairly easy. In your base class, you would have a method like this one:

```
- (void) handleNode: (NSString*)aNode withAttributes: (NSDictionary*)
    attributes
{
    NSString * sel = [NSString stringWithFormat: @"handle%@withAttributes:"
        , aNode];
    SEL selector = NSSelectorFromString(sel);
    if([self respondsToSelector: selector])
    {
        [self performSelector: selector withObject: attributes];
    }
    else
    {
        //Ignore node, or call some generic implementation.
    }
}
```

This first creates a string with the same name as the expected selector. This is then turned into a selector using the `NSSelectorFromString()` Foundation function. Next, the object checks whether it has a method that corresponds to the selector, and if it does, it calls it with the attributes as an argument. Note that it's possible to optimize this last step slightly by calling the runtime functions directly, rather than via `NSObject`, although this comes at the expense of portability.

In each subclass of this class, you would then implement individual methods to handle the child elements that you expect to receive. You would probably also implement some kind of default behavior for unrecognized nodes in a separate method called from the **`else`** clause. If you've used a language like Prolog or Erlang, you will recognize this style of programming, since it closely matches the pattern matching facilities they support. While statically typed languages like C++ allow different implementations based on the type of an argument, Objective-C lets you use a different implementation based on the value.

This is a very powerful control pattern in Objective-C. Because the dispatch mechanism is exposed to your programs, you can modify flow control in any way you choose. Adding an extra layer of indirection comes with a performance penalty, but in a program that is not CPU limited, it can greatly simplify the source code.

25.2.3 Trampolines

A trampoline is a function or method that vectors execution of your program off in a different direction. The `objc_msgSend()` function, described in detail later in this chapter, is an example of a C trampoline used to implement Objective-C messaging.

In Objective-C, a trampoline typically acts like a delegate, "bouncing" a message to another object. Good candidates for trampoline behavior are collection objects. The `NSArray` class contains a few trampoline-like methods, such as `-makeObjectsPerformSelector:`. A proper Objective-C trampoline, however, should be transparent to the caller.

A clean version of this, using a trampoline, would look more like this:

```
[[anArray allElements] doSomething];
```

In this instance, the array returns a trampoline object, which forwards every message passed to it to all of the elements in the array. This approach is known as *higher-order messaging* (*HOM*). First, we will look at the implementation of the proxy. This uses the forwarding mechanism in Objective-C to pass messages to each of the objects in the array.

The forwarding mechanism requires the implementation of two methods; `-forwardInvocation:` and `-methodSignatureForSelector:`. The return value from the second of these is used to generate the `NSInvocation` object passed to the first. The implementation of this is typically fairly simple, since forwarding is usually used to forward messages to a single class. The trampoline object, however, can't guarantee that all objects will respond to the selector, and so must iterate over the array until it finds an object that does. This must then be repeated when forwarding the invocation. The code for the trampoline and a category adding the `-allElements` method can be seen in Listing 25.2.

Listing 25.2: Array trampoline for sending messages to all elements. [from: examples/AdvancedTricks/NSArray+allElements.m]

```
#import "NSArray+allElements.h"
#import "Macros.h"

@implementation NSArrayProxy
- (id) initWithArray: (NSArray*)anArray
{
    array = [anArray retain];
    return self;
```

```
}
- (id) methodSignatureForSelector: (SEL)aSelector
{
    FOREACHI(array, object)
    {
        if([object respondsToSelector: aSelector])
        {
            return [object methodSignatureForSelector: aSelector];
        }
    }
    return [super methodSignatureForSelector: aSelector];
}
- (void) forwardInvocation: (NSInvocation*)anInvocation
{
    SEL selector = [anInvocation selector];
    FOREACHI(array, object)
    {
        if([object respondsToSelector: selector])
        {
            [anInvocation setTarget: object];
            [anInvocation invoke];
        }
    }
}
DEALLOC(
    [array release];
)
@end

@implementation NSArray (AllElements)
- (id) allElements
{
    return [[[NSArrayProxy alloc] initWithArray: self] autorelease];
}
@end
```

Note that this code uses several of the macros described earlier. This trampoline checks that each object in the destination array responds to the specified selector. If you don't do this, then you will get a runtime exception if it does not, and so it would be semantically equivalent to simply wrap the `-invoke` call in an exception handler block.

Using this trampoline mechanism is very simple. Listing 25.3 shows an example use. This creates an array of simple objects that all respond to a `-log:` message and sends it to all of them.

Listing 25.3: Sending a message to all elements in an array. [from: examples/AdvancedTricks/NSArrayExample.m]

```
#import "NSArray+allElements.h"
#import "Macros.h"

@interface Test : NSObject {
    NSString * string;
}
- (id) initWithString: (NSString*)aString;
- (void) log: (NSString*)aString;
@end
@implementation Test
- (id) initWithString: (NSString*)aString
{
    SELFINIT;
    string = [aString retain];
    return self;
}
- (void) log: (NSString*)aString
{
    printf("Object␣%s␣logging␣%s\n",
            [[string description] UTF8String]
            [[aString description] UTF8String]);
}
@end

int main(void)
{
    [[NSAutoreleasePool alloc] init];
    NSArray * array = [NSArray arrayWithObjects:
       [[Test alloc] initWithString: @"Object␣1"],
       [[Test alloc] initWithString: @"Object␣2"],
       [[Test alloc] initWithString: @"Object␣3"],
       nil];
    [[array allElements] log: @"some␣text"];
    return 0;
}
```

Running this example gives the following output:

```
$ gcc -framework Foundation NSArray+allElements.m NSArrayExample.m
$ ./a.out
Object Object 1 logging some text
Object Object 2 logging some text
```

```
Object Object 3 logging some text
```

Each object receives the same message, and produces the output. This mechanism can be easily generalized to provide map, collect, and fold operations on arrays. Doing so is left as an exercise to the reader. Note that, although the proxy is intended to be transparent, there is nothing stopping you from retaining it and reusing it for sending several messages to the same object.

25.2.4 State Machines

A lot of algorithms are very cleanly represented by state machines. The behavior of an object used to represent a state machine differs depending on what state it is in. When it receives some input, it does something and then transitions to a new state (or stays in the same state).

States, in this respect, are very similar to classes. Objects respond differently to messages depending on their classes. We can use classes to implement states using a technique known as `isa`-swizzling. We will create one class that has all of the internal state that our state machine needs to track, and methods for the default state. Other states can then be defined as a subclass of this. As long as our subclasses don't declare any new instance variables, then we can, safely, at run time, change our object to be an instance of one of the other classes simply by updating a pointer.

We can write a simple `become:` method that assumes it is safe to perform the `isa`-swizzling. After reading the runtime library section, try modifying this to check that no instance variables are declared in the destination that are not in the current class (you can do this quickly by just comparing the instance size property) and ensuring that the target class either is the base class, or is a subclass.

We will then use this to write a simple state machine that ignores all input text that is not between quotes. Our base class, `State1`, includes a public buffer used to collect every character that appears while we are between quotes. When we encounter a quote, we enter state 2, which logs every character it encounters until a closing quote is encountered.

Listing 25.4: A Simple state machine using `isa`-swizzling. [from: examples/AdvancedTricks /StateMachine.m]

```
#import <Foundation/Foundation.h>

@interface State1 : NSObject {
@public
    NSMutableString * buffer;
}
- (void) become:(Class)newState;
```

```
- (void) read:(char)aChar;
@end
@interface State2 : State1 {}
@end

@implementation State1
- (id) init
{
    if(nil == (self = [super init])) return nil;
    buffer = [[NSMutableString alloc] init];
    return self;
}
- (void) become:(Class)newState
{
    isa = newState;
}
- (void) read:(char)aChar
{
    if(aChar ==  \  )
    {
        [self become:[State2 class]];
    }
}
@end
@implementation State2
- (void) read:(char)aChar
{
    if(aChar ==  \  )
    {
        [self become:[State1 class]];
    }
    else
    {
        [buffer appendFormat:@"%c", aChar];
    }
}
@end

int main(int argc, char *argv[])
{
    [NSAutoreleasePool new];
    State1 * StateMachine = [State1 new];
    char * str = "This␣is␣a␣ test ␣string␣with␣some␣ words ␣in␣it";
    if(argc == 2)
```

```
    {
        str = argv[1];
    }
    while(*str)
    {
        [StateMachine read:*str];
        str++;
    }
    NSLog(@"Buffer: %@", StateMachine->buffer);
    return 0;
}
```

When we run this, we can see that it collects all of the text in between quotes correctly:

```
$ gcc -framework Foundation StateMachine.m && ./a.out
2009-04-13 21:33:48.672 a.out[33211:10b] Buffer: testwords
$ ./a.out "This is another  simple  test case"
2009-04-13 21:39:14.101 a.out[33222:10b] Buffer: simple
```

This specific example could be accomplished quite easily by just keeping a state variable in the class and using an **if** statement. As the number of states grows, however, this becomes increasingly complex and difficult to read.

25.3 Clean Code

One of the original motivations for Objective-C was keeping code clean and readable. Brad Cox, the inventor of the language, was a strong believer in the benefits of modular and reusable code. He used object orientation as a tool to achieve this, rather than a goal in itself. Objective-C provides a number of facilities to make this easy.

25.3.1 Toll-Free Bridging

A lot of Cocoa objects are toll-free bridged with Core Foundation types. This means that you can interact with Objective-C objects from C, as if they were C opaque data types. The mechanism used to do this is complex, but we can achieve something very similar in our own code.

If you are writing a library that needs to be called from pure-C code, but wish to use Objective-C to implement it, then this is the solution. Every Objective-C object is of type **id**, which means (from the compiler's perspective) a pointer to a C structure defined in one of the runtime library headers.

Since Objective-C objects are just pointers, there is nothing stopping you from passing them to C code. You can, for example, convert any **id** to a **void*** and pass it to a C function. Consider the following trivial Objective-C class:

```
@interface SimpleClass {
}
- (int) doSomethingWithANumber:(int)aNumber;
@end
```

This only has one method. We do, however, need to expose more than this to a C programmer for it to be useful; at the very least he or she will need +new and -release. Let's begin at the end, with what we want the C programmer to see at the end. This is a set of declarations that you might put in a header file that a C programmer can **#include** into a C source file:

```
typedef SimpleClass* SimpleClassRef;
SimpleClassRef simpleClassNew();
void simpleClassRelease(SimpleClassRef aSimpleClass);
int simpleClassDoSomethingWithANumber(SimpleClassRef aSimpleClass, int
    aNumber);
```

This defines an opaque C type that is then used by a set of three C functions that replace the Objective-C methods we wish to export. Given the Objective-C class and the C interface, all we need to do is add some glue code to join the two together. This can be quite simple, just a short wrapper function for each method:

```
SimpleClassRef simpleClassNew()
{
    return [[SimpleClass alloc] init];
}
void simpleClassRelease(SimpleClassRef aSimpleClass)
{
    [aSimpleClass release];
}
int simpleClassDoSomethingWithANumber(SimpleClassRef aSimpleClass, int
    aNumber)
{
    return [aSimpleClass doSomethingWithANumber:aNumber];
}
```

It is possible to take this even further, and call the runtime library functions directly. If you include objc/objc.h, you can use the **SEL** type from C, and call the runtime functions directly. The last function from the last example would look something like this:

```
int simpleClassDoSomethingWithANumber(SimpleClassRef aSimpleClass, int
    aNumber)
```

```
{
    SEL selector = sel_getUid("doSomethingWithANumber");
    return (int)objc_msgSend(aSimpleClass, selector, aNumber);
}
```

This version has the advantage that it can be declared **static inline** and put in a header file, allowing pure-C code to call methods inline. If you do this, then it might be better to move the selector to a global variable and have it set by a function called when the library is loaded, or in the class's +load method.

25.3.2 Multiple Inheritance

Multiple inheritance was intentionally left out of the Objective-C language, because it adds several potential problems. A program that uses multiple inheritance is often difficult to debug; when a class inherits from two classes that implement the same method, it is unclear which should be called. Multiple inheritance in C++ is tightly integrated with the type system. The version of a method that is called depends on what the caller thinks the class of the object is. This means that casting a pointer to a C++ object to a different pointer may give a different numerical value.

In spite of this, multiple inheritance is sometimes useful. Something similar can be achieved using categories, but this has the drawback that a category cannot declare new instance variables. We can, however, hack multiple inheritance into an Objective-C program by using the proxy object features of the runtime to allow aggregated objects to transparently appear like they are implemented using multiple inheritance.

If you send an unrecognized message to an object, two things happen. First, the runtime calls -methodSignatureForSelector: on the object to get the method signature. Next, it wraps the invocation up in an NSInvocation object and passes it to the -forwardInvocation: method. By default, this method simply raises an exception, but it is possible to override this behavior.

This mechanism is useful for a variety of tasks. The Distributed Object mechanism uses it to produce proxy objects when forwarding invocations to remote instances. We are going to use it as a "second-chance" mechanism for handling messages. The basic principle is simple; we will delegate all messages that we don't understand to another object by implementing these two methods:

```
- (void) forwardInvocation:(NSInvocation *)anInvocation
{
    [anInvocation setTarget:super2];
    [anInvocation invoke];
    return;
}
```

```
- (NSMethodSignature*) methodSignatureForSelector:(SEL)aSelector
{
    return [super2 methodSignatureForSelector:aSelector];
}
```

These methods expect the existence of an instance variable called `super2`, which is an instance of the second class that we wish to treat as a superclass of the current class.

This mechanism can be expanded to allow as many effective superclasses as you wish. You can use `-respondsToSelector:` to determine which object should be handling the invocations, like this:

```
- (void)forwardInvocation:(NSInvocation *)invocation
{
    SEL sel = [invocation selector];

    if ([super2 respondsToSelector:sel])
    {
        [invocation invokeWithTarget:super2];
    }
    else
    {
        [invocation invokeWithTarget:super3];
    }
}
```

This shows a version of the `-forwardInvocation:` method for an object with three superclasses. The same control structure should appear in the `-methodSignatureForSelector:` method to ensure that the correct method signatures are returned.

Make sure that you remember to create and destroy the instances of the objects implementing the extra superclasses at the correct times if you use this mechanism. Technically, this is not multiple inheritance; it is a generalized case of the *delegation pattern*. The purpose of this example is to highlight the fact that omitting multiple inheritance did not in any way reduce the expressive capabilities of Objective-C. Anything that you can do with multiple inheritance, you can also do with delegation.

Note that this implementation is very slow. Forwarding has a huge overhead compared to direct message sending. If you want something like multiple inheritance, then there are two ways of achieving the same goal. One is to define a category in a separate file, with a declaration like this:

```
@interface SOME_OBJECT (CategoryName)
```

You can then `#include` this file into different source files, redefining the `SOME_OBJECT` macro each time you include it. Alternatively, you can take methods from one class and attach them to another at run time. This only works when both classes have the same instance variable layout, and so is much more fragile, but has the advantage that you don't have to compile several copies of almost-identical methods.

With 10.6, Apple introduced a new mechanism for quickly implementing delegation. Classes can now implement a `-forwardingTargetForSelector:` method for faster forwarding. If your class does not respond to a given selector, then that selector will be passed to this method. The message will then be sent to the object that you return.

25.4 Optimization

Always be careful with optimization. The hacks in this section are all micro-optimizations. They make a small segment of your code faster, at the expense of some readability. The vast majority of the time, applying these will give no benefit to users of your code. Before using any of these, make sure you run a profiler over your code and identify the bottlenecks.

On OS X, there are several tools that you can use for profiling an application. Shark and Sampler are the two that have been around for a while, but XCode 3 introduced a new one. The Instruments application is built on Sun's DTrace framework, included with Leopard and newer releases of OS X. DTrace allows running applications to be instrumented and profiled in a wide variety of ways. Figure 25.1 shows the CPU sampler attached to TextEdit.

Using DTrace is quite complicated, but Instruments comes with a number of DTrace scripts prepackaged and ready for use. These allow you to profile an application's CPU usage, memory usage, I/O load, and a wide variety of other attributes. You can use it to help find the performance trouble spots in your code very easily.

Most programs spend 90% of their time in less than 10% of the code. Improvements in this 10% can make an entire program run a lot faster. The techniques in this section are best applied occasionally when you have identified trouble spots in performance-critical code.

25.4.1 Instance Method Pointers

Sending a message (invoking a method) in Objective-C is relatively expensive. In a static language, such as C++, methods are all hashed to an offset at compile time, and anyone invoking the method simply needs to look up the pointer to that

Figure 25.1: The CPU sampler in Instruments.

method from a table. Because Objective-C is a dynamic, late binding, language, you have to perform a more complex lookup.

When you send a message to an Objective-C object, you don't necessarily know the type of that object. Even if you explicitly cast the object, you don't know whether the object is really a sub-class of the specified class, and has had that method overridden. The runtime has to navigate the structure pointed to by the object's `isa` pointer until it finds the correct method. While some caching is done by the runtime, sending a message is still several times slower than calling a function.

Under the hood, however, an Objective-C method is just a function. The first two arguments to this function are the object and the selector, and the remainder are the arguments. The `objc_msgSend` function, the runtime function called implicitly when an Objective-C message is sent, looks up the correct function pointer and calls it directly. There is nothing stopping you from doing the same.

When using an IMP, you are bypassing the standard Objective-C behavior. As such, you should be careful with it. If you cache the IMP for a particular method on one object, and try to use it on another, then you may find yourself calling the wrong method.

One case where caching an IMP might be a good idea is in classical enumeration. This is a modified version of the typical enumeration loop, which looks up the method pointer for the -nextObject method on the enumerator and calls this directly, bypassing the lookup each time:

```
NSEnumerator * enumerator = [collection objectEnumerator];
id object;
IMP nextObjectFunction =
    [enumerator methodForSelector:@selector(nextObject)];
while((object = nextObjectFunction(enumerator, @selector(nextObject))))
{
    ...
}
```

This loop only needs to perform the dynamic lookup once. On OS X, this will not give a huge performance benefit, because the Apple runtime caches the method pointers for the last four methods to be called, but with the GNU runtime it can be a lot faster.

Another example where this can lead to significant performance improvements is when doing a lot of manipulation on NSString objects. Caching the characterAt: instance method pointer can make scanning along a string significantly faster.

25.4.2 Subverting Dynamic Dispatch

When you invoke a method in C++ or in C using something like GObject, it looks at a static dispatch table to find the address of the method and then jumps there. The last section discussed how to speed up message delivery by caching the address of the method. When you are writing an object where a method is likely to be called a lot, there is a cleaner way of doing this, involving implementing something like a C++ dispatch table yourself.

An Objective-C method is just a function, with a mapping from a selector to the address of the function stored in the object's data structure. The mapping is implemented by a fairly efficient sparse array, but we can make it even faster if we want to use a more specialized mapping.

In simple static object-oriented systems written in C, methods are implemented as function pointers in members of the structure representing the object. You would have something a little like this:

```
struct CObject
{
```

```
    void (method*)(struct CObject);
}
...
int main(void)
{
    struct CObject foo = newCObject();
    foo->method(foo);
    return 0;
}
```

In practice, the system would be likely to add a simple layer of indirection by putting all of the methods in a `CClass` structure, pointed to by a field in the `CObject` structure, but the principle is the same. In Objective-C, we can do something similar by creating public instance variables for commonly used methods. These are then set in the `-init` method. This has two advantages over the approach described in the previous section:

- The instance variable cache is only created once per object and, since it's in the object structure, will be in cache whenever the object is being accessed.
- The caller does not have to worry about subclasses having different method implementations.

Listing 25.5 shows a class with a single method set up for static dispatch. Because the `-methodForSelector` method is an instance method, and returns the mapping for the current object, the `method` instance variable will always point to the correct implementation, even in subclasses.

Listing 25.5: Static dispatch for an Objective-C method. [from: examples/AdvancedTricks/static.m]

```
#import <Foundation/Foundation.h>

@interface StaticObject : NSObject{
@public
    IMP method;
}
- (void) method;
@end

@implementation StaticObject
- (id) init
{
    if(nil == (self = [super init]))
    {
```

```
        return nil;
    }
    method = [self methodForSelector:@selector(method)];
    return self;
}
- (void) method
{
    NSLog(@"Method␣called");
}
@end
```

The following snipped shows the two ways of calling this method, using dynamic and static dispatch. The two calls are equivalent, but the second will be faster.

```
StaticObject *foo = [[StaticObject alloc] init];
[foo method];
foo->method(foo, @selector(method));
```

There are two disadvantages to using this approach. The first is that it makes quite ugly (and hard to read) code. The second is that it will break any mechanism that relies on dynamic dispatch, such as proxy use.

The best place to use this pattern is when calling commonly used methods on **self**. Rather than making the static methods public, use them in your own class to accelerate dispatch to methods within a class. This is particularly useful in a class cluster. Something like `NSString` implements most of the functionality in the base class, and has specialized subclass implementations that handle the storage of string data, and only implement a small number of methods. Caching the `IMP`s for these methods can give a significant performance improvement, since all of the higher-level methods in the base class use them.

25.4.3 Objects on the Stack

A little while ago, I encountered a criticism of Objective-C from a C++ programmer, complaining that you could not create objects on the stack with Objective-C. This was an interesting problem, and it turns out that it is possible to create Objective-C objects on the stack. It is also worth pointing out that this is almost always a bad idea, and that object pools, described in the next section, provide most of the same benefits without breaking anything.

The biggest problem with creating Objective-C objects on the stack is that most objects contain pointers to other objects, and these will be created on the heap. The second problem is that the space for the object will be deallocated when it goes out of scope, without calling the cleanup method. As such, this section should be treated as an intellectual exercise, rather than as programming advice.

If you try to create an object on the stack in the obvious way, the compiler will complain:

```
$ cat stack.m
#import <Foundation/Foundation.h>

int main(void)
{
        NSObject foo;
        return 0;
}
$ gcc stack.m
stack.m: In function  main :
stack.m:5: error: statically allocated instance of Objective-C class  NSObject
stack.m:5: error: statically allocated instance of Objective-C class  NSObject
```

We can get around this by using the **@defs** directive. This returns the C structure representing the Objective-C object, which can be placed on the stack. We define a C structure for an NSObject like this:

```
typedef struct { @defs(NSObject) } STACK_NSObject;
```

Note that `@defs()` requires the compiler to be able to get the instance variable layout at compile time. This is not possible with the modern Apple runtime. An alternative is to get the size of an instance at run time and use `alloca()` to allocate the space on the stack and then explicitly cast the return.

We can now create a `STACK_NSObject` on the stack. Allocation is only part of the problem. We also need to initialize the object, by sending it an `-init` message, as shown in Listing 25.6. Note that we need to caste the stack object, because Objective-C doesn't let us send messages to C structures.

Listing 25.6: Initializing a stack-based object. [from: examples/AdvancedTricks/stack2.m]

```
#import <Foundation/Foundation.h>

typedef struct { @defs(NSObject) } STACK_NSObject;

int main(void)
{
    STACK_NSObject foo;
    [(NSObject*)&foo init];
    return 0;
}
```

When we try to run this, it will cause a segmentation fault. The reason for this is that `+alloc` doesn't just allocate space for the object. It also sets the object's

Listing 25.7: Setting the class of a stack-based object. [from: examples/AdvancedTricks/stack3.m]

```
#import <Foundation/Foundation.h>

typedef struct { @defs(NSObject) } STACK_NSObject;

int main(void)
{
    STACK_NSObject foo;
    NSObject * bar = (NSObject*)&foo;
    foo.isa = [NSObject class];
    [bar init];
    return 0;
}
```

`isa` instance variable to point to the definition of the class. Without this, the runtime library is unable to find the location of the method. Listing 25.7 shows how to do this. We now have an NSObject allocated on the stack, which we can use.

While this mechanism is not suitable for general use, there are a few cases in which it might be feasible. To work with stack-based objects, you would need to

- Override `-retain` and `-release` so that the object never calls `-dealloc`. Ideally, you should also modify `-retain` to return a pointer to a copy of the object on the heap, rather than **`self`**.
- Create a destructor that can be called to clean up instance variables without calling `[`**`super`**` dealloc]`, if required.
- Minimize the use of dynamically allocated instance variables.

Straying slightly away from standard (Objective-)C, it turns out we can do slightly better. Part of the problem with our stack-based objects is that they are implicitly destroyed when they go out of scope. C++ handles this by having the compiler generate implicit calls to the destructor when this happens.

GCC exposes this functionality to C as well. A variable can be declared with a cleanup function that is called when it goes out of scope. The cleanup function takes a single argument, which is a pointer to the variable. We can then use this to destroy the object.

Unfortunately, calling `-dealloc` on a stack-based object gives us this warning:

```
$ ./a.out
a.out(12330) malloc: ***  Deallocation of a pointer not malloced:
0xbffff948; This could be a double free(), or free() called with
the middle of an allocated block; Try setting environment variable
MallocHelp to see tools to help debug
```

This is not ideal. It's not a huge problem, since `free()` knows to avoid freeing this memory, but it would be nice if we could avoid it. First, we need some mechanism for determining whether an object is on the stack or the heap. This is actually trivial on UNIX-like platforms due to the way in which memory is laid out. Memory allocated from the heap (by `malloc()` and friends) grows up from the bottom of the process's address space. The stack starts at the top of the process's address space and grows downward.

Since the stack grows downward, the top stack frame is actually at the bottom of the memory used for the stack. This means that a new variable created on the stack will have a lower address than any other variable on the stack, but a higher address than any variable on the heap. We can use this to create a simple test detecting whether objects are on the stack or the heap.

Listing 25.8 shows all of this put together. A category on `NSObject` replaces its `-dealloc` method with one that checks whether the pointer is on the stack or the heap, and only frees it if it's on the heap.

Listing 25.8: Stack-based objects with lifecycle management. [from: examples/AdvancedTricks/stack4.m]

```
#import <Foundation/Foundation.h>

@implementation NSObject (Stack)
- (void) dealloc
{
    int a;
    if(((id)self) > ((id)&a))
    {
        NSLog(@"Not freeing stack object at address 0x%x", self);
    }
    else
    {
        NSLog(@"Freeing heap object: %@", [self className]);
        NSDeallocateObject(self);
    }
}
@end

void dealloc(void* foo)
```

```
{
    [(id)foo dealloc];
}

#define STACK(class) __attribute__((cleanup(dealloc))) struct { @defs(class ) }
#define DECLARE_STACK(aClass, object) STACK(aClass) object## _stack ; object## _stack.isa = [aClass class]; aClass * object = (aClass*)& object## _stack

void stackTest(void)
{
    DECLARE_STACK(NSObject, bar);
    [bar init];
}
int main(void)
{
    [[NSAutoreleasePool alloc] init];
    stackTest();
    [[[NSObject alloc] init] release];
    return 0;
}
```

Compiling and running this code gives the following output:

```
$ gcc -framework Foundation stack4.m
stack4.m:16: warning: method possibly missing a [super dealloc] call
$ ./a.out
2007-09-16 14:03:21.095 a.out[12391] Not freeing stack object at
address 0xbffff948
2007-09-16 14:03:21.095 a.out[12391] Freeing heap object: NSObject
```

Note the spurious warning generated when compiling the category. GCC does not include a special case for base classes, and assumes that every object inherits from something like `NSObject` that handles the real deallocation. This is not the case in `NSObject`, and thus not the case with any category on `NSObject`.

Note that the cleanup function calls `-dealloc`, not `-release`. This is because the object's memory will be freed (or, rather, recycled) as soon as it goes out of scope irrespective of whether another object has a pointer to it. This is part of the reason why objects created on the stack were not placed in the Objective-C language in the first place: They encourage bugs. Nevertheless, this example shows a potential optimization.

The cleanup function is not limited to objects created on the stack. It can be used by objects created on the heap as well. Specifying a function that calls

-release on the object when it goes out of scope provides a nice way of handling short lifecycle objects without relying on autorelease pools.

25.4.4 Object Pools

On any operating system, malloc() is a relatively expensive operation. In the best case, it requires a short navigation of the heap. In the worst, it requires a system call to allocate more pages to the processes address space. On OS X, malloc() is particularly expensive. If you have a section of code that is creating and destroying a lot of objects in a short period of time, then you can save a lot of malloc() and free() calls by recycling the objects. Objective-C makes this particularly easy, since the allocation and initialization components of object creation are handled separately.

In the simple case, you can just keep a small collection of objects around. When an object is -dealloc'd, you just add it to the pool. The next time you +alloc an object, you see if there are any in the pool and use one of those if you can.

The disadvantage of this approach is that it wastes memory. The object pool is never freed. In general, pooling should only be used for small objects that are created and destroyed frequently; using it elsewhere can cause more performance problems than it solves.

Note that the example in this section is NOT thread safe. The locking required for thread safety in object pools is sufficiently expensive to offset any savings from not using malloc(), although it is possible to use a separate pool for each thread.

Adding and removing objects from a pool should be quick, and so we use a linked list. We could do this using an external structure, but it's easier to use an instance variable.

```
@interface PooledOjbect : NSObject {
public:
    PooledOjbect * next;
}
@end
```

We also need somewhere to store the list. In Smalltalk, this would be a class variable. In Objective-C, we use file statics for the same task:

```
static PooledObject * pool;
```

The next thing to do is override +alloc and -init to work with the pool. This gets the next object from the pool if there is one, or allocates a new one if the pool is empty:

```
+ (id)alloc
```

```
{
    if(pool != nil)
    {
        id obj = pool;
        pool = pool->next;
        return obj;
    }
    return [super alloc];
}
- (void)dealloc
{
    next = pool;
    pool = self;
    if(0) { [super dealloc]; }
}
```

The `if(0)` statement at the end of this is a small hack, which eliminates a compiler warning. GCC will complain about `-dealloc` methods that don't contain a call to `[super dealloc]`, but doesn't notice that this line is never reached.

In practice, we would probably not want to implement it quite like this. Using a separate variable to keep track of the number of objects in the pool and only adding more if it is below a certain threshold will keep memory usage down. By picking a sensible maximum, you can avoid a lot of calls to `malloc()` and `free()`, without ballooning memory usage too badly.

Another thing to watch out for is that this will break with subclasses of `PooledObject`. An implementation of these methods intended for real-world use should check that it is not being called from a subclass. Adding objects from different classes to the same pool produces some errors that are very hard to track down. (Although there's nothing stopping you from having several object pools.)

25.4.5 Inline Functions

Function calls faster than Objective-C messages, but they are still not always fast enough. Whenever you call a function in a C program, the following things happen:

1. The arguments have to be marshaled.
2. The current functions registers must be saved on the stack.
3. A new stack frame must be created.
4. The program counter must be saved onto the stack.
5. The program counter value must be set to the new function's address.

Threading and Object Pools

If you need to use object pools in multithreaded code, the best solution is to have one pool for each thread. This means that you don't need any locking, although it does require that you spend some time thinking about exactly where you are storing your pools.

Unfortunately, this solution does not often work. It is not uncommon to have one thread creating objects and another destroying them. In this case, you can create separate pools, but it won't do much good; the first thread will never have any pooled objects to use when it wants to create one, while the second will just leak memory. A solution that works reasonably well is to wait until the pool in the second thread grows to a certain size and then pass it over to the first thread. This requires some locking, but not nearly as much as a thread-safe object pool would.

6. The new function must do its works.

7. The old functions registers must be loaded from the stack.

8. The old program counter value must be loaded from the stack.

This is quite time consuming. If you have a lot of small functions, then the overhead of calling them can be greater than the overhead of actually executing them. This is not good. It is often much better to insert a copy of the function's code at the point where it is called. This is called inlining.

The C compiler does a fair job at inlining functions, but it has some significant limitations. C was created as a file-based language. As such, each source file is compiled independently. If you call a function in another source file, the compiler can't inline it.

One solution to this is to put the function in a header file. This is a bit messy (headers should contain interfaces, not implementations), but it does work. The problem then comes when you have two source files including the same header. Then, you get two copies of the same symbol and the linker gets confused trying to work out which one should be used.

You can, however, tell the compiler only to inline the code, not to create a "normal" copy of the function. This is done by specifying the `inline` keyword, as shown in listing 25.9

Listing 25.9: A function declared inline extern.

```
inline extern int add(int a, int b)
{
```

```
    return a + b;
}
```

This works well, until you try compiling your project in debugging mode, without inlining. At this point, the compiler just inserts a symbol telling the linker to insert a call to a real function. The linker, however, can't find a real copy of the function, so the whole thing fails.

To prevent this, you have to also create a source file with a copy of the code without the **extern** keyword. This will ensure that, if the inlining fails, there is a copy for the linker to fall back on. Keeping the linker happy is not the only reason to do this; you cannot have a pointer to a purely inline function.

Inlining Caveats

While inlining usually gives a speed increase, there are times when it doesn't. Inlining makes your binaries bigger, since you get multiple copies of the same code. A bigger binary means more of the CPU's instruction cache is used up. If the increased size means more instruction cache misses, then this can more than offset the speed increase from inlining. For this reason, Apple compiles with -Os, which instructs the compiler to optimize for a small binary size.

This should not discourage you from careful inlining. In general, the compiler will make good choices about what to inline if you arrange your code in such a way that it is able to. I have achieved over a 20% speed boost on some code just by re-factoring it to allow better inlining. As with other optimizations, the benefit is highly dependent on the code.

If you are using LLVM to compile your code, then you can take advantage of the link-time optimizer. This can inline function calls between modules, eliminating the need for making the method body visible in both files.

25.4.6 Avoid Objects

While this seems somewhat counter to the ideas of Objective-C, you can do a lot with plain C. In performance-critical sections of your code, it might be worth considering using plain C. Store data that you pass around in **struct**s, and try using C arrays in place of `NSArray`s. Some developers dislike this, claiming it makes the code impure in some hard-to-define way. It is worth noting that Cocoa does exactly this for ranges, sizes, points, and rectangles, which are used in a great many places.

The C99 standard relaxed the constraints on C arrays in two important ways. The first was that the size could be specified by a variable expression where C89 required a constant. The second was that variable declarations were no longer constrained to the start of a block. This allowed arrays of an arbitrary size to be created on the stack.

> ### C99
>
> Objective-C is a pure superset of C. That means that anything that is valid C, is valid Objective-C. There are, however, a number of standards for C. GCC defaults to using the 1989 version of the standard, commonly known as C89. It also supports the original version, known as K&R C after the two creators of the language, and the 1999 version, C99.
>
> A lot of nice features were introduced with C99, including the new array syntax, single line comments and variable scoping rules for **for** loops. If you are not already using it, then you should be, either by selecting it as the C dialect in XCode or by adding -std=c99 to your GCC command line.

If you use C **struct**s, then it is advisable to use either macros or inline functions to manipulate them. This allows you to retain some degree of object orientation in your code. This snippet shows the start of a pure-C version of `NSArray`:

```
typedef stuct _CArray
{
    unsigned int size;
    unsigned int elements;
    id * array;
}* CArray;

static inline id objectAtIndex(CArray array, unsigned int index)
{
    if(index >= array->elements)
    {
        return nil;
    }
    return array->array[index];
}
...
```

Here, we define a `CArray` type and an example method for manipulating the array. This gives the bounds checking of an `NSArray` at close to the cost of a C array. Other inline functions can be defined to automatically resize the array.

The Foundation framework contains two opaque C data types, `NSHashTable` and `NSMapTable`, which roughly correspond to the `NSSet` and `NSDictionary` classes. The Objective-C versions are easier to use, but come with some overhead. The plain C versions are somewhat simpler. They are also somewhat more flexible, since they allow non-objects to be used as keys and values.

When creating an `NSMapTable`, you are required to specify a hash function and a compare function, which serves the same purpose as the corresponding methods in `NSObject`. Primitive types that are smaller than a **void*** can be stored directly, without boxing or indirection.

25.5 Cross-Platform Cocoa

Cocoa is not just an OS X API. The OpenStep specification on which is is based has been mostly implemented by GNUstep, and by other open source projects. Even if you limit yourself to Apple products, the frameworks change significantly between releases, and you will often want to implement things in different ways for different releases of OS X.

The iPhone is another challenge for porting. It supports the Foundation framework, but not AppKit and not several of the other common Cocoa frameworks. Often, you will have classes that can almost be shared between the iPhone and desktop versions of Cocoa, but not quite. In this section, we'll look at how you can keep code readable and well-structured while making it portable.

While POSIX and OpenStep provide a nice abstraction layer for most things, occasionally you need some platform-specific features. The obvious way of doing this is to wrap your platform-specific code in **#ifdef** statements that detect the correct operating system. This starts looking like this:

```
#if defined LINUX
    //Some Linux-specific code
#elif defined FreeBSD
    //Some FreeBSD-specific code
#endif
```

For a small amount of code, it's not too bad. As you start to add more platforms, however, it quickly gets messy and then unmaintainable. If you have cases for three different versions of OS X on the desktop and one on the iPhone, your code will be an unreadable mess of conditional compilation directives.

A good solution is presented by the concept of categories in Objective-C. The obvious solution would be to put the platform-independent code in a class and augment this by categories for platform-specific code. Some default implementation of the platform-specific code can be placed in the class, and then overwritten by platform-specific categories.

Consider the example of a class intended to give a human-readable value of the amount of physical memory available. This could be implemented by two methods:

1. A (platform-specific) method that returns an integer value of the amount of RAM available.
2. A (platform-independent) method that converts this into a human-friendly format.

The interface to this class might look something like Listing 25.10. This declares two methods, one for getting the total as a number and another for producing a human-readable version. Only the first of these is dependent on platform-specific code.

Listing 25.10: Interface to memory info class. [from: examples/AdvancedTricks/MemoryInfo.h]

```
#import <Foundation/Foundation.h>

@interface MemoryInfo : NSObject {}
+ (unsigned int) totalMemory;
+ (NSString*) humanReadableTotalMemory;
@end
```

A basic implementation of this class is shown in Listing 25.11. Note that both methods are implemented here. The first is simply a dummy implementation, which should be overridden by a category for each supported platform. Implementing it here allows for soft failure in cases where the platform is not supported.

If you want a hard failure, GNUstep's implementation of `NSObject` adds a helpful method. Adding the following line will cause an exception to be raised indicating that the method is a dummy implementation and should not be called:

```
[self subclassResponsibility: _cmd];
```

This method is not provided by Cocoa on OS X. You can either add it yourself, or include the GNUstep Additions framework with your application. This includes most of the GNUstep extensions to OpenStep that are not part of Cocoa as categories, allowing them to be used on other OpenStep implementations.

Listing 25.11: Platform independent memory info code. [from: examples/AdvancedTricks-/MemoryInfo.m]

```
#import "MemoryInfo.h"

@interface MemoryInfo : NSObject {}
+ (unsigned long long)totalMemory
{
    return 0;
}
```

```
+ (NSString*)humanReadableTotalMemory
{
    // Ordered array of SI unit prefixes
    static const char *UnitPrefixes = "kMGTPEZY";
    unsigned long long memory = [self totalMemory];
    int prefix = 0;
    while(memory > 1024)
    {
        prefix++;
        memory >>= 10;
    }
    return [NSString stringWithFormat: @"%lld%cB",
        memory,
        UnitPrefixes[prefix]];
}
@end
```

The second method here provides a quick conversion of a 64-bit integer to a human readable string. It repeatedly divides the value by 1024, giving the total memory in the form $memory \times 10^{prefix}$. The value of `prefix` is then used as an array index to convert this to the SI prefix, which is then used for generating a human-readable string. This version is very simple, and always rounds down.

Adding a platform-specific implementation is a simple matter of providing a category implementing the first method. Listing 25.12 shows how this might be done for FreeBSD.

Listing 25.12: FreeBSD memory info code. [from: examples/AdvancedTricks/MemoryInfo_FreeBSD.m]

```
#import "MemoryInfo.h"

@interface MemoryInfo (FreeBSD)
+ (unsigned long long) totalMemory
{
    unsigned long result;
    size_t resultSize = (sizeof(result))
    sysctlbyname("hw.physmem", &result, &resultSize, NULL, 0);
    return (unsigned long long) result;
}
@end
```

The only remaining question is how you compile these different implementations. You can drop back to using **#ifdef**, wrap each file in a conditional compilation directive, and compile them all. You can use conditional **#include** statements in your implementation, pulling in the correct one there, or you can use conditional commands in your makefile.

Logical Partitioning of Code

Separating your code based on operating system is not always a good idea. For example, code handling large numbers of file descriptors might have been written using `poll()` on Linux, `kqueue()` on FreeBSD, and `select()` on NetBSD. When NetBSD gained a `kqueue()` implementation, this code would have had to mirror the FreeBSD implementation.

It is often better to write code to use specific features. In this case, by writing `poll()`, `kqueue()`, and `select()` back ends, and then detect the supported features at compile time. This also makes it easier to port to a new platform. Rather than writing a new FooOS back end, someone performing the port simply needs to edit the Makefile to let the system know that FooOS should use `select()`. Tools such as GNU Autoconf allow this process to be performed automatically.

25.6 The Runtime System

Early versions of Objective-C were implemented by a simple mechanism that translated the Objective-C code into pure C, and a set of runtime functions. This converted **@class** and definitions into the equivalent C structures and message calls into function calls to the runtime library. This shows two different ways of representing the same message send operation, one in Objective-C and the other in terms of runtime library functions:

```
[object doSomethingWith:otherObject];
objc_msgSend(object, @selector(doSomething:), otherObject);
```

Note that a real implementation of the preprocessor would replace the **@selector** with the runtime's representation of a selector. Modern Objective-C implementations have slightly more sophisticated compilers, but the principle remains the same. As we saw earlier, Objective-C messages are still delivered by a function in a runtime library written in C. These runtime functions are exposed in objc/objc-runtime.h.

There are two Objective-C runtime libraries that are commonly used with OpenStep, and GCC can generate code for both of them. Cocoa on OS X uses the NeXT (Apple) runtime, while GNUstep uses the GNU runtime. This section will cover both of them.

25.6.1 Understanding Object Implementation

The simplest object, one with no instance variables, will be compiled into a C structure of the form:

```
struct
{
    struct objc_class * isa;
};
```

If the class has any instance variables, they will be added to the structure after this pointer. This makes looking up the class of an object a very cheap operation, just dereference the object pointer. This then gives you the address of the structure that represents the class, but what is this structure? The answer is different depending on which runtime you are using. Listing 25.13 shows how the Apple legacy runtime implements classes. The modern runtime, introduced with 10.5, implements classes as an opaque type, allowing their internal structure to be changed in future versions.

Listing 25.13: Apple runtime structure representing a class.

```
struct objc_class {
    struct objc_class *isa;
    struct objc_class *super_class;
    const char *name;
    long version;
    long info;
    long instance_size;
    struct objc_ivar_list *ivars;
    struct objc_method_list **methodLists;
    struct objc_cache *cache;
    struct objc_protocol_list *protocols;
};
```

The first of these is an `isa` pointer, as with an object. This is because Objective-C classes are also objects. The GNU runtime, shown in Listing 25.14 calls this a `MetaClass`, using terminology inherited from Smalltalk (where classes were instances of metaclasses, just as objects were instances of classes); however, this is just a **typedef** introduced for clarity.

The next instance variable in both cases is a pointer to the structure defining the superclass. Any calls to **super** in an instance of an object will involve inspecting this.

There is then some metadata relating to the class. The name is used whenever something like `NSClassFromString()` is called, while the version is used for things like serialization. The `info` field is a bitfield that contains various flags relating to

Listing 25.14: GNU runtime structure representing a class.

```
typedef struct objc_class *Class;
struct objc_class {
  MetaClass             class_pointer;
  struct objc_class*  super_class;
  const char*           name;
  long                  version;
  unsigned long         info;
  long                  instance_size;
  struct objc_ivar_list* ivars;
  struct objc_method_list*  methods;
  struct sarray *    dtable;
  struct objc_class* subclass_list;
  struct objc_class* sibling_class;
  struct objc_protocol_list *protocols;
  void* gc_object_type;
};
```

the class, such as whether it has a `+initialize` method that needs to be called, or whether it was loaded from a bundle.

The `instance_size` defines the amount of space needed to create an instance of the object. As discussed earlier, creating an object is a two-step procedure, involving allocating space and setting the object's `isa` pointer. The amount of space needed to allocate is defined by `instance_size`. This size will always be greater than or equal to the equivalent field in the superclass, since any object will also contain the instance variables declared for its superclass.

The next two fields are the same on both runtimes, although they have different names. They declare lists of instance variables and methods. The instance variable lists is a linked list of structures containing the name, type, and offset of an instance variable. This is used to implement key-value coding. You can find the address of an instance variable by iterating over the list, finding the one with the matching name, and adding the provided offset to the object's address. These are stored in the same way on both runtimes, as shown in Listing 25.15. The `ivar_type` field contains an encoding of the variable type, in the same form found in various other parts of the runtime and in Cocoa classes such as `NSMethodSignature`. For example, `"@"` represents an **`id`**. The EtoileSerialise framework uses this information to automatically serialize objects.

Listing 25.15: Instance variable list structures.

```
struct objc_ivar {
```

```
    char *ivar_name;
    char *ivar_type;
    int ivar_offset;
};
struct objc_ivar_list {
    int ivar_count;
    struct objc_ivar ivar_list[1];
};
```

Methods are encoded in a similar way, with a method name, list of types, and `IMP`. The main difference comes from the need to support categories. Objective-C objects have a static structure. The compiler turns them into C structures, and nothing can alter their layout until they are recompiled. In contrast, methods can be added at run time using categories. As such, the methods are stored using a list of lists, with methods added from categories being added as a new list.

This is a slight simplification on the modern Apple runtime. This supports `non-fragile instance variables`. Each class has a static layout of instance variables, but this only refers to instance variables defined by the class itself. Instance variables inherited from a superclass are defined at load time, rather than compile time. This is implemented by storing the start offset for each class's instance variables in a global variable, which is set from the superclass' instance size when the class is loaded. For efficiency, the offsets of individual instance variables may also be cached.

Searching a linked list to find instance variables is not too much of a problem, because most classes have few instance variables, and most accesses to instance variables are computed at compile time. Searching a linked list for every message send, however, would be horrendously expensive. The runtimes optimize this by using some form of integer type to represent selectors. As each selector string is registered with the runtime, it is assigned an integer value. In both the Apple and GNU runtimes, this value is the pointer to the first string containing the selector name that the runtime encounters.

These can be aggressively cached. Here, the GNU and Apple implementations differ. When sending a message, the GNU runtime uses an efficient sparse-array structure to find the corresponding implementation information. The Apple runtime traverses the linked list, but caches the results of the last few methods to have been called on a particular class, making calling the same method several times in quick succession very fast.

Understanding these structures makes it possible to manipulate them at run time. We will see later how to use them to add or replace methods in a class at run time.

25.6.2 Enumerating All Subclasses

There are a number of cases in which it can be convenient to enumerate all of the subclasses of a particular object. A user interface option might be populated by a list of subclasses of a particular object, for example. The `objc_getClassList()` function allows us to get a list of all classes currently loaded into the runtime system.

It is worth noting that this number can be very large. The short program below is a trivial program for enumerating the number of classes loaded by the Foundation library. On OS X 10.4, this gave 506, and every subsequent release has added even more classes. If you link against AppKit and other Cocoa frameworks, then this number can get even bigger. Finally, you have to remember that any classes you write will be added to this number.

```
#import <Foundation/Foundation.h>
#import <objc/objc-runtime.h>

int main(void)
{
    NSLog(@"%d",objc_getClassList(NULL, 0));
    return 0;
}
```

When called as shown above, the `objc_getClassList()` function simply returns the number of classes loaded. While this is interesting, it is not very useful. If the first argument is not `NULL`, however, it is treated as an array that is filled in with the **`Class`** objects of the loaded classes. The second argument tells it the length of the array, to prevent buffer overflows if more classes have been added to the system since the last call.

Once you have the list of all loaded classes, it is relatively easy to test them and see which are subclasses of a particular base class, which implement a specified protocol, and which respond to a given selector. I say relatively, because there is a minor problem; not all of the classes returned will be `NSObject` subclasses. If you try sending `+isKindOfClass`, for example, to an object that is not an `NSObject` subclass (and doesn't implement the `NSObject` protocol), then it will throw an exception. To prevent this, you have to wrap it up in exception handling, to prevent this. Listing 25.16 shows how to list all subclasses of `NSObject`.

Listing 25.16: Listing all of the subclasses of NSObject. [from: examples/AdvancedTricks-/listObjects.m]

```
#import <Foundation/Foundation.h>
#import <objc/objc-runtime.h>

```

```
int main(void)
{
    [NSAutoreleasePool new];
    int classes = objc_getClassList(NULL, 0);
    //Allocate enough space
    Class * classList = calloc(classes, sizeof(Class));
    //Create an array of all classes
    objc_getClassList(classList, classes);
    for(int i=0 ; i<classes ; i++)
    {
        Class class = classList[i];
        NS_DURING
            if([class isKindOfClass:[NSObject class]])
            {
                NSLog(@"%@",[class className]);
            }
        NS_HANDLER
        NS_ENDHANDLER
    }
    return 0;
}
```

There is one other runtime library function that is useful in this setting; `class_getInstanceMethod()`. This returns a pointer to the structure representing the method implementation and its metadata. If no such method exists on that class, then it returns `NULL`. This can be used as a simple test to see whether a class responds to a particular selector, without having to rely on the class being an `NSObject` subclass. Alternatively, you could navigate the class hierarchy directly. Listing 25.17 shows how this is done. This is likely to be considerably faster, since it does not require any message sending, just a quick look up a short linked list.

Listing 25.17: Listing all of the subclasses of NSObject by inspecting the class hierarchy. [from: examples/AdvancedTricks/listObjects1.m]

```
#import <Foundation/Foundation.h>
#import <objc/objc-runtime.h>

int main(void)
{
    [NSAutoreleasePool new];
    int classes = objc_getClassList(NULL, 0);
    //Allocate enough space
    Class * classList = calloc(classes, sizeof(Class));
    //Create an array of all classes
    objc_getClassList(classList, classes);
```

```
    Class nsobject = [NSObject class];
    for(int i=0 ; i<classes ; i++)
    {
        Class class = classList[i];
        while(class != Nil)
        {
            if(class == nsobject)
            {
                NSLog(@"%s",classList[i]->name);
                break;
            }
            class = class->super_class;
        }
    }
    return 0;
}
```

The equivalent code using the GNU runtime is slightly simpler. The GNU runtime does not provide a method for getting all of the methods. Instead, it provides an enumerator method. This takes a pointer to a pointer as an argument, and uses it to store the enumerator state. Each call to the function updates this pointer (which is initialized as `NULL`) and returns the next class in the system, or `Nil` for the last one. Listing 25.18 shows the GNU runtime version of this program.

Listing 25.18: Listing all of the subclasses of NSObject with the GNU runtime.

[from: examples/AdvancedTricks/listObjectsGNU.m]

```
#import <Foundation/Foundation.h>
#import <objc/objc-api.h>

int main(void)
{
    [NSAutoreleasePool new];
    void *state = NULL;
    Class nextClass;
    Class nsobject = [NSObject class];
    while(Nil != (nextClass = objc_next_class(&state)))
    {
        Class class = nextClass;
        while(class != Nil)
        {
            if(class == nsobject)
            {
                NSLog(@"%s",nextClass->name);
                break;
```

```
            }
            class = class->super_class;
        }
    }
    return 0;
}
```

25.6.3 Adding Methods to a Class

There is a very simple way of adding methods to a class, and that is to use a category. The problem with a category is that you need to specify the class to which you intend to add methods; you can't use it to add methods to an as-yet-undefined class.

Consider the situation of loading third-party classes from a bundle. You may require these to be subclasses of a given class, but it is generally more friendly to require them to implement a give protocol. This, however, prevents you from adding on some of your own methods in a clean way.

You can create a category attached to `NSObject`, but this doesn't necessarily make sense, especially if your category calls **`self`** methods that are not part of `NSObject`. It also prevents your code from using `-respondsToSelector` on your loaded classes. What you really want to do in this case is add some methods at run time. To do this, we used to use the `class_addMethods()` runtime function with the Apple runtime.

Before doing this, we will quickly review exactly what a method is in Objective-C. At the simplest level, it's a function with the following prototype:

```
id method(id self, SEL cmd, ...);
```

This function can be accessed directly by getting the instance method pointer (`IMP`) associated with the method. On top of this, there is some metadata provided by the runtime associating a method name and some type information with the method. All we want to do is either replace the implementation of an existing method, or add a new selector to method mapping. The former can be useful for run time patching, if you know that a particular version of a class library contains a bug. The latter is useful for runtime code generation, using something like GNU Lightning or LLVM to generate the code pointed to by the `IMP`. We will add the category shown in Listing 25.19 to `NSObject`.

Listing 25.19: NSObject category for manipulating classes at run time. [from: examples/AdvancedTricks/NSObject+ReplaceMethods.h]

```
#include <Foundation/Foundation.h>

```

```
@interface NSObject (ReplaceMethods)
+ (int) replaceMethodForSelector:(SEL)aSelector with:(IMP)aMethod;
+ (int) addMethod:(IMP)aMethod forSelectorNamed:(char*)aSelector;
@end
```

There are two methods defined here. We will first look at implementing them for the GNU runtime, by manipulating the class structures directly, and then on the Apple runtime using the convenience functions provided.

The first method is shown in Listing 25.20. This finds the pointer to the method and updates it.

Listing 25.20: Replacing a method in a loaded class with the GNU runtime. [from: examples/AdvancedTricks/NSObject+ReplaceMethods_GNU.m]

```
+ (int) replaceMethodForSelector: (SEL)aSelector with: (IMP)aMethod
{
    MethodList_t methods = ((Class)self)->methods;
    NSString * selectorString = NSStringFromSelector(aSelector);
    while(methods != NULL)
    {
        for(unsigned int i=0 ; i<methods->method_count ; i++)
        {
            Method_t method = &methods->method_list[i];
            //We perform a string comparison, because == does not work on
                SEL
            if([NSStringFromSelector(method->method_name) isEqualToString:
                selectorString])
            {
                method->method_imp = aMethod;
                __objc_update_dispatch_table_for_class(self);
                return 0;
            }
        }
        methods = methods->method_next;
    }
    //Method not found
    return -1;
```

As mentioned before, methods are stored as a list of lists. For this reason, it is necessary to inspect each list in turn, which is the job of the outer loop. The inner loop looks at each method definition in a method list. These definitions contain method names (selectors), types, and implementation pointers.

For each method, we first check to see whether it has the same name as the one we are looking for. Because the GNU runtime encodes type information with selectors, the selector generated with **`@selector()`** may not actually be the selector

Listing 25.21: Adding a method to a loaded class with the GNU runtime. [from: examples/AdvancedTricks/NSObject+ReplaceMethods_GNU.m]

```
28 + (int) addMethod:(IMP)aMethod forSelectorNamed:(char*)aSelector
29 {
30     MethodList_t methods = ((Class)self)->methods;
31     //Find the last method list
32     while(methods->method_next != NULL)
33     {
34         methods = methods->method_next;
35     }
36     //Construct a new method list
37     methods->method_next = calloc(sizeof(struct objc_method_list), 1);
38     methods->method_next->method_count = 1;
39     Method_t method =  &methods->method_next->method_list[0];
40     //Add the method to the list
41     method->method_name = sel_register_name(aSelector);
42     method->method_types = NULL;
43     method->method_imp = aMethod;
44     //Update the cache
45     __objc_update_dispatch_table_for_class(self);
46     return 0;
47 }
```

we are looking for, so we perform a string comparison instead. This is slower, but this method should not be called very often, so safer is better.

Once we have found the `Method` structure corresponding to the method that we are replacing, we can simply update the `IMP`. The method has been replaced, but the runtime might miss it because it does not use these structures directly when performing method lookups. We also need to update the cache. Line 19 calls the runtime library function that updates the dispatch table, allowing methods to be quickly called.

The second method is also fairly simple, as shown in Listing 25.21.

This method simply adds a new method list containing the new method to the class. The list of method lists is a pure linked list, so all that is needed is to update the next pointer on the last element to point to our new list.

One thing to note is that in line 42 we are not correctly setting the types for the method. This can potentially cause problems for Distributed Objects, which relies on type information for efficiency. This is not a huge problem, since it will fall back to a less efficient code path using untyped selectors if no type information is available, but it means that methods added in this way will be slower in some

Listing 25.22: Adding and replacing methods with the Apple runtime. [from: examples/AdvancedTricks/NSObject+ReplaceMethods_Apple.m]

```
@implementation NSObject (ReplaceMethods)
+ (int) replaceMethodForSelector: (SEL)aSelector
                            with: (IMP)aMethod
{
    Method method = class_getInstanceMethod(self, aSelector);
    if(method != NULL)
    {
        method->method_imp = aMethod;
        _objc_flush_caches(self);
        return 0;
    }
    //Method not found
    return -1;
}
+ (int) addMethod: (IMP)aMethod
 forSelectorNamed: (char*)aSelector
{
    struct objc_method_list * methods =
        calloc(sizeof(struct objc_method_list), 1);
    methods->method_count = 1;
    Method method = methods->method_list;
    //Add the method to the list
    method->method_name = sel_getUid(aSelector);
    method->method_types = NULL;
    method->method_imp = aMethod;
    //Add the method
```

cases. We could fix this by correctly setting the type information, but it's typically not worth the effort.

The call to `sel_register_name()` in line 41 will add the selector to the runtime if it doesn't already exist. Rather than using this, we could call `sel_get_any_typed_uid()` to see if a typed selector existed already and then `sel_get_type()` to return the type information, and only use an untyped selector if this failed. This would work some of the time, but it would cause complications when registering a selector with different typed arguments but the same name as one already in use.

With the Apple runtime, the code is similar, but simpler as shown in Listing 25.22.

The first method in the Apple version is very simple, because the runtime functions do all of the work of looking up the method structure for us. The second method is very similar to the GNU version. The runtime function adds the method list and flushes the cache for us, but we are still required to create the method list manually.

With the modern runtime, this method is even simpler. All of the internal runtime structures are private with the new runtime library, and so we are not allowed to create a new method structure. To make up for this, we are given this simple convenience function:

```
Method class_addMethod(Class cls, SEL name, IMP imp,
                       const char *types);
```

This takes the class, the selector, a pointer to the method implementation, and the type string, as arguments and adds the method as a single step. These functions are used a lot more with the modern runtime than they used to be. The modern runtime deprecated class posing, which was the traditional way of replacing methods in an Objective-C class. You can use this method as a more structured alternative to class posing—and categories—when you need to replace methods in an existing class:

```
IMP class_replaceMethod(Class cls, SEL name, IMP imp,
                        const char *types);
```

This returns the old implementation, which is particularly useful if you just want to wrap the old version, rather than replace it entirely. This also helps address the case where two or more frameworks try to replace the same method in an existing class.

This mechanism can be expanded further, to allow instances of a class to be tweaked at run time in a variety of ways. You can do something similar to add instance variables to a class at run time, although this will break if instances of the class already exist, or if the class has subclasses, so is less useful.

The Objective-C runtime library is implemented in a subset of Objective-C (specifically, C) and exposed to developers. The language specification doesn't include the interface to the library, so code using it might not be portable, but the fact that it is available makes possible a lot of trick that wouldn't be possible in another language.

Index

Your purchase of ***Cocoa® Programming Developer's Handbook*** includes access to a free online edition for 45 days through the Safari Books Online subscription service. Nearly every Addison-Wesley Professional book is available online through Safari Books Online, along with more than 5,000 other technical books and videos from publishers such as Cisco Press, Exam Cram, IBM Press, O'Reilly, Prentice Hall, Que, and Sams.

SAFARI BOOKS ONLINE allows you to search for a specific answer, cut and paste code, download chapters, and stay current with emerging technologies.

Activate your FREE Online Edition at www.informit.com/safarifree

STEP 1: Enter the coupon code: BLSEHBI.

STEP 2: New Safari users, complete the brief regis
Safari subscribers, just log in.

If you have difficulty registering on Safari or accessing the online edition, please e-mail customer-service@safaribooksonline.com

AdobePress

Cisco Press

O'REILLY